MyManagementLab: Improves Student Engagement Before, During, and After Class

Prep and Engagement

Video exercises – engaging videos that bring business concepts to life and explore business topics related to the theory students are learning in class. Quizzes then assess students' comprehension of the concepts covered in each video.

Learning Catalytics – a "bring your own device" student engagement, assessment, and classroom intelligence system helps instructors analyze students' critical-thinking skills during lecture.

Dynamic Study Modules (DSMs) – through adaptive learning, students get personalized guidance where and when they need it most, creating greater engagement, improving knowledge retention, and supporting subject-matter mastery. Also available on mobile devices.

Business Today – bring current events alive in your classroom with videos, discussion questions, and author blogs. Be sure to check back often, this section changes daily.

Decision-making simulations – place your students in the role of a key decision-maker. The simulation will change and branch based on the decisions students make, providing a variation of scenario paths. Upon completion of each simulation, students receive a grade, as well as a detailed report of the choices they made during the simulation and the associated consequences of those decisions.

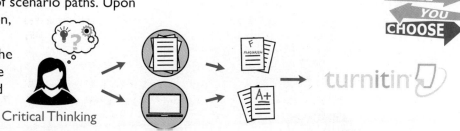

Decision Making

Critical Thinking

Writing Space – better writers make great learners—who perform better in their courses. Providing a single location to develop and assess concept mastery and critical thinking, the Writing Space offers assisted graded and create-your-own writing assignments, allowing you to exchange personalized feedback with students quickly and easily.

Writing Space can also check students' work for improper citation or plagiarism by comparing it against the world's most accurate text comparison database available from **Turnitin**.

Additional Features – included with the MyLab are a powerful homework and test manager, robust gradebook tracking, comprehensive online course content, and easily scalable and shareable content.

http://www.pearsonmylabandmastering.com

PEARSON

FROM THE LIBRARY

Thirteenth Edition
Global Edition

ESSENTIALS OF ORGANIZATIONAL BEHAVIOR

Thirteenth Edition
Global Edition

ESSENTIALS OF ORGANIZATIONAL BEHAVIOR

Stephen P. Robbins
San Diego State University

Timothy A. Judge
University of Notre Dame

BUSINESS LIBRARY

Boston   Columbus   Indianapolis   New York   San Francisco
Amsterdam   Cape Town   Dubai   London   Madrid   Milan   Munich   Paris   Montréal   Toronto
Delhi   Mexico City   São Paulo   Sydney   Hong Kong   Seoul   Singapore   Taipei   Tokyo

This book is dedicated to our friends and colleagues in
The Organizational Behavior Teaching Society
who, through their teaching, research, and commitment
to the leading process, have significantly
improved the ability of students
to understand and apply OB concepts.

100747831

Vice President, Business Publishing: Donna Battista
Editor in Chief: Stephanie Wall
Senior Editor: Kris Ellis-Levy
Senior Acquisitions Editor, Global Editions: Steven Jackson
Program Management Lead: Ashley Santora
Program Manager: Sarah Holle
Assistant Project Editor, Global Editions: Paromita Banerjee
Editorial Assistant: Bernard Ollila
Vice President, Product Marketing: Maggie Moylan
Director of Marketing, Digital Services and Products: Jeanette Koskinas
Executive Product Marketing Manager: Anne Fahlgren
Field Marketing Manager: Lenny Raper
Senior Strategic Marketing Manager: Erin Gardner
Project Management Lead: Judy Leale
Project Manager: Ann Pulido

Senior Manufacturing Controller, Global Editions: Trudy Kimber
Procurement Specialist: Carol Melville
VP, Director of Digital Strategy & Assessment: Paul Gentile
Manager of Learning Applications: Paul Deluca
Digital Editor: Brian Surette
Digital Studio Manager: Diane Lombardo
Digital Studio Project Manager: Robin Lazrus
Digital Studio Project Manager: Alana Coles
Digital Studio Project Manager: Monique Lawrence
Digital Studio Project Manager: Regina DaSilva
Media Production Manager, Global Editions: Vikram Kumar
Cover Image: © Jag_cz/Shutterstock
Cover Designer: Lumina Datamatics
Full-Service Project Management: S4Carlisle Publishing Services
Composition: S4Carlisle Publishing Services

For information regarding permissions, request forms and the appropriate contacts within the Pearson Education Global Rights & Permissions department, please visit www.pearsoned.com/permissions/.

Acknowledgements of third party content appear on the appropriate page within the text, which constitutes an extension of this copyright page

Pearson Education Limited
Edinburgh Gate
Harlow
Essex CM20 2JE
England

and Associated Companies throughout the world

Visit us on the World Wide Web at: www.pearsonglobaleditions.com

© Pearson Education Limited 2016

The rights of Stephen P. Robbins and Timothy A. Judge to be identified as authors of this work have been asserted by them in accordance with the Copyright, Designs and Patents Act 1988.

Authorized adaptation from the United States edition, entitled Essentials of Organizational Behavior, 13th Edition, ISBN 978-0-13-392081-9 by Stephen P. Robbins and Timothy A. Judge, published by Pearson Education © 2016.

All rights reserved. No part of this publication may be reproduced, stored in a retrieval system, or transmitted in any form or by any means, electronic, mechanical, photocopying, recording or otherwise, without either the prior written permission of the publisher or a license permitting restricted copying in the United Kingdom issued by the Copyright Licensing Agency Ltd, Saffron House, 6–10 Kirby Street, London EC1N 8TS.

All trademarks used herein are the property of their respective owners. The use of any trademark in this text does not vest in the author or publisher any trademark ownership rights in such trademarks, nor does the use of such trademarks imply any affiliation with or endorsement of this book by such owners.

ISBN 10: 1-292-09007-3
ISBN 13: 978-1-292-09007-8

British Library Cataloguing-in-Publication Data
A catalogue record for this book is available from the British Library

10 9 8 7 6 5 4 3 2 1

Typeset in 10/12 Times LT Std by S4Carlisle Publishing Services
Printed and bound by Courier Westford in The United States of America

BRIEF CONTENTS

CONTENTS

Chapter 8

APPLIED MOTIVATION   147

PART 4 Communicating in Groups and Teams   164

Chapter 9

COMMUNICATION AT WORK   164

Chapter 10

FROM GROUPS TO TEAMS   181

PREFACE

This book was created as an alternative to the 622- or 722-page comprehensive textbook in organizational behavior (OB). It attempts to provide balanced coverage of all the key elements comprising the discipline of OB in a style that readers will find both informative and interesting. We're pleased to say that this text has achieved a wide following in short courses and executive programs as well as in traditional courses as a companion volume with experiential, skill development, case, and readings books. It is currently used at more than 500 colleges and universities in the United States, Canada, Latin America, Europe, Australia, and Asia. It's also been translated into Spanish, Portuguese, Japanese, Chinese, Dutch, Polish, Turkish, Danish, and Bahasa Indonesian.

KEY CHANGES FOR THE THIRTEENTH EDITION

- Increased content coverage was added to include updated research, relevant discussion, and new exhibits on current issues of all aspects of organizational behavior.
- Increased integration of contemporary global issues was added into topic discussions.
- A new Implications for Managers section was created to bring chapter topics together with practical applications for managers.
- New global icons have been added to indicate material with a specific international application.
- P.I.A. (Personal Inventory Assessment) new assessment tool.
- Glossary and Index are now separate sections.

MyManagementLab® Suggested Activities

For the 13th edition, the authors are excited that Pearson's MyManagementLab® has been integrated fully into the text. These new features are outlined below. Making assessment activities available online for students to complete before coming to class will allow the professor more discussion time during the class to review areas that students are having difficulty comprehending.

CHAPTER WARM-UP
Students can be assigned the Chapter Warm-up before coming to class. Assigning these questions ahead of time will ensure that students are coming to class prepared.

WATCH IT
This feature recommends a video clip that can be assigned to students for outside classroom viewing or that can be watched in the classroom. The video corresponds to the chapter material and is accompanied by multiple-choice questions that reinforce students' comprehension of the chapter content.

Personal Inventory Assessments (PIA)

Students learn better when they can connect what they are learning to their personal experience. PIA (Personal Inventory Assessments) is a collection of online exercises designed to promote self-reflection and engagement in students, enhancing their ability to connect with concepts taught in principles of management, organizational behavior, and human resource management classes. Assessments are assignable by instructors who can then track students' completions. Student results include a written explanation along with a graphic display that shows how their results compare to the class as a whole. Instructors will also have access to this graphic representation of results to promote classroom discussion

RETAINED FROM THE PREVIOUS EDITION

What do people like about this book? Surveys of users have found general agreement about the following features. Needless to say, they've all been retained in this edition.

- **Length.** Since its inception in 1984, we've tried diligently to keep this book in the range of 350 to 400 pages. Users tell us this length allows them considerable flexibility in assigning supporting materials and projects.
- **Balanced topic coverage.** Although short in length, this book continues to provide balanced coverage of all the key concepts in OB. This

includes not only traditional topics, such as personality, motivation, and leadership, but also cutting-edge issues such as emotions, diversity, negotiation, and teamwork.

- *Writing style.* This book is frequently singled out for its fluid writing style and extensive use of examples. Users regularly tell us that they find this book "conversational," "interesting," "student friendly," and "very clear and understandable."
- *Practicality.* This book has never been solely about theory. It's about *using* theory to better explain and predict the behavior of people in organizations. In each edition of this book, we have focused on making sure that readers see the link between OB theories, research, and implications for practice.
- *Absence of pedagogy.* Part of the reason we've been able to keep this book short in length is that it doesn't include review questions, cases, exercises, or similar teaching/learning aids. It continues to provide only the basic core of OB knowledge, allowing instructors the maximum flexibility in designing and shaping their courses.
- *Integration of globalization, diversity, and ethics.* The topics of globalization and cross-cultural differences, diversity, and ethics are discussed throughout this book. Rather than being presented only in separate chapters, these topics have been woven into the context of relevant issues. Users tell us they find that this integrative approach makes these topics more fully part of OB and reinforces their importance.
- *Comprehensive supplements.* Although this book may be short in length, it's not short on supplements. It comes with a complete, high-tech support package that includes a comprehensive Instructor's Manual and Test Bank, TestGenerator, and PowerPoint slides. See below for access information.

CHAPTER-BY-CHAPTER CHANGES

Chapter 1 What Is Organizational Behavior?

- New exhibit "Employment Options"
- Major new section "Enhancing Well-Being at Work"

- New research on the importance of interpersonal skills
- Updated discussion in "Challenges and Opportunities for OB" and "Responding to Economic Pressures"
- New section "Adapting to Differing Cultural and Regulatory Norms"
- New section "Implications for Managers," with how-to tips on applying the chapter to worklife

Chapter 2 Workplace Diversity

- New research on the composition and fitness of the aging workforce
- New research and discussion on the representation of gender equality at work
- New research in "Race and Ethnicity" section
- Updated/new major section "Sexual Orientation and Gender Identity"
- Major new section "Cultural Identity"
- New research in "Attracting, Selecting, Developing, and Retaining Diverse Employees"
- New section "Implications for Managers," with how-to tips on applying the chapter to worklife

Chapter 3 Attitudes

- New research on the relationship between job satisfaction and turnover
- New research in "What Are the Major Job Attitudes?" and "Are These Job Attitudes Really All That Distinct?"
- New research and discussion in "Perceived Organizational Support"
- New research and discussion in "Employee Engagement"
- New research in "Does Behavior Always Follow from Attitudes?" and "What Causes Job Satisfaction?"
- New section "Implications for Managers," with how-to tips on applying the chapter to worklife

Chapter 4 Emotions at Work

- New exhibit "Time of Day Effects on Mood of U.S. Adults as Rated from Twitter Postings"
- New exhibit "Day-of-Week Mood Effects across Four Cultures"
- New research and discussion on the role of emotions on ethical decisions

- New research on surface acting and well-being
- Major new section "Emotion Regulation"
- New research and discussion on transformational leadership and emotional display
- New research and discussion on anger and workplace outcomes
- New section "Implications for Managers," with how-to tips on applying the chapter to worklife

Chapter 5 Values and Personality

- Major new section "The Dark Triad"
- Major new section "Personality and Situations"
- New exhibit "Trait Activation Theory: Jobs in Which Certain Big Five Traits Are More Relevant"
- Major new section "Approach–Avoidance"
- New research and discussion in "Proactive Personality"
- Major revision regarding Hofstede's model of culture and its consequences
- Updated research in "The GLOBE Framework for Assessing Cultures" and new Comparison section
- Updated discussion in "Terminal Versus Instrumental Values"
- New section "Implications for Managers," with how-to tips on applying the chapter to worklife

Chapter 6 Perception and Decision Processes

- Major new section "Creativity in Organizations"
- New exhibit "Three-Stage Model of Creativity in Organizations"
- New research and discussion in "Three Ethical Decision Criteria"
- New research on the availability bias
- New research and discussion on "Escalation of Commitment"
- New research and discussion in "The Rational Model, Bounded Rationality, and Intuition"
- New section "Implications for Managers," with how-to tips on applying the chapter to worklife

Chapter 7 The Basics of Motivation

- New research on extrinsic rewards
- New research and discussion on goal pursuit and accomplishment

- New/updated section "Equity Theory/Organizational Justice"
- New section "Implications for Managers," with how-to tips on applying the chapter to worklife

Chapter 8 Applied Motivation

- Major new section "Relational Job Design"
- New research on flextime
- New research on job sharing
- New research and discussion on telecommuting
- New research on employee involvement and participative management
- New research and discussion on pay strategies
- Updated section "Merit-Based Pay"
- New research in "Bonuses" and "Profit-Sharing Plans"
- New section "Implications for Managers," with how-to tips on applying the chapter to worklife

Chapter 9 Communication at Work

- New research and discussion in "Choosing Communication Methods"
- New research and discussion in "A Cultural Guide"
- Major new section "Choice of Communication Channel"
- New exhibit "Information Richness and Communication Channels"
- Major new section "Persuasive Communication"
- New research on nonverbal communication and information security
- New section "Implications for Managers," with how-to tips on applying the chapter to worklife

Chapter 10 From Groups to Teams

- Major new section "Multiteam Systems"
- Review of research on team decision-making strategies
- New perspectives on creativity in teams
- Presents new literature on work teams in international contexts
- New section "Implications for Managers," with how-to tips on applying the chapter to worklife

Chapter 11 Key Group Concepts

- Major new section "Faultlines"

- New research and discussion in "Deviant Workplace Behavior"
- New section "Implications for Managers," with how-to tips on applying the chapter to worklife

Chapter 12 Leadership and Trust

- Major new section "Other Contingency Theories"
- New research and discussion in "Charismatic Leadership"
- New research and discussion in "Transformational Leadership"
- New research in "Authentic Leadership: Ethics and Trust"
- New/updated section "Ethical Leadership"
- Major new section "Leading for the Future: Mentoring"
- Major new section "Finding and Creating Effective Leaders"
- New section "Implications for Managers," with how-to tips on applying the chapter to worklife

Chapter 13 Power and Organizational Politics

- Major new section "How Power Affects People"
- Major new section "Mapping Your Political Career"
- New exhibit "Drawing Your Political Map"
- New section "Implications for Managers," with how-to tips on applying the chapter to worklife

Chapter 14 Conflict and Organizations

- Major new section "Types and Loci of Conflict"
- New section "Culture in Negotiations"
- New section "Gender Differences in Negotiation"
- New research and discussion in "Personality Traits in Negotiation"
- New research and discussion in "Moods/Emotions in Negotiation"
- New section "Implications for Managers," with how-to tips on applying the chapter to worklife

Chapter 15 Organization Design

- New research in the latest trends in job specialization
- New research on centralization/decentralization
- Updated information on the simple structure

- New research and discussion on downsizing and organizational strategy
- New section "Implications for Managers," with how-to tips on applying the chapter to worklife

Chapter 16 Creating and Sustaining Culture

- New research in "Culture as a Liability"
- New research in "Keeping a Culture Alive"
- New research and discussion regarding how employees learn culture through rituals and symbols
- New research in "Emphasizing Vitality and Growth"
- New research and discussion in "Global Implications"
- New section "Implications for Managers," with how-to tips on applying the chapter to worklife

Chapter 17 Managing Change

- New research in "Forces for Change"
- New research in "Work Stress and Its Management"
- New section "Implications for Managers," with how-to tips on applying the chapter to worklife

INSTRUCTOR RESOURCES

At the Instructor Resource Center, www.pearson globaleditions.com/Robbins, instructors can easily register to gain access to a variety of instructor resources available with this text in downloadable format. If assistance is needed, our dedicated technical support team is ready to help with the media supplements that accompany this text. Visit http://247 .pearsoned.com for answers to frequently asked questions and toll-free user support phone numbers.

The following supplements are available with this text:

- Instructor's Resource Manual
- Test Bank
- TestGen® Computerized Test Bank
- PowerPoint Presentation

2015 Qualitative Business Video Library

Additional videos illustrating the most important subject topics are available in MyManagementLab®, under Instructor Resources: Business Today.

CourseSmart eTextbooks*

CourseSmart is an exciting choice for students looking to save money. As an alternative to purchasing the print textbook, students can purchase an electronic version of the same content for less than the suggested list price of the print text. With a CourseSmart eTextbook, students can search the text, make notes online, print out reading assignments that incorporate lecture notes, and bookmark important passages for later review. For more information, or to purchase access to the CourseSmart eTextbook, visit www.coursesmart.com.

---

*This product may not be available in all markets. For more details, please visit www.coursesmart.co.uk or contact your local Pearson representative.

ACKNOWLEDGMENTS

We owe a debt of gratitude to all those at Pearson Education who have supported this text over the past twenty-five years and who have worked so hard on the development of this latest edition. On the editorial side, we want to thank Editor-in-Chief Stephanie Wall, Senior Editor Kris Ellis-Levy, Program Management Lead Ashley Santora, Program Manager Sarah Holle, and Editorial Assistant Bernard Ollila. On the production side, we want to thank Project Management Lead Judy Leale and Project Manager Ann Pulido. The authors would also like to acknowledge the following contributors for the hard work they did in providing content for the MyLab activities, Nicole M. Coomber, University of Maryland; Pamela DeLotell, Kaplan University; Ryan D. Lowe, University of Delaware; and Sarah Shepler, Ivy Tech Community College. The authors express their gratitude to Lori Ehrman Tinkey for her invaluable assistance in manuscript editing and preparation. Last but not least, we would like to thank the people who promote the book to the market, Executive Product Marketing Manager Anne Fahlgren, Field Marketing Manager Lenny Raper, and Senior Strategic Marketing Manager Erin Gardner. Thank you everyone for the attention you've given this book.

ABOUT THE AUTHORS

Stephen P. Robbins
Ph.D., University of Arizona

Stephen P. Robbins is professor emeritus of management at San Diego State University and the world's best-selling textbook author in the areas of both management and organizational behavior. His books are used at more than a thousand U.S. colleges and universities, have been translated into nineteen languages, and have adapted editions for Canada, Australia, South Africa, and India. Dr. Robbins is also the author of the best-selling books *The Truth About Managing People*, 2nd ed. (Financial Times/Prentice Hall, 2008) and *Decide & Conquer* (Financial Times/Prentice Hall, 2004).

In his "other life," Dr. Robbins actively participates in masters' track competitions. Since turning fifty in 1993, he's won eighteen national championships; twelve world titles; and set numerous U.S. and world age-group records at 60, 100, 200, and 400 meters. In 2005, Dr. Robbins was elected into the USA Masters' Track & Field Hall of Fame.

Timothy A. Judge
Ph.D., University of Illinois at Urbana-Champaign

Timothy A. Judge is currently the Franklin D. Schurz Professor of Management at the Mendoza College of Business, University of Notre Dame; and Visiting Professor, Division of Psychology & Language Sciences, University College London. He has held academic positions at the University of Florida, University of Iowa, Cornell University, Charles University in the Czech Republic, Comenius University in Slovakia, and University of Illinois at Urbana-Champaign. Dr. Judge's primary research interests are in (1) personality, moods, and emotions; (2) job attitudes; (3) leadership and influence behaviors; and (4) careers (person–organization fit, career success). Dr. Judge published more than 150 articles in these and other major topics in journals such as the *Academy of Management Journal* and the *Journal of Applied Psychology*. He is a fellow of several organizations, including the American Psychological Association and the Academy of Management. Among the many professional acknowledgments of his work, most recently Dr. Judge was awarded the Academy of Management Human Resources Division's Scholarly Achievement Award for 2014. Dr. Judge is a co-author of *Organizational Behavior*, 16th ed., with Stephen P. Robbins, and *Staffing Organizations*, 8th ed., with Herbert G. Heneman III. At Notre Dame, Judge teaches undergraduate and MBA classes in management skills, organizational behavior, leadership, and staffing. He is married and has three children—a daughter who is a health care social worker, a daughter who is currently studying abroad, and a son in middle school.

1
What Is Organizational Behavior?

MyManagementLab®
⭐ Improve Your Grade!

When you see this icon ⭐, visit **www.mymanagementlab.com** for activities that are applied, personalized, and offer immediate feedback.

LEARNING OBJECTIVES

After studying this chapter, you should be able to:

1. Demonstrate the importance of interpersonal skills in the workplace.
2. Define *organizational behavior* (*OB*).
3. Show the value to OB of systematic study.
4. Identify the major behavioral science disciplines that contribute to OB.
5. Demonstrate why few absolutes apply to OB.
6. Identify the challenges and opportunities managers have in applying OB concepts.
7. Compare the three levels of analysis in this text's OB model.

⭐ Chapter Warm-up

If your professor has chosen to assign this, go to **www.mymanagementlab.com** to see what you should particularly focus on and to take the Chapter 1 warm up.

You've probably made many observations about people's behavior in your life. In a way, you are already proficient at seeing some of the major themes in organizational behavior (OB). At the same time, you probably have not had the tools to make these observations systematically. This is where OB comes into play. And, as we'll learn, OB is much more than common sense, intuition, and soothsaying.

THE IMPORTANCE OF INTERPERSONAL SKILLS

Until the late 1980s, business school curricula emphasized the technical aspects of management, focusing on economics, accounting, finance, and quantitative techniques. Course work in human behavior and people skills received relatively less attention. Since then, however, business schools have realized the significant role understanding human behavior plays in determining a manager's effectiveness. As the director of leadership at MIT's Sloan School of Business stated, "M.B.A. students may get by on their technical and quantitative skills the first couple of years out of school. But soon, leadership and communication skills come to the fore in distinguishing the managers whose careers really take off."[1]

Incorporating OB principles into the workplace can yield many important organizational outcomes. For one, companies known as good places to work—such as Starbucks, Adobe Systems, Cisco, Whole Foods, Google, American Express, Amgen, Pfizer, and Marriott—have been found to generate superior financial performance.[2] Second, developing managers' interpersonal skills helps organizations attract and keep high-performing employees, which is important since outstanding employees are always in short supply and are costly to replace. Third, there are strong associations between the quality of workplace relationships and employee job satisfaction, stress, and turnover. One large survey of hundreds of workplaces and more than 200,000 respondents showed that social relationships among coworkers and supervisors were strongly related to overall job satisfaction. Positive social relationships also were associated with lower stress at work and lower intentions to quit.[3] Further research indicates that employees who relate to their managers with supportive dialogue and proactivity find that their ideas are endorsed more often, which improves workplace satisfaction.[4] Finally, increasing the OB element in organizations can foster social responsibility awareness. Accordingly, universities have begun to incorporate social entrepreneurship education into their curriculum in order to train future leaders to use interpersonal skills to address social issues within their organizations.[5] This curriculum reflects a growing awareness of the need for understanding the means and outcomes of corporate social responsibility.[6]

We understand that in today's competitive and demanding workplace, managers can't succeed on their technical skills alone. They also have to exhibit good people skills. This text has been written to help both managers and potential managers develop those people skills with the knowledge that understanding human behavior provides.

ENTER ORGANIZATIONAL BEHAVIOR

OB's goal is to understand and predict human behavior in organizations. The complexities of human behavior are not easy to predict, but neither are they random—certain fundamental consistencies underlie the behavior of all individuals.

We've made the case for the importance of people skills. But neither this text nor the discipline on which it is based is called "people skills." The term that is widely used to describe the discipline is *organizational behavior*.

Organizational behavior (often abbreviated OB) is a field of study that investigates the impact individuals, groups, and structure have on behavior within organizations, for the purpose of applying such knowledge toward improving an organization's effectiveness. That's a mouthful, so let's break it down.

Organizational behavior is a field of study, meaning that it is a distinct area of expertise with a common body of knowledge. It studies three determinants of behavior in organizations: individuals, groups, and structure. In addition, OB applies the knowledge gained about individuals, groups, and the effect of structure on behavior in order to make organizations work more effectively.

To sum up our definition, OB is the study of what people do in an organization and how their behavior affects the organization's performance. And because OB is concerned specifically with employment-related situations, it emphasizes behavior as related to concerns such as jobs, work, absenteeism, employment turnover, productivity, human performance, and management. Although debate exists about the relative importance of each, OB includes these core topics:

- Motivation
- Leader behavior and power
- Interpersonal communication
- Group structure and processes
- Attitude development and perception
- Change processes
- Conflict and negotiation
- Work design[7]

⊛ WATCH IT

If your professor assigned this, sign into **mymanagementlab.com** to watch a video titled Herman Miller: Organizational Behavior to learn more about this topic and respond to questions.

COMPLEMENTING INTUITION WITH SYSTEMATIC STUDY

Each of us is a student of behavior. Whether you've explicitly thought about it before, you've been "reading" people almost all your life, watching their actions and trying to interpret what you see or predict what people might do under different conditions. Unfortunately, the casual or commonsense approach to reading others can often lead to erroneous predictions. However, you can improve your predictive ability by supplementing intuition with a more systematic approach.

The systematic approach in this text will uncover important facts and provide a base from which to make more accurate predictions of behavior. Underlying this systematic approach is the belief that behavior is not random. Rather, we can identify fundamental consistencies underlying the behavior of all individuals and modify them to reflect individual differences.

These fundamental consistencies are very important. Why? Because they allow predictability. Behavior is generally predictable, and the *systematic study* of behavior is a means to making reasonably accurate predictions. When we use the term **systematic study**, we mean looking at relationships, attempting to attribute causes and effects, and basing our conclusions on scientific evidence—that is, on data gathered under controlled conditions, and measured and interpreted in a rigorous manner.

Evidence-based management (EBM) complements systematic study by basing managerial decisions on the best available scientific evidence. For example, we want doctors to make decisions about patient care based on the latest available evidence, and EBM argues that managers should do the same, becoming more scientific in how they think about management problems. A manager might pose a managerial question, search for the best available evidence, and apply the relevant information to the question or case at hand. You might think it difficult to argue against this (what manager would say decisions shouldn't be based on evidence?), but the vast majority of management decisions are made "on the fly," with little systematic study of available evidence.[8]

Systematic study and EBM add to **intuition**, or those "gut feelings" about what makes others (and ourselves) "tick." Of course, the things you have come to believe in an unsystematic way are not necessarily incorrect. Jack Welch (former CEO of GE) noted, "The trick, of course, is to know when to go with your gut." But if we make *all* decisions with intuition or gut instinct, we're working with incomplete information—like making an investment decision with only half the data about the potential for risk and reward.

Big Data

It is good news for the future of business that researchers, the media, and company leaders have identified the potential of data-driven management and decision making. While "big data"—the extensive use of statistical compilation and analysis—has been applied to many areas of business, increasingly it is applied to making effective decisions and managing human resources. Let's discuss the roots of this new trend in management, which began over in the marketing department of some of the first online retailers.

It's difficult to believe it now, but it was not long ago that companies treated online shopping as a virtual point-of-sale experience: shoppers could browse websites anonymously, and sales data were tracked only on what shoppers bought. Gradually, though, online retailers began to track and act upon information on customer preferences that was uniquely available through the Internet shopping experience, information far superior to data gathered in simple store transactions. This enabled them to create more targeted marketing strategies than ever before. The bookselling industry is a case in point: Before online selling, brick-and-mortar bookstores could collect data about book sales only to create projections about consumer interests and trends. With the advent of Amazon, suddenly a vast array of information about consumer preferences became available for tracking: what customers bought, what they looked at, how they navigated the site, and what they were influenced by (such as promotions, reviews, and page presentation). The challenge for Amazon then was to identify which statistics were *persistent*, giving relatively constant outcomes over time, and *predictive*, showing steady causality between certain inputs and outcomes. The company used these statistics to develop algorithms that let it forecast which books customers would like to read next. Amazon then could base its wholesale purchase decisions on the feedback customers provided, both through passive methods and through solicited recommendations for upcoming titles.

The use of big data for managerial practices is a relatively new area but one that holds convincing promise. A manager who uses data to define objectives, develop theories of causality, and test those theories can determine which employee activities are relevant to the objectives.[9] However, we're not advising that you throw your intuition, or all the business press, out the window. In dealing with people, leaders often rely on hunches, and sometimes the outcomes are excellent. Other times, human tendencies get in the way. Research findings indicate we are likely to be biased toward information that we've heard most recently, that has been frequently repeated, or that is of personal relevance. While research findings should be viewed with the same discernment as data output, the prudent use of big data, along with an understanding of human behavioral tendencies, can contribute to sound decision making and ease natural biases. What we are advising is to use evidence as much as possible to inform your intuition and experience. That is the promise of OB.

DISCIPLINES THAT CONTRIBUTE TO THE OB FIELD

Organizational behavior is an applied behavioral science built on contributions from a number of behavioral disciplines, mainly psychology and social psychology, sociology, and anthropology. Psychology's contributions have been principally at the individual or micro level of analysis, while the other disciplines have contributed to our understanding of macro concepts such as group processes and organization. Exhibit 1-1 is an overview of the major contributions to the study of organizational behavior.

Several social science disciplines contribute to OB, but none are more important than psychology.

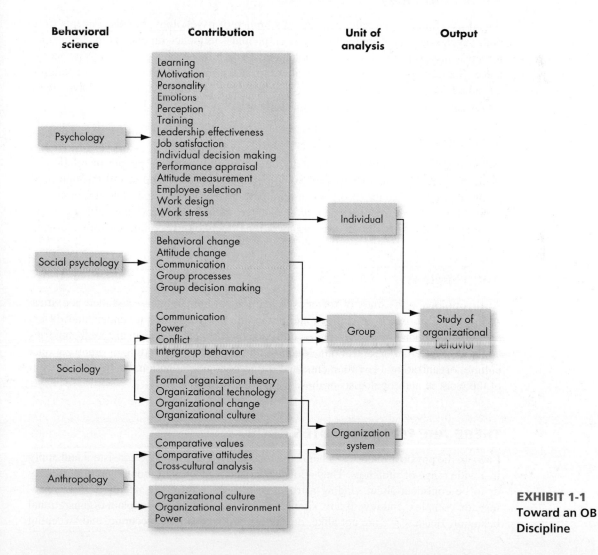

Behavioral science

Psychology

Social psychology

Sociology

Anthropology

Contribution

Learning
Motivation
Personality
Emotions
Perception
Training
Leadership effectiveness
Job satisfaction
Individual decision making
Performance appraisal
Attitude measurement
Employee selection
Work design
Work stress

Behavioral change
Attitude change
Communication
Group processes
Group decision making

Communication
Power
Conflict
Intergroup behavior

Formal organization theory
Organizational technology
Organizational change
Organizational culture

Comparative values
Comparative attitudes
Cross-cultural analysis

Organizational culture
Organizational environment
Power

Unit of analysis

Individual

Group

Organization system

Output

Study of organizational behavior

EXHIBIT 1-1
Toward an OB Discipline

Psychology

Psychology seeks to measure, explain, and sometimes change the behavior of humans and other animals. Contributors who add to the knowledge of OB are learning theorists, personality theorists, counseling psychologists, and, most important, industrial and organizational psychologists.

Early industrial/organizational psychologists studied the problems of fatigue, boredom, and other working conditions that could impede efficient work performance. More recently, their contributions have expanded to include learning, perception, personality, emotions, training, leadership effectiveness, needs and motivational forces, job satisfaction, decision-making processes, performance appraisals, attitude measurement, employee-selection techniques, work design, and job stress.

Social Psychology

Social psychology, generally considered a branch of psychology, blends concepts from both psychology and sociology to focus on peoples' influence on one another. One major study area is *change*—how to implement it and how to reduce barriers to its acceptance. Social psychologists also contribute to measuring, understanding, and changing attitudes; identifying communication patterns; and building trust. They have made important contributions to our study of group behavior, power, and conflict.

Sociology

While psychology focuses on the individual, **sociology** studies people in relation to their social environment or culture. Sociologists have contributed to OB through their study of group behavior in organizations, particularly formal and complex organizations. Perhaps most important, sociologists have studied organizational culture, formal organization theory and structure, organizational technology, communications, power, and conflict.

Anthropology

Anthropology is the study of societies to learn about human beings and their activities. Anthropologists' work on cultures and environments has helped us understand differences in fundamental values, attitudes, and behavior between people in different countries and within different organizations. Much of our current understanding of organizational culture, organizational environments, and differences among national cultures is a result of the work of anthropologists or those using their methods.

THERE ARE FEW ABSOLUTES IN OB

Laws in the physical sciences—chemistry, astronomy, physics—are consistent and apply in a wide range of situations. They allow scientists to generalize about the pull of gravity or to be confident about sending astronauts into space to repair satellites. Human beings are complex, and few, if any, simple and universal principles explain organizational behavior. Because we are not alike, our ability to make simple, accurate, and sweeping generalizations is limited. For example, not everyone is motivated by money, and people may behave differently at a religious service than they do at a party.

That doesn't mean, of course, that we can't offer reasonably accurate explanations of human behavior or make valid predictions. It does mean that OB concepts must reflect situational, or contingency, conditions. We can say x leads to y, but only under conditions specified in z—the **contingency variables**. The science of OB was developed by applying general concepts to a particular situation, person, or group. For example, OB scholars would avoid stating that everyone likes complex and challenging work (the general concept). Why? Because not everyone wants a challenging job. Some people prefer routine over varied work, or simple over complex tasks. A job attractive to one person may not be to another; its appeal is contingent on the person who holds it.

CHALLENGES AND OPPORTUNITIES FOR OB

Understanding organizational behavior has never been more important for managers. Take a quick look at the dramatic changes in organizations. The typical employee is getting older; the workforce is becoming increasingly diverse; corporate downsizing and the heavy use of temporary workers are severing the bonds of loyalty that tied many employees to their employers; and global competition requires employees to become more flexible and cope with rapid change.

As a result of these changes and others such as the rising use of technology, employment options have adapted to include new opportunities for workers. Exhibit 1-2 details some of the types of options individuals may find offered to them by organizations or for which they would like to negotiate. Under each heading in the exhibit, you will find a grouping of options from which to choose—or combine. For instance, at one point in your career you may find yourself employed full time in an office in a localized, non-union setting with a salary and bonus compensation package, while at another point you may wish to negotiate for a flex-time, virtual position and choose to work from overseas for a combination of salary and extra paid time off.

In short, today's challenges bring opportunities for managers to use OB concepts. In this section, we review some of the most critical issues confronting managers for which OB offers solutions—or at least meaningful insights toward solutions.

Responding to Economic Pressures

When the U.S. economy plunged into a deep and prolonged recession in 2008, virtually all other large economies around the world followed suit. Layoffs and job losses were widespread, and those who survived the ax were often asked to accept pay cuts. When times are bad like they were during the recession, managers are on the front lines with employees who must be fired, who are asked to make do with less, and who worry about their futures. The difference between good and bad management can be the difference between profit and loss or, ultimately, between survival and failure.

Managing employees well when times are good can be just as hard, if not harder, than when times are bad. But the OB approaches sometimes differ. In good times, understanding how to reward, satisfy, and retain employees is at a premium. In bad times, issues like stress, decision making, and coping come to the fore.

There are many reasons why it is more important than ever to learn OB concepts.

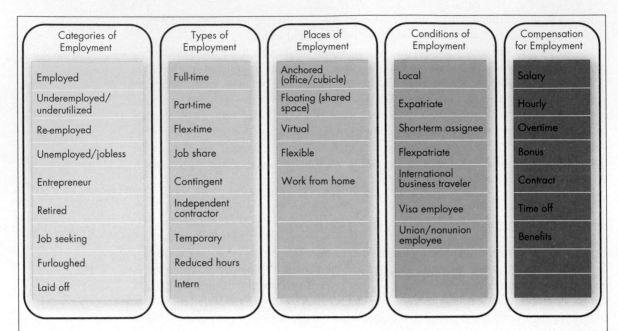

Categories of Employment	Types of Employment	Places of Employment	Conditions of Employment	Compensation for Employment
Employed	Full-time	Anchored (office/cubicle)	Local	Salary
Underemployed/ underutilized	Part-time	Floating (shared space)	Expatriate	Hourly
Re-employed	Flex-time	Virtual	Short-term assignee	Overtime
Unemployed/jobless	Job share	Flexible	Flexpatriate	Bonus
Entrepreneur	Contingent	Work from home	International business traveler	Contract
Retired	Independent contractor		Visa employee	Time off
Job seeking	Temporary		Union/nonunion employee	Benefits
Furloughed	Reduced hours			
Laid off	Intern			

Employed—working for a for-profit or nonprofit company, organization, or for an individual, either for money and/or benefits, with established expectations for performance and compensation

Underemployed/underutilized—working in a position or with responsibilities that are below one's educational or experience attainment level, or working less than full-time when one wants full-time employment

Re-employed—refers to either employees who were dismissed by a company and rehired by the same company, or to employees who left the workforce (were unemployed) and found new employment

Unemployed/jobless—currently not working; may be job seeking, either with or without government benefits/assistance, either with or without severance pay from previous job, either new to the workforce or terminated from previous employment, either short-term unemployed (months) or long-term/chronic unemployed (years)

Entrepreneur—one who runs his or her own business, either as a sole worker or as the founder of a company with employees

Retired—one who has ended his or her career in a profession, either voluntarily by choice or involuntarily by an employer's mandate

Job seeking—currently unemployed; actively looking for a job, either with or without government benefits from previous job or from disability/need, either with or without severance pay from previous job, either new to the workforce or terminated from previous employment

Furloughed—similar to a layoff; an employer-required work stoppage, temporary (weeks up to a month, usually); pay is often suspended during this time, though the person retains employment status with the company

Laid off—can be a temporary employer-required work stoppage, usually without pay, but is more often a permanent termination from the company in which the employee is recognized to be not at fault

EXHIBIT 1-2

Employment Options

Sources: J. R. Anderson Jr., et al., "Action Items: 42 Trends Affecting Benefits, Compensation, Training, Staffing and Technology," *HR Magazine* (January 2013) p. 33; M. Dewhurst, B. Hancock, and D. Ellsworth, "Redesigning Knowledge Work," *Harvard Business Review* (January–February 2013), pp. 58–64; E. Frauenheim, "Creating a New Contingent Culture," *Workforce Management* (August 2012), pp. 34–39; N. Koeppen, "State Job Aid Takes Pressure off Germany," *The Wall Street Journal* (February 1, 2013), p. A8; and M. A. Shaffer, M. L. Kraimer, Y.-P. Chen, and M. C. Bolino, "Choices, Challenges, and Career Consequences of Global Work Experiences: A Review and Future Agenda," *Journal of Management* (July 2012), pp. 1282–1327.

(continued)

Full-time—hours for full-time employment are established by companies, generally more than 30 hours per week in a set schedule, sometimes with salary pay and sometimes with hourly pay, often with a benefit package greater than that for the part-time employment category

Part-time—hours for full-time employment are established by companies, generally less than 30 hours per week in a set schedule, often with hourly pay, often with a benefit package less than that for the full-time employment category

Flex-time—an arrangement where the employee and employer create nonstandard working hours, which may be a temporary or permanent schedule; may be an expectation for a number of hours worked per week

Job share—an arrangement where two or more employees fill one job, generally by splitting the hours of a full time position that do not overlap

Contingent—the workforce of outsourced workers (including professional service firms, specialized experts, and business consultants), these employees are paid hourly or by the job and do not generally receive any company benefits and are not considered as part of the company; contingent workers may be also temporary employees or independent contractors

Independent contractor—an entrepreneur in essence, but often a specialist professional who does not aspire to create a business but who provides services or goods to a company

Temporary—individuals who may be employed directly by the organization or through an employment agency/temporary agency; their hours may be fixed per week or vary, they do not generally receive any company benefits, and are not considered as part of the company; they are employed either for a short duration or as a trial for an organization's position openings

Reduced-hours—reduction in the normal employee's work schedule by the employer, sometimes as a measure to retain employees/reduce lay-offs in economic downturns as in Germany's Kurzarbeit program, which provides government subsidies to keep workers on the job at reduced hours; employees are only paid for the time they work

Intern—short-term employment, often with an established term, designed to provide practical training to a pre-professional, either with or without pay

Anchored—an employee with an assigned office, cubicle, or desk space

Floating—an employee with a shared space workplace and no assigned working area

Virtual—an employee who works through the Internet and is not connected with any office location

Flexible—an employee who is connected with an office location but may work from anywhere

Work from home—an employee who is set up by the company to work from an office at home

Local—employees who work in one established location

Expatriate—employees who are on extended international work assignments with the expectation that they will return (repatriate) after an established term, usually a year or more; either sent by corporate request or out of self-initiated interest

Short-term assignee—employees on international assignments longer than business trips yet shorter than typical corporate expatriate assignments, usually 3 to 12 months

Flexpatriate—employees who travel for brief assignments across cultural or national borders, usually 1 to 2 months

International business traveler—employees who take multiple short international business trips for 1 to 3 weeks

Visa employee—an employee working outside of his or her country of residence who must have a work visa for employment in the current country

Union/nonunion employee—an employee who is a member of a labor union, often by trade, and subject to its protections and provisions, which then negotiates with management on certain working condition issues, or an employee who works for a nonunion facility or who sometimes elects to stay out of membership in a unionized facility

Salary—employee compensation based on a full-time workweek, where the hours are generally not kept on a time clock but where it is understood that the employee will work according to job needs

Hourly—employee compensation for each hour worked, often recorded on time sheets or by time clocks

Overtime—for hourly employees, compensation for hours worked that are greater than the standard workweek and paid at an hourly rate determined by law

Bonus—compensation in addition to standard pay, usually linked to individual or organizational performance

Contract—prenegotiated compensation for project work, usually according to a schedule as the work progresses

Time off—either paid or unpaid; negotiated time off according to the employment contract (including vacation time, sick leave, and personal days) and/or given by management as compensation for time worked

Benefits—generally stated in the employment contract or the Human Resources Employee Handbook; potentially include health insurance plans, savings plans, retirement plans, discounts, and other options available to employees at various types of employment

EXHIBIT 1-2
Employment Options (continued)

Responding to Globalization

Organizations are no longer constrained by national borders. Burger King is owned by a British firm, and McDonald's sells hamburgers in more than 100 companies in six continents. ExxonMobil, a so-called U.S. company, reported that less than 6 percent of its 2011 earnings were from gas and natural products sales in the United States. New employees at Finland-based phone maker Nokia are increasingly being recruited from India, China, and other developing countries—non-Finns now outnumber Finns at their renowned research center in Helsinki. And all major automobile makers now manufacture cars outside their borders; Honda builds cars in Ohio, Ford in Brazil, Volkswagen in Mexico, and both Mercedes and BMW in South Africa.

The world has indeed become a global village. In the process, the manager's job has changed. Effective managers will anticipate and adapt their approaches to the global issues we discuss next.

INCREASED FOREIGN ASSIGNMENTS If you're a manager, you are increasingly likely to find yourself in a foreign assignment—transferred to your employer's operating division or subsidiary in another country. Once there, you'll have to manage a workforce very different in needs, aspirations, and attitudes from those you are accustomed to back home. To be effective, you will need to understand everything you can about your new location's culture and workforce—and demonstrate your cultural sensitivity—before introducing alternate practices.

WORKING WITH PEOPLE FROM DIFFERENT CULTURES Even in your own country, you'll find yourself working with bosses, peers, and other employees born and raised in different cultures.

What motivates you may not motivate them. Or your communication style may be straightforward and open, which others may find uncomfortable and threatening. To work effectively with people from different cultures, you need to understand how their culture, geography, and religion have shaped them and how to adapt your management style to their differences.

OVERSEEING MOVEMENT OF JOBS TO COUNTRIES WITH LOW-COST LABOR It is increasingly difficult for managers in advanced nations, where minimum wages are typically $6 or more an hour, to compete against firms that rely on workers from China and other developing nations where labor is available for 30 cents an hour. In a global economy, jobs tend to flow where lower costs give businesses a comparative advantage, though labor groups, politicians, and local community leaders see the exporting of jobs as undermining the job market at home. Managers face the difficult task of balancing the interests of their organizations with their responsibilities to the communities in which they operate.

ADAPTING TO DIFFERING CULTURAL AND REGULATORY NORMS "Going global" for a business is not as simple as typing in an overseas e-mail address, shipping goods off to a foreign port, or building facilities in other countries. To be successful, managers need to know the cultural norms of the workforce in each country where they do business. For instance, in some countries a large percentage of the workforce enjoys long holidays. There will be country and local regulations to consider, too. Managers of subsidiaries abroad need to be aware of the unique financial and legal regulations applying to "guest companies" or else risk violating them. Violations can have implications for their operations in that country and also for political relations between countries. Managers also need to be cognizant of differences in regulations for competitors in that country; many times, the laws will give national companies significant financial advantages over foreign subsidiaries.

Managing Workforce Diversity

One of the most important challenges for organizations is *workforce diversity*, the concept that organizations are becoming more heterogeneous in terms of gender, age, race, ethnicity, sexual orientation, and inclusion of other diverse groups. Whereas globalization focuses on differences among people *from* different countries, workforce diversity addresses differences among people *within* given countries.

Workforce diversity acknowledges a workforce of women and men, many racial and ethnic groups, individuals with a variety of physical or psychological abilities, and people who differ in age and sexual orientation. Managing diversity is a global concern. Though we have more to say about workforce diversity later, suffice it to say here that diversity presents great opportunities and poses challenging questions for managers and employees in all countries. How can we leverage differences within groups for competitive advantage? Should we treat all employees alike? Should we recognize individual and cultural differences? How can we foster cultural awareness in employees without lapsing into stereotyped political correctness? What are the legal requirements in each country? Does diversity even matter?

Improving Customer Service

Service employees include technical support representatives, fast-food counter workers, sales clerks, nurses, automobile repair technicians, consultants, financial planners, and flight attendants. The shared characteristic of their jobs is substantial interaction with an organization's customers. OB can help managers increase the success of these interactions by showing how employee attitudes and behavior influence customer satisfaction.

Many an organization has failed because its employees failed to please customers. OB can provide considerable guidance in helping managers create customer-friendly cultures in which employees are friendly and courteous, accessible, knowledgeable, prompt in responding to customer needs, and willing to do what's necessary to please the customer.[10]

Improving People Skills

As you proceed through the chapters of this text, we'll present relevant concepts and theories that can help you explain and predict the behavior of people at work. You'll also gain insights into specific people skills you can use on the job. For instance, you'll learn ways to design motivating jobs, techniques for improving your management skills, and skills to create more effective teams.

Working in Networked Organizations

Networked organizations allow people to communicate and work together even though they may be thousands of miles apart. Independent contractors can telecommute via computer to workplaces around the globe and change employers as the demand for their services changes. Software programmers, graphic designers, systems analysts, technical writers, photo researchers, book and media editors, and medical transcribers are just a few examples of people who can work from home or other nonoffice locations.

The manager's job is different in a networked organization. Motivating and lead- ing people and making collaborative decisions online require different techniques than when individuals are physically present in a single location. As more employees do their jobs by linking to others through networks, managers must develop new skills. OB can provide valuable insights to help hone those skills.

Enhancing Employee Well-Being at Work

The typical employee in the 1960s or 1970s showed up at a specified workplace Monday through Friday and worked for clearly defined 8- or 9-hour chunks of time. That's no lon- ger true for a large segment of today's workforce as even the definition of the workplace has been expanded to include anywhere a laptop or smartphone can go. Even if employees work at home or from half a continent away, managers need to consider their well-being at work.

One of the biggest challenges to maintaining employee well-being is that organiza- tions are asking employees to put in longer hours, either in the office or online. Employees are increasingly complaining that the line between work and nonwork time has become blurred, creating personal conflicts and stress. Second, employee well-being is challenged by heavy outside commitments. Millions of single-parent households and employees with dependent parents are significantly challenged in balancing work and family responsibili- ties, for instance.

As a result of their increased responsibilities in and out of the workplace, recent studies suggest employees want jobs that give them flexibility in their work schedules so they can better manage work–life conflicts.[11] Organizations that don't help their people achieve work–life balance will find it increasingly difficult to attract and retain the most capable and motivated employees. As you'll see in later chapters, the field of OB offers a number of suggestions to guide managers in designing workplaces and jobs that can help employees reduce work–life conflicts.

Creating a Positive Work Environment

A real growth area in OB research is **positive organizational scholarship** (also called *positive organizational behavior*), which studies how organizations develop human strengths, foster vitality and resilience, and unlock potential. Researchers in this area say too much of OB research and management practice has been targeted toward identify- ing what's wrong with organizations and their employees. In response, they try to study what's *good* about them.[12] Some key independent variables in positive OB research are engagement, hope, optimism, and resilience in the face of strain.

Positive organizational scholars have studied a concept called "reflected best- self"—asking employees to think about when they were at their "personal best" in order to understand how to exploit their strengths. The idea is that we all have things at which we are unusually good, yet we too often focus on addressing our limitations and too rarely think about how to exploit our strengths.[13]

Although positive organizational scholarship does not deny the value of the negative (such as critical feedback), it does challenge researchers to look at OB through a new lens and pushes organizations to exploit employees' strengths rather than dwell on their limitations.

Improving Ethical Behavior

In an organizational world characterized by cutbacks, expectations of increasing productivity, and tough competition, it's not surprising many employees feel pressured to cut corners, break rules, and engage in other questionable practices.

Increasingly employees face **ethical dilemmas and ethical choices**, in which they are required to identify right and wrong conduct. Should they "blow the whistle" if they uncover illegal activities in their company? Do they follow orders with which they don't personally agree? Do they "play politics" to advance their career?

What constitutes ethical behavior has never been clearly defined and, in recent years, the line differentiating right from wrong has blurred. Employees see people all around them engaging in unethical practices—elected officials pad expense accounts or take bribes; corporate executives inflate profits so they can cash in lucrative stock options; and university administrators look the other way when winning coaches encourage scholarship athletes to take easy courses. When caught, these people give excuses such as "Everyone does it" or "You have to seize every advantage nowadays."

Determining the ethically correct way to behave is especially difficult in a global economy because different cultures have different perspectives on certain ethical issues.[14] Fair treatment of employees in an economic downturn varies considerably across cultures, for instance. As we'll see, perceptions of religious, ethnic, and gender diversity differ across countries. Is it any wonder employees are expressing increasing uncertainty about what is appropriate ethical behavior in their organizations?[15]

Today's manager must create an ethically healthy climate for employees where they can do their work productively with minimal ambiguity about right versus wrong behaviors. Companies that promote a strong ethical mission, encourage employees to behave with integrity, and provide strong leadership can influence employee decisions to behave ethically.[16] In upcoming chapters, we'll discuss the actions managers can take to create an ethically healthy climate and help employees sort through ambiguous situations.

COMING ATTRACTIONS: DEVELOPING AN OB MODEL

We conclude this chapter by presenting a general model that defines the field of OB and stakes out its parameters, concepts, and relationships. Through studying the model, you will have a good picture of how the topics in this text can inform your approach to management issues and opportunities.

An Overview

A **model** is an abstraction of reality, a simplified representation of some real-world phenomenon. Exhibit 1-3 presents the skeleton of our OB model. It proposes three types of variables (inputs, processes, and outcomes) at three levels of analysis (individual, group, and organizational). In the chapters to follow, we will proceed from the

**EXHIBIT 1-3
A Basic
OB Model**

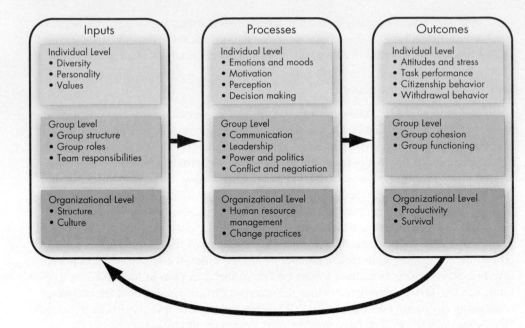

individual level (Chapters 2 through 8) to group behavior (Chapters 9 through 14) to the organizational level (Chapters 15 through 17). The model illustrates that inputs lead to processes which lead to outcomes; we will discuss these interrelationships for each level of analysis. Notice that the model also shows that outcomes can influence inputs in the future, which highlights the broad-reaching effect OB initiatives can have on an organization's future.

SUMMARY

Managers need to develop their interpersonal, or people, skills to be effective in their jobs. Organizational behavior (OB) investigates the impact that individuals, groups, and structure have on behavior within an organization, and it applies that knowledge to make organizations work more effectively.

IMPLICATIONS FOR MANAGERS

- Resist the inclination to rely on generalizations; some provide valid insights into human behavior, but many are erroneous.
- Use metrics and situational variables rather than "hunches" to explain cause-and-effect relationships.
- Work on your interpersonal skills to increase your leadership potential.
- Improve your technical skills and conceptual skills through training and staying current with organizational behavior trends like big data.
- Organizational behavior can improve your employees' work quality and productivity by showing you how to empower your employees, design and implement change programs, improve customer service, and help your employees balance work–life conflicts.

PERSONAL INVENTORY ASSESSMENT

In Personal Inventory Assessment found in MyManagementLab take assessment:
Multicultural Awareness Scale

⭐ WRITING SPACE

If your professor assigned this, sign in to **mymanagementlab.com** for the following Assisted-graded writing question:

1-1. How might managers overcome the challenges and opportunities of using OB concepts in the workplace?

2

Workplace Diversity

MyManagementLab®

✪ Improve Your Grade!

When you see this icon ✪, visit **www.mymanagementlab.com** for activities that are applied, personalized, and offer immediate feedback.

LEARNING OBJECTIVES

After studying this chapter, you should be able to:

1. Describe the two major forms of workforce diversity and give examples of how workplace discrimination undermines diversity effectiveness.
2. Identify the key biographical characteristics and describe how they are relevant to OB.
3. Define *intellectual ability* and demonstrate its relevance to OB.
4. Contrast intellectual and physical ability.
5. Describe how organizations manage diversity effectively.

✪ Chapter Warm-up

If your professor has chosen to assign this, go to **www.mymanagementlab.com** to see what you should particularly focus on and to take the Chapter 2 warm up.

Diversity in society and in organizations is complex. In this chapter, we look at how organizations work to maximize the potential contributions of a diverse workforce. We also show how demographic characteristics such as ethnicity and individual differences in the form of ability affect employee performance and satisfaction.

DIVERSITY

We aren't all the same. This is obvious enough, but managers sometimes forget they need to recognize and capitalize on differences to get the most from their employees. Effective diversity management increases an organization's access to the widest possible pool of skills, abilities, and ideas. While diversity can be a great asset, managers also need to recognize that differences among people can lead to miscommunication, misunderstanding, and conflict. In this chapter, we'll learn about how individual characteristics like age, gender, race, ethnicity, and abilities can influence employee performance. We'll also see how managers can develop awareness about these characteristics and manage a diverse workforce effectively.

Demographic Characteristics of the U.S. Workforce

In the past, OB textbooks noted that rapid change was occurring as the predominantly white, male managerial workforce gave way to a gender-balanced, multiethnic workforce. Today, that change is no longer happening: It has happened, and it is increasingly reflected in the makeup of managerial and professional jobs. In 1950, for instance, only 29.6 percent of the workforce was female.[1] By 2010, it was 46.7 percent. Women today are much more likely than ever before to be employed full time, have an advanced education, and earn wages comparable to those of men, both in the United States and abroad.[2] In addition, over the past fifty years the earnings gap between Whites and other racial and ethnic groups has decreased significantly, while differences between Whites and Asians have fluctuated.[3] By 2020, Hispanics will grow from 14.8 percent of the workforce in 2010 to 18.6 percent, blacks will increase from 11.6 to 12 percent, and Asians from 4.7 to 5.7 percent. Workers over the age of fifty-five are an increasingly large portion of the workforce as well. The 55-and-older age group, 19.5 percent of the labor force in 2010, will increase to 25.2 percent by 2020.[4] This shift toward a diverse workforce means organizations need to make diversity management a central component of their policies and practices.

A survey by the Society for Human Resources Management shows some major employer concerns and opportunities resulting from the demographic makeup of the U.S. workforce.[5] The aging of the workforce is consistently one of the most significant concerns of HR managers, along with the loss of skills resulting from the retirement of many baby boomers, increased medical costs, and the need to enhance cross-cultural understanding. Other issues include increased global competition for talent and the complexity of meeting legal HR requirements.

Levels of Diversity

Although much has been said about diversity in age, race, gender, ethnicity, religion, and disability status, experts now recognize that these demographic characteristics are just the tip of the iceberg.[6] Demographics mostly reflect **surface-level diversity**, not thoughts and feelings, and can lead employees to perceive one another through stereotypes and assumptions. However, evidence has shown that as people get to know one another, they become less concerned about demographic differences if they see themselves as sharing more important characteristics, such as personality and values, that represent **deep-level diversity**.[7]

When people first meet, they are usually perceptive of surface-level diversity characteristics, but when they get to know one another more, they become aware of deep-level diversity aspects.

To understand the difference between surface- and deep-level diversity, consider a couple of examples. Luis and Carol are managers who seem to have little in common at first glance. Luis is a young, recently hired male college graduate with a business degree, raised in a Spanish-speaking neighborhood in Miami. Carol is an older, long-tenured woman raised in rural Kansas, who started as a customer service trainee after high school and worked her way up the hierarchy. At first, these coworkers may notice their surface-level differences in education, ethnicity, regional background, and gender. However, as they get to know one another, they may find they are both deeply committed to their families, share a common way of thinking about important work problems, like to work collaboratively, and are interested in international assignments in the future. These deep-level similarities will overshadow the more superficial differences between them, and research suggests they will work well together.

As a second example, Steve and Dave are two unmarried, White, male college graduates from Oregon who recently started working together. Superficially, they seem well matched. But Steve is highly introverted, prefers to avoid risks, solicits the opinions of others before making decisions, and likes the office quiet. Dave is extroverted, risk-seeking, assertive, and likes a busy, active, and energetic work environment. Their surface-level similarity will not necessarily lead to positive interactions because they have fundamental, deep-level differences. It will be a challenge for them to collaborate regularly at work, and they'll have to make some compromises to get things done together.

Throughout this text, we will encounter differences between deep- and surface-level diversity in various contexts. Individual differences in personality and culture shape preferences for rewards, communication styles, reactions to leaders, negotiation styles, and many other aspects of behavior in organizations.

Discrimination

Although diversity presents many opportunities for organizations, effective diversity management also means working to eliminate unfair **discrimination**. To discriminate is to note a difference between things, which in itself isn't necessarily bad. Noticing one employee is more qualified than another is necessary for making hiring decisions; noticing an employee is taking on leadership responsibilities exceptionally well is necessary for making promotion decisions. Usually when we talk about discrimination, though, we mean allowing our behavior to be influenced by stereotypes about *groups* of people. Rather than looking at individual characteristics, unfair discrimination assumes everyone in a group is the same. This discrimination is often very harmful to organizations and employees.

Exhibit 2-1 provides definitions and examples of some forms of discrimination in organizations. Although many of these actions are prohibited by law, and therefore aren't part of almost any organization's official policies, the practices persist. Tens of thousands of cases of employment discrimination are documented every year, and many more incidents go unreported. As discrimination has increasingly come under both legal scrutiny and social disapproval, most overt forms have faded, which may have resulted in an increase in more covert forms like incivility or exclusion.[8]

As you can see, discrimination can occur in many ways, and its effects can be varied depending on the organizational context and the personal biases of its members. Some forms, like exclusion or incivility, are especially hard to root out because they are difficult to observe and may occur simply because the actor isn't aware of the effects of her actions. Whether intentional or not, discrimination can lead to serious negative

Type of Discrimination	Definition	Examples from Organizations
Discriminatory policies or practices	Actions taken by representatives of the organization that deny equal opportunity to perform or unequal rewards for performance.	Older workers may be targeted for layoffs because they are highly paid and have lucrative benefits.
Sexual harassment	Unwanted sexual advances and other verbal or physical conduct of a sexual nature that create a hostile or offensive work environment.	Salespeople at one company went on company-paid visits to strip clubs, brought strippers into the office to celebrate promotions, and fostered pervasive sexual rumors.
Intimidation	Overt threats or bullying directed at members of specific groups of employees.	African-American employees at some companies have found nooses hanging over their work stations.
Mockery and insults	Jokes or negative stereotypes; sometimes the result of jokes taken too far.	Arab-Americans have been asked at work whether they were carrying bombs or were members of terrorist organizations.
Exclusion	Exclusion of certain people from job opportunities, social events, discussions, or informal mentoring; can occur unintentionally.	Many women in finance claim they are assigned to marginal job roles or are given light workloads that don't lead to promotion.
Incivility	Disrespectful treatment, including behaving in an aggressive manner, interrupting the person, or ignoring varying opinions.	Female lawyers note that male attorneys frequently cut them off or do not adequately address their comments.

EXHIBIT 2-1
Forms of Discrimination

Source: J. Levitz and P. Shishkin, "More Workers Cite Age Bias after Layoffs," *Wall Street Journal* (March 11, 2009), pp. D1–D2; W. M. Bulkeley, "A Data-Storage Titan Confronts Bias Claims," *Wall Street Journal* (September 12, 2007), pp. A1, A16; D. Walker, "Incident with Noose Stirs Old Memories," *McClatchy-Tribune Business News* (June 29, 2008); D. Solis, "Racial Horror Stories Keep EEOC Busy," *Knight-Ridder Tribune Business News,* July 30, 2005, p. 1; H. Ibish and A. Stewart, *Report on Hate Crimes and Discrimination Against Arab Americans: The Post-September 11 Backlash, September 11, 2001–October 11, 2001* (Washington, DC: American-Arab Anti-Discrimination Committee, 2003); A. Raghavan, "Wall Street's Disappearing Women," *Forbes* (March 16, 2009), pp. 72–78; and L. M. Cortina, "Unseen Injustice: Incivility as Modern Discrimination in Organizations," *Academy of Management Review* 33, no. 1 (2008), pp. 55–75.

consequences for employers, including reduced productivity and organization helping or so-called citizenship behavior, negative conflicts, and increased turnover. Unfair discrimination also leaves qualified job candidates out of initial hiring and promotions. Even if an employment discrimination lawsuit is never filed, a strong business case can be made for aggressively working to eliminate unfair discrimination.

Discrimination is one of the primary factors that prevent diversity, whether the discrimination is overt or covert. On the other hand, recognizing diversity opportunities can lead to an effective diversity management program and ultimately to a better organization. *Diversity* is a broad term, and the phrase *workplace diversity* can refer to any characteristic that makes people different from one another. The following section covers some important surface-level characteristics that differentiate members of the workforce.

BIOGRAPHICAL CHARACTERISTICS

OB recognizes the factors contributing to discrimination that affect the organization.

Biographical characteristics such as age, gender, race, disability, and length of service are some of the most obvious ways employees differ. Let's begin by looking at factors that are easily definable and readily available—data that can be obtained, for the most part, from an employee's human resources (HR) file. Variations in surface-level characteristics may be the basis for discrimination against classes of employees, so it is worth knowing how closely related these surface-level characteristics actually are to important work outcomes. Many are not as important as people believe, and far more variation in work outcomes occurs *within* groups sharing biographical characteristics than between them.

Age

The relationship between age and job performance is likely to be an issue of increasing importance during the next decade for many reasons. For one, the workforce is aging worldwide; by projections, 93 percent of the growth in the labor force from 2006 to 2016 will be from workers over age fifty-four.[9] For another, U.S. legislation has, for all intents and purposes, outlawed mandatory retirement. Most workers today no longer have to retire at age seventy, and 62 percent of workers aged forty-five to sixty plan to delay retirement.[10]

Employers express mixed feelings about the older worker.[11] They see a number of positive qualities older workers bring to their jobs, such as experience, judgment, a strong work ethic, and commitment to quality. But older workers are also perceived as lacking flexibility and resisting new technology. When organizations are actively seeking individuals who are adaptable and open to change, the perceived negatives associated with age clearly hinder the initial hiring of older workers.

Now let's take a look at the evidence. What effect does age actually have on turnover, absenteeism, productivity, and satisfaction? The relationships may surprise you. Based on studies of the age–turnover relationship, the older you get, the less likely you are to quit your job.[12] This shouldn't be too surprising. As workers get older, they may have fewer alternative job opportunities because their skills may have become more specialized to certain types of work. There is also an incentive for older workers to stay in their current jobs: Longer tenure tends to provide higher wage rates, longer paid vacations, and more attractive pension benefits.

It may seem likely that age is positively correlated to absenteeism, but this isn't true. Most studies show that older employees have lower rates of avoidable absence versus younger employees and equal rates of unavoidable absence, such as sickness absence.[13] In general, the older working population is healthier than you might expect. Recent research indicates that, worldwide, older workers do not have more psychological problems or day-to-day physical health problems than younger workers.[14]

Many people believe productivity declines with age. It is often assumed that skills like speed, agility, strength, and coordination decay over time and that prolonged job boredom and lack of intellectual stimulation contribute to reduced productivity. The evidence, however, contradicts those assumptions. Reviews of the research find that age and job task performance are unrelated and that older workers are more likely to engage in organization helping behavior.[15]

Our final concern is the relationship between age and job satisfaction, where the evidence is mixed. A review of more than 800 studies found that older workers tend to be more satisfied with their work, report better relationships with coworkers, and are more committed to their employing organizations.[16] Other studies, however, have found a U-shaped relationship, meaning that job satisfaction increases up to middle age, at which point it begins to drop off. It may well be that the relationship is complex and depends on job type. When we separate the results by job type, we find that satisfaction tends to continually increase among professionals as they age, whereas it falls among nonprofessionals during middle age and then rises again in the later years. Thus an employee's enjoyment of a service-industry position or one involving manual labor may be affected by age differently than her satisfaction with a professional position.

If age has some positive and few negative effects on work effectiveness, what are the effects of discrimination against individuals on the basis of age? The indications are that age discrimination negatively affects organizational culture and overall company performance. One study of more than 8,000 employees in 128 companies found that an organizational climate favoring age discrimination was associated with lower levels of overall employee commitment to the company. This lower commitment was, in turn, related to lower levels of organizational performance.[17] Such results suggest that combating age discrimination may help achieve higher levels of organizational performance.

In sum, we can see that the surface-level characteristic of an employee's age is an unfounded basis for discrimination, and that a workforce of age-diverse employees is a benefit to an organization.

Sex

Few issues initiate more debates, misconceptions, and unsupported opinions than whether women perform as well on jobs as men do.

The best place to begin to consider this is with the recognition that few, if any, important differences between men and women affect job performance. In fact, a recent meta-analysis of job performance studies found that women scored slightly higher than men on performance measures (although, pertinent to our discussion on discrimination, men were *rated* as having higher promotion potential).[18] There are no consistent male–female differences in problem-solving ability, analytical skills, competitive drive, motivation, sociability, or learning ability.[19]

Unfortunately, stereotypic sex roles still have a detrimental effect for women. For example, while women earn 60 percent of the bachelor's degrees in the United States,[20] one recent study found that science professors still view their female undergraduate students as less competent than males with the same accomplishments and skills.[21] Research also indicates that female students are unfortunately prone to accept occupational stereotypes, and often perceive a lack of fit between themselves and traditionally male roles.[22]

In the hiring realm, research indicates that managers are still influenced by gender bias when selecting candidates for certain positions.[23] A recent study reported that once on the job, men and women may be offered a similar number of developmental experiences, but females are less likely to be assigned challenging positions by men, assignments that may help them achieve higher organizational positions.[24] Women who succeed in traditionally male domains are perceived as less likable, more hostile, and less desirable as supervisors,[25] although women at the top have been reporting that this perception can be countered by effective interpersonal skills.[26] Research also suggests that women believe sex-based discrimination is more prevalent than do male employees, and these beliefs are especially pronounced among women who work with a large proportion of men.[27]

Sex discrimination has a pervasive negative impact. Notably, women still earn less money than men for the same positions,[28] even for traditionally female positions (giving rise to the term "the glass escalator," meaning men receive faster promotions in many female-dominated occupations).[29] In a recent study, experienced managers allocated 71 percent of available pay raise funds for male employees, leaving only 29 percent for females.[30] Working mothers also face "maternal wall bias" by employers, meaning they often are not considered for new positions after they have children, and both men and women face discrimination for their family caregiving roles.[31]

Research has shown that workers who experience the worst form of overt discrimination, sexual harassment, have higher levels of psychological stress, and these feelings in turn are related to lower levels of organizational commitment and job satisfaction, and higher intentions to leave.[32] As with age discrimination, the evidence suggests that combating sex discrimination may be associated with better performance for the organization as a whole, partially since employees who are discriminated against are more likely to leave. Research continues to underline that although the reasons for employee turnover are complex, sex discrimination is detrimental to organizational performance particularly for intellectual positions, for managerial employees, in the United States, and in medium-size firms.[33]

As with the surface-level characteristic of employee age, we can see that there are many misconceptions about male and female workers. Discrimination is still an issue, but there is strong support among many organizations for a diverse workforce.

Race and Ethnicity

Race is a controversial issue in society and in organizations. We define *race* as the biological heritage people use to identify themselves; *ethnicity* is the additional set of cultural characteristics that often overlaps with race. These definitions allow each individual to define his race and ethnicity.

Race and ethnicity have been studied as they relate to employment outcomes such as hiring decisions, performance evaluations, pay, and workplace discrimination. Most research has concentrated on the differences in outcomes and attitudes between Whites and African Americans, with less study of issues relevant to Asian, Native American, and Hispanic populations. In the United States, the Bureau of the Census classifies individuals according to seven broad racial categories: American Indian and Alaska Native, Asian, Black or African American, Native Hawaiian and Other Pacific Islander, Some Other Race, White, and Two or More Races. An ethnicity distinction is also made between native English speakers and Hispanics: Hispanics can be of any race.

Let's summarize a few points from the research literature. First, in employment settings, individuals tend to slightly favor colleagues of their own race in performance evaluations, promotion decisions, and pay raises, although such differences are not found consistently, especially when highly structured methods of decision making reduce the opportunity for discrimination.[34] Second, most research shows that members of racial and ethnic minorities report higher levels of discrimination in the workplace.[35] Third, African Americans generally fare worse than Whites in employment decisions. They receive lower ratings in employment interviews, receive lower job performance ratings, are paid less, and are promoted less frequently.[36] Yet there are no statistically significant differences between African Americans and Whites in observed absence rates, applied social skills at work, or accident rates. African Americans and Hispanics also have higher turnover rates than Whites. Finally, some industries have remained less racially diverse than others. For instance, U.S. advertising and media organizations suffer a lack of racial diversity in their management ranks even though their client base is increasingly ethnically diverse.[37]

As we discussed before, discrimination—for any reason—leads to increased turnover, which is detrimental to organizational performance. While better representation of all racial groups in organizations remains a goal, recent research indicates that an individual of minority status is much less likely to leave her organization if there is a feeling of inclusiveness (a positive diversity climate).[38] Some research suggests that having a positive climate for diversity overall can also lead to increased sales, suggesting that there are organizational performance gains associated with reducing racial and ethnic discrimination.[39]

Along with age and sex discrimination, we can thus conclude that discrimination based on race/ethnicity is ungrounded and destructive to individuals and organizations. How do we move beyond racial and ethnic discrimination? The answer is in understanding one another's viewpoint. Evidence suggests that some people find interacting with other racial groups uncomfortable unless there are clear behavioral scripts to guide their behavior,[40] so creating diverse work groups focused on mutual goals could be helpful, along with developing a positive diversity climate.

Disability

With the passage of the Americans with Disabilities Act (ADA) in 1990, the representation of individuals with disabilities in the U.S. workforce rapidly increased.[41] According to the ADA, employers are required to make reasonable accommodations so their workplaces will be accessible to individuals with physical or mental disabilities. The U.S. Equal Employment Opportunity Commission (EEOC), the federal agency responsible for enforcing employment discrimination laws, classifies a person as *disabled* who has any physical or mental impairment that substantially limits one or more major life activities. Examples include missing limbs, seizure disorder, Down syndrome, deafness, schizophrenia, alcoholism, diabetes, and chronic back pain. These conditions share almost no common features, so there's no generalization about how each condition is related to employment. Some jobs obviously cannot be accommodated to some disabilities—the law and common sense recognize that a blind person could not be a bus driver, for instance. One of the most controversial aspects of the ADA is the provision that requires employers to make reasonable accommodations for people with psychiatric disabilities.[42] Due to negative employer biases, many who suffer from mental illnesses are reluctant to disclose their status, which compounds the problem.

The impact of disabilities on employment outcomes has been explored from a variety of perspectives. On the one hand, when disability status is randomly manipulated among hypothetical candidates, disabled individuals are rated as having superior personal qualities like dependability and potency.[43] Another review suggested workers with disabilities receive higher performance evaluations. However, this same review found that individuals with disabilities tend to encounter lower performance expectations and are less likely to be hired.[44] Negative employment situations are prevalent for individuals with mental disabilities, and there is some evidence to suggest mental disabilities may impair performance more than physical disabilities: Individuals with such common mental health issues as depression and anxiety are significantly more likely to be absent from work.[45]

In sum, the treatment of the disabled workforce has long been problematic, but the recognition of the talents and abilities of disabled individuals has made a difference toward reducing workplace discrimination. In addition, continuing technology and workplace advancements have greatly increased the scope of available jobs for those with all types of disabilities. Managers need to be attuned to the true requirements of employee jobs and match the skills of the individual with the requirements of the job, providing accommodations when needed for qualified disabled individuals.

Other Biographical Characteristics: Tenure, Religion, Sexual Orientation and Gender Identity, and Cultural Identity

The last set of biographical characteristics we'll look at includes tenure, religion, sexual orientation and gender identity, and cultural identity. As with the surface-level characteristics we can learn from an employee's human resources file, these biographical characteristics illustrate differences that provide opportunities for workplace diversity as long as discrimination can be overcome.

TENURE   Except for gender and racial differences, few issues are more subject to misconceptions and speculations than the impact of seniority and tenure, meaning time spent in a job, organization, or field.

Extensive reviews have been conducted of the seniority–productivity relationship.[46] If we define *seniority* as time on a particular job, evidence demonstrates a positive relationship between seniority and job productivity. So *tenure*, expressed as work experience, appears to be a good predictor of employee productivity.

The research relating tenure to absence is quite straightforward. Studies consistently show seniority to be negatively related to absenteeism.[47] Tenure is also a potent variable in explaining turnover. The longer a person is in a job, the less likely he is to quit.[48] Moreover, consistent with research suggesting past behavior is the best predictor of future behavior, evidence indicates tenure at an employee's previous job is a powerful predictor of that employee's future turnover.[49]

Research indicates tenure and job satisfaction are positively related.[50] In fact, when age and tenure are treated separately, tenure appears a more consistent and stable predictor of job satisfaction than age.

RELIGION   Not only do religious and nonreligious people question each other's belief systems; often people of different religious faiths conflict. There are few—if any—countries in which religion is a nonissue in the workplace. U.S. federal law prohibits employers from discriminating against employees based on their religion, with very few exceptions. Some other countries have similar regulations, although many have few regulations to protect individuals with minority religious viewpoints.

Perhaps the greatest religious diversity issue in the United States today revolves around Islam. There are nearly 2 million Muslims in the United States, and across the world Islam is one of the most popular religions. Yet there is evidence that people are discriminated against for their Islamic faith. For instance, research found that U.S. job applicants in Muslim-identified religious attire who applied for hypothetical retail jobs had shorter, more interpersonally negative interviews than applicants who did not wear Muslim-identified attire.[51]

Faith can be an employment issue wherever religious beliefs prohibit or encourage certain behaviors. The behavioral expectations can be informal, such as a common practice of employees leaving early on Christmas Eve. Or they may be systemic, such as the Monday to Friday workweek, which accommodates a Christian belief of not working on Sundays and a Jewish belief of not working on Saturdays. Religious individuals may also feel they have an obligation to express their beliefs in the workplace, and those who do not share those beliefs may object. Perhaps as a result of different perceptions of religion's role in the workplace, religious discrimination claims have been a growing source of discrimination claims in the United States, and an issue around the world.

SEXUAL ORIENTATION AND GENDER IDENTITY While much has changed, the full acceptance and accommodation of gay, lesbian, bisexual, and transgender employees remains a work in progress. A recent Harvard University study investigated this issue with a field experiment. The researcher sent fictitious but realistic résumés to 1,700 actual entry-level job openings. The applications were identical with one exception: Half mentioned involvement in gay organizations during college, and the other half did not. The applications without the mention received 60 percent more callbacks than the ones with it.[52] For states and municipalities that protect against discrimination based on sexual orientation, roughly as many sexual orientation discrimination claims are filed as for sex (gender) and race discrimination.[53]

Federal law does not prohibit discrimination against employees based on sexual orientation, though 21 states and more than 160 municipalities do. Recent regulatory developments suggest, however, that we may be on the cusp of change. The federal government has prohibited discrimination against government employees based on sexual orientation. The EEOC has recently held that sex-stereotyping against lesbian, gay, and bisexual individuals represents gender discrimination enforceable under the Civil Rights Act of 1964.[54] Finally, pending federal legislation against discrimination based on sexual orientation—the Employment Non-Discrimination Act (ENDA)—continues to receive more and more support in Congress.[55]

Even in the absence of federal legislation, many organizations worldwide have implemented policies and procedures protecting employees on the basis of sexual orientation.

Surveys indicate that more than 90 percent of the *Fortune* 500, for example, have policies that cover sexual orientation. As for gender identity, companies are increasingly putting in place policies to govern how their organizations treat transgender employees. In 2001, only eight companies in the *Fortune* 500 had policies on gender identity. By 2013, that number had increased to roughly half. Ken Disken, former senior vice president of defense contractor Lockheed Martin (one of the top companies in the *Fortune* 500), justified the firm's pro-tolerance policies as follows: "Lockheed Martin is committed to providing the most supportive and inclusive environment for all employees. Ensuring a positive, respectful workplace and robust set of benefits for everyone is critical to retaining employees and helping them develop to their fullest potential."[56]

Among the *Fortune* 1000, some noteworthy companies do not currently have domestic-partner benefits or nondiscrimination clauses for gay employees. These include ExxonMobil, Gannett, Goodrich, H. J. Heinz, Kohl's, Liberty Mutual, Lowe's, Nestlé, The New York Stock Exchange (NYSE), Philip Morris, RadioShack, Sherwin Williams, SYSCO, TRW, Tyson Foods, and *The Washington Post*.[57] Recently, the National Football League (NFL) acquired some unwanted publicity when it was revealed that during the NFL combine, as college players were assessed before the draft, several NFL teams inquired about players' relationships with women seemingly to ascertain the players' sexual orientation.

Thus, sexual orientation and gender identity remain individual characteristics that receive very dissimilar treatment by governments and are accepted quite differently in organizations. It is the managers' responsibility to know the policies for their organizations and to take measures to reduce discrimination.

CULTURAL IDENTITY   We have seen that people define themselves in terms of race and ethnicity, for instance. Many people carry a strong cultural identity as well, a link with the culture of family ancestry or youth that lasts a lifetime, no matter where the individual may live in the world. People choose their cultural identity, and they also choose how closely they observe the norms of that culture. Cultural norms influence the workplace, sometimes resulting in clashes. Organizations must adapt.

Workplace practices that coincided with the norms of a person's cultural identity were commonplace years ago when societies were less mobile. People looked for work near familial homes, managers thus shared the cultural identity of their employees, and organizations established holidays, observances, practices, and customs that suited the majority. Workers who struck out for other locales either looked for groups and organizations that shared their cultural identity, or they adapted their practices to the norms of their new employers. Organizations were generally not expected to accommodate each individual's preferences.

Thanks to global integration and changing labor markets, today's global companies do well to understand and respect the cultural identities of their employees, both as groups and as individuals. A U.S. company looking to do business in, say, Latin America, needs to understand that employees there expect long summer holidays. A company that requires employees to work during this culturally established break will find that resistance among employees is strong.

National labor markets are changing for many reasons, many economic. In Italy, for example, guaranteed jobs, pensions, and benefits used to be the norm. Thus, while older workers hold solid contracts providing benefits for life, the crippled economy has meant younger workers are able to find only temporary jobs despite attaining higher education levels than their parents. The financial provision that was part of the cultural identity of Italy's citizens is thus now creating a generational divide.[58]

A company seeking to be sensitive to the cultural identities of its employees should look beyond accommodating its majority groups and instead create as much of an individualized approach to practices and norms as possible. Often, managers can provide the bridge of workplace flexibility to meet both organizational goals and individual needs.

✪ WATCH IT

If your professor assigned this, sign in to **mymanagementlab.com** to watch a video titled Verizon: Diversity to learn more about this topic and respond to questions.

Ability

We've so far covered surface characteristics unlikely, on their own, to directly relate to job performance. Now we turn to deep-level abilities that *are* closely related to job performance. Contrary to what we were taught in grade school, we weren't all created equal in our abilities. Most people are to the left or the right of the median on some normally distributed ability curve. For example, regardless of how motivated you are, you may not be able to act as well as Scarlett Johansson, play basketball as well as LeBron James, or write as well as Stephen King. Of course, just because we aren't all equal in abilities does not imply that some individuals are inherently inferior. Everyone has strengths and weaknesses that make him relatively superior or inferior to others in performing certain tasks or activities. From management's standpoint, the issue is not whether people differ in terms of their abilities. They clearly do. The issue is using the knowledge that people differ to increase the likelihood an employee will perform her job well.

What does *ability* mean? As we use the term, **ability** is an individual's current capacity to perform the various tasks in a job. Overall abilities are essentially made up of two sets of factors: intellectual and physical.

INTELLECTUAL ABILITIES

Intellectual abilities are abilities needed to perform mental activities—thinking, reasoning, and problem solving. Most societies place a high value on intelligence, and for good reason. Smart people generally earn more money and attain higher levels of education. They are also more likely to emerge as leaders of groups. However, assessing and measuring intellectual ability is not always simple. People aren't consistently capable of correctly assessing their own cognitive ability.[59] IQ tests are designed to ascertain a person's general intellectual abilities, but the origins, influence factors, and testing of intelligence quotient (IQ) are controversial.[60] So, too, are popular college admission tests, such as the SAT and ACT and graduate admission tests in business (GMAT), law (LSAT), and medicine (MCAT). These testing firms don't claim their tests assess intelligence, but experts know they do.[61]

The seven most frequently cited dimensions making up intellectual abilities are number aptitude, verbal comprehension, perceptual speed, inductive reasoning, deductive reasoning, spatial visualization, and memory.[62] Exhibit 2-2 describes these dimensions.

Intelligence dimensions are positively related, so if you score high on verbal comprehension, for example, you're more likely to also score high on spatial visualization. The correlations aren't perfect, meaning people do have specific abilities that predict important work-related outcomes when considered individually.[63] However, the correlations are high enough that researchers also recognize a general factor of intelligence, **general mental ability (GMA)**. Evidence strongly supports the idea that the structures and measures of intellectual abilities generalize across cultures. Someone in Venezuela or Sudan, for instance, does not have a different set of mental abilities than a U.S. or Czech

Dimension	Description	Job Example
Number aptitude	Ability to do speedy and accurate arithmetic.	Accountant: Computing the sales tax on a set of items.
Verbal comprehension	Ability to understand what is read or heard and the relationship of words to each other.	Plant manager: Following corporate policies on hiring.
Perceptual speed	Ability to identify visual similarities and differences quickly and accurately.	Fire investigator: Identifying clues to support a charge of arson.
Inductive reasoning	Ability to identify a logical sequence in a problem and then solve the problem.	Market researcher: Forecasting demand for a product in the next time period.
Deductive reasoning	Ability to use logic and assess the implications of an argument.	Supervisor: Choosing between two different suggestions offered by employees.
Spatial visualization	Ability to imagine how an object would look if its position in space were changed.	Interior decorator: Redecorating an office.
Memory	Ability to retain and recall past experiences.	Salesperson: Remembering the names of customers.

EXHIBIT 2-2
Dimensions of Intellectual Ability

individual. There is some evidence that standard IQ scores vary to some degree across cultures, but those differences are much smaller when we take into account educational and economic differences.[64]

Jobs differ in the demands they place on intellectual abilities. The more complex a job in terms of information-processing demands, the more general intelligence and verbal abilities will be necessary to perform successfully.[65] Where employee behavior is highly routine and there are few or no opportunities to exercise discretion, a high IQ is not as important to performing well. However, that does not mean people with high IQs cannot have an impact on traditionally less complex jobs. Research consistently indicates a correlation between cognitive ability and task performance.[66]

It might surprise you that the intelligence test most widely used in hiring decisions takes only twelve minutes to complete. It's the Wonderlic Cognitive Ability Test. There are different forms of the test, but each has fifty questions and the same general construct. Here are a few questions:

- When rope is selling at $0.10 a foot, how many feet can you buy for $0.60?
- Assume the first two statements are true. Is the final one:
  1. True.
  2. False.
  3. Not certain.
     a. The boy plays baseball.
     b. All baseball players wear hats.
     c. The boy wears a hat.

The Wonderlic measures both speed (almost nobody has time to answer every question) and power (the questions get harder as you go along), so the average score is quite low—about 21 of 50. Because the Wonderlic is able to provide valid information cheaply (for $5 to $10 per applicant), more companies are using it in hiring decisions. The Factory Card & Party Outlet, with 182 stores nationwide, uses it. So do Subway, Peoples Flowers, Security Alarm, Workforce Employment Solutions, and many others. Most of these companies don't give up other hiring tools, such as application forms or interviews. Rather, they add the Wonderlic for its ability to provide valid data on applicants' intelligence levels.

While intelligence is a big help in performing a job well, it doesn't make people happier or more satisfied with their jobs. The correlation between intelligence and job satisfaction is about zero. Why? Research suggests that although intelligent people perform better and tend to have more interesting jobs, they are also more critical when evaluating their job conditions. Thus, smart people have it better, but they also expect more.[67]

PHYSICAL ABILITIES

Though the changing nature of work suggests intellectual abilities are increasingly important for many jobs, **physical abilities** have been and will remain valuable. Research on hundreds of jobs has identified nine basic abilities needed in the performance of physical tasks.[68] These are described in Exhibit 2-3. Individuals differ in the extent to which they have each of these abilities. Not surprisingly, there is also little relationship among them: a high score on one is no assurance of a high score on others. High employee performance is likely to be achieved when management has ascertained the extent to which a job requires each of the nine abilities and then ensures that employees in that job have those abilities.

Strength Factors	
1. Dynamic strength	Ability to exert muscular force repeatedly or continuously over time.
2. Trunk strength	Ability to exert muscular strength using the trunk (particularly abdominal) muscles.
3. Static strength	Ability to exert force against external objects.
4. Explosive strength	Ability to expend a maximum of energy in one or a series of explosive acts.
Flexibility Factors	
5. Extent flexibility	Ability to move the trunk and back muscles as far as possible.
6. Dynamic flexibility	Ability to make rapid, repeated flexing movements.
Other Factors	
7. Body coordination	Ability to coordinate the simultaneous actions of different parts of the body.
8. Balance	Ability to maintain equilibrium despite forces pulling off balance.
9. Stamina	Ability to continue maximum effort requiring prolonged effort over time.

EXHIBIT 2-3
Nine Basic
Physical Abilities

The Role of Disabilities

The importance of ability at work obviously creates problems when we attempt to formulate workplace policies that recognize diversity in terms of disability status. As we have noted, recognizing that individuals have different abilities that can be taken into account when making hiring decisions is not problematic. However, it is discriminatory to make blanket assumptions about people on the basis of a disability. It is also possible to make accommodations for disabilities.

IMPLEMENTING DIVERSITY MANAGEMENT STRATEGIES

A diversity management strategy is necessary to realize the potential benefits of a diverse workforce and to minimize discrimination.

Having discussed a variety of ways in which people differ, we now look at how a manager can and should manage these differences. **Diversity management** makes everyone more aware of and sensitive to the needs and differences of others. This definition highlights the fact that diversity programs include and are meant for everyone. Diversity is much more likely to be successful when we see it as everyone's business than if we believe it helps only certain groups of employees.

Attracting, Selecting, Developing, and Retaining Diverse Employees

One method of enhancing workforce diversity is to target recruiting messages to specific demographic groups underrepresented in the workforce. This means placing advertisements in publications geared toward specific demographic groups; recruiting at colleges, universities, and other institutions with significant numbers of underrepresented minorities; and forming partnerships with associations like the Society of Women Engineers or the National Minority Supplier Development Council.

Research has shown that women and minorities do have greater interest in employers that make special efforts to highlight a commitment to diversity in their recruiting materials. Diversity advertisements that fail to show women and minorities in positions of organizational leadership send a negative message about the diversity climate at an organization.[69] Of course, in order to show the pictures, organizations must have diversity in their management ranks. Some companies have been actively working toward recruiting less-represented groups. Google, for instance, has been making sure female candidates meet other women during interviews and offering family benefits that may appeal to them.[70] Etsy, an online retailer, hosts engineering classes and provides grants for aspiring women coders, then hires the best.[71] McKinsey & Co., Bain & Co., Boston Consulting Group, and Goldman Sachs Group have been actively recruiting women who left the workforce to start families by offering phase-in programs and other benefits.[72]

The selection process is one of the most important places to apply diversity efforts. Managers who hire need to value fairness and objectivity in selecting employees and focus on the productive potential of new recruits. When managers use a well-defined protocol for assessing applicant talent and the organization clearly prioritizes nondiscrimination policies, qualifications become far more important in determining who gets hired than demographic characteristics.[73]

Similarity in personality appears to affect career advancement, and those whose personality traits are similar to those of their coworkers are more likely to be promoted than those whose personalities are different.[74] There's an important qualifier to these findings: In collectivistic cultures, similarity to supervisors is more important for predicting advancement, whereas in individualistic cultures, similarity to peers is more important. Either way, managers need to create a diversity climate where individuals look beyond surface-level characteristics to find deep-level personality similarities.

Individuals who are demographically different from their coworkers may be more likely to feel low commitment and to turn over, but a positive diversity climate can be helpful. Many diversity training programs are available to employers, and research efforts are focusing on identifying the most effective initiatives. It seems that the best programs are inclusive of all employees in their design and implementation, rather than targeted to special groups of employees.[75] What we know is that a positive diversity climate should be the goal. All workers appear to prefer an organization that values diversity.

Diversity in Groups

Most contemporary workplaces require extensive work in group settings. When people work in groups, they need to establish a common way of looking at and accomplishing the major tasks, and they need to communicate with one another often. If they feel little sense of membership and cohesion in their groups, all group attributes are likely to suffer.

Does diversity hurt or help group performance? The answer is "yes." In some cases, diversity in traits can hinder team performance, whereas in others diversity can facilitate performance.[76] Whether diverse or homogeneous teams are more effective depends on the characteristic of interest. Demographic diversity (in gender, race, and ethnicity) does not appear to either hurt or help team performance in general. On the other hand, teams of individuals who are highly intelligent, conscientious, and interested in working in team settings are more effective. Thus, diversity on these variables is likely to be a bad thing—it makes little sense to try to form teams that mix in members who are lower in intelligence, lower in conscientiousness, and uninterested in teamwork. In other cases, differences can be a strength. Groups of individuals with different types of expertise and education are more effective than homogeneous groups. Similarly, a group made entirely of assertive people who want to be in charge, or a group whose members all prefer to follow the lead of others, will be less effective than a group that mixes leaders and followers.

Regardless of the composition of the group, differences can be leveraged to achieve superior performance. The most important factor is to emphasize the similarities among members.[77] Groups of diverse individuals will be much more effective if leaders can show how members have a common interest in the group's success. Evidence also shows leaders who emphasize goals and values in their leadership style are more effective in managing diverse teams.[78]

Effective Diversity Programs

Organizations use a variety of efforts to capitalize on diversity, including recruiting and selection policies, as well as training and development practices. Effective, comprehensive workforce programs encouraging diversity have three distinct components. First, they teach managers about the legal framework for equal employment opportunity and encourage fair treatment of all people regardless of their demographic characteristics. Second, they teach managers how a diverse workforce will be better able to serve a diverse market of customers and clients. Third, they foster personal development practices that bring out the skills and abilities of all workers, acknowledging how differences in perspective can be a valuable way to improve performance for everyone.[79]

Much concern about diversity has to do with fair treatment.[80] Most negative reactions to employment discrimination are based on the idea that discriminatory treatment is unfair. Regardless of race or gender, people are generally in favor of diversity-oriented programs, including affirmative action, if they believe the policies ensure everyone a fair opportunity to show their skills and abilities.

A major study of the consequences of diversity programs concluded that organizations with diversity training were not consistently more likely to have women and minorities in upper management positions than organizations that without diversity training.[81] Why might this be? Experts have long known one-shot training sessions without strategies to encourage diversity management back on the job are not likely to be very effective. Ongoing diversity strategies should include measuring the representation of women and minorities in managerial positions, and holding managers accountable for achieving more demographically diverse management teams. Researchers also suggest that diversity experiences are more likely to lead to positive adaptation for all parties if (1) the diversity experience undermines stereotypical attitudes, (2) the perceiver is motivated and able to consider a new perspective on others, (3) the perceiver engages in stereotype suppression and generative thought in response to the diversity experience, and (4) the positive experience of stereotype undermining is repeated frequently.[82] Diversity programs based on these principles are likely to be more effective than traditional classroom learning.

Organizational leaders should examine their workforce to determine whether target groups have been underutilized. If groups of employees are not proportionally represented in top management, managers should look for any hidden barriers to advancement. Managers can often improve recruiting practices, make selection systems more transparent, and provide training for those employees who have not had adequate exposure to certain material in the past. The organization should also clearly communicate its policies to employees so they can understand how and why certain practices are followed. Communications should focus as much as possible on qualifications and job performance; emphasizing certain groups as needing more assistance could well backfire. Research indicates a tailored approach will be needed for international companies. For instance, a case study of the multinational Finnish company TRANSCO found it was possible to develop a consistent global philosophy for diversity management. However, differences in legal and cultural factors across nations forced TRANSCO to develop unique policies to match the cultural and legal frameworks of each country in which it operated.[83]

SUMMARY

This chapter looked at diversity from many perspectives. We paid particular attention to three variables—biographical characteristics, ability, and diversity programs. Diversity management must be an ongoing commitment that crosses all levels of the organization. Policies to improve the climate for diversity can be effective, so long as they are designed to acknowledge all employees' perspectives.

IMPLICATIONS FOR MANAGERS

- Understand your organization's antidiscrimination policies thoroughly and share them with all employees.

- Assess and challenge your stercotype beliefs to increase your objectivity.
- Look beyond readily observable biographical characteristics and consider the individual's capabilities before making management decisions.
- Fully evaluate what accommodations a person with disabilities will need and then fine-tune the job to that person's abilities.
- Seek to understand and respect the unique biographical characteristics of each individual; a fair but individualistic approach yields the best performance.

PERSONAL INVENTORY ASSESSMENT

In Personal Inventory Assessment found in MyManagementLab take assessment: Intercultural Sensitivity Scale

⭐ WRITING SPACE

If your professor assigned this, sign in to **mymanagementlab.com** for the following Assisted-graded writing question:

2-1. How might managers maximize workplace diversity and minimize workplace discrimination?

3

Attitudes

MyManagementLab®
⭐ Improve Your Grade!

When you see this icon ⭐, visit **www.mymanagementlab.com** for activities that are applied, personalized, and offer immediate feedback.

LEARNING OBJECTIVES

After studying this chapter, you should be able to:

1. Contrast the three components of an attitude.
2. Summarize the relationship between attitudes and behavior.
3. Compare and contrast the major job attitudes.
4. Define *job satisfaction* and show how we can measure it.
5. Identify four employee responses to dissatisfaction.

⭐ Chapter Warm-up

If your professor has chosen to assign this, go to **www.mymanagementlab.com** to see what you should particularly focus on and to take the Chapter 3 warm up.

We seem to have attitudes toward everything, whether it's about our leaders, our college or university, our families, or ourselves. In this chapter, we look at attitudes, their link to behavior, and how employees' satisfaction or dissatisfaction with their jobs affects the workplace.

⭐ WATCH IT

If your professor assigned this, sign in to **mymanagementlab.com** to watch a video titled Gawker Media: Attitudes and Job Satisfaction to learn more about this topic and respond to questions.

ATTITUDES

Attitudes are evaluative statements—either favorable or unfavorable—about objects, people, or events. They reflect how we feel about something. When you say "I like my job," you are expressing your attitude about work.

Attitudes are complex. If you ask people about their attitude toward religion, Miley Cyrus, or the organization they work for, you may get a simple response, but the underlying reasons are probably complicated. In order to fully understand attitudes, we must consider their fundamental properties or components.

What Are the Main Components of Attitudes?

Typically, researchers have assumed that attitudes have three components: cognition, affect, and behavior.[1] Let's look at each.

The statement "My pay is low" is the **cognitive component** of an attitude—a description of or belief in the way things are. It sets the stage for the more critical part of an attitude—its **affective component**. Affect is the emotional or feeling segment of an attitude and is reflected in the statement "I am angry over how little I'm paid." Finally, affect is often an immediate precursor to behavior. The **behavioral component** of an attitude describes an intention to behave in a certain way toward someone or something—to continue the example, "I'm going to look for another job that pays better."

Viewing attitudes as having three components—cognition, affect, and behavior—is helpful in understanding the complexity and potential relationship between attitudes and behavior. Keep in mind that these components are closely related, and cognition and affect in particular are inseparable in many ways. For example, imagine you realized that someone has just treated you unfairly. Aren't you likely to have feelings about that, occurring virtually instantaneously with the realization? Thus, cognition and affect are intertwined.

Exhibit 3-1 illustrates how the three components of an attitude are related. In this example, an employee didn't get a promotion he thought he deserved; a coworker got it instead. The employee's attitude toward his supervisor is illustrated as follows: The employee thought he deserved the promotion (cognition), he strongly dislikes his supervisor (affect), and he has complained and taken action (behavior). Although we often think cognition causes affect, which then causes behavior, in reality these components are difficult to separate.

In organizations, attitudes are important for their behavioral component. If workers believe, for example, that supervisors, auditors, bosses, and time-and-motion engineers are all in conspiracy to make employees work harder for the same or less money, it makes sense to try to understand how these attitudes formed, how they relate to actual job behavior, and how they might be changed.

Does Behavior Always Follow from Attitudes?

Early research on attitudes assumed they were causally related to behavior—that is, the attitudes people hold determine what they do. Common sense, too, suggests a relationship. Isn't it logical that people watch television programs they like, or that employees try to avoid assignments they find distasteful?

EXHIBIT 3-1
The Components of an Attitude

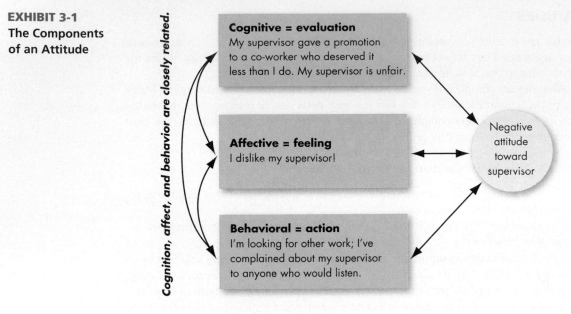

Cognition, affect, and behavior are closely related.

Cognitive = evaluation
My supervisor gave a promotion to a co-worker who deserved it less than I do. My supervisor is unfair.

Affective = feeling
I dislike my supervisor!

Behavioral = action
I'm looking for other work; I've complained about my supervisor to anyone who would listen.

Negative attitude toward supervisor

However, in the late 1960s, a review of the research challenged this assumed effect of attitudes on behavior.[2] One researcher—Leon Festinger—argued that attitudes *follow* behavior. Subsequent researchers have agreed that attitudes predict future behavior and confirmed Festinger's idea that moderating variables can strengthen the link.[3]

Did you ever notice how people change what they say so it doesn't contradict what they do? Perhaps a friend of yours consistently argued that his apartment complex was better than yours until another friend in your complex asked him to move in with him; once he moved to your complex, you noticed his attitude toward his former apartment became more critical. Festinger proposed that cases of attitude following behavior illustrate the effects of **cognitive dissonance**,[4] any incompatibility an individual might perceive between two or more attitudes or between behavior and attitudes.

Research has generally concluded that people do seek consistency among their attitudes and between their attitudes and their behavior.[5] As Festinger argued, any form of inconsistency is uncomfortable and individuals will therefore attempt to reduce it. People will seek a stable state, which is a minimum of dissonance. They either alter the attitudes or the behavior, or they develop a rationalization for the discrepancy.

No individual, of course, can completely avoid dissonance. You know texting and driving is unsafe, but you do it anyway and hope nothing bad happens. Or you give someone advice you have trouble following yourself. Festinger proposed that the desire to reduce dissonance depends on three factors, including the *importance* of the elements creating it and the degree of *influence* we believe we have over them. The third factor is the *rewards* of dissonance; high rewards accompanying high dissonance tend to reduce the tension inherent in the dissonance (the dissonance is less distressing if accompanied by something good, such as a higher pay raise than expected). Individuals will be more motivated to reduce dissonance when the attitudes are important or when they believe the dissonance is due to something they can control.

Moderating Variables

The most powerful moderators of the attitudes relationship are the *importance* of the attitude, its *correspondence to behavior*, its *accessibility*, the presence of *social pressures*, and whether a person has *direct experience* with the attitude.[6] Let's review each of these in turn.

Important attitudes reflect our fundamental values, self-interest, or identification with individuals or groups we value. These attitudes tend to show a strong relationship to our behavior.

Specific attitudes tend to predict specific behaviors, whereas general attitudes tend to predict general behaviors. For instance, asking someone about her intention to stay with an organization for the next six months is likely to better predict turnover for that person than asking her how satisfied she is with her job overall. On the other hand, overall job satisfaction would better predict a general pattern of behavior, such as whether the individual was engaged in her work or motivated to contribute to her organization.[7]

You're more likely to remember attitudes you frequently express, and attitudes that our memories can easily access are more likely to predict our behavior. Discrepancies between attitudes and behaviors tend to occur when social pressures to behave in certain ways hold exceptional power, as in most organizations. Finally, the attitude–behavior relationship is likely to be much stronger if an attitude refers to something with which we have direct personal experience.

WHAT ARE THE MAJOR JOB ATTITUDES?

We each have thousands of attitudes, but OB focuses on a very limited number of work-related attitudes that tap positive or negative evaluations employees hold about their work environments. Much of the research has looked at three attitudes: job satisfaction, job involvement, and organizational commitment.[8] Other important attitudes include perceived organizational support and employee engagement.

Individuals have many kinds of attitudes about their jobs. Of the main job attitudes, organizational commitment and job satisfaction are the most widely studied.

Job Satisfaction

When people speak of employee attitudes, they usually mean **job satisfaction**, which describes a positive feeling about a job, resulting from an evaluation of its characteristics. A person with a high level of job satisfaction holds positive feelings about his job, while a person with a low level holds negative feelings. Because OB researchers give job satisfaction high importance, we'll review this attitude in detail later.

Job Involvement

Related to job satisfaction is **job involvement**,[9] which measures the degree to which people identify psychologically with their jobs and consider their perceived performance levels important to self-worth.[10] Employees with a high level of job involvement strongly identify with and really care about the kind of work they do. Another closely related concept is **psychological empowerment**, employees' beliefs in the degree to which they influence their work environments, their competencies, the meaningfulness of their jobs, and their perceived autonomy.[11] Research suggests that empowerment initiatives need to be tailored to the culture and desired behavioral outcomes. One study of nursing managers in Singapore found that good leaders empower their employees by fostering their self-perception of competence—through involving them in decisions, making them feel their work is important, and giving them discretion to "do their own thing."[12] Another study found, however, that for teachers in India, the self-perception of competence does not affect innovative behavior.[13]

As with job satisfaction, high levels of both job involvement and psychological empowerment are positively related to citizenship behavior, discussed later in this chapter, and job performance.[14]

Organizational Commitment

An employee with **organizational commitment** identifies with a particular organization and its goals and wishes to remain a member. Most research has focused on emotional attachment to an organization and belief in its values as the "gold standard" for employee commitment.[15]

A positive relationship appears to exist between organizational commitment and job productivity, but it is a modest one.[16] A review of twenty-seven studies suggested the relationship between organizational commitment and performance is strongest for new employees and considerably weaker for more experienced employees.[17] Research indicates that employees who feel their employers fail to keep promises to them feel less committed, and these reductions in commitment, in turn, lead to lower levels of creative performance.[18] And, as with job involvement, the research evidence demonstrates negative relationships between organizational commitment and both absenteeism and turnover.[19]

Theoretical models propose that employees who are committed will be less likely to engage in work withdrawal even if they are dissatisfied because they have a sense of organizational loyalty or attachment. On the other hand, employees who are not committed, who feel less loyal to the organization, will tend to show lower levels of attendance at work across the board. Research confirms this theoretical proposition.[20] It does appear that even if employees are not currently happy with their work, they are willing to make sacrifices for the organization if they are committed enough.

Perceived Organizational Support

Perceived organizational support (POS) is the degree to which employees believe the organization values their contributions and cares about their well-being. An excellent example has been related by R&D engineer John Greene. When Greene was diagnosed with leukemia, CEO Marc Benioff and 350 fellow Salesforce.com employees covered all out-of-pocket costs for his care, staying in touch with him throughout his recovery. No doubt POS stories like this are part of the reason Salesforce.com is on *Fortune*'s 100 Best Companies to Work For list.[21]

Research shows that people perceive their organizations as supportive when rewards are deemed fair, when employees have a voice in decisions, and when they see their supervisors as supportive.[22] Employees with strong POS perceptions have been found more likely to have higher levels of citizenship behaviors, lower levels of tardiness, and better customer service.[23] This seems to hold true mainly in countries where the power distance, the degree to which people in a country accept that power in institutions and organizations is distributed unequally, is lower. In low power-distance countries like the United States, people are more likely to view work as an exchange than as a moral obligation, so employees look for reasons to feel supported by their organizations. In high power-distance countries like China, employee POS perceptions are not as based on demonstrations of fairness, support, and encouragement. POS can be a predictor anywhere on a situation-specific basis, of course. One study found POS predicted the job performance and citizenship behaviors of Chinese employees who were untraditional or low power-distance in their orientation.[24]

Employee Engagement

A relatively new concept is **employee engagement**, an individual's involvement with, satisfaction with, and enthusiasm for, the work she does. To evaluate engagement, we might ask employees whether they have access to resources and the opportunities to learn new skills, whether they feel their work is important and meaningful, and whether their interactions with coworkers and supervisors are rewarding.[25] Highly engaged employees have a passion for their work and feel a deep connection to their companies; disengaged employees have essentially checked out—putting time but not energy or attention into their work. Engagement becomes a real concern for most organizations because surveys indicate that few employees—between 17 percent and 29 percent—are highly engaged by their work.

Engagement levels determine many measurable outcomes. A study of nearly 8,000 business units in 36 companies found that units whose employees reported high-average levels of engagement achieved higher levels of customer satisfaction, were more productive, brought in higher profits, and experienced lower levels of turnover and accidents than other business units.[26] Molson Coors, for example, found that engaged employees were five times less likely to have safety incidents, and when an accident did occur it was much less serious and less costly for the engaged employee than for a disengaged one ($63 per incident versus $392). Caterpillar set out to increase employee engagement and recorded a resulting 80 percent drop in grievances and a 34 percent increase in highly satisfied customers.[27]

Such promising findings have earned employee engagement a following in business organizations and management consulting firms. However, the concept is relatively new and still generates active debate about its usefulness. Part of the reason for this is the difficulty of identifying what creates job engagement. For instance, two top reasons for job engagement that participants gave in a recent study were (1) having a good manager they enjoy working for and (2) feeling appreciated by their supervisor. Because both factors relate to work relationships, it would be easy to conclude that this proves the case for job engagement. Yet, in this same study, individuals ranked "liking and respecting my coworkers" lower on the list, below career advancement concerns.[28]

One review of the job engagement literature concluded, "The meaning of employee engagement is ambiguous among both academic researchers and among practitioners who use it in conversations with clients." Another reviewer called engagement "an umbrella term for whatever one wants it to be."[29] More recent research has set out to clarify the dimensions of employee engagement. For instance, a study in Australia found that emotional intelligence is linked to job satisfaction and well-being, and to employee engagement.[30] Another recent study suggested that engagement fluctuates partially due to daily challenge-seeking and demands.[31]

It is clear that the debate about the determinants and dimensions of job engagement are far from settled, but it is also clear that job engagement yields important organizational outcomes.

ARE THESE JOB ATTITUDES REALLY ALL THAT DISTINCT?   You might wonder whether the preceding job attitudes are really distinct. If people feel deeply engaged by their job (high job involvement), isn't it probable they like it, too (high job satisfaction)? Won't people who think their organization is supportive (high perceived organizational support) also feel committed to it (strong organizational commitment)? Evidence suggests these attitudes *are* highly related, perhaps to a troubling degree that makes one wonder whether there are useful distinctions to be made among them.

There is some distinctiveness among attitudes, but they overlap greatly for various reasons, including the employee's personality. If you as a manager know someone's level of job satisfaction, you know most of what you need to know about how that person sees the organization. Recent research suggests that managers tend to identify their employees as belonging to one of four distinct categories: enthusiastic stayers, reluctant stayers, enthusiastic leavers (planning to leave), and reluctant leavers (not planning to leave but should leave).[32]

JOB SATISFACTION

We have already discussed job satisfaction briefly. Now let's dissect the concept more carefully. How do we measure job satisfaction? What causes an employee to have a high level of job satisfaction? How do dissatisfied and satisfied employees affect an organization? Understanding the inputs and outcomes of job satisfaction is an important tool toward managing your best organizational asset, your employees.

Measuring Job Satisfaction

Our definition of **job satisfaction**—a positive feeling about a job resulting from an evaluation of its characteristics—is clearly broad. Yet that breadth is appropriate. A job is more than shuffling papers, writing programming code, waiting on customers, or driving a truck. Jobs require interacting with coworkers and bosses, following organizational rules and policies, meeting performance standards, living with less than ideal working conditions, and the like.[33] An employee's assessment of his satisfaction with the job is thus a complex summation of many discrete elements. How, then, do we measure it?

Two approaches are popular. The single global rating is a response to one question, such as "All things considered, how satisfied are you with your job?" Respondents circle a number between 1 and 5 on a scale from "highly satisfied" to "highly dissatisfied." The second method, the summation of job facets, is more sophisticated. It identifies key elements in a job such as the nature of the work, supervision, present pay, promotion opportunities, and relationships with coworkers.[34] Respondents rate these on a standardized scale, and researchers add the ratings to create an overall job satisfaction score.

Is one of these approaches superior? Intuitively, summing up responses to a number of job factors seems likely to achieve a more accurate evaluation of job satisfaction. Research, however, doesn't support the intuition.[35] This is one of those rare instances in which simplicity seems to work as well as complexity, making one method essentially as valid as the other. The best explanation is that the concept of job satisfaction is so broad, a single question captures its essence. The summation of job facets may also leave out some important facets that are encompassed in the broader question. Both methods are helpful. The single global rating method isn't very time consuming, thus freeing time for other tasks, and the summation of job facets helps managers zero in on problems and deal with them faster and more accurately.

How Satisfied Are People in Their Jobs?

Are most people satisfied with their jobs? The answer seems to be a qualified "yes" in the United States and most other developed countries. Independent studies conducted among U.S. workers over the past thirty years generally indicate more workers are satisfied with their jobs than not. Thus it shouldn't surprise you that recent research found that average job satisfaction levels were consistently high from 1972 to 2006.[36] But a caution is in order. A dramatic drop-off in average job satisfaction levels from the economic contraction began in late 2007, so that only about half of workers reported being satisfied with their jobs in 2010.[37] Early indications are that job satisfaction levels have not recovered well since then.[38]

Research shows satisfaction levels vary a lot, depending on which facet of job satisfaction you're talking about. As shown in Exhibit 3-2, people have typically been more satisfied with their jobs overall, with the work itself, and with their supervisors and coworkers than they have been with their pay and with promotion opportunities. It's not really clear why people dislike their pay and promotion possibilities more than other aspects of their jobs.[39]

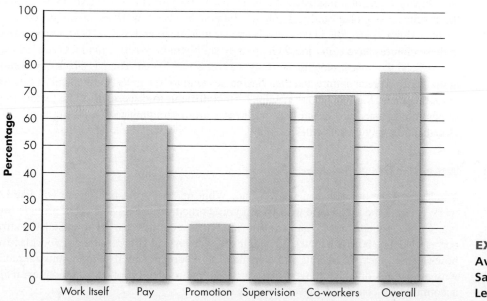

**EXHIBIT 3-2
Average Job
Satisfaction
Levels by Facet**

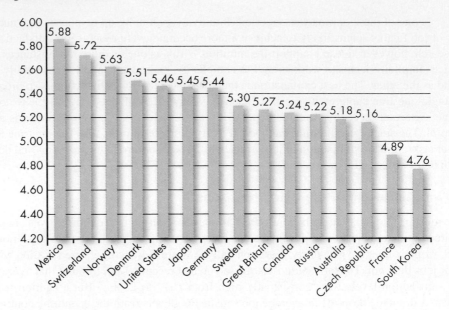

EXHIBIT 3-3
Average Levels of Employee Job Satisfaction by Country

Source: J. H. Westover, "The Impact of Comparative State-Directed Development on Working Conditions and Employee Satisfaction," *Journal of Management & Organization* (July 2012), pp. 537–554.

Although job satisfaction appears relevant across cultures, that doesn't mean there are no cultural differences in job satisfaction. Evidence suggests employees in Western cultures have higher levels of job satisfaction than those in Eastern cultures.[40] Exhibit 3-3 provides the results of a global study of job satisfaction levels of workers in fifteen countries. As the exhibit shows, the highest levels appear in Mexico and Switzerland. Do employees in these cultures have better jobs? Or are they simply more positive (and less self-critical)? Conversely, the lowest score in the study was for South Korea. There is a lack of autonomy in the South Korean culture and their businesses tend to be rigidly hierarchical in structure. Does this make for low job satisfaction?[41] It is difficult to discern all of the factors in the scores, but considering if and how businesses are responding to changes brought on by globalization may give us clues.

What Causes Job Satisfaction?

Think about the best job you've ever had. What made it so? Chances are you liked the work you did and the people with whom you worked. Interesting jobs that provide training, variety, independence, and control satisfy most employees.[42] There is also a strong correspondence between how well people enjoy the social context of their workplace and how satisfied they are overall. Interdependence, feedback, social support, and interaction with coworkers outside the workplace are strongly related to job satisfaction, even after accounting for characteristics of the work itself.[43]

You've probably noticed that pay comes up often when people discuss job satisfaction. For people who are poor or who live in poor countries, pay does correlate with job satisfaction and overall happiness. But that changes once an individual reaches a standard level of comfortable living. A meta-analysis of the research literature found little relationship between pay levels and satisfaction, and subsequent research generally concurs with this conclusion. Satisfaction does rise incrementally with pay, but the effect is very small. People who earn $80,000 are, on average, no happier with their jobs than those who earn closer to $40,000.[44] The job satisfaction—pay relationship is a complex matter of perspective. For example, recent research indicates that job satisfaction may be higher for employees who enter the workforce during lean economic times, even when they earn less pay. This higher job satisfaction appears to last throughout the individual's career, no matter what pay and economic conditions ensue.[45]

Money does motivate people, as we will discover in Chapter 6. But what motivates us is not necessarily what makes us happy. One study found that many factors other than money led to employee job satisfaction, including the nature of the work (employees whose jobs involved caregiving, and those who worked in skilled trades, were more satisfied), structural characteristics of the job (people who worked for companies with fewer than 100 employees, and people whose jobs involved supervising others, were more satisfied), and even demographics (employees were least job satisfied when in their forties).[46] Personality also plays a role. Research has shown that people who have positive **core self-evaluations (CSEs)**—who believe in their inner worth and basic competence—are more satisfied with their jobs than those with negative core self-evaluations.

THE IMPACT OF SATISFIED AND DISSATISFIED EMPLOYEES ON THE WORKPLACE

What happens when employees like their jobs, and when they dislike their jobs? One theoretical model—the exit–voice–loyalty–neglect framework—is helpful in understanding the consequences of dissatisfaction. Exhibit 3-4 illustrates the framework's four

Most employees are satisfied with their jobs; when they're not, however, a host of actions in response to the dissatisfaction might be expected.

EXHIBIT 3-4
Responses to Dissatisfaction

	Constructive	Destructive
Active	VOICE	EXIT
Passive	LOYALTY	NEGLECT

responses, which differ along two dimensions: constructive/destructive and active/passive. The responses are as follows:[47]

- *Exit.* The **exit response** directs behavior toward leaving the organization, including looking for a new position as well as resigning. To measure the effects of this response to dissatisfaction, researchers study individual terminations and *collective turnover*, the total loss to the organization of employee knowledge, skills, abilities, and other characteristics.[48]
- *Voice.* The **voice response** includes actively and constructively attempting to improve conditions, including suggesting improvements, discussing problems with superiors, and undertaking some forms of union activity.
- *Loyalty.* The **loyalty response** means passively but optimistically waiting for conditions to improve, including speaking up for the organization in the face of external criticism and trusting the organization and its management to "do the right thing."
- *Neglect.* The **neglect response** passively allows conditions to worsen and includes chronic absenteeism or lateness, reduced effort, and increased error rate.

Exit and neglect behaviors encompass our performance variables—productivity, absenteeism, and turnover. But this model expands employee response to include voice and loyalty—constructive behaviors that allow individuals to tolerate unpleasant situations or revive satisfactory working conditions. It helps us understand situations, such as we sometimes find among unionized workers. Union members often express dissatisfaction through the grievance procedure or formal contract negotiations. These voice mechanisms allow them to continue in their jobs while convincing themselves they are acting to improve the situation.

As helpful as this framework is, it's quite general. We now discuss more specific outcomes of job satisfaction and dissatisfaction in the workplace.

Job Satisfaction and Job Performance

As several studies have concluded, happy workers are more likely to be productive workers. Some researchers used to believe the relationship between job satisfaction and job performance was a myth. But a review of 300 studies suggested the correlation is quite strong.[49] As we move from the individual to the organizational level, we also find support for the satisfaction–performance relationship.[50] When we gather satisfaction and productivity data for the organization as a whole, we find organizations with more satisfied employees tend to be more effective than organizations with fewer satisfied employees.

Job Satisfaction and OCB

It seems logical to assume job satisfaction should be a major determinant of an employee's organizational citizenship behavior (known as OCB and also discussed as simply citizenship behavior).[51] Satisfied employees would seem more likely to talk positively about their organizations, help others, and go beyond the normal expectations in their jobs, perhaps because they want to reciprocate their positive experiences. Consistent with this thinking, evidence suggests job satisfaction *is* moderately correlated with OCB; people who are more satisfied with their jobs are more likely to engage in OCB.[52] Why? Fairness perceptions help explain the relationship.[53] Individuals who feel their coworkers support them are more likely to engage in helpful behaviors, whereas those who have antagonistic relationships with coworkers are less likely to do so.[54] Individuals with certain personality traits are also more satisfied with their work, which in turn leads them to engage in more OCB.[55] Finally, research shows that when people are in a good mood, they are more likely to engage in OCB.[56]

Job Satisfaction and Customer Satisfaction

As we noted in Chapter 1, employees in service jobs often interact with customers. Because service organization managers should be concerned with pleasing customers, it is reasonable to ask, Is employee satisfaction related to positive customer outcomes? For frontline employees who have regular customer contact, the answer is "yes." Satisfied employees appear to increase customer satisfaction and loyalty.[57]

A number of companies are acting on this evidence. The first core value of online retailer Zappos, "Deliver WOW through service," seems fairly obvious, but the way in which Zappos delivers exceptional customer service is not clearly prescribed. Zappos employees are directed to "create fun and a little weirdness" and are given unusual discretion in making customers satisfied. Zappos is so committed to finding only customer service employees who are satisfied with the job that it offers a $2,000 bribe to quit the company after training.[58]

Job Satisfaction and Absenteeism

We find a consistent negative relationship between satisfaction and absenteeism, but the relationship is moderate to weak.[59] While it certainly makes sense that dissatisfied employees are more likely to miss work, other factors affect the relationship. Organizations that provide liberal sick leave benefits are encouraging all their employees—including those who are highly satisfied—to take days off. You can find work satisfying yet still want to enjoy a 3-day weekend if the extra break comes free with no penalties. When numerous alternative jobs are available, dissatisfied employees have high absence rates, but when there are few alternatives, dissatisfied employees have the same (low) rate of absence as satisfied employees.[60]

Job Satisfaction and Turnover

The relationship between job satisfaction and turnover is stronger than between satisfaction and absenteeism.[61] Recent research suggests that managers looking to determine who might be likely to leave should focus on employees' job satisfaction levels over time, because levels do change. A pattern of lowered job satisfaction is a predictor of possible intent to leave. Job satisfaction has an environmental connection too. If the climate within an employee's immediate workplace is one of low job satisfaction, there will be a "contagion effect." This research suggests managers should consider the job satisfaction patterns of coworkers when assigning new workers to a new area.[62]

The satisfaction–turnover relationship also is affected by alternative job prospects. If an employee is presented with an unsolicited job offer, job dissatisfaction is less predictive of turnover because the employee is more likely leaving in response to "pull" (the lure of the other job) than "push" (the unattractiveness of the current job). Similarly, job dissatisfaction is more likely to translate into turnover when employment opportunities are plentiful because employees perceive that it is easy to move. Also, when employees have high "human capital" (high education, high ability), job dissatisfaction is more likely to translate into turnover because they have, or perceive, many available alternatives.[63] Finally, employees' embeddedness in their jobs and communities can help lower the probability of turnover, particularly in collectivist cultures.[64] Embedded employees seem less likely to want to consider alternative job prospects.

Job Satisfaction and Workplace Deviance

Job dissatisfaction and antagonistic relationships with coworkers predict a variety of behaviors organizations find undesirable, including unionization attempts, substance abuse, stealing at work, undue socializing, and tardiness. Researchers argue these behaviors are indicators of a broader syndrome called *deviant behavior in the workplace* (or *counterproductive behavior* or *employee withdrawal*).[65] If employees don't like their work environment, they'll respond somehow, though it is not always easy to forecast exactly *how*. One worker might quit. Another might use work time to surf the Internet or take work supplies home for personal use. In short, workers who don't like their jobs "get even" in various ways. Because those ways can be quite creative, controlling only one behavior such as with an absence policy leaves the root cause untouched. To effectively control the undesirable consequences of job dissatisfaction, employers should attack the source of the problem—the dissatisfaction—rather than try to control the different responses.

Managers Often "Don't Get It"

Given the evidence we've just reviewed, it should come as no surprise that job satisfaction can affect the bottom line. One study by a management consulting firm separated large organizations into high morale (more than 70 percent of employees expressed overall job satisfaction) and medium or low morale (fewer than 70 percent). The stock prices of companies in the high-morale group grew 19.4 percent, compared with 10 percent for the medium- or low-morale group. Despite these results, many managers are unconcerned about employee job satisfaction. Still others overestimate how satisfied employees are with their jobs, so they don't think there's a problem when there is. In one study of 262 large employers, 86 percent of senior managers believed their organization treated its employees well, but only 55 percent of employees agreed. Another study found 55 percent of managers thought morale was good in their organization, compared to only 38 percent of employees.[66]

Regular surveys can reduce gaps between what managers *think* employees feel and what they *really* feel. This can impact the bottom line in small franchise sites as well as large companies. For instance, Jonathan McDaniel, manager of a KFC restaurant in Houston, surveyed his employees every three months. Some results led him to make changes, such as giving employees greater say about which workdays they have off. However, McDaniel believed the process itself was valuable. "They really love giving their opinions," he said. "That's the most important part of it—that they have a voice and that they're heard." Surveys are no panacea, but if job attitudes are as important as we believe, organizations need to find out how job attitudes can be improved.[67]

SUMMARY

Managers should be interested in their employees' attitudes because attitudes give warnings of potential problems and influence behavior. Creating a satisfied workforce is hardly a guarantee of successful organizational performance, but evidence strongly suggests that whatever managers can do to improve employee attitudes will likely result in positive outcomes including greater organizational effectiveness, higher customer satisfaction, and increased profits.

Job satisfaction is related to organizational effectiveness—a large study found that business units whose employees had high-average levels of engagement had higher levels of customer satisfaction and lower levels of turnover and accidents. All else equal, it clearly behooves organizations to have a satisfied workforce.

IMPLICATIONS FOR MANAGERS

- Pay attention to your employees' job satisfaction levels as determinants of their performance, turnover, absenteeism, and withdrawal behaviors.
- Measure employee job attitudes objectively and at regular intervals in order to determine how employees are reacting to their work.
- To raise employee satisfaction, evaluate the fit between the employee's work interests and the intrinsic parts of the job to create work that is challenging and interesting to the individual.
- Consider the fact that high pay alone is unlikely to create a satisfying work environment.

PERSONAL INVENTORY ASSESSMENT

In Personal Inventory Assessment found in MyManagementLab take assessment: Core Self Evaluation Scale

⭐ WRITING SPACE

If your professor assigned this, sign in to **mymanagementlab.com** for the following Assisted-graded writing question:

3-1. What outcomes do job satisfaction influence? What implication does this have for management?

4

Emotions at Work

MyManagementLab®
✪ Improve Your Grade!
When you see this icon ✪, visit **www.mymanagementlab.com** for activities that are applied, personalized, and offer immediate feedback.

LEARNING OBJECTIVES

After studying this chapter, you should be able to:

1. Differentiate between emotions and moods.
2. Discuss whether emotions are rational and what functions they serve.
3. Describe the validity of potential sources of emotions and moods.
4. Show the impact emotional labor has on employees.
5. Describe affective events theory and its applications.
6. Contrast the evidence for and against the existence of emotional intelligence.
7. Identify strategies for emotion regulation and their likely effects.
8. Apply concepts about emotions and moods to specific OB issues.

✪ Chapter Warm-up
If your professor has chosen to assign this, go to **www.mymanagementlab.com** to see what you should particularly focus on and to take the Chapter 4 warm up.

G iven the obvious role emotions play in our lives, it might surprise you that the field of OB has not given the topic of emotions much attention.[1] Why? Generally, because emotions in the workplace were historically thought to be detrimental. Both managers and researchers rarely viewed emotions as constructive or contributing to performance. Although managers knew emotions were an inseparable part of everyday life, they tried to create organizations that were emotion-free. Researchers tended to focus on strong negative emotions—especially anger—that interfered with an employee's ability to work effectively.

Thankfully, this thinking is changing. Certainly some emotions, particularly exhibited at the wrong time, can hinder performance. Other emotions are neutral, and some are constructive. Employees bring their emotions to work every day, so no study of OB would be comprehensive without considering their role in workplace behavior.

WHAT ARE EMOTIONS AND MOODS?

In our analysis, we'll need three terms that are closely intertwined: *affect, emotions,* and *moods.*

Affect is a generic term that covers a broad range of feelings people experience, including both emotions and moods.[2] **Emotions** are intense feelings directed at someone or something.[3] **Moods** are less intense feelings than emotions that often arise without a specific event acting as a stimulus.[4] Exhibit 4-1 shows the relationships among affect, emotions, and moods.

First, as the exhibit shows, *affect* is a broad term that encompasses emotions and moods. Second, there are differences between emotions and moods. Emotions are more likely to be caused by a specific event, and emotions are more fleeting than moods. Also, some researchers speculate that emotions may be more action-oriented—they may lead us to some immediate action—while moods may be more cognitive, meaning they may cause us to think or brood for a while.[5] Finally, as the exhibit shows, emotions and moods are closely connected and can influence each other. A specific emotion may lead to a generally bad or good mood, and moods can influence how particular events stimulate specific emotions.

Affect, emotions, and moods are separable in theory; in practice the distinction isn't always crystal clear. When we review the OB topics on emotions and moods, you

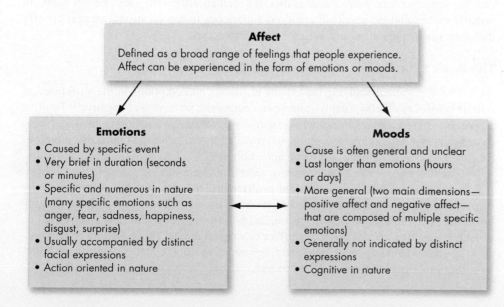

Affect
Defined as a broad range of feelings that people experience. Affect can be experienced in the form of emotions or moods.

Emotions
- Caused by specific event
- Very brief in duration (seconds or minutes)
- Specific and numerous in nature (many specific emotions such as anger, fear, sadness, happiness, disgust, surprise)
- Usually accompanied by distinct facial expressions
- Action oriented in nature

Moods
- Cause is often general and unclear
- Last longer than emotions (hours or days)
- More general (two main dimensions— positive affect and negative affect— that are composed of multiple specific emotions)
- Generally not indicated by distinct expressions
- Cognitive in nature

EXHIBIT 4-1
Affect, Emotions, and Moods

may see more information about emotions in one area and about moods in another. This is simply the state of the research. Let's start with a review of the basic emotions.

The Basic Emotions

How many emotions are there? There are dozens, including anger, contempt, enthusiasm, envy, fear, frustration, disappointment, embarrassment, disgust, happiness, hate, hope, jealousy, joy, love, pride, surprise, and sadness. Numerous researchers have tried to limit them to a fundamental set.[6] But some scholars argue that it makes no sense to think in terms of "basic" emotions because even emotions we rarely experience, such as shock, can have a powerful effect on us.[7]

Psychologists have tried to identify the basic emotions by studying facial expressions but have found the process difficult.[8] One problem is that some emotions are too complex to be easily represented on our faces. Cultures also have norms that govern emotional expression, so the way we *experience* an emotion isn't always the same as the way we *show* it. People in the United States and the Middle East recognize a smile as indicating happiness, for example, but in the Middle East a smile is more likely to be seen as a sign of sexual attraction, so women have learned not to smile at men. In collectivist countries, people are more likely to believe another's emotional displays have something to do with the relationship between them, while people in individualistic cultures don't think others' emotional expressions are directed at them.

It's unlikely that psychologists or philosophers will ever completely agree on a set of basic emotions, or even on whether there is such a thing. Still, many researchers agree on six essentially universal emotions—anger, fear, sadness, happiness, disgust, and surprise.[9] Some even plot them along a continuum: happiness—surprise—fear—sadness—anger—disgust.[10] The closer two emotions are to each other on this continuum, the more likely people will confuse them. We sometimes mistake happiness for surprise, but rarely do we confuse happiness and disgust.

Emotions can be fleeting, but moods can endure . . . quite a while. Because moods can last longer and be more durable, they are studied differently than are emotions. In order to understand the impact of emotions and moods in organizations, we next classify the many distinct emotions into broader mood categories.

The Basic Moods: Positive and Negative Affect

As a first step toward studying the effects of moods and emotions in the workplace, it will be helpful to classify emotions into two categories: positive and negative.[11] Positive emotions—such as joy and gratitude—express a favorable evaluation or feeling. Negative emotions—such as anger or guilt—express the opposite. Keep in mind that emotions can't be neutral. Being neutral is being nonemotional.[12]

The two categories of emotions now represent overall mood states, known as positive and negative affect. We can think of **positive affect** as a mood dimension consisting of positive emotions such as excitement, enthusiasm, and elation at the high end (high positive affect), and boredom, depression, and fatigue at the low end (low positive affect, or lack of positive affect). **Negative affect** is a mood dimension consisting of nervousness, stress, and anxiety at the high end (high negative affect), and contentedness, calmness, and serenity at the low end (low negative affect, or lack of negative affect).

Experiencing Moods and Emotions

As if it weren't complex enough to consider the many distinct emotions and moods a person can identify, the reality is that we all experience moods and emotions differently. Our broader categorizations (positive and negative) can thus be helpful in finding commonalities. For most people, for instance, positive moods are somewhat more common than negative moods. Indeed, research finds a **positivity offset**, meaning that at zero input (when nothing in particular is going on), most individuals experience a mildly positive mood.[13] This appears to be true for employees in a wide range of job settings. One study of customer-service representatives in a British call center revealed that people reported experiencing positive moods 58 percent of the time.[14] Another research finding is that negative emotions are likely to become negative moods. Perhaps this happens because people think about events that created strong negative emotions five times as long as they do about events that created strong positive ones.[15]

Does the degree to which people experience positive and negative emotions vary across cultures? Yes. In China, people report experiencing fewer positive and negative emotions than people in other cultures, and the emotions they experience are less intense. Compared with Mainland Chinese, Taiwanese are more like U.S. workers in their experience of emotions: in one study, they reported more positive and fewer negative emotions than their Chinese counterparts.[16] This isn't because people of different cultures are inherently different: People in most cultures appear to have certain positive and negative emotions in common, and people interpret negative and positive emotions in much the same way worldwide. We all view negative emotions such as hate, terror, and rage as dangerous and destructive, and we desire positive emotions such as joy, love, and happiness. However, an individual's experience of emotions appears to be culturally shaped. Some cultures value certain emotions more than others, which leads individuals to change their perspective on experiencing those emotions. There is much to be learned in exploring the value differences. For instance, U.S. culture values enthusiasm, while the Chinese consider negative emotions—while not always pleasant—as potentially more useful and constructive than do people in the United States.

In this value, the Chinese may be right. Recent research has suggested that negative affect has many benefits. Visualizing the worst-case scenario often allows people to accept present circumstances and cope, for instance.[17] Negative affect can allow managers to think more critically and fairly, other research indicates.[18]

Now that we've identified the basic emotions, the basic moods, and our experience of them, we will next explore the function of emotions and moods, particularly in the workplace.

THE FUNCTION OF EMOTIONS AND MOODS

In some ways, emotions are a mystery. What function do they serve? As we discussed, researchers and managers determined for many years that emotions serve no purpose in the workplace. Psychologists have always said otherwise, insisting that emotions serve a function in any human situation. Organizational behaviorists have been finding that emotions can be critical to an effectively functioning workplace. Let's discuss two critical areas—rationality and ethicality—in which emotions can enhance performance.

Do Emotions Make Us Irrational?

How often have you heard someone say, "Oh, you're just being emotional"? You might have been offended. Observations like this suggest that rationality and emotion are in conflict and that if you exhibit emotion, you are likely to act irrationally. The perceived association between emotionality and irrationality is so strong that some researchers argue that displaying emotions such as sadness to the point of crying is toxic to a career and we should leave the room rather than allow others to witness it.[19] This perspective suggests the demonstration or even experience of emotions can make us weak, brittle, or irrational. However, this is wrong.

Research is increasingly indicating that emotions are critical to rational thinking. Brain injury studies in particular suggest we must have the ability to experience emotions to be rational. Why? Because our emotions provide a context for how we understand the world around us. For instance, a recent study indicated that individuals in a negative mood are better able to discern truthful information than people in a happy mood.[20] Therefore, if we have a concern about someone telling the truth, shouldn't we conduct an inquiry while we are actively concerned, rather than wait until we cheer up? There may be benefits to this, or maybe not, depending on all the factors including the range of our emotions. The keys are to acknowledge the effect that emotions and moods are having on us, and to not discount our emotional responses as irrational or invalid.

Do Emotions Make Us Ethical?

A growing body of research has begun to examine the relationship between emotions and moral attitudes.[21] It was previously believed that, like decision making in general, most ethical decision making was based on higher-order cognitive processes, but research on moral emotions increasingly questions this perspective. Examples of moral emotions include sympathy for the suffering of others, guilt about our own immoral behavior, anger about injustice done to others, contempt for those who behave unethically, and disgust at violations of moral norms. Numerous studies suggest that moral judgments are largely based on feelings rather than on cognition. However, we tend to see our moral boundaries as logical and reasonable, not as emotional. We therefore must be careful to objectively analyze our ethical decisions.

When we study emotions and moods in relation to ethics and organizational behavior, it is tempting to focus on the categorization and work outcome aspects, which might lead us to some useful conclusions for managers. However, the sources of emotions and moods should not be overlooked, because when we identify sources, we are better able to predict behavior and manage people well.

SOURCES OF EMOTIONS AND MOODS

Have you ever said, "I got up on the wrong side of the bed today"? Have you ever snapped at a coworker or family member for no particular reason? If you have, you probably wonder where emotions and moods come from. Here we discuss some of the primary influences.

Potential Influences on Moods and Emotions

PERSONALITY   Moods and emotions have a personality trait component: Most people have built-in tendencies to experience certain moods and emotions more frequently than others do. People also experience the same emotions with different intensities, which is called **affect intensity**.[22] Affectively intense people experience both positive and negative emotions more deeply: when they're sad, they're really sad, and when they're happy, they're really happy.

TIME OF THE DAY   People vary in their moods by the time of day. However, research suggests most of us actually follow the same pattern, and the nature of this pattern may surprise you. Exhibit 4-2 illustrates moods analyzed from 509 million Twitter messages posted by 2.4 million individuals across 84 countries.[23] As you can see, levels of positive affect are the greatest in the evening, and the lowest in the early morning, on most days of the week. Levels of negative affect are also the highest in the overnight hours, but the lowest point is later in the morning than for positive affect.

DAY OF THE WEEK   Are people in their best moods on the weekends? In most cultures that is true—for example, U.S. adults tend to experience their highest positive affect on Friday, Saturday, and Sunday, and their lowest on Monday.[24] As shown in Exhibit 4-3, the trend tends to be true in several other cultures as well.

WEATHER   Many people believe their mood is tied to the weather. However, a fairly large and detailed body of evidence conducted by multiple researchers suggests weather has little effect on mood, at least for most people.[25] **Illusory correlation**, which occurs when we associate two events that in reality have no connection, explains why people tend to *think* nice weather improves their mood.

STRESS   As you might imagine, stressful events at work (a nasty e-mail, an impending deadline, the loss of a big sale, a reprimand from the boss) negatively affect moods. The effects of stress also build over time. Mounting levels of stress can worsen our moods, and we experience more negative emotions. Although sometimes we thrive on stress, most of us find stress takes a toll on our mood.

SOCIAL ACTIVITIES   For most people, social activities increase positive moods and have little effect on negative moods. The type of social interaction does appear to matter. Research suggests activities that are physical (skiing or hiking with friends), informal (going to a party), or epicurean (eating with others) are more strongly associated with increases in positive mood than events that are formal (attending a meeting) or sedentary (watching TV with friends).[26]

SLEEP   Sleep quality affects mood, and increased fatigue puts workers at health risks of disease, injury, and depression.[27] According to one study, poor sleep impairs job satisfaction because people feel fatigued, irritable, and less alert.[28] This is a big problem, since according to researchers and public health specialists, 41 million U.S. workers are able to sleep less than six hours per night.

EXHIBIT 4-2
Time-of-Day Effects on Mood of U.S. Adults as Rated from Twitter Postings

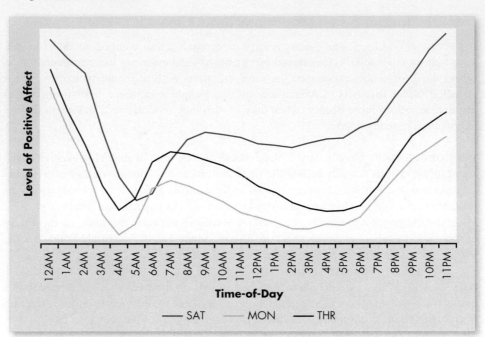

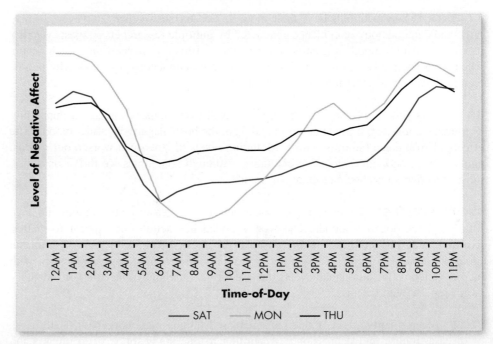

Sources: Based on S. A. Golder and M. W. Macy, "Diurnal and Seasonal Mood Vary with Work, Sleep, and Daylength Across Diverse Cultures," *Science* 333 (2011), pp. 1878–1881; and A. Elejalde-Ruiz, "Seize the day," *Chicago Tribune* (September 5, 2012), downloaded June 20, 2013 from http://articles.chicagotribune.com/.

Note: Based on analysis of U.S. Twitter postings and coding of words that represent positive feelings (delight, enthusiasm) and negative feelings (fear, guilt). Lines represent percent of total words in Twitter post that convey these moods.

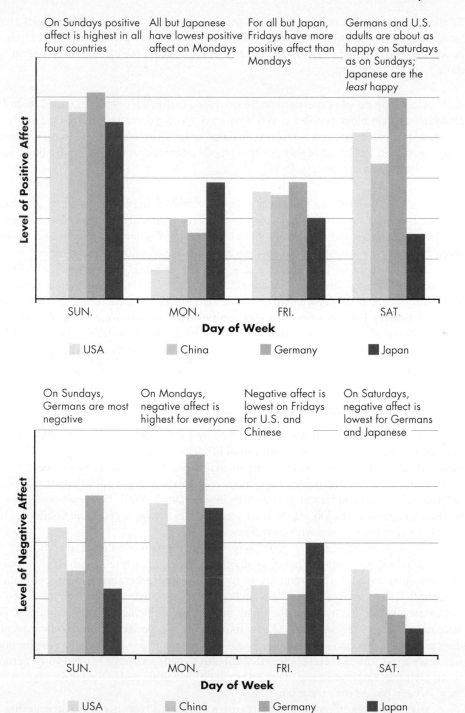

On Sundays positive affect is highest in all four countries

All but Japanese have lowest positive affect on Mondays

For all but Japan, Fridays have more positive affect than Mondays

Germans and U.S. adults are about as happy on Saturdays as on Sundays; Japanese are the *least* happy

On Sundays, Germans are most negative

On Mondays, negative affect is highest for everyone

Negative affect is lowest on Fridays for U.S. and Chinese

On Saturdays, negative affect is lowest for Germans and Japanese

EXHIBIT 4-3
Day-of-Week Mood Effects across Four Cultures

Sources: Based on S. A. Golder and M. W. Macy, "Diumal and Seasonal Mood Vary with Work, Sleep, and Daylength Across Diverse Cultures," *Science* 333 (2011), pp. 1878–1881; and A. Elejalde-Ruiz, "Seize the Day," *Chicago Tribune* (September 5, 2012), downloaded June 20, 2013 from http://articles.chicagotribune.com/.

EXERCISE   You often hear that people should exercise to improve their mood. Does "sweat therapy" really work? It appears so. Research consistently shows exercise enhances people's positive mood.[29] While not terribly strong overall, the effects are strongest for those who are depressed.

AGE   Do young people experience more extreme positive emotions (so-called youthful exuberance) than older people? If you answered "yes," you were wrong. One study of people ages eighteen to ninety-four revealed that negative emotions seem to occur less as people get older. Periods of highly positive moods lasted longer for older individuals, and bad moods faded more quickly.[30]

SEX   Many people believe women are more emotional than men. Is there any truth to this? Evidence does confirm women are more emotionally expressive than men,[31] experience emotions more intensely, tend to "hold onto" emotions longer, and display more frequent expressions of both positive and negative emotions, except anger.[32]

It might seem by now that we all—leaders, managers, and employees alike—operate as unwitting slaves to our emotions and moods. On an internal experiential level, this may be true. Yet we know from our workplace experiences that people aren't expressing every brief emotion that flits through their consciousness. On the way toward applying what we've discussed to specific OB applications, let's put together what we've learned about emotions and moods with workplace behaviors, beginning with emotional labor.

EMOTIONAL LABOR

Employees expend physical and mental labor by putting body and mind, respectively, into the job. But jobs also require **emotional labor**, an employee's expression of organizationally desired emotions during interpersonal transactions at work. Emotional labor is a key component of effective job performance. We expect flight attendants to be cheerful, funeral directors to be sad, and doctors emotionally neutral. But emotional labor is relevant to almost every job. At the least your managers expect you to be courteous, not hostile, in your interactions with coworkers.

The way we experience an emotion is obviously not always the same as the way we show it. To analyze emotional labor, we divide emotions into *felt* or *displayed emotions*.[33] **Felt emotions** are our actual emotions. In contrast, **displayed emotions** are those that the organization requires workers to show and considers appropriate in a given job. They're not innate; they're learned, and they may or may not coincide with felt emotions. For instance, research suggests that in U.S. workplaces, it is expected that we should typically display positive emotions like happiness and excitement, and suppress negative emotions like fear, anger, disgust, and contempt.[34] Effective managers have learned to be serious when giving an employee a negative performance evaluation and to hide their anger when they've been passed over for promotion.

Displaying fake emotions requires us to suppress real ones. **Surface acting** is hiding inner feelings and emotional expressions in response to display rules. A worker who smiles at a customer even when he doesn't feel like it is surface acting. **Deep acting** is trying to modify our true inner feelings based on display rules. Surface acting deals with *displayed* emotions, and deep acting deals with *felt* emotions.

Displaying emotions we don't really feel can be exhausting. When employees have to project one emotion while feeling another, this disparity is called **emotional dissonance**. Emotional dissonance is like cognitive dissonance discussed in the previous chapter, except that emotional dissonance concerns feelings rather than thinking. Bottled-up feelings of frustration, anger, and resentment can lead to emotional exhaustion. Long-term emotional dissonance is a predictor for job burnout, declines in job performance, and lower job satisfaction.[35]

It is important to counteract the effects of emotional labor and emotional disso- nance. Research in the Netherlands and Belgium indicated that surface acting is stressful to employees, while *mindfulness* (learning to objectively evaluate our emotional situation in the moment, akin to deep acting) is beneficial to employee well-being.[36] It is also important to give employees who engage in surface displays a chance to relax and recharge. A study that looked at how cheerleading instructors spent their breaks from teaching found those who used the time to rest and relax were more effective after their breaks. Instructors who did chores during their breaks were only about as effective after their break as they were before.[37]

The concept of emotional labor makes intuitive and organizational sense. Affective events theory, discussed in the next section, fits a job's emotional labor requirements into a construct that leads to work events, emotional reactions, and, finally, to job satisfaction and job performance.

AFFECTIVE EVENTS THEORY

We've seen that emotions and moods are an important part of our personal lives and our work lives. But how do they influence our job performance and satisfaction? A model called **affective events theory (AET)** demonstrates that employees react emotionally to things that happen to them at work, and this reaction influences their job performance and satisfaction.[38]

Exhibit 4-4 summarizes AET. The theory begins by recognizing that emotions are a response to an event in the work environment. The work environment includes every-thing surrounding the job—the variety of tasks and degree of autonomy, job demands, and requirements for emotional labor. This environment creates work events that can be hassles, uplifting events, or both. Examples of hassles are colleagues who refuse to carry their share of work, conflicting directions from different managers, and excessive time pressures. Uplifting events include meeting a goal, getting support from a colleague, and receiving recognition for an accomplishment.[39]

Work events trigger positive or negative emotional reactions, to which employees' personalities and moods predispose them to respond with greater or lesser intensity. People who score low on emotional stability are more likely to react strongly to negative events, and our emotional response to a given event can change depending on mood. Finally, emotions influence a number of performance and satisfaction variables, such as organizational citizenship behavior, organizational commitment, level of effort, intention to quit, and workplace deviance.

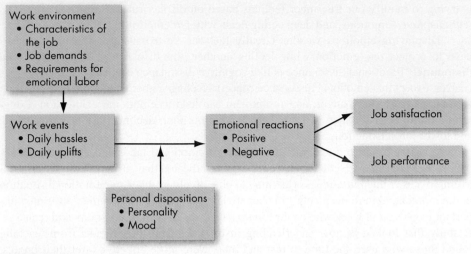

EXHIBIT 4-4
Affective Events Theory

Source: Based on N. M. Ashkanasy and C. S. Daus, "Emotion in the Workplace: The New Challenge for Managers," *Academy of Management Executive* (February 2002), p. 77.

AET provides us with valuable insights into the role emotions play in primary organizational outcomes of job satisfaction and job performance. Employees and managers therefore shouldn't ignore emotions or the events that cause them.[40] Emotional intelligence is another framework that helps us understand the impact of emotions on job performance, so we will look at that next.

EMOTIONAL INTELLIGENCE

People who know their own emotions and are good at reading others' emotions may be more effective in their jobs.

Emotional intelligence (EI) is a person's ability to (1) perceive emotions in the self and others, (2) understand the meaning of these emotions, and (3) regulate one's emotions accordingly in a cascading model, as shown in Exhibit 4-5. People who know their own emotions and are good at reading emotional cues—for instance, knowing why they're angry and how to express themselves without violating norms—are most likely to be effective.[41]

Several studies suggest EI plays an important role in job performance. However, EI has been a controversial concept in OB, with supporters and detractors. In the following sections, we review the arguments for and against its viability.

The Case for EI

The arguments in favor of EI include its intuitive appeal, the fact that it predicts criteria that matter, and the idea that it is biologically based.

INTUITIVE APPEAL Intuition suggests that people who can detect emotions in others, control their own emotions, and handle social interactions well have an advantage in the business world.

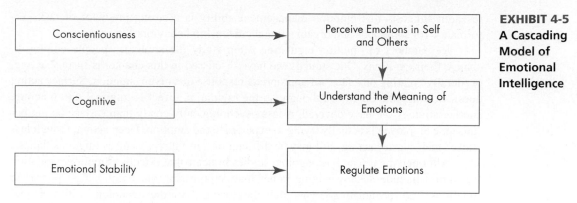

**EXHIBIT 4-5
A Cascading
Model of
Emotional
Intelligence**

EI PREDICTS CRITERIA THAT MATTER   Evidence suggests a high level of EI means a person will perform well on the job.

EI IS BIOLOGICALLY BASED   There is evidence that EI is genetically influenced, further supporting the idea that it measures a real underlying biological factor.[42]

The Case Against EI

For all its supporters, EI has just as many critics who say it is vague and impossible to measure, and they question its validity.

EI RESEARCHERS DO NOT AGREE ON DEFINITIONS   To many researchers, it's not clear what EI is, because researchers use different definitions of it.[43]

EI CAN'T BE MEASURED   The measures of EI are diverse, and researchers have not subjected them to as much rigorous study as they have measures of personality and general intelligence.[44]

EI IS NOTHING BUT PERSONALITY WITH A DIFFERENT LABEL   Some critics argue that because EI is so closely related to intelligence and personality, once you control for these factors, it has nothing unique to offer. To some extent, researchers have resolved this issue by noting that EI is a construct partially determined by traits like cognitive intelligence, conscientiousness, and neuroticism, so it makes sense that EI is correlated with these characteristics.[45]

Although the field is progressing in its understanding of EI, many questions have not been answered. EI is wildly popular among consulting firms and in the popular press, and while it has accumulated some support in the research literature, critics remain. Love it or hate it, one thing is for sure—EI is here to stay. So may be our next topic, emotion regulation, which is part of the EI literature but is increasingly studied as an independent concept.[46]

EMOTION REGULATION

Have you ever tried to cheer yourself up when you're feeling down, or calm yourself when you're feeling angry? If so, you have engaged in *emotion regulation*. The central idea behind emotion regulation is to identify and modify the emotions you feel. Recent research suggests that emotion management ability is a strong predictor of task performance for some jobs and organizational citizenship behaviors.[47]

Researchers of emotion regulation often study the strategies people employ to change their emotions. One strategy we have discussed in this chapter is surface acting, or literally "putting on a face" of appropriate response to a given situation. Surface acting doesn't change the emotions, though, so the regulation effect is minimal. Deep acting, another strategy we have covered, is less psychologically costly than surface acting because the employee is actually trying to experience the emotion. Deep acting, though less "false" than surface acting, still may be difficult because it represents acting nonetheless.

Although the research is ongoing, studies indicate that effective emotion regulation techniques include acknowledging rather than suppressing our emotional responses to situations, and reevaluating events after they occur.[48]Another technique with potential is venting. Research shows that open expression of emotions can be helpful to the individual, as opposed to keeping emotions "bottled up." Caution must be exercised, though, because venting, or expressing your frustration outwardly, touches other people.

As you might suspect, not everyone is equally good at regulating his emotions. Individuals who are higher in the personality trait of neuroticism have more trouble with emotion regulation and often find their moods are beyond their ability to control. Individuals who have lower levels of self-esteem are less likely to try to improve their sad moods, perhaps because they are less likely than others to feel they deserve to be in a good mood.[49]

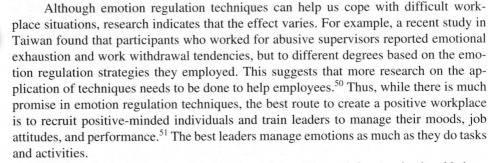

Although emotion regulation techniques can help us cope with difficult workplace situations, research indicates that the effect varies. For example, a recent study in Taiwan found that participants who worked for abusive supervisors reported emotional exhaustion and work withdrawal tendencies, but to different degrees based on the emotion regulation strategies they employed. This suggests that more research on the application of techniques needs to be done to help employees.[50] Thus, while there is much promise in emotion regulation techniques, the best route to create a positive workplace is to recruit positive-minded individuals and train leaders to manage their moods, job attitudes, and performance.[51] The best leaders manage emotions as much as they do tasks and activities.

Now that we have studied the role of emotions and moods in organizational behavior, let's consider the opportunities for more specific applications that our understanding provides.

✪ WATCH IT

If your professor assigned this, sign in to **mymanagementlab.com** to watch a video titled East Haven Fire Department: Emotions and Moods to learn more about this topic and respond to questions.

OB APPLICATIONS OF EMOTIONS AND MOODS

Positive emotions can increase problem-solving skills and help us understand and analyze new information.

Our understanding of emotions and moods can impact the selection process, decision making, creativity, motivation, leadership, negotiation, customer service, job attitudes, deviant workplace behavior, and safety.

Selection

Research indicates that employers should consider EI a factor in selecting employees, especially for jobs that demand a high degree of social interaction. More employers have started to use EI measures in their hiring processes and are finding high-scoring EI employees outperform low-scoring employees for recruiting and sales positions. It also makes sense for managers to select members who are predisposed to positive moods for teamwork because positive moods transmit from team member to team member. One study of professional cricket teams, for instance, found players' happy moods affected the moods of their team members and positively influenced their performance.[52]

Decision Making

Moods and emotions have effects on decision making that managers should understand. Positive emotions and moods seem to help people make sound decisions. Positive emotions furthermore enhance problem-solving skills, so positive people find better solutions to problems.[53]

OB researchers continue to debate the role of negative emotions and moods in decision making. Although one major study suggested that depressed people reach more accurate judgments,[54] more recent evidence hints that they make poorer decisions. Why? Because depressed people are slower at processing information and tend to weigh all possible options rather than the most likely ones.[55] They search for the perfect solution, when there rarely is one.

Creativity

As we see throughout this text, one goal of leadership is to maximize employee productivity. Creativity is influenced by emotions and moods, but there are two schools of thought on the relationship. Much research suggests that people in good moods tend to be more creative than people in bad moods.[56] People in good moods produce more ideas and more options, and others think their ideas are original.[57] They are more flexible and open in their thinking, which may explain why they're more creative.[58] This research suggests that supervisors should try to keep employees happy because doing so creates more good moods, which in turn leads people to be more creative.[59] Other researchers do not believe a positive mood enhances creativity. They argue that when people are in positive moods, they may relax ("If I'm in a good mood, things must be going okay, and I must not need to think of new ideas") and not engage in the critical thinking necessary for some forms of creativity.[60]

The research findings may not be as conflicting as they seem. Rather than looking at positive or negative affect, it's possible to conceptualize moods as active feelings like anger, fear, or elation, and contrast these with deactivating moods like sorrow, depression, or serenity. All the activating moods, whether positive *or* negative, seem to lead to more creativity, whereas deactivating moods lead to less.[61] This would suggest managers should try to increase the energy in the workplace rather than focus on enhancing positive moods.

Motivation

Several studies have highlighted the importance of moods and emotions on motivation. One study found that a group in a good mood was more motivated in a problem-solving task than a group in a neutral mood.[62] Another study found that giving people performance feedback—whether real or fake—influenced their mood, which then influenced their motivation.[63] One other study in Taiwan found that employees in a good mood were more helpful and felt better about themselves, which led to superior performance.

So, a cycle can be created in which positive moods cause people to be more creative, which leads to positive feedback from those observing their work. This positive feedback further reinforces the positive mood, which may make people perform even better, and so on. Overall, the findings suggest a manager may enhance employee motivation—and performance—by encouraging good moods.

Leadership

Research indicates that in leadership, putting people in a good mood makes good sense. Leaders who focus on inspirational goals generate greater optimism and enthusiasm in employees, which leads to more positive social interactions with coworkers and customers.[64] A study with Taiwanese military participants further indicates that by sharing emotions, leaders can inspire positive emotions in their followers that lead to higher task performance.[65]

Research indicates that when leaders are in good moods, group members are more positive; as a result, they cooperate better.[66] But what about when leaders are sad? A recent study found that leader displays of sadness increased the analytic performance of followers through emotional contagion, perhaps because followers attended more closely to the tasks at hand. This study also indicated that leaders are perceived as more effective when they share positive emotions, and followers are more creative in a positive emotional environment.[67]

Corporate executives, who set the tone for an organizational culture, know emotional content is critical for employees to buy into their vision of the company's future and accept change. When higher-ups offer new visions, especially with vague or distant goals, it is often difficult for employees to accept the changes they'll bring. By arousing emotions and linking them to an appealing vision, leaders increase the likelihood that managers and employees alike will accept change.[68]

Negotiation

Negotiation is more of an emotional process than we may care to admit, but have you considered the potential of using emotions and moods to enhance your negotiation skills? For example, several studies suggest that a negotiator who feigns anger has an advantage over her opponent. Why? Because when a negotiator shows anger, the opponent concludes the negotiator has conceded all she can and so he gives in.[69] However, anger should be used selectively in negotiation: angry negotiators who have less information or less power than their opponents have significantly worse outcomes.[70]

Like the use of any emotion, context matters. Displaying a negative emotion (such as anger) can be effective, but feeling bad about your performance appears to impair future negotiations. Individuals who do poorly in a negotiation experience negative emotions, develop negative perceptions of their counterparts, and are less willing to share information or be cooperative in future negotiations.[71]

Altogether, the best negotiators are probably the ones who remain emotionally detached. One study of people who had suffered damage to the emotional centers of their brains suggested that unemotional people may be the best negotiators because they're not likely to overcorrect when faced with negative outcomes.[72]

Customer Service

Workers' emotional states influence customer service, which influences levels of repeat business and customer satisfaction.[73] This is primarily due to **emotional contagion**—the "catching" of emotions from others. When someone experiences positive emotions and laughs and smiles at you, you tend to respond positively. Of course, the opposite is true as well.

Studies indicate a matching effect between employee emotions and customer emotions.[74] In the employee-to-customer direction, research finds that customers who catch the positive emotions of employees shop longer. In the other direction, when an employee feels unfairly treated by a customer, it's harder for him to display the positive emotions his organization expects of him.[75] High-quality customer service makes demands on employees because it often puts them in a state of emotional dissonance, which can be deleterious to the employee and the organization. Managers can interrupt negative contagion by fostering positive moods.

Job Attitudes

There is good news and bad news about the relationship between moods and job attitudes. The good news is that it appears that a positive mood at work can spill over to your off-work hours, and a negative mood at work can be restored to a positive mood after a break. Several studies have shown people who had a good day at work tend to be in a better mood at home that evening, and vice versa.[76] Other research has found that although people do emotionally take their work home with them, by the next day the effect is usually gone.[77] The bad news is that the moods of your household may interfere. As you might expect, one study found if one member of a couple was in a negative mood during the workday, the negative mood spilled over to the spouse at night.[78] Thus, the relationship between moods and job attitudes is reciprocal—how our workday goes colors our moods, but our moods also affect how we see our job.

Deviant Workplace Behaviors

Anyone who has spent much time in an organization realizes people sometimes behave in ways that violate established norms and threaten the organization, its members, or both. As we saw in Chapter 3, these actions are called *deviant workplace behaviors*.[79] Many can be traced to negative emotions.

Evidence suggests that people who feel negative emotions are more likely than others to engage in short-term deviant behavior at work such as gossiping or searching the Internet.[80] Of concern, a recent study in Pakistan found that anger correlated with more aggressive counterproductive behaviors such as abuse against others and production deviance, while sadness did not. Neither anger nor sadness predicted workplace withdrawal, which suggests that managers need to take employee expressions of anger seriously because employees may stay with an organization and continue to act aggressively toward others.[81] Managers therefore need to stay connected with their employees to gauge emotions and emotion intensity levels.

Safety and Injury at Work

Research relating negative affectivity to increased injuries at work suggests employers might improve health and safety (and reduce costs) by ensuring workers aren't engaged in potentially dangerous activities when they're in a bad mood. Bad moods can contribute to injury at work in several ways.[82] Individuals in negative moods tend to be more anxious, which can make them less able to cope effectively with hazards. A person who is always fearful will be more pessimistic about the effectiveness of safety precautions because she feels she'll just get hurt anyway, or she might panic or freeze up when confronted with a threatening situation. Negative moods also make people more distractible, and distractions can lead to careless behaviors.

SUMMARY

Emotions and moods are similar in that both are affective in nature. But they're also different—moods are more general than emotions. Events impact emotions and moods. The time of day, stressful situations, and sleep patterns are some of the factors that influence emotions and moods. OB research on emotional labor, affective events theory, emotional intelligence, and emotional regulation helps us understand how people deal with emotions. Emotions and moods have proven relevant for virtually every work outcome, with implications for effective managerial practices.

IMPLICATIONS FOR MANAGERS

- Recognize that emotions are a natural part of the workplace and good management does not mean creating an emotion-free environment.
- To foster effective decision making, creativity, and motivation in employees, model positive emotions and moods as much as is authentically possible.
- Provide positive feedback to increase the positivity of the workplace.
- In the service sector, encourage positive displays of emotion, which make customers feel more positive and thus improve customer service interactions and negotiations.
- Managers who understand the role of emotions and moods will significantly improve their ability to explain and predict their coworkers' and employees' behavior.

PERSONAL INVENTORY ASSESSMENT

In Personal Inventory Assessment found in MyManagementLab take assessment: Emotional Intelligence Assessment

⭐ WRITING SPACE

If your professor assigned this, sign in to **mymanagementlab.com** for the following Assisted-graded writing question:

4-1. How might managers use their own emotional intelligence (FI) to increase their leadership abilities?

5

Values and Personality

MyManagementLab®

⊛ Improve Your Grade!

When you see this icon ⊛, visit **www.mymanagementlab.com** for activities that are applied, personalized, and offer immediate feedback.

LEARNING OBJECTIVES

After studying this chapter, you should be able to:

1. Describe personality, the way it is measured, and the factors that shape it.

2. Describe the Myers-Briggs Type Indicator (MBTI) personality framework and the Big Five model, and describe their strengths and weaknesses.

3. Identify the three traits of the Dark Triad, and describe the contrasting ideas of the approach–avoidance framework.

4. Discuss how the concepts of core self-evaluation (CSE), self-monitoring, and proactive personality contribute to the understanding of personality.

5. Describe how the situation affects whether personality predicts behavior.

6. Contrast terminal and instrumental values.

7. Describe the differences between person–job fit and person–organization fit.

8. Identify Hofstede's five value dimensions of national culture.

⊛ Chapter Warm-up

If your professor has chosen to assign this, go to **www.mymanagementlab.com** to see what you should particularly focus on and to take the Chapter 5 warm up.

We all have different personalities. In the first half of this chapter, we review the research on personality and its relationship to behavior. People also differ in their values. In the latter half of the chapter, we look at how values shape many of our work-related behaviors, and how values tend to vary by national culture.

PERSONALITY

Why are some people quiet and passive, while others are loud and aggressive? Are certain personality types better adapted than others for certain jobs? Before we can answer these questions, we need to address a more basic one: What is personality?

What Is Personality?

When we talk of someone's personality, we don't mean a person has charm or is constantly smiling. When psychologists talk of personality, they mean a dynamic concept of the growth and development of a person's whole psychological system. First we will define personality, and then discuss personality measurement methods and determinants.

DEFINING PERSONALITY   The definition of *personality* we most frequently use was produced by Gordon Allport over 70 years ago. Allport said personality is "the dynamic organization within the individual of those psychophysical systems that determine his unique adjustments to his environment."[1] For our purposes, you should think of **personality** as the sum total of ways in which an individual reacts to and interacts with others. We most often describe it in terms of the measurable traits a person exhibits.

MEASURING PERSONALITY   The most important reason managers need to know how to measure personality is that research has shown personality tests are useful in hiring decisions and help managers forecast who is best for a job.[2] The most common means of measuring personality is through self-report surveys in which individuals evaluate themselves on a series of factors, such as "I worry a lot about the future." Though self-report measures work when well-constructed, the respondent might lie or practice impression management to create a good impression. When people know their personality scores are going to be used for hiring decisions, they rate themselves as about half a standard deviation more conscientious and emotionally stable than if they are taking the test to learn more about themselves.[3] Another problem is accuracy; a candidate who is in a bad mood when taking the survey may have inaccurate scores.

Personality—the sum total of ways in which an individual reacts to and interacts with others—is partly genetic in origin; yet, personality can be easily measured by various survey methods, including self-report surveys.

PERSONALITY DETERMINANTS   An early debate in personality research centered on whether an individual's personality is the result of heredity or environment. Personality appears to be a result of both; however, research tends to support the importance of heredity over the environment.

Heredity refers to factors determined at conception. Physical stature, facial features, gender, temperament, muscle composition and reflexes, energy level, and biological rhythms are generally considered to be either completely or substantially influenced by parentage—by your biological parents' genetic, physiological, and psychological makeup. The heredity approach argues that the ultimate explanation of an individual's personality is the molecular structure of the genes, located in the chromosomes.

Researchers in many different countries have studied thousands of sets of identical twins who were separated at birth and raised apart.[4] If heredity played little or no part in determining personality, you would expect to find few similarities between separated twins. Researchers have found, however, that genetics accounts for about 50 percent of the personality similarities between twins and more than 30 percent of shared occupational and leisure interests. One set of twins who were separated for thirty-nine years and raised forty-five miles apart were found to drive the same model and color car. Although they had never met, they chain-smoked the same brand of cigarette, owned dogs with the same name, and regularly vacationed within three blocks of each other in a beach community 1,500 miles away.

Interestingly, twin studies have suggested parents don't add much to personality development. The personalities of identical twins raised in different households were far more similar to each other than to the personalities of siblings with whom the twins were raised. Ironically, the most important contribution our parents may make to our personalities is giving us their genes!

This is not to suggest that personality never changes. People's scores on dependability tend to increase over time, as when young adults start families and establish careers. However, strong individual differences in dependability remain; everyone tends to change by about the same amount, so their rank order stays roughly the same.[5] An analogy to intelligence may make this clearer. Children become smarter as they age, so nearly everyone is smarter at age twenty than at age ten. Still, if Keisha is smarter than Blake at age ten, she is likely to be smarter than he is at age twenty, too. Research has shown that personality is more changeable in adolescence and more stable among adults.[6]

Early work on personality tried to identify and label enduring characteristics that describe an individual's behavior, including shy, aggressive, submissive, lazy, ambitious, loyal, and timid. When someone exhibits these characteristics in a large number of situations, we call them the **personality traits** of that person.[7] The more consistent the characteristic over time, and the more frequently it occurs in diverse situations, the more important that trait is in describing the individual.

Early efforts to identify and classify the primary traits that govern behavior[8] often produced long lists that were difficult to generalize from and provided little practical guidance to organizational decision makers. Two exceptions are the Myers-Briggs Type Indicator and the Big Five Model, now the dominant frameworks for assessing an individual's personality traits. Let's discuss each of them in turn.

DOMINANT PERSONALITY FRAMEWORKS

Throughout history, people have sought to understand what makes individuals behave in myriad ways. Many of our behaviors stem from our personalities, so understanding the components of personality helps us predict behavior. Important theoretical frameworks and assessment tools, discussed next, help us categorize and study the dimensions of personality.

The Myers-Briggs Type Indicator

The **Myers-Briggs Type Indicator (MBTI)** is the most widely used personality-assessment instrument in the world.[9] It is a 100-question personality test that asks people how they usually feel or act in situations. Respondents are classified as extraverted or introverted (E or I), sensing or intuitive (S or N), thinking or feeling (T or F), and judging or perceiving (J or P):

- *Extraverted (E) versus Introverted (I).* Extraverted individuals are outgoing, sociable, and assertive. Introverts are quiet and shy.
- *Sensing (S) versus Intuitive (N).* Sensing types are practical, prefer routine and order, and focus on details. Intuitives rely on unconscious processes and look at the "big picture."
- *Thinking (T) versus Feeling (F).* Thinking types use reason and logic to handle problems. Feeling types rely on their personal values and emotions.
- *Judging (J) versus Perceiving (P).* Judging types want control and prefer order and structure. Perceiving types are flexible and spontaneous.

These classifications describe personality types by identifying one trait from each of the four pairs. For example, Introverted/Intuitive/Thinking/Judging (INTJ) people are visionaries with original minds and great drive. They are skeptical, critical, independent, determined, and often stubborn. ENFJs are natural teachers and leaders. They are relational, motivational, intuitive, idealistic, ethical, and kind. ESTJs are organizers. They are realistic, logical, analytical, and decisive, perfect for business or mechanics. The ENTP type is innovative, individualistic, versatile, and attracted to entrepreneurial ideas. This person tends to be resourceful in solving challenging problems but may neglect routine assignments.

According to the Myers & Briggs Foundation, introverts account for over 50 percent of the E/I responses in the U.S. population. Indeed, two of the three most common MBTI types are introverts: ISFJ and ISTJ. ISFJs are nurturing and responsible, and ISTJs are dutiful and logical. The least common types are INFJ (insightful and protective) and ENTJ (focused and decisive).[10]

The MBTI has been widely used by organizations including Apple Computer, AT&T, Citigroup, GE, and 3M Co.; many hospitals and educational institutions; and even the U.S. Armed Forces. It is taken by over 2.5 million people each year and 89 of the *Fortune* 100 companies use it.[11] Evidence is mixed about its validity as a measure of personality, however; most of the evidence is against it.[12] One problem is that the model forces a person into one type or another; that is, you're either introverted or extraverted. There is no in-between, though most people are both extraverted and introverted to some degree. Another problem is with the reliability of the measure: When people retake the assessment, they often receive different results. An additional problem is in the difficulty of interpretation. There are levels of importance for each of the MBTI facets, and separate meanings for certain combinations of facets, all of which require trained interpretation that can leave room for error. Finally, results from the MBTI tend to be unrelated to job performance. The MBTI can thus be a valuable tool for increasing self-awareness and providing career guidance, but managers should consider using the Big Five Personality Model, discussed next, as the personality selection test for job candidates instead.

The Big Five Personality Model

The MBTI may lack strong supporting evidence, but an impressive body of research supports the thesis of the **Big Five Model**—that five basic dimensions underlie all others and encompass most of the significant variation in human personality.[13] Test scores of the Big

Five traits do a very good job of predicting how people behave in a variety of real-life situations.[14] These are the Big Five factors:

- *Extraversion.* The **extraversion** dimension captures our comfort level with relationships. Extraverts tend to be gregarious, assertive, and sociable. Introverts tend to be reserved, timid, and quiet.
- *Agreeableness.* The **agreeableness** dimension refers to an individual's propensity to defer to others. Highly agreeable people are cooperative, warm, and trusting. People who score low on agreeableness are cold, disagreeable, and antagonistic.
- *Conscientiousness.* The **conscientiousness** dimension is a measure of reliability. A highly conscientious person is responsible, organized, dependable, and persistent. Those who score low on this dimension are easily distracted, disorganized, and unreliable.
- *Emotional stability.* The **emotional stability** dimension—often labeled by its converse, neuroticism—taps a person's ability to withstand stress. People with positive emotional stability tend to be calm, self-confident, and secure. Those with high negative scores tend to be nervous, anxious, depressed, and insecure.
- *Openness to experience.* The **openness to experience** dimension addresses range of interests and fascination with novelty. Open people are creative, curious, and artistically sensitive. Those at the other end of the category are conventional and find comfort in the familiar.

> The Big Five personality traits are related to many OB criteria; each of the five traits has proven its usefulness to understanding individual behavior in organizations.

HOW DO THE BIG FIVE TRAITS PREDICT BEHAVIOR AT WORK?   Research has found relationships between the Big Five personality dimensions and job performance.[15] As the authors of the most-cited review observed, "The preponderance of evidence shows that individuals who are dependable, reliable, careful, thorough, able to plan, organized, hardworking, persistent, and achievement-oriented tend to have higher job performance in most if not all occupations."[16] Employees who score higher in conscientiousness develop higher levels of job knowledge, probably because highly conscientious people learn more (a review of 138 studies revealed conscientiousness was related to GPA).[17] Higher levels of job knowledge contribute to higher levels of job performance. There can be "too much of a good thing," however, as extremely conscientious individuals typically do not perform better than those who are simply above average in conscientiousness.[18]

Conscientiousness is important to organizational success. A study of the personality scores of 313 CEO candidates in private equity companies (of whom 225 were hired; their company's performance was later correlated with their personality scores) found conscientiousness—in the form of persistence, attention to detail, and setting of high standards—was more important than other traits.

Interestingly, conscientious people live longer; they take better care of themselves and engage in fewer risky behaviors like smoking, drinking and drugs, and unsafe sexual or driving behaviors.[19] They don't adapt as well to changing contexts, however. They are generally performance oriented and may have more trouble learning complex skills early in the training process because their focus is on performing well rather than on learning. Finally, they are often less creative than less conscientious people, especially artistically.[20]

Although conscientiousness is most consistently related to job performance, the other Big Five traits are also related to aspects of performance and have other implications for work and for life. Let's look at them one at a time. Exhibit 5-1 summarizes.

EXHIBIT 5-1
Model of How Big Five Traits Influence OB Criteria

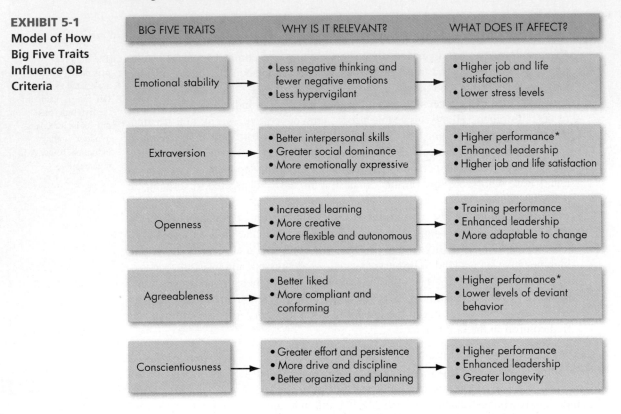

BIG FIVE TRAITS	WHY IS IT RELEVANT?	WHAT DOES IT AFFECT?
Emotional stability	• Less negative thinking and fewer negative emotions • Less hypervigilant	• Higher job and life satisfaction • Lower stress levels
Extraversion	• Better interpersonal skills • Greater social dominance • More emotionally expressive	• Higher performance* • Enhanced leadership • Higher job and life satisfaction
Openness	• Increased learning • More creative • More flexible and autonomous	• Training performance • Enhanced leadership • More adaptable to change
Agreeableness	• Better liked • More compliant and conforming	• Higher performance* • Lower levels of deviant behavior
Conscientiousness	• Greater effort and persistence • More drive and discipline • Better organized and planning	• Higher performance • Enhanced leadership • Greater longevity

Of the Big Five traits, emotional stability is most strongly related to life satisfaction, job satisfaction, and low stress levels. High scorers are more likely to be positive and optimistic and experience fewer negative emotions; they are generally happier than low scorers. Low scorers are hypervigilant (looking for problems or impending signs of danger) and are vulnerable to the physical and psychological effects of stress.

Extraverts tend to be happier in their jobs and in their lives. They experience more positive emotions than do introverts, and they more freely express these feelings. Extraverts also tend to perform better in jobs with significant interpersonal interaction. They usually have more social skills and friends. Finally, extraversion is a relatively strong predictor of leadership emergence in groups; extraverts are more socially dominant, "take charge" people and usually more assertive than introverts.[21] Extraverts are more impulsive than introverts; they are more likely to be absent from work and engage in risky behaviors such as unprotected sex, drinking, and other sensation-seeking acts.[22] One study also found extraverts were more likely than introverts to lie during job interviews.[23]

High scorers for openness to experience are more creative in science and art than low scorers. Because creativity is important to leadership, open people are more likely to be effective leaders—and more comfortable with ambiguity. They cope better with organizational change and are more adaptable in varying contexts. As for the downside, evidence suggests they are susceptible to workplace accidents.[24]

You might expect agreeable people to be happier than disagreeable people. They are, but only slightly. When people choose romantic partners, friends, or organizational team members, agreeable individuals are usually first choice. Agreeable individuals are better liked than disagreeable people; they tend to do better in interpersonally oriented jobs such as customer service. Agreeable people also are more compliant and rule abiding, less likely to get into accidents, and more satisfied in their jobs. They contribute to organizational performance by engaging in citizenship behavior[25] and are less likely to engage in organizational deviance. Agreeableness, however, is associated with lower levels of career success (especially earnings), perhaps because agreeable people are less willing to promote their self-interests.

The Big Five personality factors appear in almost all cross-cultural studies,[26] including China, Israel, Germany, Japan, Spain, Nigeria, Norway, Pakistan, and the United States. Generally, the findings corroborate what has been found in U.S. research: Of the Big Five traits, conscientiousness is the best predictor of job performance.

OTHER PERSONALITY FRAMEWORKS

Research indicates the Big Five traits have the most verifiable linkages to important organizational outcomes, but neither are they the only traits a person exhibits nor are they the only ones with organizational behavior implications. Let's discuss some other traits, known collectively as the Dark Triad, and the Approach–Avoidance framework, which describes personality traits in terms of motivation.

The Dark Triad

With the exception of neuroticism, the Big Five traits are what we call socially desirable, meaning we might be glad to score high on them. Researchers have found that three other socially *undesirable* traits, which we all have in varying degrees, are relevant to organizational behavior: Machiavellianism, narcissism, and psychopathy. Owing to their negative nature, researchers have labeled these three traits the **Dark Triad**—though, of course, they do not always occur together.[27]

MACHIAVELLIANISM   Hao is a young bank manager in Shanghai. He's received three promotions in the past four years and makes no apologies for the aggressive tactics he's used to propel his career upward. "My name means clever, and that's what I am—I do whatever I have to do to get ahead," he says. Hao would be termed Machiavellian.

The personality characteristic of **Machiavellianism** (often abbreviated *Mach*) is named after Niccolo Machiavelli, who wrote in the sixteenth century on how to gain and use power. An individual high in Machiavellianism is pragmatic, maintains emotional distance, and believes ends can justify means. "If it works, use it" is consistent with a high-Mach perspective. A considerable amount of research has found high Machs manipulate more, win more, are persuaded less, and persuade others more than do low Machs.[28] They are more likely to act aggressively and engage in other counterproductive work behaviors as well. A recent review of the literature revealed that Machiavellianism does not significantly predict overall job performance.[29] High-Mach employees, by manipulating others to their advantage, may win in the short term, but they lose those gains in the long term because they are not well liked.

The effects of Machiavellianism depend somewhat on the context. The reason, in part, is that individuals' personalities affect the situations they choose. One study showed that high-Mach job seekers were less positively affected by knowing an organization engaged in a high level of corporate social responsibility (CSR).[30] Another study found that Machs' ethical leadership behaviors were less likely to translate into followers' work engagement because followers "see through" these behaviors and realize it is a case of surface acting.[31]

NARCISSISM   Sabrina likes to be the center of attention. She often looks at herself in the mirror, has extravagant dreams, and considers herself a person of many talents. Sabrina is a narcissist. The trait is named for the Greek myth of Narcissus, a youth so vain and proud he fell in love with his own image. In psychology, **narcissism** describes a person who has a grandiose sense of self-importance, requires excessive admiration, has a sense of entitlement, and is arrogant. Evidence suggests narcissists are more charismatic than others.[32] Both leaders and managers tend to score higher on narcissism, suggesting that a certain self-centeredness is needed to succeed. Some evidence suggests that narcissists are more adaptable and make better business decisions than others when the decision is complex.[33] One study of Norwegian bank employees found that those scoring high on narcissism enjoyed their work more.[34]

While narcissism seems to have little relationship with overall job performance, it is fairly strongly related to increased counterproductive work behaviors and is linked to other negative outcomes. A study found that while narcissists thought they were *better* leaders than their colleagues, their supervisors rated them as *worse*. In highly ethical contexts, narcissistic leaders are likely to be perceived as ineffective and unethical.[35] A study of Swiss Air Force officers found that narcissists were particularly likely to be irritated by feeling under-benefited, meaning that when narcissists don't get what they want, they are more stressed by that than others.[36]

Special research attention has been paid to the narcissism of CEOs. An executive described Oracle's CEO Larry Ellison as follows: "The difference between God and Larry is that God does not believe he is Larry."[37] A study of narcissistic CEOs revealed that they make more acquisitions, pay higher premiums for those acquisitions, respond less clearly to objective measures of performance, and respond to media praise by making even more acquisitions.[38] Research using data compiled over 100 years has shown that narcissistic CEOs of baseball organizations generate higher levels of manager turnover, although members of external organizations see them as more influential.[39]

Narcissism and its effects are not confined to CEOs or celebrities. Like the effects of Machiavellianism, those of narcissism vary by context, but are represented in all areas of life. For example, narcissists are more likely to post self-promoting material on their Facebook pages.[40]

PSYCHOPATHY   Psychopathy is part of the Dark Triad, but in organizational behavior it does not connote insanity. In the OB context, **psychopathy** is defined as a lack of concern for others, and a lack of guilt or remorse when their actions cause harm.[41] Measures of psychopathy attempt to assess the person's motivation to comply with social norms; willingness to use deceit to obtain desired ends and the effectiveness of those efforts; impulsivity; and disregard, that is, lack of empathic concern, for others.

The literature is not consistent about whether psychopathy or other aberrant personality traits are important to work behavior. One review found little correlation between measures of psychopathy and job performance or counterproductive work behaviors. A recent study found that antisocial personality, which is closely related to psychopathy, was positively related to advancement in the organization but unrelated to other aspects of career success and effectiveness.[42] Still other research suggests that psychopathy is related to the use of hard influence tactics (threats, manipulation) and bullying work behavior (physical or verbal threatening).[43] The cunning displayed by people who score high on psychopathy may help them gain power in an organization, but keep them from using that power toward healthy ends for themselves or their organizations.

Given the relative newness of research on the Dark Triad, using psychopathology scores for employment decisions may carry more risks for now than rewards. Organizations wishing to assess psychopathy or other aberrant traits need to exercise caution. The Americans with Disabilities Act (ADA) prohibits discrimination against individuals with "a physical or mental impairment." This does not mean organizations must hire every mentally ill person who applies, or that they cannot consider mental illness in hiring decisions. However, if they do, the ADA places specific guidelines on when it is a permissible factor, such as when the illness prevents or severely restricts effective performance, and when it cannot be reasonably accommodated.[44]

As the name implies, the Dark Triad represents three traits that can present significant downsides for individuals and organizations. It would be easy to make quick conclusions on them as managers, but it is important to keep discussions on personality in perspective. The degrees of each trait—the Big Five, the Dark Triad, and other traits—in a person, and the combination of the traits, matter a great deal to organizational outcomes. So does the person's approach–avoidance motivation, which we discuss next.

Approach–Avoidance

The MBTI, the Big Five, and the Dark Triad are not the only theoretical frameworks for personality. Recently, the **approach–avoidance framework** has cast personality traits as motivations. Approach and avoidance motivation represent the degree to which we react to stimuli whereby approach motivation is our attraction to positive stimuli, and avoidance motivation is our aversion to negative stimuli.

The approach–avoidance framework organizes traits and may help explain how they predict work behavior. One study showed, for instance, that approach and avoidance motivation can help explain how core self-evaluations affect job satisfaction.[45] The framework also addresses our multiple motives when we act. For example, competitive pressures tend to invoke both approach motivation (people work harder to win) and avoidance motivation (people are distracted and demotivated by fear of losing). The way an individual performs depends on which of these motivations dominates.[46] Another study found that when newcomers joined IT companies in India, they received support from their supervisor (who helped the newcomer by doing a special favor), but also verbal aggression (the supervisor made fun of new ideas). The support they received provoked approach behavior (the newcomer asked the supervisor for feedback on performance). The aggression provoked avoidance behavior (the newcomer avoided speaking with the supervisor unless absolutely necessary). The net effect on performance depended on which of these dominated.[47]

While the approach–avoidance framework has provided some important insights into behavior in organizations, there are several unresolved issues. First, is the framework simply a way of categorizing positive and negative traits, such as conscientiousness and neuroticism? Second, what traits fit into the framework? Nearly all the traits reviewed in this text do—including the Big Five, the Dark Triad, and others—yet these traits are quite different. Do we gain enough from aggregating them to make up for possibly missing other insights into behavior that are unique to each? Further research and evaluation are needed. For now, it is helpful to consider our approach–avoidance tendencies while we explore some other relevant personality traits in the next section.

OTHER PERSONALITY TRAITS RELEVANT TO OB

As we've discussed, studies of the Big Five traits, the Dark Triad, and approach–avoidance tendencies have much to offer to the field of OB. Now we'll look at other attributes that are powerful predictors of behavior in organizations: core self-evaluations, self-monitoring, and proactive personality.

Core Self-Evaluations

People who have positive **core self-evaluations (CSE)** like themselves and see themselves as effective, capable, and in control of their environment. Those with negative CSE tend to dislike themselves, question their capabilities, and view themselves as powerless over their environment.[48] We discussed in Chapter 3 that core self-evaluations relate to job satisfaction because people positive on this trait see more challenge in their jobs and actually attain more complex jobs.

People with positive CSE perform better than others because they set more ambitious goals, are more committed to their goals, and persist longer in attempting to reach them. One study of life insurance agents found core self-evaluations were critical predictors of performance. In fact, this study showed the majority of successful salespersons did have positive CSE.[49] Ninety percent of life insurance sales calls end in rejection, so an agent has to believe in herself to persist. People who have high CSE provide better customer service, are more popular coworkers, and have careers that begin on better footing and ascend more rapidly over time.[50] They perform especially well if they feel their work provides meaning and is helpful to others.[51]

What happens when someone thinks he is capable but is actually incompetent? One study found that many *Fortune* 500 CEOs are overconfident, and their perceived infallibility often causes them to make bad decisions.[52] These CEOs may be *over*confident and have high CSE, but people with lower CSE may sell themselves short and be less happy and effective than they could be because of it. If people decide they can't do something, they may not try, thus reinforcing their self-doubts.

Self-Monitoring

Zoe is always in trouble at work. Although she's competent, hardworking, and productive, she is rated no better than average in performance reviews, and she seems to have made a career of irritating her bosses. Zoe's problem is that she's politically inept. She's unable to adjust her behavior to fit changing situations. As she said, "I'm true to myself. I don't remake myself to please others." Zoe is a low self-monitor.

Self-monitoring describes an individual's ability to adjust her behavior to external, situational factors.[53] High self-monitors show considerable adaptability in adjusting their behavior to external situational factors. They are highly sensitive to external cues and can behave differently in varying situations, sometimes presenting striking contradictions between their public persona and their private self. Low self-monitors like Zoe can't disguise themselves in that way. They tend to display their true dispositions and attitudes in every situation; hence, there is high behavioral consistency between who they are and what they do.

Evidence indicates high self-monitors pay closer attention to the behavior of others and are more capable of conforming than are low self-monitors.[54] High self-monitors also receive better performance ratings, are more likely to emerge as leaders, and show less commitment to their organizations.[55] In addition, high self-monitor managers tend to be more mobile in their careers, receive more promotions (both internal and cross-organizational), and be more likely to occupy central positions in organizations.[56]

Proactive Personality

Did you ever notice that some people actively take the initiative to improve their current circumstances or create new ones? These are proactive personalities.[57] Those with a **proactive personality** identify opportunities, show initiative, take action, and persevere until meaningful change occurs, compared to others who passively react to situations. Proactive individuals have many desirable behaviors that organizations covet. They also have higher levels of job performance and career success.[58]

Proactive personality may be important for work teams. One study of 95 R&D teams in 33 Chinese companies revealed that teams with high-average levels of proactive personality were more innovative.[59] Like other traits, proactive personality is affected by the context. One study of bank branch teams in China found that if a team's leader was not proactive, the potential benefits of the team's proactivity will lie dormant or, worse, be suppressed by the leader.[60]

Are there downsides to having a proactive personality? There may be. A recent study of 231 Flemish unemployed individuals found that proactive individuals abandoned their job searches sooner. It may be that proactivity includes knowing when to step back and reconsider alternatives in the face of failure.[61]

In short, while proactive personality may be important to individual and team performance, like all traits it may have downsides, and its effectiveness may depend on the context. This brings us to the study of context and personality. Do you think personality changes in various situations? Let's explore this possibility.

PERSONALITY AND SITUATIONS

Earlier we discussed how research shows that heredity is more important than the environment in developing our personalities. The environment is not irrelevant, though. Some personality traits like the Big Five tend to be effective in almost any environment or situation. For example, research indicates that conscientiousness is helpful in the performance of most jobs, and extraversion is related to emergence as a leader in most situations.

Increasingly, we are learning that the effect of particular traits on organizational behavior depends on the situation. Two theoretical frameworks, situation strength and trait activation, help explain how this works.

Situation Strength Theory

Imagine you are in a meeting with your department. How likely are you to walk out in the middle of the meeting, shout at someone, turn your back on the group, or fall asleep? It's probably highly unlikely. Now imagine working from home. You might work in your pajamas, listen to loud music, or take a catnap.

Situation strength theory proposes that the way personality translates into behavior depends on the strength of the situation. By *situation strength*, we mean the degree to which norms, cues, or standards dictate appropriate behavior. Strong situations pressure us to exhibit the right behavior, clearly show us what that behavior is, and discourage the wrong behavior. In weak situations, conversely, "anything goes," and thus we are freer to express our personality in our behaviors. Thus, research suggests that personality traits better predict behavior in weak situations than in strong ones.

Researchers have analyzed situation strength in organizations in terms of four elements:[62]

1. *Clarity*, or the degree to which cues about work duties and responsibilities are available and clear. Jobs high in clarity produce strong situations because individuals can readily determine what to do, thus increasing the chances that everyone behaves similarly. For example, the job of janitor probably provides higher clarity about what needs to be done than the job of nanny.
2. *Consistency*, or the extent to which cues regarding work duties and responsibilities are compatible with one another. Jobs with high consistency represent strong situations because all the cues point toward the same desired behavior. The job of acute care nurse, for example, probably has higher consistency than the job of manager.
3. *Constraints*, or the extent to which individuals' freedom to decide or act is limited by forces outside their control. Jobs with many constraints represent strong situations because an individual has limited discretion. Bank examiner, for example, is probably a job with stronger constraints than forest ranger.
4. *Consequences*, or the degree to which decisions or actions have important implications for the organization or its members, clients, supplies, and so on. Jobs with important consequences represent strong situations because the environment is probably heavily structured to guard against mistakes. A surgeon's job, for example, has higher consequences than a foreign-language teacher's.

Some researchers have speculated that organizations are, by definition, strong situations because they impose rules, norms, and standards that govern behavior. These constraints are usually appropriate. For example, we would not want an employee to feel free to engage in sexual harassment, to follow questionable accounting procedures, or to come to work only when the mood strikes.

But that does not mean it is always desirable for organizations to create strong situations for their employees. First, jobs with myriad rules and tightly controlled processes can be dull or demotivating. Imagine that all work was executed with an assembly-line approach. Most of us prefer having some freedom to decide how to do our work. Second, people do differ, so what works well for one person might work poorly for another. Third, strong situations might suppress the creativity, initiative, and discretion prized by some cultures. One recent study, for example, found that in weak organizational situations, employees were more likely to behave proactively in accordance with their values.[63]

Finally, work is increasingly complex and interrelated globally. Creating strong rules to govern complex, interrelated, and culturally diverse systems might be not only difficult but unwise. Managers need to recognize the role of situation strength in the workplace and find the appropriate balance.

Trait Activation Theory

Another important theoretical framework toward understanding situational activators for personality is **trait activation theory (TAT)**. TAT predicts that some situations, events, or interventions "activate" a trait more than others. For example, a commission-based compensation plan would likely activate individual differences in extraversion because extraversion is more reward-sensitive, than, say, openness. Conversely, in jobs that allow expression of individual creativity, individual differences in openness may better predict creative behavior than individual differences in extraversion. See Exhibit 5-2 for specific examples.

A recent study found that people learning online responded differently when their behavior was electronically monitored. Those who had high fear of failure had higher evaluation apprehension than others and learned significantly less. In this case, a feature of the environment (electronic monitoring) activated a trait (fear of failing), and the combination of the two meant lowered job performance.[64] TAT can also work in a positive

Detail Orientation Required	Social Skills Required	Competitive Work	Innovation Required	Dealing with Angry People	Time Pressure (Deadlines)
Jobs scoring high (the traits listed here should predict behavior in these jobs)					
Air traffic controller Accountant Legal seceratary	Clergy Therapist Concierge	Coach/scout Financial manager Sales representative	Actor Systems analyst Advertising writer	Correctional officer Telemarketer Flight attendant	Broadcast news analyst Editor Airline pilot
Jobs scoring low (the traits listed here should not predict behavior in these jobs)					
Forester Masseuse Model	Software engineer Pump operator Broadcast technician	Postal clerk Historian Nuclear reactor operator	Court reporter Archivist Medical technician	Composer Biologist Satistician	Skincare specialist Mathematician Fitness trainer
Jobs that score high activate these traits (make them more relevant to predicting behavior)					
Conscientious-ness (+)	Extraversion (+) Agreeable-ness (+)	Extraversion (+) Agreeable-ness (−)	Openness (+)	Extraversion (+) Agreeable-ness (+) Neuroticism (−)	Conscientious-ness (+) Neuroticism (−)

EXHIBIT 5-2

Trait Activation Theory: Jobs in Which Certain Big Five Traits Are More Relevant

Note: A plus (+) sign means individuals who score high on this trait should do better in this job. A minus (−) sign means individuals who score low on this trait should do better in this job.

way. A recent study applying TAT found that individual differences in the tendency to behave prosocially mattered more when coworkers were not supportive. In other words, in a supportive environment, everyone behaves prosocially, but in an environment that is not so nice, whether an individual has the personality to behave prosocially makes a major difference.[65]

Together, situation strength and trait activation theories show that the debate over nature versus nurture might best be framed as nature *and* nurture. Not only does each affect behavior, but they interact with one another. Put another way, personality affects work behavior and the situation affects work behavior, but when the situation is right, the power of personality to predict behavior is even higher.

Having discussed personality traits—the enduring characteristics that describe a person's behavior—we now turn to values. Values are often very specific and describe belief systems rather than behavioral tendencies. Some beliefs or values say little about a person's personality, and we don't always act consistently with our values.

VALUES

Is capital punishment right or wrong? Is a desire for power good or bad? The answers to these questions are value-laden.

Values represent basic convictions that "a specific mode of conduct or end-state of existence is personally or socially preferable to an opposite or converse mode of conduct or end-state of existence."[66] Values contain a judgmental element because they carry an individual's ideas about what is right, good, or desirable. They have both content and intensity attributes. The content attribute says a mode of conduct or end-state of existence is *important*. The intensity attribute specifies *how important* it is. When we rank values in terms of intensity, we obtain that person's **value system**. We all have a hierarchy according to the relative importance we assign to values such as freedom, pleasure, self-respect, honesty, obedience, and equality.

Values tend to be relatively stable and enduring.[67] Many of the values we hold are established in our early years—by parents, teachers, friends, and others. As children, we are told certain behaviors or outcomes are *always* desirable or *always* undesirable, with few gray areas. You were never taught to be just a little bit honest or a little bit responsible, for example. It is this absolute, black-or-white characteristic of values that ensures their stability and endurance. If we question our values, they may change, but more often they are reinforced. There is also evidence linking personality to values, implying our values may be partly determined by genetically transmitted traits.[68] Open people, for example, may be more politically liberal, whereas conscientious people may place a greater value on rules ensuring safe or ethical conduct. To explore the topic further, we will discuss the importance and organization of values next.

The Importance and Organization of Values

Values lay the foundation for our understanding of people's attitudes and motivation, and they influence our perceptions. We enter an organization with preconceived notions of what "ought" and "ought not" to be. These notions are not value-free; on the contrary, they contain our interpretations of right and wrong and our preference for certain behaviors or outcomes over others. While values can sometimes augment decision making, at times they can also cloud objectivity and rationality.[69] Regardless of whether they clarify or bias our judgment, our values do influence our attitudes and behaviors at work.

Suppose you enter an organization with the view that allocating pay on the basis of performance is right, while allocating pay on the basis of seniority is wrong. How will you react if you find the organization you've just joined rewards seniority and not performance? You're likely to be disappointed—this can lead to job dissatisfaction and a decision not to exert a high level of effort because "It's probably not going to lead to more money anyway." Would your attitudes and behavior be different if your values aligned with the organization's pay policies? Most likely.

✪ WATCH IT

If your professor assigned this, sign in to **mymanagementlab.com** to watch a video titled Honest Tea: Ethics – Company Mission and Values to learn more about this topic and respond to questions.

Terminal versus Instrumental Values

How can we organize values? One researcher—Milton Rokeach—argued that we can separate values into two categories. One set, called **terminal values**, refers to desirable end-states. These are the goals a person would like to achieve during his lifetime. The other set, called **instrumental values**, refers to preferable modes of behavior, or means of achieving the terminal values. Some examples of terminal values are prosperity and economic success, freedom, health and well-being, world peace, and meaning in life. Examples of instrumental values are autonomy and self-reliance, personal discipline, kindness, and goal-orientation. Each of us places value on both the ends (terminal values) and the means (instrumental values). A balance between the two is important, as well as an understanding of how to strike this balance. Which terminal and instrumental values are especially key vary by the person.

So far, we've discussed personality and values separately, including some organizational implications for each. As you can see, finding a fit between an individual person and an optimal work situation is complex. A few theories we discuss in the next section help link an individual's personality and values to jobs and organizations.

LINKING AN INDIVIDUAL'S PERSONALITY AND VALUES TO THE WORKPLACE

Thirty years ago, organizations were concerned only with personality because their primary focus was to match individuals to specific jobs. That concern has expanded to include how well the individual's personality *and* values match the organization. Why? Because managers today are less interested in an applicant's ability to perform a *specific* job than with the applicant's *flexibility* to meet changing situations and commitment to the organization.

We'll now discuss person–job fit and person–organization fit in more detail.

Person–Job Fit

The effort to match job requirements with personality characteristics is best articulated in John Holland's **personality–job fit theory**.[70] Holland presents six personality types

Type	Personality Characteristics	Congruent Occupations
Realistic: Prefers physical activities that require skill, strength, and coordination	Shy, genuine, persistent, stable, conforming, practical	Mechanic, drill press operator, assemblyline worker, farmer
Investigative: Prefers activities that involve thinking, organizing, and understanding	Analytical, original, curious, independent	Biologist, economist, mathematician, news reporter
Social: Prefers activities that involve helping and developing others	Sociable, friendly, cooperative, understanding	Social worker, teacher, counselor, clinical psychologist
Conventional: Prefers rule-regulated, orderly, and unambiguous activities	Conforming, efficient, practical, unimaginative, inflexible	Accountant, corporate manager, bank teller, file clerk
Enterprising: Prefers verbal activities in which there are opportunities to influence others and attain power	Self-confident, ambitious, energetic, domineering	Lawyer, real estate agent, public relations specialist, small business manager
Artistic: Prefers ambiguous and unsystematic activities that allow creative expression	Imaginative, disorderly, idealistic, emotional, impractical	Painter, musician, writer, interior decorator

EXHIBIT 5-3
Holland's Typology of Personality and Congruent Occupations

and proposes that satisfaction and the propensity to leave a position depend on how well individuals match their personalities to a job. Exhibit 5-3 describes the six types, their personality characteristics, and examples of the congruent occupations for each.

Holland developed the Vocational Preference Inventory questionnaire, which contains 160 occupational titles. Respondents indicate which they like or dislike, and their answers form personality profiles. Research supports the resulting hexagonal diagram shown in Exhibit 5-4.[71] The closer two fields or orientations are in the hexagon, the more compatible they are. Adjacent categories are quite similar, whereas diagonally opposite ones are highly dissimilar.

What does all this mean? Personality–job fit theory argues that satisfaction is highest and turnover lowest when personality and occupation are in agreement. A realistic person in a realistic job is in a more congruent situation than a realistic person in an investigative job. A realistic person in a social job is in the most incongruent situation possible. The key point of this model is that people in jobs congruent with their personality should be more satisfied and less likely to voluntarily resign than people in incongruent jobs.

Person–Organization Fit

We've noted that researchers have looked at matching people to organizations and jobs. If an organization faces a dynamic and changing environment and needs employees able to

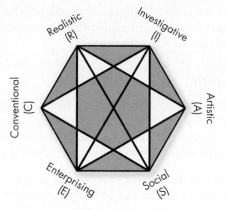

EXHIBIT 5-4
Relationships Among Occupational Personality Types

Source: Reprinted by special permission of the publisher, Psychological Assessment Resources, Inc., from Making Vocational Choices, copyright 1973, 1985, 1992 by Psychological Assessment Resources, Inc. All rights reserved.

readily change tasks and move easily between teams, it's more important that employees' personalities fit with the overall organization's culture than with the characteristics of any specific job.

The *person–organization fit* theory essentially argues that people are attracted to and selected by organizations that match their values, and they leave organizations that are not compatible with their personalities.[72] Using the Big Five terminology, for instance, we could expect that people high on extraversion fit well with aggressive and team-oriented cultures, people high on agreeableness match up better with a supportive organizational climate than one focused on aggressiveness, and people high on openness to experience fit better in organizations that emphasize innovation rather than standardization.[73] Following these guidelines at the time of hiring should identify new employees who fit better with the organization's culture, which should, in turn, result in higher employee satisfaction and reduced turnover. Research on person–organization fit has also looked at whether people's values match the organization's culture. This match predicts job satisfaction, commitment to the organization, and low turnover.[74]

Are person–job fit and person–organization fit more applicable in some countries than others? Apparently yes. Research indicated that person–job fit was a strong predictor of lower turnover in the United States, but a combination of person–organization fit and other factors strongly predicted lower turnover in India.[75] These findings may be generalizable for individualistic countries like the United States, and collectivistic countries like India, but more research is needed to understand the exact relationship.

INTERNATIONAL VALUES

Unlike personality, which as we have seen is largely genetically determined, values are learned from our environments. Values are also shared between people and passed down from one generation to the next. For these reasons, different value systems have

Values do appear to vary across cultures, meaning that, on average, people's values in one nation tend to differ from those in another; however, there is substantial variability in values within a culture.

developed over time in each national culture. As researchers have sought to understand the national value system differences, two important frameworks that have emerged are from Geert Hofstede and the GLOBE studies.

Hofstede's Framework

One of the most widely referenced approaches for analyzing variations among cultures was done in the late 1970s by Geert Hofstede.[76] Hofstede surveyed more than 116,000 IBM employees in 40 countries about their work-related values and found that managers and employees vary on five value dimensions of national culture:

- *Power distance.* **Power distance** describes the degree to which people in a country accept that power in institutions and organizations is distributed unequally. A high rating on power distance means that large inequalities of power and wealth exist and are tolerated in the culture, as in a class or caste system that discourages upward mobility. A low power distance rating characterizes societies that stress equality and opportunity.
- *Individualism versus collectivism.* **Individualism** is the degree to which people prefer to act as individuals rather than as members of groups and believe in individual rights above all else. **Collectivism** emphasizes a tight social framework in which people expect others in groups of which they are a part to look after them and protect them.
- *Masculinity versus femininity.* Hofstede's construct of **masculinity** is the degree to which the culture favors traditional masculine roles such as achievement, power, and control, as opposed to viewing men and women as equals. A high masculinity rating indicates the culture has separate roles for men and women, with men dominating the society. A high **femininity** rating means the culture sees little differentiation between male and female roles and treats women as the equals of men in all respects.
- *Uncertainty avoidance.* The degree to which people in a country prefer structured over unstructured situations defines their **uncertainty avoidance**. In cultures that score high on uncertainty avoidance, people have an increased level of anxiety about uncertainty and ambiguity and use laws and controls to reduce uncertainty. People in cultures low on uncertainty avoidance are more accepting of ambiguity, are less rule oriented, take more risks, and more readily accept change.
- *Long-term versus short-term orientation.* This newer addition to Hofstede's typology measures a society's devotion to traditional values. People in a culture with **long-term orientation** look to the future and value thrift, persistence, and tradition. In a **short-term orientation**, people value the here and now; they accept change more readily and don't see commitments as impediments to change.

How do different countries score on Hofstede's dimensions? Exhibit 5-5 shows the ratings for the countries for which data are available. For example, power distance is higher in Malaysia than in any other country, and lowest in Austria. The United States is very individualistic; in fact, it's the most individualistic nation of all (closely followed by Australia and Great Britain). Guatemala is the most collectivistic nation. The country with the highest masculinity rank by far is Japan, and the country with the highest femininity rank is Sweden. Greece scores the highest in uncertainty avoidance, while

Country	Power Distance		Individualism versus Collectivism		Masculinity versus Femininity		Uncertainty Avoidance		Long- versus Short-Term Orientation	
	Index	Rank	Index	Rank	Index	Rank	Index	Rank	Index	Rank
Argentina	49	35–36	46	22–23	56	20–21	86	10–15		
Australia	36	41	90	2	61	16	51	37	31	22–24
Austria	11	53	55	18	79	2	70	24–25	31	22–24
Belgium	65	20	75	8	54	22	94	5–6	38	18
Brazil	69	14	38	26–27	49	27	76	21–22	65	6
Canada	39	39	80	4–5	52	24	48	41–42	23	30
Chile	63	24–25	23	38	28	46	86	10–15		
Colombia	67	17	13	49	64	11–12	80	20		
Costa Rica	35	42–44	15	46	21	48–49	86	10–15		
Denmark	18	51	74	9	16	50	23	51	46	10
Ecuador	78	8–9	8	52	63	13–14	67	28		
El Salvador	66	18–19	19	42	40	40	94	5–6		
Finland	33	46	63	17	26	47	59	31–32	41	14
France	68	15–16	71	10–11	43	35–36	86	10–15	39	17
Germany	35	42–44	67	15	66	9–10	65	29	31	22–24
Great Britain	35	42–44	89	3	66	9–10	35	47–48	25	28–29
Greece	60	27–28	35	30	57	18–19	112	1		
Guatemala	95	2–3	6	53	37	43	101	3		
Hong Kong	68	15–16	25	37	57	18–19	29	49–50	96	2
India	77	10–11	48	21	56	20–21	40	45	61	7
Indonesia	78	8–9	14	47–48	46	30–31	48	41–42		
Iran	58	29–30	41	24	43	35–36	59	31–32		
Ireland	28	49	70	12	68	7–8	35	47–48	43	13
Israel	13	52	54	19	47	29	81	19		
Italy	50	34	76	7	70	4–5	75	23	34	19
Jamaica	45	37	39	25	68	7–8	13	52		
Japan	54	33	46	22–23	95	1	92	7	80	4
Korea (South)	60	27–28	18	43	39	41	85	16–17	75	5
Malaysia	104	1	26	36	50	25–26	36	46		
Mexico	81	5–6	30	32	69	6	82	18		
The Netherlands	38	40	80	4–5	14	51	53	35	44	11–12
New Zealand	22	50	79	6	58	17	49	39–40	30	25–26
Norway	31	47–48	69	13	8	52	50	38	44	11–12
Pakistan	55	32	14	47–48	50	25–26	70	24–25	0	34
Panama	95	2–3	11	51	44	34	86	10–15		

(Continued)

EXHIBIT 5-5
Hofstede's Cultural Values by Nation

Source: Copyright Geert Hofstede BV, hofstede@bart.nl. Reprinted with permission.

Country	Power Distance		Individualism versus Collectivism		Masculinity versus Femininity		Uncertainty Avoidance		Long- versus Short-Term Orientation	
	Index	Rank	Index	Rank	Index	Rank	Index	Rank	Index	Rank
Peru	64	21–23	16	45	42	37–38	87	9		
Philippines	94	4	32	31	64	11–12	44	44	19	31–32
Portugal	63	24–25	27	33–35	31	45	104	2	30	25–26
Singapore	74	13	20	39–41	48	28	8	53	48	9
South Africa	49	35–36	65	16	63	13–14	49	39–40		
Spain	57	31	51	20	42	37–38	86	10–15	19	31–32
Sweden	31	47–48	71	10–11	5	53	29	49–50	33	20
Switzerland	34	45	68	14	70	4–5	58	33	40	15–16
Taiwan	58	29–30	17	44	45	32–33	69	26	87	3
Thailand	64	21–23	20	39–41	34	44	64	30	56	8
Turkey	66	18–19	37	28	45	32–33	85	16–17		
United States	40	38	91	1	62	15	46	43	29	27
Uruguay	61	26	36	29	38	42	100	4		
Venezuela	81	5–6	12	50	73	3	76	21–22		
Yugoslavia	76	12	27	33–35	21	48–49	88	8		
Regions:										
Arab countries	80	7	38	26–27	53	23	68	27		
East Africa	64	21–23	27	33–35	41	39	52	36	25	28–29
West Africa	77	10–11	20	39–41	46	30–31	54	34	16	33

EXHIBIT 5-5 (*Continued*)

Note: Scores range from 0 = extremely low on dimension to 100 = extremely high.

1 = highest rank. LTO ranks: 1 = China; 15–16 = Bangladesh; 21 = Poland; 34 = lowest.

Singapore scores the lowest. Hong Kong has one of the longest-term orientations; Pakistan has the shortest-term orientation.

Hofstede's culture dimensions have been enormously influential on OB researchers and managers, and he has been one of the most widely cited social scientists ever. Nevertheless, Hofstede's research has been criticized. First, although the data has been updated, the original work is more than forty years old and was based on a single company (IBM). A lot has happened on the world scene since then. Some of the most obvious changes include the fall of the Soviet Union, the transformation of central and eastern Europe, the end of apartheid in South Africa, the rise of China as a global power, and the advent of a world-wide recession. These changes would more than likely shift some of the cultural values that Hofstede's framework assesses. Second, few researchers have read the details of Hofstede's methodology closely and are therefore unaware of the many decisions and judgment calls he had to make (for example, reducing the number of cultural values to just five).

Research across 598 studies with more than 200,000 respondents investigated the relationship between Hofstede's cultural values and a variety of organizational criteria at both the individual and national level of analysis.[77] Overall, the five original culture dimensions were found to be equally strong predictors of relevant outcomes. The researchers also found that measuring individual scores resulted in much better predictions of most outcomes than assigning all people in a country the same cultural values. In sum, this research suggests that Hofstede's framework may be a valuable way of thinking about differences among people, but we should be cautious about assuming all people from a country have the same values.

The GLOBE Framework

Begun in 1993, the Global Leadership and Organizational Behavior Effectiveness (GLOBE) research program is an ongoing cross-cultural investigation of leadership and national culture. Using data from 825 organizations in 62 countries, the GLOBE team has identified nine dimensions on which national cultures differ.[78] Some dimensions— such as power distance, individualism/collectivism, uncertainty avoidance, gender differentiation (similar to masculinity versus femininity), and future orientation (similar to long-term versus short-term orientation)—resemble the Hofstede dimensions. The main difference is that the GLOBE framework added dimensions, such as humane orientation (the degree to which a society rewards individuals for being altruistic, generous, and kind to others) and performance orientation (the degree to which a society encourages and rewards group members for performance improvement and excellence).

Comparison of Hofstede's Framework and the GLOBE Framework

Which framework is better, Hofstede's or the GLOBE? That's hard to say, and each has its supporters. We give more emphasis to Hofstede's dimensions here because they have stood the test of time and the GLOBE study confirmed them. For example, a review of the organizational commitment literature found that both the Hofstede and GLOBE individualism/collectivism dimensions operated similarly. Specifically, both frameworks suggest that organizational commitment (discussed earlier) tends to be lower in individualistic countries.[79] Both frameworks thus have a great deal in common, and each has something unique to offer.

SUMMARY

Personality matters to organizational behavior. It does not explain all behavior, but it sets the stage. Emerging theory and research reveal how personality matters more in some situations than in others. The Big Five has been a particularly important advancement; the Dark Triad and other traits matter as well. Every trait has advantages and disadvantages for work behavior, and there is no perfect constellation of traits that is ideal for every situation. Personality can help you to understand why people (including yourself!) act, think, and feel the way we do, and the astute manager can put that understanding to use by taking care to place employees in situations that best fit their personality.

  Why is it important to know an individual's values? Values often underlie and explain attitudes, behaviors, and perceptions. Values tend to vary internationally along dimensions that can predict organizational outcomes; however, an individual may or may not hold values that are consistent with the values of the national culture. Knowledge of an individual's value system can provide insight into what makes the person "tick."

IMPLICATIONS FOR MANAGERS

- Consider screening job candidates for high conscientiousness—as well as the other Big Five traits, depending on the criteria your organization finds most important. Other traits, such as core self-evaluation or narcissism, may be relevant in certain situations.
- Although the MBTI has faults, you can use it in training and development to help employees better understand themselves, help team members better understand each other, and open up communication in work groups and possibly reduce conflicts.
- You need to evaluate your employees' jobs, their work groups, and your organization to determine the optimal personality fit.
- Take into account employees' situational factors when evaluating their observable personality traits, and lower the situation strength to better ascertain personality characteristics.
- The findings from Hofstede's work and the GLOBE program underscore the need for managers to understand the cultural values of their employees. The more you take into consideration people's different cultures, the better you will be able to determine their work behavior and create a positive organizational climate that performs well.

PERSONAL INVENTORY ASSESSMENT

In Personal Inventory Assessment found in MyManagementLab take assessment: Personality Style Indicator

⭐ WRITING SPACE

If your professor assigned this, sign in to **mymanagementlab.com** for the following Assisted-graded writing question:

5-1. What do you feel are the pros and cons of extraversion and introversion for your work life? Can you increase desirable traits?

6
Perception and Decision Processes

MyManagementLab®
✪ Improve Your Grade!

When you see this icon ✪, visit **www.mymanagementlab.com** for activities that are applied, personalized, and offer immediate feedback.

LEARNING OBJECTIVES

After studying this chapter, you should be able to:

1. Define *perception*, and explain the factors that influence it.
2. Explain attribution theory, and describe the common shortcuts used in judging others.
3. Explain the link between perception and decision making.
4. Contrast the rational model of decision making with bounded rationality and intuition.
5. Identify the common decision biases or errors.
6. Explain how individual differences and organizational constraints affect decision making.
7. Contrast the three ethical decision criteria.
8. Define *creativity*, and describe the three-stage model of creativity.

✪ Chapter Warm-up

If your professor has chosen to assign this, go to **www.mymanagementlab.com** to see what you should particularly focus on and to take the Chapter 6 warm up.

Any discussion of individual decision making must take into account the role of how we perceive people and situations. In this chapter, we will discuss various factors in the individual decision-making process—factors like perception and biases that shape how we are likely to make decisions, and factors like ethics and creativity that we should consider in order to make the best decisions.

WHAT IS PERCEPTION?

Perception is a process by which individuals organize and interpret sensory impressions in order to give meaning to their environment. However, what we perceive can be substantially different from objective reality. For example, all employees in a firm may view it as a great place to work—favorable working conditions, interesting job assignments, good pay, excellent benefits, understanding and responsible management—but, as most of us know, it's very unusual to find such agreement.

Why is perception important in the study of OB? Simply because people's behavior is based on their perception of what reality is, not on reality itself. As you've surely found in your own experiences, what we perceive can be substantially different from objective reality. *The world as it is perceived is the world that is behaviorally important.* To understand what we have in common in our interpretations of reality, we need to begin with the factors that influence our perceptions.

Factors That Influence Perception

People have inherent biases in how they see others (perception) and in how they make decisions (decision making). We can better understand people by understanding these biases.

A number of factors shape and sometimes distort perception. These factors can reside in the *perceiver*; in the object, or *target*, being perceived; or in the *situation* in which the perception is made.

When you look at a target, your interpretation of what you see is influenced by your personal characteristics—attitudes, personality, motives, interests, past experiences, and expectations. For instance, if you expect police officers to be authoritative, you may perceive them as such, regardless of their actual traits.

The characteristics of the target also affect what we perceive. Loud people are more likely to be noticed than quiet ones. So, too, are extremely attractive or unattractive individuals. Because we don't look at targets in isolation, the relationship of a target to its background influences perception, as does our tendency to group close things and similar things together. We often perceive women, men, Whites, African Americans, Asians, or members of any other group that has clearly distinguishable characteristics as alike in other, unrelated ways as well.

Context matters, too. The time at which we see an object or event can influence our attention, as can location, light, heat, or situational factors. For instance, at a club on Saturday night you may not notice someone "decked out." Yet that same person so attired for your Monday morning management class would certainly catch your attention. Neither the perceiver nor the target has changed between Saturday night and Monday morning, but the situation is different.

✪ WATCH IT

If your professor assigned this, sign in to **mymanagementlab.com** to watch a video titled Orpheus Group Casting: Social Perception and Attribution to learn more about this topic and respond to questions.

PERSON PERCEPTION: MAKING JUDGMENTS ABOUT OTHERS

Now we turn to the application of perception concepts most relevant to OB—*person perception*, or the perceptions people form about each other. We begin with a discussion of attribution theory, a construct that helps to explain how we form perceptions of other people.

Attribution Theory

Nonliving objects such as desks, machines, and buildings are subject to the laws of nature, but they have no beliefs, motives, or intentions. People do. When we observe people, we attempt to explain their behavior. Our perception and judgment of a person's actions are influenced by the assumptions we make about that person's state of mind.

Attribution theory tries to explain the ways we judge people differently, depending on the meaning we attribute to a behavior.[1] It suggests that when we observe an individual's behavior, we attempt to determine whether it was internally or externally caused. That determination depends largely on three factors: (1) distinctiveness, (2) consensus, and (3) consistency. Let's clarify the differences between internal and external causation, and then we'll discuss the determining factors.

Internally caused behaviors are those an observer believes to be under the personal control of another individual. *Externally* caused behavior is what we imagine the situation forced the individual to do. For example, if one of your employees is late for work, you might attribute that to his overnight partying and subsequent oversleeping. This is an internal attribution. But if you attribute his tardiness to an automobile accident that tied up traffic, you are making an external attribution.

Now let's discuss the three determining factors. *Distinctiveness* refers to whether an individual displays different behaviors in different situations. Is the employee who arrives late today also one who regularly "blows off" other kinds of commitments? What we want to know is whether this behavior is unusual. If it is, we are likely to give it an external attribution. If it's not, we will probably judge the behavior to be internal.

If everyone who faces a similar situation responds in the same way, the behavior shows *consensus*. The behavior of our tardy employee meets this criterion if all employees who took the same route were also late. From an attribution perspective, if consensus is high, you would probably give an external attribution to the employee's tardiness, whereas if other employees who took the same route made it to work on time, you would attribute his lateness to an internal cause.

Finally, an observer looks for *consistency* in a person's actions. Does the person respond the same way over time? Coming in ten minutes late for work is not perceived in the same way for an employee who hasn't been late for several months as it is for an employee who is late three times a week. The more consistent the behavior, the more we are inclined to attribute it to internal causes.

Exhibit 6-1 summarizes the key elements in attribution theory. It tells us, for instance, that if an employee, Katelyn, generally performs at about the same level on related tasks as she does on her current task (low distinctiveness); other employees frequently perform differently—better or worse—than Katelyn on that task (low consensus); and Katelyn's performance on this current task is consistent over time (high consistency), anyone judging Katelyn's work will likely hold her primarily responsible for her task performance (internal attribution).

EXHIBIT 6-1
Attribution
Theory

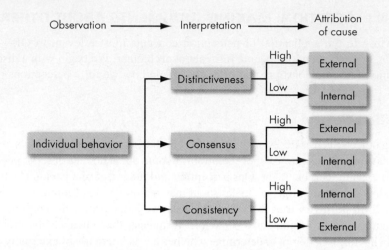

One of the findings from attribution theory research is that errors or biases distort attributions. When we make judgments about the behavior of other people, we tend to underestimate the influence of external factors and overestimate the influence of internal or personal factors.[2] This **fundamental attribution error** can explain why a sales manager is prone to attribute the poor performance of her sales agents to laziness rather than to a competitor's innovative product line. Individuals and organizations tend to attribute their own successes to internal factors such as ability or effort, while blaming failure on external factors such as bad luck or unproductive coworkers. People also tend to attribute ambiguous information as relatively flattering, accept positive feedback, and reject negative feedback. This is **self-serving bias**.[3]

The evidence on cultural differences in perception is mixed, but most suggests there *are* differences across cultures in the attributions people make.[4] One study found Korean managers were less prone to self-serving bias—they tended to accept responsibility for group failure "because I was not a capable leader" instead of attributing failure to group members.[5] On the other hand, in other research Asian managers are more likely to blame institutions or whole organizations, whereas Western observers believe individual managers should get blame or praise.[6] That probably explains why U.S. newspapers feature the names of individual executives when firms do poorly, whereas Asian media cover how the firm as a whole has failed. This tendency to make group-based attributions also explains why individuals from Asian cultures are more likely to make group-based stereotypes.[7] Attribution theory was developed based on experiments with U.S. and Western European workers. But the studies suggest caution in making attribution theory predictions in non-Western societies, especially in countries with strong collectivist traditions.

Differences in attribution tendencies don't mean the basic concepts of attribution completely differ across cultures, though. Self-serving biases may be less common in East Asian cultures, but evidence suggests they still operate across cultures.[8] Studies indicate Chinese managers assess blame for mistakes using the same distinctiveness, consensus, and consistency cues Western managers use.[9] They also become angry and punish those deemed responsible for failure, a reaction shown in many studies of Western managers. This means the basic process of attribution applies across cultures, but that it takes more evidence for Asian managers to conclude that someone else should be blamed.

The concept of attribution theory significantly advances our understanding of people perception by helping us identify why we may draw certain conclusions from people's behavior. Having discussed person perception in particular, now let's take a more general look at the common shortcuts we use to simplify our processing of others' behavior.

Common Shortcuts in Judging Others

The shortcuts for judging others often allow us to form perceptions rapidly and provide valid data for making predictions. However, shortcuts can and do sometimes result in significant distortions.

SELECTIVE PERCEPTION   Any characteristic that makes a person, an object, or an event stand out will increase the probability that we will perceive it. Why? Because it is impossible for us to assimilate everything we see; we can take in only certain stimuli. Thus, you are more likely to notice cars like your own, and your boss may reprimand some people and not others doing the same thing. Because we can't observe everything going on around us, we use **selective perception**. But we don't choose randomly: We select according to our interests, background, experience, and attitudes. Selective perception allows us to speed-read others, but not without the risk of drawing an inaccurate or incomplete picture. Seeing what we want to see, we can draw unwarranted conclusions from an ambiguous situation.

HALO EFFECT   When we draw an impression about an individual on the basis of a single characteristic, such as intelligence, sociability, or appearance, a **halo effect** is operating.[10] The halo effect was confirmed in a classic study in which subjects were given a list of traits such as intelligent, skillful, practical, industrious, determined, and warm and asked to evaluate the person to whom those traits applied.[11] With these qualities in mind, subjects also then judged the person to be wise, humorous, popular, and imaginative. When the same list substituted the word "cold" for "warm," a completely different picture emerged; subjects did not judge the person as holding positive qualities. Clearly, the subjects were allowing a single trait to influence their overall impression of the person they were judging. As managers, we need to be careful not to draw inferences from small clues.

CONTRAST EFFECTS   An old adage among entertainers is "Never follow an act that has kids or animals in it." Why? Audiences love children and animals so much that you'll look bad in comparison. This example demonstrates how a **contrast effect** can distort perceptions. We don't evaluate a person in isolation. Our reaction is influenced by other persons we have recently encountered.

STEREOTYPING   When we judge someone on the basis of our perception of the group to which he belongs, we are **stereotyping**.[12]

We deal with an unmanageable number of stimuli from our complex world by using *heuristics* or stereotypes to make decisions quickly. For example, it does make sense to assume that Allison from finance will be able to help you figure out a forecasting problem. The problem occurs when we generalize inaccurately or too much. In organizations, we frequently hear comments that represent stereotypes based on gender, age, race, religion, ethnicity, and even weight (see Chapter 2):[13] "Men aren't interested in child care," "Older workers can't learn new skills," "Asian immigrants are hardworking and conscientious." Research suggests stereotypes operate emotionally and often below the level of conscious awareness, making them particularly hard to challenge and change.[14]

Stereotypes can be deeply ingrained and powerful enough to influence life-and-death decisions. One study, controlling for a wide array of factors (such as aggravating or mitigating circumstances), showed that the degree to which Black defendants in murder trials looked "stereotypically black" essentially doubled their odds of receiving a death sentence if convicted.[15] Another study found that students who read scenarios describing leaders tended to assign higher scores for leadership potential and effective leadership to Whites than to minorities even though the content of the scenarios was equivalent, supporting the idea of a stereotype of Whites as better leaders.[16]

One problem of stereotypes is that they *are* widespread generalizations, though they may not contain a shred of truth when applied to a particular person or situation. We have to monitor ourselves to make sure we're not unfairly applying a stereotype in our evaluations and decisions. Stereotypes are an example of the warning, "The more useful, the more danger from misuse."

It should be obvious by now that our perceptions, many of which are near-instantaneous and without conscious deliberation, color our outlook. Sometimes our perceptions have little impact on anyone, but more often our perceptions greatly influence our decisions. The first step toward increasing the effectiveness of organizational decision making is to understand the process on an individualized level, discussed next.

THE LINK BETWEEN PERCEPTION AND INDIVIDUAL DECISION MAKING

Individuals make **decisions**, choices from among two or more alternatives. Ideally, decision making would be an objective process, but the way individuals make decisions and the quality of their choices are largely influenced by their perceptions. Individual decision making is an important factor of behavior at all levels of an organization. Top managers determine their organization's goals, what products or services to offer, how best to finance operations, or where to locate a new manufacturing plant. Middle- and lower-level managers set production schedules, select new employees, and decide how to allocate pay raises. Organizations sometimes give their nonmanagerial employees decision-making authority historically reserved for managers alone, but even in traditional settings, nonmanagerial employees make decisions that affect the organization.

Decision making occurs as a reaction to a **problem**.[17] That is, a discrepancy exists between the current state of affairs and some desired state, requiring us to consider alternative courses of action. If your car breaks down and you rely on it to get to work, you have a problem that requires a decision on your part. Unfortunately, most problems do not come neatly labeled as such. One person's *problem* is another person's *satisfactory state of affairs*. One manager may view her division's 2 percent decline in quarterly sales to be a serious problem requiring immediate action on her part. Her counterpart in another division, who also had a 2 percent sales decrease, might consider that quite acceptable. So awareness that a problem exists and that a decision might or might not be needed is a perceptual issue.

Every decision requires us to interpret and evaluate information. We typically receive data from multiple sources we need to screen, process, and interpret. Which data are relevant to the decision, and which are not? Our perceptions will answer that question. We also need to develop alternatives and evaluate their strengths and weaknesses. Again, our perceptual process will affect the final outcome. Throughout the decision-making process, perceptual errors often surface that can bias analyses and conclusions.

DECISION MAKING IN ORGANIZATIONS

Business schools train students to follow rational decision-making models. While such rationalistic models have merit, they don't always describe how people make decisions. OB improves the way we make decisions in organizations by addressing the decision-making errors people commit in addition to the perception errors we've discussed. First, we will describe some decision-making constructs, and then we will describe a few of the most common errors.

The Rational Model, Bounded Rationality, and Intuition

In OB, there are generally accepted constructs of decision making each of us employs to make determinations: rational decision making, bounded rationality, and intuition. Though their processes make sense, they may not lead to the most accurate (or best) decisions. More importantly, there are times when one strategy may lead to a better outcome than another in a given situation.

RATIONAL DECISION MAKING   We often think the best decision maker is **rational** and makes consistent, value-maximizing choices within specified constraints.[18] These decisions often follow a six-step **rational decision-making model**.[19] The six steps are listed in Exhibit 6-2.

The rational decision-making model assumes that the decision maker has complete information, is able to identify all the relevant options in an unbiased manner, and chooses the option with the highest utility.[20] In reality, though, most decisions don't follow the rational model; people are usually content to find an acceptable or reasonable solution to a problem rather than an optimal one. We tend to limit our choices to the neighborhood of the problem's symptom and the current alternative at hand. As one expert in decision making put it, "Most significant decisions are made by judgment, rather than by a defined prescriptive model."[21] Unfortunately, people are remarkably unaware of making suboptimal decisions.[22]

1. Define the problem.
2. Identify the decision criteria.
3. Allocate weights to the criteria.
4. Develop the alternatives.
5. Evaluate the alternatives.
6. Select the best alternative.

EXHIBIT 6-2
Steps in Rational Decision-Making Model

BOUNDED RATIONALITY Often, we don't follow the rational decision-making model for a reason: Our limited information-processing capability makes it impossible to assimilate all the information necessary to optimize.[23] Many problems don't have an optimal solution because they are too complicated to fit the rational decision-making model, so people *satisfice*; they seek solutions that are satisfactory and sufficient. We tend to reduce complex problems to a level we can readily understand. When you considered which college to attend, did you look at every viable alternative? Did you carefully identify all the criteria that were important in your decision? Did you evaluate each alternative against the criteria in order to find the optimal college? The answers are probably "no." Don't feel bad; few people make their college choice this way. Instead of optimizing, you probably satisficed.

Because the human mind cannot formulate and solve complex problems with full rationality, we operate within the confines of **bounded rationality**. We construct simplified models that extract the essential features from problems without capturing all their complexity.[24] We can then behave rationally within the limits of the simple model.

How does bounded rationality work for the typical individual? Once we've identified a problem, we begin to search for criteria and alternatives. The criteria are unlikely to be exhaustive. We identify alternatives that are highly visible and that usually represent familiar criteria and tried-and-true solutions. Next, we begin reviewing the alternatives, focusing on choices that differ little from the current state until we identify one that is "good enough"—that meets an acceptable level of performance. Thus ends our search. Therefore, the solution represents a satisficing choice—the first *acceptable* one we encounter—rather than an optimal one.

Satisficing is not always bad—a simple process may frequently be more sensible than the traditional rational decision-making model.[25] To use the rational model, you need to gather a great deal of information about all the options, compute applicable weights, and then calculate values across a huge number of criteria. All these processes can cost time, energy, and money. If there are many unknown weights and preferences, the fully rational model may not be any more accurate than a best guess. Sometimes a fast-and-frugal process of solving problems might be your best option.

INTUITION Perhaps the least rational way of making decisions is **intuitive decision making**, a nonconscious process created from distilled experience.[26] Intuitive decision making occurs outside conscious thought; relies on holistic associations, or links between disparate pieces of information; is fast; and is *affectively charged*, meaning it engages the emotions.[27]

While intuition isn't rational, it isn't necessarily wrong. Nor does it always contradict rational analysis; the two can complement each other. Nor is intuition superstition, or the product of some magical or paranormal sixth sense. Intuition is complex and based on years of experience and learning.

Does intuition help effective decision making? Researchers are divided, but most experts are skeptical, in part because intuition is hard to measure and analyze. Probably the best advice from one expert is, "Intuition can be very useful as a way of setting up a hypothesis but is unacceptable as 'proof.'" Use hunches derived from your experience to speculate, yes, but always make sure to test those hunches with objective data and rational, dispassionate analysis.[28]

As you can see, the more objective processes for decision making we use may correct some of the problems with our perceptual process. Just as there are biases and errors in the perceptual process, it stands to reason there are identifiable biases and errors in our decision making, which we will outline next.

COMMON BIASES AND ERRORS IN DECISION MAKING

Decision makers engage in bounded rationality, but they also allow systematic biases and errors to creep into their judgments.[29] To minimize effort and avoid trade-offs, people tend to rely too heavily on experience, impulses, gut feelings, and rules of thumb. Shortcuts can be helpful; however, they can distort rationality. Following are the most common biases in decision making. Exhibit 6-3 provides some suggestions for how to avoid falling into these biases and errors.

> Perceptual and decision-making biases and heuristics are not necessarily bad. They allow us to process information more quickly and efficiently. The key is to be self-aware enough to see when a bias or shortcut may be counterproductive.

Overconfidence Bias

Recent research continues to conclude that we tend to be overconfident about our abilities and about the abilities of others, and that we are usually not aware of this bias.[30] It's been said that "no problem in judgment and decision making is more prevalent and more potentially catastrophic than overconfidence."[31] When we're given factual questions and

---

Focus on Goals.

Without goals, you can't be rational, you don't know what information you need, you don't know which information is relevant and which is irrelevant, you'll find it difficult to choose between alternatives, and you're far more likely to experience regret over the choices you make. Clear goals make decision making easier and help you eliminate options that are inconsistent with your interests.

Look for Information That Disconfirms Your Beliefs.

One of the most effective means for counteracting overconfidence and the confirmation and hindsight biases is to actively look for information that contradicts your beliefs and assumptions. When we overtly consider various ways we could be wrong, we challenge our tendencies to think we're smarter than we actually are.

Don't Try to Create Meaning Out of Random Events.

The educated mind has been trained to look for cause-and-effect relationships. When something happens, we ask why. And when we can't find reasons, we often invent them. You have to accept that there are events in life that are outside your control. Ask yourself if patterns can be meaningfully explained or whether they are merely coincidence. Don't attempt to create meaning out of coincidence.

Increase Your Options.

No matter how many options you've identified, your final choice can be no better than the best of the option set you've selected. This argues for increasing your decision alternatives and for using creativity in developing a wide range of diverse choices. The more alternatives you can generate, and the more diverse those alternatives, the greater your chance of finding an outstanding one.

**EXHIBIT 6-3
Reducing Bias and Errors**

Source: S. P. Robbins, *Decide & Conquer: Making Winning Decisions and Taking Control of Your Life* (Upper Saddle River, NJ: Financial Times/Prentice Hall, 2004), pp 164–168.

asked to judge the probability that our answers are correct, we tend to be overly optimistic. When people say they're 90 percent confident about the range a certain number might take, their estimated ranges contain the correct answer only about 50 percent of the time—and experts are no more accurate in setting up confidence intervals than are novices.[32]

Individuals whose intellectual and interpersonal abilities are *weakest* are most likely to overestimate their performance and ability.[33] There's also a negative relationship between entrepreneurs' optimism and performance of their new ventures: the more optimistic, the less successful.[34] The tendency to be too confident about their ideas might keep some from planning how to avoid problems that arise.

Anchoring Bias

Anchoring bias is a tendency to fixate on initial information and fail to adequately adjust for subsequent information.[35] In other words, our mind appears to give a disproportionate amount of emphasis to the first information it receives. Anchors are widely used by people in professions in which persuasion skills are important—advertising, management, politics, real estate, and law. Anytime a negotiation takes place, so does anchoring. When a prospective employer asks how much you made in your prior job, your answer typically anchors the employer's offer. (Remember this when you negotiate your salary, but set the anchor only as high as you truthfully can.) The more precise your anchor, the smaller the adjustment. Some research suggests people think of making an adjustment after an anchor is set as rounding off a number: If you suggest a salary of $55,000, your boss will consider $50,000 to $60,000 a reasonable range for negotiation, but if you mention $55,650, your boss is more likely to consider $55,000 to $56,000 the range of likely values.[36]

Confirmation Bias

The rational decision-making process assumes we objectively gather information. But we don't. We *selectively* gather it. **Confirmation bias** represents a case of selective perception: we seek out information that reaffirms our past choices, and we discount information that contradicts them.[37] We also tend to accept at face value information that confirms our preconceived views, while we are skeptical of information that challenges them. Therefore, the information we gather is typically biased toward supporting views we already hold. We even tend to seek sources most likely to tell us what we want to hear, and we give too much weight to supporting information and too little to contradictory. We are most prone to confirmation bias when we believe we have good information and have strong opinions. Fortunately, those who feel there is a need to be accurate in making a decision are less prone to confirmation bias.

Availability Bias

More people fear flying than fear driving in a car. But if flying on a commercial airline were as dangerous as driving, the equivalent of two 747s filled to capacity would crash every week, killing all aboard. Because the media give more attention to air accidents, we tend to overstate the risk of flying and understate the risk of driving.

Availability bias is our tendency to base judgments on information readily available. Recent research indicates that a combination of readily available information and our previous direct experience with similar information is particularly impactful to our decision making. Events that evoke emotions, that are particularly vivid, or that are more recent tend to be more available in our memory, leading us to overestimate the chances of unlikely events such as being in an airplane crash, suffering complications from medical treatment, or getting fired.[38] Availability bias can also explain why managers give more weight in performance appraisals to employee behaviors on which they took notes—even if those notes represent a small sample of all the employee's actions.

Escalation of Commitment

Another distortion that creeps into decisions is a tendency to escalate commitment, often for increasingly nonrational reasons.[39] **Escalation of commitment** refers to our staying with a decision even if there is clear evidence it's wrong. Consider a friend who has been dating someone for several years. Although he admits things aren't going too well, he says he is still going to marry her. His justification: "I have a lot invested in the relationship!"

When is escalation most likely to occur? Evidence indicates that it occurs when individuals view themselves as responsible for the outcome. The fear of personal failure even biases the way we search for and evaluate information so that we choose only information that supports our dedication. We might, for example, weight opinions in favor of reinvestment as more credible than opinions for divestment.[40]

Risk Aversion

Mathematically, we should find a 50–50 flip of the coin for $100 to be worth as much as a sure promise of $50. After all, the expected value of the gamble over a number of trials is $50. However, nearly everyone but committed gamblers would rather have the sure thing than a risky prospect.[41] For many people, a 50–50 flip of a coin even for $200 might not be worth as much as a sure promise of $50, even though the gamble is mathematically worth twice as much! This tendency to prefer a sure thing over a risky outcome is **risk aversion**.

Risk aversion has important implications. To offset the risks inherent in a commission-based wage, companies pay commissioned employees considerably more than they do those on straight salaries. Risk-averse employees will stick with the established way of doing their jobs, rather than taking a chance on innovative methods. Sticking with a strategy that has worked in the past minimizes risk, but it will lead to stagnation. Ambitious people with power that can be taken away (most managers) appear to be especially risk averse, perhaps because they don't want to lose on a gamble everything they've worked so hard to achieve.[42] CEOs at risk of termination are exceptionally risk averse, even when a riskier investment strategy is in their firms' best interests.[43]

Hindsight Bias

Hindsight bias is the tendency to believe falsely, after the outcome is known, that we would have accurately predicted it.[44] When we have feedback on the outcome, we seem good at concluding it was obvious.

For instance, the home video rental industry collapsed when online distribution outlets ate away at the market.[45] Hollywood Video declared bankruptcy in May 2010 and began liquidating its assets; Blockbuster filed for bankruptcy in September 2010. Some have suggested that if these organizations had leveraged their brand and distribution resources effectively, developed web-based delivery sooner, as Netflix did, and added low-cost distribution in grocery and convenience stores, which Redbox offers, they could have avoided failure. While that seems obvious now in hindsight, tempting us to think we would have predicted it, many experts with good information failed to predict these two major trends that would upend the industry.

After the fact, it is easy to see that a combination of automated and mail-order distribution would outperform the traditional brick-and-mortar movie rental business. Similarly, in the recent housing bubble, former Merrill Lynch CEO John Thain—and other Wall Street executives—missed what now seems obvious—that housing prices were inflated, too many risky loans were granted, and the values of many "securities" were based on fragile assumptions. Though criticisms of decision makers may have merit, as Malcolm Gladwell, author of *Blink* and *The Tipping Point*, writes, "What is clear in hindsight is rarely clear before the fact."[46]

We are all susceptible to biases like hindsight bias, but are we all susceptible to the same degree? Much of OB research centers on answering this type of question. Our individual differences do play a significant role in our decision-making processes, while our organizations constrain the range of our available decision choices.

ORGANIZATIONAL CONSTRAINTS ON DECISION MAKING

Having examined the rational decision-making model, bounded rationality, and some of the most salient biases and errors in decision making, we turn now to a discussion of organizational constraints. Organizations can constrain decision makers, creating deviations from the rational model. Managers shape decisions to reflect the organization's performance evaluation and reward systems, to comply with formal regulations, and to meet organizationally imposed time constraints. Precedent can also influence decisions.

Performance Evaluation

Managers are influenced by the criteria on which they are evaluated. If a division manager believes the manufacturing plants under her responsibility are operating best when she hears nothing negative, we would find her plant managers spending a good part of their time ensuring that negative information doesn't reach her.

Reward Systems

The organization's reward system influences decision makers by suggesting which choices have better personal payoffs. If the organization rewards risk aversion, managers are more likely to make conservative decisions. For instance, for over half a century (the 1930s through the mid-1980s), General Motors consistently gave promotions and bonuses to managers who kept a low profile and avoided controversy. Their executives became adept at dodging tough issues and passing controversial decisions on to committees, which detrimentally influenced the organization over time.

Formal Regulations

David, a shift manager at a Taco Bell restaurant in San Antonio, Texas, describes constraints he faces on his job: "I've got rules and regulations covering almost every decision I make—from how to make a burrito to how often I need to clean the restrooms. My job doesn't come with much freedom of choice." David's situation is not unique. All but the smallest organizations create rules and policies to program decisions and get individuals to act in the intended manner. In doing so, they limit decision choices.

System-Imposed Time Constraints

Almost all important decisions come with explicit deadlines. A report on new-product development may have to be ready for executive committee review by the first of the month. Such conditions often make it difficult, if not impossible, for managers to gather all the information before making a final choice.

Historical Precedents

Decisions aren't made in a vacuum; they have a context. Individual decisions are points in a stream of choice; those made in the past are like ghosts that haunt and constrain current choices. It's common knowledge that the largest determinant of the size of any given year's budget is last year's budget. Choices made today are largely a result of choices made over the years.

WHAT ABOUT ETHICS IN DECISION MAKING?

Ethical considerations should be an important criterion in all organizational decision making. In this section, we present three ways to frame decisions ethically.[47] Managers also need to understand the important role creativity should play in the decision process; the best managers employ strategies to increase the creative potential of their employees and harvest the ideas for organizational application.

Three Ethical Decision Criteria

The first ethical yardstick is **utilitarianism**, which proposes making decisions solely on the basis of their *outcomes*, ideally to provide the greatest good for the greatest number. This view dominates business decision making. It is consistent with goals such as efficiency, productivity, and high profits.

Another ethical criterion is to make decisions consistent with fundamental liberties and privileges, as set forth in documents such as the Bill of Rights. An emphasis on *rights* in decision making means respecting and protecting the basic rights of individuals, such as the right to privacy, free speech, and due process. This criterion protects **whistle-blowers** when they reveal an organization's unethical practices to the press or government agencies, using their right to free speech.

A third criterion is to impose and enforce rules fairly and impartially to ensure *justice* or an equitable distribution of benefits and costs. Union members typically favor this view because it justifies paying people the same wage for a given job regardless of performance differences, and using seniority as the primary determination in layoff decisions.

Each criterion has advantages and liabilities. A focus on utilitarianism promotes efficiency and productivity, but it can sideline the rights of some individuals, particularly those with minority representation. The use of rights protects individuals from injury and is consistent with freedom and privacy, but it can create a legalistic environment that hinders productivity and efficiency. A focus on justice protects the interests of the underrepresented and less powerful, but it can encourage a sense of entitlement that reduces risk taking, innovation, and productivity.

Decision makers, particularly in for-profit organizations, feel comfortable with utilitarianism. The "best interests" of the organization and its stockholders can justify a lot of questionable actions, such as large layoffs. But many critics feel this perspective needs to change. Public concern about individual rights and social justice suggests managers should develop ethical standards based on nonutilitarian criteria. This presents a challenge because satisfying individual rights and social justice creates far more ambiguities than utilitarian effects on efficiency and profits. However, while raising prices, selling products with questionable effects on consumer health, closing down inefficient plants, laying off large numbers of employees, and moving production overseas to cut costs can be justified in utilitarian terms, there may no longer be a single measure by which good decisions are judged.

Increasingly, researchers are turning to **behavioral ethics**—an area of study that analyzes how people behave when confronted with ethical dilemmas. Their research tells us that while ethical standards exist collectively (society and organizations) and individually (personal ethics), individuals do not always follow ethical standards promulgated by their organizations, and we sometimes violate our own standards. Our ethical behavior varies widely from one situation to the next.

CREATIVITY IN ORGANIZATIONS

Although the rational decision-making model will often improve decisions, a decision maker also needs **creativity**, the ability to produce novel and useful ideas. Novel ideas are different from what's been done before but are appropriate for the problem.

Although all aspects of organizational behavior have complexities, that is especially true for creativity. To simplify, Exhibit 6-4 provides a **three-stage model of**

EXHIBIT 6-4
Three-Stage Model of Creativity in Organizations

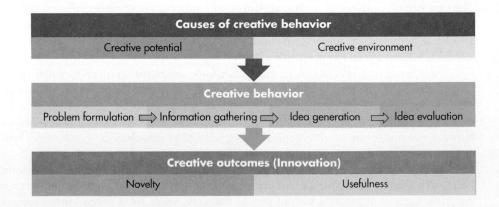

Causes of creative behavior — Creative potential | Creative environment

Creative behavior — Problem formulation ⇨ Information gathering ⇨ Idea generation ⇨ Idea evaluation

Creative outcomes (Innovation) — Novelty | Usefulness

creativity in organizations. The core of the model is *creative behavior*, which has both *causes* (predictors of creative behavior) and *effects* (outcomes of creative behavior). In this section, we discuss the three stages of creativity, starting with the center, creative behavior.

Creative Behavior

Creative behavior occurs in four steps, each of which leads to the next:

1. *Problem formulation.* Any act of creativity begins with a problem that the behavior is designed to solve. Thus, **problem formulation** is defined as the stage of creative behavior in which we identify a problem or opportunity that requires a solution as yet unknown. For example, artist/entrepreneur Marshall Carbee and businessperson John Bennett founded Eco Safety Products after discovering that even paints declared safe by the Environmental Protection Agency (EPA) emit hazardous chemical compounds. Thus, Bennett's development of artist-safe soy based paint began with identifying a safety problem with paints currently on the market.[48]

2. *Information gathering.* Given a problem, the solution is rarely directly at hand. We need time to learn more and to process that learning. Thus, **information gathering** is the stage of creative behavior when possible solutions to a problem incubate in an individual's mind. Niklas Laninge of Hoa's Tool Shop, a Stockholm-based company that helps organizations become more innovative, argues that creative information gathering means thinking beyond usual routines and comfort zones. For example, have lunch with someone outside your field to discuss the problem. "It's so easy, and you're forced to speak about your business and the things that you want to accomplish in new terms. You can't use buzzwords because people don't know what you mean," Laninge says.[49]

3. *Idea generation.* Once we have collected the relevant information, it is time to translate knowledge into ideas. Thus, **idea generation** is the process of creative behavior in which we develop possible solutions to a problem from relevant information and knowledge. Increasingly, idea generation is collaborative. For example, when NASA engineers developed the idea for landing a spacecraft on Mars, they did so collaboratively. Before coming up with the Curiosity—an SUV-sized rover that lands on Mars from a sky crane—the team spent three days scribbling potential ideas on whiteboards.[50]

4. *Idea evaluation.* Finally, it's time to choose from the ideas we have generated. Thus, **idea evaluation** is the process of creative behavior in which we evaluate potential solutions to identify the best one. Sometimes the method of choosing can be innovative. When Dallas Mavericks owner Mark Cuban was unhappy with the team's uniforms, he asked fans to help design and choose the best uniform. Cuban said, "What's the best way to come up with creative ideas? You ask for them. So we are going to crowd source the design and colors of our uniforms."[51] Generally, you want those who evaluate ideas to be different from those who generate them, to eliminate the obvious biases.

Causes of Creative Behavior

Having defined creative behavior, the main stage in the three-stage model, we now look back to the causes of creativity: creative potential and creative environment.

CREATIVE POTENTIAL   Is there such a thing as a creative personality? Indeed. While creative genius—whether in science (Albert Einstein), art (Pablo Picasso), or business (Steve Jobs)—is scarce, most people have some of the characteristics shared by exceptionally creative people. The more of these characteristics we have, the higher our creative potential.

Intelligence is related to creativity. Smart people are more creative because they are better at solving complex problems. However, intelligent individuals may also be more creative because they have greater "working memory"; that is, they can recall more information that is related to the task at hand.[52]

The Big Five personality trait of openness to experience (see Chapter 5) correlates with creativity, probably because open individuals are less conformist in action and more divergent in thinking.[53] Other traits of creative people include proactive personality, self-confidence, risk taking, tolerance for ambiguity, and perseverance.[54]

Expertise is the foundation for all creative work and thus is the single most important predictor of creative potential. Film writer, producer, and director Quentin Tarantino spent his youth working in a video rental store, where he built up an encyclopedic knowledge of movies. The potential for creativity is enhanced when individuals have abilities, knowledge, proficiencies, and similar expertise to their field of endeavor. For instance, you wouldn't expect someone with minimal knowledge of programming to be very creative as a software engineer.

CREATIVE ENVIRONMENT   Most of us have creative potential we can learn to apply, but as important as creative potential is, by itself it is not enough. We need to be in an environment where creative potential can be realized. What environmental factors affect whether creative potential translates into creative behaviors?

First and perhaps most important is *motivation*. If you aren't motivated to be creative, it is unlikely you will be. A review of twenty-six studies revealed that intrinsic motivation, or the desire to work on something because it's interesting, exciting, satisfying, and challenging (discussed in more detail in the next chapter), correlates fairly strongly with creative outcomes. This link is true regardless of whether we are talking about student creativity or employee creativity.[55]

It is also valuable to work in an environment that rewards and recognizes creative work. The organization should foster the free flow of ideas, including providing fair and constructive judgment. Freedom from excessive rules encourages creativity; employees should have the freedom to decide what work is to be done and how to do it. One study of 385 employees working for several drug companies in China revealed that both structural empowerment (in which the structure of the work unit allows sufficient employee freedom) and psychological empowerment (which lets the individual feel personally empowered) were related to employee creativity.[56]

Creative Outcomes (Innovation)

The final stage in our model of creativity is the outcome. Creative behavior does not always produce a creative or innovative outcome. An employee might generate a creative idea and never share it. Management might reject a creative solution. Teams might squelch creative behaviors by isolating those who propose different ideas. One study showed that most people have a bias against accepting creative ideas because ideas create uncertainty. When people feel uncertain, their ability to see any idea as creative is blocked.[57]

We can define *creative outcomes* as ideas or solutions judged to be novel and useful by relevant stakeholders. Novelty itself does not generate a creative outcome if it isn't useful. Thus, "off-the-wall" solutions are creative only if they help solve the problem. The usefulness of the solution might be self-evident (the iPad), or it might be considered successful by stakeholders before the actual success can be known.[58]

Creative ideas do not implement themselves; translating them into creative outcomes is a social process that requires utilizing other concepts addressed in this text, including power and politics, leadership, and motivation.

SUMMARY

Individuals base their behavior not on the way their external environment actually is, but rather on the way they see it or believe it to be. An understanding of the way people make decisions can help us explain and predict behavior, but few important decisions are simple or unambiguous enough for the rational model's assumptions to apply. We find individuals looking for solutions that satisfice rather than optimize, injecting biases and prejudices into the decision-making process, and relying on intuition. Managers should encourage creativity in employees and teams to create a route to innovative decision making.

IMPLICATIONS FOR MANAGERS

- Behavior follows perception, so to influence behavior at work, assess how people perceive their work. Often behaviors we find puzzling can be explained by understanding the initiating perceptions.
- Make better decisions by recognizing perceptual biases and decision-making errors we tend to commit. Learning about these problems doesn't always prevent us from making mistakes, but it does help. Exhibit 6-3 offers some suggestions.
- Adjust your decision-making approach to the national culture you're operating in and to the criteria your organization values. If you're in a country that doesn't value rationality, don't feel compelled to follow the decision-making model or to try to make your decisions appear rational. Adjust your decision approach to ensure compatibility with the organizational culture.
- Combine rational analysis with intuition. These are not conflicting approaches to decision making. By using both, you can actually improve your decision-making effectiveness.
- Try to enhance your creativity. Actively look for novel solutions to problems, attempt to see problems in new ways, use analogies, and hire creative talent. Try to remove work and organizational barriers that might impede your creativity.

PERSONAL INVENTORY ASSESSMENT

In Personal Inventory Assessment found in MyManagementLab take assessment: How Creative Are You?

⭐ WRITING SPACE

If your professor assigned this, sign in to **mymanagementlab.com** for the following Assisted-graded writing question:

6-1. As a manager, how can you best create a format for decision making for complex decisions?

7

The Basics of Motivation

MyManagementLab®

✪ Improve Your Grade!

When you see this icon ✪, visit **www.mymanagementlab.com** for activities that are applied, personalized, and offer immediate feedback.

LEARNING OBJECTIVES

After studying this chapter, you should be able to:

1. Describe the three key elements of motivation.
2. Evaluate the applicability of early theories of motivation.
3. Contrast the elements of self-determination theory and goal-setting theory.
4. Demonstrate the differences between self-efficacy theory, equity theory, and expectancy theory.
5. Identify the implications of employee job engagement for management.

✪ Chapter Warm-up

If your professor has chosen to assign this, go to **www.mymanagementlab.com** to see what you should particularly focus on and to take the Chapter 7 warm up.

Motivating employees is one of the most important, and one of the most challenging, aspects of management. As we will see, there is no shortage of advice about how to do it. Motivation is not simply about working hard—it also reflects your view of your own abilities.

Motivation is one of the most frequently researched topics in OB.[1] A Gallup poll revealed one reason—added to the majority of U.S. employees who are not actively engaged in their work (neither engaged nor disengaged), another portion (17 percent) are actively disengaged.[2] In another survey, 69 percent of workers reported wasting time at work every day, and nearly a quarter said they waste between thirty and sixty minutes each day. How? Usually by surfing the Internet (checking the news and visiting social network sites) and chatting with coworkers.[3] So, though times change, the problem of motivating a workforce stays the same.

In this chapter, we'll review the basics of motivation, assess motivation theories, and provide an integrative model that fits theories together.

DEFINING MOTIVATION

Some individuals seem driven to succeed. The same student who struggles to read a textbook for more than twenty minutes may devour a *Harry Potter* book in a day. The difference is the situation. As we analyze the concept of motivation, keep in mind that the level of motivation varies both between individuals and within individuals at different times.

We define **motivation** as the processes that account for an individual's *intensity, direction*, and *persistence* of effort toward attaining a goal.[4] While general motivation is concerned with effort toward *any* goal, we'll narrow the focus to *organizational* goals toward work-related behavior.

Intensity describes how hard a person tries. This is the element most of us focus on when we talk about motivation. However, high intensity is unlikely to lead to favorable job-performance outcomes unless the effort is channeled in a *direction* that benefits the organization. Therefore, we consider the quality of effort as well as its intensity. Effort directed toward, and consistent with, the organization's goals is the kind of effort we should be seeking. Finally, motivation has a *persistence* dimension. This measures how long a person can maintain effort. Motivated individuals stay with a task long enough to achieve their goals.

✪ WATCH IT

If your professor assigned this, sign in to **mymanagementlab.com** to watch a video titled Motivation (TWZ Role Play) to learn more about this topic and respond to questions.

EARLY THEORIES OF MOTIVATION

Four theories of employee motivation formulated during the 1950s, although now of questionable validity, are probably the best known. We discuss more valid explanations later, but these four represent a foundation, and practicing managers still use their terminology.

Hierarchy of Needs Theory

The best-known theory of motivation is Abraham Maslow's **hierarchy of needs**.[5] Maslow hypothesized that within every human being, there exists a hierarchy of five needs:

1. *Physiological.* Includes hunger, thirst, shelter, sex, and other bodily needs.
2. *Safety.* Security and protection from physical and emotional harm.
3. *Social.* Affection, belongingness, acceptance, and friendship.

EXHIBIT 7-1
Maslow's Hierarchy of Needs

Source: A. H. Maslow, *Motivation and Personality*, 3rd ed., R. D. Frager and J. Fadiman (eds.). © 1997. Adapted by permission of Pearson Education, Inc., Upper Saddle River, New Jersey.

4. ***Esteem.*** Internal factors such as self-respect, autonomy, and achievement, and external factors such as status, recognition, and attention.
5. ***Self-actualization.*** Drive to become what we are capable of becoming; includes growth, achieving our potential, and self-fulfillment.

According to Maslow, as each need becomes substantially satisfied, the next one becomes dominant. So if you want to motivate someone, you need to understand what level of the hierarchy that person is currently on and focus on satisfying that need, moving up the steps in Exhibit 7-1.

Maslow's theory has received wide recognition, particularly among practicing managers. It is intuitively logical and easy to understand. Unfortunately, however, research does not validate it. Maslow provided no empirical substantiation, and several studies that sought to validate it found no support for it.[6] But old theories, especially intuitively logical ones, die hard.

Some researchers have attempted to revive components of the needs hierarchy concept, using principles from evolutionary psychology.[7] They propose that lower-level needs are the chief concern of immature animals or those with primitive nervous systems, whereas higher needs are more frequently observed in mature animals with more developed nervous systems. They also note distinct underlying biological systems for different types of needs. Time will tell whether revisions to Maslow's hierarchy will be useful for practicing managers.

Theory X and Theory Y

One theory that is consistent with the needs hierarchy is Douglas McGregor's Theory X and Theory Y.[8] Under **Theory X**, managers believe employees inherently dislike work and must therefore be directed or even coerced into performing it (thus assuming that lower-order needs dominate). Under **Theory Y**, in contrast, managers assume employees can view work as being as natural as rest or play, and therefore the average person can learn to accept, and even seek, responsibility (thus assuming that higher-order needs motivate). McGregor believed Theory Y assumptions were more valid, and thus proposed motivating through participative decision making, challenging work, and good group

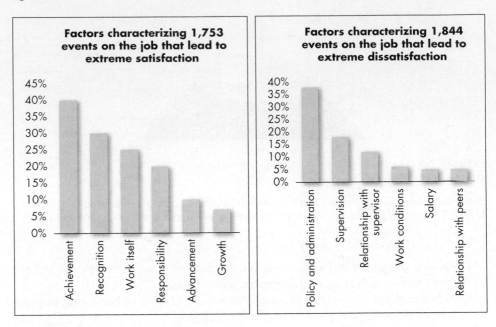

EXHIBIT 7-2

Comparison of Satisfiers and Dissatisfiers

Source: Based on Harvard Business Review. "Comparison of Satisfiers and Dissatisfiers." An exhibit from One More Time: How Do You Motivate Employees? by Fredrick Herzberg, January 2003. Copyright © 2003 by the Harvard Business School Publishing Corporation. All rights reserved.

relations. Unfortunately, like the needs hierarchy, little evidence confirms that *either* set of assumptions is valid or that acting on Theory Y assumptions will lead to more motivated workers.

Two-Factor Theory

Believing an individual's relationship to work is basic, and that the attitude toward work can determine success or failure, psychologist Frederick Herzberg wondered, "What do people want from their jobs?" He asked people to describe, in detail, situations in which they felt exceptionally *good* or *bad* about their jobs. The responses differed significantly and led Herzberg to his **two-factor theory**—also called *motivation-hygiene theory.*[9]

As shown in Exhibit 7-2, intrinsic factors such as advancement, recognition, responsibility, and achievement seem related to job satisfaction. Respondents who felt good about their work tended to attribute these factors to themselves, while dissatisfied respondents tended to cite extrinsic factors such as supervision, pay, company policies, and working conditions.

To Herzberg, the data suggest that the opposite of satisfaction is not dissatisfaction, as was traditionally believed. Removing dissatisfying characteristics from a job does not necessarily make the job satisfying. Herzberg proposed a dual continuum: The opposite of "satisfaction" is "no satisfaction," and the opposite of "dissatisfaction" is "no dissatisfaction."

According to Herzberg, the factors that lead to job satisfaction are separate and distinct from those that lead to job dissatisfaction. Therefore, managers who seek to eliminate factors that can create job dissatisfaction may bring about peace, but not necessarily motivation. They will be placating rather than motivating their workers. As a result, Herzberg characterized conditions such as quality of supervision, pay, company policies, physical working conditions, relationships with others, and job security as **hygiene factors**. When they're adequate, people will not be dissatisfied; neither will they be satisfied. If we want to *motivate* people in their jobs, Herzberg suggested emphasizing factors associated with the work itself or with outcomes directly derived from it, such as promotional opportunities, personal growth opportunities, recognition, responsibility, and achievement. These are the characteristics people find intrinsically rewarding.

Like Maslow's needs hierarchy and McGregor's Theory X and Theory Y, the two-factor theory has not been well supported in research and has many detractors.[10] Criticisms center on Herzberg's original methodology, and his assumptions such as the statement that satisfaction is strongly related to productivity. Subsequent research has tended to show that if hygiene and motivational factors are equally important to a person, both are capable of motivating people.

Regardless of the criticisms, Herzberg's theory has been quite influential, and few managers are unfamiliar with its recommendations.

McClelland's Theory of Needs

You have one beanbag and five targets set up in front of you, each farther away than the last. Target A sits almost within arm's reach. If you hit it, you get $2. Target B is a bit farther out, but about 80 percent of the people who try can hit it. It pays $4. Target C pays $8, and about half the people who try can hit it. Very few people can hit Target D, but the payoff is $16 for those who do. Finally, Target E pays $32, but it's almost impossible to achieve. Which would you try for? If you selected C, you're likely to be a high achiever. Why? Read on.

McClelland's theory of needs was developed by David McClelland and his associates.[11] It looks at three needs:

- **Need for achievement (nAch)** is the drive to excel, to achieve in relationship to a set of standards.
- **Need for power (nPow)** is the need to make others behave in a way they would not have otherwise.
- **Need for affiliation (nAff)** is the desire for friendly and close interpersonal relationships.

McClelland and subsequent researchers focused most of their attention on nAch. High achievers perform best when they perceive their probability of success as 0.5—that is, a 50–50 chance. They dislike gambling with high odds because they feel no achievement satisfaction from success that comes by pure chance. Similarly, they dislike low odds (high probability of success) because then there is no challenge to their skills. They like to set goals that require stretching themselves a little.

Relying on an extensive amount of research, we can predict some relationships between achievement need and job performance. First, when jobs have a high degree of personal responsibility, feedback, and an intermediate degree of risk, high achievers are strongly motivated. They are successful in entrepreneurial activities such as running their own businesses, for example, and managing self-contained units within large organizations.[12] Second, a high need to achieve does not necessarily make someone a good manager, especially in large organizations. People with a high achievement need are interested in how well they do personally, and not in influencing others to do well. High-nAch salespeople do not necessarily make good sales managers, and the good general manager in a large organization does not typically have a high need to achieve.[13] Third, needs for affiliation and power tend to be closely related to managerial success. The best managers are high in their need for power and low in their need for affiliation.[14] In fact, a high power motive may be a requirement for managerial effectiveness.[15]

The view that a high achievement need acts as an internal motivator presupposes two cultural characteristics—willingness to accept a moderate degree of risk (which excludes countries with strong uncertainty-avoidance characteristics) and concern with performance (which applies to countries with strong achievement characteristics). This combination is found in Anglo-American countries such as the United States, Canada, and Great Britain,[16] and much less in more collectivistic societies like Chile and Portugal.

Among the early theories of motivation, McClelland's has garnered the best research support. Unfortunately, it has less practical effect than the others. Because McClelland argued that the three needs are subconscious—we may rank high on them but not know it—measuring them is not easy. In the most common approach, a trained expert presents pictures to individuals, asks them to tell a story about each, and then scores the responses in terms of the three needs. However, the process is time consuming and expensive, and few organizations have been willing to invest in employing McClelland's concept.

CONTEMPORARY THEORIES OF MOTIVATION

Early theories of motivation either have not held up under close examination or have fallen out of favor. In contrast, contemporary theories have one thing in common: Each has a reasonable degree of valid supporting documentation. This doesn't mean they are unquestionably right. We call them "contemporary theories" because they represent the current state of thinking in explaining employee motivation.

Self-Determination Theory

"It's strange," said Marcia. "I started work at the humane society as a volunteer. I put in fifteen hours a week helping people adopt pets. And I loved coming to work. Then, three months ago, they hired me full-time at $11 an hour. I'm doing the same work I did before. But I'm not finding it nearly as much fun."

Does Marcia's reaction seem counterintuitive? There's an explanation for it. It's called **self-determination theory**, which proposes that people prefer to feel they have control over their actions, so anything that makes a previously enjoyed task feel more like an obligation than a freely chosen activity will undermine motivation.[17] Much research on self-determination theory in OB has focused on **cognitive evaluation theory**, a complementary theory that hypothesizes that extrinsic rewards will reduce intrinsic interest in a task. When people are paid for work, it feels less like something they *want* to do and more like something they *have* to do. Self-determination theory proposes that in addition to being driven by a need for autonomy, people seek ways to achieve competence and positive connections to others. A large number of studies support self-determination theory.[18] Its major implications relate to work rewards.

When organizations use extrinsic rewards as payoffs for superior performance, employees feel they are doing a good job less because of their own intrinsic desire to excel than because that's what the organization wants. Eliminating extrinsic rewards can shift an individual's perception of why he works on a task from an external to an internal explanation. If you're reading a novel a week because your English literature instructor requires you to, you can attribute your reading behavior to an external source. However, if you find yourself continuing to read a novel a week after the course is over, your natural inclination is to say, "I must enjoy reading novels because I'm still reading one a week." Applying extrinsic rewards is therefore all in the approach.

Studies examining how extrinsic rewards increase motivation for creative tasks suggest we might need to place cognitive evaluation theory's predictions into a broader context.[19] Goal setting is more effective in improving motivation, for instance, when we provide rewards for achieving the goals. The original authors of self-determination theory acknowledged that extrinsic rewards such as verbal praise and feedback about competence could improve intrinsic motivation under specific circumstances. Deadlines and specific work standards do, too, if people believe they are in control of their behavior.[20] This is consistent with the central theme of self-determination theory: Rewards and deadlines diminish motivation if people see them as coercive or controlling.

What does self-determination theory suggest for providing rewards? It suggests some caution in the use of extrinsic rewards to motivate. Specifically, self-determination theory suggests that pursuing goals out of intrinsic motives (such as a strong interest in the work itself) is more sustaining to human motivation than extrinsic rewards. Similarly, cognitive evaluation theory suggests that providing extrinsic incentives may, in many cases, undermine intrinsic motivation. As an example, if a computer programmer values writing code because she likes to solve problems, an organizational extrinsic reward for writing a certain number of lines of code every day could feel coercive, and her intrinsic motivation would suffer. She would be less interested in the task and might reduce her effort.

A more recent outgrowth of self-determination theory is **self-concordance**, which considers how strongly people's reasons for pursuing goals are consistent with their interests and core values. Across cultures, if individuals pursue goals because of intrinsic interest, they are more likely to attain goals, are happier when they do, and are happy even if they do not.[21] Why? Because the process of striving towards goals is fun whether or not the goal is achieved.[22] The opposite appears true as well. Recent research reveals that when people do *not* enjoy their work for intrinsic reasons, those who work because they feel obligated to do so can still perform well, though they experience higher levels of strain as a result.[23]

What does all this mean? For individuals, it means choose your job for reasons other than extrinsic rewards. For organizations, it means managers should provide intrinsic as well as extrinsic incentives. Managers need to make the work interesting, provide recognition, and support employee growth and development. Employees who feel what they do is within their control and a result of free choice are likely to be more motivated by their work and committed to their employers.[24]

Goal-Setting Theory

In general, managers should make goals specific and difficult—managers should set the highest goals to which employees will commit.

Gene Broadwater, former coach of the Hamilton High School cross-country team, gave his squad these last words before they approached the starting line for the league championship race: "Each one of you is physically ready. Now, get out there and do your best. No one can ever ask more of you than that."

You've heard the sentiment a number of times yourself: "Just do your best. That's all anyone can ask." But what does "do your best" mean? Do we ever know whether we've achieved that vague goal? Would the cross-country runners have recorded faster times if Coach Broadwater had given each a specific goal? Research on **goal-setting theory** reveals impressive effects of goal specificity, challenge, and feedback on performance.

In the late 1960s, Edwin Locke proposed that intentions to work toward a goal are a major source of work motivation.[25] That is, goals tell an employee what needs to be done and how much effort is needed.[26] Evidence strongly suggests that specific goals increase performance; that difficult goals, when accepted, result in higher performance than do easy goals; and that feedback leads to higher performance than does non-feedback.[27]

In general, specific goals produce a higher level of output than the generalized goal "do your best." Why? Specificity itself seems to act as an internal stimulus. When a trucker commits to making twelve round-trip hauls between Toronto and Buffalo, New York each week, this intention gives him a specific objective to attain. All things being equal, he will outperform a counterpart with no goals or the generalized goal "do your best."

If factors such as acceptance of goals are held constant, the more difficult the goal, the higher the level of performance. Of course, it's logical to assume easier goals are more likely to be accepted. But once a hard task is accepted, we can expect the employee to exert a high level of effort to try to achieve it.

Why are people motivated by difficult goals?[28] First, challenging goals get our attention and help us focus. Second, difficult goals energize us because we have to work harder to attain them. Do you study as hard for an easy exam as you do for a difficult one? Probably not. Third, when goals are difficult, people persist in trying to attain them. Finally, difficult goals lead us to discover strategies that help us perform the job or task more effectively. If we have to struggle to solve a difficult problem, we often think of a better way to go about it.

People do better when they get feedback on how well they are progressing toward their goals because it helps identify discrepancies between what they have done and what they want to do next—that is, feedback guides behavior. But all feedback is not equally potent. Self-generated feedback—with which employees are able to monitor their own progress or receive feedback from the task process itself—is more powerful than externally generated feedback.[29]

If employees can participate in setting their own goals, will they try harder? The evidence is mixed. In some cases, participatively set goals yielded superior performance; in others, individuals performed best when assigned goals by their boss. But a major advantage of participation may be that it increases acceptance of the goal as a desirable one toward which to work.[30] Without participation, the individual pursuing the goal needs to clearly understand its purpose and importance.[31]

In addition to feedback, three other factors influence the goals–performance relationship: *goal commitment*, *task characteristics*, and *national culture*. Goal-setting theory assumes an individual is *committed* to the goal and determined not to lower or abandon it. The individual (1) believes he can achieve the goal and (2) wants to achieve it.[32] Goal commitment is most likely to occur when goals are made public, when the individual has an internal locus of control, when the goals are self-set rather than assigned, and when goals are based at least partially on individual ability.[33]

Goals seem to affect performance more strongly when *tasks* are simple rather than complex, well learned rather than novel, independent rather than interdependent, and are on the high end of achievability.[34] On interdependent tasks, group goals are preferable.

Setting specific, difficult, individual goals may have different effects in different *cultures*. Most goal-setting research has been done in the United States and Canada, where individual achievement and performance are most highly valued. Research has not shown that group-based goals are more effective in collectivist than in individualist cultures. In collectivistic and high power-distance cultures, achievable moderate goals can be more highly motivating than difficult ones.[35] Finally, assigned goals appear to generate greater goal commitment in high than in low power-distance cultures.[36] More research is needed to assess how goal constructs might differ across cultures.

Although goal setting has positive outcomes, it is not unequivocally beneficial. For example, some goals may be *too* effective.[37] When learning something is important, goals related to performance undermine adaptation and creativity because people become too focused on outcomes and ignore changing conditions. A goal to learn and generate alternative solutions will be more effective than a goal to perform. In addition, some authors argue that goals can lead employees to focus on a single standard and exclude all others. For example, a goal to boost short-term stock prices may lead organizations to ignore long-term success and even to engage in unethical behavior such as "cooking the books" to meet the goal. Other studies show that employees low in conscientiousness and emotional stability experience greater emotional exhaustion when their leaders set goals.[38] Finally, individuals may fail to give up on an unattainable goal, even when it might be beneficial to do so. Despite differences of opinion, most researchers agree that goals are powerful in shaping behavior. Managers should make sure goals are aligned with company objectives.

Research has found that people differ in the way they regulate their thoughts and behaviors during goal pursuit. Generally, people fall into one of two categories, though they could belong to both. Those with a **promotion focus** strive for advancement and accomplishment, and they approach conditions that move them closer toward desired goals. Those with a **prevention focus** strive to fulfill duties and obligations and avoid conditions that pull them away from desired goals. Although you would be right in noting that both strategies are in the service of goal accomplishment, the manner in which they get there is quite different. As an example, consider studying for an exam. You could engage in promotion-focused activities such as reading class materials and notes, or you could engage in prevention-focused activities such as refraining from things that would get in the way of studying, such as playing video games or going out with friends. Or, you could do both activities. Ideally, it's probably best to be both promotion *and* prevention oriented.[39]

IMPLEMENTING GOAL-SETTING THEORY How do managers make goal-setting theory operational? That's often left up to the individual. Some managers set aggressive performance targets—what General Electric called "stretch goals." Some CEOs, such as

**EXHIBIT 7-3
Cascading of
Objectives**

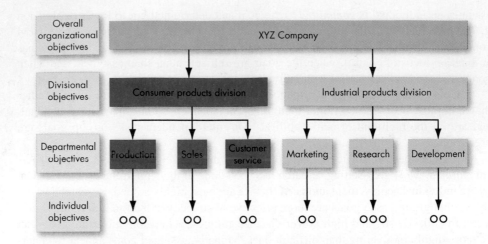

Procter & Gamble's A. G. Lafley and Best Buy's Hubert Joly, are known for demanding performance goals. But many managers don't set goals. When asked whether their jobs had clearly defined goals, only a minority of employees in a survey said yes.[40]

A more systematic way to utilize goal setting is with **management by objectives (MBO)**, an initiative most popular in the 1970s, but still used today. MBO emphasizes participatively set goals that are tangible, verifiable, and measurable. As in Exhibit 7-3, the organization's overall objectives are translated into specific objectives for each level (divisional, departmental, individual). But because lower-unit managers jointly participate in setting their own goals, MBO works from the bottom up as well as from the top down. The result is a hierarchy that links objectives from one level to those at the next. For the individual employee, MBO provides specific personal performance objectives.

Four ingredients are common to MBO programs: goal specificity, participation in decision making (including the setting of goals or objectives), an explicit time period, and performance feedback.[41] Many elements in MBO programs match propositions of goal-setting theory. For example, having an explicit time period to accomplish objectives matches goal-setting theory's emphasis on goal specificity. Similarly, we noted earlier that feedback about goal progress is a critical element of goal-setting theory. The only area of possible disagreement between MBO and goal-setting theory is participation: MBO strongly advocates participation, whereas goal-setting theory demonstrates that managers' assigned goals are usually just as effective.

OTHER CONTEMPORARY THEORIES OF MOTIVATION

Self-Efficacy Theory

Managers will increase employees' motivation by increasing their confidence in successfully completing the task (self-efficacy).

Self-efficacy theory, also known as *social cognitive theory* or *social learning theory*, refers to an individual's belief that he is capable of performing a task.[42] The higher your self-efficacy, the more confidence you have in your ability to succeed. So, in difficult situations, people with low self-efficacy are more likely to lessen their effort or give up altogether, while those with high self-efficacy will try harder to master the challenge.[43] Self-efficacy can create a positive spiral in which those with high efficacy become more

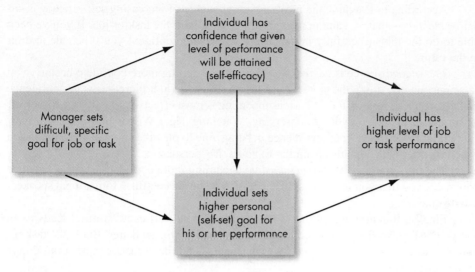

EXHIBIT 7-4

Joint Effects of Goals and Self-Efficacy on Performance

Source: Based on E. A. Locke and G. P. Latham, "Building a Practically Useful Theory of Goal Setting and Task Motivation: A 35-Year Odyssey," *American Psychologist* (September 2002), pp. 705–717.

engaged in their tasks and then, in turn, increase their performance, which increases efficacy further.[44] Changes in self-efficacy over time are related to changes in creative performance as well.[45] Individuals high in self-efficacy also seem to respond to negative feedback with increased effort and motivation, while those low in self-efficacy are likely to lessen their effort after negative feedback.[46] How can managers help their employees achieve high levels of self-efficacy? By bringing goal-setting theory and self-efficacy theory together.

Goal-setting theory and self-efficacy theory don't compete; they complement each other. As Exhibit 7-4 shows, employees whose managers set difficult goals for them will have a higher level of self-efficacy and set higher goals for their own performance. Why? Setting difficult goals for people communicates your confidence in them. Imagine you learn that your boss sets a higher goal for you than for your coworkers. How would you interpret this? As long as you didn't feel you were being picked on, you would probably think, "Well, I guess my boss thinks I'm capable of performing better than others." This sets in motion a psychological process in which you're more confident in yourself (higher self-efficacy) and you set higher personal goals, performing better both inside and outside the workplace.

The researcher who developed self-efficacy theory, Albert Bandura, proposes four ways self-efficacy can be increased:[47]

1. Enactive mastery.
2. Vicarious modeling.
3. Verbal persuasion.
4. Arousal.

According to Bandura, the most important source of increasing self-efficacy is *enactive mastery*—that is, gaining relevant experience with the task or job. If you've been able to do the job successfully in the past, you're more confident you'll be able to do it in the future.

The second source is *vicarious modeling*—becoming more confident because you see someone else doing the task. If your friend slims down, it increases your confidence that you can lose weight, too. Vicarious modeling is most effective when you see yourself as similar to the person you are observing. Watching Tiger Woods play a difficult golf shot might not increase your confidence in being able to play the shot yourself, but if you watch a golfer with a handicap similar to yours, it's persuasive.

The third source is *verbal persuasion*: becoming more confident because someone convinces you that you have the skills necessary to be successful. Motivational speakers use this tactic.

Finally, Bandura argues that *arousal* increases self-efficacy. Arousal leads to an energized state, so the person gets "psyched up" and performs better. But if the task requires a steady, lower-key perspective (say, carefully editing a manuscript), arousal may in fact hurt performance.

The best way for a manager to use verbal persuasion is through the *Pygmalion effect* or the *Galatea effect*. The Pygmalion effect is a form of self-fulfilling prophecy in which believing something can make it true. In some studies, teachers were told their students had very high IQ scores when, in fact, they spanned a range from high to low. Consistent with the Pygmalion effect, the teachers spent more time with the students they *thought* were smart, gave them more challenging assignments, and expected more of them—all of which led to higher student self-efficacy and better grades.[48] This strategy has been used successfully in the workplace.[49] Also, sailors who were told convincingly that they would not get seasick were in fact much less likely to do so.[50]

What are the OB implications of self-efficacy theory? Well, it's a matter of applying Bandura's sources of self-efficacy to the work setting. Training programs often make use of enactive mastery by having people practice and build their skills. In fact, one reason training works is that it increases self-efficacy.[51] Individuals with higher levels of self-efficacy also appear to reap more benefits from training programs and are more likely to use their training on the job.[52]

Intelligence and personality are absent from Bandura's list, but they can increase self-efficacy.[53] People who are intelligent, conscientiousness, and emotionally stable are so much more likely to have high self-efficacy that some researchers argue self-efficacy is less important than prior research would suggest.[54] They believe self-efficacy is partially a by-product in a smart person with a confident personality. Although Bandura strongly disagrees with this conclusion, more research is needed.

Equity Theory/Organizational Justice

Ainsley is a student at State University working toward a bachelor's degree in finance. In order to gain some work experience and increase her marketability, she has accepted a summer internship in the finance department at a pharmaceutical company. She is quite pleased at the pay: $15 an hour is more than other students in her cohort were receiving for their summer internships. At work she meets Josh, a recent graduate of State

University working as a middle manager in the same finance department. Josh makes $30 an hour.

On the job, Ainsley could be described as a go-getter. She's engaged, satisfied, and always seems willing to help others. Josh is quite the opposite. He often seems disinterested in his job and even has thoughts about quitting. When pressed one day about why he is unhappy, Josh cites his pay as the main reason. Specifically, he tells Ainsley that, compared to managers at other pharmaceutical companies, he makes much less. "It isn't fair," he complains. "I work just as hard as they do, yet I don't make as much. Maybe I should go work for the competition."

How could someone making $30 an hour be less satisfied with his pay and less motivated than someone making $15 an hour? The answer lies in **equity theory** and, more broadly, in principles of organizational justice. According to equity theory, employees compare what they get from their job (their "outcomes," such as pay, promotions, recognition, or having the corner office) to what they put into it (their "inputs," such as effort, experience, and education). They take the ratio of their outcomes to their inputs and compare it to the ratio of others, usually someone similar like a coworker or someone doing the same job. This is shown in Exhibit 7-5. If we believe our ratio to be equal to those with whom we compare ourselves, a state of equity exists and we perceive the situation as fair.

Based on equity theory, employees who perceive inequity will make one of six choices:[55]

1. Change inputs (exert less effort if underpaid or more if overpaid).
2. Change outcomes (individuals paid on a piece-rate basis can increase their pay by producing a higher quantity of units of lower quality).
3. Distort perceptions of self ("I used to think I worked at a moderate pace, but now I realize I work a lot harder than everyone else.").
4. Distort perceptions of others ("Mike's job isn't as desirable as I thought.").
5. Choose a different referent ("I may not make as much as my brother-in-law, but I'm doing a lot better than my Dad did when he was my age.").
6. Leave the field (quit the job).

Some of these propositions have been supported, but others haven't.[56] First, inequities created by overpayment do not seem to significantly affect behavior in most work

EXHIBIT 7-5
Equity Theory

Ratio Comparisons*	Perception
$\dfrac{O}{I_A} < \dfrac{O}{I_B}$	Inequity due to being underrewarded
$\dfrac{O}{I_A} = \dfrac{O}{I_B}$	Equity
$\dfrac{O}{I_A} > \dfrac{O}{I_B}$	Inequity due to being overrewarded

*Where $\dfrac{O}{I_A}$ represents the employee; and $\dfrac{O}{I_B}$ represents relevant others
O = outcomes and I = Inputs

situations. So don't expect an employee who feels overpaid to give back part of her salary or put in more hours to make up for the inequity. Although individuals may sometimes perceive that they are overrewarded, they restore equity by rationalizing their situation ("I'm worth it because I work harder than everyone else."). Second, not everyone is equity-sensitive.[57] A few actually prefer outcome–input ratios lower than the referent comparisons. Predictions from equity theory are not likely to be very accurate about these "benevolent types."

Although equity theory's propositions have not all held up, the hypothesis served as an important precursor to the study of **organizational justice**, or more simply, fairness, in the workplace.[58] Organizational justice is concerned with how employees feel authorities and decision makers treat them. For the most part, employees evaluate how fairly they are treated along four dimensions, shown in Exhibit 7-6.

Distributive justice is concerned with the fairness of the outcomes, such as pay and recognition that employees receive. Outcomes can be allocated in many ways. For example, we could distribute raises equally among employees, or we could base them on

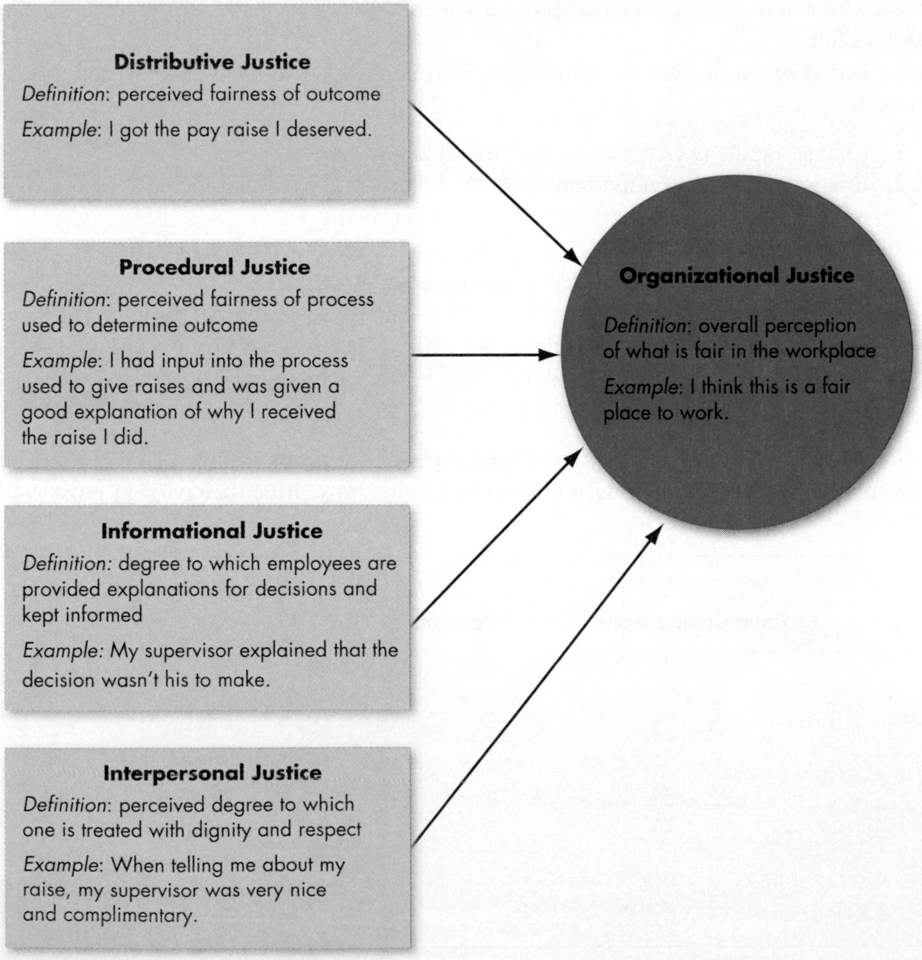

Distributive Justice
Definition: perceived fairness of outcome
Example: I got the pay raise I deserved.

Procedural Justice
Definition: perceived fairness of process used to determine outcome
Example: I had input into the process used to give raises and was given a good explanation of why I received the raise I did.

Informational Justice
Definition: degree to which employees are provided explanations for decisions and kept informed
Example: My supervisor explained that the decision wasn't his to make.

Interpersonal Justice
Definition: perceived degree to which one is treated with dignity and respect
Example: When telling me about my raise, my supervisor was very nice and complimentary.

Organizational Justice
Definition: overall perception of what is fair in the workplace
Example: I think this is a fair place to work.

EXHIBIT 7-6
Model of Organizational Justice

which employees need money the most. However, as we discussed about equity theory, employees tend to perceive their outcomes are fairest when they are distributed equitably.

Does the same logic apply to teams? At first glance, it would seem that distributing rewards equally among team members is best for boosting morale and teamwork—that way, no one is favored more than another. A recent study of National Hockey League teams suggests otherwise. Differentiating the pay of team members on the basis of their inputs (how well they performed in games) attracted better players to the team, made it more likely they would stay, and increased team performance.[59]

The way we have described things so far, it would seem that distributive justice and equity are gauged in a rational, calculative way as individuals compare their outcome–input ratios to others. But the experience of justice, and especially injustice, is often not so cold and calculated. Instead, people base distributive judgments on a feeling or an emotional reaction to the way they think they are being treated relative to others, and their reactions are often "hot" and emotional rather than rational.[60]

Although employees care a lot about *what* outcomes are distributed (distributive justice), they also care a lot about *how* outcomes are distributed. While distributive justice looks at *what* outcomes are allocated, **procedural justice** examines *how* outcomes are allocated.[61] What makes procedures more or less fair? There are several factors. For one, employees perceive that procedures are fairer when they are given a say in the decision-making process. Having direct influence over how decisions are made, or at the very least being able to present your opinion to decision makers, creates a sense of control and makes us feel empowered (we discuss empowerment more in the next chapter). Employees perceive that procedures are fairer when decision makers follow several "rules." These include making decisions in a consistent manner (across people and over time), avoiding bias (not favoring one group or person over another), using accurate information, considering the groups or people their decisions affect, acting ethically, and remaining open to appeals or correction.

To promote fairness in the workplace, managers should consider openly sharing information on how allocation decisions are made. Fair and open procedures are especially important when the outcome is likely to be viewed negatively by some or all employees.

It turns out that procedural and distributive justice combine to influence people's perceptions of fairness. If outcomes are favorable and individuals get what they want, they care less about the process, so procedural justice doesn't matter as much when distributions are perceived to be fair. It's when outcomes are unfavorable that people pay close attention to the process. If the process is judged to be fair, then employees are more accepting of unfavorable outcomes.[62] Why is this the case? It's likely that employees believe that fair procedures, which often have long-lasting effects, will eventually result in a fair outcome, even if the immediate outcome is unfair. Think about it. If you are hoping for a raise and your manager informs you that you did not receive one, you'll probably want to know how raises were determined. If it turns out that your manager allocated raises based on merit, and you were simply outperformed by a coworker, then you're more likely to accept your manager's decision than if raises were based on favoritism. Of course, if you get the raise in the first place, then you'll be less concerned with how the decision was made.

Beyond outcomes and procedures, research has shown that employees care about two other types of fairness that have to do with the way they are treated during interactions with others. The first type is **informational justice**, which reflects whether managers provide employees with explanations for key decisions and keep them informed of important organizational matters. The more detailed and candid managers are with employees, the more fairly treated those employees feel.

Though it may seem obvious that managers should be honest with their employees and not keep them in the dark about organizational matters, many managers are hesitant to share information. This is especially the case with bad news, which is uncomfortable for both the manager delivering it and the employee receiving it. For example, managers may fail to provide an adequate explanation for bad news such as a layoff or temporary pay cut out of a fear of being blamed, worries about making the situation worse, or concerns about triggering legal action.[63] In fact, research has linked the *absence* of explanations to increased litigation intentions by employees who have been laid off.[64] Explanations for bad news are beneficial when they take the form of post hoc excuses ("I know this is bad, and I wanted to give you the office, but it wasn't my decision") rather than justifications ("I decided to give the office to Sam, but having it isn't a big deal").[65]

The second type of justice relevant to interactions between managers and employees is **interpersonal justice**, which reflects whether employees are treated with dignity and respect. Compared to the three other forms of justice we've discussed, interpersonal justice is unique in that it can occur in everyday interactions between managers and employees.[66] This quality allows managers to take advantage of (or miss out on) opportunities to make their employees feel fairly treated. Many managers may view treating employees politely and respectfully as too "soft," choosing more aggressive tactics out of a belief that doing so will be more motivating. Although displays of negative emotions such as anger may be motivating in some cases,[67] managers sometimes take this too far. Consider the recent firing of the Rutgers University men's basketball coach, Mike Rice, who was terminated after video surfaced of him verbally and even physically abusing players.[68]

After all this talk about types of justice, how much does justice really matter to employees? A great deal, as it turns out. When employees feel fairly treated, they respond in a number of positive ways. All four types of justice discussed in this section have been linked to higher levels of task performance and citizenship behaviors such as helping coworkers, as well as lower levels of counterproductive behaviors such as shirking job duties. Distributive and procedural justice are more strongly associated with task performance, while informational and interpersonal justice are more strongly associated with citizenship behavior. Even more physiological outcomes, such as how well employees sleep and the state of their health, have been linked to fair treatment.[69]

Why does justice have these positive effects? First, fair treatment enhances commitment to the organization and makes employees feel it cares about their well-being. In addition, employees who feel fairly treated trust their supervisors more, which reduces uncertainty and fear of being exploited by the organization. Finally, fair treatment elicits positive emotions, which in turn prompt citizenship behaviors.[70]

Studies suggest that managers are motivated to foster employees' perceptions of justice because they wish to ensure compliance, maintain a positive identity, and establish fairness at work.[71] To enhance perceptions of justice, managers should realize that employees are especially sensitive to unfairness in procedures when bad news has to be communicated (that is, when distributive justice is low). Thus, it's important to openly share information about how allocation decisions are made, follow consistent and unbiased procedures, and engage in practices to increase the perception of procedural justice. However, it may be that managers are constrained in how much they can affect distributive and procedural justice because of formal organizational policies or cost constraints. Interpersonal and informational justice are less likely to be governed by these mechanisms because providing information and treating employees with dignity are practically "free." In such cases, managers wishing to promote fairness could focus their efforts more on informational and interpersonal justice.[72]

Despite all attempts to enhance fairness, perceived injustices are likely to occur. Fairness is often subjective; what one person sees as unfair, another may see as perfectly appropriate. In general, people see allocations or procedures favoring themselves as fair.[73] So, when addressing perceived injustices, managers need to focus their actions on the source of the problem. In addition, if employees feel they have been treated unjustly, having opportunities to express their frustration has been shown to reduce their desire for retribution.[74]

In terms of cultural differences, meta-analytic evidence shows individuals in both individualistic and collectivistic cultures prefer an equitable distribution of rewards over an equal division (everyone gets paid the same regardless of performance).[75] Across nations, the same basic principles of procedural justice are respected, and workers around the world prefer rewards based on performance and skills over rewards based on seniority.[76] However, in collectivist cultures employees expect rewards to reflect their individual needs as well as their performance.[77] Other research suggests that inputs and outcomes are valued differently in various cultures.[78] Some cultures emphasize status over individual achievement as a basis for allocating resources. Materialistic cultures are more likely to see cash compensation and rewards as the most relevant outcomes of work, whereas relational cultures will see social rewards and status as important outcomes. International managers must consider the cultural preferences of each group of employees when determining what is "fair" in different contexts.

Expectancy Theory

One of the most widely accepted explanations of motivation is Victor Vroom's **expectancy theory**.[79] Although it has its critics, most of the evidence supports the theory.[80]

Expectancy theory argues that the strength of our tendency to act a certain way depends on the strength of our expectation of a given outcome and its attractiveness. In practical terms, employees will be motivated to exert a high level of effort when they believe it will lead to a good performance appraisal; that a good appraisal will lead to organizational rewards, such as salary increases and/or intrinsic rewards; and that the rewards will satisfy the employees' personal goals. The theory, therefore, focuses on three relationships (see Exhibit 7-7).

1. *Effort–performance relationship.* The probability perceived by the individual that exerting a given amount of effort will lead to performance.
2. *Performance–reward relationship.* The degree to which the individual believes performing at a particular level will lead to the attainment of a desired outcome.
3. *Rewards–personal goals relationship.* The degree to which organizational rewards satisfy an individual's personal goals or needs and the attractiveness of those potential rewards for the individual.[81]

Expectancy theory helps explain why a lot of workers aren't motivated on their jobs and do only the minimum necessary to get by. Let's frame the theory's three relationships as questions employees need to answer in the affirmative if their motivation is to be maximized.

EXHIBIT 7-7
Expectancy
Theory

Effort–performance relationship
Performance–reward relationship
Rewards–personal goals relationship

First, *if I give a maximum effort, will it be recognized in my performance appraisal?* For many employees, the answer is "no." Why? Their skill level may be deficient, which means no matter how hard they try, they're not likely to be high performers. The organization's performance appraisal system may be designed to assess non-performance factors such as loyalty, initiative, or courage, which means more effort won't necessarily result in a higher evaluation. Another possibility is that employees, rightly or wrongly, perceive the boss doesn't like them. As a result, they expect a poor appraisal, regardless of effort. These examples suggest that people will be motivated only if they perceive a link between their effort and their performance.

Second, *if I get a good performance appraisal, will it lead to organizational rewards?* Many organizations reward things besides performance. When pay is based on factors such as having seniority, being cooperative, or "kissing up" to the boss, employees are likely to see the performance–reward relationship as weak and demotivating.

Finally, *if I'm rewarded, are the rewards attractive to me?* The employee works hard in the hope of getting a promotion but gets a pay raise instead. Or the employee wants a more interesting and challenging job but receives only a few words of praise. Unfortunately, many managers are limited in the rewards they can distribute, which makes it difficult to tailor rewards to individual employee needs. Some managers incorrectly assume that all employees want the same thing, thus overlooking the motivational effects of differentiating rewards. Whenever the offered rewards are not attractive to the employee, employee motivation is submaximized.

As a vivid example of how expectancy theory can work, consider stock analysts. They make their living trying to forecast a stock's future price; the accuracy of their buy, sell, or hold recommendations is what keeps them in work or gets them fired. But it's not quite that simple. Analysts place few sell ratings on stocks, although in a steady market, by definition, as many stocks are falling as are rising. Expectancy theory provides an explanation: Analysts who place a sell rating on a company's stock have to balance the benefits they receive by being accurate against the risks they run by drawing that company's ire. What are these risks? Risks include public rebuke, professional blackballing, and exclusion from information. When analysts place a buy rating on a stock, they face no such trade-off because, obviously, companies love it when analysts recommend that investors buy their stocks. So the incentive structure suggests the expected outcome of buy ratings is higher than the expected outcome of sell ratings, and that's why buy ratings vastly outnumber sell ratings.[82]

Does expectancy theory work? Some critics suggest it has only limited use and is more valid where individuals clearly perceive effort–performance and performance–reward linkages.[83] Because few individuals do, the theory tends to be idealistic. If organizations actually rewarded individuals for performance rather than seniority, effort, skill level, and job difficulty, expectancy theory might be much more valid. However, rather than invalidating it, this criticism can explain why a significant segment of the workforce exerts low effort on the job.

WORKPLACE MOTIVATION

Job Engagement

When Joseph reports to his job as a hospital nurse, it seems that everything else in his life goes away, and he becomes completely absorbed in what he is doing. His emotions, thoughts, and behavior are all directed toward patient care. In fact, he can get so caught up in work that he isn't even aware of how long he's been there. As a result of this total commitment, he is more effective in providing patient care and feels uplifted by his time at work.

Joseph has a high level of **job engagement**, the investment of an employee's physical, cognitive, and emotional energies into job performance.[84] Practicing managers and scholars have become interested in facilitating job engagement, believing factors deeper than liking a job or finding the work interesting drive performance. Studies attempt to measure this deeper level of commitment.

The Gallup organization has been using twelve questions to assess the extent to which employee engagement is linked to positive work outcomes for millions of employees over the past thirty years.[85] There are far more engaged employees in highly successful than in average organizations, and groups with more engaged employees have higher levels of productivity, fewer safety incidents, and lower turnover. Academic studies have also found positive outcomes. One study examined multiple business units for their level of engagement and found a positive relationship with a variety of practical outcomes.[86] Another study reviewed ninety-one distinct investigations and found higher levels of engagement associated with task performance and citizenship behavior.[87]

What makes people more likely to be engaged in their jobs? One key is the degree to which an employee believes it is meaningful to engage in work. This is partially determined by job characteristics and access to sufficient resources to work effectively.[88] Another factor is a match between the individual's values and those of the organization.[89] Leadership behaviors that inspire workers to a greater sense of mission also increase employee engagement.[90]

One of the critiques of engagement theory is that the construct is partially redundant with job attitudes like satisfaction or stress.[91] Other critics note there may be a "dark side" to engagement, as evidenced by a positive relationship between engagement and work–family conflict.[92] For instance, individuals might grow so engaged in their work roles that family responsibilities become an unwelcome intrusion. An overly high level of engagement can lead to a loss of perspective and, ultimately, burnout. Further research exploring how engagement relates to negative outcomes may help clarify whether some highly engaged employees might be getting "too much of a good thing."

SUMMARY

The motivation theories in this chapter differ in their predictive strength. Maslow's hierarchy, Theory X and Theory Y, Two-Factor Theory, and McClelland's Theory focus on needs. None has found widespread support, although McClelland's is the strongest, particularly regarding the relationship between achievement and productivity. Self-determination theory and cognitive evaluation theory have merits to consider. Goal-setting theory can be helpful but does not cover absenteeism, turnover, or job satisfaction. Reinforcement theory can be helpful, but not regarding employee satisfaction or the decision to quit. Equity theory's strongest legacy is that it provided the spark for research on organizational justice, which has more support in the literature. Expectancy theory can be helpful, but assumes employees have few constraints on decision making, such as bias or incomplete information, and this limits its applicability. Job engagement goes a long way toward explaining various degrees of employee commitment, although the outcomes of high engagement may not all be desirable.

IMPLICATIONS FOR MANAGERS

- Make sure extrinsic rewards for employees are not viewed as coercive, and recognize the importance of intrinsic motivators that appeal to employees' desires for autonomy, relatedness, and competence.
- Consider goal-setting theory: Within reason, clear and difficult goals often lead to higher levels of employee productivity.
- In accordance with self-efficacy theory, efforts you make to help your employees feel successful in completing tasks will result in their increased motivation.
- As suggested by justice theory, ensure that employees feel fairly treated; sensitivity to processes and interactions are particularly important when rewards are distributed unequally.
- Expectancy theory offers a partial means of enhancing employee productivity, absenteeism, and turnover: Employees are more motivated to engage in behaviors they think they can perform, which in turn lead to valued rewards.

PERSONAL INVENTORY ASSESSMENT

In Personal Inventory Assessment found in MyManagementLab take assessment: Work Motivation Indicator

⭐ WRITING SPACE

If your professor assigned this, sign in to **mymanagementlab.com** for the following Assisted-graded writing question:

7-1. As a manager, how would you seek to increase your employees' levels of job engagement?

8
Applied Motivation

MyManagementLab®
✪ Improve Your Grade!

When you see this icon ✪, visit **www.mymanagementlab.com** for activities that are applied, personalized, and offer immediate feedback.

LEARNING OBJECTIVES

After studying this chapter, you should be able to:

1. Describe the job characteristics model and the way it motivates by changing the work environment.
2. Compare the main ways jobs can be redesigned.
3. Explain how specific alternative work arrangements can motivate employees.
4. Describe how employee involvement measures can motivate employees.
5. Demonstrate how the different types of variable-pay programs can increase employee motivation.
6. Show how flexible benefits turn benefits into motivators.
7. Identify the motivational benefits of intrinsic rewards such as employee recognition programs.

✪ Chapter Warm-up

If your professor has chosen to assign this, go to **www.mymanagementlab.com** to see what you should particularly focus on and to take the Chapter 8 warm up.

Pay is not the only motivator for working individuals. Pay is a central means of motivation, but what you're actually doing for the money matters, too. In Chapter 7, we focused on motivation theories. In this chapter, we apply motivation concepts to practices.

While it's important to understand the foundational concepts, it's even more important to see how, as a manager, you can use them.

MOTIVATING BY JOB DESIGN: THE JOB CHARACTERISTICS MODEL

Increasingly, research on motivation focuses on approaches that link motivational concepts to the way work is structured. Research in **job design** suggests that the way the elements of a job are organized can influence employee effort. We'll discuss the job characteristics model and investigate ways jobs can be redesigned. We'll then explore alternative work arrangements.

The Job Characteristics Model

Developed by J. Richard Hackman and Greg Oldham, the **job characteristics model** (**JCM**) describes jobs by five core dimensions:[1]

Although there are individual differences, most people respond well to intrinsic job characteristics; the job characteristics model summarizes what intrinsic job characteristics might be altered to make the work more interesting and intrinsically motivating for employees.

1. **Skill variety** is the degree to which a job requires different activities using specialized skills and talents. The work of a garage owner-operator who does electrical repairs, rebuilds engines, does bodywork, and interacts with customers scores high on skill variety. The job of a bodyshop worker who sprays paint eight hours a day scores low on this dimension.
2. **Task identity** is the degree to which a job requires completion of a whole and identifiable piece of work. A cabinetmaker who designs furniture, selects the wood, builds the object, and finishes it has a job that scores high on task identity. A job scoring low on this dimension is operating a lathe to make table legs.
3. **Task significance** is the degree to which a job affects the lives or work of other people. The job of a nurse helping patients in a hospital intensive care unit scores high on task significance; sweeping floors in a hospital scores low.
4. **Autonomy** is the degree to which a job provides the worker freedom, independence, and discretion in scheduling work and determining the procedures for carrying it out. A sales manager who schedules his own work and the sales approach for each customer without supervision has a highly autonomous job. An account representative who is required to follow a standardized sales script with potential customers while under supervision has a job low on autonomy.
5. **Feedback** is the degree to which carrying out work activities generates direct and clear information about your own performance. A job with high feedback is testing and inspecting iPads. Assembling components of an iPad as they move down an assembly line would provide low feedback.

Exhibit 8-1 presents the job characteristics model (JCM). Note how the first three dimensions—skill variety, task identity, and task significance—combine to create meaningful work the employee will view as important, valuable, and worthwhile. Jobs with high autonomy give employees a feeling of personal responsibility for results; feedback will show employees how effectively they are performing. The JCM proposes that individuals obtain internal rewards when they learn (knowledge of results) that they personally have performed well (experienced responsibility) on a task they care about

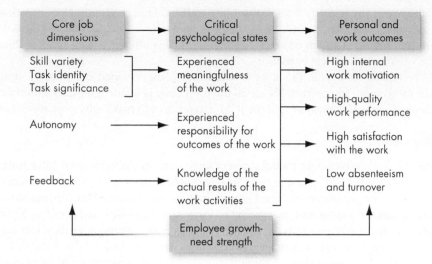

EXHIBIT 8-1
The Job Characteristics Model

Source: Adaptation of Job Characteristics Model, pp. 78–80 from J. Richard Hackman & Greg R. Oldham, *Work Redesign*, 1st Edition, © 1980. Adapted by permission of Pearson Education, Inc., Upper Saddle River, NJ.

(experienced meaningfulness).[2] The more these three psychological states are present, the greater will be employees' motivation, performance, and satisfaction, and the lower their absenteeism and likelihood of leaving. As Exhibit 8-1 indicates, individuals with a high growth need are likely to experience the critical psychological states when their jobs are enriched—and respond to them positively.

In general, research concurs with the factors of the JCM, although studies have introduced potential modifiers. One study suggested that when employees were "other oriented" (concerned with the welfare of others at work), the relationship between intrinsic job characteristics and job satisfaction was weaker. A few studies have tested the JCM in different cultures, but the results aren't consistent. The fact that the JCM is relatively individualistic (it considers the relationship between the employee and her work) suggests job enrichment strategies may not have the same effects in collectivistic cultures as in individualistic cultures (such as the United States).[3] However, another study suggested the degree to which jobs offered intrinsic motivators predicted job satisfaction and job involvement equally well for U.S., Japanese, and Hungarian employees.[4]

HOW CAN JOBS BE REDESIGNED?

"Every day was the same thing," Frank said. "Stand on that assembly line. Wait for an instrument panel to be moved into place. Unlock the mechanism and drop the panel into the Jeep Liberty as it moved by on the line. Then I plugged in the harnessing wires. I repeated that for eight hours a day. I don't care that they were paying me twenty-four dollars an hour. I was going crazy. Finally, I just said . . . this isn't going to be the way I'm going to spend the rest of my life. My brain was turning to JELL-O . . . so I quit. Now I work in a print shop and I make less than fifteen dollars an hour. But let me tell you, the work I do is really interesting. The job changes all the time, I'm continually learning new things, and the work really challenges me!"

The repetitive tasks in Frank's job at the Jeep plant provided little variety, autonomy, or motivation. In contrast, his job in the print shop is challenging and stimulating. Let's look at some of the ways to put the JCM into practice to make jobs more motivating.

Job Rotation

If employees suffer from over-routinization of their work, one alternative is **job rotation**, or the periodic shifting of an employee from one task to another with similar skill requirements at the same organizational level (also called *cross-training*). Many manufacturing firms have adopted job rotation as a means of increasing flexibility and avoiding layoffs. Managers at these companies train workers on all their equipment so they can move around as needed in response to incoming orders. International evidence from Italy, Britain, and Turkey shows that job rotation is associated with higher levels of organizational performance in manufacturing settings.[5] Although job rotation was originally conceptualized for assembly line and manufacturing employees, many organizations use job rotation for new managers and others to help them get a picture of the whole business.[6] At Singapore Airlines, for instance, a ticket agent may take on the duties of a baggage handler. Extensive job rotation is among the reasons Singapore Airlines is rated one of the best airlines in the world.[7]

The strengths of job rotation are that it reduces boredom, increases motivation, and helps employees understand how their work contributes to the organization. However, job rotation has drawbacks. Work that is done repeatedly may become habitual and "routine," which makes decision making more automatic and efficient. Training costs increase as each rotation necessitates a round of training, and moving a worker into a new position reduces productivity for that role. Job rotation also creates disruptions when members of the work group have to adjust to new employees. And supervisors may have to spend more time answering questions and monitoring the work of recently rotated employees.

Job Enrichment

Job enrichment expands jobs by increasing the degree to which the worker controls the planning, execution, and evaluation of the work. An enriched job allows the worker to do a complete activity, increases the employee's freedom and independence, increases responsibility, and provides feedback so individuals can assess and correct their own performance.[8]

How does management enrich an employee's job? Exhibit 8-2 offers suggested guidelines based on the JCM. *Combining tasks* puts fractionalized tasks back together to form a new and larger module of work. *Forming natural work units* makes an employee's tasks an identifiable and meaningful whole. *Establishing client relationships* increases the direct relationships between workers and their clients (clients can be internal as well as outside the organization). *Expanding jobs vertically* gives employees responsibilities and control formerly reserved for management. *Opening feedback channels* lets employees know how well they are doing and whether their performance is improving, deteriorating, or remaining constant.

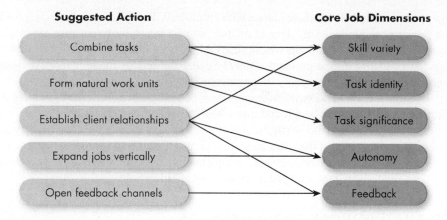

Suggested Action   **Core Job Dimensions**

Combine tasks   Skill variety

Form natural work units   Task identity

Establish client relationships   Task significance

Expand jobs vertically   Autonomy

Open feedback channels   Feedback

EXHIBIT 8-2
Guidelines for Enriching a Job

Source: "Guidelines for Enriching a Job" Source: J. R. Hackman and J. L. Suttle (eds.),
Improving Life at Work (Glenview, IL: Scott Foresman, 1977), p. 138. Reprinted by permission
of Richard Hackman and J. Lloyd Suttle.

Another method for improving the meaningfulness of work is providing employees
with mutual assistance programs.[9] Employees who can help each other directly through
their work come to see themselves, and the organizations for which they work, in more positive, pro-social terms. This, in turn, can increase employee commitment to the organization.

The evidence on job enrichment indicates that it reduces absenteeism and turnover
costs and increases satisfaction, but not all programs are equally effective.[10] A review of
eighty-three organizational interventions designed to improve performance management
found that frequent, specific feedback on solving problems was linked to consistently
higher performance, but infrequent feedback that focused more on past problems than
future solutions was much less effective.[11] Thus, job enrichment can be effective when
accompanied by practices—such as feedback—that support it. To some degree, its effectiveness also depends on the person. One study found employees with a higher preference
for challenging work experienced larger reductions in stress following job redesign than
individuals who did not prefer challenging work.[12]

Relational Job Design

While redesigning jobs on the basis of job characteristics theory is likely to make work
more intrinsically motivating, contemporary research is focusing on how to make jobs
more prosocially motivating to people. In other words, how can managers design work
so employees are motivated to promote the well-being of the organization's beneficiaries
(customers, clients, patients, and employees)? This view of job design shifts the spotlight
from the employee to those whose lives are affected by the job that employee performs.[13]

One way to make jobs more prosocially motivating is to better connect employees
with the beneficiaries of their work by relating stories from customers who have found
the company's products or services to be helpful. The medical device manufacturer
Medtronic invites people to describe how Medtronic products have improved, or even

saved, their lives and shares these stories with employees during annual meetings, providing a powerful reminder of the impact of their work. One study found that radiologists who saw photographs of patients whose scans they were examining made more accurate diagnoses of their medical problems. Why? Seeing the photos made it more personal, which elicited feelings of empathy in the radiologists.[14]

Even better, in some cases managers may be able to connect employees directly with beneficiaries. Researchers found that when university fundraisers briefly interacted with the undergraduates who would receive the scholarship money they raised, they persisted 42 percent longer in their fundraising, and raised nearly twice as much money, as those who didn't interact with potential recipients.[15] The positive impact was apparent even when fundraisers met with just a single scholarship recipient.

ALTERNATIVE WORK ARRANGEMENTS

Another approach to motivation is to consider alternative work arrangements such as flextime, job sharing, or telecommuting. These are likely to be especially important for a diverse workforce of dual-earner couples, single parents, and employees caring for a sick or aging relative.

Flextime

Susan is the classic "morning person." She rises at 5:00 A.M. sharp each day, full of energy. However, as she puts it, "I'm usually ready for bed right after the 7:00 P.M. news."

Susan's work schedule as a claims processor at the Hartford Financial Services Group is flexible. Her office opens at 6:00 A.M. and closes at 7:00 P.M., and she schedules her eight-hour day within this thirteen-hour period. Because Susan is a morning person whose seven-year-old son gets out of school at 3:00 P.M., she opts to work from 6:00 A.M. to 3:00 P.M. "My work hours are perfect. I'm at the job when I'm mentally most alert, and I can be home to take care of my son after he gets out of school."

Susan's schedule is an example of **flextime**, short for "flexible work time." Employees must work a specific number of hours per week but may vary their hours of work within limits. As in Exhibit 8-3, each day consists of a common core, usually 6 hours, with a flexibility band surrounding it. The core may be 9:00 A.M. to 3:00 P.M., with the office opening at 6:00 A.M. and closing at 6:00 P.M. Employees must be at their jobs during the common core period, but they may accumulate their other two hours around that. Some flextime programs allow employees to accumulate extra hours and turn them into a free day off each month.

Flextime has become extremely popular. According to a recent survey, a majority (53 percent) of organizations now offer some form of flextime.[16] This is not a U.S. phenomenon. In Germany, for instance, 73 percent of businesses offer flextime, and flextime is becoming more widespread in Japan as well.[17] In Germany, Belgium, the Netherlands, and France, by law employers are not allowed to refuse an employee's request for either a part-time or a flexible work schedule as long as the reason is reasonable, such as to care for an infant.[18]

Claimed benefits include reduced absenteeism, increased productivity, reduced overtime expenses, reduced hostility toward management, reduced traffic congestion around work sites on commute paths, elimination of tardiness, and increased autonomy and responsibility for employees—any of which may increase employee job satisfaction.[19] But what is flextime's actual record?

EXHIBIT 8-3
Possible Flextime
Staff Schedules

Schedule 1	
Percent Time:	100% = 40 hours per week
Core Hours:	9:00 A.M.–5:00 P.M., Monday through Friday (1-hour lunch)
Work Start Time:	Between 8:00 A.M. and 9:00 A.M.
Work End Time:	Between 5:00 P.M. and 6:00 P.M.
Schedule 2	
Percent Time:	100% = 40 hours per week
Work Hours:	8:00 A.M.–6:30 P.M., Monday through Thursday (1/2-hour lunch) Friday off
Work Start Time:	8:00 A.M.
Work End Time:	6:30 P.M.
Schedule 3	
Percent Time:	90% = 36 hours per week
Work Hours:	8:30 A.M.–5:00 P.M., Monday through Thursday (1/2-hour lunch) 8:00 A.M.–Noon Friday (no lunch)
Work Start Time:	8:30 A.M. (Monday–Thursday); 8:00 A.M. (Friday)
Work End Time:	5:00 P.M. (Monday–Thursday); Noon (Friday)
Schedule 4	
Percent Time:	80% = 32 hours per week
Work Hours:	8:00 A.M.–6:00 P.M., Monday through Wednesday (1/2-hour lunch) 8:00 A.M.–11:30 A.M. Thursday (no lunch) Friday off
Work Start Time:	Between 8:00 A.M. and 9:00 A.M.
Work End Time:	Between 5:00 P.M. and 6:00 P.M.

Most of the evidence stacks up favorably. Flextime tends to reduce absenteeism and frequently improves worker productivity,[20] probably for several reasons. Employees can schedule their work hours to align with personal demands, reducing tardiness and absences, and they can work when they are most productive. Flextime can also help employees balance work and family lives; it is a popular criterion for judging how "family friendly" a workplace is.

Flextime's major drawback is that it's not applicable to every job or every worker. It works well with clerical tasks when an employee's interaction with people outside his department is limited. It is often not a viable option for receptionists or sales personnel in retail stores—anyone whose jobs require them to be at their workstations at predetermined times. It also appears that people who have a strong desire to separate their work and family lives are less prone to use flextime.[21] Overall, employers need to consider the appropriateness of both the work and the workers before implementing flextime schedules.

Job Sharing

Job sharing allows two or more individuals to split a traditional forty-hour-a-week job. One employee might perform the job from 8:00 A.M. to noon and another from 1:00 P.M. to 5:00 P.M., or they could work full but alternate days. For example, top Ford engineers Julie Levine and Julie Rocco engaged in a job-sharing program that allowed both of them to spend time with their families while redesigning the Explorer crossover. Typically, one of them would work late afternoons and evenings and the other worked mornings. They agreed that the program worked well, although making the job share work required a great deal of time and preparation.[22]

Only 12 percent of large organizations offer job sharing, a significant decline from 18 percent in 2008.[23] Reasons it is not more widely adopted include the difficulty of finding compatible partners to job share and the historically negative perceptions of individuals not completely committed to their jobs and employers. However, decreasing job sharing for these reasons may be short-sighted. Job sharing allows an organization to draw on the talents of more than one individual for a given job. It opens the opportunity to acquire skilled workers—for instance, women with young children and retirees—who might not be available on a full-time basis. From the employee's perspective, job sharing can increase motivation and satisfaction.

An employer's decision to use job sharing is sometimes based on economics and national policy. Two part-time employees sharing a job can be less expensive than one full-time employee, but experts suggest this is not the case because training, coordination, and administrative costs can be high. In the United States, the national Affordable Care Act may create an incentive for companies to increase job sharing arrangements in order to avoid the fees employees must pay the government for full-time employees.[24] Many German and Japanese[25] firms have been using job sharing—but for a very different reason. Germany's Kurzarbeit program, which is now close to 100 years old, has kept employment levels from plummeting throughout the economic crisis by switching full-time workers to part-time job sharing work.[26]

Ideally, employers should consider each employee and job separately, seeking to match up the skills, personalities, and needs of each employee with the tasks required for the job to look for potential job sharing matches.

Telecommuting

It might be close to the ideal job for many people: no rush hour traffic, flexible hours, freedom to dress as you please, and fewer interruptions. It's called **telecommuting**, or working at home at least two days a week on a computer linked to the employer's office.[27] (A closely related term—the *virtual office*—describes working from home on a relatively permanent basis.) While telecommuting would seem to mesh with a transition to knowledge work (which often can be performed anywhere), it has been a popular topic lately not for its potential, but rather for reconsideration. Recently, large companies such as Yahoo! and Best Buy have eliminated this form of flexible work.[28] Yahoo! CEO Marissa Mayer discussed how telecommuting may undermine corporate culture, noting "People are more productive when they're alone, but they're more collaborative and innovative when they're together."[29]

While the movement away from telecommuting for some companies like Yahoo! has made the headlines, it appears that for most, the movement continues to grow.

The U.S. Department of the Census estimated there was a 25 percent increase in self-employed home-based workers from 1999 to 2005 and a 20 percent increase in employed workers who work exclusively from home.[30] One recent survey of nearly 500 organizations found that 57 percent of organizations offered telecommuting, with 36 percent allowing employees to telecommute at least part of the time and 20 percent allowing employees to telecommute full-time, and these percentages have remained relatively stable since 2008.[31] Organizations that actively encourage telecommuting include AT&T, IBM, American Express, Sun Microsystems, and a number of U.S. government agencies.[32]

What kinds of jobs lend themselves to telecommuting? There are three categories: routine information-handling tasks, mobile activities, and professional and other knowledge-related tasks.[33] Writers, attorneys, analysts, and employees who spend the majority of their time on computers or the telephone—including telemarketers, customer-service representatives, reservation agents, and product-support specialists—are candidates. As telecommuters, they can access information on their computers at home as easily as in the office.

Telecommuting has several potential benefits. These include a larger labor pool from which to select, higher productivity, less turnover, improved morale, and reduced office-space costs. A positive relationship exists between telecommuting and supervisor performance ratings, but a relationship between telecommuting and potentially lower turnover intentions has not been substantiated in research.[34] Beyond the benefits to employees and organizations, telecommuting has potential benefits to society. One study estimated that, in the United States, if people telecommuted half the time, carbon emissions would be reduced by approximately 51 metric tons per year. Environmental savings could come about from lower office energy consumption, fewer traffic jams that emit greenhouse gasses, and fewer road repairs.[35]

Telecommuting has several downsides. The major one for management is less direct employee supervision. In today's team-focused workplace, telecommuting may make it more difficult to coordinate teamwork and can reduce knowledge transfer in organizations.[36] From the employee's standpoint, telecommuting can increase feelings of isolation and reduce job satisfaction. Telecommuters are also vulnerable to the "out of sight, out of mind" effect.[37] Employees who aren't at their desks, who miss meetings, and who don't share in day-to-day informal workplace interactions may be at a disadvantage when it comes to raises and promotions because they're perceived as not putting in the requisite "face-time."

Telecommuting is a contemporary reality, particularly in the minds of employees. Telecommuting certainly does appear to make sense given changes in technology, the nature of work, and preferences of younger workers. Yet as the Yahoo! experience shows, some leaders do not think those benefits outweigh the costs.

EMPLOYEE INVOLVEMENT

Employee involvement is a participative process that uses employees' input to increase their commitment to organizational success. If workers are engaged in decisions that increase their autonomy and control over their work lives, they will become more motivated, more committed to the organization, more productive, and more satisfied with their jobs. These benefits don't stop with individuals—when teams are given more control over their work, morale and performance increase as well.[38]

To be successful, employee involvement programs should be tailored to country norms.[39] A study of four countries, including the United States and India, confirmed the importance of modifying practices to reflect national culture.[40] While U.S. employees readily accepted employee involvement programs, managers in India who tried to empower their employees were rated low by those employees. These reactions are consistent with India's high power–distance culture, which accepts and expects differences in authority. Similarly, Chinese workers who were very accepting of traditional Chinese values showed few benefits from participative decision making, but workers who were less traditional were more satisfied and had higher performance ratings under participative management.[41] Another study conducted in China found that involvement increased employees' thoughts and feelings of job security, enhancing their well-being.[42]

Examples of Employee Involvement Programs

Let's look at two major forms of employee involvement—participative management and representative participation—in more detail.

PARTICIPATIVE MANAGEMENT Common to all **participative management** programs is joint decision making, in which subordinates share a significant degree of decision-making power with their immediate superiors. Participative management has, at times, been considered a panacea for poor morale and low productivity. In reality, for participative management to be effective, followers must have trust and confidence in their leaders. Leaders should refrain from coercive techniques and instead stress the organizational consequences of decisions to their followers.[43]

Studies of the participation–performance relationship have yielded mixed findings.[44] Organizations that institute participative management report higher stock returns, lower turnover rates, and higher labor productivity, although these effects are typically not large.[45] Research at the individual level indicates participation has only a modest influence on employee productivity, motivation, and job satisfaction. This doesn't mean participative management isn't beneficial. However, it is not a sure means for improving performance.

REPRESENTATIVE PARTICIPATION Most countries in western Europe require companies to practice **representative participation**, called "the most widely legislated form of employee involvement around the world."[46] Representative participation redistributes power within an organization, putting labor on a more equal footing with the interests of management and stockholders by letting workers be represented by a small group of employees who participate in decision making.

The two most common forms of representation are works councils and board representatives.[47] Works councils are groups of nominated or elected employees who must be consulted when management makes decisions about employees. Board representatives are employees who sit on a company's board of directors and represent employees' interests.

The influence of representative participation on working employees seems to be minimal.[48] Works councils are dominated by management and have little impact on employees or the organization. While participation might increase the motivation and satisfaction of employee representatives, there is little evidence that this trickles down to the employees they represent. Overall, "the greatest value of representative participation is symbolic. If one is interested in changing employee attitudes or in improving organizational performance, representative participation would be a poor choice."[49]

Linking Employee Involvement Programs and Motivation Theories

Employee involvement draws on a number of the motivation theories we discussed in Chapter 7. Theory Y is consistent with participative management and Theory X with the more traditional autocratic style of managing. In terms of two-factor theory, employee involvement programs could provide intrinsic motivation by increasing opportunities for growth, responsibility, and involvement in the work itself. The opportunity to make and implement decisions—and then see them work out—can help satisfy an employee's needs for responsibility, achievement, recognition, growth, and enhanced self-esteem. Extensive employee involvement programs have the potential to increase intrinsic motivation. And giving employees control over key decisions, along with ensuring that their interests are represented, can augment feelings of procedural justice.

> As opposed to research on the job characteristics model and work redesign, which is mostly favorable, the research evidence on employee involvement programs is decidedly mixed. It is not clear that employee involvement programs have fulfilled their promise.

USING PAY TO MOTIVATE EMPLOYEES

As we saw in Chapter 3, pay is not a primary factor driving job satisfaction. However, it does motivate people, and companies often underestimate its importance. One study found that while 45 percent of employers thought pay was a key factor in losing top talent, 71 percent of top performers called it a strong reason.[50]

Given that pay is so important, will the organization lead, match, or lag the market in pay? How will individual contributions be recognized? In this section, we consider (1) what to pay employees (decided by establishing a pay structure), (2) how to pay individual employees (decided through variable-pay plans and skill-based pay plans), (3) what benefits and choices to offer (such as flexible benefits), and (4) how to construct employee recognition programs.

What to Pay: Establishing a Pay Structure

There are many ways to pay employees. The process of initially setting pay levels entails balancing *internal equity*—the worth of the job to the organization (usually established through a technical process called job evaluation)—and *external equity*—the competitiveness of an organization's pay relative to pay in its industry (usually established through pay surveys). Obviously, the best system pays what the job is worth while also paying competitively relative to the labor market.

Some organizations prefer to pay above the market, while some may lag the market because they can't afford to pay market rates, or they are willing to bear the costs of paying below market (namely, higher turnover as people are lured to better-paying jobs). Some companies who have realized impressive gains in income and profit margins have done so partially by holding down employee wages, such as Comcast, Walt Disney, McDonald's, and AT&T.[51]

Pay more, and you may get better-qualified, more highly motivated employees who will stay with the organization longer. A study covering 126 large organizations found employees who believed they were receiving a competitive pay level had higher morale and were more productive, and customers were more satisfied as well.[52] But pay is often the highest single operating cost for an organization, which means paying too much can make the organization's products or services too expensive.

Establishing a pay structure thus has broad implications for employees and for the organization as a whole. Finding the right balance can be an art and a science, handled best when leaders understand the implications of pay decisions.

How to Pay: Rewarding Individual Employees through Variable-Pay Programs

Variable-pay plans, when properly designed and administered, do appear to enhance employee motivation.

"Why should I put any extra effort into this job?" asked Anne, a fourth-grade elementary schoolteacher in Denver, Colorado. "I can excel or I can do the bare minimum. It makes no difference. I get paid the same. Why do anything above the minimum to get by?" Comments like Anne's have been voiced by schoolteachers for decades because pay increases were tied to seniority. Recently, however, a number of states have revamped their compensation systems to motivate teachers by linking pay levels to results in the classroom, and other states are considering such programs.[53] Many organizations, public and private, are moving away from pay based on seniority or credentials.

Piece-rate, merit-based, bonus, skill-based, profit sharing, gain-sharing, and employee stock ownership plans are all forms of a **variable-pay program**, which bases a portion of an employee's pay on some individual and/or organizational measure of performance.[54] Variable-pay plans have long been used to compensate salespeople and executives, but the scope of variable-pay jobs has broadened. Recent research indicates that 26 percent of U.S. companies have either increased or plan to increase the proportion of variable pay in employee pay programs, and another 40 percent have already recently increased the proportion of variable pay.[55]

Globally, around 80 percent of companies offer some form of variable-pay plan. In Latin America, more than 90 percent of companies offer some form of variable-pay plan. Latin American companies also have the highest percentage of total payroll allocated to variable pay, at nearly 18 percent. European and U.S. companies are relatively lower, at about 12 percent.[56] When it comes to executive compensation, Asian companies are outpacing Western companies in their use of variable pay.[57]

A recent study of 415 companies in South Korea suggested that group-based pay-for-performance plans can have a strong, positive effect on organizational performance.[58] Unfortunately, not all employees see a strong connection between pay and performance. Therefore, the results of pay-for-performance plans are mixed; the context and the receptivity of the individual to the plans play a large role.

Let's examine the different types of variable-pay programs in more detail.

PIECE-RATE PAY   The **piece-rate pay plan** has long been popular as a means of compensating production workers with a fixed sum for each unit of production. A pure piece-rate plan provides no base salary and pays the employee only for what he or she produces. Ballpark workers selling peanuts are frequently paid piece-rate. If they sell forty bags of peanuts at $1 each for their earnings, their take is $40. The more peanuts they sell, the more they earn. The limitation of these plans is that they're not feasible for many jobs. An emergency room (ER) doctor and nurse can earn significant salaries regardless of the number of patients seen or their patients' outcomes. Would it be better to pay them only if their patients fully recover? It seems unlikely that most would accept such a deal, and it might cause unanticipated consequences as well (such as ERs avoiding patients with chronic or terminal conditions). So, although piece-rate incentives are motivating and relevant for some jobs, it is unrealistic to think they can constitute all employees' pay.

MERIT-BASED PAY   A **merit-based pay plan** pays for individual performance based on performance appraisal ratings. A main advantage is that high performers can get bigger raises. If designed correctly, merit-based plans let individuals perceive a strong relationship between their performance and their rewards.[59]

Although you might think a person's average level of performance is the key factor in merit pay decisions, recent research indicates that the projected level of future performance also plays a role. One study found that National Basketball Association (NBA) players whose performance was on an upward trend were paid more than their average performance would have predicted. Managers of all organizations may unknowingly be basing merit pay decisions on how they *think* employees will perform, which may result in overly optimistic (or pessimistic) pay decisions.[60]

Despite their intuitive appeal, merit pay plans have several limitations. One is that they are typically based on an annual performance appraisal and thus are only as valid as the performance ratings. Another limitation is that the pay-raise pool of available funds fluctuates on economic or other conditions that have little to do with individual performance. For instance, a colleague at a top university who performed very well in teaching and research was given a pay raise of $300. Why? Because the pay-raise pool was very small. Yet that is hardly pay-for-performance. Lastly, a move away from merit pay is coming from organizational leaders who don't feel it separates high and low performers enough.

The concept and intention of merit pay—that employees are paid for performance—is sound. For employee motivation purposes, however, merit pay should be only one part of a performance recognition program.

BONUSES   An annual **bonus** is a significant component of total compensation for many jobs. The incentive effects of performance bonuses should be higher than those of merit pay because, rather than paying for performance years ago that has rolled into current base pay, bonuses reward recent performance. When times are bad, firms can cut bonuses to reduce compensation costs. Workers on Wall Street, for example, saw their average bonus drop by more than a third in 2012 as their firms faced greater scrutiny.[61]

Although admittedly a bit manipulative sounding, taking rewards and bonuses and splitting them into multiple categories—even if those categories are meaningless—may increase motivation.[62] Why? Because, research indicates, people are more likely to feel they "missed out" on a reward if they don't receive all from each category.

SKILL-BASED PAY   **Skill-based pay** (also called *competency-based* or *knowledge-based pay*) is an alternative to job-based pay that centers pay levels on how many skills employees have or how many jobs they can do.[63] For employers, the lure of skill-based pay plans is increased workforce flexibility: Staffing is easier when employees possess a wide range of usable skills. Skill-based pay also facilitates communication because people gain a better understanding of the skills used for other organizational jobs. One study found that across 214 different organizations, skill-based pay was related to higher levels of workforce flexibility, positive attitudes, membership behaviors, and productivity.[64] Another study found that over five years, a skill-based pay plan was associated with higher levels of individual skill change and skill maintenance.[65] These results suggest that skill-based pay plans are effective.

What about the downsides? People can "top out"—that is, they can learn all the skills the program calls for them to learn. This can frustrate employees after they've been challenged by an environment of learning, growth, and continual pay raises. Plus, skill-based plans don't address overall performance but only whether someone can manage the skills. Perhaps reflecting these weaknesses, one study of ninety-seven U.S. companies using skill-based pay plans found that 39 percent had switched to a more traditional market-based pay plan seven years later.[66] A skill-based pay plan may thus help an organization increase the scope of skills of its workforce, but may be limited to a prescribed number of development years. A skill-based plan would rarely be a good overall motivational strategy.

PROFIT-SHARING PLANS   A **profit-sharing plan** distributes compensation based on some established formula designed around a company's profitability. Compensation can be direct cash outlays or, particularly for top managers, allocations of stock options. When you read about executives like Oracle's Larry Ellison, the top-earning U.S. CEO, earning $96.2 million, much of it ($90.7 million) comes from stock options previously granted based on company profit performance.[67] Or, take Facebook's Mark Zuckerberg, who despite accepting a $1 salary, made $2.3 billion in 2012 after cashing out 60,000 stock options.[68] Of course, the vast majority of profit-sharing plans are not so grand in scale. Jacob started his own lawn-mowing business at age thirteen. Jacob employed his brother, Isaiah, and friend Marcel, and paid them each 25 percent of the profits he made on each yard. Profit-sharing plans at the organizational level appear to have positive impacts on employee attitudes; employees report a greater feeling of psychological ownership.[69] Obviously, profit sharing does not work when there is no reported profit per se, such as in nonprofit organizations, or often in the public sector. However, profit sharing may make sense for many organizations, large or small.

GAINSHARING   **Gainsharing**[70] is a formula-based group incentive plan that uses improvements in group productivity from one period to another to determine the total amount of money allocated. Its popularity seems narrowly focused among large manufacturing companies, although some health care organizations have experimented with it as a cost-saving mechanism. Gainsharing differs from profit sharing in tying rewards to productivity gains rather than profits, so employees can receive incentive awards even when the organization isn't profitable. Because the benefits accrue to groups of workers, high performers pressure weaker ones to work harder, improving performance for the group as a whole.[71]

EMPLOYEE STOCK OWNERSHIP PLANS   An **employee stock ownership plan (ESOP)** is a company-established benefit plan in which employees acquire stock, often at below-market prices, as part of their benefits. Research on ESOPs indicates they increase employee satisfaction and innovation.[72] Their impact on performance is less clear. ESOPs have the potential to increase employee job satisfaction and work motivation, but employees need to psychologically experience ownership.[73] That is, in addition to their granted financial stake in the company, they need to be kept regularly informed of the status of the business and have the opportunity to influence its performance.[74]

ESOPs for top management can reduce unethical behavior. CEOs are less likely to manipulate firm earnings reports to make themselves look good in the short run when they have an ownership share.[75] Of course, ESOPs are not wanted by all companies, and they won't work in all situations, but they can be an important part of an organization's motivational strategy.

EVALUATION OF VARIABLE PAY Do variable-pay programs increase motivation and productivity? Studies generally support the idea that organizations with profit-sharing plans have higher levels of profitability than those without them.[76] Profit-sharing plans have also been linked to higher levels of employee commitment to the organization, especially in small organizations.[77] Thus, economist Ed Lazear was generally right when he said, "Workers respond to prices just as economic theory predicts. Claims by sociologists and others that monetizing incentives may actually reduce output are unambiguously refuted by the data." But that doesn't mean everyone responds positively to variable-pay plans.[78] One study found that whereas piece-rate pay plans stimulated higher levels of productivity, this positive affect was not observed for risk-averse employees.

You'd probably think individual pay systems such as merit pay or pay-for-performance work better in individualistic cultures such as the United States or that group-based rewards such as gainsharing or profit sharing work better in collectivistic cultures. Unfortunately, there isn't much research on the issue. One study did suggest that employee beliefs about the fairness of a group incentive plan were more predictive of pay satisfaction in the United States than in Hong Kong. One interpretation is that U.S. employees are more critical in appraising group pay plans, and therefore it's more important that the plans are communicated clearly and administered fairly.[79]

USING BENEFITS TO MOTIVATE EMPLOYEES

As with pay, benefits are both an employee provision and an employee motivator. Whereas organizations of yesteryear took a "one size fits all" approach to benefits, meaning a standard package was issued to every employee, contemporary leaders understand that each individual employee values the components of a benefits package differently. A flexible program turns the benefits package into a motivational tool.

Flexible Benefits: Developing a Benefits Package

Consistent with expectancy theory's thesis that organizational rewards should be linked to each employee's goals, **flexible benefits** individualize rewards by allowing individuals to choose the compensation package that best satisfies his current needs and situation. These plans replace the "one-benefit-plan-fits-all" programs designed for a male with a wife and two children at home that dominated organizations for more than fifty years.[80] Fewer than 10 percent of employees now fit this image: About 25 percent are single, and one-third are part of two-income families with no children. Flexible benefits can accommodate differences in employee needs based on age, marital status, partner's benefit status, and the number and age of dependents.

Today, almost all major corporations in the United States offer flexible benefits. Flexible benefits are becoming the norm in other countries and in small companies, too. A recent survey of 211 Canadian organizations found that 60 percent offer flexible benefits, up from 41 percent in 2005.[81] A similar survey of firms in the United Kingdom found that nearly all major organizations were offering flexible benefits programs, with options ranging from private supplemental medical insurance to holiday trading (with coworkers), discounted bus travel, and child care assistance.[82]

USING INTRINSIC REWARDS TO MOTIVATE EMPLOYEES

We have discussed motivating employees through job design and by the extrinsic rewards of pay and benefits. On an organizational level, are those the only ways to motivate employees? Not at all! We would be remiss to overlook intrinsic rewards organizations can provide such as employee recognition programs, discussed next.

Employee Recognition Programs

Laura makes $8.50 per hour working at her fast-food job in Pensacola, Florida, and the job isn't very challenging or interesting. Yet Laura talks enthusiastically about the job, her boss, and the company that employs her. "What I like is the fact that Guy [her supervisor] appreciates the effort I make. He compliments me regularly in front of the other people on my shift, and I've been chosen Employee of the Month twice in the past six months. Did you see my picture on that plaque on the wall?"

Organizations are increasingly recognizing what Laura knows: Work rewards can be both intrinsic and extrinsic. Rewards are intrinsic in the form of employee recognition programs and extrinsic in the form of compensation systems. Employee recognition programs range from a spontaneous and private thank-you to widely publicized formal programs in which specific types of behavior are encouraged and the procedures for attaining recognition are clearly identified.

As companies and government organizations face tighter budgets, nonfinancial incentives become more attractive. Everett Clinic in Washington State uses a combination of local and centralized initiatives to encourage managers to recognize employees.[83] Employees and managers give "Hero Grams" and "Caught in the Act" cards to colleagues for exceptional accomplishments at work. Part of the incentive is simply to receive recognition, but there are also drawings for prizes based on the number of cards a person receives. Managers are trained to use the programs frequently and effectively to reward good performance. Multinational corporations like Symantec Corporation have also increased their use of recognition programs. Centralized programs across offices in different countries can help ensure that all employees, regardless of where they work, can be recognized for their contribution to the work environment.[84] Recognition programs are common in Canadian and Australian firms as well.[85]

Some research suggests that financial incentives may be more motivating in the short term, but in the long run nonfinancial incentives motivate best.[86] A few years ago, 1,500 employees were surveyed in a variety of work settings to find out what they considered the most powerful workplace motivator. Their response? Recognition, recognition, and more recognition.

An obvious advantage of recognition programs is that they are inexpensive because praise is free.[87] Recognition programs with or without financial rewards can be highly motivating to employees. Despite the increased popularity of recognition programs, critics argue they are highly susceptible to political manipulation by management. When applied to jobs for which performance factors are relatively objective, such as sales, recognition programs are likely to be perceived by employees as fair. However, in most jobs, the criteria for good performance aren't self-evident, which allows managers to manipulate the system and recognize their favorites. Abuse can undermine the value of recognition programs and demoralize employees. Where formal recognition programs are used, care must be taken to ensure fairness. Where they are not used, it is important to motivate employees by recognizing their performance efforts.

✪ WATCH IT

If your professor assigned this, sign in to **mymanagementlab.com** to watch a video titled Zappos: Motivating Employees Through Company Culture to learn more about this topic and respond to questions.

SUMMARY

As we've seen in this chapter, understanding what motivates individuals is key to organizational performance. Employees whose differences are recognized, who feel valued, and who have the opportunity to work in jobs tailored to their strengths and interests will be motivated to perform at the highest levels. Employee participation and recognition can increase employee productivity, commitment to work goals, motivation, and job satisfaction.

IMPLICATIONS FOR MANAGERS

- *Recognize individual differences.* Spend the time necessary to understand what's important to each employee. Design jobs to align with individual needs and maximize their motivation potential.
- *Use goals and feedback.* You should give employees firm, specific goals, and they should receive feedback on how well they are faring in pursuit of those goals.
- *Allow employees to participate in decisions that affect them.* Employees can contribute to setting work goals, choosing their own benefits packages, and solving productivity and quality problems.
- *Link rewards to performance.* Rewards should contain a performance component, and employees must find the process to be fair. Recognize the power of both extrinsic and intrinsic rewards.
- *Check the system for equity.* Employees should perceive that experience, skills, abilities, effort, and job requirements explain differences in pay, job assignments, and other rewards.

PERSONAL INVENTORY ASSESSMENT

In Personal Inventory Assessment found in MyManagementLab take assessment: Diagnosing the Need for Team Building

✪ WRITING SPACE

If your professor assigned this, sign in to **mymanagementlab.com** for the following Assisted-graded writing question:

8-1. How would you design a pay program that might appeal to new entrants to the workforce?

9

Communication at Work

MyManagementLab®

⭐ Improve Your Grade!

When you see this icon ⭐, visit **www.mymanagementlab.com** for activities that are applied, personalized, and offer immediate feedback.

LEARNING OBJECTIVES

After studying this chapter, you should be able to:

1. Describe the communication process and formal and informal communication.
2. Contrast downward, upward, and lateral communication.
3. Compare and contrast formal small-group networks and the grapevine.
4. Contrast oral, written, and nonverbal communication.
5. Show how channel richness underlies the choice of communication channel.
6. Differentiate between automatic and controlled processing of persuasive messages.
7. Identify common barriers to effective communication.
8. Show how to overcome the potential problems in cross-cultural communication.

⭐ Chapter Warm-up

If your professor has chosen to assign this, go to **www.mymanagementlab.com** to see what you should particularly focus on and to take the Chapter 9 warm up.

One of the many challenges in organizations is communication. In this chapter, we'll analyze communication and ways in which we can make it more effective. Communication is powerful: no group or organization can exist without sharing meaning among its members.

Communication must include both the *transfer* and *the understanding of meaning.* Communicating is more than merely imparting meaning; that meaning must also be understood. It is only thus that we can convey information and ideas. In perfect communication, if it existed, a thought would be transmitted so the receiver understood the same mental picture the sender intended. Though it sounds elementary, perfect communication is never achieved in practice, for reasons we shall see later.

First let's describe the communication process.

THE COMMUNICATION PROCESS

For communication to take place, a message needs to be conveyed between a sender and a receiver. The sender encodes the message (converts it to a symbolic form) and passes it through a medium (channel) to the receiver, who decodes it. The result is the transfer of meaning from one person to another.[1]

Exhibit 9-1 depicts the **communication process**. The key parts of this model are (1) the sender, (2) encoding, (3) the message, (4) the channel, (5) decoding, (6) the receiver, (7) noise, and (8) feedback.

The *sender* initiates a message by encoding a thought. The *message* is the actual physical product of the sender's *encoding*. When we speak, the speech is the message. When we write, the writing is the message. When we gesture, our movements and expressions are the message. The *channel* is the medium through which the message travels. The sender selects it, determining whether to use a formal or informal channel. **Formal channels** are established by the organization and transmit messages related to the professional activities of members. They traditionally follow the authority chain within the organization. Other forms of messages, such as personal or social messages, follow **informal channels**, which are spontaneous and determined by individual choice.[2] The *receiver* is the person(s) to whom the message is directed, who must first translate the symbols into understandable form. This step is the *decoding* of the message. *Noise* represents communication barriers that distort the clarity of the message, such as perceptual problems, information overload, semantic difficulties, or cultural differences. The final link in the communication process is a feedback loop. *Feedback* is the check on how successful we have been in transferring our messages as originally intended. Feedback determines whether understanding has been achieved.

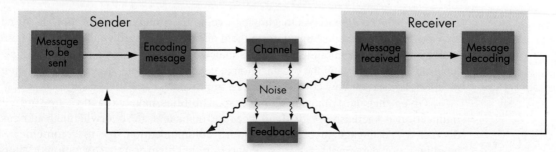

EXHIBIT 9-1
The Communication Process

DIRECTION OF COMMUNICATION

Communication can flow vertically or laterally. We subdivide the vertical dimension into downward and upward directions.[3]

Downward Communication

Downward, upward, and lateral directions of communication have their own challenges; understand and manage these unique challenges.

Communication that flows from one level of a group or organization to a lower level is *downward communication*. Group leaders and managers use it to assign goals, provide job instructions, explain policies and procedures, point out problems that need attention, and offer feedback.

In downward communication, managers must explain the reasons *why* a decision was made. One study found employees were twice as likely to be committed to changes when the reasons behind them were fully explained. Although this may seem like common sense, many managers feel they are too busy to explain things or that explanations will raise too many questions. Evidence clearly indicates, though, that explanations increase employee commitment and support of decisions.[4] Managers might think that sending a message one time is enough to get through to lower-level employees, but research suggests managerial communications must be repeated several times and through a variety of different media to be truly effective.[5]

Another problem in downward communication is its one-way nature; generally, managers inform employees but rarely solicit their advice or opinions. A study revealed that nearly two-thirds of employees say their boss rarely or never asks their advice. The study noted, "Organizations are always striving for higher employee engagement, but evidence indicates they unnecessarily create fundamental mistakes. People need to be respected and listened to." Companies like cell phone maker Nokia actively listen to employee suggestions, a practice the company thinks is especially important to innovation.[6] Research indicates the way advice is solicited also matters. Employees will not provide input, even when conditions are favorable, if doing so seems against their best interests.[7]

The best communicators explain the reasons behind their downward communications but also solicit communication from the employees they supervise. That leads us to the next direction: upward communication.

Upward Communication

Upward communication flows to a higher level in the group or organization. It's used to provide feedback to higher-ups, inform them of progress toward goals, and relay current problems. Upward communication keeps managers aware of how employees feel about their jobs, coworkers, and the organization in general. Managers rely on upward communication for ideas on how conditions can be improved.

Given that most managers' job responsibilities have expanded, upward communication is increasingly difficult because managers are overwhelmed and easily distracted. To engage in effective upward communication, try to communicate in headlines not paragraphs (short summaries rather than long explanations), support your headlines with actionable items, and prepare an agenda to make sure you use your boss's attention well.[8]

Lateral Communication

When communication occurs between members of a work group, members at the same level in separate work groups, or any other horizontally equivalent workers, we describe it as *lateral communication.*

Lateral communication saves time and facilitates coordination. Some lateral relationships are formally sanctioned. More often, they are informally created to short-circuit the vertical hierarchy and expedite action. From management's viewpoint, lateral communication can be good or bad. Because strictly adhering to the formal vertical structure can be inefficient, lateral communication with management's support can be beneficial. But dysfunctional conflict can result when formal vertical channels are breached, when members go above or around their superiors, or when bosses find decisions were made without their knowledge.

ORGANIZATIONAL COMMUNICATION

Formal Small-Group Networks

Formal organizational networks can be complicated, including hundreds of people and a half-dozen or more hierarchical levels. To simplify, we've condensed these networks into three common small groups of five people each (see Exhibit 9-2): chain, wheel, and all channel.

The *chain* rigidly follows the formal chain of command; this network approximates the communication channels you might find in a rigid three-level organization. The *wheel* relies on a central figure to act as the conduit for all group communication; it simulates the communication network you would find on a team with a strong leader. The *all-channel* network permits group members to actively communicate with each other; it's most often characterized in practice by self-managed teams, in which group members are free to contribute and no one person takes a leadership role.

As Exhibit 9-3 demonstrates, the effectiveness of each network depends on the dependent variable that concerns you. The structure of the wheel facilitates the emergence of a leader, the all-channel network is best if you desire high member satisfaction, and the chain is best if accuracy is most important. Exhibit 9-3 leads us to the conclusion that no single network will be best for all occasions.

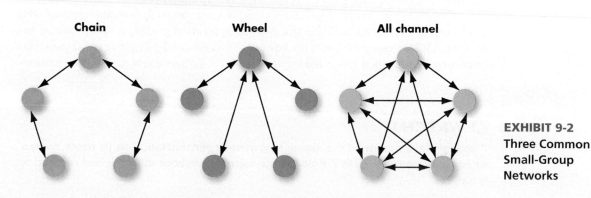

Chain   **Wheel**   **All channel**

EXHIBIT 9-2
Three Common Small-Group Networks

EXHIBIT 9-3
Small-Group
Networks and
Effective Criteria

Criteria	Chain	Networks Wheel	All Channel
Speed	Moderate	Fast	Fast
Accuracy	High	High	Moderate
Emergence of a leader	Moderate	High	None
Member satisfaction	Moderate	Low	High

The Grapevine

The informal communication network in a group or organization is called the **grapevine**.[9] Although rumors and gossip transmitted through the grapevine may be informal, it's still an important source of information for employees. Grapevine or word-of-mouth information about a company also has an impact on whether job applicants join an organization.[10]

Rumors emerge as a response to situations that are *important* to us, when there is *ambiguity*, and under conditions that arouse *anxiety*.[11] The fact that work situations frequently contain these three elements explains why rumors flourish in organizations. The secrecy and competition that typically prevail—around the appointment of new bosses, the relocation of offices, downsizing decisions, or the realignment of work assignments—encourage and sustain rumors on the grapevine. A rumor will persist until either the wants and expectations creating the uncertainty are fulfilled, or the anxiety has been reduced.

The grapevine is an important part of any group or organization communication network. It gives managers a feel for the morale of their organizations, identifies issues employees consider important, and helps tap into employee anxieties. The grapevine also serves employees' needs: small talk creates a sense of closeness and friendship among those who share information, although research suggests it often does so at the expense of the "out" group.[12] Evidence also indicates that gossip is driven largely by employee social networks that managers can study to learn more about how positive and negative information is flowing through the organization.[13] Thus, while the grapevine may not be sanctioned or controlled by the organization, it can be understood.

Can managers entirely eliminate rumors? No, nor should they want to; rumors serve some purposes. Research indicates that even some forms of gossip provide prosocial motivation.[14] What managers should do, however, is minimize the negative consequences of rumors by limiting their range and impact. Exhibit 9-4 offers a few practical suggestions.

✪ WATCH IT

If your professor assigned this, sign in to **mymanagementlab.com** to watch a video titled Communication (TWZ Role Play) to learn more about this topic and respond to questions.

> 1. **Provide** information—in the long run, the best defense against rumors is a good offense (in other words, rumors tend to thrive in the absence of formal communication).
> 2. **Explain** actions and decisions that may appear inconsistent, unfair, or secretive.
> 3. **Refrain** from shooting the messenger—rumors are a natural fact of organizational life, so respond to them calmly, rationally, and respectfully.
> 4. **Maintain** open communication channels—constantly encourage employees to come to you with concerns, suggestions, and ideas.

EXHIBIT 9-4
Suggestions for Reducing the Negative Consequences of Rumors

Source: Based on L. Hirschhorn, "Managing Rumors," in L. Hirschhorn (ed.), *Cutting Back* (San Francisco: Jossey-Bass, 1983), pp. 54–56.

MODES OF COMMUNICATION

How do group members transfer meaning among each other? They rely on oral, written, and nonverbal communication.

Oral Communication

A primary means of conveying messages is oral communication. Speeches, formal one-on-one and group discussions, and the informal rumor mill or grapevine are popular forms of oral communication.

    The advantages of oral communication are speed and feedback. We can convey a verbal message and receive a response in minimal time. If the receiver is unsure of the message, rapid feedback allows the sender to quickly detect and correct it. As one professional put it, "Face-to-face communication on a consistent basis is still the best way to get information to and from employees."[15]

    One major disadvantage of oral communication surfaces whenever a message has to pass through a number of people: the more people, the greater the potential distortion. If you've ever played the game "Telephone," you know the problem. Each person interprets the message in her own way. The message's content, when it reaches its destination, is often very different from the original.

Oral, written, and nonverbal communication forms or mediums of communication have their unique purposes, and specific limitations; utilize each medium when optimal, and try to avoid their limitations.

Written Communication

Written communication includes any method that conveys written words or symbols. As such, the earliest forms of written communication date back thousands of years, and since we have samples from these earliest writings, written communication is thus the longest-lasting form of communication. Written business communication today is usually conducted via letters, e-mail, instant messaging, text messaging, social media, and blogs.

Nonverbal Communication

Every time we deliver a verbal message, we also impart a nonverbal message.[16] No discussion of communication would thus be complete without consideration of *nonverbal communication*—which includes body movements, the intonations or emphasis we give to words, facial expressions, and the physical distance between the sender and receiver. Nonverbal body language can either enhance the sender's verbal message (when the body language concurs with the message) or detract from the message (when the nonverbal cues tell a different story than the message). Sometimes nonverbal communication may stand alone without a verbal message.

We could argue that every *body movement* has meaning, and no movement is accidental (though some are unconscious). We act out our state of being with nonverbal body language. We can smile to project trustworthiness, uncross our arms to appear approachable, and stand to signal authority.[17]

Body language can convey status, level of engagement, and emotional state.[18] Body language adds to, and often complicates, verbal communication. A body position or movement can communicate something of the emotion behind a message, but when it is linked with spoken language, it gives fuller meaning to a sender's message. Studies indicate that people read much more about another's attitude and emotions from their nonverbal cues than their words. If the nonverbal cues conflict with the speaker's verbal message, the nonverbal cues are sometimes more likely to be believed by the listener.[19]

If you read the minutes of a meeting, you wouldn't grasp the impact of what was said the same way as if you had been there or could see the meeting on video. Why? There is no record of nonverbal communication. The emphasis given to words or phrases is missing; *intonations* can change the meaning of a message. *Facial expressions* also convey meaning. Facial expressions, along with intonations, can show arrogance, aggressiveness, fear, shyness, and other characteristics.

Physical distance also has meaning. What is considered proper spacing between people largely depends on cultural norms. A business-like distance in some European countries feels intimate in many parts of North America. If someone stands closer to you than is considered appropriate, it may indicate aggressiveness or sexual interest; if farther away, it may signal disinterest or displeasure with what is being said.

CHOICE OF COMMUNICATION CHANNEL

Why do people choose one channel of communication over another? A model of media richness helps explain channel selection among managers.[20]

Channel Richness

Channels differ in their capacity to convey information. Some are *rich* in that they can (1) handle multiple cues simultaneously, (2) facilitate rapid feedback, and (3) be very personal. Others are *lean* in that they score low on these factors. As Exhibit 9-5 illustrates, face-to-face conversation scores highest in **channel richness** because it transmits the most information per communication episode—multiple information cues (words, postures, facial expressions, gestures, intonations), immediate feedback (both verbal and nonverbal), and the personal touch of being physically present. Impersonal written media such as formal reports and bulletins rate lowest in richness.

Choosing Communication Methods

The choice of channel depends on whether the message is routine. Routine messages tend to be straightforward and have minimal ambiguity, so channels low in richness can carry

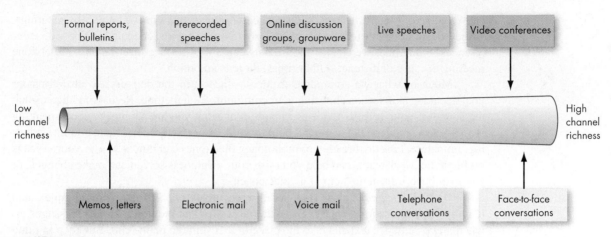

EXHIBIT 9-5
Information Richness and Communication Channels

Sources: Based on R. H. Lengel and R. L. Daft, "The Selection of Communication Media as an Executive Skill," *Academy of Management Executive* (August 1988), pp. 225–232; and R. L. Daft and R. H. Lengel, "Organizational Information Requirements, Media Richness, and Structural Design," *Managerial Science* (May 1996), pp. 554–572. Reproduced from R. L. Daft and R. A. Noe, *Organizational Behavior* (Fort Worth, TX: Harcourt, 2001), p. 311.

them efficiently. Non-routine communications are likely to be complicated and have the potential for misunderstanding. Managers can communicate them effectively only by selecting rich channels.

Often, a variety of modes of communication work best to convey important ideas. For example, when tough times hit Manpower Business Solutions during the recent economic recession, the company elected to communicate with employees daily using a variety of media to ensure that everyone remained informed.[21] Employees were given updates about the company's plans for dealing with economic problems, including advance warning before layoffs. The company believes its strategy of using rich communication channels for non-routine information has paid off by reducing employee anxiety and increasing employee engagement with the organization.

Channel richness is a helpful framework for choosing your mode of communication. It is not always easy to know when to choose oral rather than written communication, for instance. Experts say oral communication or "face time" with coworkers, clients, and upper management is key to success. However, if you seek out the CEO just to say hello, you may be remembered as an annoyance rather than a star, and signing up for every meeting on the calendar to increase your face time is counterproductive to getting the work of the organization done. Your communication choice is worth a moment's thought: Is the message you need to communicate better suited to a discussion, or a diagram?

Whenever you need to gauge the receiver's receptivity, *oral communication* is usually the better choice. The marketing plan for a new product may need to be worked out with clients in person, so you can see their reactions to each idea you are proposing. Also consider the receiver's preferred mode of communication; some individuals focus on content better over the phone than in meetings. The pace of your work environment matters too. If your manager requests a meeting with you, you may not want to ask for an exchange of e-mails instead. A fast-paced workplace may thrive on pop-by meetings, while a deadline-heavy team project may progress faster with scheduled Skype videoconferences. Sometimes we cannot choose between a face-to-face meeting and a telephone meeting because of distance. Other times, there is an option.

Much of what we communicate face-to-face is in the delivery, so also consider your speaking skills when choosing your communication method. Research indicates that the sound of your voice is twice as important as what you are saying. A good speaking voice—clear, moderated—can be a help to your career, while loud, questioning, irritating, immature, falsetto, breathy, or monotone voice tones can hinder you. If your voice is problematic, work teams can help you raise your awareness so you can make changes, or you may benefit from the help of a voice coach.[22]

Written communication is generally the most reliable mode for complex and lengthy communications, and it can be the most efficient method for short messages, as when a two-sentence text can take the place of a 10-minute phone call. But keep in mind that written communication can be limited in its emotional expression.

Choose written communication when you want the information to be tangible and verifiable. Both you and the receiver(s) will have a record of the message. People are usually forced to think more thoroughly about what they want to convey in a written message than in a spoken one, so written communications can be well thought out, logical, and clear. But be aware that, as with oral communication, your delivery is just as important as the content. Managers report that grammar mistakes and lack of business formality are unprofessional . . . and unacceptable. "People get passionate about grammar," corporate writing instructor and author Jack Appleman noted, and a recent study found that 45 percent of employers were adding training programs to teach grammar and communication skills. Other experts argue that the use of social media jargon and abbreviations are good for business. James Grimes, marketing vice president of software firm RescueTime, advocates that his employees stay culturally relevant. He says, "Those who can be sincere, and still text and Twitter . . . those are the ones who are going to succeed." Of course, his advice might be best suited to his computer-based industry. For your professional success, know your audience when possible, and use good grammar.

Finally, in choosing a communication channel it's important to be alert to *nonverbal* aspects of communication and consider your body language cues as well as the literal meaning of your words. You should particularly be aware of contradictions between the verbal and nonverbal messages, as a sender and as a receiver. Someone who frequently glances at her smartphone is giving the message that she would prefer to terminate the conversation no matter what she actually says, for instance. We misinform others when we express one message verbally, such as trust, but nonverbally communicate a contradictory message that reads, "I don't have confidence in you."

Information Security

Security is a huge concern for nearly all organizations with private or proprietary information about clients, customers, and employees. Organizations worry about the security of the electronic information they seek to protect, such as hospital patient data; the physical information they still keep in file cabinets, which is decreasing but still important; and the security of the information they entrust their employees with knowing, such as

Apple's project groups that are given information only on a need-to-know basis. The recent adoption of cloud-based electronic data storage has brought a new level of worry; 51 percent of managers in a recent survey were considering cloud-based human resources software. Early research indicates that fears about cloud computing seem unwarranted, so its business use will likely increase.[23] As we've discussed, most companies actively monitor employee Internet use and e-mail records, and some even use video surveillance and record phone conversations. Necessary though they may be, such practices can seem invasive to employees. An organization can relieve employee concerns by engaging them in the creation of information-security policies and giving them some control over how their personal information is used.[24]

PERSUASIVE COMMUNICATION

We've discussed a number of methods for communication up to this point. Now we turn our attention to one of the functions of communication and the features that might make messages more or less persuasive to an audience.

Automatic and Controlled Processing

To understand the process of communication, it is useful to consider two different ways that we process information.[25] Consider the last time you bought a can of soda. Did you carefully research brands, or did you choose the can that had the most appealing advertising images? If we're honest, we'll admit glitzy ads and catchy slogans do indeed influence our choices as consumers. We often rely on **automatic processing**, a relatively superficial consideration of evidence and information making use of heuristics. Automatic processing takes little time and minimal effort, so it makes sense to use it for processing persuasive messages related to topics you don't care much about. The disadvantage is that it lets us be easily fooled by a variety of tricks, like a cute jingle or a glamorous photo.

Now consider the last time you chose a place to live. You probably researched the area, gathered information about prices from a variety of sources, and considered the costs and benefits of renting versus buying. Here, you're relying on more effortful **controlled processing**, a detailed consideration of evidence and information relying on facts, figures, and logic. Controlled processing requires effort and energy, but it's harder to fool someone who has taken the time and effort to engage in it. So what makes someone engage in either automatic or controlled processing? There are a few rules of thumb for determining what types of processing an audience will use.

Interest Level

One of the best predictors of whether people will use an automatic or controlled process for reacting to a persuasive message is their level of interest in the outcome.[26] Interest levels reflect the impact a decision is going to have on your life. When people are very interested in the outcome of a decision, they're more likely to process information carefully. That's probably why people look for so much more information when deciding about something important (like where to live) than something relatively unimportant (like which soda to drink).

Prior Knowledge

People who are very well informed about a subject area are more likely to use controlled processing strategies. They have already thought through various arguments for or against a specific course of action, and therefore they won't readily change their position unless very good, thoughtful reasons are provided. On the other hand, people who are poorly informed about a topic can change their minds more readily, even in the face of fairly superficial arguments presented without a great deal of evidence. Overall, then, a better-informed audience is likely to be much harder to persuade.

Personality

Do you always read at least five reviews of a movie before deciding whether to see it? Perhaps you even research recent films by the same stars and director. If so, you are probably high in *need for cognition*, a personality trait of individuals who are most likely to be persuaded by evidence and facts.[27] Those who are lower in need for cognition are more likely to use automatic processing strategies, relying on intuition and emotion to guide their evaluation of persuasive messages.

Message Characteristics

Another factor that influences whether people use an automatic or controlled processing strategy is the characteristics of the message itself. Messages provided through relatively lean communication channels, with little opportunity for users to interact with the content of the message, encourage automatic processing. Conversely, messages provided through richer communication channels tend to encourage more deliberative processing.

The most important implication is to match your persuasive message to the type of processing your audience is likely to use. When the audience is not interested in a persuasive message topic, when they are poorly informed, when they are low in need for cognition, and when information is transmitted through relatively lean channels, they'll be more likely to use automatic processing. In these cases, use messages that are more emotionally laden and associate positive images with your preferred outcome. On the other hand, when the audience is interested in a topic, when they are high in need for cognition, or when the information is transmitted through rich channels, then it is a better idea to focus on rational arguments and evidence to make your case.

BARRIERS TO EFFECTIVE COMMUNICATION

A number of barriers can slow or distort effective communication. In this section, we highlight the most important.

Filtering

Filtering refers to a sender's purposely manipulating information so the receiver will see it more favorably. A manager who tells his boss what he feels the boss wants to hear is filtering information.

The more vertical levels in the organization's hierarchy, the more opportunities there are for filtering. But some filtering will occur wherever there are status differences.

Factors such as fear of conveying bad news and the desire to please the boss often lead employees to tell their superiors what they think they want to hear, thus distorting upward communications.

Selective Perception

Selective perception, discussed in Chapter 6, is important because the receivers in the communication process selectively see and hear based on their needs, motivations, experience, background, and other personal characteristics. Receivers also project their interests and expectations into communications as they decode them. An employment interviewer who expects a female job applicant to put her family ahead of her career is likely to see that in all female applicants, regardless of whether they actually feel that way. As receivers, we don't see reality; we interpret what we see and call it reality.

Information Overload

Individuals have a finite capacity for processing data. When the information we have to work with exceeds our processing capacity, the result is information overload. We've seen that dealing with copious amounts of information has become a huge challenge for individuals and for organizations.

What happens when individuals have more information than they can sort and use? They tend to select, ignore, pass over, or forget. Or they may put off further processing until the overload situation ends. In any case, this results in lost information and less effective communication, making it all the more important to deal well with overload.

Emotions

You may interpret the same message differently when you're angry or distraught than when you're happy. For example, individuals in positive moods are more confident about their opinions after reading a persuasive message, so well-designed arguments have stronger impacts on their opinions.[28] People in negative moods are more likely to scrutinize messages in greater detail, whereas those in positive moods tend to accept communications at face value.[29] Extreme emotions such as jubilation or depression are most likely to hinder effective communication. In such instances, we are most prone to abandon our rational and objective thinking processes and substitute emotional judgments.

Language

Even when we're communicating in the same language, words mean different things to different people. Age and context are two of the biggest factors that influence such differences.

Age and context factors are often at play when people from different generations and backgrounds interact. For instance, when business consultant Michael Schiller asked his fifteen-year-old daughter where she was going with friends, he said, "You need to recognize your ARAs and measure against them." Schiller said that in response, his daughter "looked at him like he was from outer space." (For the record, ARA stands for accountability, responsibility, and authority.) Those new to corporate lingo may find acronyms such as ARA, words such as *deliverables* (verifiable outcomes of a project), and phrases such as *get the low-hanging fruit* (deal with the easiest parts first) bewildering, in the same way parents may be mystified by teen slang.[30]

Our use of language is far from uniform even when we think we are speaking plainly. If we knew how each of us defines and interprets words we select, we could minimize communication difficulties, but we usually don't know. Senders tend to incorrectly assume the words and terms they use mean the same to the receiver as to them.

Silence

It's easy to ignore silence or lack of communication because it is defined by the absence of information. This is often a mistake—silence itself can be the message to communicate noninterest or inability to deal with a topic. Silence can also be a simple outcome of information overload, or a delaying period for considering a response. For whatever reasons, research suggests using silence and withholding communication are common and problematic.[31] One survey found that more than 85 percent of managers reported remaining silent about at least one issue of significant concern.[32] The impact of silence can be organizationally detrimental. Employee silence can mean managers lack information about ongoing operational problems. Silence regarding discrimination, harassment, corruption, and misconduct can mean top management will not take action to eliminate problematic behavior.

Silence is less likely to occur where minority opinions are treated with respect, workgroup identification is high, and high procedural justice prevails.[33] Practically, this means managers must make sure they behave in a supportive manner when employees voice divergent opinions or concerns, and they must take these under advisement. One act of ignoring an employee for expressing concerns may well lead the employee to withhold important future communication.

Communication Apprehension

An estimated 5 to 20 percent of the population suffers debilitating **communication apprehension**, or social anxiety.[34] These people experience undue tension and anxiety in oral communication, written communication, or both.[35] They may find it extremely difficult to talk with others face-to-face or may become extremely anxious when they have to use the phone, relying on memos or e-mails when a phone call would be faster and more appropriate.

Oral-communication apprehensives avoid situations, such as teaching, for which oral communication is a dominant requirement.[36] But almost all jobs require *some* oral communication. Of greater concern is evidence that high oral-communication apprehensives distort the communication demands of their jobs in order to minimize the need for communication. Be aware that some people severely limit their oral communication and rationalize their actions by telling themselves communicating isn't necessary for them to do their jobs effectively.

Lying

The final barrier to effective communication is outright misrepresentation of information, or lying. People differ in their definition of a lie. For example, is deliberately withholding information about a mistake a lie, or do you have to actively deny your role in the mistake to pass the threshold? While the definition of a lie befuddles ethicists and social scientists, there is no denying the prevalence of lying. In one diary study, the average person reported telling one to two lies per day, with some individuals telling considerably more.[37] Compounded across a large organization, this is an enormous amount of deception happening every single day. Evidence shows that people are more comfortable lying over the phone than face-to-face and more comfortable lying in e-mails than when they have to write with pen and paper.[38]

Can you detect liars? The literature suggests most people are not very good at detecting deception in others.[39] The problem is there are no nonverbal or verbal cues unique to lying—averting your gaze, pausing, and shifting your posture can also be signals of nervousness, shyness, or doubt. Most people who lie take steps to guard against being detected, so they might look a person in the eye when lying because they know that direct eye contact is (incorrectly) assumed to be a sign of truthfulness. Finally, many lies are embedded in truths; liars usually give a somewhat true account with just enough details changed to avoid detection.

In sum, the frequency of lying and the difficulty in detecting liars makes this an especially strong barrier to effective communication.

GLOBAL IMPLICATIONS

Effective communication is difficult under the best of conditions. Cross-cultural factors clearly create the potential for increased communication problems. A gesture that is well understood and acceptable—either oral, written, or nonverbal—in one culture can be meaningless or lewd in another. Only 18 percent of companies have documented strategies for communicating with employees across cultures, and only 31 percent require that corporate messages be customized for consumption in other cultures. Procter & Gamble seems to be an exception; more than half the company's employees don't speak English as their first language, so the company focuses on simple messages to make sure everyone knows what's important.[40]

Cultural Barriers

Researchers have identified a number of problems related to language difficulties in cross-cultural communications.[41]

First are *barriers caused by semantics*. Words mean different things to different people, particularly people from different national cultures. Some words simply don't translate between cultures. For instance, the new capitalists in Russia may have difficulty communicating with British or Canadian counterparts because English terms such as *efficiency*, *free market*, and *regulation* have no direct Russian equivalents.

Second are *barriers caused by word connotations*. Words imply different things in different languages. Negotiations between U.S. and Japanese executives can be difficult because the Japanese word *hai* translates as "yes," but its connotation is "Yes, I'm listening" rather than "Yes, I agree."

Third are *barriers caused by tone differences*. In some cultures, language is formal; in others, it's informal. The tone can also change depending on the context: People speak differently at home, in social situations, and at work. Using a personal, informal style when a more formal style is expected can be inappropriate.

Fourth are *differences in tolerance for conflict and methods for resolving conflicts*. People from individualist cultures tend to be more comfortable with direct conflicts and

A number of barriers—such as culture—often retard or distort effective communication; understand these barriers as a means of overcoming them.

will make the source of their disagreements overt. Collectivists are more likely to acknowledge conflict only implicitly and avoid emotionally charged disputes. They may attribute conflicts to the situation more than to the individuals and therefore may not require explicit apologies to repair relationships, whereas individualists prefer explicit statements accepting responsibility for conflicts and public apologies to restore relationships.

Cultural Context

Cultures tend to differ in the degree to which context influences the meaning individuals take from communication.[42] In **high-context cultures** such as China, Korea, Japan, and Vietnam, people rely heavily on nonverbal and subtle situational cues in communicating with others, and a person's official status, place in society, and reputation carry considerable weight. What is *not* said may be more significant than what *is* said. In contrast, people from Europe and North America reflect their **low-context cultures**. They rely essentially on spoken and written words to convey meaning; body language and formal titles are secondary.

Contextual differences mean quite a lot in terms of communication. Communication in high-context cultures implies considerably more trust by both parties. What may appear to be casual and insignificant conversation in fact reflects the desire to build a relationship and create trust. Oral agreements imply strong commitments in high-context cultures. And who you are—your age, seniority, rank in the organization—is highly valued and heavily influences your credibility. But in low-context cultures, enforceable contracts tend to be in writing, precisely worded, and highly legalistic. Similarly, low-context cultures value directness. Managers are expected to be explicit and precise in conveying intended meaning. It's quite different in high-context cultures, in which managers tend to "make suggestions" rather than give orders.

A Cultural Guide

Much can be gained from business intercultural communications. It is safe to assume every single one of us has a different viewpoint that is culturally shaped. Because we do have differences, we have an opportunity to reach the most creative solutions possible with the help of others if we communicate effectively.

According to Fred Casmir, a leading expert in intercultural communication research, we often do not communicate well with people outside of our culture because we tend to generalize from only knowing their cultural origin. This can be insensitive and potentially disastrous, especially when we make assumptions based on observable characteristics. Many of us have a richly varied ethnic background and would be offended if someone addressed us according to what culture our physical features might favor, for instance. Also, attempts to be culturally sensitive to another person are often based on stereotypes propagated by media. These stereotypes usually do not have a correct or current relevance.

Casmir noted that because there are far too many cultures for anyone to understand completely, and individuals interpret their own cultures differently, intercultural communication should be based on sensitivity and pursuit of common goals. He found the ideal condition is an ad hoc "third culture" a group can form when seeking to incorporate aspects of each member's cultural communication preferences. The norms this subculture establishes through appreciating individual differences creates a common ground for effective communication. Intercultural groups that communicate effectively can be highly productive and innovative.

When communicating with people from a different culture, what can you do to reduce misinterpretations? Casmir and other experts offer the following suggestions:

1. *Know Yourself.* Recognizing your own cultural identity and biases is critical to understanding the unique viewpoint of others.
2. *Foster a Climate of Mutual Respect, Fairness, and Democracy.* Clearly establish an environment of equality and mutual concern. This will be your "third culture" context for effective intercultural communication that transcends each person's cultural norms.
3. *Learn the Cultural Context of Each Person.* You may find more similarities or differences to your own frame of reference than you might expect. Be careful not to categorize them, however.
4. *When in Doubt, Listen.* If you speak your opinions too early, you may be more likely to offend the other person. You will also want to listen first to better understand the other person's intercultural language fluency and familiarity with your culture.
5. *State Facts, Not Your Interpretation.* Interpreting or evaluating what someone has said or done draws more on your own culture and background than on the observed situation. If you state only facts, you will have the opportunity to benefit from the other person's interpretation. Delay judgment until you've had sufficient time to observe and interpret the situation from the differing perspectives of all concerned.
6. *Consider the Other Person's Viewpoint.* Before sending a message, put yourself in the recipient's shoes. What are his values, experiences, and frames of reference? What do you know about his education, upbringing, and background that can give you added insight? Try to see the people in the group as they really are first, and take a collaborative problem-solving approach whenever potential conflicts arise.
7. *Proactively Maintain the Identity of the Group.* Like any culture, the establishment of a common-ground "third culture" for effective intercultural communication takes time and nurturing. Remind members of the group of your common goals, mutual respect, and need to adapt to individual communication preferences.[43]

SUMMARY

You've probably discovered the link between communication and employee satisfaction in this chapter: the less uncertainty, the greater the satisfaction. Distortions, ambiguities, and incongruities between oral, written, and nonverbal messages all increase uncertainty and reduce satisfaction. Since everyone's perspective is different, the more you can understand your employees, the better you can respond. Cultural sensitivity is an important organizational component for establishing communications understanding.

IMPLICATIONS FOR MANAGERS

- Remember that your communication mode will partly determine your communication effectiveness.
- Obtain feedback from your employees to make certain your messages—however they are communicated—are understood.
- Remember that written communication creates more misunderstandings than oral communication; communicate with employees through in-person meetings when possible.
- Make sure you use communication strategies appropriate to your audience and the type of message you're sending.
- Keep in mind communication barriers such as gender and culture.

PERSONAL INVENTORY ASSESSMENT

In Personal Inventory Assessment found in MyManagementLab take assessment: Communication Styles

⊛ WRITING SPACE

If your professor assigned this, sign in to **mymanagementlab.com** for the following Assisted-graded writing question:

9-1. As a manager of an international work group, what might be the best way to develop a communications strategy for employees who work overseas?

10

From Groups to Teams

MyManagementLab®

✪ Improve Your Grade!

When you see this icon ✪, visit **www.mymanagementlab.com** for activities that are applied, personalized, and offer immediate feedback.

LEARNING OBJECTIVES

After studying this chapter, you should be able to:

1. Analyze the growing popularity of teams in organizations.
2. Contrast groups and teams.
3. Contrast the five types of teams.
4. Identify the characteristics of effective teams.
5. Show how organizations can create team players.
6. Decide when to use individuals instead of teams.

✪ Chapter Warm-up

If your professor has chosen to assign this, go to **www.mymanagementlab.com** to see what you should particularly focus on and to take the Chapter 10 warm up.

Teams are increasingly the primary means for organizing work in contemporary business firms. In fact, there are few more damaging insults than "not a team player." Do you think you're a team player?

Decades ago, when companies such as W. L. Gore, Volvo, and General Foods introduced teams into their production processes, it made news because no one else was doing it. Today, the organization that *doesn't* use teams has become newsworthy. Teams are everywhere.

WHY HAVE TEAMS BECOME SO POPULAR?

How do we explain the popularity of teams? As organizations have restructured to compete more efficiently, they have turned to teams as a way to optimize employee talents. Teams are more flexible and responsive to changing events than traditional departments or other forms of permanent groupings. They can quickly assemble, deploy, refocus, and disband. Another explanation for the popularity of teams is that they are an effective means for management to democratize organizations, facilitate employee participation in operating decisions, and increase employee involvement.

The fact that organizations have turned to teams doesn't necessarily mean they're always effective. Team members, as humans, can be swayed by fads and herd mentality that can lead them astray from the best decisions. Are teams truly effective? What conditions affect their potential? How do members work together? These are some of the questions we'll answer in this chapter.

DIFFERENCES BETWEEN GROUPS AND TEAMS

Groups and teams are not the same thing. In this section, we define and clarify the difference between work groups and work teams.[1]

In Chapter 11, we define a *group* as two or more individuals, interacting and interdependent, who have come together to achieve particular objectives. A **work group** is a group that interacts primarily to share information and make decisions to help each member perform within that member's area of responsibility.

Work groups have no need or opportunity to engage in collective work with joint effort, so the group's performance is merely the summation of each member's individual contribution. There is no positive synergy to create an overall level of performance greater than the sum of the inputs. A work group is a collection of individuals doing their work, albeit with interaction and/or interdependency.

A **work team**, on the other hand, generates positive synergy through coordinated effort. The individual efforts result in a level of performance greater than the sum of those individual inputs.

In both work groups and work teams, there are often behavioral expectations of members, collective normalization efforts, active group dynamics, and some level of decision making (even if just informally about the scope of membership). Both work groups and work teams may generate ideas, pool resources, or coordinate logistics such as work schedules; for the work group, however, this effort will be limited to information gathering for decision makers outside the group. Whereas we can think of a work team as a subset of a work group, the team is constructed to be purposeful (symbiotic) in its member interaction. The distinction between a work group and a work team should be kept even when the terms are mentioned interchangeably in differing contexts. Exhibit 10-1 highlights the differences between work groups and work teams.

The definitions help clarify why organizations structure work processes by teams. Management is looking for positive synergy that will allow the organizations to increase performance. The extensive use of teams creates the *potential* for an organization to generate greater outputs with no increase in employee headcount. Notice, however, that we said *potential*. There is nothing magical that ensures the achievement of positive synergy

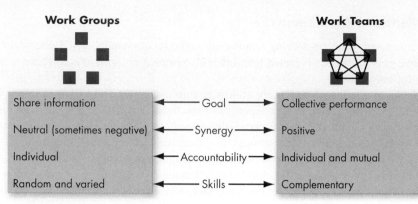

EXHIBIT 10-1
Comparing Work Groups and Work Teams

Work Groups		Work Teams
Share information	← Goal →	Collective performance
Neutral (sometimes negative)	← Synergy →	Positive
Individual	← Accountability →	Individual and mutual
Random and varied	← Skills →	Complementary

in the creation of teams. Merely calling a *group* a *team* doesn't automatically improve its performance. As we show later in this chapter, effective teams have certain common characteristics. If management hopes to gain increases in organizational performance through the use of teams, its teams must possess these characteristics.

TYPES OF TEAMS

Teams can make products, provide services, negotiate deals, coordinate projects, offer advice, and make decisions.[2] In this section, first we describe four common types of teams in organizations: *problem-solving teams*, *self-managed work teams*, *cross-functional teams*, and *virtual teams* (see Exhibit 10-2). Then we will discuss *multiteam systems*, a "team of teams."

Problem-Solving Teams

In the past, teams were typically composed of 5 to 12 hourly employees from the same department who met for a few hours each week to discuss ways of improving quality, efficiency, and the work environment.[3] These **problem-solving teams** rarely have the authority to unilaterally implement any of their suggestions, but if their recommendations are paired with implementation processes, some significant improvements can be realized. For instance, brokerage firm Merrill Lynch used a problem-solving team to brainstorm ways to reduce the number of days needed to open a new cash management account.[4] By finding ways to cut the number of steps from 46 to 36, the team—and eventually the firm—reduced the average number of days from 15 to 8.

   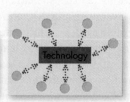

Problem-solving Self-managed   Cross-functional   Virtual

EXHIBIT 10-2
Four Types of Teams

Self-Managed Work Teams

As we discussed, problem-solving teams only make recommendations. Some organizations have gone further and created teams that also implement solutions and take responsibility for outcomes.

Self-managed work teams are groups of employees (typically 10 to 15 in number) who perform highly related or interdependent jobs; these teams take on some supervisory responsibilities.[5] Typically, the responsibilities include planning and scheduling work, assigning tasks to members, making operating decisions, taking action on problems, and working with suppliers and customers. Fully self-managed work teams even select their own members and evaluate each other's performance. When self-managed work teams are established, former supervisory positions take on decreased importance and are sometimes eliminated.

Research on the effectiveness of self-managed work teams has not been uniformly positive.[6] Some research indicates that self-managed work teams may be more or less effective based on the degree to which team-promoting behaviors are rewarded. One study of 45 self-managing factory teams found that when members perceived that economic rewards such as pay were dependent on input from their teammates, performance improved for both individuals and the team as a whole.[7]

A second area of research focus has been the effect of conflict on self-managed work team effectiveness. Some research indicates that self-managed teams are not effective when there is conflict. When disputes arise, members often stop cooperating and power struggles ensue, which leads to lower group performance.[8] However, other research indicates that when members feel confident they can speak up without being embarrassed, rejected, or punished by other team members—in other words, when they feel psychologically safe—conflict can be beneficial and boost team performance.[9]

Thirdly, research has explored the effect of self-managed work teams on member behavior. Here again the findings are mixed. Although individuals on teams report higher levels of job satisfaction than other individuals, studies indicate they sometimes have higher absenteeism and turnover rates. One large-scale study of labor productivity in British establishments found that although using teams improved individual (and overall) labor productivity, no evidence supported the claim that *self-managed* teams performed better than traditional teams with less decision-making authority.[10] On the whole, it appears that for self-managing teams to be advantageous, a number of facilitating factors must be in place.

Cross-Functional Teams

Starbucks created a team of individuals from production, global PR, global communications, and U.S. marketing to develop the Via brand of instant coffee. The team's suggestions resulted in a product that was cost-effective to produce and distribute, and marketed with a tightly integrated, multifaceted strategy.[11] This example illustrates the use of **cross-functional teams**, made up of employees from about the same hierarchical level but different work areas who come together to accomplish a task.

Cross-functional teams are an effective means of allowing people from diverse areas to exchange information, develop new ideas, solve problems, and coordinate complex projects. Due to the high need for coordination, cross-functional teams are not simple to manage. Their early stages of development are often long, as members learn to work with the diversity and complexity. And it takes time to build trust and teamwork, especially among people from varying backgrounds with different experiences and perspectives.

Organizations have used horizontal, boundary-spanning teams for decades, and we would be hard-pressed to find a major organization or product launch that did not employ cross-functional teams. Most of the major automobile manufacturers—Toyota, Honda, Nissan, BMW, GM, Ford, and Chrysler—use these teams to coordinate complex projects. Network equipment corporation Cisco Systems relies on cross-functional teams to identify new business opportunities in the field and then implement them from the bottom up.[12]

In sum, the strength of traditional cross-functional teams is the face-to-face collaborative efforts of individuals with diverse skills from a variety of disciplines. When the unique perspectives of these members is considered, these teams can be very effective.

Virtual Teams

Cross-functional teams do their collaborative work primarily face-to-face, whereas **virtual teams** use computer technology to unite physically dispersed members to achieve a common goal.[13] Virtual teams collaborate online—using communication links such as wide area networks, corporate social media, videoconferencing, and e-mail—whether members are nearby or continents apart. Virtual teams are so pervasive that it's a bit of a misnomer to call them "virtual." Nearly all teams today do at least some of their work remotely.

For virtual teams to be effective, management should ensure that (1) trust is established among members (one inflammatory remark in an e-mail can severely undermine trust), (2) team progress is monitored closely (so the team doesn't lose sight of its goals and no team member "disappears"), and (3) the efforts and products of the team are publicized throughout the organization (so the team does not become invisible).[14]

Virtual teams face special challenges. They may suffer because there is less social rapport and direct interaction among members, leaving some members feeling isolated. One study showed that team leaders can reduce the feeling of isolation, however, by communicating frequently and consistently with team members so none feel unfairly disfavored.[15] Another challenge is to correctly disperse information. Evidence from 94 studies involving more than 5,000 groups found that virtual teams are better at sharing unique information (information held by individual members, not the entire group), but they tend to share less information overall.[16] A further challenge is finding the best amount of communication. Low levels of virtual communication in teams result in higher levels of information sharing, but high levels of virtual communication hinder it.

Thus, it is a mistake to think that virtual teams are an easy substitute for face-to-face teams. While the geographical reach and immediacy of virtual communication makes virtual teams a natural development, managers must make certain this type of team is the optimal choice for the desired outcome and then maintain an oversight role throughout the collaboration.

Multiteam Systems

The types of teams we've described so far are typically smaller, standalone teams, though their activities relate to the broader objectives of the organization. As tasks become more complex, teams often grow in size. Increases in team size are accompanied by higher coordination demands, creating a tipping point at which the addition of another member does more harm than good. To solve this problem, organizations are employing **multiteam systems**, collections of two or more interdependent teams that share a superordinate goal. In other words, multiteam systems are a "team of teams."[17]

To picture a multiteam system, imagine the coordination of response needed after a major car accident. There is the emergency medical services team, which responds first and transports the injured to the hospital. An emergency room team then takes over, providing medical care, followed by a recovery team. Although the emergency services team, the emergency room team, and the recovery team are technically independent, their activities are interdependent, and the success of one depends on the success of the others. Why? Because they all share the higher goal of saving lives.

Some factors that make smaller, more traditional teams effective do not necessarily apply to multiteam systems and can even hinder their performance. One study showed that multiteam systems performed better when they had "boundary spanners" whose job was to coordinate with members of the other subteams. This reduced the need for some team member communication. Restricting the lines of communication was helpful because it reduced coordination demands.[18] Research on smaller, stand-alone teams tends to find that opening up all lines of communication is better for coordination, but when it comes to multiteam systems, the same rules do not always apply.

In general, a multiteam system is the best choice when either a team has become too large to be effective, or when teams with distinct functions need to be highly coordinated.

✪ WATCH IT

If your professor assigned this, sign in to **mymanagementlab.com** to watch a video titled Teams (TWZ Role Play) to learn more about this topic and respond to questions.

CREATING EFFECTIVE TEAMS

Many researchers have tried to identify factors related to team effectiveness. To help, some studies have organized what was once a large list of characteristics into a relatively focused model.[19] Exhibit 10-3 summarizes what we currently know about what makes teams effective. As you'll see, the model builds on many of the group concepts introduced earlier.

In considering the team effectiveness model, keep in mind three points. First, teams differ in form and structure. The model attempts to generalize across all varieties of teams, but avoids rigidly applying its predictions to all teams.[20] Use it as a guide. Second, the model assumes teamwork is preferable to individual work. Creating "effective" teams when individuals can do the job better is like perfectly solving the wrong problem. Third, let's consider what *team effectiveness* means in this model. Typically, team effectiveness includes objective measures of the team's productivity, managers' ratings of the team's performance, and aggregate measures of member satisfaction.

We can organize the key components of effective teams into three general categories. First are the resources and other *contextual* influences that make teams effective. The second relates to the team's *composition*. Finally, *process* variables are events within the team that influence effectiveness. We will discuss each of these components next.

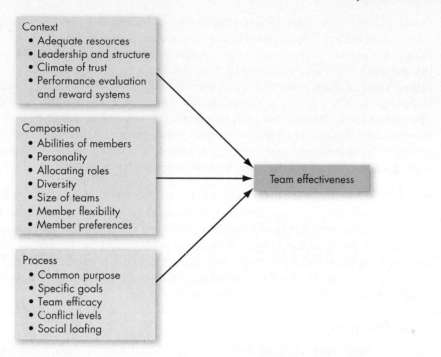

EXHIBIT 10-3
Team
Effectiveness
Model

Context: What Factors Determine Whether Teams Are Successful

The four contextual factors most significantly related to team performance are adequate resources, effective leadership, a climate of trust, and a performance evaluation and reward system that reflects team contributions.

ADEQUATE RESOURCES   Teams are part of a larger organization system; every work team relies on resources outside the group to sustain it. A scarcity of resources directly reduces the ability of a team to perform its job effectively and achieve its goals. As one study concluded after looking at 13 factors related to group performance, "perhaps one of the most important characteristics of an effective work group is the support the group receives from the organization."[21] This support includes timely information, proper equipment, adequate staffing, encouragement, and administrative assistance.

LEADERSHIP AND STRUCTURE   Teams can't function if they can't agree on who is to do what and ensure all members share the workload. Agreeing on the specifics of work and how they fit together to integrate individual skills requires leadership and structure, either from management or from the team members themselves. It's true in self-managed teams that team members absorb many of the duties typically assumed by managers. A manager's job then becomes managing *outside* (rather than inside) the team.

Leadership is especially important in multiteam systems. Here, leaders need to empower teams by delegating responsibility to them, and management plays the role of facilitator, making sure teams work together rather than against one another.[22] Teams that establish shared leadership by effectively delegating it are more effective than teams with a traditional single-leader structure.[23]

CLIMATE OF TRUST Members of effective teams trust each other. They also exhibit trust in their leaders.[24] Interpersonal trust among team members facilitates cooperation, reduces the need to monitor each others' behavior, and bonds individuals by the belief that members won't take advantage of them. Members are more likely to take risks and expose vulnerabilities when they trust others on their team. Trust is the foundation of leadership; it allows a team to accept and commit to the leader's goals and decisions. The overall level of trust in a team is important, but how trust is dispersed among team members also matters. Trust levels that are asymmetric and imbalanced between team members can mitigate the performance advantages of a high overall level of trust—in such cases, coalitions form that often undermine the team as a whole.[25]

PERFORMANCE EVALUATION AND REWARD SYSTEMS Individual performance evaluations and incentives may interfere with the development of high-performance teams. So, in addition to evaluating and rewarding employees for their individual contributions, management should utilize hybrid performance systems that incorporate an individual member component and a group reward to recognize positive team outcomes.[26] Group-based appraisals, profit sharing, gainsharing, small-group incentives, and other system modifications can reinforce team effort and commitment.

Team Composition

Team composition matters—the optimal way to construct teams depends on the ability, skill, or trait under consideration.

The team composition category includes variables that relate to how teams should be staffed—the abilities and personalities of team members, allocation of roles, diversity, size of the team, and members' preference for teamwork.

ABILITIES OF MEMBERS Part of a team's performance depends on the knowledge, skills, and abilities of individual members.[27] It's true we occasionally read about an athletic team of mediocre players who, because of excellent coaching, determination, and precision teamwork, beat a far more talented group. But such cases make the news precisely because they are unusual. A team's performance is not merely the summation of its individual members' abilities. However, these abilities set limits on what members can do and how effectively they will perform on a team.

Research reveals some insights into team composition and performance. First, when the task entails solving a complex problem such as reengineering an assembly line, high-ability teams—composed of mostly intelligent members—do better than lower-ability teams. High-ability teams are also more adaptable to changing situations; they can more effectively apply existing knowledge to new problems.

Finally, the ability of the team's leader matters. Smart team leaders help less intelligent team members when they struggle with a task. A less intelligent leader can actually neutralize the effect of a high-ability team.[28]

PERSONALITY OF MEMBERS We demonstrated in Chapter 5 that personality significantly influences individual behavior. Some dimensions identified in the Big Five personality model are relevant to team effectiveness.[29] Specifically, teams that rate higher on mean levels of conscientiousness and openness to experience tend to perform better, and the minimum level of team member agreeableness also matters: teams did worse when they had one or more highly disagreeable members. Perhaps one bad apple *can* spoil the whole bunch!

Research provides us with a good idea about why personality traits are important to teams. Conscientious people are good at backing up other team members, and they're good at sensing when their support is truly needed. Conscientious teams also have other advantages—one study found that specific behavioral tendencies such as personal organization, achievement-orientation, and endurance were all related to higher levels of team performance.[30] Open team members communicate better with one another and throw out more ideas, which makes teams composed of open people more creative and innovative.[31]

Team composition can be based on individual personalities to good effect. Suppose an organization needs to create 20 teams of 4 people each and has 40 highly conscientious people and 40 who score low on conscientiousness. Would the organization be better off (1) forming 10 teams of highly conscientious people and 10 teams of members low on conscientiousness, or (2) "seeding" each team with 2 people who scored high and 2 who scored low on conscientiousness? Perhaps surprisingly, evidence suggests option 1 is the best choice; performance across the teams will be higher if the organization forms 10 highly conscientious teams and 10 teams low in conscientiousness. The reason is that a team with varying conscientiousness levels will not work to the peak performance of the highly conscientious members. Instead, a group normalization dynamic (or simple resentment) will complicate interactions and force the highly conscientious members to lower their expectations, reducing the group's performance. In cases like this, it does appear to make sense to "put all of one's eggs [conscientious team members] into one basket [into teams with other conscientious members]."[32]

ALLOCATION OF ROLES   Members should be selected to ensure all the various team roles are filled. A study of 778 major league baseball teams over a twenty-one-year period highlights the importance of assigning roles appropriately.[33] As you might expect, baseball teams with more experienced and skilled members performed better. However, the experience and skill of players in core roles who handled more of the workflow of the team, and who were central to all work processes (pitchers and catchers), were especially vital. Based on this study and many other research findings, managers should assign the most able, experienced, and conscientious workers to the central roles in a team.

We can identify nine potential team roles. Successful work teams have selected people to play all these roles based on their skills and preferences.[34] (On many teams, individuals will play multiple roles.) To increase the likelihood that team members will work well together, managers need to understand the individual strengths each person can bring to a team, select members with their strengths in mind, and allocate work assignments that fit with members' preferred styles.

> By matching individual preferences with team role demands, managers increase the likelihood that the team members will work well together.

DIVERSITY OF MEMBERS   In Chapter 11, we will discuss research on the effect of diversity on groups. How does *team* diversity affect *team* performance? The degree to which members of a work unit (group, team, or department) share a common demographic attribute, such as age, sex, race, educational level, or length of service in the organization is the subject of **organizational demography**. Organizational demography suggests that diversity in attributes such as age or the date of joining should help us predict turnover. The logic goes like this: Turnover will be greater among those with dissimilar backgrounds because communication is more difficult and conflict is more likely. Increased conflict makes membership less attractive, so employees are more likely to quit. Similarly, the losers of a conflict are more apt to leave voluntarily or be forced out.[35]

The conclusion would be that diversity, at least on these two characteristics, negatively affects team performance.

We have discussed research on team diversity in race or gender. But what about diversity created by national differences? Like the aforementioned research, evidence here indicates elements of national diversity interfere with team processes, at least in the short term.[36] Cultural diversity does seem to be an asset for tasks that call for a variety of viewpoints. But culturally heterogeneous teams have more difficulty learning to work with each other and solving problems. The good news is that these difficulties seem to dissipate with time. Although newly formed culturally diverse teams underperform newly formed culturally homogeneous teams, the differences disappear after about three months.[37]

SIZE OF TEAMS   Most experts agree that keeping teams small is key to improving group effectiveness.[38] Generally speaking, the most effective teams have five to nine members. Experts suggest using the smallest number of people who can do the task. Unfortunately, managers often err by making teams too large. It may require only four or five members to develop an array of views and skills, while coordination problems can increase exponentially as team members are added. When teams have excess members, cohesiveness and mutual accountability decline, social loafing increases, and people communicate less. Members of large teams have trouble coordinating with one another, especially under time pressure. When a natural working unit is larger and you want a team effort, consider breaking the group into subteams.[39]

MEMBER PREFERENCES   Not every employee is a team player. Given the option, many employees will select themselves *out* of team participation. When people who prefer to work alone are required to team up, there is a direct threat to the team's morale and to individual member satisfaction.[40] This suggests that, when selecting team members, managers should consider individual preferences along with abilities, personalities, and skills. High-performing teams are likely to be composed of people who prefer working as part of a group.

Team Processes

The final category related to team effectiveness includes process variables such as member commitment to a common purpose, establishment of specific team goals, team efficacy, mental models, a managed level of conflict, and minimized social loafing. These will be especially important in larger teams and in teams that are highly interdependent.[41]

Why are processes important to team effectiveness? Teams should create outputs greater than the sum of their inputs, as when a diverse group develops creative alternatives. Exhibit 10-4 illustrates how group processes can have an impact on a group's actual effectiveness.[42] Teams are often used in research laboratories because they can draw on the diverse skills of various individuals to produce more meaningful research than researchers working independently—that is, they produce positive synergy, and their process gains exceed their process losses.

EXHIBIT 10-4
Effects of Group Processes

COMMON PLAN AND PURPOSE Effective teams begin by analyzing the team's mission, developing goals to achieve that mission, and creating strategies for achieving the goals. Teams that consistently perform better have established a clear sense of what needs to be done and how.[43] This sounds obvious, but it is surprising how many teams ignore this fundamental process.

Members of successful teams put a tremendous amount of time and effort into discussing, shaping, and agreeing on a purpose that belongs to them both collectively and individually. This common purpose, when accepted by the team, becomes what GPS is to a ship captain: It provides direction and guidance under any conditions. Like a ship following the wrong course, teams that don't have good planning skills are doomed, executing the wrong plan.[44] Teams should agree on whether their goal is to learn about and master a task or simply to perform the task; evidence suggests that different perspectives on learning versus performance goals lead to lower levels of team performance overall.[45] It appears that these differences in goal orientation produce their effects by reducing the sharing of information. In sum, having all employees on a team strive for the same *type* of goal is important.

Effective teams show **reflexivity**, meaning they reflect on and adjust their master plan when necessary. A team has to have a good plan, but it also has to be willing and able to adapt when conditions call for it.[46] Interestingly, some evidence suggests that teams high in reflexivity are better able to adapt to conflicting plans and goals among team members.[47]

SPECIFIC GOALS Successful teams translate their common purpose into specific, measurable, and realistic performance goals. Specific goals facilitate clear communication. They help teams maintain their focus on getting results.

Consistent with the research on individual goals, team goals should be challenging. Difficult but achievable goals raise team performance on those criteria at which they're aiming. So, for instance, goals for quantity tend to raise quantity, goals for accuracy raise accuracy, and so on.[48]

TEAM EFFICACY Effective teams have confidence in themselves; they believe they can succeed. We call this *team efficacy*.[49] Teams that have been successful raise their beliefs about future success, which, in turn, motivates them to work harder. In addition, teams that have a shared knowledge of individual capabilities can strengthen the link between team members' self-efficacy and their individual creativity because members can more effectively solicit opinions from their teammates.[50] What can management do to increase team efficacy? Two options are helping the team achieve small successes that build confidence, and providing training to improve members' technical and interpersonal skills. The greater the abilities of team members, the more likely the team will develop confidence and the ability to deliver on that confidence.

MENTAL MODELS Effective teams share accurate **mental models**—organized mental representations of the key elements within a team's environment that team members share.[51] (If team mission and goals pertain to *what* a team needs to do to be effective, mental models pertain to *how* a team does it work.) If team members have the wrong mental models, which is particularly likely in teams under acute stress, their performance suffers.[52] The similarity of team members' mental models matters, too. If team members

Effective teams maintain a common plan and purpose to their actions that concentrates their energies.

have different ideas about how to do things, the team will fight over methods rather than focus on what needs to be done.[53] One review of 65 independent studies of team cognition found that teams with shared mental models engaged in more frequent interactions with one another, were more motivated, had more positive attitudes toward their work, and had higher levels of objectively rated performance.[54]

 CONFLICT LEVELS Conflict on a team isn't necessarily bad. Conflict has a complex relationship with team performance. *Relationship conflicts*—those based on interpersonal incompatibility, tension, and animosity toward others—are almost always dysfunctional. However, when teams are performing nonroutine activities, disagreements about task content—called *task conflicts*—stimulate discussion, promote critical assessment of problems and options, and can lead to better team decisions. The timing of conflict matters, too. A study conducted in China found that moderate levels of task conflict during the initial phases of team performance were positively related to team creativity, but both very low and very high levels of task conflict were negatively related to team performance.[55] In other words, both too much and too little disagreement about how a team should initially perform a creative task can inhibit performance.

The way conflicts are resolved can make the difference between effective and ineffective teams. A study of ongoing comments made by 37 autonomous work groups showed that effective teams resolved conflicts by explicitly discussing the issues, whereas ineffective teams experienced conflicts focused more on personalities and the way things were said.[56]

SOCIAL LOAFING As we noted earlier, individuals can engage in social loafing and coast on the group's effort when their particular contributions can't be identified. Effective teams undermine this tendency by making members individually and jointly accountable for the team's purpose, goals, and approach.[57] Therefore, members should be clear on what they are individually responsible for and what they are jointly responsible for on the team.

TURNING INDIVIDUALS INTO TEAM PLAYERS

We've made a case for the value and growing popularity of teams. But many people are not inherently team players, and many organizations have historically nurtured individual accomplishments. Teams fit well in countries that score high on collectivism, but what if an organization wants to introduce teams into a work population of individuals born and raised in an individualistic society? A veteran employee of a large company, who had done well working in an individualistic company in an individualist country, described the experience of joining a team: "I'm learning my lesson. I just had my first negative performance appraisal in 20 years."[58]

So what can organizations do to enhance team effectiveness—to turn individual contributors into team members? Here are options for managers trying to turn individuals into team players.

Selecting: Hiring Team Players

Some people already possess the interpersonal skills to be effective team players. When hiring team members, be sure candidates can fulfill their team roles as well as technical requirements.[59]

Creating teams often means resisting the urge to hire top talent no matter what. For example, the New York Knicks professional basketball player Carmelo Anthony scores a lot of points for his team, but statistics show he scores many of them by taking more shots than other highly paid players in the league, which means fewer shots for his teammates.[60]

As a final consideration, personal traits appear to make some people better candidates for working in diverse teams. Teams of members who like to work through difficult mental puzzles also seem more effective and able to capitalize on the multiple points of view that arise from diversity in age and education.[61]

Training: Creating Team Players

Training specialists conduct exercises that allow employees to experience the satisfaction teamwork can provide. Workshops help employees improve their problem-solving, communication, negotiation, conflict-management, and coaching skills. L'Oréal, for example, found that successful sales teams required much more than being staffed with high-ability salespeople: Management had to focus much of its efforts on team building. "What we didn't account for was that many members of our top team in sales had been promoted because they had excellent technical and executional skills," said L'Oréal Senior VP David Waldock. As a result of the focus on team training, Waldock said, "We are no longer a team just on paper, working independently. We have a real group dynamic now, and it's a good one."[62] Developing an effective team doesn't happen overnight—it takes time.

Rewarding: Providing Incentives to Be a Good Team Player

An organization's reward system must be reworked to encourage cooperative efforts rather than competitive ones.[63] Hallmark Cards Inc. added to its basic individual-incentive system an annual bonus based on achievement of team goals. Whole Foods directs most of its performance-based rewards toward team performance. As a result, teams select new members carefully so they will contribute to team effectiveness (and, thus, team bonuses).[64] It is usually best to set a cooperative tone as soon as possible in the life of a team. Teams that switch from a competitive to a cooperative system do not immediately share information, and they still tend to make rushed, poor-quality decisions.[65] Apparently, the low trust typical of the competitive group will not be readily replaced by high trust with a quick change in reward systems.

Promotions, pay raises, and other forms of recognition should be given to individuals who work effectively as team members by training new colleagues, sharing information, helping resolve team conflicts, and mastering needed skills. This doesn't mean individual contributions should be ignored; rather, they should be balanced with the contributions to the team.

Finally, don't forget the intrinsic rewards, such as camaraderie, that employees can receive from teamwork. It's exciting to be part of a successful team. The opportunity for personal development of self and teammates can be a very satisfying and rewarding experience.

BEWARE! TEAMS AREN'T ALWAYS THE ANSWER

Teamwork takes more time and often more resources than individual work. Teams have increased communication demands, conflicts to manage, and meetings to run. So, the benefits of using teams have to exceed the costs, and that's not always possible.[66] Before you rush to implement teams, carefully assess whether the work will benefit from a collective effort.

How do you know whether the work of your group would be done better in teams? You can apply three tests.[67] First, can the work be done better by more than one person? A good indicator is the complexity of the work and the need for different perspectives. Simple tasks that don't require diverse input are probably better left to individuals. Second, does the work create a common purpose or set of goals for the people in the group that is more than the aggregate of individual goals? Many service departments of new-vehicle dealers have introduced teams that link customer-service people, mechanics, parts specialists, and sales representatives. Such teams can better manage collective responsibility for ensuring that customer needs are properly met.

The final test is to determine whether the members of the group are interdependent. Using teams makes sense when there is interdependence among tasks—the success of the whole depends on the success of each one, *and* the success of each one depends on the success of the others. Soccer, for instance, is an obvious *team* sport. Success requires a great deal of coordination between interdependent players. Conversely, except possibly for relays, swim teams are not really teams. They're groups of individuals performing individually, whose total performance is merely the aggregate summation of their individual performances.

SUMMARY

Few trends have influenced jobs as much as the massive movement to introduce teams into the workplace. The shift from working alone to working on teams requires employees to cooperate with others, share information, confront differences, and sublimate personal interests for the greater good of the team.

IMPLICATIONS FOR MANAGERS

- Effective teams have common characteristics. They have adequate resources, effective leadership, a climate of trust, and a performance evaluation and reward system that reflects team contributions. These teams have individuals with technical expertise as well as problem-solving, decision-making, and interpersonal skills, as well as the right traits, especially conscientiousness and openness.
- Effective teams tend to be small—fewer than ten people, preferably of diverse backgrounds. They have members who fill role demands and who prefer to be part of a group. The work that these members do provides freedom and autonomy, the opportunity to use different skills and talents, the ability to complete a whole and identifiable task or product, and work that has a substantial impact on others.
- Effective teams have members who believe in the team's capabilities and are committed to a common plan and purpose, have an accurate shared mental model of what is to be accomplished, share specific team goals, maintain a manageable level of conflict, and show a minimal degree of social loafing.

- Because individualistic organizations and societies attract and reward individual accomplishments, it can be difficult to create team players in these environments. To make the conversion, try to select individuals who have the interpersonal skills to be effective team players, provide training to develop teamwork skills, and reward individuals for cooperative efforts.

PERSONAL INVENTORY ASSESSMENT

In Personal Inventory Assessment found in MyManagementLab take assessment: Team Development Behaviors

⭐ WRITING SPACE

If your professor assigned this, sign in to **mymanagementlab.com** for the following Assisted-graded writing question:

10-1. As a manager, what do you think are the characteristics of an optimally successful team?

11
Key Group Concepts

MyManagementLab®

⭐ **Improve Your Grade!**

When you see this icon ⭐, visit **www.mymanagementlab.com** for activities that are applied, personalized, and offer immediate feedback.

LEARNING OBJECTIVES

After studying this chapter, you should be able to:

1. Define *group*, and identify the five stages of group development.
2. Show how role requirements change in different situations.
3. Demonstrate how norms exert influence on an individual's behavior.
4. Discuss the dynamics of status in group behavior.
5. Show how group size affects group performance.
6. Contrast the benefits and disadvantages of cohesive groups.
7. Explain the implications of diversity for group effectiveness.
8. Contrast the strengths and weaknesses of group decision making.
9. Compare the effectiveness of interacting, brainstorming, and the nominal group technique.

⭐ **Chapter Warm-up**

If your professor has chosen to assign this, go to **www.mymanagementlab.com** to see what you should particularly focus on and to take the Chapter 11 warm up.

Groups have their place—and their pitfalls. The objectives of this chapter and Chapter 10 are to introduce you to basic group concepts, provide you with a foundation for understanding how groups work, and show you how to create effective teams. Let's begin by defining a *group* and explaining why people join groups.

DEFINING AND CLASSIFYING GROUPS

A **group** is two or more individuals, interacting and interdependent, who have come together to achieve particular objectives. Groups can be either formal or informal; both affect employee behavior and performance. A **formal group** is defined by the organization's structure, with designated work assignments establishing tasks. In formal groups, the behaviors team members should engage in are stipulated by and directed toward organizational goals. The six members of an airline flight crew are a formal group, for example. In contrast, an **informal group** is neither formally structured nor organizationally determined. Informal groups in the work environment meet the need for social contact. Three employees from different departments who regularly have lunch together are an informal group. These types of interactions among individuals, though informal, deeply affect their behavior and performance.

Groups can be formal as well as informal; regardless of the type of group, group norms, roles, and identities have powerful effects on individuals' behavior.

⭐ WATCH IT

If your professor assigned this, sign in to **mymanagementlab.com** to watch a video titled Witness.org: Managing Groups & Teams to learn more about this topic and respond to questions.

Groups generally pass through a predictable sequence in their evolution. In this section, we describe the five-stage model and an alternative for temporary groups with deadlines.

The Five-Stage Model

As shown in Exhibit 11-1, the **five-stage group-development model** characterizes groups as proceeding through the distinct stages of forming, storming, norming, performing, and adjourning.[1]

The first stage, the **forming stage**, is characterized by uncertainty about the group's purpose, structure, and leadership. Members determine acceptable behavior for themselves in the group by trial and error. This stage is complete when members have begun to think of themselves as part of a group.

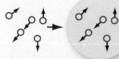

| Prestage I | Stage I Forming | Stage II Storming | Stage III Norming | Stage IV Performing | Stage V Adjourning |

EXHIBIT 11-1
Stages of Group Development

The **storming stage** is one of intragroup conflict. Members accept the group but resist the constraints it imposes on individuality. There is conflict over who will control the group. When this stage is complete, there will be a relatively clear hierarchy of leadership.

In the third stage, close relationships develop and the group demonstrates cohesiveness. There is a strong sense of group identity and camaraderie. This **norming stage** is complete when the group structure solidifies and the group has assimilated a common set of expectations of what constitutes correct member behavior.

The fourth stage is **performing**. The structure is now fully functional. Group energy has advanced from understanding each other to performing the task at hand.

For permanent work groups, performing is the last stage in development. For committees, teams, task forces, and similar groups that have a limited scope of work, the **adjourning stage** is for wrapping up activities and preparing to disband. Some group members are upbeat, basking in the group's accomplishments. Others may be depressed over the loss of camaraderie sustained during the work group's life.

Many interpreters of the five-stage model have assumed that a group becomes more and more effective as it progresses through the first four stages. Although this may be generally true, what makes a group effective is actually more complex.[2] First, groups proceed through the stages of group development at different rates. Groups with a strong sense of purpose and strategy rapidly achieve high performance and improve over time, whereas those with less sense of purpose see their performance worsen over time. Similarly, groups that begin with a positive social focus achieve the "performing" stage more rapidly. It's also true that groups do not always proceed clearly from one stage to the next. Storming and performing can occur simultaneously, and groups can regress to previous stages.

An Alternative Model for Temporary Groups with Deadlines

Temporary groups with finite deadlines[3] don't seem to follow the usual five-stage model. Studies indicate they have their own unique sequencing of actions (or inaction): (1) Their first meeting sets the group's direction, (2) the first phase of group activity is one of inertia and thus slower progress, (3) a transition takes place exactly when the group has used up half its allotted time,[4] (4) this transition initiates major changes, (5) a second phase of inertia follows the transition, and (6) the group's last meeting is characterized by markedly accelerated activity.[5] This pattern, called the **punctuated-equilibrium model**, is shown in Exhibit 11-2.

The first meeting sets the group's direction, and then a framework of behavioral patterns and assumptions through which the group will approach its project emerges,

EXHIBIT 11-2
The Punctuated-Equilibrium Model

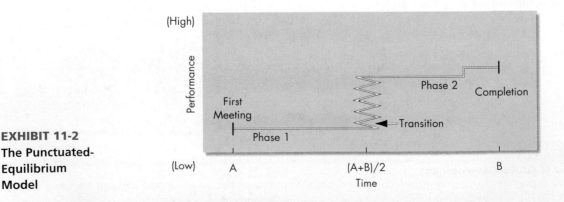

sometimes in the first few seconds of the group's existence. Once set, the group's direction is solidified and is unlikely to be reexamined throughout the first half of its life. This is a period of inertia—the group tends to stand still or become locked into a fixed course of action even if it gains new insights that challenge initial patterns and assumptions.

One of the most interesting discoveries in work team studies[6] was that groups experienced their transition precisely halfway between the first meeting and the official deadline—whether members spent an hour on their project or 6 months. The midpoint appears to work like an alarm clock, heightening members' awareness that their time is limited and they need to get moving. This transition ends phase 1 and is characterized by a concentrated burst of changes, dropping of old patterns, and adoption of new perspectives. The transition sets a revised direction for phase 2, a new equilibrium or period of inertia in which the group executes plans created during the transition period.

The group's last meeting is characterized by a final burst of activity to finish its work. In summary, the punctuated-equilibrium model characterizes groups as exhibiting long periods of inertia interspersed with brief revolutionary changes triggered primarily by members' awareness of time and deadlines. Keep in mind, however, that this model doesn't apply to all groups but is suited to the finite quality of temporary task groups working under a time deadline.[7]

GROUP PROPERTY 1: ROLES

Work groups shape members' behavior and help explain individual behavior as well as the performance of the group itself. Some of the defining group properties are roles, norms, status, size, cohesiveness, and diversity. Let's begin with the first group property, roles.

Shakespeare said, "All the world's a stage, and all the men and women merely players." Using the same metaphor, all group members are actors, each playing a **role**, a set of expected behavior patterns attributed to someone occupying a given position in a social unit. We are required to play a number of diverse roles, both on and off our jobs. As we'll see, one of the tasks in understanding behavior is grasping the role a person is currently playing.

Bill is a plant manager with EMM Industries, an electrical equipment manufacturer in Phoenix. At his job, Bill fulfills a number of roles—employee, member of middle management, electrical engineer, and primary company spokesperson in the community. Off the job, Bill holds more roles: husband, father, Catholic, tennis player, member of the Thunderbird Country Club, and president of his homeowners' association. Many of these roles are compatible; some create conflicts. How does Bill's religious commitment influence his managerial decisions regarding layoffs, expense padding, and provision of accurate information to government agencies? A recent offer of promotion requires Bill to relocate, yet his family wants to stay in Phoenix. Can the role demands of his job be reconciled with the demands of his husband and father roles?

Different groups impose different role requirements on individuals. Like Bill, we all play a number of roles, and our behavior varies with each.

Role Perception

Our view of how we're supposed to act in a given situation is a **role perception**. We get role perceptions from stimuli all around us—for example, friends, books, films, and television, such as when we form an impression of the work of doctors from watching *Grey's Anatomy.* Apprenticeship programs allow beginners to watch an expert so they can learn to act as they should.

Role Expectations

Role expectations are the way others believe you should act in a given context. A U.S. federal judge is viewed as having propriety and dignity, while a football coach is seen as aggressive, dynamic, and inspiring to his players.

Role Conflict

When compliance with one role requirement may make it difficult to comply with another, the result is **role conflict**.[8] At the extreme, two or more role expectations can be completely contradictory. For example, if you were to provide a performance evaluation on a person you mentored, your roles as evaluator and mentor may conflict.

GROUP PROPERTY 2: NORMS

Did you ever notice that golfers don't speak while others are putting or that employees don't criticize their bosses in public? Why not? The answer is norms.

All groups have established **norms**—acceptable standards of behavior shared by their members that express what they ought and ought not to do under certain circumstances. When agreed to by the group, norms influence behavior with a minimum of external controls. Different groups, communities, and societies have different norms, but they all have them.[9]

Norms can cover any aspect of group behavior.[10] Probably the most common is a *performance norm*, providing explicit cues about how hard members should work, how to do the job, what level of tardiness is appropriate, and the like. These norms are capable of greatly affecting behavior and performance, if they are internalized. Other norms include *appearance norms* (dress codes, unspoken rules about when to look busy), *social arrangement norms* (with whom to eat lunch, whether to form friendships on and off the job), and *resource allocation norms* (assignment of difficult jobs, distribution of resources like pay or equipment).

Norms and Behavior

As we've mentioned, norms in the workplace significantly influence employee behavior. This may seem intuitive, but full appreciation of the influence of norms on worker behavior did not occur until the Hawthorne Studies undertaken between 1924 and 1932 at the Western Electric Company's Hawthorne Works in Chicago.[11]

The Hawthorne researchers began by examining the relationship between the physical environment and productivity. As they increased the light level for the experimental group of workers, output rose for that unit and the control group. But as they dropped the light level in the experimental group, productivity continued to increase in both groups. In fact, productivity in the experimental group decreased only when the light intensity had been reduced to that of moonlight, leading researchers to believe that group dynamics influenced behavior.

The researchers next isolated a small group of women assembling telephone relays from the main work group so their behavior could be more carefully observed. Over the next several years, this small group's output increased steadily, and the number of personal and sick absences was approximately one-third of the regular production department. It became evident this group's performance was significantly influenced by its "special" status. The members thought they were in an elite group, and that management showed concern about their interests by engaging in experimentation. In essence, workers in both the illumination and assembly experiments were really reacting to the increased attention they received.

A wage incentive plan was introduced to a group of workers in the bank wiring observation room. The most important finding was that employees did not individually maximize their output. Rather, their role performance became controlled by a group norm. Members were afraid that if they significantly increased their output, the unit incentive rate might be cut, the expected daily output might be increased, layoffs might occur, or slower workers might be reprimanded. So the group established its idea of a fair output—neither too much nor too little. Members helped each other ensure their reports were nearly level, and the norms the group established included a number of behavioral "don'ts." *Don't* be a rate-buster, turning out too much work. *Don't* be a chiseler, turning out too little work. *Don't* squeal on any of your peers. The group enforced their norms with name-calling, ridicule, ostracism, and even punches to the upper arm of violators. The group thus operated well below its capability, using norms that were tightly established and strongly enforced.

Conformity

As a member of a group, you desire acceptance by the group. Thus, you are susceptible to conforming to the group's norms. Considerable evidence suggests that groups can place strong pressures on individual members to change their attitudes and behaviors to conform to the group's standard.[12] There are numerous reasons for conformity, with recent research highlighting the importance of a desire to develop meaningful social relationships with others or to maintain a favorable self-concept.

The impact that group pressures for **conformity** can have on an individual member's judgment was demonstrated in studies by Solomon Asch.[13] Asch made up groups of seven or eight people who were asked to compare two cards held by the experimenter. One card had one line, and the other had three lines of varying length, one of which was identical to the line on the one-line card, as Exhibit 11-3 shows. The difference in line length was quite obvious; in fact, under ordinary conditions, subjects made fewer than 1 percent errors in announcing aloud which of the three lines matched the single line. But what happens if members of the group begin giving incorrect answers? Would pressure to conform cause an unsuspecting subject (USS) to alter an answer? Asch arranged the group so only the USS was unaware the experiment was rigged. The seating was prearranged so the USS was one of the last to announce a decision.

The experiment began with several sets of matching exercises. All the subjects gave the right answers. On the third set, however, the first subject gave an obviously wrong answer—for example, saying "C" in Exhibit 11-3. The next subject gave the same

Conformity is a problem with groups; managers should encourage group leaders to actively seek input from all members and avoid expressing their own opinions, especially in the early stages of deliberation.

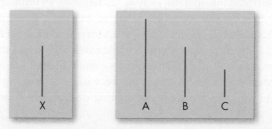

EXHIBIT 11-3
Examples of Cards Used in Asch's Study

wrong answer, and so did the others. Now the dilemma confronting the USS was this: publicly state a perception that differs from the announced position of the others in the group, or give an incorrect answer in order to agree with the others.

The results over many experiments and trials showed 75 percent of subjects gave at least one answer that conformed—that they knew was wrong but was consistent with the replies of other group members—and the average conformer gave wrong answers 37 percent of the time. What meaning can we draw from these results? They suggest group norms press us toward conformity. We desire to be one of the group and therefore avoid being visibly different.

This research was conducted more than 50 years ago. Has time altered the conclusions' validity? And should we consider them generalizable across cultures? Evidence indicates levels of conformity have steadily declined since Asch's studies in the early 1950s, and his findings *are* culture-bound to the United States.[14] Conformity to social norms is even higher in collectivist cultures, but it is still a powerful force in groups in individualist countries.

Do individuals conform to the pressures of all groups to which they belong? Obviously not, because people belong to many groups, and their norms vary and sometimes are contradictory. People conform to the important groups to which they belong or hope to belong. These important groups are **reference groups**, in which a person is aware of other members, defines himself as a member or would like to be a member, and feels group members are significant to him. The implication, then, is that all groups do not impose equal conformity pressures on their members, since their importance is in the eye of the perceiver.

Deviant Workplace Behavior

LeBron is frustrated by a coworker who constantly spreads malicious and unsubstantiated rumors about him. Debra is tired of a member of her work team who, when confronted with a problem, takes out his frustration by yelling and screaming at her and other members. And Mi-Cha recently quit her job as a dental hygienist after being constantly sexually harassed by her employer.

What do these three illustrations have in common? They represent employees exposed to acts of deviant workplace behavior.[15] **Deviant workplace behavior** (also called *antisocial behavior* or *workplace incivility*) is voluntary behavior that violates significant organizational norms and, in doing so, threatens the well-being of the organization or its members. Exhibit 11-4 provides a typology of deviant workplace behaviors, with examples of each.

Few organizations will admit to creating or condoning conditions that encourage and maintain deviant norms. Yet they exist. Employees report an increase in rudeness and disregard toward others by bosses and coworkers in recent years. And nearly half of employees who have suffered this incivility say it has led them to think about changing jobs; 12 percent actually quit because of it.[16] A study of nearly 1,500 respondents found that in addition to increasing turnover intentions, incivility at work increased reports of psychological stress and physical illness.[17] Recent research also suggests that lack of sleep, which hinders a person's ability to regulate emotions and behaviors, can lead to deviant behavior. As organizations have tried to do more with less, pushing their employees to work extra hours, they may indirectly be facilitating deviant behavior.[18]

Category	Examples
Production	Leaving early
	Intentionally working slowly
	Wasting resources
Property	Sabotage
	Misusing equipment
	Stealing from the organization
Political	Showing favoritism
	Gossiping and spreading rumors
	Blaming coworkers
Personal aggression	Sexual harassment
	Verbal abuse
	Stealing from coworkers

EXHIBIT 11-4

Typology of Deviant Workplace Behavior

Sources: Based on S. L. Robinson and R. J. Bennett, "A Typology of Deviant Workplace Behaviors: A Multidimensional Scaling Study," *Academy of Management Journal* (April 1995), p. 565. Copyright 1995 by Academy of Management (NY); S. H. Appelbaum, G. D. Iaconi, and A. Matousek, "Positive and Negative Deviant Workplace Behaviors: Causes, Impacts, and Solutions," *Corporate Governance* 7, no. 5 (2007), pp. 586–598; and R. W. Griffin and A. O'Leary-Kelly, *The Dark Side of Organizational Behavior* (New York: Wiley, 2004).

Like norms in general, individual employees' antisocial actions are shaped by the group context within which they work. Evidence demonstrates deviant workplace behavior is likely to occur when supported by group norms.[19] For example, workers who socialize either at or outside work with people who are frequently absent from work are more likely to be absent themselves as they begin to identify with that possible group norm.[20] Thus when deviant workplace norms surface, employee cooperation, commitment, and motivation are likely to suffer.

What are the consequences of workplace deviance for teams? Some research suggests a chain reaction occurs in groups with high levels of dysfunctional behavior.[21] The process begins with negative behaviors like shirking, undermining coworkers, or being generally uncooperative. As a result, the team collectively starts to experience negative moods. These negative moods result in poor coordination of effort and lower levels of group performance.

GROUP PROPERTY 3: STATUS

Status—a socially defined position or rank given to groups or group members by others—permeates every society. Even the smallest group will show differences in member status over time. Status is a significant motivator and has major behavioral consequences when individuals perceive a disparity between what they believe their status is and what others perceive it to be.

What Determines Status?

According to **status characteristics theory**, status tends to derive from one of three sources:[22]

1. *The Power a Person Wields Over Others.* Because they likely control the group's resources, people who control the group outcomes tend to be perceived as high status.
2. *A Person's Ability to Contribute to Group Goals.* People whose contributions are critical to the group's success tend to have high status. Some thought NBA star Kobe Bryant had more say over player decisions than his coaches did (though not as much as Bryant wanted!).
3. *An Individual's Personal Characteristics.* Someone whose personal characteristics are positively valued by the group (good looks, intelligence, money, or a friendly personality) typically has higher status than someone with fewer valued attributes.

Status and Norms

Status has some interesting effects on the power of norms and pressures to conform. High-status individuals are often given more freedom to deviate from norms than are other group members.[23] For instance, physicians resist administrative decisions made by lower-ranking insurance company employees.[24] High-status people are also better able to resist conformity pressures than their lower-status peers. Research indicates an individual who is highly valued by a group but doesn't need or care about the group's social rewards is particularly able to disregard conformity norms.[25] In general, bringing high-status members into a group may improve performance, but only up to a point, perhaps because they may introduce counterproductive norms.[26]

Status and Group Interaction

High-status people tend to be more assertive group members.[27] They speak out more often, criticize more, state more commands, and interrupt others more often. Lower-status members tend to participate less actively in group discussions. When they possess expertise and insights that could aid the group, failure to fully utilize these members reduces the group's overall creativity and performance. Perhaps this is partly why large differences in status within groups are associated with poorer individual performance, lower health, and higher intentions to leave the group.[28]

GROUP PROPERTY 4: SIZE

Does the size of a group affect the group's overall behavior? Yes, but the effect depends on what dependent variables we examine. Groups with a dozen or more members are good for gaining diverse input. If the goal is fact-finding, larger groups should be more effective. Smaller groups of about seven members are better at doing something productive.

One of the most important findings about the size of a group concerns **social loafing**, the tendency for individuals to expend less effort when working collectively than alone.[29] It directly challenges the assumption that the productivity of the group as a whole should at least equal the sum of the productivity of the individuals in it.

Does team spirit spur individual effort and enhance a group's overall productivity? German psychologist Max Ringelmann compared the results of individual and group performance on a rope-pulling task.[30] He expected that three people pulling together should exert three times as much pull on a rope as one person, and eight people eight times as much. One person pulling on a rope alone exerted an average of 63 kilograms of force. But in groups of three, the per-person force dropped to 53 kilograms. And in groups of eight, it fell to only 31 kilograms per person.

Replications of Ringelmann's research with similar tasks have generally supported his findings.[31] Total group performance increases with group size, but the addition of new members has diminishing returns on individual productivity. So more may be better in that total productivity of a group of four is greater than that of three, but the individual productivity of each member declines. More is not always better when it comes to getting the most out of every individual.

What causes social loafing? It may be a belief that others in the group are not carrying their fair share. If you see others as lazy or inept, you can reestablish equity by reducing your effort. But simply failing to contribute may not be enough to be labeled a "free rider." Instead, the group must believe the social loafer is acting in an exploitive manner (benefitting at the expense of other team members).[32] Another explanation for social loafing is the diffusion of responsibility. Because group results cannot be attributed to any single person, the relationship between an individual's input and the group's output is clouded. Individuals may then be tempted to become free riders and coast on the group's efforts. The implications for OB are significant. When managers use collective work situations to enhance morale and teamwork, they must also be able to identify individual efforts. Otherwise, they must weigh the potential losses in productivity from using groups against the possible gains in worker satisfaction.[33]

Social loafing appears to have a Western bias. It's consistent with individualist cultures, such as the United States and Canada, that are dominated by self-interest. It is *not* consistent in collectivist societies, in which individuals are motivated by in-group goals. In studies comparing U.S. employees with employees from the People's Republic of China and Israel (both collectivist societies), the Chinese and Israelis showed no propensity to engage in social loafing and actually performed better in a group than alone.

Recent research indicates that the stronger an individual's work ethic is, the less likely that person is to engage in social loafing.[34] There are ways to prevent social loafing: (1) set group goals, so the group has a common purpose to strive toward; (2) increase intergroup competition, which focuses on the shared outcome; (3) engage in peer evaluation, so each person evaluates each other person's contribution; (4) select members who have high motivation and prefer to work in groups; and (5) if possible, base group rewards in part on each member's unique contributions.[35] Although no magic bullet will prevent social loafing in all cases, these steps should help minimize its effect.

GROUP PROPERTY 5: COHESIVENESS

Groups differ in their **cohesiveness**—the degree to which members are attracted to each other and motivated to stay in the group. Some work groups are cohesive because the members have spent a great deal of time together, the group's small size or purpose facilitates high interaction, or external threats have brought members close together.

Cohesiveness affects group productivity. Studies consistently show that the relationship between cohesiveness and productivity depends on the group's performance-related norms.[36] If norms for quality, output, and cooperation with outsiders are high, for instance, a cohesive group will be more productive than will a less cohesive group. But if cohesiveness is high and performance norms are low, productivity will be low. If cohesiveness is low and performance norms are high, productivity increases, but less than in the high-cohesiveness/high-norms situation. When cohesiveness and performance-related norms are both low, productivity tends to fall into the low-to-moderate range.

What can you do to encourage group cohesiveness? (1) Make the group smaller, (2) encourage agreement with group goals, (3) increase the time members spend together, (4) increase the group's status and the perceived difficulty of attaining membership, (5) stimulate competition with other groups, (6) give rewards to the group rather than to individual members, and (7) physically isolate the group.[37]

GROUP PROPERTY 6: DIVERSITY

The final property of groups we consider is **diversity** in the group's membership, or the degree to which members of the group are similar to, or different from, one another. A great deal of research focuses on how diversity influences group performance. Some research looks at cultural diversity and some at racial, gender, and other differences. Overall, studies identify both costs and benefits from group diversity.

Diversity appears to increase group conflict, especially in the early stages of a group's tenure, which often lowers group morale and raises dropout rates. One study compared groups that were culturally diverse (composed of people from different countries) and homogeneous (composed of people from the same country). On a wilderness survival exercise, the groups performed equally well, but the members from the diverse groups were less satisfied with their groups, were less cohesive, and had more conflict.[38] Another study examined the effect of differences in tenure on the performance of 67 engineering research and development groups.[39] When people had roughly the same level of tenure, performance was high, but as tenure diversity increased, performance dropped off. There was an important qualifier: Higher levels of tenure diversity were not related to lower performance for groups when there were effective team-oriented human resources practices. Teams in which members' values or opinions differ tend to experience more conflict, but leaders who can get the group to focus on the task at hand and encourage group learning are able to reduce these conflicts and enhance discussion of group issues.[40] It seems diversity can be bad for performance even in creative teams, but appropriate organizational support and leadership might offset the problems.

Culturally and demographically diverse groups may perform better over time—if they can get over their initial conflicts. Why might this be so?

Surface-level diversity—in observable characteristics such as national origin, race, and gender—alerts people to possible deep-level diversity—in underlying attitudes, values, and opinions. One researcher argued, "The mere presence of diversity you can see, such as a person's race or gender, actually cues a team that there's likely to be differences of opinion."[41] Although those differences can lead to conflict, they also provide an opportunity to solve problems in unique ways.

One study of jury behavior found diverse juries more likely to deliberate longer, share more information, and make fewer factual errors when discussing evidence. Two studies of MBA student groups found surface-level diversity led to greater openness. Surface-level diversity may subconsciously cue team members to be more open-minded in their views.[42]

The impact of diversity on groups is mixed. It is difficult to be in a diverse group in the short term. However, if members can weather their differences, over time diversity may help them be more open-minded, creative, and to do better. But even positive effects are unlikely to be especially strong. As one review stated, "The business case (in terms of demonstrable financial results) for diversity remains hard to support based on the extant research."[43]

Faultlines

One possible side effect of diverse teams—especially those that are diverse in terms of surface-level characteristics—is **faultlines**, or perceived divisions that split groups into two or more subgroups based on individual differences such as sex, race, age, work experience, and education.

For example, let's say group A is composed of three men and three women. The three men have approximately the same amount of work experience and backgrounds in marketing. The three women have about the same amount of work experience and backgrounds in finance. Group B also has three men and three women, but they all differ in terms of their experience and backgrounds. Two of the men are relatively experienced, while the other is new. One of the women has worked at the company for several years, while the other two are new. In addition, two of the men and one woman in group B have backgrounds in marketing, while the other man and the remaining two women have backgrounds in finance. It is thus likely that a faultline will result in subgroups of males and females in group A but not in group B based on the differentiating characteristics.

Research on faultlines has shown that splits are generally detrimental to group functioning and performance. Subgroups may wind up competing with each other, which takes time away from core tasks and harms group performance. Groups that have subgroups learn more slowly, make more risky decisions, are less creative, and experience higher levels of conflict. Subgroups are less likely to trust each other. Finally, although the overall group's satisfaction is lower when faultlines are present, satisfaction with subgroups is generally high.[44]

Are faultlines ever a good thing? One study suggested that faultlines based on differences in skill, knowledge, and expertise could be beneficial when the groups were in organizational cultures that strongly emphasized results. Why? A results-driven culture focuses people's attention on what's important to the company rather than on problems arising from subgroups.[45] Another study showed that problems stemming from strong faultlines based on gender and educational major were counteracted when their roles were cross-cut and the group as a whole was given a common goal to strive for. Together, these strategies force collaboration between members of subgroups and focus their efforts on accomplishing a goal that transcends the boundary imposed by the faultline.[46]

Overall, although research on faultlines suggests that diversity in groups is a potential double-edged sword, recent work indicates they can be strategically employed to improve performance.

GROUP DECISION MAKING

The belief—characterized by juries—that two heads are better than one has long been accepted as a basic component of the U.S. legal system and those of many other countries. Many decisions in organizations are made by groups, teams, or committees. We'll discuss the advantages of group decision making, along with the unique challenges group dynamics bring to the decision-making process. Finally, we'll offer some techniques for maximizing the group decision-making opportunity.

Groups versus the Individual

Decision-making groups may be widely used in organizations, but are group decisions preferable to those made by an individual alone? The answer depends on a number of factors. Let's begin by looking at the strengths and weaknesses of group decision making.[47]

Group decision making is not always better than individual decision making.

STRENGTHS OF GROUP DECISION MAKING Groups generate *more complete information and knowledge.* By aggregating the resources of several individuals, groups bring more input as well as heterogeneity into the decision process. They offer *increased diversity of views.* This opens up the opportunity to consider more approaches and alternatives. Finally, groups lead to increased *acceptance of a solution.* Group members who participated in making a decision are more likely to enthusiastically support and encourage others to accept it.

WEAKNESSES OF GROUP DECISION MAKING Group decisions are time consuming because groups typically take more time to reach a solution. There are *conformity pressures.* The desire by group members to be accepted and considered an asset to the group can squash any overt disagreement. Group discussion can be *dominated by one or a few members.* If they're low- and medium-ability members, the group's overall effectiveness will suffer. Finally, group decisions suffer from *ambiguous responsibility.* In an individual decision, it's clear who is accountable for the final outcome. In a group decision, the responsibility of any single member is diluted.

EFFECTIVENESS AND EFFICIENCY Whether groups are more effective than individuals depends on how you define effectiveness. Group decisions are generally more *accurate* than the decisions of the average individual in a group, but less accurate than the judgments of the most accurate person.[48] In terms of *speed*, individuals are superior. If *creativity* is important, groups tend to be more effective. And if effectiveness means the degree of *acceptance* the final solution achieves, the nod again goes to the group.[49]

But we cannot consider effectiveness without also assessing efficiency. With few exceptions, group decision making consumes more work hours than an individual tackling the same problem alone. The exceptions tend to be instances in which, to achieve comparable quantities of diverse input, the single decision maker must spend a great deal of time reviewing files and talking to other people. In deciding whether to use groups, then, managers must assess whether increases in effectiveness are more than enough to offset the reductions in efficiency.

Groupthink and Groupshift

Two by-products of group decision making, groupthink and groupshift, potentially affect a group's ability to appraise alternatives objectively and achieve high-quality solutions.

Groupthink relates to norms and describes situations in which group pressures for conformity deter the group from critically appraising unusual, minority, or unpopular views. Groupthink attacks many groups and can dramatically hinder their performance. **Groupshift** describes the way group members tend to exaggerate their initial positions when discussing alternatives and arriving at a solution. In some situations, caution dominates and there is a conservative shift, while in other situations groups tend toward a risky shift. Let's look at each phenomenon in detail.

GROUPTHINK Have you ever felt like speaking up in a meeting, a classroom, or an informal group but decided against it? One reason may have been shyness. Or you may have been a victim of groupthink. The individual's mental efficiency, reality testing, and moral judgment deteriorate as a result of group pressures.[50]

We have all seen the symptoms of groupthink:

1. Members rationalize any resistance to the assumptions they've made. No matter how strongly the evidence may contradict their basic assumptions, they reinforce them.
2. Members apply direct pressure on those who express doubts about any of the group's shared views, or who question the validity of arguments supporting the alternative favored by the majority.
3. Members who have doubts or differing points of view seek to avoid deviating from what appears to be group consensus by keeping silent about misgivings and even minimizing to themselves the importance of their doubts.
4. There is an illusion of unanimity. If someone doesn't speak, it's assumed she is in full accord. Abstention becomes a "yes" vote.[51]

Groupthink appears closely aligned with the conclusions Solomon Asch drew in his experiments with a lone dissenter. Individuals who hold a position different from that of the dominant majority are under pressure to suppress, withhold, or modify their true feelings and beliefs. As members, we find it more pleasant to be in agreement—to be a positive part of the group—than to be a disruptive force, even if disruption would improve effectiveness. Groups more focused on performance than learning are especially likely to fall victim to groupthink and to suppress the opinions of those who do not agree with the majority.[52]

Does groupthink attack all groups? No. It seems to occur most often when there is a clear group identity, when members hold a positive image of their group that they want to protect, and when the group perceives a collective threat to this positive image.[53] So groupthink is not a dissenter-suppression mechanism as much as a means for a group to protect its positive image. One study showed that those influenced by groupthink were more confident about their course of action early on.[54] Groups that believe too strongly in the correctness of their course of action are more likely to suppress dissent and encourage conformity than are groups that are more skeptical about their course of action.

What can managers do to minimize groupthink?[55] First, they can monitor group size. People grow more intimidated and hesitant as group size increases, and although there is no magic number that will eliminate groupthink, individuals are likely to feel less personal responsibility when groups get larger than about 10 members. Managers should also encourage group leaders to play an impartial role. Leaders should actively seek input from all members and avoid expressing their own opinions, especially in the early stages of deliberation. In addition, managers should appoint one group member to play the role of devil's advocate, overtly challenging the majority position and offering divergent perspectives. Yet another suggestion is to use exercises that stimulate active discussion of diverse alternatives without threatening the group or intensifying identity protection. Have group members delay discussion of possible gains so they can first talk about the dangers or risks inherent in a decision. Requiring members to initially focus on the negatives of an alternative makes the group less likely to stifle dissenting views and more likely to gain an objective evaluation.

GROUPSHIFT OR GROUP POLARIZATION There are differences between group decisions and the individual decisions of group members.[56] As discussed previously, what appears to happen in groups is that the discussion leads members toward a more extreme view of the position they already held. Conservatives become more cautious, and more aggressive types take on more risk. The group discussion tends to exaggerate the initial position of the group.

We can view group polarization as a special case of groupthink. The group's decision reflects the dominant decision-making norm that develops during discussion. Whether the shift in the group's decision is toward greater caution or more risk depends on the dominant pre-discussion norm.

The shift toward polarization has several explanations.[57] It's been argued, for instance, that discussion makes members more comfortable with each other and thus more willing to express extreme versions of their original positions. Another argument is that the group diffuses responsibility. Group decisions free any single member from accountability for the group's final choice, so a more extreme position can be taken. It's also likely that people take on extreme positions because they want to demonstrate how different they are from the outgroup.[58] People on the fringes of political or social movements take on ever-more extreme positions just to prove they are really committed to the cause, whereas those who are more cautious tend to take moderate positions to demonstrate how reasonable they are.

So how should you use the findings on groupshift? Recognize that group decisions exaggerate the initial position of the individual members, that the shift has been shown more often to be toward greater risk, and that which way a group will shift is a function of the members' pre-discussion inclinations.

We now turn to the techniques by which groups make decisions. These reduce some of the dysfunctional aspects of group decision making.

GROUP DECISION-MAKING TECHNIQUES

The most common form of group decision making takes place in **interacting groups**. Members meet face to face and rely on both verbal and nonverbal interaction to communicate. But as our discussion of groupthink demonstrated, interacting groups often censor themselves and pressure individual members toward conformity of opinion. Brainstorming and the nominal group technique can reduce problems inherent in the traditional interacting group.

Brainstorming can overcome the pressures for conformity that dampen creativity[59] by encouraging any and all alternatives while withholding criticism. In a typical brainstorming session, a half-dozen to a dozen people sit around a table. The group leader states the problem in a clear manner so all participants understand. Members then freewheel as many alternatives as they can in a given length of time. To encourage members to "think the unusual," no criticism is allowed, even of the most bizarre suggestions, and all ideas are recorded for later discussion and analysis.

Brainstorming may indeed generate ideas—but not in a very efficient manner. Research consistently shows individuals working alone generate more ideas than a group in a brainstorming session. One reason for this is "production blocking." When people are generating ideas in a group, many are talking at once, which blocks the thought process and eventually impedes the sharing of ideas.[60] The nominal group technique goes further than brainstorming by helping groups arrive at a preferred solution.[61]

The **nominal group technique** restricts discussion or interpersonal communication during the decision-making process, hence the term *nominal*. Group members are all

EXHIBIT 11-5
Evaluating Group
Effectiveness

	Type of Group		
Effectiveness Criteria	**Interacting**	**Brainstorming**	**Nominal**
Number and quality of ideas	Low	Moderate	High
Social pressure	High	Low	Moderate
Money costs	Low	Low	Low
Speed	Moderate	Moderate	Moderate
Task orientation	Low	High	High
Potential for interpersonal conflict	High	Low	Moderate
Commitment to solution	High	Not applicable	Moderate
Development of group cohesiveness	High	High	Moderate

physically present, as in a traditional committee meeting, but they operate independently. Specifically, a problem is presented and then the group takes the following steps:

1. Before any discussion takes place, each member independently writes down ideas on the problem.
2. After this silent period, each member presents one idea to the group. No discussion takes place until all ideas have been presented and recorded.
3. The group discusses the ideas for clarity and evaluates them.
4. Each group member silently and independently rank-orders the ideas. The idea with the highest aggregate ranking determines the final decision.

The chief advantage of the nominal group technique is that it permits a group to meet formally but does not restrict independent thinking, as does an interacting group. Research generally shows nominal groups outperform brainstorming groups.[62]

Each of the group-decision techniques has its own set of strengths and weaknesses. The choice depends on what criteria you want to emphasize and the cost–benefit trade-off. As Exhibit 11-5 indicates, an interacting group is good for achieving commitment to a solution, brainstorming develops group cohesiveness, and the nominal group technique is an inexpensive means for generating a large number of ideas.

SUMMARY

We can draw several implications from our discussion of groups. First, norms control behavior by establishing standards of right and wrong. The norms of a given group can help explain members' behaviors for managers. Second, status inequities create frustration and can adversely influence productivity and willingness to remain with an organization. Third, the impact of size on a group's performance depends on the type of task. Larger groups are associated with lower satisfaction. Fourth, cohesiveness may influence a group's level of productivity, depending on the group's performance-related norms. Fifth, diversity appears to have a mixed impact on group performance, with some studies suggesting that diversity can help performance and others suggesting it can hurt it. Sixth, role conflict is associated with job-induced tension and job dissatisfaction.[63] Lastly, people generally prefer to communicate with others at their own status level or a higher one, rather than with those below them.[64]

IMPLICATIONS FOR MANAGERS

- Recognize that groups can dramatically affect individual behavior in organizations, to either positive or negative effect. Therefore, pay special attention to roles, norms, and cohesion—to understand how these are operating within a group is to understand how the group is likely to behave.
- To decrease the possibility of deviant workplace activities, ensure that group norms do not support antisocial behavior.
- Pay attention to the organizational status levels of the employee groups you create. Because lower-status people tend to participate less in group discussions, groups with high status differences are likely to inhibit input from lower-status members and reduce their potential.
- When forming employee groups, use larger groups for fact-finding activities and smaller groups for action-taking tasks. When creating larger groups, you should also provide measures of individual performance.
- To increase employee satisfaction, work on making certain your employees perceive their job roles the same way you perceive their roles.

PERSONAL INVENTORY ASSESSMENT

In Personal Inventory Assessment found in MyManagementLab take assessment: Communicating Supportively

⭐ WRITING SPACE

If your professor assigned this, sign in to **mymanagementlab.com** for the following Assisted-graded writing question:

11-1. As a manager, how might you set up a work group to minimize the common pitfalls discussed in this chapter?

12

Leadership and Trust

MyManagementLab®

✪ Improve Your Grade!

When you see this icon ✪, visit **www.mymanagementlab.com** for activities that are applied, personalized, and offer immediate feedback.

LEARNING OBJECTIVES

After studying this chapter, you should be able to:

1. Contrast leadership and management.
2. Summarize the conclusions of trait theories of leadership.
3. Identify the central tenets and main limitations of behavioral theories.
4. Assess contingency theories of leadership by their level of support.
5. Contrast *charismatic* and *transformational leadership*.
6. Describe the roles of ethics and trust in *authentic leadership*.
7. Demonstrate the role mentoring plays in our understanding of leadership.
8. Address challenges to the effectiveness of leadership.
9. Describe how organizations can find or create effective leaders.

✪ Chapter Warm-up

If your professor has chosen to assign this, go to **www.mymanagementlab.com** to see what you should particularly focus on and to take the Chapter 12 warm up.

In this chapter, we look at what differentiates leaders from nonleaders. First, we'll present trait theories of leadership. Then, we'll discuss challenges to the meaning and importance of leadership. But before we review these approaches, let's clarify what we mean by the term *leadership*.

WHAT IS LEADERSHIP?

In today's dynamic world, leadership has the ability to influence a group toward the achievement of a vision or set of goals.

We define **leadership** as the ability to influence a group toward the achievement of a vision or set of goals. The source of influence may be formal, such as that provided by managerial rank in an organization. But not all managers are leaders, nor are all leaders managers. Just because an organization provides its managers with certain formal rights is no assurance they will lead effectively. Leaders can emerge from within a group as well as by formal appointment. Nonsanctioned leadership—the ability to influence that arises outside the formal structure of the organization—is often as important or more important than formal positions of influence.

Organizations need strong leadership *and* strong management for optimal effectiveness. We need leaders to challenge the status quo, create visions of the future, and inspire organizational members to achieve these visions. We need managers to formulate detailed plans, create efficient organizational structures, and oversee day-to-day operations.

⭐ WATCH IT

If your professor assigned this, sign in to **mymanagementlab.com** to watch a video titled Leadership (TWZ Role Play) to learn more about this topic and respond to questions.

TRAIT THEORIES

Throughout history, strong leaders have been described by their traits. Therefore, leadership research has long sought to identify the personality, social, physical, or intellectual attributes that differentiate leaders from non-leaders. In recent research, the **trait theories of leadership** focus on personal qualities and characteristics, some of which have been shown to be particularly predictive of leadership ability.

The trait approach using the Big Five framework offers insight into the relationship between personality traits and leadership. A comprehensive review of the leadership literature organized around the Big Five personality framework (see Chapter 5) has found extraversion to be the most predictive trait of leadership.[1] However, extraversion relates more to the way leaders emerge than to their effectiveness. Sociable and dominant people are more likely to assert themselves in group situations, which can help extraverts be identified as leaders, but effective leaders are not domineering. One study found leaders who scored very high on assertiveness were actually less effective than those who scored moderately high.[2] Unlike agreeableness and emotional stability, conscientiousness and openness to experience also predict leadership, especially leader effectiveness. In general, leaders who like being around people and are able to assert themselves (extraverted), who are disciplined and able to keep commitments they make (conscientious), and who are creative and flexible (open) do have an apparent advantage when it comes to leadership.

Based on the latest findings, we offer two conclusions. First, we can say that traits can predict leadership. Second, traits do a better job predicting the emergence of leaders and the appearance of leadership than distinguishing between effective and ineffective leaders.[3] The fact that an individual exhibits the right traits and that others consider him a leader does not necessarily mean that he will be an effective leader, successful at getting the group to achieve its goals.

Trait theories help us predict leadership, but they don't help us explain leadership. What do successful leaders *do* that makes them effective? Are there different types of leader behaviors that are equally effective? Behavioral theories, discussed next, help us define the parameters of leadership.

BEHAVIORAL THEORIES

Trait research provides a basis for *selecting* the right people for leadership. But you probably noticed trait theories don't adequately explore the way leaders *behave*. **Behavioral theories of leadership** imply that we can determine leadership effectiveness by leader behavior, and perhaps train people to be leaders.

The most comprehensive behavioral theories in use today resulted from the Ohio State Studies,[4] which sought to identify independent dimensions of leader behavior. Beginning with more than a thousand behaviors, the studies narrowed the list to two dimensions that substantially accounted for most of the effective leadership behavior described by employees: *initiating structure* and *consideration.*

Initiating structure is the extent to which a leader is likely to define and construct her role and those of employees in the search for goal attainment. It includes behavior that attempts to organize work, work relationships, and goals. A leader high in initiating structure is someone task-oriented who "assigns group members to particular tasks," "expects workers to maintain definite standards of performance," and "emphasizes the meeting of deadlines."

Consideration is the extent to which a person's job relationships are characterized by mutual trust, respect for employees' ideas, and regard for their feelings. A leader high in consideration helps employees with personal problems, is friendly and approachable, treats all employees as equals, and expresses appreciation and support (people-oriented). Most of us want to work for considerate leaders—when asked to indicate what most motivated them at work, 66 percent of U.S. employees surveyed mentioned appreciation.[5]

Leadership studies at the University of Michigan's Survey Research Center had similar objectives to the Ohio State Studies: to locate behavioral characteristics of leaders that related to performance effectiveness. The Michigan group identified two behavioral types: the **employee-oriented leader** emphasized interpersonal relationships by taking a personal interest in employees' needs and accepting individual differences, and the **production-oriented leader** emphasized technical or task aspects of jobs, focusing on accomplishing the group's tasks. These dimensions are closely related to the Ohio State dimensions. Employee-oriented leadership is similar to consideration, and production-oriented leadership is similar to initiating structure. In fact, most researchers use the terms synonymously.[6]

The results of behavioral theory studies have been mixed. However, a review of 160 studies found the followers of leaders high in consideration were more satisfied with their jobs, were more motivated, and had more respect for their leaders. Initiating structure was more strongly related to higher levels of group and organization productivity and more positive performance evaluations.

The reason for some of the mixed results from behavioral theory tests may partly lie in follower preferences, particularly cultural preferences. Research from the GLOBE program—a study of 18,000 leaders from 825 organizations in 62 countries discussed in Chapter 5—suggested there are international differences in the preference for initiating structure and consideration.[7] The study found that leaders high in consideration succeeded best in countries where the cultural values did not favor unilateral decision making, such as Brazil. As one Brazilian manager noted, "We do not prefer leaders who take self-governing decisions and act alone without engaging the group. That's part of who we are." A U.S. manager leading a team in Brazil would therefore need to be high in consideration—team oriented, participative, and humane—to be effective. In contrast, the French have a more bureaucratic view of leaders and are less likely to expect them to be humane and considerate. A leader high in initiating structure (relatively task-oriented) will do best and can make decisions in a relatively autocratic manner in this culture. On the other hand, a manager who scores high on consideration (people-oriented) may find his style backfires in France. In other cultures, both may be important—Chinese culture emphasizes being polite, considerate, and unselfish, but it has a high performance orientation. Thus, consideration and initiating structure may both be important for a manager to be effective in China.

Summary of Trait Theories and Behavioral Theories

In general, research indicates there is validity for both the trait and behavioral theories. Parts of each theory can help explain facets of leadership emergence and effectiveness. The first difficulty is in correctly identifying whether a trait or a behavior predicts a certain outcome. The second difficulty is in exploring which combinations of traits and behaviors yield certain outcomes. The third challenge is to determine the causality of traits to behaviors so that predictions toward desirable leadership outcomes can be made. We've discussed some of these complex determinations as they are currently understood. Leaders who have certain traits desirable to their positions and who display culturally appropriate initiating structure and consideration behaviors do appear to be more effective. Some of the other determinations are less clear. For example, perhaps you're wondering whether conscientious leaders (trait) are more likely to be structuring (behavior), and extraverted leaders (trait) to be considerate (behavior). Unfortunately, we are not sure there is a connection. Future research is needed to determine the exact nature of these relationships.

As important as traits and behaviors are in identifying effective or ineffective leaders, they do not guarantee success. Some leaders may have the right traits or display the right behaviors and still fail. As we've mentioned, context matters, too, which has given rise to the contingency theories we discuss next.

CONTINGENCY THEORIES

Some tough-minded leaders seem to gain a lot of admirers when they take over struggling companies and lead them out of crises. However, predicting leadership success is more complex than finding a few hero examples. Also, the leadership style that works in very bad times doesn't necessarily translate into long-term success. When researchers looked at situational influences, it appeared that under condition a, leadership style x would be appropriate, whereas style y was more suitable for condition b, and style z for condition c. But what *were* conditions a, b, and c? We next consider the Fiedler model, one approach to isolating situational variables.

The Fiedler Model

Fred Fiedler developed the first comprehensive contingency model for leadership, still in use today.[8] The **Fiedler contingency model** proposes that effective group performance depends on the proper match between the leader's style and the degree to which the situation gives the leader control.

IDENTIFYING LEADERSHIP STYLE With the Fiedler model, a key factor in leadership success is the individual's leadership style, which is assumed to be permanent. The model's **least preferred co-worker (LPC) questionnaire** identifies leadership style by measuring whether a person is *task-oriented* or *relationship-oriented*. The LPC questionnaire asks respondents to think of all the coworkers they have ever had and describe the one they *least enjoyed* working with, on a scale of 1 to 8, for 16 sets of contrasting adjectives (such as pleasant–unpleasant, efficient–inefficient, open–guarded, supportive–hostile). If you describe the person you are least able to work with in favorable terms (a high LPC score), you are relationship-oriented. If you rate your least-preferred coworker in unfavorable terms (a low LPC score), you are primarily interested in productivity and are task-oriented. About 16 percent of respondents score in the middle range[9] and thus fall outside the theory's predictions. Our discussion thus pertains to the 84 percent who score in the high or low range of the LPC questionnaire.

DEFINING THE SITUATION With the Fiedler model, a fit must be found between the organizational situation and the leader's style for there to be leadership effectiveness. If a situation requires a task-oriented leader and the person in the leadership position is relationship oriented, either the situation has to be modified or the leader has to be replaced to achieve optimal effectiveness. We can assess the situation in terms of three contingency or situational dimensions:

1. **Leader–member relations** is the degree of confidence, trust, and respect members have in their leader.
2. **Task structure** is the degree to which the job assignments are procedurized (that is, structured or unstructured).
3. **Position power** is the degree of influence a leader has over power variables such as hiring, firing, discipline, promotions, and salary increases.

According to Fiedler's model, the higher the task structure becomes, the more procedures are added; and the stronger the position power, the more control the leader has. A very favorable situation (in which the leader has a great deal of control) might include a payroll manager who has the respect and confidence of his employees (good leader–member relations); activities that are clear and specific—such as wage computation, check writing, and report filing (high task structure); and considerable freedom to reward and punish employees (strong position power). The favorable situations are on the left-hand side of the model in Exhibit 12-1. An unfavorable situation, to the right in the model, might be that of the disliked chairperson of a volunteer United Way fundraising team (low leader–member relations, low task structure, low position power). In this job, the leader has very little control.

MATCHING LEADERS AND SITUATIONS Combining the three contingency dimensions yields eight possible categories of leadership situations. The Fiedler model proposes

EXHIBIT 12-1
Findings from the Fiedler Model

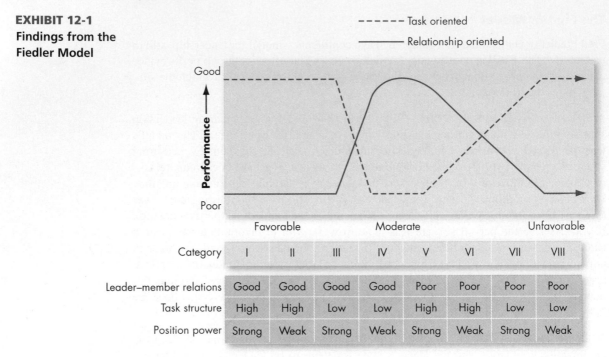

Category	I	II	III	IV	V	VI	VII	VIII
Leader–member relations	Good	Good	Good	Good	Poor	Poor	Poor	Poor
Task structure	High	High	Low	Low	High	High	Low	Low
Position power	Strong	Weak	Strong	Weak	Strong	Weak	Strong	Weak

matching an individual's LPC score and these eight situations to achieve maximum leadership effectiveness.[10] Let's walk through an example. By the model, task-oriented leaders (represented by the dotted line) perform better in situations that are either very favorable to them and or are very unfavorable, but not as well in moderately favorable situations. So, when faced with a category I, II, III, VII, or VIII situation, task-oriented leaders perform better. Relationship-oriented leaders (represented by the solid line), however, perform better in moderately favorable situations—categories IV and V especially.

Note that each of the categories shows us what creates a favorable or unfavorable situation for each leadership style. Fiedler later condensed these eight situations down to three, with the same general findings:[11] Task-oriented leaders perform best in situations of high and low control, while relationship-oriented leaders perform best in moderate control situations.

How would you apply Fiedler's findings? You would match leaders—in terms of their LPC scores—with situations—in terms of leader–member relationships, task structure, and position power. But remember that the model considers an individual's leadership style as fixed. Therefore, there are only two ways to improve leader effectiveness.

First, you can change the leader to fit the situation—in the same way a baseball manager puts a right- or left-handed pitcher into the game depending on whether the hitter is right- or left-handed. If a group situation rates as highly unfavorable but is currently led by a relationship-oriented manager, for example, the group's performance could be improved under a manager who is task-oriented. The second alternative is to change the situation to fit the leader by restructuring tasks, or increasing or decreasing the leader's power to control factors such as salary increases, promotions, and disciplinary actions.

EVALUATION   Studies testing the overall validity of the Fiedler model find considerable evidence to support substantial parts of it.[12] If we use Fiedler's later three situation categories rather than the original eight, ample evidence supports his conclusions.[13] But the logic underlying the LPC questionnaire is not well understood, and respondents' scores are not stable.[14] The contingency variables are also complex and difficult for practitioners to assess.[15] Therefore, while the Fiedler model is widely known and referenced, and its concepts should be understood in organizations, its practical application is sometimes problematic.

Other Contingency Theories

Although the Fiedler model is the most researched contingency theory, two others deserve discussion: situational leadership theory and path–goal theory.

SITUATIONAL LEADERSHIP THEORY   **Situational leadership theory (SLT)** focuses on the followers. It says successful leadership depends on selecting the right leadership style contingent on the followers' *readiness,* the extent to which followers are willing and able to accomplish a specific task. A leader should choose one of four behaviors depending on follower readiness.

If followers are *unable* and *unwilling* to do a task, the leader needs to give clear and specific directions. If followers are *unable* but *willing,* the leader needs to display high task orientation to compensate for followers' lack of ability, and high relationship orientation to get them to "buy into" the leader's desires. If followers are *able* but *unwilling,* the leader needs to use a supportive and participative style; if they are both *able* and *willing,* the leader doesn't need to do much.

SLT has intuitive appeal. It acknowledges the importance of followers and builds on the logic that leaders can compensate for followers' limited ability and motivation. Yet research efforts to test and support the theory have generally been disappointing.[16] Why? Possible explanations include internal ambiguities and inconsistencies in the model itself as well as problems with research methodology. So, despite its intuitive appeal and wide popularity, any endorsement must be cautious for now.

PATH–GOAL THEORY   Developed by Robert House, **path–goal theory** extracts elements from the Ohio State leadership research on initiating structure and consideration, and the expectancy theory of motivation.[17] Path–goal theory suggests it's the leader's job to provide followers with information, support, or other resources necessary to achieve goals. (The term *path–goal* implies that effective leaders clarify followers' paths to their work goals and make the journey easier by reducing roadblocks.) The theory predicts:

- Directive leadership yields greater satisfaction when tasks are ambiguous or stressful than when they are highly structured and well laid out.
- Supportive leadership results in high performance and satisfaction when employees are performing structured tasks.
- Directive leadership is likely to be perceived as redundant by employees with high ability or considerable experience.

Of course, this is a simplification. The match between leadership style and situation can be individualistic and mercurial. Some tasks may be both stressful and highly structured, and employees may have high ability or experience in some tasks and not others. Studies indicate that leaders who set goals enable conscientious followers to achieve higher performance but may cause stress for workers who are low in conscientiousness.

Altogether, the foundation of path-goal theory has merit. Directive or supportive leadership does matter to followers' performance, and leaders need to be aware of their important facilitating role. Additionally, path–goal theory, like SLT and other contingency theories, reminds us that the effectiveness of leaders depends to a large degree on their followers.

CHARISMATIC LEADERSHIP AND TRANSFORMATIONAL LEADERSHIP

Do you think that leaders are born not made, or do you think they are made not born? True, an individual may be literally born into a leadership position (think family heirs with surnames like Ford and Hilton), be endowed with a leadership position due to past accomplishments (like CEOs who worked their way up the organizational ranks), or be informally acknowledged as a leader (like a Microsoft employee who knows everything because he was "there at the start"). But here we are talking not about the inputs into leadership role attainment; rather, we are focused on what makes great leaders extraordinary. Two contemporary leadership theories—charismatic leadership and transformational leadership—share a common theme in the great leader debate: They view leaders as individuals who inspire followers through words, ideas, and behaviors.

Charismatic Leadership

Martin Luther King Jr., Ronald Reagan, Mary Kay Ash (founder of Mary Kay Cosmetics), and Steve Jobs (co-founder of Apple Computer) are frequently cited as charismatic leaders. What do they have in common?

WHAT IS CHARISMATIC LEADERSHIP? Sociologist Max Weber defined *charisma* (from the Greek for "gift") more than a century ago as "a certain quality of an individual personality, by virtue of which he or she is set apart from ordinary people and treated as endowed with supernatural, superhuman, or at least specifically exceptional powers or qualities. These are not accessible to the ordinary person and are regarded as of divine origin or as exemplary, and on the basis of them the individual concerned is treated as a leader."[18]

The first researcher to consider charismatic leadership in terms of OB was Robert House. According to House's **charismatic leadership theory**, followers attribute heroic or extraordinary leadership abilities when they observe certain behaviors and tend to give these leaders power.[19] A number of studies have attempted to identify the characteristics of charismatic leaders: They have a vision, are willing to take personal risks to achieve that vision, are sensitive to follower needs, and exhibit extraordinary behaviors[20] (see Exhibit 12-2).

ARE CHARISMATIC LEADERS BORN OR MADE? Are charismatic leaders born with their qualities? Or can people actually learn to be charismatic leaders? Yes, and yes.

1. *Vision and articulation.* Has a vision—expressed as an idealized goal—that proposes a future better than the status quo; and is able to clarify the importance of the vision in terms that are understandable to others.
2. *Personal risk.* Willing to take on high personal risk, incur high costs, and engage in self-sacrifice to achieve the vision.
3. *Sensitivity to follower needs.* Perceptive of others' abilities and responsive to their needs and feelings.
4. *Unconventional behavior.* Engages in behaviors that are perceived as novel and counter to norms.

EXHIBIT 12-2

Key Characteristics of a Charismatic Leader

Source: Based on J. A. Conger and R. N. Kanungo, *Charismatic Leadership in Organizations* (Thousand Oaks, CA: Sage, 1998), p. 94.

Individuals *are* born with traits that make them charismatic. In fact, studies of identical twins found that twins scored similarly on charismatic leadership measures, even if they were raised in different households and never met. Personality is also related to charismatic leadership; charismatic leaders are likely to be extraverted, self-confident, and achievement-oriented.[21] Consider Presidents Barack Obama, Bill Clinton, and Ronald Reagan, and Prime Minister Margaret Thatcher: Like them or not, they are often compared because they all possess the qualities of charismatic leaders.

Recent research indicates that charismatic leadership is not only the province of world leaders—all of us can develop, within our own limitations, a more charismatic leadership style. If you stay active and central in your leadership roles, you will naturally communicate your vision for achieving goals to your followers, which increases the likelihood that you will be seen as charismatic.[22] To further develop an aura of charisma, use your passion as a catalyst for generating enthusiasm. Speak in an animated voice, reinforce your message with eye contact and facial expression, and gesture for emphasis. Bring out the potential in followers by tapping into their emotions, and create a bond that inspires them. Remember, enthusiasm is contagious!

HOW CHARISMATIC LEADERS INFLUENCE FOLLOWERS   How do charismatic leaders actually influence followers? By articulating an appealing **vision**, a long-term strategy for attaining a goal by linking the present with a better future for the organization. Desirable visions fit the times and circumstances and reflect the uniqueness of the organization. Thus, followers are inspired not only by how passionately the leader communicates—there must be an underlying vision that appeals to followers as well.

A vision needs an accompanying **vision statement**, a formal articulation of an organization's vision or mission. Charismatic leaders may use vision statements to imprint on followers an overarching goal and purpose. These leaders also set a tone of cooperation and mutual support. They build followers' self-esteem and confidence with high performance expectations and the belief that followers can attain them. Through words and actions, the leader conveys values and sets an example for followers to imitate. Finally, the charismatic leader engages in emotion-inducing and often unconventional behavior to demonstrate courage and conviction about the vision.

Research indicates that charismatic leadership strategies work as followers "catch" the emotions and values their leader is conveying.[23] A study of 115 U.S. government employees found they had a stronger sense of personal belonging at work when they had charismatic leaders, increasing their willingness to engage in helping and compliance-oriented behavior.[24] When followers mirror the desirable behaviors, the effectiveness of these leaders is heightened. One study of Israeli bank employees also showed charismatic leaders were more effective because their employees personally identified with them.

DOES EFFECTIVE CHARISMATIC LEADERSHIP DEPEND ON THE PERSON AND THE SITUATION? Charismatic leadership has positive effects across many contexts. There are, however, characteristics of followers, and of the situation, that enhance or somewhat limit its effects.

One factor that enhances charismatic leadership is stress. People are especially receptive to charismatic leadership when they sense a crisis, when they are under stress, or when they fear for their lives. We may be more receptive to charismatic leadership under crises because we think bold leadership is needed. Some of it, however, may be more primal. When people are psychologically aroused, even in laboratory studies, they are more likely to respond to charismatic leaders.[25] This may explain why, when charismatic leaders surface, it's likely to be in politics or religion, during wartime, or when a business is in its infancy or facing a life-threatening crisis. Charismatic leaders are able to reduce stress for their followers, perhaps because they help make work seem more meaningful and interesting.[26]

You may wonder whether a situational factor limiting charisma is the level in the organization. Top executives create vision. It is more difficult to utilize a person's charismatic leadership qualities in lower-level management jobs or to align her vision with the specific top-management goals of the organization. While charismatic leadership may be more important in the upper echelons of organizations, it is also clear that its effects are not confined to high-level leaders, as it can be effective from a distance, or from close range.

Some personalities are especially susceptible to charismatic leadership.[27] For instance, an individual who lacks self-esteem and questions his self-worth is more likely to absorb a leader's direction rather than establish his own way of leading or thinking. For these people, the situation may matter much less than the charismatic qualities of the leader.

THE DARK SIDE OF CHARISMATIC LEADERSHIP Unfortunately, charismatic leaders who are larger than life don't necessarily act in the best interests of their organizations.[28] Research has shown that individuals who are narcissistic are also higher in some behaviors associated with charismatic leadership.[29] Many charismatic—but corrupt—leaders have allowed their personal goals to override the goals of the organization. Leaders at Enron, Tyco, WorldCom, and HealthSouth recklessly used organizational resources for their personal benefit and violated laws and ethics to inflate stock prices, and then cashed in millions of dollars in personal stock options. Some charismatic leaders—Hitler, for example—are all too successful at convincing their followers to pursue a vision that can be disastrous. If charisma is power, then that power can be used for good—and for ill.

It's not that charismatic leadership isn't effective; overall, it is. But a charismatic leader isn't always the answer. Success depends, to some extent, on the situation, on the leader's vision, and on the organizational checks and balances in place to monitor the outcomes.

Transformational Leadership

Charismatic leadership theory relies on leaders' ability to inspire followers to believe in them. In contrast, Fiedler's model, situational leadership theory, and path–goal theory describe **transactional leaders**, who guide their followers toward established goals by clarifying role and task requirements. A stream of research has focused on differentiating transactional from **transformational leaders**,[30] who inspire followers to transcend their self-interests for the good of the organization. Transformational leaders can have an extraordinary effect on their followers. Recent research suggests that transformational leaders are most effective when their followers are able to see the positive impact of their work through direct interaction with customers or other beneficiaries.[31] Exhibit 12-3 briefly identifies and defines characteristics that differentiate transactional from transformational leaders.

Transactional and transformational leadership complement each other; they aren't opposing approaches to leadership effectiveness.[32] The best leaders are transactional *and* transformational. Transformational leadership *builds on* transactional leadership and produces levels of follower effort and performance beyond what transactional leadership alone can do. But the reverse isn't true. If you are a good transactional leader but do not have transformational qualities, you'll likely be only a mediocre leader. A model of leader behaviors indicates increasing effectiveness as a leader moves from passive, transactional behaviors to active, transformational behaviors (see Exhibit 12-4).

TRANSACTIONAL LEADER

Contingent Reward. Contracts exchange of rewards for effort, promises rewards for good performance, recognizes accomplishments.

Management by Exception (active). Watches and searches for deviations from rules and standards, takes correct action.

Management by Exception (passive). Intervenes only if standards are not met.

Laissez-Faire. Abdicates responsibilities, avoids making decisions.

TRANSFORMATIONAL LEADER

Idealized Influence. Provides vision and sense of mission, instills pride, gains respect and trust.

Inspirational Motivation. Communicates high expectations, uses symbols to focus efforts, expresses important purposes in simple ways.

Intellectual Stimulation. Promotes intelligence, rationality, and careful problem solving.

Individualized Consideration. Gives personal attention, treats each employee individually, coaches, advises.

EXHIBIT 12-3

Characteristics of Transactional and Transformational Leaders

Sources: Based on A. H. Eagly, M. C. Johannesen-Schmidt, and M. L. Van Engen, "Transformational, Transactional, and Laissez-faire Leadership Styles: A Meta-Analysis Comparing Women and Men," *Psychological Bulletin* 129, no. 4 (2003), pp. 569–591; and T. A. Judge and J. E. Bono, "Five Factor Model of Personality and Transformational Leadership," *Journal of Applied Psychology* 85, no. 5 (2000), pp. 751–765.

**EXHIBIT 12-4
Full Range
of Leadership
Model**

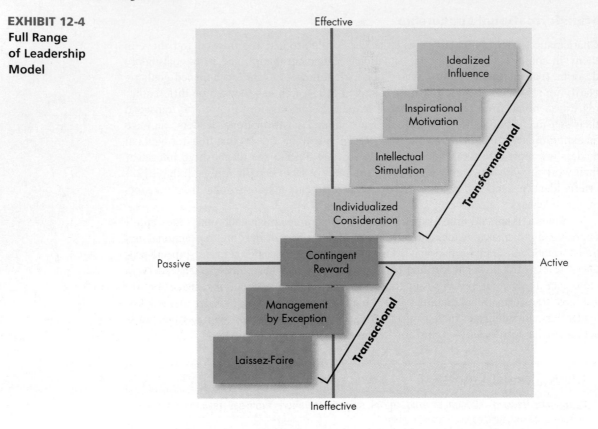

FULL RANGE OF LEADERSHIP MODEL   Exhibit 12-4 shows the full range of leadership model. Laissez-faire, which literally means "let it be" (do nothing), is the most passive and therefore least effective of leader behaviors.[33] Management-by-exception, where leaders primarily "put out fires" when there are crisis exceptions to normal operating procedures, means they are often too late to be effective. Contingent reward leadership, where predetermined rewards are given for employee efforts, can be an effective style of leadership but will not get employees to go above and beyond the call of duty.

Only with the four remaining styles—all aspects of transformational leadership—are leaders able to motivate followers to perform above expectations and transcend their self-interest for the sake of the organization. Individualized consideration, intellectual stimulation, inspirational motivation, and idealized influence (known as the "four I's") all result in extra effort from workers, higher productivity, higher morale and satisfaction, higher organizational effectiveness, lower turnover, lower absenteeism, and greater organizational adaptability. Based on this model, leaders are generally most effective when they regularly use the four I's.

EVALUATION OF TRANSFORMATIONAL LEADERSHIP   Transformational leadership has been supported at diverse job levels and occupations (school principals, teachers, marine commanders, ministers, presidents of MBA associations, military cadets, union shop stewards, sales reps). In general, organizations perform better when they have transformational leaders.

Companies with transformational leaders show greater agreement among top managers about the organization's goals, which yields superior organizational performance.[34]

The effect of transformational leadership on performance can vary by the situation. In general, transformational leadership has a greater impact on the bottom line in smaller, privately held firms than in more complex organizations,[35] which decentralization and corporate entrepreneurship can mediate. Transformational leadership can also vary depending on whether work is evaluated at the team or individual level.[36] Individual-focused transformational leadership is behavior that empowers individual followers to develop, enhance their abilities, and increase self-efficacy. Team-focused transformational leadership emphasizes group goals, shared values and beliefs, and unified efforts.

Just as vision helps explain how charismatic leadership works, it also explains part of the effectiveness of transformational leadership. One study found vision was even more important than a charismatic (effusive, dynamic, lively) communication style in explaining the success of entrepreneurial firms.[37] Vision is the most important element of transformational leadership in any culture, according to the GLOBE study.[38] The GLOBE team concluded that "effective business leaders in any country are expected by their subordinates to provide a powerful and proactive vision to guide the company into the future, strong motivational skills to stimulate all employees to fulfill the vision, and excellent planning skills to assist in implementing the vision."[39]

Although vision is important in any culture, the way it is formed and communicated may need to be adapted. Transformational leadership may be more effective when leaders can directly interact with the workforce to make decisions than when they report to an external board of directors or deal with a complex bureaucratic structure. One study showed transformational leaders were more effective in improving group potency in teams higher in power distance and collectivism.[40] Other research using a sample of employees both in China and the United States found that transformational leadership had a more positive relationship with perceived procedural justice among individuals who were lower in power-distance orientation, which suggests that transformational leadership may work in many cultures as long as the leaders interact directly with followers.[41]

Transformational leaders are more effective because they are creative, but also because they encourage those who follow them to be creative, too.[42] Creativity and empowerment are key to organizational success, and transformational leaders are able to increase follower self-efficacy, giving the group a "can do" spirit.[43] Empowered followers are more likely to pursue ambitious goals, agree on the strategic objectives of the organization, and believe the goals they are pursuing are personally important.[44]

Like charisma, transformational leadership can be learned. One study of Canadian bank managers found branches managed by those who underwent transformational leadership training performed significantly better than branches whose managers did not receive training.

TRANSFORMATIONAL LEADERSHIP AND TRANSACTIONAL LEADERSHIP We have seen that transformational leadership yields many desirable organizational outcomes. When comparing transformational leadership with transactional leadership, research indicates transformational leadership is more strongly correlated than transactional leadership with lower turnover rates, higher productivity, lower employee stress and burnout, and higher employee satisfaction. However, transformational leadership theory is not perfect.

The full range of leadership model shows a clear division between transactional and transformational leadership that may not fully exist in effective leadership. And contrary to the model, research suggests the four I's of transformational leadership are not always superior in effectiveness to transactional leadership.[45] Specifically, contingent reward leadership sometimes works as well as transformational leadership. More research is needed, but the general supportable conclusion is that transformational leadership is desirable and effective, given the right application.

TRANSFORMATIONAL LEADERSHIP AND CHARISMATIC LEADERSHIP In considering transformational and charismatic leadership, you will have noticed some commonalities. And indeed there are. Yet there are differences, too. Charismatic leadership places somewhat more emphasis on *how* leaders communicate (are they passionate and dynamic) while transformational leadership focuses more on *what* is communicated (especially a compelling vision); the theories are more alike than different. At their heart, both theories focus on the ability of leaders to inspire followers, and some of the ways they do this are the same in both theories. Because of this, some researchers believe the concepts are interchangeable.

AUTHENTIC LEADERSHIP: ETHICS AND TRUST

If we're looking for the best possible leader, it is not enough to be charismatic or visionary—one must also be ethical and authentic.

Although theories have increased our understanding of effective leadership, they do not explicitly deal with the role of ethics and trust, which are essential to complete the picture. Here, we consider these two concepts under the rubric of authentic leadership.[46]

What Is Authentic Leadership?

Authentic leadership focuses on the moral aspects of being a leader. **Authentic leaders** know who they are, know what they believe in, and act on those values and beliefs openly and candidly. Their followers consider them ethical people. The primary quality produced by authentic leadership is trust. Authentic leaders share information, encourage open communication, and stick to their ideals. The result: People have faith in them.

There has been limited research on authentic leadership. However, recent research indicated that authentic leadership, especially when shared among top management team members, created a positive energizing effect that heightened firm performance.[47] Transformational or charismatic leaders can have a vision and communicate it persuasively, but sometimes the vision is wrong (as in the case of Hitler), or the leaders are more concerned with their own needs or pleasures, as were Dennis Kozlowski (ex-CEO of Tyco), Jeff Skilling (ex-CEO of Enron), and Raj Rajaratnam (founder of the Galleon Group).[48]

Ethical Leadership

For better or worse, leadership is not value-free. In assessing leadership effectiveness, we need to address the *means* a leader uses to achieve goals as well as the content of those goals. The role of the leader in creating the ethical expectations for all members is crucial.[49] Therefore, although every member of an organization is responsible for ethical behavior, many initiatives aimed at increasing organizational ethical behavior are focused on the leaders. A recent study of 2,572 U.S. Army soldiers underscored that ethical leadership among the top brass influences not only their direct followers, but all the way down the command structure as well, because top leaders create an ethical culture and expect lower-level leaders to behave along ethical guidelines.[50]

Ethics and authentic leadership intersect at a number of junctures. Leaders who treat their followers with fairness, especially by providing honest, frequent, and accurate information, are seen as more effective.[51] Related to this is the concept of humbleness, another characteristic ethical leaders often exhibit as part of being authentic. Research indicates that leaders who model humility help followers to understand the growth process for their own development.[52] Leaders rated as highly ethical also tend to have followers who engage in more organizational citizenship behaviors and who are more willing to bring problems to the leaders' attention.[53] Recent research also found that ethical leadership reduced interpersonal conflicts.[54]

Ethical considerations are inherent to transformational and charismatic leadership. Transformational leadership has ethical implications since these leaders change the way followers think. Charisma, too, has an ethical component. Unethical leaders use their charisma to enhance power over followers, directed toward self-serving ends. To integrate ethical and charismatic leadership, scholars have advanced the idea of **socialized charismatic leadership**—leadership that conveys other-centered (not self-centered) values by leaders who model ethical conduct.[55] Socialized charismatic leaders are able to bring employee values in line with their own values through their words and actions.[56]

Leaders can build on a foundation of trust to show their character, enhance a sense of unity, and create buy-in from followers. Research findings suggest that organizations should invest in ethical leadership training programs, especially in industries with few regulations. Ethical leadership training programs to teach cultural values should especially be mandated for leaders who take foreign assignments or manage multicultural work teams.[57]

Servant Leadership

Scholars have recently considered ethical leadership from a new angle by examining **servant leadership**.[58] Servant leaders go beyond their self-interest and focus on opportunities to help followers grow and develop. They don't use power to achieve ends; they emphasize persuasion. Characteristic behaviors include listening, empathizing, persuading, accepting stewardship, and actively developing followers' potential. Because servant leadership emphasizes serving the needs of others, research has focused on its outcomes for the well-being of followers. Perhaps not surprisingly, a recent study of 126 CEOs found that servant leadership is negatively correlated with the trait of narcissism.[59]

What are the effects of servant leadership? One study of 123 supervisors found servant leadership resulted in higher levels of commitment to the supervisor, self-efficacy, and perceptions of justice, which all were related to organizational citizenship behavior (OCB).[60] This relationship between servant leadership and follower OCB appears to be stronger when followers are focused on being dutiful and responsible.[61] Second, servant leadership increases team potency (a belief that one's team has above-average skills and abilities), which in turn leads to higher levels of group performance.[62] Third, a study with a nationally representative sample found a higher level of OCB was associated with a focus on growth and advancement, which in turn was associated with a higher level of creative performance.[63]

Servant leadership may be more prevalent and more effective in certain cultures.[64] When asked to draw images of leaders, for example, U.S. subjects tended to draw them in front of the group, giving orders to followers. Singaporeans tended to draw leaders at the back of the group, acting more to gather a group's opinions together and then unify them from the rear. This suggests the East Asian prototype is more like a servant leader, which might mean servant leadership is more effective in these cultures.

Trust and Leadership

Trust is a psychological state that exists when you agree to make yourself vulnerable to another person because you have positive expectations about how things are going to turn out.[65] Although you aren't completely in control of the situation, you are willing to take a chance that the other person will come through for you. Trust is a primary attribute associated with leadership; breaking it can have serious adverse effects on a group's performance.[66]

Followers who trust a leader are confident their rights and interests will not be abused.[67] Transformational leaders create support for their ideas in part by arguing that their direction will be in everyone's best interests. People are unlikely to look up to or follow someone they perceive as dishonest or may take advantage of them. Thus, as you might expect, transformational leaders generate higher levels of trust from their followers, which relate to higher levels of team confidence and, ultimately, higher levels of team performance.[68]

In a simple contractual exchange of goods and services, your employer is legally bound to pay you for fulfilling your job description. But today's rapid reorganizations, diffusion of responsibility, and collaborative team-based work style mean employment relationships are not stable long-term contracts with explicit terms. Rather, they are based more on trusting relationships than ever before. You have to trust that if you show your supervisor a creative project you've been working on, she won't steal the credit behind your back. You have to trust that the extra work you've been doing will be recognized in your performance appraisal. In contemporary organizations, where work is less closely documented and specified, voluntary employee contribution based on trust is absolutely necessary. Only a trusted leader will be able to encourage employees to reach beyond themselves to a transformational goal.

What Are the Consequences of Trust?

Trust between supervisors and employees has a number of advantages. Here are just a few that research has shown:

- *Trust encourages taking risks.* Whenever employees decide to deviate from the usual way of doing things, or to take their supervisors' word on a new direction, they are taking a risk. In both cases, a trusting relationship can facilitate that leap.
- *Trust facilitates information sharing.* One big reason employees fail to express concerns at work is that they don't feel psychologically safe revealing their views. When managers demonstrate they will give employees' ideas a fair hearing and actively make changes, employees are more willing to speak out.[69]
- *Trusting groups are more effective.* When a leader sets a trusting tone in a group, members are more willing to help each other and exert extra effort, which increases

trust. Members of mistrusting groups tend to be suspicious of each other, constantly guard against exploitation, and restrict communication with others in the group. These actions tend to undermine and eventually destroy the group.

- *Trust enhances productivity.* The bottom-line interest of companies appears to be positively influenced by trust. Employees who trust their supervisors tend to receive higher performance ratings.[70] People respond to mistrust by concealing information and secretly pursuing their own interests.

One potentially significant opportunity for building trust within an organization is to encourage positive relationships between leaders and would-be leaders. Mentoring programs, discussed next, allow individuals from different organizational levels to get to know one another and create bonds of trust.

LEADING FOR THE FUTURE: MENTORING

Leaders often take responsibility for developing future leaders. Let's consider what makes mentoring valuable as well as its potential pitfalls.

Mentoring

A **mentor** is a senior employee who sponsors and supports a less experienced employee, a protégé. Successful mentors are good teachers. They present ideas clearly, listen well, and empathize with protégés' problems. Mentoring relationships, whether formal or informal, serve career functions and psychosocial functions.[71]

In formal mentoring relationships, protégé candidates are identified according to assessments of leadership potential, and then they are matched with leaders in corresponding organizational functions. Informal mentoring relationships happen much the same, but organically: first, a less experienced, lower-level employee who appears to have potential for future development is identified.[72] The protégé is often then tested with a particularly challenging assignment. If performance is acceptable, the leader will develop the mentoring relationship. In both formal and informal mentoring, the goal is to show the protégé how the organization *really* works outside its formal structures and procedures.

Are all employees in an organization likely to participate in a mentoring relationship? Unfortunately, no.[73] However, research indicates that employers should establish mentoring programs because they benefit both mentors and protégés. A recent study in Korea, for instance, found that mentors achieved higher levels of transformational leadership abilities as a result of the process, while organizational commitment and well-being increased for both mentors and protégés.[74]

Although begun with the best intentions, formal mentoring relationships are not as effective as informal ones,[75] perhaps due to poor planning, design, and communication. Mentors must see the relationship as beneficial to themselves and the protégé, and the protégé must feel he has input into the relationship.[76] Formal mentoring programs are also most likely to succeed if they appropriately match the work style, needs, and skills of protégé and mentor.[77]

You might assume mentoring is valuable for objective outcomes like compensation and job performance, but research suggests the gains are primarily psychological. Research further indicates that while mentoring can have an impact on career success, it is not as much of a contributing factor as ability and personality. It may *feel* nice to have a mentor, but it doesn't appear that having a good mentor, or any mentor, is critical to your career. Mentors may be effective not because of the functions they provide, but because of the resources they can obtain; a mentor connected to a powerful network can build relationships that will help the protégé advance. Network ties, whether built through a mentor or not, are a significant predictor of career success.[78] If a mentor is not well connected or not a very strong performer, the best mentoring advice in the world will not be very beneficial.

CHALLENGES TO THE LEADERSHIP CONSTRUCT

"In the 1500s, people ascribed all events they didn't understand to God. Why did the crops fail? God. Why did someone die? God. Now our all-purpose explanation is leadership."[79] This may be an astute observation from management consulting, but of course much of an organization's success or failure is due to factors outside the influence of leadership. Sometimes it's a matter of being in the right or wrong place at a given time. In this section, we present challenges to the accepted beliefs about the value of leadership.

Leadership as an Attribution

As you may remember from Chapter 6, attribution theory examines how people try to make sense of cause-and-effect relationships. The **attribution theory of leadership** says leadership is merely an attribution people make about other individuals.[80] We attribute the following to leaders: intelligence, outgoing personality, strong verbal skills, aggressiveness, understanding, and industriousness.[81] At the organizational level, we tend, rightly or wrongly, to see leaders as responsible for both extremely negative and extremely positive performance.[82]

One study of 128 major U.S. corporations found that whereas perceptions of CEO charisma did not lead to objectively better company performance, company performance did lead to perceptions of charisma.[83] Employee perceptions of leaders' behaviors are significant predictors of whether they blame the leader for failure, regardless of how the leader assesses himself.[84] A study of more than 3,000 employees from western Europe, the United States, and the Middle East found people who tended to "romanticize" leadership in general were more likely to believe their own leaders were transformational.[85]

Attribution theory suggests it is important to project the *appearance* of being a leader rather than focusing on *actual accomplishments*. Leader-wannabes who can shape the perception that they're smart, personable, verbally adept, aggressive, hardworking, and consistent in their style can increase the probability their bosses, colleagues, and employees will view them as effective leaders.

Substitutes for and Neutralizers of Leadership

One theory of leadership suggests that in many situations, leaders' actions are irrelevant.[86] Experience and training are among the **substitutes** that can replace the need for a leader's support or ability to create structure. Recently, companies such as video game producer Valve Corporation, Gore-Tex maker W. L. Gore, and collaboration-software

Defining Characteristics	Relationship-Oriented Leadership	Task-Oriented Leadership
Individual		
Experience/training	No effect on	Substitutes for
Professionalism	Substitutes for	Substitutes for
Indifference to rewards	Neutralizes	Neutralizes
Job		
Highly structured task	No effect on	Substitutes for
Provides its own feedback	No effect on	Substitutes for
Intrinsically satisfying	Substitutes for	No effect on
Organization		
Explicit formalized goals	No effect on	Substitutes for
Rigid rules and procedures	No effect on	Substitutes for
Cohesive work groups	Substitutes for	Substitutes for

EXHIBIT 12-5

Substitutes for and Neutralizers of Leadership

Source: Based on S. Kerr and J. M. Jermier, "Substitutes for Leadership: Their Meaning and Measurement," *Organizational Behavior and Human Performance* (December 1978), p. 378.

firm GitHub have experimented with eliminating leaders and management. Governance in the "bossless" work environment is achieved through accountability to coworkers, who determine team composition and even sometimes pay.[87] Organizational characteristics such as explicit formalized goals, rigid rules and procedures, and cohesive work groups can replace formal leadership, while indifference to organizational rewards can neutralize its effects. **Neutralizers** make it impossible for leader behavior to make any difference to follower outcomes (see Exhibit 12-5).

Sometimes the difference between substitutes and neutralizers is fuzzy. If I'm working on a task that's intrinsically enjoyable, theory predicts leadership will be less important because the task provides motivation. But does that mean intrinsically enjoyable tasks neutralize leadership effects, or substitute for them, or both? Another problem is that while substitutes for leadership (such as employee characteristics, the nature of the task, etc.) matter to performance, we can't infer that leadership doesn't matter.[88]

FINDING AND CREATING EFFECTIVE LEADERS

How can organizations find or create effective leaders? Let's try to answer that question.

Selecting Leaders

The process organizations go through to fill management positions is an exercise in the identification of effective leaders. You might begin by reviewing the knowledge, skills, and abilities needed to do the job effectively. Personality tests can identify traits associated with leadership—extraversion, conscientiousness, and openness to experience. High self-monitors are better at reading situations and adjusting their behavior accordingly. Candidates with high emotional intelligence should have an advantage, especially in situations requiring transformational leadership.[89] Experience is a poor predictor of leader effectiveness, but situation-specific experience is relevant.

Training Leaders

Organizations spend billions of dollars on leadership training and development.[90] These take many forms, including $50,000 executive leadership programs offered by universities such as Harvard, to sailing experiences offered by the Outward Bound program. Business schools and companies are placing renewed emphasis on leadership development.

How can managers get the most from their leadership-training budgets? First, leadership training is likely to be more successful with high self-monitors. Such individuals have the flexibility to change their behavior. Second, organizations can teach implementation skills. Third, we can teach skills such as trust building and mentoring. Leaders can be taught situational-analysis skills. They can learn how to evaluate situations, modify them to better fit their style, and assess which leader behaviors might be most effective in given situations.

Fourth, behavioral training through modeling exercises can increase an individual's ability to exhibit charismatic leadership qualities. Fifth, leaders should engage in regularly reviewing their leadership after key organizational events. These after-event reviews are especially effective for leaders who are high in conscientiousness and openness to experience, and who are emotionally stable (low in neuroticism).[91] Finally, leaders can be trained in transformational leadership skills that have bottom-line results.

SUMMARY

Leadership plays a central part in understanding group behavior because it's the leader who usually directs us toward our goals. Knowing what makes a good leader should thus be valuable in improving group performance. The early search for a set of universal leadership traits failed. However, recent efforts using the Big Five personality framework show strong and consistent relationships between leadership and extraversion, conscientiousness, and openness to experience. The behavioral approach's major contribution was narrowing leadership into task-oriented (initiating structure) and people-oriented (consideration) styles. By considering the situation in which the leader operates, contingency theories promised to improve on the behavioral approach. Research on charismatic and transformational leadership has made major contributions to our understanding of leadership effectiveness. The concept of authentic leadership encompasses the dimensions of ethics and trust that characterize the best leadership practices, although the need for leadership to increase performance is not always certain.

IMPLICATIONS FOR MANAGERS

- For maximum leadership effectiveness, ensure that your preferences on the initiating structure and consideration dimensions are a match for your work dynamics and culture.

- Hire candidates who exhibit transformational leadership qualities and who have demonstrated success in working through others to meet a long-term vision. Personality tests can reveal candidates higher in extraversion, conscientiousness, and openness, which may indicate leadership readiness.
- For management roles, hire candidates whom you believe are ethical and trustworthy, and train current managers in your organization's ethical standards in order to increase leadership effectiveness.
- Seek to develop trusting relationships with followers because, as organizations have become less stable and predictable, strong bonds of trust are replacing bureaucratic rules in defining expectations and relationships.
- Consider investing in leadership training such as formal courses, workshops, rotating job responsibilities, coaching, and mentoring.

PERSONAL INVENTORY ASSESSMENT

In Personal Inventory Assessment found in MyManagementLab take assessment: Ethical Leadership Assessment

⭐ WRITING SPACE

If your professor assigned this, sign in to **mymanagementlab.com** for the following Assisted-graded writing question:

12-1. What are your suggestions for creating ethical leadership in organizations?

13

Power and Organizational Politics

MyManagementLab®
✪ Improve Your Grade!

When you see this icon ✪, visit **www.mymanagementlab.com** for activities that are applied, personalized, and offer immediate feedback.

LEARNING OBJECTIVES

After studying this chapter, you should be able to:

1. Define *power*.
2. Contrast leadership and power.
3. Describe the five bases of power.
4. Identify nine power or influence tactics and their contingencies.
5. Determine how power affects people.
6. Define *organizational politics* and describe why politics exist in organizations.
7. Identify the causes and consequences of political behavior.
8. Determine whether a political action is ethical.
9. Describe the political mapping process and its advantages.

✪ Chapter Warm-up

If your professor has chosen to assign this, go to **www.mymanagementlab.com** to see what you should particularly focus on and to take the Chapter 13 warm up.

In both research and practice, *power* and *politics* have been described as dirty words. It is easier for most of us to talk about sex or money than about power or political behavior. People who have power deny it, people who want it try not to look like they're seeking it, and those who are good at getting it are secretive about how they do so.[1]

In this chapter, we show that power determines what goals a group will pursue and how the group's resources will be distributed among its members. Further, we show how group members with good political skills use their power to influence the distribution of resources in their favor.

✪ WATCH IT

If your professor assigned this, sign in to **mymanagementlab.com** to watch a video titled Power and Political Behavior to learn more about this topic and respond to questions.

A DEFINITION OF POWER

Power refers to a capacity that *A* has to influence the behavior of *B* so *B* acts in accordance with *A*'s wishes.[2] Someone can thus have power but not use it; it is a capacity or potential. Probably the most important aspect of power is that it is a function of **dependence**. The greater *B*'s dependence on *A,* the greater *A*'s power is in the relationship. Dependence, in turn, is based on alternatives that *B* perceives and the importance *B* places on the alternative(s) *A* controls. A person can have power over you only if he controls something you desire. If you want a college degree and have to pass a certain course to get it, and your current instructor is the only faculty member in the college who teaches that course, he has power over you. Your alternatives are highly limited, and you place a high degree of importance on the outcome. Similarly, if you're attending college on funds provided by your parents, you probably recognize the power they hold over you. You're dependent on them for financial support. But once you're out of school, have a job, and are making a good income, your parents' power is reduced significantly. Who among us has not known or heard of a rich relative who is able to control a large number of family members merely through the implicit or explicit threat of "writing them out of the will"?

In a disturbing example of the power of dependence, Wall Street portfolio manager Ping Jiang allegedly was able to coerce analyst Andrew Tong into taking female hormones and wearing lipstick and makeup. Why such power? Jiang controlled Tong's access to day trading. That's how much power dependency can bring.[3]

Money is often a dependence factor in power and politics, but it is not the only means by which one person or group creates dependence from another. Before we examine the ways power is gained and exercised, let's be certain we understand the important differences between leadership and power.

CONTRASTING LEADERSHIP AND POWER

A careful comparison of our description of power with our description of leadership in Chapter 12 reveals the concepts are closely intertwined. Leaders use power as a means of attaining group goals.

How are the two terms different? Power does not require goal compatibility, merely dependence. Leadership, on the other hand, requires some congruence between the goals of the leader and those being led. A second difference relates to the direction of influence. Leadership research focuses on the downward influence on followers. It minimizes the importance of lateral and upward influence patterns. Power research takes all factors into consideration. For a third difference, leadership research often emphasizes style. It seeks answers to questions such as: How supportive should a leader be? How much decision making should be shared with followers? In contrast, the research on power focuses on tactics for gaining compliance. Lastly, leadership concentrates on the individual leader's influence, while the study of power acknowledges that groups as well as individuals can use power to control other individuals or groups.

You may have noted that for a power situation to exist, one person or group needs to have control over resources the other person or group values. This is usually the case in established leadership situations. However, it is important to remember that power relationships exist potentially in all areas of life and power can be obtained in many ways. Let's explore the various sources of power next.

BASES OF POWER

Where does power come from? What gives an individual or a group influence over others? We answer by dividing the bases or sources of power into two general groupings—formal and personal—and then breaking each of these down into more specific categories.[4]

Formal Power

Formal power is based on an individual's position in an organization. It can come from the ability to coerce or reward, or from formal authority.

COERCIVE POWER   The **coercive power** base depends on fear of the negative results from failing to comply. On the physical level, coercive power rests on the application, or the threat of application, of bodily distress through the infliction of pain, the restriction of movement, or the withholding of basic physiological or safety needs.

At the organizational level, *A* has coercive power over *B* if *A* can dismiss, suspend, or demote *B*, assuming *B* values his job. If *A* can assign *B* work activities *B* finds unpleasant, or treat *B* in a manner *B* finds embarrassing, *A* possesses coercive power over *B*. Coercive power can also come from withholding key information. People in an organization who have knowledge others need can make others dependent on them.

REWARD POWER   The opposite of coercive power is **reward power**, with which people comply because it produces positive benefits; someone who can distribute rewards others view as valuable will have power over them. These rewards can be either financial—such as controlling pay rates, raises, and bonuses—or nonfinancial, including recognition, promotions, interesting work assignments, friendly colleagues, and preferred work shifts or sales territories.[5]

LEGITIMATE POWER   In formal groups and organizations, probably the most common access to one or more of the power bases is through **legitimate power**. It represents the formal authority to control and use organizational resources based on structural position in the organization.

Legitimate power is broader than the power to coerce and reward. Specifically, it includes members' acceptance of the authority of a position. We associate power so closely with the concept of hierarchy that just drawing longer lines in an organization chart leads people to infer the leaders are especially powerful.[6] When school principals, bank presidents, or army captains speak, teachers, tellers, and first lieutenants listen and usually comply.

Personal Power

Many of the most competent and productive chip designers at Intel have power, but they aren't managers and have no formal power. What they have is *personal power*, which comes from an individual's unique characteristics. There are two bases of personal power: expertise, and the respect and admiration of others.

EXPERT POWER **Expert power** is influence wielded as a result of expertise, special skills, or knowledge. As jobs become more specialized, we become increasingly dependent on experts to achieve goals. It is generally acknowledged that physicians have expertise and hence expert power: Most of us follow our doctor's advice. Computer specialists, tax accountants, economists, industrial psychologists, and other specialists wield power as a result of their expertise.

REFERENT POWER **Referent power** is based on identification with a person who has desirable resources or personal traits. If I like, respect, and admire you, you can exercise power over me because I want to please you.

Referent power develops out of admiration of another and a desire to be like that person. It helps explain, for instance, why celebrities are paid millions of dollars to endorse products in commercials. Marketing research shows people such as LeBron James and Tom Brady have the power to influence your choice of athletic shoes and credit cards. With a little practice, you and I could probably deliver as smooth a sales pitch as these celebrities, but the buying public doesn't identify with you and me. Some people who are not in formal leadership positions nonetheless have referent power and exert influence over others because of their charismatic dynamism, likability, and emotional effects on us.

Which Bases of Power Are Most Effective?

Of the three bases of formal power (coercive, reward, legitimate) and two bases of personal power (expert, referent), which is most important to have? Research suggests pretty clearly that the personal sources of power are most effective. Both expert and referent power are positively related to employees' satisfaction with supervision, their organizational commitment, and their performance, whereas reward and legitimate power seem to be unrelated to these outcomes. One source of formal power—coercive power—is negatively related to employee satisfaction and commitment.[7]

Consider Steve Stoute's company, Translation, which matches pop-star spokespersons with corporations that want to promote their brands. Stoute has paired Gwen Stefani with HP, Justin Timberlake with McDonald's, Beyoncé Knowles with Tommy Hilfiger, and Jay-Z with Reebok. Stoute's business seems to be all about referent power. His firm aims to use the credibility of artists and performers to reach youth culture.[8] In other words, Stoute is expecting the buying public to identify and emulate his spokespersons and therefore think highly of his brands.

No matter which base of power is planned, it will be effective only if the power tactics are effective. Let's explore the concept of power tactics more fully.

> Formal power can come from the ability to coerce or reward, or it can come from formal authority. However, evidence suggests that informal expert and referent power are the most important to acquire.

POWER TACTICS

Political behaviors are one important means of gaining power and influence. The most effective influence behaviors—consultation and inspirational appeal—tend to be the least widely used. You should make these influence tactics part of your repertoire.

What **power tactics** do people use to translate power bases into specific action? What options do they have for influencing their bosses, coworkers, and employees? Following are some popular tactical options and the conditions that may make one option more effective than another. Research has identified nine distinct influence tactics:[9]

1. *Legitimacy.* Relying on your authority position, or saying that a request accords with organizational policies or rules.
2. *Rational persuasion.* Presenting logical arguments and factual evidence to demonstrate that a request is reasonable.
3. *Inspirational appeals.* Developing emotional commitment by appealing to a target's values, needs, hopes, and aspirations.
4. *Consultation.* Increasing support by involving the target in deciding how you will accomplish your plan.
5. *Exchange.* Rewarding the target with benefits or favors in exchange for following a request.
6. *Personal appeals.* Asking for compliance based on friendship or loyalty.
7. *Ingratiation.* Using flattery, praise, or friendly behavior prior to making a request.
8. *Pressure.* Using warnings, repeated demands, and threats.
9. *Coalitions.* Enlisting the aid or support of others to persuade the target to agree.

Some tactics are more effective than others. Rational persuasion, inspirational appeals, and consultation tend to be the most effective, especially when the audience is highly invested in the outcomes of a decision process. The pressure tactic tends to backfire and is typically the least effective of the nine tactics.[10] You can increase your chance of success by using two or more tactics together or sequentially, as long as your choices are compatible.[11] Using both ingratiation and legitimacy can lessen negative reactions, but only when the audience does not really care about the outcome of a decision process or the policy is routine.[12]

Let's consider the most effective way of getting a raise. You can start with a rational approach—figure out how your pay compares to that of your organizational peers, land a competing job offer, gather data that testify to your performance, or use salary calculators like Salary.com to compare your pay with others in your occupation—and share your results with your manager. Kitty Dunning, a vice president at Don Jagoda Associates, landed a 16 percent raise when she e-mailed her boss numbers showing she had increased sales.[13]

While rational persuasion may work for you, the effectiveness of some influence tactics depends on the direction of influence.[14] As Exhibit 13-1 shows, rational persuasion is the only tactic effective across organizational levels. Inspirational appeals work best as a downward-influencing tactic with subordinates. When pressure works, it's generally downward only. Personal appeals and coalitions are most effective as lateral influence. Other factors that impact the effectiveness of influence include the sequencing of tactics, a person's skill in using the tactic, and the organizational culture.

You're more likely to be effective if you begin with "softer" tactics that rely on personal power, such as personal and inspirational appeals, rational persuasion, and consultation. If these fail, you can move to "harder" tactics, such as exchange, coalitions, and pressure, which emphasize formal power and incur greater costs and risks.[15] Interestingly, a single soft tactic

Upward Influence	Downward Influence	Lateral Influence
Rational persuasion	Rational persuasion	Rational persuasion
	Inspirational appeals	Consultation
	Pressure	Ingratiation
	Consultation	Exchange
	Ingratiation	Legitimacy
	Exchange	Personal appeals
	Legitimacy	Coalitions

EXHIBIT 13-1
Preferred
Power Tactics
by Influence
Direction

is more effective than a single hard tactic, and combining two soft tactics or a soft tactic and rational persuasion is more effective than any single tactic or combination of hard tactics.[16] The effectiveness of tactics depends on the audience.[17] People especially likely to comply with soft power tactics tend to be more reflective and intrinsically motivated; they have high self-esteem and a greater desire for control. Those likely to comply with hard power tactics are more action-oriented and extrinsically motivated, and are more focused on getting along with others than on getting their own way.

People in different countries prefer different power tactics.[18] Those from individualistic countries tend to see power in personalized terms and as a legitimate means of advancing their personal ends, whereas those in collectivistic countries see power in social terms and as a legitimate means of helping others.[19] A study comparing managers in the United States and China found that U.S. managers preferred rational persuasion, whereas Chinese managers preferred coalition tactics.[20] These differences tend to be consistent with the values in these two countries. Reason-based tactics are consistent with the U.S. preference for direct confrontation and rational persuasion to influence others and resolve differences, while coalition tactics align with the Chinese preference for meeting difficult or controversial requests with indirect approaches.

People differ in their **political skill**, or their ability to influence others to enhance their own objectives. The politically skilled are more effective users of all the influence tactics. Political skill is also more effective when the stakes are high, such as when the individual is accountable for important organizational outcomes. Finally, the politically skilled are able to exert their influence without others detecting it, a key element in being effective (it's damaging to be labeled as political).[21] However, these individuals are most able to use their political skills in environments marked by low levels of procedural and distributive justice. When an organization is run with open and fairly applied rules, free of favoritism or biases, political skill is actually negatively related to job performance ratings.[22]

Lastly, we know cultures within organizations differ markedly—some are warm, relaxed, and supportive; others are formal and conservative. Some encourage participation and consultation, some encourage reason, and still others rely on pressure. People who fit the culture of the organization tend to obtain more influence.[23] Specifically, extraverts tend to be more influential in team-oriented organizations, and highly conscientious people are more influential in organizations that value working alone on technical tasks. People who fit the culture are influential because they can perform especially well in the domains deemed most important for success. In other words, they are influential because they are competent. Thus, the organization itself will influence which subset of power tactics is viewed as acceptable for use.

HOW POWER AFFECTS PEOPLE

To this point, we've discussed what power is and how it is acquired. But we've not yet answered one important question: Does power corrupt?

There is certainly evidence that there are corrupting aspects of power. Research suggests that power leads people to place their own interests ahead of others. Why does this happen? Interestingly, research suggests that power not only leads people to focus on their self-interests because they can, but it also liberates people to focus inward and thus come to place greater weight on their goals and interests. Power also appears to lead individuals to "objectify" others (to see them as tools to obtain their instrumental goals) and to see relationships as more peripheral.[24]

That's not all. Powerful people react—especially negatively—to any threats to their competence. They're more willing to denigrate others. People given power are more likely to make self-interested decisions when faced with a moral hazard (such as when hedge fund managers take more risks with other people's money because they're rewarded for gains but less often punished for losses). Power also leads to overconfident decision making.[25]

Frank Lloyd Wright, perhaps America's greatest architect, is a good example of power's corrupting effects. Early in his career, Wright worked for and was mentored by renowned architect Louis Sullivan (sometimes known as "the father of the skyscraper"). Before Wright achieved greatness, he was copious in his praise for Sullivan. Later in his career, that praise faded, and Wright even took credit for one of Sullivan's noted designs. Wright was never a benevolent man, but as his power accumulated, so did his potential to behave in a "monstrous" way toward others.[26]

So, yes, power does appear to have some important disturbing effects on us. But that is hardly the whole story—it's more complicated than that. Power doesn't affect everyone in the same way, and there are even positive effects of power. Let's consider each of these in turn.

First, the toxic effects of power depend on one's personality. Research suggests that if we have an anxious personality, power does not corrupt us because we are less likely to think that using power benefits us.[27] Second, the corrosive effect of power can be contained by organizational systems. One study found, for example, that while power made people behave in a self-serving manner, when accountability of this behavior was initiated, the self-serving behavior stopped. Third, forgive the pun, but we have the power to blunt the negative effects of power. One study showed that simply expressing gratitude toward powerful others made them less likely to aggress against us. Finally, remember the aphorism that those with little power grab and abuse what little they have? There appears to be some truth to this in that the people most likely to abuse power are those who are low in status and gain power. Why is this the case? It appears that having low status is threatening, and this fear is used in negative ways if power is given.[28]

As you can see, there are factors that can ameliorate the negative effects of power. But there also appear to be general positive effects. Power energizes and leads to approach motivation (that is, more motivation to achieve goals). It also can enhance people's motivation to help others, at least for certain people. One study found, for example, that values toward helping others translated into actual work behavior only when people felt a sense of power.[29]

This study points to an important insight about power. It is not so much that power corrupts as it *reveals*. Supporting this line of reasoning, another study revealed that power led to self-interested behavior only for those with a weak moral identity (the degree to which morals are core to one's identity). For those with a strong moral identity, power actually enhanced their moral awareness.[30]

POLITICS: POWER IN ACTION

When people get together in groups, power will be exerted. People want to carve out a niche from which to exert influence, earn rewards, and advance their careers. When employees in organizations convert their power into action, we describe them as being engaged in *politics*. Those with good political skills have the ability to use their bases of power effectively.[31]

Definition of Organizational Politics

There is no shortage of definitions of *organizational politics*. Essentially, this type of politics focuses on the use of power to affect decision making in an organization, or on self-serving and organizationally unsanctioned behaviors.[32] For our purposes, **political behavior** in organizations consists of activities that are not required as part of an individual's formal role but that influence, or attempt to influence, the distribution of advantages and disadvantages within the organization.[33]

This definition encompasses what most people mean when they talk about organizational politics. Political behavior is outside specified job requirements. It requires some attempt to use power bases. It includes efforts to influence the goals, criteria, or processes used for decision making. Our definition is broad enough to include varied political behaviors such as withholding key information from decision makers, joining a coalition, whistle-blowing, spreading rumors, leaking confidential information to the media, exchanging favors with others in the organization for mutual benefit, and lobbying on behalf of or against a particular individual or decision alternative.

The Reality of Politics

Interviews with experienced managers show that most believe political behavior is a major part of organizational life.[34] Many managers report some use of political behavior is both ethical and necessary, as long as it doesn't directly harm anyone else. They describe politics as a necessary evil and believe someone who *never* uses political behavior will have a hard time getting things done. Most also indicate they have never been trained to use political behavior effectively. But why, you may wonder, must politics exist? Isn't it possible for an organization to be politics-free? It's *possible*—but unlikely.

Organizations are made up of individuals and groups with different values, goals, and interests.[35] This sets up the potential for conflict over the allocation of limited resources such as departmental budgets, space, project responsibilities, and salary adjustments.[36] If resources were abundant, then all constituencies within the organization could satisfy their goals. But because they are limited, not everyone's interests can be satisfied.

Furthermore, gains by one individual or group are often *perceived* as coming at the expense of others within the organization (whether they are or not). These forces create real competition among members for the organization's limited resources.

Maybe the most important factor leading to politics within organizations is the realization that most of the "facts" used to allocate the limited resources are open to interpretation. What, for instance, is *good* performance? What's an *adequate* improvement? What constitutes an *unsatisfactory* job? One person's "selfless effort to benefit the organization" is seen by another as a "blatant attempt to further one's interest."[37] The manager of any major league baseball team knows a .400 hitter is a high performer and a .125 hitter is a poor performer. You don't need to be a baseball genius to know you should play your .400 hitter and send the .125 hitter back to the minors. But what if you have to choose between players who hit .280 and .290? Then less objective factors come into play: fielding expertise, attitude, potential, ability to perform in a clutch, loyalty to the team, and so on. More managerial decisions resemble the choice between a .280 and a .290 hitter than between a .125 hitter and a .400 hitter. It is in this large and ambiguous middle ground of organizational life—where the facts *don't* speak for themselves—that politics flourish.

Finally, because most decisions have to be made in a climate of ambiguity—where facts are rarely fully objective and thus are open to interpretation—people within organizations will use whatever influence they can to taint the facts to support their goals and interests. That, of course, creates the activities we call *politicking*.

Therefore, to answer the question of whether it is possible for an organization to be politics-free, we can say "yes"—if all members of that organization hold the same goals and interests, if organizational resources are not scarce, and if performance outcomes are completely clear and objective. But that doesn't describe the organizational world in which most of us live.

CAUSES AND CONSEQUENCES OF POLITICAL BEHAVIOR

Factors Contributing to Political Behavior

Not all groups or organizations are equally political. In some organizations, for instance, politicking is overt and rampant, while in others, politics play a small role in influencing outcomes. Why this variation? Recent research and observation have identified a number of factors that appear to encourage political behavior. Some are individual characteristics, derived from the unique qualities of the people the organization employs; others are a result of the organization's culture or internal environment. Both individual and organizational factors can increase political behavior and provide favorable outcomes (increased rewards and averted punishments) for individuals and groups in the organization.

INDIVIDUAL FACTORS   At the individual level, researchers have identified certain personality traits, needs, and other factors likely to be related to political behavior. In terms of traits, we find that employees who are high self-monitors, possess an internal locus of control, and have a high need for power are more likely to engage in political behavior.[38] The high self-monitor is more sensitive to social cues, exhibits higher levels of social conformity, and is more likely to be skilled in political behavior than the low self-monitor. Because they believe they can control their environment, individuals with an internal locus of control are more prone to take a proactive stance and attempt to manipulate situations in their favor. Not surprisingly, the Machiavellian personality—characterized by the will to manipulate and the desire for power—is comfortable using politics as a means to further personal interests.

In addition, an individual's investment in the organization, perceived alternatives, and expectations of success influence the degree to which she will pursue illegitimate means of political action.[39] The more a person expects increased future benefits from the organization, and the more that person has to lose if forced out, the less likely that individual is to use illegitimate means. Conversely, the more alternative job opportunities an individual has—due to a favorable job market, the possession of scarce skills or knowledge, a prominent reputation, or influential contacts outside the organization—the more likely he is to risk illegitimate political actions. Finally, an individual with low expectations of success from illegitimate means is unlikely to use them. High expectations of success from such measures are most likely to be the province of experienced and powerful individuals with polished political skills, as well as inexperienced and naïve employees who misjudge their chances.

ORGANIZATIONAL FACTORS   Although we acknowledge the role individual differences can play, the evidence more strongly suggests that certain situations and cultures promote politics. Specifically, when an organization's resources are declining, when the existing pattern of resources is changing, and when there is opportunity for promotions, politicking is more likely to surface.[40] When organizations downsize to improve efficiency, resources must be reduced, and people may engage in political actions to safeguard what they have. But *any* changes, especially those that imply a significant reallocation of resources within the organization, are likely to stimulate conflict and increase politicking. The opportunity for promotions or advancement has consistently been found to encourage competition for a limited resource as people try to positively influence the decision outcome.

Cultures characterized by low trust, role ambiguity, unclear performance evaluation systems, zero-sum (win–lose) reward allocation practices, democratic decision making, high pressure for performance, and self-serving senior managers will create breeding grounds for politicking.[41] The less trust within the organization, the higher the level of political behavior and the more likely it will be of the illegitimate kind. So, high trust should suppress political behavior in general and inhibit illegitimate actions in particular.

Role ambiguity means the prescribed employee behaviors are not clear. There are, therefore, fewer limits to the scope and functions of the employee's political actions. Because political activities are defined as those not required as part of the employee's formal role, the greater the role ambiguity, the more employees can engage in unnoticed political activity.

Performance evaluation is far from a perfect science. The more organizations use subjective criteria in the appraisal, emphasize a single outcome measure, or allow significant time to pass between the time of an action and its appraisal, the greater the likelihood that an employee can get away with politicking. Subjective performance criteria create ambiguity. The use of a single outcome measure encourages individuals to do whatever is necessary to "look good" on that measure, but often at the cost of good performance on other important parts of the job that are not being appraised.

The more an organization's culture emphasizes the zero-sum or win–lose approach to reward allocations, the more employees will be motivated to engage in politicking. The **zero-sum approach** treats the reward "pie" as fixed, so any gain one person or group achieves has to come at the expense of another person or group. If $15,000 in annual raises is to be distributed among five employees, any employee who gets more than $3,000 takes money away from one or more of the others. Such a practice encourages making others look bad and increasing the visibility of what you do.

Finally, when employees see the people on top engaging in political behavior, especially doing so successfully and being rewarded for it, a climate is created that supports politicking. Politicking by top management in a sense gives those lower in the organization permission to play politics by implying that such behavior is acceptable.

How Do People Respond to Organizational Politics?

Trish loves her job as a writer on a weekly television comedy series but hates the internal politics. "A couple of the writers here spend more time kissing up to the executive producer than doing any work. And our head writer clearly has his favorites. While they pay me a lot and I get to really use my creativity, I'm sick of having to be on alert for backstabbers and constantly having to self-promote my contributions. I'm tired of doing most of the work and getting little of the credit." Are Trish's comments typical of people who work in highly politicized workplaces? We all know friends or relatives who regularly complain about the politics at their jobs. But how do people in general react to organizational politics? Let's look at the evidence.

In our earlier discussion in this chapter of factors that contribute to political behavior, we focused on the favorable outcomes. But for most people—who have modest political skills or are unwilling to play the politics game—outcomes tend to be predominantly negative. Exhibit 13-2 summarizes the extensive research (mostly conducted in the United States) on the relationship between organizational politics and individual outcomes.[42] Very strong evidence indicates, for instance, that perceptions of organizational politics are negatively related to job satisfaction.[43] The perception of politics also tends to increase job anxiety and stress, possibly because people believe they may be losing ground to others who are active politickers or, conversely, because they feel additional pressures from entering into and competing in the political arena.[44] Politics may lead to self-reported declines in employee performance, perhaps because employees perceive political environments to be unfair, which demotivates them.[45] Not surprisingly, when politicking becomes too much to handle, it can lead employees to quit.[46]

Researchers have noted several interesting qualifiers. First, the politics–performance relationship appears to be moderated by an individual's understanding of the "hows" and

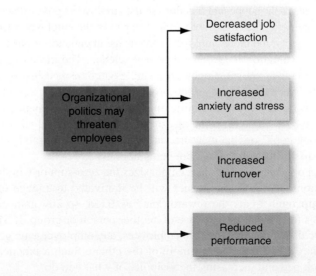

**EXHIBIT 13-2
Employee
Responses to
Organizational
Politics**

"whys" of organizational politics. "An individual who has a clear understanding of who is responsible for making decisions and why they were selected to be the decision makers would have a better understanding of how and why things happen the way they do than someone who does not understand the decision-making process in the organization."[47] When both politics and understanding are high, performance is likely to increase because the individual will see political actions as an opportunity. This is consistent with what you might expect among individuals with well-honed political skills. But when understanding is low, individuals are more likely to see politics as a threat, which can have a negative effect on job performance.[48]

Second, political behavior at work moderates the effects of ethical leadership.[49] One study found that male employees were more responsive to ethical leadership and showed the most citizenship behavior when levels of both politics and ethical leadership were high. Women, on the other hand, appeared most likely to engage in citizenship behavior when the environment was consistently ethical and *apolitical*.

Third, when employees see politics as a threat, they often respond with **defensive behaviors**—reactive and protective behaviors to avoid action, blame, or change.[50] (Exhibit 13-3 provides some examples of these behaviors.) Defensive behaviors are often associated with negative feelings toward the job and work environment.[51] In the short

---

AVOIDING ACTION

Overconforming. Strictly interpreting your responsibility by saying things like "The rules clearly state . . ." or "This is the way we've always done it."

Buck passing. Transferring responsibility for the execution of a task or decision to someone else.

Playing dumb. Avoiding an unwanted task by falsely pleading ignorance or inability.

Stretching. Prolonging a task so that one person appears to be occupied—for example, turning a two week task into a four month job.

Stalling. Appearing to be more or less supportive publicly while doing little or nothing privately.

AVOIDING BLAME

Buffing. This is a nice way to refer to "covering your rear." It describes the practice of rigorously documenting activity to project an image of competence and thoroughness.

Playing safe. Evading situations that may reflect unfavorably. It includes taking on only projects with a high probability of success, having risky decisions approved by superiors, qualifying expressions of judgment, and taking neutral positions in conflicts.

Justifying. Developing explanations that lessen one's responsibility for a negative outcome and/or apologizing to demonstrate remorse, or both.

Scapegoating. Placing the blame for a negative outcome on external factors that are not entirely blameworthy.

Misrepresenting. Manipulation of information by distortion, embellishment, deception, selective presentation, or obfuscation.

AVOIDING CHANGE

Prevention. Trying to prevent a threatening change from occurring.

Self-protection. Acting in ways to protect one's self-interest during change by guarding information or other resources.

EXHIBIT 13-3
Defensive Behaviors

run, employees may find that defensiveness protects their self-interest, but in the long run it wears them down. People who consistently rely on defensiveness find that, eventually, it is the only way they know how to behave. At that point, they lose the trust and support of their peers, bosses, employees, and clients.

Impression Management

Impression management is a specific type of political behavior, designed to alter other's immediate perceptions of us; evidence suggests that the effectiveness of impression management techniques depends on the setting (e.g., self-promotion works better in interviews than in performance evaluations).

We know people have an ongoing interest in how others perceive and evaluate them. For example, North Americans spend billions of dollars on diets, health club memberships, cosmetics, and plastic surgery—all intended to make them more attractive to others. Being perceived positively by others should have benefits for people in organizations. It might, for instance, help them initially to get the jobs they want in an organization and, once hired, to get favorable evaluations, superior salary increases, and more rapid promotions. In a political context, it might help sway the distribution of advantages in their favor. The process by which individuals attempt to control the impression others form of them is called **impression management (IM)**.[52]

Who might we predict will engage in IM? No surprise here. It's our old friend, the high self-monitor.[53] Low self-monitors tend to present images of themselves that are consistent with their personalities, regardless of the beneficial or detrimental effects for them. In contrast, high self-monitors are good at reading situations and molding their appearances and behavior to fit each situation. If you want to control the impression others form of you, what IM techniques can you use? Exhibit 13-4 summarizes some of the most popular and provides an example of each.

Keep in mind that when people engage in IM, they are sending a false message that might be true under other circumstances.[54] Excuses, for instance, may be offered with sincerity. Referring to the example in Exhibit 13-4, you can *actually* believe that ads contribute little to sales in your region. But misrepresentation can have a high cost. If you "cry wolf" once too often, no one is likely to believe you when the wolf really comes. So the impression manager must be cautious not to be perceived as insincere or manipulative.[55] Consider the effect of implausible name-dropping as an example of this principle. Participants in a study in Switzerland disliked an experimental confederate who claimed to be a personal friend of the well-liked Swiss tennis star Roger Federer, but they generally liked confederates who just said they were fans.[56] Another study found that when managers attributed an employee's citizenship behaviors to impression management, they actually felt angry (probably because they felt manipulated) and gave the subordinate lower performance ratings. When managers attributed the same behaviors to prosocial values and concern about the organization, they felt happy and gave higher performance ratings.[57] In sum, people don't like to feel others are manipulating them through impression management, so such tactics should be employed with caution.

Most of the studies undertaken to test the effectiveness of IM techniques have related it to two criteria: interview success and performance evaluations. Let's consider each of these.

The evidence indicates most job applicants use IM techniques in interviews and that it works.[58] In one study, for instance, interviewers felt applicants for a position as a customer service representative who used IM techniques performed better in the interview, and the interviewers seemed somewhat more inclined to hire these people.[59] Moreover, when the researchers considered applicants' credentials, they concluded it was

CONFORMITY

Agreeing with someone else's opinion to gain his approval is a *form of ingratiation.*
Example: A manager tells his boss, "You're absolutely right on your reorganization plan for the western regional office. I couldn't agree with you more."

FAVORS

Doing something nice for someone to gain that person's approval is a *form of ingratiation.*
Example: A salesperson says to a prospective client, "I've got two tickets to the theater tonight that I can't use. Take them. Consider it a thank-you for taking the time to talk with me."

EXCUSES

Explanations of a predicament-creating event aimed at minimizing the apparent severity of the predicament is a *defensive IM technique.*
Example: A sales manager says to her boss, "We failed to get the ad in the paper on time, but no one responds to those ads anyway."

APOLOGIES

Admitting responsibility for an undesirable event and simultaneously seeking to get a pardon for the action is a *defensive IM technique.*
Example: An employee says to his boss, "I'm sorry I made a mistake on the report. Please forgive me."

SELF-PROMOTION

Highlighting one's best qualities, downplaying one's deficits, and calling attention to one's achievements is a *self-focused IM technique.*
Example: A salesperson tells her boss, "Matt worked unsuccessfully for three years to try to get that account. I sewed it up in six weeks. I'm the best closer this company has."

ENHANCEMENT

Claiming that something you did is more valuable than most other members of the organizations would think is a *self-focused IM technique.*
Example: A journalist tells his editor, "My work on this celebrity divorce story was really a major boost to our sales" (even though the story only made it to page 3 in the entertainment section).

FLATTERY

Complimenting others about their virtues in an effort to make oneself appear perceptive and likeable is an *assertive IM technique.*
Example: A new sales trainee says to her peer, "You handled that client's complaint so tactfully! I could never have handled that as well as you did."

EXEMPLIFICATION

Doing more than you need to in an effort to show how dedicated and hard working you are is an *assertive IM technique.*
Example: An employee sends e-mails from his work computer when he works late so that his supervisor will know how long he's been working.

EXHIBIT 13-4
Impression Management (IM) Techniques

Sources: Based on B. R. Schlenker, *Impression Management* (Monterey, CA: Brooks/Cole, 1980); M. C. Bolino, K. M. Kacmar, W. H. Turnley, and J. B. Gilstrap, "A Multi-Level Review of Impression Management Motives and Behaviors," *Journal of Management* 34, no. 6 (2008), pp. 1080–1109; and R. B. Cialdini, "Indirect Tactics of Image Management Beyond Basking," in R. A. Giacalone and P. Rosenfeld (eds.), *Impression Management in the Organization* (Hillsdale, NJ: Lawrence Erlbaum, 1989), pp. 45–71.

the IM techniques alone that influenced the interviewers—that is, it didn't seem to matter whether applicants were well or poorly qualified. If they used IM techniques, they did better in the interviews.

Some IM techniques work better in interviews than others. Researchers have compared applicants whose IM techniques focused on promoting their accomplishments (*self-promotion*) to those who focused on complimenting the interviewer and finding areas of agreement (such as flattery, conformity, or favors). In general, applicants appear to use self-promotion more than ingratiatory tactics such as flattery.[60] What's more, self-promotion may be more important to interviewing success. Applicants who work to create an appearance of competence by enhancing their accomplishments, taking credit for successes, and explaining away failures do better in interviews. These effects reach beyond the interview: Applicants who use more self-promotion also seem to get more follow-up job-site visits, even after adjusting for grade-point average, gender, and job type. Ingratiation also works well in interviews; applicants who compliment the interviewer, agree with his opinions, and emphasize areas of fit do better than those who don't.[61]

In terms of performance ratings, the picture is quite different. Ingratiation is positively related to performance ratings, meaning those who ingratiate themselves with their supervisors get higher performance evaluations. However, self-promotion appears to backfire: Those who self-promote actually seem to receive *lower* performance evaluations.[62] There is an important qualifier to this general result. It appears that individuals high in political skill are able to translate IM into higher performance appraisals, whereas those lower in political skill are more likely to be hurt by their IM attempts.[63] A study of 760 boards of directors found that individuals who ingratiate themselves with current board members (express agreement with the director, point out shared attitudes and opinions, and compliment the director) increase their chances of landing on a board.[64]

What explains these results? If you think about them, they make sense. Ingratiating always works because everyone—both interviewers and supervisors—likes to be treated nicely. However, self-promotion may work only in interviews and backfire on the job because, whereas the interviewer has little idea whether you're blowing smoke about your accomplishments, the supervisor knows because it's her job to observe you. Thus, if you're going to self-promote, remember that what works in an interview won't always work once you're on the job, and stick to the truth.

Are our conclusions about responses to politics globally valid? Should we expect employees in Israel, for instance, to respond the same way to workplace politics that employees in the United States do? Almost all our conclusions on employee reactions to organizational politics are based on studies conducted in North America. The few studies that have included other countries suggest some minor modifications.[65] One study of managers in U.S. culture and three Chinese cultures (People's Republic of China, Hong Kong, and Taiwan) found U.S. managers evaluated "gentle persuasion" tactics such as consultation and inspirational appeals as more effective than did their Chinese counterparts.[66] Other research suggests that effective U.S. leaders achieve influence by focusing on personal goals of group members and the tasks at hand (an analytical approach), whereas influential East Asian leaders focus on relationships among group members and meeting the demands of the people around them (a holistic approach).[67]

As another example, Israelis and the British seem to generally respond as North Americans do—their perception of organizational politics relates to decreased job satisfaction and increased turnover.[68] In countries that are more politically unstable, employees seem to demonstrate greater tolerance of intense political processes in the workplace, perhaps because they are used to power struggles and have more experience in coping with them.[69] This suggests that people from politically turbulent countries in the Middle East or Latin America might be more accepting of organizational politics, and more willing to use aggressive political tactics in the workplace, than people from countries such as Great Britain or Switzerland.

THE ETHICS OF BEHAVING POLITICALLY

Although there are no clear-cut ways to differentiate ethical from unethical politicking, there are some questions you should consider. For example, what is the utility of engaging in politicking? Sometimes we do it for little good reason. Major league baseball player Al Martin claimed he played football at USC when in fact he never did. As a baseball player, he had little to gain by pretending to have played football. Outright lies like this may be a rather extreme example of impression management, but many of us have at least distorted information to make a favorable impression. One thing to keep in mind is whether it's really worth the risk. Another question to ask is this: How does the utility of engaging in the political behavior balance out any harm (or potential harm) it will do to others? Complimenting a supervisor on his appearance in order to curry favor is probably much less harmful than grabbing credit for a project that others deserve.

Finally, does the political activity conform to standards of equity and justice? Sometimes it is difficult to weigh the costs and benefits of a political action, but its ethicality is clear. The department head who inflates the performance evaluation of a favored employee and deflates the evaluation of a disfavored employee—and then uses these evaluations to justify giving the former a big raise and nothing to the latter—has treated the disfavored employee unfairly.

Unfortunately, powerful people can become very good at explaining self-serving behaviors in terms of the organization's best interests. They can persuasively argue that unfair actions are really fair and just. Our point is that immoral people can justify almost any behavior. Those who are powerful, articulate, and persuasive are most vulnerable to ethical lapses because they are likely to be able to get away with unethical practices successfully. When faced with an ethical dilemma regarding organizational politics, try to consider whether playing politics is worth the risk and whether others might be harmed in the process. If you have a strong power base, recognize the ability of power to corrupt. Remember that it's a lot easier for the powerless to act ethically, if for no other reason than they typically have very little political discretion to exploit.

MAPPING YOUR POLITICAL CAREER

As we have seen, politics are not just for politicians. You can use the concepts presented in this chapter in some very tangible ways we have outlined. However, there is another application: You.

One of the most useful ways to think about power and politics is in terms of your own career. Think about your career in your organization of choice. What are your ambitions?

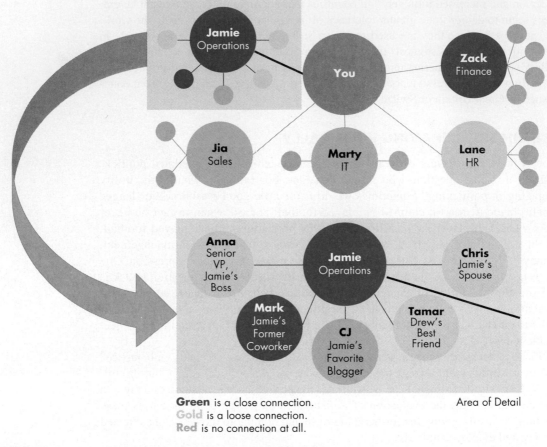

Green is a close connection.
Gold is a loose connection.
Red is no connection at all.

Area of Detail

EXHIBIT 13-5
Drawing Your Political Map

Source: Based on Clark, "A Campaign Strategy for Your Career," *Harvard Business Review* (November 2012), pp. 131–134.

Who has the power to help you get there? What is your relationship with these people? The best way to answer these questions is with a political map, which can help you sketch out your relationships with the people upon whom your career depends. Exhibit 13-5 contains such a political map.[70] Let's walk through it.

Assume that your future promotion depends on five people, including Jamie, your immediate supervisor. As you can see in the exhibit, you have a close relationship with Jamie (you would be in real trouble otherwise). You also have a close relationship with Zack in finance. However, for the others, you either have a loose relationship (Lane), or none at all (Jia, Marty). One obvious implication of this map is to formulate a plan for more influence over, and a closer relationship with, these people. How might you do that?

The map also provides for a useful way to think about the power network. Assume that the five individuals have their own networks. In this case, though, assume these aren't so much power networks, but influence networks representing your knowledge of the people who influence the individuals in power positions.

One of the best ways to influence people is indirectly. What if you played in a tennis league with Mark, Jamie's former coworker who you know remains friends with Jamie? To influence Mark, in many cases, may also be to influence Jamie. Why not post an entry on CJ's blog? This same analysis can then be completed with the other four decision makers.

Of course, this map doesn't show you everything you need to know—no map does. For example, rarely would all five people have the same amount of power. Moreover, maps are harder to construct in the era of large social networks. Try to keep this basic, to the people who *really* matter to your career.

All of this may seem a bit Machiavellian to you. However, remember, only one person gets the promotion, and your competition may have a map of his own. As we noted in the early part of the chapter, power and politics are a part of organizational life. To decide not to play is deciding not to be effective. Better to be explicit about it with a political map than to proceed as if power and politics didn't matter.

SUMMARY

An effective manager accepts the political nature of organizations. Some people are significantly more politically astute than others, meaning that they are aware of the underlying politics and can manage impressions. Those who are good at playing politics can be expected to get higher performance evaluations and, hence, larger salary increases and more promotions than the politically naïve or inept. The politically astute are also likely to exhibit higher job satisfaction and be better able to neutralize job stressors.

Few employees relish being powerless in their job and organization. People respond differently to the various power bases. Expert and referent power are derived from an individual's personal qualities. In contrast, coercion, reward, and legitimate power are essentially organizationally derived. Competence especially appears to offer wide appeal, and its use as a power base results in high performance by group members.

IMPLICATIONS FOR MANAGERS

If you want to get things done in a group or an organization, it helps to have power. Here are several suggestions for how to deal with power in your own work life:

- As a manager who wants to maximize your power, you will want to increase others' dependence on you. You can, for instance, increase your power in relation to your boss by developing knowledge or a skill she needs and for which she perceives no ready substitute.
- You will not be alone in attempting to build your power bases. Others, particularly employees and peers, will be seeking to increase your dependence on them, while you are trying to minimize it and increase their dependence on you. The result is a continual battle.
- Try to avoid putting others in a position where they feel they have no power.

- By assessing behavior in a political framework, you can better predict the actions of others and use that information to formulate political strategies that will gain advantages for you and your work unit.
- Consider that employees who have poor political skills or are unwilling to play the politics game generally relate perceived organizational politics to lower job satisfaction and self-reported performance, increased anxiety, and higher turnover. Therefore, if you are adept at organizational politics, help others understand the importance of becoming politically savvy.

PERSONAL INVENTORY ASSESSMENT

In Personal Inventory Assessment found in MyManagementLab take assessment: Gaining Power and Influence

✪ WRITING SPACE

If your professor assigned this, sign in to **mymanagementlab.com** for the following Assisted-graded writing question:

13-1. What do you think are some tasks in an organization that a top executive should never delegate to others, and why?

14

Conflict in Organizations

MyManagementLab®

⭐ Improve Your Grade!

When you see this icon ⭐, visit **www.mymanagementlab.com** for activities that are applied, personalized, and offer immediate feedback.

LEARNING OBJECTIVES

After studying this chapter, you should be able to:

1. Differentiate between the traditional and interactionist views of conflict.
2. Describe the three types of conflict and the three loci of conflict.
3. Outline the conflict process.
4. Contrast distributive and integrative bargaining.
5. Apply the five steps of the negotiation process.
6. Show how individual differences influence negotiations.

⭐ Chapter Warm-up

If your professor has chosen to assign this, go to **www.mymanagementlab.com** to see what you should particularly focus on and to take the Chapter 14 warm up.

Conflict and negotiation are often complex—and controversial—interpersonal processes. While we generally see conflict as a negative topic and negotiation as a positive one, what we deem positive or negative depends on our perspective.

Conflict can often turn personal. It can create chaotic conditions that make it nearly impossible for employees to work as a team. However, conflict also has a less well-known positive side. We'll explain the difference between negative and positive conflicts in this chapter and provide a guide to help you understand how conflicts develop. We'll also present a topic closely akin to conflict: negotiation.

A DEFINITION OF CONFLICT

Conflict is an inherent part of organizational life. Indeed, some level of conflict is probably necessary for optimal organizational functioning.

There has been no shortage of definitions of *conflict*,[1] but common to most is the idea that conflict is a perception. If no one is aware of a conflict, then it is generally agreed no conflict exists. Also needed to begin the conflict process are opposition or incompatibility, and interaction.

We define **conflict** broadly as a process that begins when one party perceives another party has negatively affected or is about to negatively affect something the first party cares about.[2] Conflict describes the point in ongoing activity when interaction becomes interparty disagreement. People experience a wide range of conflicts in organizations: incompatibility of goals, differences over interpretations of facts, disagreements based on behavioral expectations, and the like. Our definition covers the full range of conflict levels from overt and violent acts to subtle forms of disagreement.

There has been disagreement over the role of conflict in groups and organizations. One school of thought argues that conflict must be avoided—that conflict indicates a malfunction within the group. We call this the *traditional* view. Another perspective proposes not only that conflict can be a positive force in a group but that some conflict is absolutely necessary for a group to perform effectively. We label this the *interactionist* view. Let's take a closer look at each.

The Traditional View of Conflict

The **traditional view of conflict** was consistent with attitudes about group behavior that prevailed in the 1930s and 1940s. Conflict was seen as a dysfunctional outcome resulting from poor communication, a lack of openness and trust between people, and the failure of managers to be responsive to the needs and aspirations of their employees. Conflict was discussed with the terms *violence*, *destruction*, and *irrationality*.

While the idea that all conflict is bad and should be avoided certainly offers a simple approach to looking at the behavior of people who create disagreements, researchers realized that some level of conflict was inevitable. We need merely study the causes of conflict and correct the malfunctions to improve group and organizational performance.

The Interactionist View of Conflict

The **interactionist view of conflict** encourages conflict on the grounds that a harmonious, peaceful, tranquil, and cooperative group is prone to becoming static, apathetic, and unresponsive to needs for change and innovation.[3] The major contribution of this view is recognizing that a minimal level of conflict can help keep a group viable, self-critical, and creative.

The interactionist view does not propose that all conflicts are good. Rather, **functional conflict** supports the goals of the group, improves its performance, and is thus a constructive form of conflict. Conflict that hinders group performance is destructive or **dysfunctional conflict**. What differentiates functional from dysfunctional conflict? To a large degree, this depends on the *type* of conflict and the *locus* of conflict. We will review each of these in turn.

TYPES AND LOCI OF CONFLICT

Types of Conflict

One means of understanding conflict is to identify the *type* of disagreement, or what the conflict is about. Is it a disagreement about goals? Is it about people who just rub one another the wrong way? Or is it about the best way to get things done? Although each conflict is unique, researchers have classified conflicts into three categories: task, relationship, and process. **Task conflict** relates to the content and goals of the work. **Relationship conflict** focuses on interpersonal relationships. **Process conflict** is about how the work gets done.

Studies demonstrate that relationship conflicts, at least in work settings, are almost always dysfunctional.[4] Why? It appears that the friction and interpersonal hostilities inherent in relationship conflicts increase personality clashes and decrease mutual understanding, which hinders the completion of organizational tasks. Of the three types, relationship conflicts also appear to be the most psychologically exhausting to individuals.[5] Because they tend to revolve around personalities, you can see how relationship conflicts can become destructive. After all, we can't expect to change our coworkers' personalities, and we would generally take offense at criticisms directed at who we *are* as opposed to how we behave.

While scholars agree that relationship conflict is dysfunctional, there is considerably less agreement as to whether task and process conflicts are functional. Early research suggested that task conflict within groups was associated with higher group performance, but a recent review of 116 studies found that task conflict was essentially unrelated to group performance. However, there were factors that could create a relationship between conflict and performance.[6]

One such factor was whether the conflict included top management or occurred lower in the organization. Task conflict among top management teams was positively associated with their performance, whereas conflict lower in the organization was negatively associated with group performance. This review also found that it mattered whether other types of conflict were occurring at the same time. If task and relationship conflict occurred together, task conflict was more likely negative, whereas if task conflict occurred by itself, it was more likely positive. Finally, some scholars have argued that the strength of the conflict is important—if task conflict is very low, people aren't really engaged or addressing the important issues. If task conflict is too high, however, infighting will quickly degenerate into relationship conflict. According to this view, moderate levels of task conflict are optimal. Supporting this argument, one study in China found that moderate levels of task conflict in the early development stage increased creativity in groups, but high levels decreased team performance.[7]

Finally, the personalities of the teams appear to matter. A recent study demonstrated that teams made up of individuals who are, on average, high in openness and emotional stability are better able to turn task conflict into increased group performance.[8] The reason may be that open and emotionally stable teams can put task conflict in perspective and focus on how the variance in ideas can help solve the problem, rather than letting it degenerate into relationship conflict.

What about process conflict? Researchers found that process conflict revolves around delegation and roles. Conflicts over delegation often revolve around shirking, and

> Task conflict is more constructive than process or, especially, relationship conflict.

conflicts over roles can leave some group members feeling marginalized. Thus, process conflict often becomes highly personalized and quickly devolves into relationship conflict. It's also true, of course, that arguing about how to do something takes time away from actually doing it. We've all been part of groups in which the arguments and debates about roles and responsibilities seem to go nowhere.

Loci of Conflict

Another way to understand conflict is to consider its *locus*, or where the conflict occurs. Here, too, there are three basic types. **Dyadic conflict** is conflict between two people. **Intragroup conflict** occurs *within* a group or team. **Intergroup conflict** is conflict *between* groups or teams.

Nearly all the literature on task, relationship, and process conflict considers intragroup conflict (within the group). That makes sense given that groups and teams often exist only to perform a particular task. However, it doesn't necessarily tell us about the other loci of conflict. For example, research has found that for intragroup task conflict to influence performance within the team, it is important that the teams have a supportive climate in which mistakes aren't penalized and every team member "[has] the other's back."[9] But is this concept useful for understanding the effects of intergroup conflict for the organization? Think about, say, NFL football. For a team to adapt and improve, perhaps a certain amount of task conflict is good for team performance, especially when the team members support one another. But would we care whether members from one team supported members from another team? Probably not. In fact, if groups are competing with one another so that only one team can "win," intergroup conflict seems almost inevitable. When is that helpful, and when is it a concern?

One study that focused on intergroup conflict found an interplay between an individual's position within a group and the way that individual managed conflict between groups. Group members who were relatively peripheral in their own group were better at resolving conflicts between their group and another one. But this happened only when those peripheral members were still accountable to their group.[10] Thus, being at the core of your work group does not necessarily make you the best person to manage conflict with other groups.

Another intriguing question about loci is whether conflicts interact or buffer one another. Assume, for example, that Dana and Scott are on the same team. What happens if they don't get along interpersonally (dyadic conflict) *and* their team also has high personality conflict? What happens to their team if two other team members, Shawna and Justin, do get along well? It's also possible to ask this question at the intragroup and intergroup level. Intense intergroup conflict can be quite stressful to group members and might well affect the way they interact. One study found, for example, that high levels of conflict between teams caused individuals to focus on complying with norms within their teams.[11]

Thus, understanding functional and dysfunctional conflict requires not only that we identify the type of conflict; we also need to know where it occurs. It's possible that while the concepts of task, relationship, and process conflict are useful in understanding intragroup or even dyadic conflict, they are less useful in explaining the effects of intergroup conflict.

In sum, the traditional view that all conflict should be eliminated is short-sighted. The interactionist view that conflict can stimulate active discussion without spilling over into negative, disruptive emotions is incomplete. Thinking about conflict in terms of type and locus helps us realize that conflict is probably inevitable in most organizations. When conflict does occur, we can seek to manage the variables of the conflict process, discussed next, to make the resolution as productive as possible.

THE CONFLICT PROCESS

The **conflict process** has five stages: potential opposition or incompatibility, cognition and personalization, intentions, behavior, and outcomes (see Exhibit 14-1).

Stage I: Potential Opposition or Incompatibility

The first stage of conflict is the appearance of conditions—causes or sources—that create opportunities for it to arise. These conditions *need not* lead directly to conflict, but one of them is necessary if it is to surface. We group the conditions into three general categories: communication, structure, and personal variables.

COMMUNICATION   Communication can be a source of conflict[12] arising from semantic difficulties, misunderstandings, and "noise" in the communication channel (Chapter 9). These factors, along with jargon and insufficient information, can be barriers to communication and potential antecedent conditions to conflict. The potential for conflict has also been found to increase with too little or *too much* communication. Communication is functional up to a point, after which it is possible to overcommunicate, increasing the potential for conflict.

STRUCTURE   The term *structure* in this context includes variables such as size of group, degree of specialization in tasks assigned to group members, jurisdictional clarity, member–goal compatibility, leadership styles, reward systems, and degree of dependence between groups. The larger the group and the more specialized its activities, the greater the likelihood for conflict. Tenure and conflict are inversely related; potential for conflict is greatest when group members are younger and when turnover is high. The greater the ambiguity about where responsibility for actions lies, the greater the potential for conflict. Jurisdictional ambiguities increase fighting for control of resources and territory. Diversity of goals among groups is also a major source of conflict. Reward systems, too, create conflict when one member's gain comes at another's expense. Finally, if a group is dependent on another group (in contrast to the two being mutually independent), or if interdependence allows one group to gain at another's expense, opposing forces are stimulated.

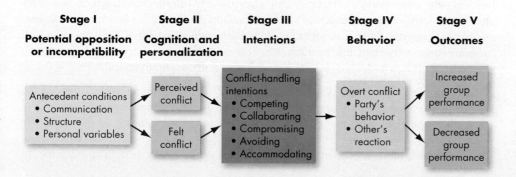

EXHIBIT 14-1
The Conflict Process

PERSONAL VARIABLES   Our last category of potential sources of conflict is personal variables, which include personality, emotions, and values. People high in the personality traits of disagreeableness, neuroticism, or self-monitoring are prone to tangle with other people more often—and to react poorly when conflicts occur.[13] Emotions can also cause conflict even when they are not directed at others. An employee who shows up to work irate from her hectic morning commute may carry that anger into her workday and create a tension-filled meeting.[14] People are furthermore more likely to cause conflict when their values are opposed.

Stage II: Cognition and Personalization

If the conditions cited in Stage I negatively affect something one party cares about, then the potential for opposition or incompatibility becomes actualized in the second stage.

As we noted in our definition of conflict, one or more of the parties must be aware that antecedent conditions exist. However, because a disagreement is a **perceived conflict** does not mean it is personalized. In other words, "*A* may be aware that *B* and *A* are in serious disagreement . . . but it may not make *A* tense or anxious, and it may have no effect whatsoever on *A*'s affection toward *B*."[15] It is at the **felt conflict** level, when individuals become emotionally involved, that they experience anxiety, tension, frustration, or hostility.

Keep in mind two points. First, Stage II is important because it's where conflict issues tend to be defined, where the parties decide what the conflict is about.[16] The definition of conflict is important because it delineates the set of possible settlements.

Second, emotions play a major role in shaping perceptions.[17] Negative emotions allow us to oversimplify issues, lose trust, and put negative interpretations on the other party's behavior.[18] In contrast, positive feelings increase our tendency to see potential relationships among elements of a problem, take a broader view of the situation, and develop innovative solutions.[19]

Stage III: Intentions

Intentions intervene between people's perceptions and emotions, and their overt behavior. They are decisions to act in a given way.[20]

Intentions are a distinct stage because we have to infer the other's intent to know how to respond to this behavior. Many conflicts escalate simply because one party attributes the wrong intentions to the other. There is slippage between intentions and behavior, so behavior does not always accurately reflect a person's intentions.

Using two dimensions—*cooperativeness* (the degree to which one party attempts to satisfy the other party's concerns) and *assertiveness* (the degree to which one party attempts to satisfy her own concerns)—we can identify five conflict-handling intentions: *competing* (assertive and uncooperative), *collaborating* (assertive and cooperative), *avoiding* (unassertive and uncooperative), *accommodating* (unassertive and cooperative), and *compromising* (midrange on both assertiveness and cooperativeness).[21]

1. *Competing.* When one person seeks to satisfy his own interests regardless of the impact on the other parties to the conflict, that person is **competing**. You compete when you place a bet that only one person can win, for example.
2. *Collaborating.* When parties in conflict each desire to fully satisfy the concerns of all parties, there is cooperation and a search for a mutually beneficial outcome. In

collaborating, parties intend to solve a problem by clarifying differences rather than by accommodating various points of view. If you attempt to find a win–win solution that allows both parties' goals to be completely achieved, that's collaborating.

3. *Avoiding.* A person may recognize a conflict exists and want to withdraw from or suppress it. Examples of **avoiding** include trying to ignore a conflict and avoiding others with whom you disagree.

4. *Accommodating.* A party who seeks to appease an opponent may be willing to place the opponent's interests above his own, sacrificing to maintain the relationship. We refer to this intention as **accommodating**. Supporting someone else's opinion despite your reservations about it, for example, is accommodating.

5. *Compromising.* In **compromising**, there is no winner or loser. Rather, there is a willingness to ration the object of the conflict and accept a solution with incomplete satisfaction of both parties' concerns. The distinguishing characteristic of compromising, therefore, is that each party intends to give up something.

Intentions are not always fixed. During the course of a conflict, intentions might change if the parties are able to see the other's point of view or to respond emotionally to the other's behavior. People generally have preferences among the five conflict-handling intentions. We can predict a person's intentions rather well from a combination of intellectual and personality characteristics.

Stage IV: Behavior

When most people think of conflict, they tend to focus on Stage IV because this is where conflicts become visible. The behavior stage includes statements, actions, and reactions made by conflicting parties, usually as overt attempts to implement their own intentions. As a result of miscalculations or unskilled enactments, overt behaviors sometimes deviate from original intentions.[22]

Stage IV is a dynamic process of interaction. For example, you make a demand on me, I respond by arguing, you threaten me, I threaten you back, and so on. Exhibit 14-2 provides a way of visualizing conflict behavior. All conflicts exist somewhere along this

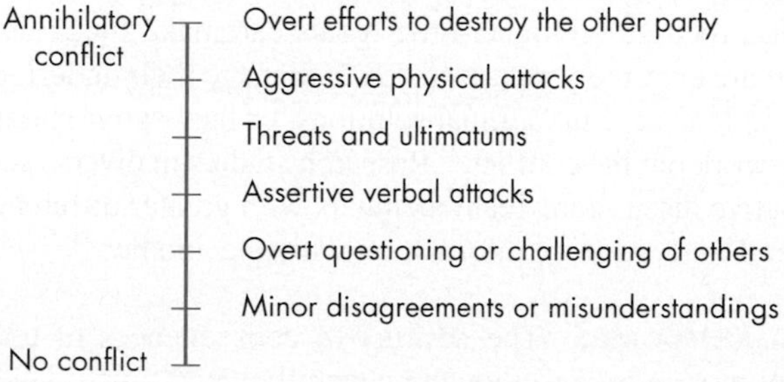

Annihilatory conflict — Overt efforts to destroy the other party

Aggressive physical attacks

Threats and ultimatums

Assertive verbal attacks

Overt questioning or challenging of others

Minor disagreements or misunderstandings

No conflict

EXHIBIT 14-2
Conflict-Intensity Continuum

Sources: Based on S. P. Robbins, *Managing Organizational Conflict: A Nontraditional Approach* (Upper Saddle River, NJ: Prentice Hall, 1974), pp. 93–97; and F. Glasi, "The Process of Conflict Escalation and the Roles of Third Parties," in G. B. J. Bomers and R. Peterson (eds.), *Conflict Management and Industrial Relations* (Boston: Kluwer-Nijhoff, 1982), pp. 119–140.

continuum. At the lower end are conflicts characterized by subtle, indirect, and highly controlled forms of tension, such as a student questioning in class a point the instructor has just made. Conflict intensities escalate as they move upward along the continuum until they become highly destructive. Strikes, riots, and wars clearly fall in this upper range. Conflicts that reach the upper ranges of the continuum are almost always dysfunctional. Functional conflicts are typically confined to the lower range of the continuum.

If a conflict is dysfunctional, what can the parties do to de-escalate it? Or, conversely, what options exist if conflict is too low and needs to be increased? This brings us to techniques of **conflict management**. We have already described several techniques as part of conflict-handling intentions. Under ideal conditions, a person's intentions should translate into comparable behaviors.

Stage V: Outcomes

The action–reaction interplay between conflicting parties creates consequences. As our model demonstrates (see Exhibit 14-1), these outcomes may be functional, if the conflict improves the group's performance, or dysfunctional, if it hinders performance.

FUNCTIONAL OUTCOMES How might conflict act as a force to increase group performance? It is hard to visualize a situation in which open or violent aggression could be functional. But it's possible to see how low or moderate levels of conflict could improve group effectiveness. Note that all our examples focus on task and process conflicts and exclude the relationship variety.

Conflict is constructive when it improves the quality of decisions, stimulates creativity and innovation, encourages interest and curiosity among group members, provides the medium for problems to be aired and tensions released, and fosters self-evaluation and change.

Conflict is an antidote for groupthink (see Chapter 11). Conflict doesn't allow the group to passively rubber-stamp decisions that may be based on weak assumptions, inadequate consideration of relevant alternatives, or other debilities. Conflict challenges the status quo and furthers the creation of new ideas, promotes reassessment of group goals and activities, and increases the probability that the group will respond to change. An open discussion focused on higher-order goals can make functional outcomes more likely. Groups that are extremely polarized do not manage their underlying disagreements effectively and tend to accept suboptimal solutions, or they avoid making decisions altogether rather than work out the conflict.[23] Research studies in diverse settings confirm the functionality of active discussion. Team members with greater differences in work styles and experience tend to share more information with one another.[24]

DYSFUNCTIONAL OUTCOMES The destructive consequences of conflict on the performance of a group or an organization are generally well known: Uncontrolled opposition breeds discontent, which acts to dissolve common ties and eventually leads to the destruction of the group. And, of course, a substantial body of literature documents how dysfunctional conflicts can reduce group effectiveness.[25] Among the undesirable consequences are poor communication, reductions in group cohesiveness, and subordination of group goals to the primacy of infighting among members. All forms of conflict—even the functional varieties—appear to reduce group member satisfaction and trust.[26] When active discussions turn into open conflicts between members, information sharing between members decreases significantly.[27] At the extreme, conflict can bring group functioning to a halt and threaten the group's survival.

MANAGING FUNCTIONAL CONFLICT If managers recognize that in some situations conflict can be beneficial, what can they do to manage conflict effectively in their organizations? Let's look at some approaches organizations are using to encourage their people to challenge the system and develop fresh ideas.

One of the keys to minimizing counterproductive conflict is recognizing when there really is a disagreement. Many apparent conflicts are due to people using a different language to discuss the same general course of action. For example, someone in marketing might focus on "distribution problems," while someone from operations will talk about "supply chain management" to describe essentially the same issue. Successful conflict management recognizes these different approaches and attempts to resolve them by encouraging open, frank discussion focused on interests rather than issues (we'll have more to say about this when we contrast distributive and integrative bargaining styles later in the chapter). Another approach is to have opposing groups pick the issues that are most important to them and then focus on how each side can get its top needs satisfied. Neither side may get exactly what it wants, but each side will get the most important parts of its agenda.[28]

Groups that resolve conflicts successfully discuss differences of opinion openly and are prepared to manage conflict when it arises.[29] The most disruptive conflicts are those that are never addressed directly. An open discussion makes it much easier to develop a shared perception of the problems at hand; it also allows groups to work toward a mutually acceptable solution. Managers need to emphasize shared interests in resolving conflicts, so groups that disagree with one another don't become too entrenched in their points of view and start to take the conflicts personally. Groups with cooperative conflict styles and a strong underlying identification to the overall group goals are more effective than groups with a competitive style.[30]

Differences across countries in conflict resolution strategies may be based on collectivistic tendencies and motives.[31] Collectivist cultures see people as deeply embedded in social situations, whereas individualist cultures see them as autonomous. As a result, collectivists are more likely to seek to preserve relationships and promote the good of the group as a whole. They will avoid the direct expression of conflicts, preferring indirect methods for resolving differences of opinion. Collectivists may also be more interested in demonstrations of concern and working through third parties to resolve disputes, whereas individualists will be more likely to confront differences of opinion directly and openly.

Some research supports this theory. Compared to collectivist Japanese negotiators, their more individualist U.S. counterparts are more likely to see offers from their counterparts as unfair and to reject them. Another study revealed that whereas U.S. managers were more likely to use competing tactics in the face of conflict, compromise and avoidance are the most preferred methods of conflict management in China.[32] Interview data, however, suggest that top management teams in Chinese high-technology firms prefer collaboration even more than compromising and avoiding.[33]

Having considered conflict—its nature, causes, and consequences—we now turn to negotiation, which often resolves conflict.

☆ WATCH IT

If your professor assigned this, sign in to **mymanagementlab.com** to watch a video titled Gordon Law Group: Conflict and Negotiation to learn more about this topic and respond to questions.

NEGOTIATION

The most effective negotiators utilize different tactics for distributive and integrative bargaining; the chapter provides clear ways for you to improve each type of bargaining.

Negotiation permeates the interactions of almost everyone in groups and organizations. There's the obvious: Labor bargains with management. There's the not-so-obvious: Managers negotiate with employees, peers, and bosses; salespeople negotiate with customers; purchasing agents negotiate with suppliers. And there's the subtle: An employee agrees to cover for a colleague for a few minutes in exchange for future benefit. In today's loosely structured organizations, in which members work with colleagues over whom they have no direct authority and with whom they may not even share a common boss, negotiation skills are critical.

We can define **negotiation** as a process that occurs when two or more parties decide how to allocate scarce resources.[34] Although we commonly think of the outcomes of negotiation in one-shot economic terms, like negotiating over the price of a car, every negotiation in organizations also affects the relationship between negotiators and the way negotiators feel about themselves.[35] Depending on how much the parties are going to interact with one another, sometimes maintaining the social relationship and behaving ethically will be just as important as achieving an immediate outcome of bargaining. Note that we use the terms *negotiation* and *bargaining* interchangeably. Next, we contrast two bargaining strategies, provide a model of the negotiation process, and ascertain the role of individual differences in negotiation effectiveness.

Bargaining Strategies

There are two general approaches to negotiation—*distributive bargaining* and *integrative bargaining*.[36] As Exhibit 14-3 shows, the approaches differ in their goal and motivation, focus, interests, information sharing, and duration of relationship. Let's define each and illustrate the differences.

DISTRIBUTIVE BARGAINING   You see a used car advertised for sale online that looks great. You go see the car. It's perfect, and you want it. The owner tells you the asking price. You don't want to pay that much. The two of you negotiate. The negotiating strategy you're engaging in is called **distributive bargaining**. Its identifying feature is that it operates under zero-sum conditions—that is, any gain I make is at your expense, and vice versa. Every dollar you can get the seller to cut from the car's price is a dollar you save, and every dollar the seller can get from you comes at your expense. The essence of distributive bargaining is negotiating over who gets what share of a fixed pie. By **fixed pie**, we mean a set amount of goods or services to be divvied up. When the pie is fixed, or the parties believe it is, they tend to bargain distributively.

The most widely cited example of distributive bargaining may be labor–management negotiations over wages. Typically, labor's representatives come to the bargaining table determined to get as much money as possible from management. Because every cent labor negotiates increases management's costs, each party bargains aggressively and treats the other as an opponent to defeat.

EXHIBIT 14-3
Distributive Versus Integrative Bargaining

Bargaining Characteristic	Distributive Bargaining	Integrative Bargaining
Goal	Get as much of the pie as possible	Expand the pie so that both parties are satisfied
Motivation	Win–lose	Win–win
Focus	Positions ("I can't go beyond this point on this issue.")	Interests ("Can you explain why this issue is so important to you?")
Interests	Opposed	Congruent
Information sharing	Low (Sharing information will only allow other party to take advantage)	High (Sharing information will allow each party to find ways to satisfy interests of each party)
Duration of relationship	Short term	Long term

The essence of distributive bargaining is depicted in Exhibit 14-4. Parties *A* and *B* represent two negotiators. Each has a *target point* that defines what she would like to achieve. Each also has a *resistance point*, which marks the lowest acceptable outcome—the point below which the party would break off negotiations rather than accept a less favorable settlement. The area between these two points makes up each party's aspiration range. As long as there is some overlap between *A*'s and *B*'s aspiration ranges, there exists a settlement range in which each one's aspirations can be met.

When you are engaged in distributive bargaining, one of the best things you can do is make the first offer, and make it an aggressive one. Making the first offer shows power; individuals in power are much more likely to make initial offers, speak first at meetings, and thereby gain the advantage. Another reason this is a good strategy is the anchoring bias, mentioned in Chapter 6. People tend to fixate on initial information. Once that anchoring point is set, they fail to adequately adjust it based on subsequent information. A savvy negotiator sets an anchor with the initial offer, and scores of negotiation studies show that such anchors greatly favor the person who sets them.[37]

INTEGRATIVE BARGAINING   Jake was a Chicago luxury boutique owned by Jim Wetzel and Lance Lawson. In the early days of the business, Wetzel and Lawson moved millions of dollars of merchandise from many up-and-coming designers. They developed such a good rapport that many designers would send allotments to Jake without requiring

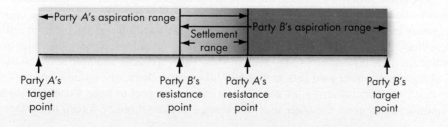

EXHIBIT 14-4
Staking Out the Bargaining Zone

advance payment. When the economy soured in 2008, Jake had trouble selling inventory, and designers were not being paid for what they had shipped to the store. Despite the fact that many designers were willing to work with the store on a delayed payment plan, Wetzel and Lawson stopped returning their calls. Lamented one designer, Doo-Ri Chung, "You kind of feel this familiarity with people who supported you for so long. When they have cash-flow issues, you want to make sure you are there for them as well."[38] Chung's attitude shows the promise of **integrative bargaining**. In contrast to distributive bargaining, integrative bargaining assumes that one or more of the possible settlements can create a win–win solution. Of course, as the boutique example shows and we'll highlight later, both parties must be engaged for integrative bargaining to work.

In terms of intraorganizational behavior, integrative bargaining is preferable to distributive bargaining because the former builds long-term relationships. Integrative bargaining bonds negotiators and allows them to leave the bargaining table feeling that they have achieved a victory. Distributive bargaining, however, leaves one party a loser. It tends to build animosity and deepen divisions when people have to work together on an ongoing basis. Research shows that over repeated bargaining episodes, a losing party who feels positive about the negotiation outcome is much more likely to bargain cooperatively in subsequent negotiations. This points to an important advantage of integrative negotiations: Even when you win, you want your opponent to feel good about the negotiation.[39]

Why, then, don't we see more integrative bargaining in organizations? The answer lies in the conditions necessary for it to succeed. These include opposing parties who are open with information and candid about concerns, are sensitive to the other's needs, and maintain flexibility.[40] Because these conditions seldom exist in organizations, negotiations often take on a win-at-any-cost dynamic.

Individuals who bargain in teams reach more integrative agreements than those who bargain individually because more ideas are generated when more people are at the bargaining table.[41] Another way to achieve higher joint-gain settlements is to put more issues on the table. The more negotiable issues introduced into a negotiation, the more opportunity for "logrolling," where issues are traded off according to individual preferences. This creates better outcomes for each side than if they negotiated each issue individually.[42] Focus also on the underlying interests of both sides rather than on issues. In other words, it is better to concentrate on *why* an employee wants a raise rather than to focus just on the raise amount—some unseen potential for integrative outcomes may arise if both sides concentrate on what they really want rather than on specific items they're bargaining over. Typically, it's easier to concentrate on underlying interests when parties stay focused on broad, overall goals rather than on immediate outcomes of a specific decision.[43] Negotiations when both parties are focused on learning and understanding the other side tend to yield higher joint outcomes than those in which parties are more interested in their individual bottom-line outcomes.[44]

Compromise may be your worst enemy in negotiating a win–win agreement. Compromising reduces the pressure to bargain integratively. After all, if you or your opponent caves in easily, no one needs to be creative to reach a settlement. People then settle for less than they could have obtained if they had been forced to consider the other party's interests, trade off issues, and be creative.[45] Consider a classic example in which two sisters are arguing over who gets an orange. Unknown to them, one sister wants the orange to drink the juice, whereas the other wants the orange peel to bake a cake. If one sister capitulates and gives the other sister the orange, they will not be forced to explore their reasons for wanting the orange, and thus they will never find the win–win solution: They could *each* have the orange because they want different parts!

THE NEGOTIATION PROCESS

Exhibit 14-5 provides a simplified model of the negotiation process. It views negotiation as made up of five steps: (1) preparation and planning, (2) definition of ground rules, (3) clarification and justification, (4) bargaining and problem solving, and (5) closure and implementation.[46]

Steps in the Negotiation Process

PREPARATION AND PLANNING   Before you start negotiating, do your homework. What's the nature of the conflict? What's the history leading up to this negotiation? Who's involved and what are their perceptions of the conflict? What do you want from the negotiation? What are *your* goals? If you're a supply manager at Dell Computer, for instance, and your goal is to get a significant cost reduction from your supplier of keyboards, make sure this goal stays paramount in discussions and doesn't get overshadowed by other issues. It helps to put your goals in writing and develop a range of outcomes—from "most hopeful" to "minimally acceptable"—to keep your attention focused.

You should assess what you think are the other party's goals. What are they likely to ask? How entrenched is their position likely to be? What intangible or hidden interests may be important to them? On what might they be willing to settle? When you can anticipate your opponent's position, you are better equipped to counter arguments with facts and figures that support your position.

Relationships change as a result of negotiation, so take that into consideration. If you could "win" a negotiation but push the other side into resentment or animosity, it might be wiser to pursue a more compromising style. If preserving the relationship will make you seem easily exploited, you may consider a more aggressive style. As an

EXHIBIT 14-5
The Negotiation

example of how the tone of a relationship set in negotiations matters, people who feel good about the *process* of a job offer negotiation are more satisfied with their jobs and less likely to turn over a year later regardless of their actual *outcomes* from these negotiations.[47]

Once you've gathered your information, develop a strategy. For example, expert chess players know how they will respond to any given situation. You should determine your and the other side's **b**est **a**lternative **t**o a **n**egotiated **a**greement, or **BATNA**.[48] Your BATNA determines the lowest value acceptable to you for a negotiated agreement. Any offer you receive that is higher than your BATNA is better than an impasse. Conversely, you shouldn't expect success in your negotiation effort unless you're able to make the other side an offer it finds more attractive than its BATNA. If you go into your negotiation having a good idea of what the other party's BATNA is, you might be able to elicit a change even if you're not able to meet it. Think carefully about what the other side is willing to give up. People who underestimate their opponent's willingness to give on key issues before the negotiation even starts end up with lower outcomes from a negotiation.[49]

DEFINITION OF GROUND RULES   Once you've done your planning and developed a strategy, you're ready to begin defining with the other party the ground rules and procedures of the negotiation itself. Who will do the negotiating? Where will it take place? What time constraints, if any, will apply? To what issues will negotiation be limited? Will you follow a specific procedure if an impasse is reached? During this phase, the parties will also exchange their initial proposals or demands.

CLARIFICATION AND JUSTIFICATION   When you have exchanged initial positions, you and the other party will explain, amplify, clarify, bolster, and justify your original demands. This step needn't be confrontational. Rather, it's an opportunity for educating each other on the issues, why they are important, and how you arrived at your initial demands. Provide the other party with any documentation that supports your position.

BARGAINING AND PROBLEM SOLVING   The essence of the negotiation process is the actual give-and-take in trying to hash out an agreement. This is where both parties need to make concessions.

CLOSURE AND IMPLEMENTATION   The final step in the negotiation process is formalizing your agreement and developing procedures necessary for implementing and monitoring it. For major negotiations—from labor–management negotiations to bargaining over lease terms—this requires hammering out the specifics in a formal contract. For other cases, closure of the negotiation process is nothing more formal than a handshake.

In negotiations, individual differences do matter. Differences in personalities, moods and emotions, culture, and gender influence our negotiation effectiveness.

INDIVIDUAL DIFFERENCES IN NEGOTIATION EFFECTIVENESS

Are some people better negotiators than others? The answer is complex. Four factors influence how effectively individuals negotiate: personality, moods/emotions, culture, and gender.

Personality Traits in Negotiation

Can you predict an opponent's negotiating tactics if you know something about his personality? Because personality and negotiation outcomes are related but only weakly, the answer is, at best, "sort of." Most research has focused on the Big Five trait of agreeableness, for obvious reasons—agreeable individuals are cooperative, compliant, kind, and conflict-averse. We might think such characteristics make agreeable individuals easy prey in negotiations, especially distributive ones. The evidence suggests, however, that overall agreeableness is weakly related to negotiation outcomes. Why is this the case?

It appears that the degree to which agreeableness, and personality more generally, affects negotiation outcomes depends on the situation. The importance of being extraverted in negotiations, for example, will depend very much on how the other party reacts to someone who is assertive and enthusiastic. One complicating factor for agreeableness is that it has two facets: The tendency to be cooperative and compliant is one, but so is the tendency to be warm and empathetic.[50] It may be that while the former is a hindrance to negotiating favorable outcomes, the latter helps. Empathy, after all, is the ability to take the perspective of another person and to gain insight/understanding of them. We know so-called perspective-taking benefits integrative negotiations, so perhaps the null effect for agreeableness is due to the two tendencies pulling against one another.

Moods/Emotions in Negotiation

Do moods and emotions influence negotiation? They do, but the way they work depends on the emotion as well as the context. A negotiator who shows anger generally induces concessions, for instance, because the other negotiator believes no further concessions from the angry party are possible. One factor that governs this outcome, however, is power—you should show anger in negotiations only if you have at least as much power as your counterpart. If you have less, showing anger actually seems to provoke "hardball" reactions from the other side.[51] Another factor is how genuine your anger is—"faked" anger, or anger produced from so-called surface acting (see Chapter 4), is not effective, but showing anger that is genuine (so-called deep acting) does.[52] It also appears that having a history of showing anger, rather than sowing the seeds of revenge, actually induces more concessions because the other party perceives the negotiator as "tough."[53] Finally, culture seems to matter. For instance, one study found that when East Asian participants showed anger, it induced more concessions than when the negotiator expressing anger was from the United States or Europe, perhaps because of the stereotype of East Asians as refusing to show anger.[54]

Another relevant emotion is disappointment. Generally, a negotiator who perceives disappointment from her counterpart concedes more because disappointment makes many negotiators feel guilty. In one study, Dutch students were given 100 chips to bargain over. Negotiators who expressed disappointment were offered 14 more chips than those who didn't. In a second study, showing disappointment yielded an average concession of 12 chips. Unlike a show of anger, the relative power of the negotiators made no difference in either study.[55]

Anxiety also appears to have an impact on negotiation. For example, one study found that individuals who experienced more anxiety about a negotiation used more deceptions in dealing with others.[56] Another study found that anxious negotiators expect lower outcomes, respond to offers more quickly, and exit the bargaining process more quickly, leading them to obtain worse outcomes.[57]

As you can see, emotions—especially negative ones—matter to negotiation. Even emotional unpredictability affects outcomes; researchers have found that negotiators who express positive and negative emotions in an unpredictable way extract more concessions because it makes the other party feel less in control.[58] As one negotiator put it, "Out of the blue, you may have to react to something you have been working on in one way, and then something entirely new is introduced, and you have to veer off and refocus."[59]

Culture in Negotiations

Do people from different cultures negotiate differently? The simple answer is the obvious one: Yes, they do. However, there are many nuances in the way this works. It isn't as simple as "U.S. negotiators are the best"; indeed, success in negotiations depends on the context.

So what can we say about culture and negotiations? First, it appears that people generally negotiate more effectively within cultures than between them. For example, a Colombian is apt to do better negotiating with a Colombian than with a Sri Lankan. Second, it appears that in cross-cultural negotiations, it is especially important that the negotiators be high in openness. This suggests choosing cross-cultural negotiators who are high on openness to experience, but also avoiding factors—such as time pressures—that tend to inhibit learning to understand the other party.[60]

Finally, because emotions are culturally sensitive, negotiators need to be especially aware of the emotional dynamics in cross-cultural negotiation. One study, for example, explicitly compared how U.S. and Chinese negotiators reacted to an angry counterpart. Chinese negotiators increased their use of distributive negotiating tactics, whereas U.S. negotiators decreased their use of these tactics. That is, Chinese negotiators began to drive a harder bargain once they saw that their negotiation partner was becoming angry, whereas U.S. negotiators actually capitulated somewhat in the face of angry demands. Why the difference? It may be that individuals from East Asian cultures feel that using anger to get their way in a negotiation is not a legitimate tactic, so they respond by refusing to cooperate when their opponents become upset.[61]

Gender Differences in Negotiations

There are many areas of organizational behavior in which men and women are not that different. Negotiation is not one of them. It seems fairly clear that men and women negotiate differently, and these differences affect outcomes.

A popular stereotype is that women are more cooperative and pleasant in negotiations than are men. Though this is controversial, there is some merit to it. Men tend to place a higher value on status, power, and recognition, whereas women tend to place a higher value on compassion and altruism. Moreover, women tend to value relationship outcomes more than men, and men tend to value economic outcomes more than women.[62]

These differences affect both negotiation behavior and negotiation outcomes. Compared to men, women tend to behave in a less assertive, less self-interested, and more accommodating manner. As one review concluded, women "are more reluctant to initiate negotiations, and when they do initiate negotiations, they ask for less, are more willing to accept [the] offer, and make more generous offers to their negotiation partners than men do."[63] A study of MBA students at Carnegie-Mellon University found that male MBA students took the step of negotiating their first offer 57 percent of the time, compared to 4 percent for female MBA students. The net result? A $4,000 difference in starting salaries.[64]

Evidence suggests women's own attitudes and behaviors hurt them in negotiations. Managerial women demonstrate less confidence than men in anticipation of negotiating and are less satisfied with their performance afterward, even when their performance and the outcomes they achieve are similar to those for men.[65] Women are also less likely than men to see an ambiguous situation as an opportunity for negotiation. Women may unduly penalize themselves by failing to engage in negotiations that would be in their best interests. Some research suggests that women are less aggressive in negotiations because they are worried about backlash from others. There is an interesting qualifier to this result: Women are more likely to engage in assertive negotiations when they are bargaining on behalf of someone else than when they are bargaining on their own behalf.[66]

SUMMARY

While many people assume conflict lowers group and organizational performance, this assumption is frequently incorrect. Conflict can be either constructive or destructive to the functioning of a group or unit. As shown in Exhibit 14-6, levels of conflict can be either too high or too low to be constructive. Either extreme hinders performance. An optimal level is one that prevents stagnation, stimulates creativity, allows tensions to be released, and initiates the seeds of change without being disruptive or preventing coordination of activities. Negotiation often resolves conflict, particularly if the negotiators seek integrative solutions and constructively work through the negotiation process. Negotiations can be further improved when the parties take their individual differences into account.

IMPLICATIONS FOR MANAGERS

- Choose an authoritarian management style in emergencies, when unpopular actions need to be implemented (such as cost cutting, enforcement of unpopular rules, discipline), and when the issue is vital to the organization's welfare. Be certain to communicate your logic to ensure that employees remain engaged and productive.
- Seek integrative solutions when your objective is to learn, when you want to merge insights from people with different perspectives, when you need to gain commitment by incorporating concerns into a consensus, and when you need to work through feelings that have interfered with a relationship.
- You can build trust by accommodating others when you find you're wrong, when you need to demonstrate reasonableness, when other positions need to be heard, when issues are more important to others than to yourself, when you want to satisfy others and maintain cooperation, when you can build social credits for later issues, to minimize loss when you are outmatched and losing, and when employees should learn from their own mistakes.
- Consider compromising when goals are important but not worth potential disruption, when opponents with equal power are committed to mutually exclusive goals, and when you need temporary settlements to complex issues.
- Make sure you set aggressive negotiating goals and try to find creative ways to achieve the objectives of both parties, especially when you value the long-term relationship with the other party. That doesn't mean sacrificing your self-interest; rather, it means trying to find creative solutions that give both parties what they really want.

**EXHIBIT 14-6
Conflict and Unit
Performance**

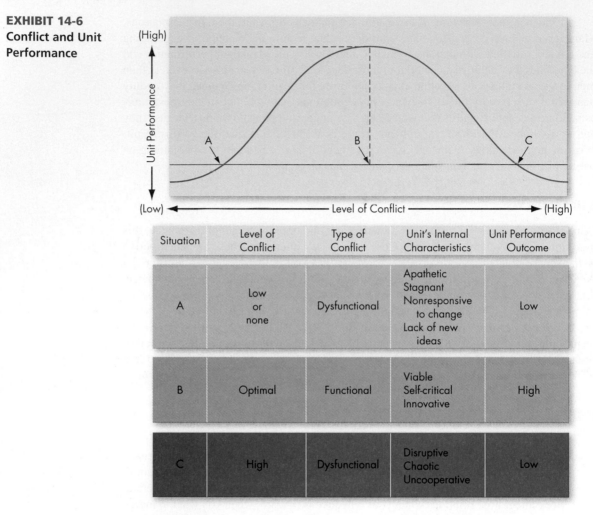

Situation	Level of Conflict	Type of Conflict	Unit's Internal Characteristics	Unit Performance Outcome
A	Low or none	Dysfunctional	Apathetic Stagnant Nonresponsive to change Lack of new ideas	Low
B	Optimal	Functional	Viable Self-critical Innovative	High
C	High	Dysfunctional	Disruptive Chaotic Uncooperative	Low

PERSONAL INVENTORY ASSESSMENT

In Personal Inventory Assessment found in MyManagementLab take assessment:
Strategies for Handling Conflict

⭐ WRITING SPACE

If your professor assigned this, sign in to **mymanagementlab.com** for the following Assisted-graded writing question:

14-1. If you were advising union and management representatives about how to negotiate an agreement, drawing from the concepts in this chapter, what would you tell them?

15
Organization Design

MyManagementLab®

✪ Improve Your Grade!

When you see this icon ✪, visit **www.mymanagementlab.com** for activities that are applied, personalized, and offer immediate feedback.

After studying this chapter, you should be able to:

1. Identify the six elements of an organization's structure.
2. Identify the characteristics of the three most common organizational designs.
3. Describe the characteristics of the virtual organization, the boundaryless organization, and leaner organizations.
4. Demonstrate how organizational structures differ, and contrast mechanistic and organic structural models.
5. Analyze the behavioral implications of different organizational designs.

✪ Chapter Warm-up

If your professor has chosen to assign this, go to **www.mymanagementlab.com** to see what you should particularly focus on and to take the Chapter 15 warm up.

Even for a start-up company with only a few employees, organizational structure is far more than simply deciding who's the boss and how many employees will be needed. The organization's structure will determine what relationships form, the formality of those relationships, and many work outcomes. The structure may also change as organizations grow and shrink, as management trends dictate, and as research uncovers better ways of maximizing productivity. In this chapter, we'll explore how structure impacts employee behavior and the organization as a whole.[1]

EXHIBIT 15-1
Key Design Questions and Answers for Designing the Proper Organizational Structure

The Key Question	The Answer Is Provided by
1. To what degree are activities subdivided into separate jobs?	Work specialization
2. On what basis will jobs be grouped together?	Departmentalization
3. To whom do individuals and groups report?	Chain of command
4. How many individuals can a manager efficiently and effectively direct?	Span of control
5. Where does decision-making authority lie?	Centralization and decentralization
6. To what degree will there be rules and regulations to direct employees and managers?	Formalization

WHAT IS ORGANIZATIONAL STRUCTURE?

An **organizational structure** defines how job tasks are formally divided, grouped, and coordinated. Managers need to address six key elements when they design their organization's structure: work specialization, departmentalization, chain of command, span of control, centralization and decentralization, and formalization.[2] Exhibit 15-1 presents each of these elements as an answer to an important structural question, and the following sections describe them.

Work Specialization

Early in the twentieth century, Henry Ford became rich by building automobiles on an assembly line. Every Ford worker was assigned a specific, repetitive task such as putting on the right front wheel or installing the right front door. By dividing jobs into small standardized tasks that could be performed over and over, Ford was able to produce a car every 10 seconds, using employees who had relatively limited skills.

Ford demonstrated that work can be performed more efficiently if employees are allowed to specialize. Today, we use the term **work specialization**, or *division of labor*, to describe the degree to which activities in the organization are divided into separate jobs. The essence of work specialization is to divide a job into a number of steps, each completed by a separate individual. Individuals specialize in doing part of an activity rather than the entirety.

By the late 1940s, most manufacturing jobs in industrialized countries featured high work specialization. Because not all employees in an organization have the same skills, management saw specialization as a means of making the most efficient use of its employees' skills and successfully improving them through repetition. Less time is spent in changing tasks, putting away tools and equipment from a prior step, and getting ready for another. Equally important, it's easier and less costly to find and train workers to do specific and repetitive tasks, especially in highly sophisticated and complex operations. Could Cessna produce one Citation jet a year if one person had to build the entire plane alone? Not likely! Finally, work specialization increases efficiency and productivity by encouraging the creation of customized inventions and machinery.

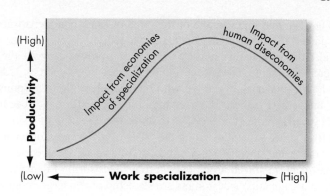

EXHIBIT 15-2
Economies and
Diseconomies
of Work
Specialization

Thus, for much of the first half of the twentieth century, managers viewed work specialization as an unending source of increased productivity. And they were probably right. When specialization was not widely practiced, its introduction almost always generated higher productivity. But by the 1960s, it increasingly seemed a good thing could be carried too far. Human diseconomies from specialization began to surface in the form of boredom, fatigue, stress, low productivity, poor quality, increased absenteeism, and high turnover, which more than offset the economic advantages (see Exhibit 15-2). Managers could increase productivity now by enlarging, rather than narrowing, the scope of job activities. Giving employees a variety of activities to do, allowing them to do a whole and complete job, and putting them into teams with interchangeable skills often achieved significantly higher output, with increased employee satisfaction.

Most managers today recognize the economies specialization provides in certain jobs and the problems when it's carried too far. High work specialization helps McDonald's make and sell hamburgers and fries efficiently and aids medical specialists in most health maintenance organizations. Amazon's Mechanical Turk program, TopCoder, and others like it have facilitated a new trend in microspecialization in which extremely small pieces of programming, data processing, or evaluation tasks are delegated to a global network of individuals by a program manager who then assembles the results.[3] For example, a manager who has a complex but routine computer program to write might send a request for specific subcomponents of the code to be written and tested by dozens of subcontracted individuals in the network (which spans the entire globe), enabling the project to be completed far more quickly than if a single programmer were writing the parts. This emerging trend suggests that there still may be advantages to be had in specialization, particularly for offices where job sharing and part-time work are prevalent.[4]

Departmentalization

Once jobs have been divided through work specialization, they must be grouped so common tasks can be coordinated. The basis by which jobs are grouped is called **departmentalization**.

One of the most popular ways to group activities is by the *functions* performed. A manufacturing manager might organize a plant into engineering, accounting, manufacturing, personnel, and supply specialists departments. A hospital might have departments devoted to research, surgery, intensive care, accounting, and so forth. A professional football franchise might have departments for personnel, ticket sales, and travel and accommodations. The major advantage of this type of functional departmentalization is the efficiency gained from putting like specialists together.

We can also departmentalize jobs by the type of *product* or *service* the organization produces. Procter & Gamble places each major product line—such as Tide, CoverGirl, Charmin, and Iams—under an executive who has complete global responsibility for it. The major advantage here is increased accountability for performance because all activities related to a specific product or service are under the direction of a single manager.

When a firm is departmentalized on the basis of *geography*, or territory, the sales function, for instance, may have western, southern, midwestern, and eastern regions, each in effect a department organized around geography. This form of departmentalization is valuable when an organization's customers are scattered over a large geographic area and have similar needs based on their location. For this reason, Toyota recently changed its management structure into geographic regions "so that they may develop and deliver ever better products," said CEO Akio Toyoda.[5]

Process departmentalization works for processing customers as well as products. If you've ever been to a state motor vehicle office to get a driver's license, you probably went through several departments before receiving your license. In one typical state, applicants go through three steps, each handled by a separate department: (1) validation by the motor vehicles division, (2) processing by the licensing department, and (3) payment collection by the treasury department.

A final category of departmentalization uses the particular *type* of customer the organization seeks to reach. Microsoft, for example, is organized around four customer markets: consumers, large corporations, software developers, and small businesses. Customers from each market have a common set of problems and needs best met by having specialists for each.

Chain of Command

While the chain of command was once a basic cornerstone in the design of organizations, it has far less importance today.[6] But contemporary managers should still consider its implications, particularly for industries that deal with potential life-or-death situations. The **chain of command** is an unbroken line of authority that extends from the top of the organization to the lowest echelon and clarifies who reports to whom.

We can't discuss the chain of command without also discussing *authority* and *unity of command*. **Authority** refers to the rights inherent in a managerial position to give orders and expect them to be obeyed. To facilitate coordination, each managerial position is given a place in the chain of command, and each manager is given a degree of authority in order to meet his responsibilities. The principle of **unity of command** helps preserve the concept of an unbroken line of authority. It says a person should have one and only one superior to whom she is directly responsible. If the unity of command is broken, an employee might have to cope with conflicting demands or priorities from several superiors, as is often the case in organization chart dotted-line reporting relationships.

Times change, and so do the basic tenets of organizational design. A low-level employee today can access information in seconds that was available only to top managers a generation ago, and many employees are empowered to make decisions previously reserved for management. Add the popularity of self-managed and cross-functional teams as well as the creation of new structural designs that include multiple bosses, and you can see why authority and unity of command may appear to hold less relevance. Many organizations do still find they can be most productive by enforcing the chain of command. Indeed, one survey of more than 1,000 managers found that 59 percent of them agreed with the statement, "There is an imaginary line in my company's organizational chart. Strategy is created by people above this line, while strategy is executed by people below the line."[7] However, this same survey found that lower-level employees' buy-in to the organization's strategy was inhibited by their reliance on the hierarchy for decision making.

Span of Control

How many employees can a manager efficiently and effectively direct? This question of **span of control** is important because it largely determines the number of levels and managers an organization creates. All things being equal, the wider or larger the span, the more efficient the organization.

Assume two organizations each have about 4,100 operative-level employees. One has a uniform span of four and the other a span of eight. As Exhibit 15-3 illustrates, the wider span will have two fewer levels and approximately 800 fewer managers. If the average manager makes $50,000 a year, the wider span will save $40 million a year in management salaries! Obviously, wider spans are more efficient in terms of cost. However, at some point when supervisors no longer have time to provide the necessary leadership and support, they reduce effectiveness and employee performance suffers.

Narrow or small spans have their advocates. By keeping the span of control to five or six employees, a manager can maintain close control.[8] But narrow spans have three major drawbacks. First, they're expensive because they add levels of management. Second, they make vertical communication in the organization more complex. The added levels of hierarchy slow down decision making and tend to isolate upper management. Third, narrow spans encourage overly tight supervision and discourage employee autonomy.

The trend in recent years has been toward wider spans of control. They're consistent with firms' efforts to reduce costs, cut overhead, speed decision making, increase flexibility, get closer to customers, and empower employees. However, to ensure performance doesn't suffer because of these wider spans, organizations have been investing

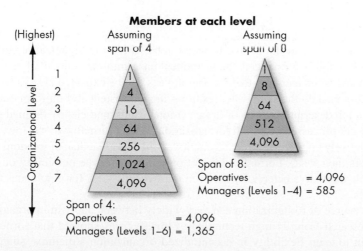

Members at each level

(Highest)

Organizational level

1
2
3
4
5
6
7

Assuming span of 4

1
4
16
64
256
1,024
4,096

Assuming span of 8

1
8
64
512
4,096

Span of 8:
Operatives   = 4,096
Managers (Levels 1–4) = 585

Span of 4:
Operatives   = 4,096
Managers (Levels 1–6) = 1,365

EXHIBIT 15-3
Contrasting
Spans of Control

heavily in employee training. Managers recognize that they can handle a wider span best when employees know their jobs inside and out or can turn to coworkers when they have questions.

Centralization and Decentralization

Centralization refers to the degree to which decision making is concentrated at a single point in the organization. In *centralized* organizations, top managers make all the decisions, and lower-level managers merely carry out their directives. In organizations at the other extreme, *decentralized* decision making is pushed down to the managers closest to the action or even to work groups.

The concept of centralization includes only formal authority—that is, the rights inherent to a position. An organization characterized by centralization is inherently different structurally from one that's decentralized. A decentralized organization can act more quickly to solve problems, more people provide input into decisions, and employees are less likely to feel alienated from those who make decisions that affect their work lives. Recent research indicates that the effects of centralization and decentralization can be predicted: Centralized organizations are better for avoiding commission errors (bad choices), while decentralized organizations are better for avoiding omission errors (lost opportunities).[9]

Management efforts to make organizations more flexible and responsive have produced a recent trend toward decentralized decision making by lower-level managers, who are closer to the action and typically have more detailed knowledge about problems than top managers. Sears and JCPenney have given their store managers considerably more discretion in choosing what merchandise to stock. This allows the stores to compete more effectively against local merchants. Similarly, when Procter & Gamble empowered small groups of employees to make decisions about new-product development independent of the usual hierarchy, it was able to rapidly increase the proportion of new products ready for market.[10] Research investigating a large number of Finnish organizations demonstrated that companies with decentralized research and development offices in multiple locations were better at producing innovation than companies that centralized all research and development in a single office.[11]

Formalization

Formalization refers to the degree to which jobs within the organization are standardized. If a job is highly formalized, the incumbent has a minimal amount of discretion over what to do and when and how to do it. Employees can be expected always to handle the same input in exactly the same way, resulting in a consistent and uniform output. There are explicit job descriptions, lots of organizational rules, and clearly defined procedures covering work processes with high formalization. Where formalization is low, job behaviors are relatively unprogrammed, and employees have a great deal of freedom to exercise discretion in their work. Formalization not only eliminates the possibility of employees engaging in alternative behaviors, but even removes the need for employees to consider alternatives.

The degree of formalization can vary widely between and within organizations. In general, research from 94 high-technology Chinese firms showed that formalization is a detriment to team flexibility in decentralized organization structures, suggesting that formalization does not work as well where duties are inherently interactive, or where there is a need to be flexible and innovative.[12] For example, publishing representatives who call on college professors to inform them of their company's new publications have a great deal of freedom in their jobs. They have only a general sales pitch, which they tailor as needed, and rules and procedures governing their behavior may be little more than the requirement to submit a weekly sales report and suggestions on what to emphasize about forthcoming titles. At the other extreme, clerical and editorial employees in the same publishing houses may need to be at their desks by 8:00 A.M. and follow a set of precise procedures dictated by management. To review, we have discussed in detail each of the six key elements of organizational structure that managers must address for their organizations: work specialization, departmentalization, chain of command, span of control, centralization and decentralization, and formalization. You probably have some personal experience with at least some of the issues and opportunities that arise from the decisions leaders have made in your school or workplace on these factors, but it may not always be easy to discern their intentions. The organizational design, which can be depicted by a drawing of an organizational chart, can help you clarify leadership intentions. We discuss the common organizational designs in the next section.

COMMON ORGANIZATIONAL DESIGNS

We now turn to three of the more common organizational designs: the *simple structure*, the *bureaucracy*, and the *matrix structure*.

The Simple Structure

What do a small retail store, an electronics firm run by a hard-driving entrepreneur, and an airline's "war room" in the midst of a pilot's strike have in common? They probably all use the **simple structure**.

The simple structure has a low degree of departmentalization, wide spans of control, authority centralized in a single person, and little formalization.

We can think of the simple structure in terms of what it is *not* rather than what it is. The simple structure is not elaborate. It has a low degree of departmentalization, wide spans of control, authority centralized in a single person, and little formalization. It is a "flat" organization; it usually has only two or three vertical levels, a loose body of employees, and one individual in whom decision-making authority is centralized. For this reason, the simple structure allows for the fastest possible decision making, which is why this organizational design is appropriate for "war room"–type situations.

Most companies start as a simple structure, and many innovative technology-based firms with short expected lifespans like cell phone app development firms remain compact by design.[13] The simple structure is most widely adopted in small businesses in which the manager and owner are one and the same. Consider a retail men's store owned and managed by Jack Gold. Jack employs five full-time salespeople, a cashier, and extra workers for weekends and holidays, but he "runs the show." Though he is typical for a small business, large companies in times of crisis often simplify their structures as a means of focusing their resources.

The strength of the simple structure lies in its simplicity. It's fast, flexible, inexpensive to operate, and accountability is clear. One major weakness is that it becomes increasingly inadequate as an organization grows because its low formalization and high centralization tend to create information overload at the top. As size increases, decision making typically becomes slower and can eventually come to a standstill as the single executive tries to continue making all the decisions. This proves the undoing of many small businesses. If the structure isn't changed and made more elaborate, the firm often loses momentum and can eventually fail. The simple structure's other weakness is that it's risky—everything depends on one person. One illness can literally destroy the organization's information and decision-making center.

The Bureaucracy

Standardization! That's the key concept that underlies all bureaucracies. Consider the bank where you keep your checking account; the department store where you buy clothes; or the government offices that collect your taxes, enforce health regulations, or provide local fire protection. They all rely on standardized work processes for coordination and control.

The **bureaucracy** is characterized by highly routine operating tasks achieved through specialization, strictly formalized rules and regulations, tasks grouped into functional departments, centralized authority, narrow spans of control, and decision making that follows the chain of command. *Bureaucracy* is a dirty word in many people's minds. However, it does have advantages. Its primary strength is its ability to perform standardized activities in a highly efficient manner. Putting like specialties together in functional departments results in economies of scale, minimum duplication of people and equipment, and employees who can speak "the same language" among their peers. Bureaucracies can get by with less talented—and hence less costly—middle- and lower-level managers because rules and regulations substitute for managerial discretion. Standardized operations and high formalization allow decision making to be centralized. There is little need for innovative and experienced decision makers below the level of senior executives.

Listen in on a dialogue among four executives in one company: "You know, nothing happens in this place until we *produce* something," said the production executive. "Wrong," commented the research and development manager. "Nothing happens until we *design* something!" "What are you talking about?" asked the marketing executive. "Nothing happens here until we *sell* something!" The exasperated accounting manager responded, "It doesn't matter what you produce, design, or sell. No one knows what happens until we *tally up the results!*" This conversation highlights the fact that bureaucratic specialization can create conflicts in which functional-unit goals override the overall goals of the organization.

The other major weakness of a bureaucracy is something we've all witnessed: obsessive concern with following the rules. When cases don't precisely fit the rules, there is no room for modification. The bureaucracy is efficient only as long as employees confront familiar problems with programmed decision rules.

The Matrix Structure

You'll find the **matrix structure** in advertising agencies, aerospace firms, research and development laboratories, construction companies, hospitals, government agencies, universities, management consulting firms, and entertainment companies.[14] It combines two forms of departmentalization: functional and product. Companies that use matrix-like structures include ABB, Boeing, BMW, IBM, and Procter and Gamble.

The strength of functional departmentalization is putting like specialists together, which minimizes the number necessary while allowing the pooling and sharing of specialized resources across products. Its major disadvantage is the difficulty of coordinating the tasks of diverse functional specialists on time and within budget. Product departmentalization has exactly the opposite benefits and disadvantages. It facilitates coordination among specialties to achieve on-time completion and meet budget targets. It provides clear responsibility for all activities related to a product, but with duplication of activities and costs. The matrix attempts to gain the strengths of each while avoiding their weaknesses.

The most obvious structural characteristic of the matrix is that it breaks the unity-of-command concept. Employees in the matrix have two bosses: their functional department managers and their product managers.

Exhibit 15-4 shows the matrix form in a college of business administration. The academic departments of accounting, decision and information systems, marketing, and so forth are functional units. Overlaid on them are specific programs (that is, products). Thus, members in a matrix structure have a dual chain of command: to their functional department and to their product group. A professor of accounting teaching an undergraduate course may report to the director of undergraduate programs as well as to the chairperson of the accounting department.

The strength of the matrix is its ability to facilitate coordination when the organization has a number of complex and interdependent activities. Direct and frequent contact between different specialties in the matrix can let information permeate the organization and more quickly reach the people who need it. The matrix reduces "bureaupathologies"— the dual lines of authority reduce people's tendency to become so busy protecting their little worlds that the organization's goals become secondary.[15] A matrix also achieves economies of scale and facilitates the allocation of specialists by providing both the best resources and an effective way of ensuring their efficient deployment.

The major disadvantages of the matrix lie in the confusion it creates, its tendency to foster power struggles, and the stress it places on individuals.[16] Without the unity-of-command concept, ambiguity about who reports to whom is significantly increased and often leads to conflict. It's not unusual for product managers to fight over getting the best specialists assigned to their products. Bureaucracy reduces the potential for power grabs by defining the rules of the game. When those rules are "up for grabs" in a matrix, power struggles between functional and product managers result. For individuals who desire security and absence of ambiguity, this work climate can be stressful. Reporting to more

Academic Departments / Programs	Undergraduate	Master's	Ph.D.	Research	Executive Development	Community Service
Accounting						
Finance						
Decision and Information Systems						
Management						
Marketing						

EXHIBIT 15-4
Matrix Structure for a College of Business Administration

than one boss introduces role conflict, and unclear expectations introduce role ambiguity. The comfort of bureaucracy's predictability is replaced by insecurity and stress.

Did you recognize any of your organizations as having a simple, bureaucracy, or matrix structure? It wouldn't be surprising if you said no. Increasingly, leaders have been exploring new design options for their organizations, which we will discuss next.

NEW DESIGN OPTIONS

Senior managers in a number of organizations have been developing new structural options with fewer layers of hierarchy and more emphasis on opening the boundaries of the organization.[17] In this section, we describe two such designs: the *virtual organization* and the *boundaryless organization*. We'll also discuss how efforts to reduce bureaucracy and increase strategic focus have made downsizing routine.

The Virtual Organization

Why own when you can rent? This question captures the essence of the **virtual organization** (also sometimes called the *network*, or *modular*, organization), typically a small, core organization that outsources its major business functions.[18] In structural terms, the virtual organization is highly centralized, with little or no departmentalization.

The prototype of the virtual structure is today's movie-making organization. In Hollywood's golden era, movies were made by huge, vertically integrated corporations. Studios such as MGM, Warner Brothers, and 20th Century Fox owned large movie lots and employed thousands of full-time specialists—set designers, camera people, film editors, directors, and even actors. Today, most movies are made by a collection of individuals and small companies who come together and make films project by project.[19] This structural form allows each project to be staffed with the talent best suited to its demands, rather than just with the people employed by the studio. It minimizes bureaucratic overhead because there is no lasting organization to maintain. And it lessens long-term risks and their costs because there *is* no long term—a team is assembled for a finite period and then disbanded.

Philip Rosedale co-founded a virtual company called LoveMachine (now called SendLove) that lets employees send brief electronic messages to one another to acknowledge a job well done; the messages can be then used to facilitate company bonuses. The company has no full-time software development staff—instead, the company outsources assignments to freelancers who submit bids for projects like debugging software or designing new features. Programmers work from around the world, including Russia, India, Australia, and the United States.[20] Similarly, Newman's Own, the food products company founded by actor Paul Newman, sells hundreds of millions of dollars in food every year, yet employs only 32 people.[21] This is possible because it outsources almost everything: manufacturing, procurement, shipping, and quality control.

Exhibit 15-5 shows a virtual organization in which management outsources all the primary functions of the business. The core of the organization is a small group of executives whose job is to oversee directly any activities done in-house and to coordinate relationships with the other organizations that manufacture, distribute, and perform crucial functions for the virtual organization. The dotted lines represent the relationships typically maintained under contracts. In essence, managers in virtual structures spend most of their time coordinating and controlling external relations, typically by way of computer network links.

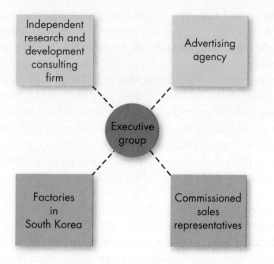

**EXHIBIT 15-5
A Virtual
Organization**

The major advantage of the virtual organization is its flexibility, which allows individuals with an innovative idea and little money to successfully compete against larger, more established organizations. Virtual organizations also save a great deal of money by eliminating permanent offices and hierarchical roles.[22]

Virtual organizations' drawbacks have become increasingly clear as their popularity has grown.[23] They are in a state of perpetual flux and reorganization, which means roles, goals, and responsibilities are unclear, setting the stage for political behavior. Cultural alignment and shared goals can be lost because of the low degree of interaction among members. Team members who are geographically dispersed and communicate infrequently find it difficult to share information and knowledge, which can limit innovation and slow response time. Ironically, some virtual organizations are less adaptable and innovative than those with well-established communication and collaboration networks. A leadership presence that reinforces the organization's purpose and facilitates communication is thus especially valuable.

The Boundaryless Organization

General Electric's former chairman, Jack Welch, coined the term **boundaryless organization** to describe what he wanted GE to become: a "family grocery store."[24] That is, in spite of GE's monstrous size (2013 revenues were $142.5 billion),[25] Welch wanted to eliminate *vertical* and *horizontal* boundaries within the company and break down *external* barriers between the company and its customers and suppliers. The boundaryless organization seeks to eliminate the chain of command, have limitless spans of control, and replace departments with empowered teams. Although GE has not yet achieved this boundaryless state—and probably never will—it has made significant progress toward that end. So have other companies, such as Hewlett-Packard, AT&T, Motorola, and 3M. Let's see what a boundaryless organization looks like and what some firms are doing to make it a reality.

By removing vertical boundaries, management flattens the hierarchy and minimizes status and rank. Cross-hierarchical teams (which include top executives, middle managers, supervisors, and operative employees), participative decision-making practices, and the use of 360-degree performance appraisals (in which peers and others above and below the employee evaluate performance) are examples of what GE does to break down vertical boundaries.

Functional departments create horizontal boundaries that stifle interaction among functions, product lines, and units. The way to reduce them is to replace functional departments with cross-functional teams and organize activities around processes. Xerox develops new products through multidisciplinary teams that work on a single process instead of on narrow functional tasks. Some AT&T units prepare annual budgets based not on functions or departments but on processes, such as the maintenance of a worldwide telecommunications network. Another way to lower horizontal barriers is to rotate people through different functional areas using lateral transfers. This approach turns specialists into generalists.

When fully operational, the boundaryless organization breaks down geographic barriers. Today, most large U.S. companies see themselves as global corporations; many, like Coca-Cola and McDonald's, do as much business overseas as in the United States, and others are working to incorporate new geographic regions into their structure. The boundaryless organization approach is sometimes need-based. Such is the case for Chinese companies, which have made 93 acquisitions in the oil and gas industry since 2008 to meet the forecasted demand their resources in China cannot meet.[26] The boundaryless organization provides one solution because it considers geography more of a tactical, logistical issue than a structural one. In short, the goal is to break down cultural barriers.

One way to do so is through strategic alliances.[27] Firms such as NEC Corporation, Boeing, and Apple have strategic alliances or joint partnerships with dozens of companies. These alliances blur the distinction between one organization and another as employees work on joint projects. Research from 119 international joint ventures (IJVs) in China indicated that the partnerships allowed firms to learn from each other and obtain higher new product performance, especially where a strong learning culture existed.[28] Other companies allow customers to perform functions previously done by management. Some AT&T units receive bonuses based on customer evaluations of the teams that serve them. Finally, telecommuting is blurring organizational boundaries. The security analyst with Merrill Lynch who does her job from her ranch in Montana, or the software designer in Boulder, Colorado who works for a San Francisco firm are just two of the millions of workers operating outside the physical boundaries of their employers' premises.

The Leaner Organization: Downsizing

The goal of the new organizational forms we've described is to improve agility by creating a lean, focused, and flexible organization. *Downsizing* is a systematic effort to make an organization leaner by closing locations, reducing staff, or selling off business units that don't add value.

The radical shrinking of Motorola Mobility in 2012 and 2013 is a case of downsizing to survive after its merger with Google. In response to declining demand for its smartphones, Motorola cut the workforce by 20 percent in August 2012. When the company posted a $350 million fourth-quarter loss for 2012, with a 40 percent revenue decline, it cut the workforce again by 10 percent. Google calls this "rightsizing" and hopes a new Motorola phone will save the company from further layoffs.[29]

Other firms downsize to direct all their efforts toward their core competencies. American Express claims to have been doing this in a series of layoffs over more than a decade: 7,700 jobs in 2001; 6,500 jobs in 2002; 7,000 jobs (10 percent of its workforce) in 2008; and 4,000 jobs in 2009. The 2013 cut of 5,400 jobs (8.5 percent of the remaining workforce) represents "its biggest retrenchment in a decade." Each layoff has been accompanied by a restructuring to reflect changing customer preferences away from personal customer service and toward online customer service. According to CEO Ken Chennault, these "restructuring initiatives" were "designed to make American Express more nimble, more efficient, and more effective in using our resources to drive growth . . . and to maintain marketing and promotion investments."[30]

Some companies focus on lean management techniques as part of downsizing efforts to reduce bureaucracy and speed decision making. Starbucks adopted lean initiatives in 2009, which encompassed all levels of management and also focused on faster barista techniques and manufacturing processes. Customers have generally applauded the shortened wait times and product consistency at this well-run corporation, while the company has capitalized on strategic downsizing opportunities. Starbucks continues to reap returns from its lean initiatives, posting notable revenue gains each quarter.[31]

Despite the advantages of being a lean organization, the impact of downsizing on organizational performance has been a source of controversy.[32] Reducing the size of the workforce has an immediately positive outcome in the form of lower wage costs. Companies downsizing to improve strategic focus often see positive effects on stock prices after the announcement. A recent example of this is Russia's Gorky Automobile Factory (GAZ), which realized a profit for the first time in many years after President Bo Andersson fired 50,000 workers, half the workforce.[33] On the other hand, among companies that only cut employees but don't restructure, profits and stock prices usually decline. Part of the problem is the effect of downsizing on employee attitudes. Employees who remain often feel worried about future layoffs and may be less committed to the organization.[34] Stress reactions can lead to increased sickness absences, lower concentration on the job, and lower creativity. In companies that don't invest much in their employees, downsizing can lead to more voluntary turnover, so vital human capital is lost. The result is a company that is more anemic than lean.

Companies can reduce negative impacts by preparing in advance, thus alleviating some employee stress and strengthening support for the new direction.[35] Here are some effective strategies for downsizing. Most are closely linked to the principles for organizational justice we've discussed previously.

- *Investment.* Companies that downsize to focus on core competencies are more effective when they invest in high-involvement work practices afterward.
- *Communication.* When employers make efforts to discuss downsizing with employees early, employees are less worried about the outcomes and feel the company is taking their perspective into account.
- *Participation.* Employees worry less if they can participate in the process in some way. Voluntary early-retirement programs or severance packages can help achieve leanness without layoffs.
- *Assistance.* Severance pay and packages, extended health care benefits, and job search assistance demonstrate that a company cares about its employees and honors their contributions.

In short, companies that make themselves lean can be more agile, efficient, and productive—but only if they make cuts carefully and help employees through the process.

No doubt you are well aware by now that there is considerable variation in the structures an organization may choose. Let's take a moment to next consider why structures differ and what organizational strategies may be most conducive to certain structures.

WHY DO STRUCTURES DIFFER?

We've described organizational designs ranging from the highly structured bureaucracy to the amorphous boundaryless organization. The other designs we discussed exist somewhere in between.

Exhibit 15-6 recaps our discussions by presenting two extreme models of organizational design. One we'll call the **mechanistic model**. It's generally synonymous with bureaucracy in that it has highly standardized processes for work, high formalization, and more managerial hierarchy. The other extreme, the **organic model**, looks a lot like the boundaryless organization. It's flat, has fewer formal procedures for making decisions, has multiple decision makers, and favors flexible practices.[36]

With these two models in mind, let's ask a few questions: Why are some organizations structured along more mechanistic lines, whereas others follow organic characteristics? What forces influence the choice of design? In this section, we present the major causes or determinants of an organization's structure.[37]

Organizational Strategies

Because structure is a means to achieve objectives, and objectives derive from the organization's overall strategy, it's only logical that structure should follow strategy. If management

The Mechanistic Model

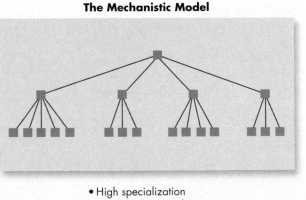

- High specialization
- Rigid departmentalization
- Clear chain of command
- Narrow spans of control
- Centralization
- High formalization

The Organic Model

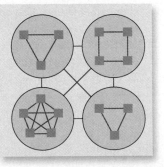

- Cross-functional teams
- Cross-hierarchical teams
- Free flow of information
- Wide spans of control
- Decentralization
- Low formalization

EXHIBIT 15-6
Mechanistic Versus Organic Models

significantly changes the organization's strategy, the structure must change to accommodate.[38] Most current strategy frameworks focus on three strategy dimensions—innovation, cost minimization, and imitation—and the structural design that works best with each.[39]

To what degree does an organization introduce major new products or services? An **innovation strategy** strives to achieve meaningful and unique innovations. Obviously, not all firms pursue innovation. Apple and 3M do, but conservative retailer Marks & Spencer doesn't. Innovative firms will use competitive pay and benefits to attract top candidates and motivate employees to take risks. Some degree of mechanistic structure can actually benefit innovation. Well-developed communication channels, policies for enhancing long-term commitment, and clear channels of authority all may make it easier for rapid changes to occur smoothly.

An organization pursuing a **cost-minimization strategy** tightly controls costs, refrains from incurring unnecessary expenses, and cuts prices in selling a basic product. This describes the strategy pursued by Walmart and the makers of generic or store-label grocery products. Cost-minimizing organizations pursue fewer policies meant to develop commitment among their workforce.

Organizations following an **imitation strategy** try to both minimize risk and maximize opportunity for profit, moving new products or entering new markets only after innovators have proven their viability. Mass-market fashion manufacturers that copy designer styles follow this strategy, as do firms such as Hewlett-Packard and Caterpillar. They follow smaller and more innovative competitors with their products, but only after competitors have demonstrated the market is there. Italy's Moleskine SpA, a small maker of fashionable notebooks, is another example of imitation strategy, but in the reverse; looking to open more retail shops around the world, it is employing the expansion strategies of larger, successful fashion companies Salvatore Ferragamo SpA and Brunello Cucinelli.[40]

Organization Size

An organization's size significantly affects its structure. Organizations that employ 2,000 or more people tend to have more specialization, more departmentalization, more vertical levels, and more rules and regulations than do small organizations. However, size becomes less important as an organization expands. Why? At around 2,000 employees, an organization is already fairly mechanistic; 500 more employees won't have much impact. But adding 500 employees to an organization of only 300 is likely to significantly shift it toward a more mechanistic structure.

Technology

Technology describes the way an organization transfers inputs into outputs. Every organization has at least one technology for converting financial, human, and physical resources into products or services. Ford Motor Company uses an assembly-line process to make its products. Colleges may use a number of instructional technologies—the ever-popular lecture method, case analyses, experiential exercises, programmed learning, online instruction, and distance learning. Regardless, organizational structures adapt to their technology.

Numerous studies have examined the technology–structure relationship.[41] What differentiates technologies is their *degree of routineness.* Routine activities are characterized by automated and standardized operations. Examples are injection-mold production of plastic knobs, automated processing of sales transactions, and the printing and binding of books. Nonroutine activities are customized and require frequent revision and updating. They include furniture restoring, custom shoemaking, genetic research, and the writing and editing of books. In general, organizations engaged in nonroutine activities tend to prefer organic structures, whereas those performing routine activities prefer mechanistic structures.

Environment

An organization's **environment** includes outside institutions or forces that can affect its performance, such as suppliers, customers, competitors, government regulatory agencies, and public pressure groups. Dynamic environments create significantly more uncertainty for managers than do static ones. To minimize uncertainty in key market arenas, managers may broaden their structure to sense and respond to threats. For example, most companies, including Pepsi and Southwest Airlines, have added social networking departments to counter negative information posted on blogs. Or companies may form strategic alliances with other companies.

Any organization's environment has three dimensions: capacity, volatility, and complexity.[42] *Capacity* refers to the degree to which the environment can support growth. Rich and growing environments generate excess resources, which can buffer the organization in times of relative scarcity.

Volatility describes the degree of instability in the environment. A dynamic environment with a high degree of unpredictable change makes it difficult for management to make accurate predictions. Because information technology changes at such a rapid pace, for instance, more organizations' environments are becoming volatile.

Finally, *complexity* is the degree of heterogeneity and concentration among environmental elements. Simple environments—like the tobacco industry where the methods of production, competitive and regulatory pressures, and the like haven't changed in quite some time—are homogeneous and concentrated. Environments characterized by heterogeneity and dispersion—like the broadband industry—are complex and diverse, with numerous competitors.

Given this three-dimensional definition of *environment*, we can offer some general conclusions about environmental uncertainty and structural arrangements. The more scarce, dynamic, and complex the environment, the more organic a structure should be. The more abundant, stable, and simple the environment, the more the mechanistic structure will be preferred.

While factors such as the organization's environment can provide clues as to which type of structure may be most effective, the best structure for any organization is one that fits the organization's strategy . . . and its people. To conclude our exploration on the foundations of organization structure, we will focus on the effects of structure on behavior.

ORGANIZATIONAL DESIGNS AND EMPLOYEE BEHAVIOR

We opened this chapter by implying that an organization's structure can have significant effects on its members. What might those effects be?

A review of the evidence leads to a pretty clear conclusion: You can't generalize! Not everyone prefers the freedom and flexibility of organic structures. Different factors stand out in different structures. In highly formalized, heavily structured, mechanistic organizations, the level of fairness in formal policies and procedures is a very important predictor of satisfaction. In more personal, individually adaptive organic organizations, employees value interpersonal justice more.[43] Some people are most productive and satisfied when work tasks are standardized and ambiguity minimized—that is, in mechanistic structures. So, any discussion of the effect of organizational design on employee behavior has to address individual differences. To do so, let's consider employee preferences for work specialization, span of control, and centralization.[44]

The evidence generally indicates that *work specialization* contributes to higher employee productivity—but at the price of reduced job satisfaction. However, work specialization is not an unending source of higher productivity. Problems start to surface, and productivity begins to suffer, when the human diseconomies of doing repetitive and narrow tasks overtake the economies of specialization. As the workforce has become more highly educated and desirous of jobs that are intrinsically rewarding, we seem to reach the point at which productivity begins to decline as a function of specialization more quickly than in the past. While decreased productivity often prompts companies to add oversight and inspection roles, the better answer may be to reorganize work functions and accountability.[45]

A segment of the workforce still prefers the routine and repetitiveness of highly specialized jobs. Some individuals want work that makes minimal intellectual demands and provides the security of routine; for them, high work specialization is a source of job satisfaction. The question, of course, is whether they represent 2 percent of the workforce or 52 percent. Research suggests the "real" answer is closer to 2 percent than 52 percent. Given that some self-selection operates in the choice of careers, we might conclude that negative behavioral outcomes from high specialization are most likely to surface in professional jobs occupied by individuals with high needs for personal growth and diversity.

It is probably safe to say no evidence supports a relationship between *span of control* and employee satisfaction or performance. Although it is intuitive that large spans might lead to higher employee performance because they provide more distant supervision and more opportunity for personal initiative, the research fails to support this notion. Some people like to be left alone; others prefer the security of a boss who is quickly available at all times. Consistent with several of the contingency theories of leadership discussed in Chapter 12, we would expect factors such as employees' experiences and abilities and the degree of structure in their tasks to explain when wide or narrow spans of control are likely to contribute to their performance and job satisfaction. However, some evidence indicates that a *manager's* job satisfaction increases as the number of employees supervised increases.

We find fairly strong evidence linking *centralization* and job satisfaction. In general, less centralized organizations have a greater amount of autonomy. And autonomy appears positively related to job satisfaction. But, again, while one employee may value freedom, another may find autonomous environments frustratingly ambiguous.

Our conclusion: To maximize employee performance and satisfaction, managers must take individual differences, such as experience, personality, and the work task, into account. Culture should factor in, too.

We can draw one obvious insight: other things equal, people don't select employers randomly. They are attracted to, are selected by, and stay with organizations that suit their personal characteristics.[46] Job candidates who prefer predictability are likely to seek out and take employment in mechanistic structures, and those who want autonomy are more likely to end up in an organic structure. Thus, the effect of structure on employee behavior is undoubtedly reduced when the selection process facilitates proper matching of individual characteristics with organizational characteristics. Furthermore, companies should strive to establish, promote, and maintain the unique identities of their structures since skilled employees may quit as a result of dramatic changes.[47]

Globalization, strategic alliances, customer-organization links, and telecommuting are all examples of practices that reduce external boundaries.

Research suggests that national culture influences the preference for structure.[48] Organizations that operate with people from high power–distance cultures, such as Greece, France, and most of Latin America, find their employees are much more accepting of mechanistic structures than are employees from low power–distance countries. So consider cultural differences along with individual differences when predicting how structure will affect employee performance and satisfaction.

SUMMARY

The theme of this chapter is that an organization's internal structure contributes to explaining and predicting behavior. That is, in addition to individual and group factors, the structural relationships in which people work have a bearing on employee attitudes and behavior. What's the basis for this argument? To the degree that an organization's structure reduces ambiguity for employees and clarifies concerns such as "What am I supposed to do?" "How am I supposed to do it?" "To whom do I report?" and "To whom do I go if I have a problem?" it shapes their attitudes and facilitates and motivates them to higher levels of performance.

IMPLICATIONS FOR MANAGERS

- Specialization can make operations more efficient, but remember that excessive specialization can create dissatisfaction and reduced motivation.
- Avoid designing rigid hierarchies that overly limit employees' empowerment and autonomy.
- Balance the advantages of virtual and boundaryless organizations against the potential pitfalls before adding flexible workplace options.
- Downsize your organization to realize major cost savings, and focus the company around core competencies—but only if necessary because downsizing can have a significant negative impact on employee affect.
- Consider the scarcity, dynamism, and complexity of the environment, and balance the organic and mechanistic elements when designing an organizational structure.

✪ WATCH IT

If your professor assigned this, sign in to **mymanagementlab.com** to watch a video titled ZipCar: Organizational Structure to learn more about this topic and respond to questions.

PERSONAL INVENTORY ASSESSMENT

In Personal Inventory Assessment found in MyManagementLab take assessment: Organizational Structure Assessment

✪ WRITING SPACE

If your professor assigned this, sign in to **mymanagementlab.com** for the following Assisted-graded writing question:

15-1.   Which organizational designs do you think are best suited to incorporate employees who work from home? Why?

16
Creating and Sustaining Culture

MyManagementLab®
⭐ Improve Your Grade!

When you see this icon ⭐, visit **www.mymanagementlab.com** for activities that are applied, personalized, and offer immediate feedback.

LEARNING OBJECTIVES

After studying this chapter, you should be able to:

1. Describe the common characteristics of organizational culture.
2. Compare the functional and dysfunctional effects of organizational culture on people and the organization.
3. Identify the factors that create and sustain an organization's culture.
4. Show how culture is transmitted to employees.
5. Demonstrate how an ethical culture can be created.
6. Describe a positive organizational culture.
7. Show how national culture can affect the way organizational culture is interpreted.

⭐ Chapter Warm-up

If your professor has chosen to assign this, go to **www.mymanagementlab.com** to see what you should particularly focus on and to take the Chapter 16 warm up.

⭐ WATCH IT

If your professor assigned this, sign in to **mymanagementlab.com** to watch a video titled Organizational Culture (TWZ Role Play) to learn more about this topic and respond to questions.

A strong organizational culture provides stability to an organization. For some organizations, culture can be a major barrier to change. In this chapter, we show that every organization has a culture that, depending on its strength, can have a significant influence on the attitudes and behaviors of organization members.

The culture of any organization, although it may be hard to measure precisely, nevertheless exists and is generally recognized by its employees. We call this variable *organizational culture.* Just as tribal cultures have totems and taboos that dictate how each member should act toward fellow members and outsiders, organizations have cultures that govern how members behave. In this chapter, we'll discuss just what organizational culture is, how it affects employee attitudes and behavior, where it comes from, and whether or not it can be changed.

WHAT IS ORGANIZATIONAL CULTURE?

An executive once was asked what he thought *organizational culture* meant. He gave essentially the same answer U.S. Supreme Court Justice Potter Stewart gave in defining pornography: "I can't define it, but I know it when I see it." In this section, we propose one definition of organizational culture and review several related ideas.

A Definition of Organizational Culture

Organizational culture refers to a system of shared meaning held by members that distinguishes the organization from other organizations.[1] Seven primary characteristics seem to capture the essence of an organization's culture:[2]

> An organization's culture develops over many years and is rooted in deeply held values to which employees are strongly committed.

1. *Innovation and Risk Taking.* The degree to which employees are encouraged to be innovative and take risks.
2. *Attention to Detail.* The degree to which employees are expected to exhibit precision, analysis, and attention to detail.
3. *Outcome Orientation.* The degree to which management focuses on results or outcomes rather than on the techniques and processes used to achieve them.
4. *People Orientation.* The degree to which management decisions take into consideration the effect of outcomes on people within the organization.
5. *Team Orientation.* The degree to which work activities are organized around teams rather than individuals.
6. *Aggressiveness.* The degree to which people are aggressive and competitive rather than easygoing.
7. *Stability.* The degree to which organizational activities emphasize maintaining the status quo in contrast to growth.

Each of these characteristics exists on a continuum from low to high. Appraising the organization on these seven dimensions, then, gives a composite picture of its culture and a basis for the shared understanding members have about the organization, how things are done in it, and the way they are supposed to behave.

Culture Is a Descriptive Term

Organizational culture shows how employees perceive the characteristics of an organization not whether they like them—that is, it's a descriptive term. Research on organizational culture has sought to measure how employees see the organization: Does it encourage teamwork? Does it reward innovation? Does it stifle initiative? In contrast, job satisfaction seeks to measure how employees feel about the organization's expectations, reward practices, and the like. Although the two terms have overlapping characteristics, keep in mind that *organizational culture* is descriptive, whereas *job satisfaction* is evaluative.

Do Organizations Have Uniform Cultures?

Organizational culture represents a perception the organization's members hold in common. We should therefore expect individuals with different backgrounds or at different levels in the organization to describe its culture in similar terms.[3]

That doesn't mean, however, that there are no subcultures. Most large organizations have a dominant culture and numerous subcultures.[4] A **dominant culture** expresses the **core values** a majority of members share and that give the organization its distinct personality.[5] **Subcultures** tend to develop in large organizations to reflect common problems or experiences members face in the same department or location. The purchasing department can have a subculture that includes the core values of the dominant culture plus additional values unique to members of that department.

If organizations were composed only of numerous subcultures, organizational culture as an independent variable would be significantly less powerful. It is the "shared meaning" aspect of culture that makes it such a potent device for guiding and shaping behavior. That's what allows us to say, for example, that the Zappos culture values customer care and dedication over speed and efficiency, and to use that information to better understand the behavior of Zappos executives and employees.[6]

Strong Versus Weak Cultures

It's possible to differentiate between strong and weak cultures.[7] If most employees (responding to management surveys) have the same opinions about the organization's mission and values, the culture is strong; if opinions vary widely, the culture is weak.

In a **strong culture**, the organization's core values are both intensely held and widely shared.[8] The more members who accept the core values and the greater their commitment, the stronger the culture and the greater its influence on member behavior. This is because the high degree of shared values and intensity create a climate of high behavioral control. Nordstrom employees know in no uncertain terms what is expected of them, for example, and these expectations go a long way in shaping their behavior. In contrast, Nordstrom competitor Macy's, which has struggled through an identity crisis, is working to remake its culture.

A strong culture should reduce employee turnover because it demonstrates high agreement about what the organization represents. Such unanimity of purpose builds cohesiveness, loyalty, and organizational commitment. These qualities, in turn, lessen employees' propensity to leave.[9] One study found that the more employees agreed on customer orientation in a service organization, the higher the profitability of the business unit.[10] Another study found that when team managers and team members disagreed about perceptions of organizational support, there were more negative moods among team members, and the performance of teams was lower.[11] These negative effects are especially strong when managers believe the organization provides more support than employees think it does.

Culture Versus Formalization

We've seen that high formalization creates predictability, orderliness, and consistency. A strong culture achieves the same end without the need for written documentation.[12] Therefore, we should view formalization and culture as two different roads to a common destination. The stronger an organization's culture, the less management needs to be concerned with developing formal rules and regulations to guide employee behavior. Those guides will be internalized in employees when they accept the organization's culture.

WHAT DO CULTURES DO?

Let's review the role culture performs and whether it can ever be a liability for an organization.

The Functions of Culture

First, culture has a boundary-defining role: It creates distinctions between organizations. Second, it conveys a sense of identity for organization members. Third, culture facilitates commitment to something larger than individual self-interest. Fourth, it enhances the stability of the social system. Culture is the social glue that helps hold the organization together by providing standards for what employees should say and do. Finally, it is a sense-making and control mechanism that guides and shapes employees' attitudes and behavior. This last function is of particular interest to us.[13] Culture defines the rules of the game.

Today's trend toward decentralized organizations makes culture more important than ever, but ironically it also makes establishing a strong culture more difficult. When formal authority and control systems are reduced, culture's *shared meaning* can point everyone in the same direction. However, employees organized in teams may show greater allegiance to their team and its values than to the organization as a whole. In virtual organizations, the lack of frequent face-to-face contact makes establishing a common set of norms very difficult. Strong leadership that communicates frequently about common goals and priorities is especially important in innovative organizations.[14]

Individual–organization "fit"—that is, whether the applicant's or employee's attitudes and behavior are compatible with the culture—strongly influences who gets a job offer, a favorable performance review, or a promotion. It's no coincidence that Disney theme park employees appear almost universally attractive, clean, and wholesome with bright smiles. The company selects employees who will maintain that image. On the job, a strong culture supported by formal rules and regulations ensures employees will act in a relatively uniform and predictable way.

Culture Creates Climate

If you've worked with someone whose positive attitude inspired you to do your best, or with a lackluster team that drained your motivation, you've experienced the effects of climate. **Organizational climate** refers to the shared perceptions organizational members have about their organization and work environment.[15] This aspect of culture is like team spirit at the organizational level. When everyone has the same general feelings about what's important or how well things are working, the effect of these attitudes will be more than the sum of the individual parts. One meta-analysis found that across dozens of different samples, psychological climate was strongly related to individuals' level of job satisfaction, involvement, commitment, and motivation.[16] A positive overall work-place climate has been linked to higher customer satisfaction and financial performance as well.[17]

Dozens of dimensions of climate have been studied, including innovation, creativity, communication, warmth and support, involvement, safety, justice, diversity, and customer service.[18] A person who encounters a positive climate for performance will think about doing a good job more often and will believe others support her success. Someone who encounters a positive climate for diversity will feel more comfortable collaborating with coworkers regardless of their demographic background. Climates can interact with one another to produce behavior. For example, a positive climate for worker empowerment can lead to higher levels of performance in organizations that also have a climate for personal accountability.[19] Climate also influences habits. If the climate for safety is positive, everyone wears safety gear and follows safety procedures even if individually they wouldn't normally think very often about being safe—indeed, many studies have shown that a positive safety climate decreases the number of documented injuries on the job.[20]

Culture as a Liability

Culture can enhance organizational commitment and increase the consistency of employee behavior, which clearly benefits an organization. Culture is valuable to employees too, because it spells out how things are done and what's important. But we shouldn't ignore the potentially dysfunctional aspects of culture, especially a strong one, on an organization's effectiveness. Hewlett-Packard, once known as a premier computer manufacturer, has been rapidly losing market share and profits as the dysfunction of its top management team has trickled down, leaving employees disengaged, uncreative, unappreciated, and polarized.[21]

INSTITUTIONALIZATION When an organization undergoes **institutionalization** and becomes *institutionalized*—that is, it is valued for itself and not for the goods or services it produces—it takes on a life of its own, apart from its founders or members.[22] Institutionalized organizations often don't go out of business even if the original goals are no longer relevant. Acceptable modes of behavior become largely self-evident to members, and although this isn't entirely negative, it does mean behaviors and habits go unquestioned, which can stifle innovation and make maintaining the organization's culture an end in itself.

BARRIERS TO CHANGE Culture is a liability when the shared values don't agree with those that further the organization's effectiveness. This is most likely when an organization's environment is undergoing rapid change, and its entrenched culture may no longer be appropriate.[23] Consistency of behavior, an asset in a stable environment, may then burden the organization and make it difficult to respond to changes.

BARRIERS TO DIVERSITY Hiring new employees who differ from the majority in race, age, gender, disability, or other characteristics creates a paradox:[24] Management wants to demonstrate support for the differences these employees bring to the workplace, but newcomers who wish to fit in must accept the organization's core culture. Second, because diverse behaviors and unique strengths are likely to diminish as people assimilate, strong cultures can become liabilities when they eliminate the advantages of diversity. Third, a strong culture that condones prejudice, supports bias, or becomes insensitive to differences can undermine formal diversity policies.

BARRIERS TO ACQUISITIONS AND MERGERS Historically, when management looked at acquisition or merger decisions, the key factors were financial advantage and product synergy. In recent years, cultural compatibility has become the primary concern.[25] All things being equal, whether the acquisition actually works seems to have much to do with how well the two organizations' cultures match up.

A survey by consulting firm A. T. Kearney revealed that 58 percent of mergers failed to reach their financial goals.[26] As one expert commented, "Mergers have an unusually high failure rate, and it's always because of people issues"—in other words, because of conflicting organizational cultures. The $183 billion merger between America Online (AOL) and Time Warner in 2001 was the largest in U.S. corporate history. It was also a disaster. Only 2 years later, the stock had fallen an astounding 90 percent, and the new company reported what was then the largest financial loss in U.S. history. Culture clash is commonly argued to be one of the causes of AOL Time Warner's problems.

CREATING AND SUSTAINING CULTURE

An organization's culture doesn't pop out of thin air, and once established it rarely fades away. What influences the creation of a culture? What reinforces and sustains it once in place?

How a Culture Begins

An organization's current customs, traditions, and general way of doing things are largely due to what it has done before and how successful it was in doing it. This leads us to the ultimate source of an organization's culture: the founders.[27] Free of previous customs or ideologies, founders have a vision of what the organization should be, and the firm's small size makes it easy to impose that vision on all members.

Culture creation occurs in three ways.[28] First, founders hire and keep only employees who think and feel the same way they do. Second, they indoctrinate and socialize employees to their way of thinking and feeling. And finally, the founders' own behavior encourages employees to identify with them and internalize their beliefs, values, and assumptions. When the organization succeeds, the founders' personality becomes embedded in the culture.

The fierce, competitive style and disciplined, authoritarian nature of Hyundai, the giant Korean conglomerate, exhibits the same characteristics often used to describe founder Chung Ju-Yung. Other founders with immeasurable impact on their organization's culture include Bill Gates at Microsoft, Ingvar Kamprad at IKEA, Herb Kelleher at Southwest Airlines, Fred Smith at FedEx, and Richard Branson at the Virgin Group.

Keeping a Culture Alive

Once a culture is in place, practices within the organization maintain it by giving employees a set of similar experiences.[29] The selection process, performance evaluation criteria, training and development activities, and promotion procedures ensure those hired fit in with the culture, reward those who support it, and penalize (or even expel) those who challenge it. Three forces play a particularly important part in sustaining a culture: selection practices, actions of top management, and socialization methods. Let's look at each.

SELECTION The explicit goal of the selection process is to identify and hire individuals with the knowledge, skills, and abilities to perform successfully. The final decision, because it is significantly influenced by the decision maker's judgment of how well the candidates will fit into the organization, identifies people whose values are essentially consistent with at least a good portion of the organization's.[30] Selection also provides information to applicants. Individuals who perceive a conflict between their values and those of the organization can remove themselves from the applicant pool. Selection thus becomes a two-way street, allowing employer or applicant to avoid a mismatch and sustaining an organization's culture by removing those who might attack or undermine its core values.

W. L. Gore & Associates, the maker of Gore-Tex fabric used in outerwear, prides itself on its democratic culture and teamwork. There are no job titles, bosses, or chains of command. All work is done in teams. In Gore's selection process, teams put job applicants through extensive interviews to ensure they can deal with the level of uncertainty, flexibility, and teamwork that's normal in Gore plants. Not surprisingly, W. L. Gore appears regularly on *Fortune*'s list of 100 Best Companies to Work For (number 21 in 2013).[31]

TOP MANAGEMENT The actions of top management also have a major impact on the organization's culture.[32] Through words and behavior, senior executives establish norms that filter through the organization about, for instance, whether risk taking is desirable, how much freedom managers give employees, what is appropriate dress, and what actions earn pay raises, promotions, and other rewards.

The culture of supermarket chain Wegmans—which believes driven, happy, and loyal employees are more eager to help one another and provide exemplary customer service—is a direct result of the beliefs of the Wegman family. The chain began in 1930 when brothers John and Walter Wegman opened their first grocery store in Rochester, New York. Their focus on fine foods quickly separated Wegmans from other grocers— a focus maintained by the company's employees, many of whom were hired based on their interest in food. In 1950, Walter's son Robert became president and added generous employee benefits such as profit sharing and fully paid medical coverage. Now Robert's son Danny is president, and he has continued the Wegmans tradition of taking care of employees. To date, Wegmans has paid more than $90 million in scholarships for more than 28,400 employees. Pay is well above market average, making annual turnover for full-time employees a mere 3.6 percent (the industry average is 24 percent). Wegmans regularly appears on *Fortune*'s list as well (number 5 in 2013).[33]

SOCIALIZATION No matter how good a job the organization does in recruiting and selection, new employees need help adapting to the prevailing culture. That help is **socialization**.[34] For example, all Marines must go through boot camp, where they prove their commitment and learn the "Marine way." The consulting firm Booz Allen Hamilton begins its process of bringing new employees on board even before they start their first day of work. New recruits go to an internal web portal to learn about the company and engage in some activities that help them understand the culture of the organization. After they start work, they continue to learn about the organization through an ongoing social networking application that links new workers with more established members of the firm and helps ensure that culture is transmitted over time.[35] Clear Channel Communications, Facebook, Google, and other companies are adopting fresh onboarding (new hire) procedures, including assigning "peer coaches," holding socializing events, personalizing orientation programs, and giving out immediate work assignments. "When we can stress the personal identity of people, and let them bring more of themselves to work, they are more satisfied with their job and have better results," researcher Francesca Gino of Harvard said.[36]

We can think of socialization as a process with three stages: prearrival, encounter, and metamorphosis.[37] This process, shown in Exhibit 16-1, has an impact on the new employee's work productivity, commitment to the organization's objectives, and eventual decision to stay with the organization.

The **prearrival stage** recognizes that each individual arrives with a set of values, attitudes, and expectations about both the work and the organization. One major purpose of a business school, for example, is to socialize business students to the attitudes and behaviors business firms want. Newcomers to high-profile organizations with a strong market position will make their own assumptions about what it must be like to work there.[38] Most new recruits will expect Nike to be dynamic and exciting, a prestigious law firm to be high in pressure and rewards, and the Marine Corps to require both discipline and courage. No matter how well managers think they can socialize newcomers, however, the most important predictor of future behavior is past behavior. What people know before they join the organization, and how proactive their personality is, are critical predictors of how well they adjust to a new culture.[39]

One way to capitalize on prehire characteristics in socialization is to use the selection process to inform prospective employees about the organization as a whole. We've also seen how the selection process ensures the inclusion of the "right type"—those who will fit in.

On entry into the organization, the new member enters the **encounter stage** and confronts the possibility that expectations—about the job, coworkers, the boss, and the organization in general—may differ from reality. If expectations were fairly accurate, this stage merely cements earlier perceptions. However, this is often not the case. At the extreme, a new member may become disillusioned enough to resign. Proper recruiting and selection should significantly reduce that outcome, along with encouraging friendship

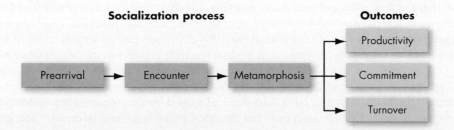

**EXHIBIT 16-1
A Socialization
Model**

EXHIBIT 16-2
Entry Socialization
Options

FORMAL VS. INFORMAL The more a new employee is segregated from the ongoing work setting and differentiated in some way to make explicit his newcomer's role, the more socialization is formal. Specific orientation and training programs are examples. Informal socialization puts the new employee directly into the job, with little or no special attention.

INDIVIDUAL VS. COLLECTIVE New members can be socialized individually. This describes how it's done in many professional offices. They can also be grouped together and processed through an identical set of experiences, as in military boot camp.

FIXED VS. VARIABLE This refers to the time schedule in which newcomers make the transition from outsider to insider. A fixed schedule establishes standardized stages of transition. This characterizes rotational training programs. It also includes probationary periods, such as the 8- to 10-year "associate" status used by accounting and law firms before deciding on whether or not a candidate is made a partner. Variable schedules give no advance notice of their transition timetable. Variable schedules describe the typical promotion system, in which one is not advanced to the next stage until one is "ready."

SERIAL VS. RANDOM Serial socialization is characterized by the use of role models who train and encourage the newcomer. Apprenticeship and mentoring programs are examples. In random socialization, role models are deliberately withheld. New employees are left on their own to figure things out.

INVESTITURE VS. DIVESTITURE Investiture socialization assumes that the newcomer's qualities and qualifications are the necessary ingredients for job success, so these qualities and qualifications are confirmed and supported. Divestiture socialization tries to strip away certain characteristics of the recruit. Fraternity and sorority "pledges" go through divestiture socialization to shape them into the proper role.

ties in the organization—newcomers are more committed when friends and coworkers help them "learn the ropes."[40]

Finally, to work out any problems discovered during the encounter stage, the new member changes or goes through the **metamorphosis stage**. The options presented in Exhibit 16-2 are alternatives designed to bring about the desired metamorphosis. Most research suggests there are two major "bundles" of socialization practices. The more management relies on formal, collective, sequential, fixed, and serial socialization programs and emphasizes divestiture, the more likely newcomers' differences will be stripped away and replaced by standardized predictable behaviors. These *institutional* practices are common in police departments, fire departments, and other organizations that value rule following and order. Programs that are informal, individual, random, variable, and disjunctive and that emphasize investiture are more likely to give newcomers an innovative sense of their roles and methods of working. Creative fields, such as research and development, advertising, and filmmaking, rely on these *individual* practices. Most research suggests that high levels of institutional practices encourage person–organization fit and high levels of commitment, whereas individual practices produce more role innovation.[41]

The three-part entry socialization process is complete when new members have internalized and accepted the norms of the organization and their work group, are confident in their competence, and feel trusted and valued by their peers. They understand the system—not only their own tasks but the rules, procedures, and informally accepted practices as well. Finally, they know what is expected of them and what criteria will be used to measure and evaluate their work. As Exhibit 16-2 showed, successful metamorphosis should have a positive impact on new employees' productivity and their commitment to the organization, and reduce their propensity to leave the organization.

Researchers have begun to examine how employees change during socialization by measuring attitudes at several points over the first few months. One study has documented patterns of "honeymoons" and "hangovers" for new workers, showing that the period of initial adjustment is often marked by decreases in job satisfaction as idealized hopes come into contact with the reality of organizational life.[42] Other research suggests that role conflict and role overload for newcomers rise over time, and workers with the largest increases in these role problems experience the largest decreases in commitment and satisfaction.[43] It may be that the initial adjustment period for newcomers presents increasing demands and difficulties, at least in the short term.

Summary: How Cultures Form

Exhibit 16-3 summarizes how an organization's culture is established and sustained. The original culture derives from the founders' philosophy and strongly influences hiring criteria as the firm grows. Top managers' actions set the general climate, including what is acceptable behavior and what is not. The way employees are socialized will depend both on the degree of success achieved in matching new employees' values to those of the organization in the selection process, and on top management's preference for socialization methods.

HOW EMPLOYEES LEARN CULTURE

Culture is transmitted to employees in a number of forms, the most potent being stories, rituals, material symbols, and language.

Stories

When Henry Ford II was chairman of Ford Motor Company, you would have been hard pressed to find a manager who hadn't heard how he reminded his executives, when they got too arrogant, "It's my name that's on the building." The message was clear: Henry Ford II ran the company.

A number of senior Nike executives spend much of their time serving as corporate storytellers.[44] When they tell how co-founder (and Oregon track coach) Bill Bowerman went to his workshop and poured rubber into a waffle iron to create a better running shoe, they're talking about Nike's spirit of innovation. When new hires hear tales of Oregon

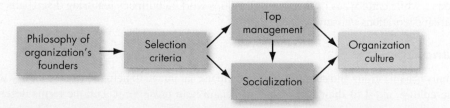

EXHIBIT 16-3
How
Organization
Cultures Form

running star Steve Prefontaine's battles to make running a professional sport and attain better performance equipment, they learn of Nike's commitment to helping athletes.

Stories such as these circulate through many organizations, anchoring the present in the past and legitimating current practices. They typically include narratives about the organization's founders, rule breaking, rags-to-riches successes, reductions in the workforce, relocation of employees, reactions to past mistakes, and organizational coping.[45] Employees also create their own narratives about how they came to either fit or not fit with the organization during the process of socialization, including first days on the job, early interactions with others, and first impressions of organizational life.[46]

Rituals

Rituals are repetitive sequences of activities that express and reinforce the key values of the organization—what goals are most important, which people are important, and which are expendable.[47] One of the best known rituals is Walmart's company chant. Begun by the company's founder, the late Sam Walton, as a way to motivate his workforce, "Gimme a W, gimme an A, gimme an L, gimme a squiggle, give me an M, A, R, T!" became a ritual to bond workers together and reinforce Walton's belief that employees made the company successful. Other companies have nontraditional rituals to help support the values of their cultures. Kimpton Hotels & Restaurants, one of *Fortune*'s 100 Best Companies to Work For, maintains its customer-oriented culture with traditions like a Housekeeping Olympics that includes blindfolded bedmaking and vacuum races, for instance.[48]

Symbols

The layout of corporate headquarters, the types of automobiles top executives are given, and the presence or absence of corporate aircraft are a few examples of **material symbols**. Others include the size of offices, and the elegance of furnishings, perks, and attire.[49] These convey to employees who is important, the degree of egalitarianism top management desires, and the kinds of behavior that are appropriate, such as risk-taking, conservative, authoritarian, participative, individualistic, or social.

One example is the Texas electric company Dynegy. Dynegy's headquarters doesn't look like your typical head-office operation. There are few individual offices, even for senior executives. The space is essentially made up of cubicles, common areas, and meeting rooms. This informality conveys to employees that Dynegy values openness, equality, creativity, and flexibility. Some corporations provide their top executives with chauffeur-driven limousines and a corporate jet. Other CEOs drive the company car themselves and travel in the economy section. At some firms, like Chicago shirtmaker Threadless, an "anything goes" atmosphere helps emphasize a creative culture. Meetings are held in an Airstream camper parked inside the company's converted FedEx warehouse, while employees in shorts and flip-flops work in bullpens featuring disco balls and garish decorations chosen by each team.[50]

Language

Many organizations and subunits within them use language to help members identify with the culture, attest to their acceptance of it, and help preserve it. Unique terms describe equipment, officers, key individuals, suppliers, customers, or products that relate to the business. New employees may at first be overwhelmed by acronyms and jargon that, once assimilated, act as a common denominator to unite members of a given culture or subculture.

Since culture is key to the essence of an organization, and is perceived both inside and outside the organization, it is important to establish a culture that reflects the values of its founders and top management. Let's next explore the ways an ethical, positive culture can be created and transmitted around the world.

CREATING AN ETHICAL ORGANIZATIONAL CULTURE

The organizational culture most likely to shape high ethical standards among its members is high in risk tolerance, low to moderate in aggressiveness, and focused on means as well as outcomes.[51] This type of culture takes a long-term perspective and balances the rights of multiple stakeholders, including employees, stockholders, and the community. Managers are supported for taking risks and innovating, discouraged from engaging in unbridled competition, and guided to heed not just *what* goals are achieved but also *how*.

If the culture is strong and supports high ethical standards, it should have a very powerful and positive influence on employee behavior. Examples of organizations that have failed to establish proper codes of ethical conduct can be found in the media nearly every day. Some actively deceive customers or clients. Others produce products that harm consumers or the environment, or they harass or discriminate against certain groups of employees. Others are more subtle and cover up or fail to report wrongdoing. The negative consequences of a systematic culture of unethical behavior can be severe and include customer boycotts, fines, lawsuits, and government regulation of an organization's practices.

What can managers do to create a more ethical culture? They can adhere to the following principles:[52]

- *Be a Visible Role Model.* Employees will look to the actions of top management as a benchmark for appropriate behavior. Send a positive message.
- *Communicate Ethical Expectations.* Minimize ethical ambiguities by sharing an organizational code of ethics that states the organization's primary values and ethical rules employees must follow.
- *Provide Ethical Training.* Set up seminars, workshops, and training programs to reinforce the organization's standards of conduct, clarify what practices are permissible (or impermissible), and address potential ethical dilemmas.
- *Visibly Reward Ethical Acts and Punish Unethical Ones.* Appraise managers on how their decisions measure up against the organization's code of ethics. Review the means as well as the ends. Visibly reward those who act ethically and conspicuously punish those who don't.
- *Provide Protective Mechanisms.* Provide formal mechanisms so employees can discuss ethical dilemmas and report unethical behavior without fear of reprimand. These might include ethical counselors, ombudspeople, or ethical officers.

The work of setting a positive ethical climate has to start at the top of the organization.[53] A study of 195 managers demonstrated that when top management emphasizes

It is possible to form ethical cultures and positive organizational cultures, but the means by which such cultures are attained are quite different.

strong ethical values, supervisors are more likely to practice ethical leadership. Positive attitudes transfer down to line employees, who show lower levels of deviant behavior and higher levels of cooperation and assistance. A study involving auditors found perceived pressure from organizational leaders to behave unethically was associated with increased intentions to engage in unethical practices.[54] Clearly the wrong type of organizational culture can negatively influence employee ethical behavior. Finally, employees whose ethical values are similar to those of their department are more likely to be promoted, so we can think of ethical culture as flowing from the bottom up as well.[55]

CREATING A POSITIVE ORGANIZATIONAL CULTURE

At first blush, creating a positive culture may sound hopelessly naïve or like a Dilbert-style conspiracy. The one thing that makes us believe this trend is here to stay, however, are signs that management practice and OB research are converging.

A **positive organizational culture** emphasizes building on employee strengths, rewards more than it punishes, and emphasizes individual vitality and growth.[56] Let's consider each of these areas.

Building on Employee Strengths

Although a positive organizational culture does not ignore problems, it does emphasize showing workers how they can capitalize on their strengths. As management guru Peter Drucker said, "Most Americans do not know what their strengths are. When you ask them, they look at you with a blank stare, or they respond in terms of subject knowledge, which is the wrong answer." Wouldn't it be better to be in an organizational culture that helped you discover your strengths and learn how to make the most of them?

As CEO of Auglaize Provico, an agribusiness based in Ohio, Larry Hammond used this approach when you'd least expect it: during his firm's darkest days. In the midst of the firm's worst financial struggles, when it had to lay off one-quarter of its workforce, Hammond tried a different approach. Rather than dwell on what was wrong, he took advantage of what was right. "If you really want to [excel], you have to know yourself—you have to know what you're good at, and you have to know what you're not so good at," said Hammond. With the help of Gallup consultant Barry Conchie, Hammond focused on discovering and using employee strengths, and helped the company turn itself around. "You ask Larry [Hammond] what the difference is, and he'll say that it's individuals using their natural talents," said Conchie.[57]

Rewarding More Than Punishing

Although most organizations are sufficiently focused on extrinsic rewards such as pay and promotions, they often forget about the power of smaller (and cheaper) rewards such as praise. Part of creating a positive organizational culture is "catching employees doing something right." Many managers withhold praise because they're afraid employees will coast or because they think praise is not valued. Employees generally don't ask for praise, and managers usually don't realize the costs of failing to give it.

Consider Elżbieta Górska-Kolodziejczyk, a plant manager for International Paper's facility in Kwidzyn, Poland. Employees worked in a bleak windowless basement. Staffing became roughly one-third its prior level, while production tripled. These challenges had done in the previous three managers. So when Górska-Kolodziejczyk took over, although she had many ideas about transforming the organization, at the top were recognition and praise. She initially found it difficult to give praise to those who weren't used to it, especially men. "They were like cement at the beginning," she said. "Like cement." Over time, however, she found they valued and even reciprocated praise. One day a department supervisor pulled her over to tell her she was doing a good job. "This I do remember, yes," she said.[58]

Emphasizing Vitality and Growth

No organization will get the best from employees who see themselves as mere cogs in the machine. A positive culture recognizes the difference between a job and a career. It supports not only what the employee contributes to organizational effectiveness but also how the organization can make the employee more effective—personally and professionally. Top companies recognize the value of helping people grow. Safelite AutoGlass, *Workforce Management*'s 2012 Optima award winner for Competitive Advantage, attributes its success in part to its People First Plan talent development initiative. "The only way we can stand out is if we have the best people," says Senior Vice President Steve Miggo.[59]

Although it may take more creativity to encourage employee growth in other industries, consider the food industry. At Masterfoods in Belgium, Philippe Lescornez led a team of employees including Didier Brynaert, who worked in Luxembourg, nearly 150 miles away. Brynaert was considered a good sales promoter who was meeting expectations when Lescornez decided Brynaert's job could be made more important if he were seen less as just another sales promoter and more as an expert on the unique features of the Luxembourg market. So Lescornez asked Brynaert for information he could share with the home office. He hoped that by raising Brynaert's profile, he could create in him a greater sense of ownership for his remote sales territory. "I started to communicate much more what he did to other people [within the company], because there's quite some distance between the Brussels office and the section he's working in. So I started to communicate, communicate, communicate. The more I communicated, the more he started to provide material," said Lescornez. As a result, "Now he's recognized as the specialist for Luxembourg—the guy who is able to build a strong relationship with the Luxembourg clients," says Lescornez. What's good for Brynaert was, of course, also good for Lescornez, who got credit for helping Brynaert grow and develop.[60]

Limits of Positive Culture

Is a positive culture a cure-all? Though many companies have embraced aspects of a positive organizational culture, it is a new enough idea for us to be uncertain about how and when it works best.

Not all national cultures value being positive as much as U.S. culture does, and, even within U.S. culture, there surely are limits to how far U.S. companies should go. The limits may need to be dictated by the culture and the industry. For example, Admiral, a British insurance company, has established a Ministry of Fun in its call centers to organize poem writing, foosball, conker (a British game involving chestnuts), and fancy-dress days, while other companies in the insurance industry have maintained more serious cultures. When does the pursuit of a positive culture start to seem coercive or even Orwellian?

As one critic notes, "Promoting a social orthodoxy of positiveness focuses on a particular constellation of desirable states and traits but, in so doing, can stigmatize those who fail to fit the template."[61] There may be benefits to establishing a positive culture, but an organization also needs to be objective and not pursue it past the point of effectiveness.

GLOBAL IMPLICATIONS

Organizational culture and national culture are not the same thing, though to some degree, an organization's culture reflects the dominant values of its host country.

We considered global cultural values (collectivism–individualism, power distance, and so on) in Chapter 5. Here our focus is a bit narrower: How is organizational culture affected by a global context? Organizational culture is so powerful it often transcends national boundaries. But that doesn't mean organizations should, or could, ignore local cultures.

Organizational cultures often reflect national culture. The culture at AirAsia, a Malaysian-based airline, emphasizes openness and friendships. The carrier has lots of parties, participative management, and no private offices, reflecting Malaysia's relatively collectivistic culture. The culture of many U.S. airlines does not reflect the same degree of informality. If U.S. airlines were to merge with AirAsia, they would need to take these cultural differences into account. Organizational culture differences are not always due to international cultures differences, however. One of the chief challenges of the merger between US Airways and American Airlines is the integration of US Airway's "open-collar" culture with American's "button-down" culture.[62]

One of the primary things U.S. managers can do is be culturally sensitive. The United States is a dominant force in business and in culture—and with that influence comes a reputation. "We are broadly seen throughout the world as arrogant people, totally self-absorbed and loud," says one U.S. executive. Some ways in which U.S. managers can be culturally sensitive include talking in a low tone of voice, speaking slowly, listening more, and avoiding discussions of religion and politics.

The management of ethical behavior is one area where national culture can rub up against corporate culture.[63] U.S. managers endorse the supremacy of anonymous market forces and implicitly or explicitly view profit maximization as a moral obligation for business organizations. This worldview sees bribery, nepotism, and favoring personal contacts as highly unethical. Any action that deviates from profit maximization may indicate that inappropriate or corrupt behavior may be occurring. In contrast, managers in developing economies are more likely to see ethical decisions as embedded in a social environment. That means that doing special favors for family and friends is not only appropriate but possibly even an ethical responsibility. Managers in many nations also view capitalism skeptically and believe the interests of workers should be put on a par with the interests of shareholders.

U.S. employees are not the only ones who need to be culturally sensitive. Three times a week, employees at the Canadian unit of Japanese videogame maker Koei begin the day by standing next to their desks, facing their boss, and saying "Good morning" in unison. Employees then deliver short speeches on topics that range from corporate principles to 3D game engines. Koei also has employees punch a time clock and asks women to serve tea to top executive guests. Although these practices are consistent with Koei's culture, they do not fit the Canadian culture very well. "It's kind of like school," said one Canadian employee.[64]

SUMMARY

Employees form an overall subjective perception of the organization based on factors such as degree of risk tolerance, team emphasis, and support of individuals. This overall perception becomes, in effect, the organization's culture or personality and affects employee performance and satisfaction, with stronger cultures having greater impact.

IMPLICATIONS FOR MANAGERS

- Realize that an organization's culture is relatively fixed in the short term. To effect change, involve top management and strategize a long-term plan.
- Hire individuals whose values align with those of the organization; these employees will tend to remain committed and satisfied. Not surprisingly, "misfits" have considerably higher turnover rates.
- Understand that employees' performance and socialization depend to a considerable degree on their knowing what to do and not do. Train your employees well and keep them informed of changes to their job roles.
- As a manager, you can shape the culture of your work environment, sometimes as much as it shapes you. All managers can especially do their part to create an ethical culture.
- Be aware that your company's organizational culture may not be "transportable" to other countries. Understand the cultural relevance of your organization's norms before introducing new plans or initiatives overseas.

PERSONAL INVENTORY ASSESSMENT

In Personal Inventory Assessment found in MyManagementLab take assessment: Comfort with Change Scale

⭐ WRITING SPACE

If your professor assigned this, sign in to **mymanagementlab.com** for the following Assisted-graded writing question:

16-1.   How can you determine when a line has been crossed between a fun and informal culture, and one that is offensive and inappropriate?

17
Managing Change

MyManagementLab®
⊛ Improve Your Grade!

When you see this icon ⊛, visit **www.mymanagementlab.com** for activities that are applied, personalized, and offer immediate feedback.

LEARNING OBJECTIVES

After studying this chapter, you should be able to:

1. Identify forces that act as stimulants to change.
2. Describe the sources of resistance to change.
3. Compare the four main approaches to managing organizational change.
4. Demonstrate two ways of creating a culture for change.
5. Identify the potential sources and consequences of stress, and describe techniques for managing stress.

⊛ Chapter Warm-up

If your professor has chosen to assign this, go to **www.mymanagementlab.com** to see what you should particularly focus on and to take the Chapter 17 warm up.

This chapter is about change and stress. We describe environmental forces that require firms to change, why people and organizations often resist change, and how this resistance can be overcome. We review processes for managing organizational change.

With change often comes stress. Stress is an important topic for organizations to address in strengthening and retaining talented individuals. We will discuss the topic of stress and its consequences. In closing, we will explore what individuals and organizations can do to better manage stress levels.

FORCES FOR CHANGE

No company today is in a particularly stable environment. Even those with dominant market share must change, sometimes radically. The car market, for instance, is particularly volatile. The Toyota Camry and the Honda Accord have been market leaders in the midsize division, but their sales have not been as strong since the Great Recession, while sales for the Ford Fusion climbed 66 percent in four years. In the compact class, Chevrolet saw strong growth for the Cruze until it was plagued by recalls (following reports of the steering wheel breaking away from the steering column during motion) and poor reliability. In each car market segment, then, producers must constantly adapt and change in order to compete.[1]

"Change or die!" is the rallying cry among today's managers worldwide. In a number of places in this text, we've discussed the *changing nature of the workforce.* Almost every organization must adjust to a multicultural environment, demographic changes, immigration, and outsourcing. *Technology* is continually changing jobs and organizations. It is not hard to imagine the very idea of an office becoming an antiquated concept in the near future.

The housing and financial sectors experienced extraordinary *economic shocks* leading to the elimination, bankruptcy, or acquisition of some of the best-known U.S. companies, including Bear Stearns, Merrill Lynch, Lehman Brothers, Countrywide Financial, Washington Mutual, and Ameriquest. Tens of thousands of jobs were lost and may never return. After years of declining numbers and bankruptcies, the global recession caused the bankruptcy of auto manufacturers General Motors and Chrysler, retailers Borders and Sharper Image, and myriad other organizations.

Competition is changing. Competitors are as likely to come from across the ocean as from across town. Successful organizations will be fast on their feet, capable of developing new products rapidly and getting them to market quickly. They will be flexible and will require an equally flexible and responsive workforce. Sometimes, government regulations affect organizational behavior decisions. For instance, increasingly in the United States and Europe, the government regulates business practices, including executive pay.

Social trends don't remain static. Consumers who are otherwise strangers now meet and share product information in chat rooms and blogs. Companies must continually adjust product and marketing strategies to be sensitive to changing social trends, as Liz Claiborne did when it sold off fashion brands such as Ellen Tracy, de-emphasized large vendors such as Macy's, streamlined operations, and cut staff. Consumers, employees, and organizational leaders are increasingly sensitive to environmental concerns. "Green" practices are quickly becoming expected rather than optional.

Not even globalization's strongest proponents could have imagined how *world politics* would change in recent years. We've seen a major set of financial crises that have rocked global markets, a dramatic rise in the power and influence of China, and intense shakeups in governments in the Middle East. Throughout the industrialized world, businesses—particularly in the financial, transportation, and energy sectors—have come under new scrutiny.

One of the most well-documented findings from studies of individual and organizational behavior is that organizations and their members resist change.

RESISTANCE TO CHANGE

Our egos are fragile, and we often see change as threatening. One study showed that even when employees are shown data that suggest they need to change, they latch onto whatever data they can find that suggest they are okay and don't need to change.[2] Employees who have negative feelings about a change cope by not thinking about it, increasing their use of sick time or quitting. These reactions can sap the organization of vital energy when it is most needed.[3]

Resistance to change can be positive if it leads to open discussion and debate.[4] Open dialogue responses are usually preferable to apathy or silence and can indicate that members of the organization are engaged in the process, which then provides change agents an opportunity to explain the change effort. When members treat resistance only as a threat to be internalized, rather than as a point of discussion, they may increase dysfunctional conflict. Change agents can use the points of resistance they hear about to modify the change to fit the preferences of members of the organization.

Resistance doesn't necessarily surface in standardized ways. It can be overt, implicit, immediate, or deferred. Management can most easily deal with overt and immediate resistance, such as complaints, a work slowdown, or a strike threat. The greater challenge is managing resistance that is implicit or deferred. These responses—loss of loyalty or motivation, increased errors or absenteeism—are more subtle and more difficult to recognize for what they are. Deferred actions may surface weeks, months, or even years later and thus cloud the link between the change and the reaction to it. A single change of little inherent impact may be the straw that breaks the camel's back because resistance to earlier changes has been deferred and stockpiled.

Exhibit 17-1 summarizes major forces for resistance to change, categorized by their sources. Individual sources reside in human characteristics such as perceptions, personalities, and needs. Organizational sources reside in the structural makeup of organizations themselves.

It's worth noting that not all change is good. Speed can lead to bad decisions, and sometimes those initiating change fail to realize the full magnitude of the effects or their true costs. Rapid, transformational change is risky, and some organizations have collapsed for this reason.[5] JCPenney, under a new CEO, decided to radically change its pricing strategy (eliminate "permanent" sales that cut into margins). After its sales and stock price dropped roughly one-third, it reversed course, but has not yet recovered to its pre-change levels. The lesson? Change *can* be good, but change agents need to carefully think through the implications.

Overcoming Resistance to Change

Eight tactics can help change agents deal with resistance to change.[6] Let's review them briefly.

EDUCATION AND COMMUNICATION   Communicating the logic of a change can reduce employee resistance on two levels. First, it fights the effects of misinformation and poor communication: If employees receive the full facts and clear up misunderstandings, resistance should subside. One study of an organization in the Philippines found that formal change information sessions decreased employees' anxiety about the change, while providing high-quality information about the change increased their commitment to it.[7] Second, communication can help "sell" the need for change by packaging it properly.[8] For example, a study of German companies revealed changes are most effective when a company communicates a rationale that balances the interests of various stakeholders (shareholders, employees, community, and customers) rather than considering the viewpoint of shareholders only.[9]

EXHIBIT 17-1
Sources of
Resistance to
Change

INDIVIDUAL SOURCES

Habit. To cope with life's complexities, we rely on habits or programmed responses. But when confronted with change, this tendency to respond in our accustomed ways becomes a source of resistance.

Security. People with a high need for security are likely to resist change because it threatens feelings of safety.

Economic factors. Changes in job tasks or established work routines can arouse economic fears if people are concerned that they won't be able to perform the new tasks or routines to their previous standards, especially when pay is closely tied to productivity.

Fear of the unknown. Change substitutes ambiguity and uncertainty for the unknown.

Selective information processing. Individuals are guilty of selectively processing information in order to keep their perceptions intact. They hear what they want to hear and they ignore information that challenges the world they've created.

ORGANIZATIONAL SOURCES

Structural inertia. Organizations have built-in mechanisms—like their selection processes and formalized regulations—to produce stability. When an organization is confronted with change, this structural inertia acts as a counterbalance to sustain stability.

Limited focus of change. Organizations are made up of a number of interdependent subsystems. One can't be changed without affecting the others. So limited changes in subsystems tend to be nullified by the larger system.

Group inertia. Even if individuals want to change their behavior, group norms may act as a constraint.

Threat to expertise. Changes in organizational patterns may threaten the expertise of specialized groups.

Threat to established power relationships. Any redistribution of decision-making authority can threaten long-established power relationships within the organization.

PARTICIPATION It's difficult to resist a change decision in which we've participated. Assuming participants have the expertise to make a meaningful contribution, their involvement can reduce resistance, obtain commitment, and increase the quality of the change decision. However, against these advantages are the negatives: potential for a poor solution and great consumption of time.

BUILDING SUPPORT AND COMMITMENT When employees' fear and anxiety are high, counseling and therapy, new-skills training, or a short paid leave of absence may facilitate adjustment. When managers or employees have low emotional commitment to change, they favor the status quo and resist it.[10] Employees are also more accepting of changes when they are committed to the organization as a whole.[11] So, firing up employees and emphasizing their commitment to the organization overall can help them emotionally commit to the change rather than embrace the status quo.

DEVELOP POSITIVE RELATIONSHIPS People are more willing to accept changes if they trust the managers implementing them.[12] One study surveyed 235 employees from a large housing corporation in the Netherlands that was experiencing a merger. Those who had a more positive relationship with their supervisors, and who felt that the work environment supported development, were much more positive about the change process.[13] Another set of studies found that individuals who were dispositionally resistant to change felt more positive about the change if they trusted the change agent.[14] This research suggests that if managers are able to facilitate positive relationships, they may be able to overcome resistance to change even among those who ordinarily don't like changes.

IMPLEMENTING CHANGES FAIRLY   One way organizations can minimize negative impact is to make sure change is implemented fairly. As we saw in Chapter 7, procedural fairness is especially important when employees perceive an outcome as negative, so it's crucial that employees see the reason for the change and perceive its implementation as consistent and fair.[15]

MANIPULATION AND COOPTATION   *Manipulation* refers to covert influence attempts. Twisting facts to make them more attractive, withholding information, and creating false rumors to get employees to accept change are all examples of manipulation. If management threatens to close a manufacturing plant whose employees are resisting an across-the-board pay cut, and if the threat is actually untrue, management is using manipulation. *Cooptation*, on the other hand, combines manipulation and participation. It seeks to "buy off" the leaders of a resistance group by giving them a key role, seeking their advice not to find a better solution but to get their endorsement. Both manipulation and cooptation are relatively inexpensive ways to gain the support of adversaries, but they can backfire if the targets become aware they are being tricked or used. Once discovered, the change agent's credibility may drop to zero.

SELECTING PEOPLE WHO ACCEPT CHANGE   One study of managers in the United States, Europe, and Asia found those with a positive self-concept and high risk tolerance coped better with organizational change. Research suggests that the ability to easily accept and adapt to change is related to personality—some people simply have more positive attitudes about change than others.[16] Such individuals are open to experience, are willing to take risks, and are flexible in their behavior. A study of 258 police officers found those who were higher in growth-needs, internal locus of control, and internal work motivation had more positive attitudes about organizational change efforts.[17] Individuals higher in general mental ability are also better able to learn and adapt to changes in the workplace.[18] In sum, an impressive body of evidence shows organizations can facilitate change by selecting people predisposed to accept it.

Besides selecting individuals who are willing to accept changes, it is also possible to select teams that are more adaptable. Studies have shown that teams that are strongly motivated by learning about and mastering tasks are better able to adapt to changing environments.[19] This research suggests it may be necessary to consider not just individual motivation, but also group motivation when trying to implement changes.

COERCION   Last on the list of tactics is *coercion*, the application of direct threats or force on the dissenters. If management really is determined to close a manufacturing plant whose employees don't acquiesce to a pay cut, the company is using coercion. Other examples of coercion tools are forced transfers, loss of promotions, negative performance evaluations, and a poor letter of recommendation. The advantages and drawbacks of coercion are approximately the same as for manipulation and cooptation.

APPROACHES TO MANAGING ORGANIZATIONAL CHANGE

Now we turn to several approaches to managing change: Lewin's classic three-step model of the change process, Kotter's eight-step plan, and organizational development.

Lewin's Three-Step Model

Kurt Lewin argued that successful change in organizations should follow three steps: **unfreezing** the status quo, **movement** to a desired end state, and **refreezing** the new change to make it permanent[20] (see Exhibit 17-2).

The status quo is an equilibrium state. To move from equilibrium—to overcome the pressures of both individual resistance and group conformity—unfreezing must happen in one of three ways (see Exhibit 17-3). The **driving forces**, which direct behavior away from the status quo, can be increased. The **restraining forces**, which hinder movement away from equilibrium, can be decreased. A third alternative is to combine the first two approaches. Companies that have been successful in the past are likely to encounter restraining forces because people question the need for change.[21] Similarly, research shows that companies with strong cultures excel at incremental change but are overcome by restraining forces against radical change.[22]

Research on organizational change has shown that, to be effective, the actual change has to happen quickly.[23] Organizations that build up to change do less well than those that get to and through the movement stage quickly.

Once change has been implemented, to be successful the new situation must be refrozen so it can be sustained over time. Without this last step, change will likely be short-lived, and employees will attempt to revert to the previous equilibrium state. The objective of refreezing, then, is to stabilize the new situation by balancing the driving and restraining forces.

Kotter's Eight-Step Plan for Implementing Change

John Kotter of Harvard Business School built on Lewin's three-step model to create a more detailed approach for implementing change.[24] Kotter began by listing common

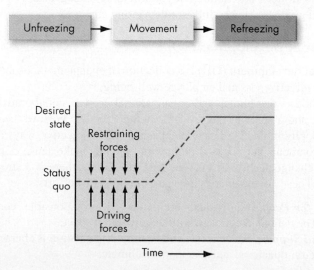

EXHIBIT 17-2
Lewin's Three-Step Change Model

EXHIBIT 17-3
Unfreezing the Status Quo

Establish a sense of urgency by creating a compelling reason for why change is needed.

Form a coalition with enough power to lead the change.

Create a new vision to direct the change and strategies for achieving the vision.

Communicate the vision throughout the organization.

Empower others to act on the vision by removing barriers to change and encouraging risk taking and creative problem solving.

Plan for, create, and reward short-term "wins" that move the organization toward the new vision.

Consolidate improvements, reassess changes, and make necessary adjustments in the new programs.

Reinforce the changes by demonstrating the relationship between new behaviors and organizational success.

EXHIBIT 17-4
Kotter's Eight-Step Plan for Implementing Change

Source: Based on M. du Plessis, "Re-implementing an Individual Performance Management System as a Change Intervention at Higher Education Institutions - Overcoming Staff Resistance," *Proceedings of the 7th European Conference on Management Leadership and Governance* (2011), pp. 105–115.

mistakes managers make when trying to initiate change. They may fail to create a sense of urgency about the need for change, to create a coalition for managing the change process, to have a vision for change and effectively communicate it, to remove obstacles that could impede the vision's achievement, to provide short-term and achievable goals, and/or to anchor the changes into the organization's culture. They may also declare victory too soon.

Kotter then established eight sequential steps to overcome these problems. They're listed in Exhibit 17-4. Notice how Kotter's first four steps essentially describe Lewin's "unfreezing" stage. Steps 5, 6, and 7 represent "movement," and the final step works on "refreezing." So Kotter's contribution lies in providing managers and change agents with a more detailed guide for successfully implementing change.

Organizational Development

Organizational development (OD) is a collection of change methods that try to improve organizational effectiveness and employee well-being.[25]

OD methods value human and organizational growth, collaborative and participative processes, and a spirit of inquiry.[26] Contemporary OD borrows heavily from postmodern philosophy in placing heavy emphasis on the subjective ways in which people see their environment. The focus is on how individuals make sense of their work environment. The change agent may take the lead in OD, but there is a strong emphasis on collaboration. These are the underlying values in most OD efforts:

1. *Respect for People.* Individuals are perceived as responsible, conscientious, and caring. They should be treated with dignity and respect.
2. *Trust and Support.* An effective and healthy organization is characterized by trust, authenticity, openness, and a supportive climate.

3. *Power Equalization.* Effective organizations de-emphasize hierarchical authority and control.
4. *Confrontation.* Problems should be openly confronted, not swept under the rug.
5. *Participation.* The more engaged in the decisions they are, the more people affected by a change will be committed to implementing it.

What are some OD techniques or interventions for bringing about change? Here are five.

1. *Survey Feedback.* One tool for assessing attitudes held by organizational members, identifying discrepancies among member perceptions, and solving these differences is the **survey feedback** approach.[27] Everyone in an organization can participate in survey feedback, but of key importance is the organizational "family"—the manager of any given unit and the employees who report directly to her. All usually complete a questionnaire about their perceptions and attitudes on a range of topics, including decision-making practices; communication effectiveness; coordination among units; and satisfaction with the organization, job, peers, and immediate supervisor.

   Data from this questionnaire are tabulated with data pertaining to an individual's specific "family" and to the entire organization. These data become the springboard for identifying problems and clarifying issues that may be creating difficulties for people. Particular attention is given to encouraging discussion and ensuring that it focuses on issues and ideas, and not on attacking individuals. For instance, are people listening? Are new ideas being generated? Can decision making, interpersonal relations, or job assignments be improved? Answers should lead the group to commit to various remedies for the problems identified.

2. *Process Consultation.* Managers often sense their unit's performance can be improved but are unable to identify what to improve and how. The purpose of **process consultation (PC)** is for an outside consultant to assist a client, usually a manager, "to perceive, understand, and act upon process events" with which the manager must deal.[28]

   PC is similar to sensitivity training in assuming that we can improve organizational effectiveness by dealing with interpersonal problems and by emphasizing involvement. But PC is more task directed, and consultants are there to "give the client 'insight' into what is going on around him, within him, and between him and other people."[29] The consultants do not solve the organization's problems, but rather guide or coach the client to solve the problems alone after *jointly* diagnosing what needs improvement. The client develops the skill to analyze processes within the organizational unit to solve current and future problems.

3. *Team Building.* We've noted throughout this text that organizations increasingly rely on teams to accomplish work tasks. **Team building** uses high-interaction group activities to increase trust and openness among team members, improve coordinative efforts, and increase team performance.[30] Team building typically includes goal-setting, development of interpersonal relations among team members, role analysis to clarify each member's role and responsibilities, and team process analysis. It may emphasize or exclude certain activities, depending on the purpose of the development effort and the specific problems with which the team is confronted.

4. *Intergroup Development.* A major area of concern in OD is dysfunctional conflict among groups. **Intergroup development** seeks to change groups' attitudes,

stereotypes, and perceptions about each other. Here, training sessions closely resemble diversity training (in fact, diversity training largely evolved from intergroup development in OD), except rather than focusing on demographic differences, they focus on differences among occupations, departments, or divisions within an organization.

Among several approaches for improving intergroup relations, a popular one emphasizes problem solving.[31] Each group meets independently to list its perceptions of itself and of the other group and how it believes the other group perceives it. The groups share their lists, discuss similarities and differences, and look for the causes of disparities. Once they have identified the causes of the difficulty, the groups move to the integration phase—developing solutions to improve relations between them. Subgroups can be formed of members from each of the conflicting groups to conduct further diagnoses and formulate alternative solutions.

5. *Appreciative Inquiry.* Most OD approaches are problem centered. They identify a problem or set of problems, then look for a solution. **Appreciative inquiry (AI)** instead accentuates the positive.[32] Rather than looking for problems to fix, it seeks to identify the unique qualities and special strengths of an organization, which members can build on to improve performance. That is, AI focuses on an organization's successes rather than its problems. The AI process consists of four steps—discovery, dreaming, design, and destiny—often played out in a large-group meeting over a 2- or 3-day time period and overseen by a trained change agent. *Discovery* sets out to identify what people think are the organization's strengths. Employees recount times they felt the organization worked best or when they specifically felt most satisfied with their jobs. In *dreaming*, employees use information from the discovery phase to speculate on possible futures, such as what the organization will be like in five years. In *design*, participants find a common vision of how the organization will look in the future and agree on its unique qualities. For the fourth step, participants seek to define the organization's *destiny* or how to fulfill their dream, and they typically write action plans and develop implementation strategies.

CREATING A CULTURE FOR CHANGE

Various approaches can be used to manage organizational change and for developing a culture for change; it is unlikely one approach is always best in every situation.

We've considered how organizations can *adapt* to change. But recently, some OB scholars have focused on a more proactive approach—how organizations can *embrace* change by transforming their cultures.

Stimulating a Culture of Innovation

How can an organization become more innovative? An excellent model is W. L. Gore, the $2.6-billion-per-year company best known as the maker of Gore-Tex fabric.[33] Gore has established a reputation as one of the most innovative U.S. companies by developing a stream of diverse products—including guitar strings, dental floss, medical devices, and fuel cells.

What's the secret of Gore's success? What can other organizations do to duplicate its track record for innovation? Although there is no guaranteed formula, certain characteristics surface repeatedly when researchers study innovative organizations. We consider the characteristics as structural, cultural, and human resources. Change agents should consider introducing these characteristics into their organization to create an innovative climate. Let's start by clarifying what we mean by innovation.

DEFINITION OF *INNOVATION* We said change refers to making things different. **Innovation**, a more specialized kind of change, is a new idea applied to initiating or improving a product, process, or service.[34] So all innovations imply change, but not all changes necessarily introduce new ideas or lead to significant improvements. Innovations can range from small incremental improvements, such as tablets, to radical breakthroughs, such as Soylent, a liquid food product that is cheaper and more environmentally sustainable than nearly every other food source.[35]

SOURCES OF INNOVATION *Structural variables* have been the most studied potential source of innovation.[36] A comprehensive review of the structure–innovation relationship leads to the following conclusions:[37]

1. Organic structures positively influence innovation. Because they're lower in vertical differentiation, formalization, and centralization, organic organizations facilitate the flexibility, adaptation, and cross-fertilization that make the adoption of innovations easier.
2. Long tenure in management is associated with innovation. Managerial tenure apparently provides legitimacy and knowledge of how to accomplish tasks and obtain desired outcomes.
3. Innovation is nurtured when there are slack resources. Having an abundance of resources allows an organization to afford to purchase innovations, bear the cost of instituting them, and absorb failures.
4. Interunit communication is high in innovative organizations.[38] These organizations are high users of committees, task forces, cross-functional teams, and other mechanisms that facilitate interaction across departmental lines.

Innovative organizations tend to have similar *cultures*. They encourage experimentation. They reward both successes and failures. They celebrate mistakes. Unfortunately, in too many organizations, people are rewarded for the absence of failures rather than for the presence of successes. Such cultures extinguish risk-taking and innovation. People will suggest and try new ideas only when they feel such behaviors exact no penalties. Managers in innovative organizations recognize that failures are a natural by-product of venturing into the unknown.

Within the *human resources* category, innovative organizations actively promote the training and development of their members so they keep current, offer high job security so employees don't fear getting fired for making mistakes, and encourage individuals to become champions of change. Once a new idea is developed, **idea champions** actively and enthusiastically promote it, build support, overcome resistance, and ensure it is implemented.[39] Champions have common personality characteristics: extremely high self-confidence, persistence, energy, and a tendency to take risks. They also display characteristics associated with transformational leadership—they inspire and energize others with their vision of an innovation's potential and their strong personal conviction about their mission. Idea champions are good at gaining the commitment of others, and their jobs provide considerable decision-making discretion; this autonomy helps them introduce and implement innovations.[40]

Do successful idea champions do things differently in different cultures? Yes.[41] People in collectivist cultures prefer appeals for cross-functional support for innovation efforts; people in high power distance cultures prefer champions to work closely with those in authority to approve innovative activities before work is begun; and the higher the uncertainty avoidance of a society, the more champions should work within the organization's rules and procedures to develop the innovation. These findings suggest that effective managers will alter their organization's championing strategies to reflect cultural values. So, for instance, although idea champions in Russia might succeed by ignoring budgetary limitations and working around confining procedures, champions in Austria, Denmark, Germany, or other cultures high in uncertainty avoidance will be more effective by closely following budgets and procedures.

WORK STRESS AND ITS MANAGEMENT

Change is often stressful to individuals but researchers are beginning to accept that not all stress is harmful.

Friends say they're stressed from greater workloads and longer hours because of downsizing at their companies. Parents worry about the lack of job stability and reminisce about a time when a job with a large company implied lifetime security. We read surveys in which employees complain about the stress of trying to balance work and family responsibilities.[42] Harris, Rothenberg International, a leading provider of employee assistance programs (EAPs), finds that employees are having mental breakdowns and needing professional help at higher rates than ever.[43] Indeed, work is, for most people, the most important source of stress in life. What are the consequences of stress, and what can individuals and organizations do to reduce it?

What Is Stress?

Stress is a dynamic condition in which an individual is confronted with an opportunity, demand, or resource related to what the individual desires and for which the outcome is perceived to be both uncertain and important.[44] This is a complicated definition. Let's look at its components more closely.

Although stress is typically discussed in a negative context, it is not necessarily bad in and of itself; it also has a positive value.[45] In response to stress, your nervous system, hypothalamus, pituitary, and adrenal glands supply you with stress hormones to cope. Your heartbeat and breathing accelerate to increase oxygen, while your muscles tense for action.[46] This is an opportunity when it offers potential gain. Consider, for example, the superior performance an athlete or stage performer gives in a "clutch" situation. Athletes often use stress positively to rise to the occasion and perform at their maximum. Similarly, many professionals see the pressures of heavy workloads and deadlines as positive challenges that enhance the quality of their work and the satisfaction they get from their job. However, when the situation is negative, stress is harmful and may hinder your progress by elevating your blood pressure uncomfortably and creating an erratic heart rhythm as you struggle to speak and think logically.[47]

Researchers have argued that **challenge stressors**—stressors associated with workload, pressure to complete tasks, and time urgency—operate quite differently from **hindrance stressors**—stressors that keep you from reaching your goals (for example, red tape, office politics, confusion over job responsibilities). Evidence suggests that challenge stressors produce less strain than hindrance stressors.[48]

Researchers have sought to clarify the conditions under which each type of stress exists. It appears that employees who have stronger commitment to their organizations can transfer psychological stress into greater focus and higher sales performance, whereas employees with low levels of commitment perform worse under stress.[49] And when challenge stress increases, those with high levels of organizational support have higher role-based performance, but those with low levels of organizational support do not.[50]

More typically, stress is associated with **demands** and **resources**. Demands are responsibilities, pressures, obligations, and uncertainties individuals face in the workplace. Resources are things within an individual's control that he can use to resolve the demands. Let's discuss what this demands–resources model means.[51]

When you take a test at school or undergo your annual performance review at work, you feel stress because you confront opportunities and performance pressures. A good performance review may lead to a promotion, greater responsibilities, and a higher salary. A poor review may prevent you from getting a promotion. An extremely poor review might even result in your being fired. To the extent you can apply resources to the demands on you—such as being prepared, placing the exam or review in perspective, or obtaining social support—you will feel less stress.

Research suggests that adequate resources help reduce the stressful nature of demands if demands and resources match. If emotional demands are stressing you, having emotional resources in the form of social support is especially important. If the demands are cognitive—say, information overload—then job resources in the form of computer support or information are more important. Thus, under the demands–resources perspective, coping resources are just as important in offsetting stress as demands are in increasing stress.[52]

Consequences of Stress

Stress shows itself in a number of ways, such as high blood pressure, ulcers, irritability, difficulty making routine decisions, loss of appetite, accident proneness, and the like. These symptoms fit under three general categories: physiological, psychological, and behavioral.

PHYSIOLOGICAL SYMPTOMS Most early concern with stress was directed at physiological symptoms because most researchers were specialists in the health and medical sciences. Their work led to the conclusion that stress could create changes in metabolism, increase heart and breathing rates and blood pressure, bring on headaches, and induce heart attacks.

Evidence clearly suggests that stress may have harmful physiological effects. One study linked stressful job demands to increased susceptibility to upper-respiratory illnesses and poor immune system functioning, especially for individuals with low self-efficacy.[53] A long-term study conducted in the United Kingdom found that job strain was associated with higher levels of coronary heart disease.[54] Still another study conducted with Danish human services workers found that higher levels of psychological burnout at the work-unit level were related to significantly higher levels of sickness absence.[55] Many other studies have shown similar results linking work stress to a variety of indicators of poor health.

PSYCHOLOGICAL SYMPTOMS Job dissatisfaction is an obvious cause of stress. But stress shows itself in other psychological states including tension, anxiety, irritability, boredom, and procrastination. For example, a study that tracked responses of employees over time found that stress due to high workloads was related to lower emotional well-being.[56]

Jobs that make multiple and conflicting demands or that lack clarity about the incumbent's duties, authority, and responsibilities increase both stress and dissatisfaction.[57] Similarly, the less control people have over the pace of their work, the greater their stress and dissatisfaction. Jobs that provide a low level of variety, significance, autonomy, feedback, and identity appear to create stress and reduce satisfaction and involvement in the job.[58] Not everyone reacts to autonomy in the same way, however. For those with an external locus of control, increased job control increases the tendency to experience stress and exhaustion.[59]

BEHAVIORAL SYMPTOMS Research on behavior and stress has been conducted across several countries and over time, and the relationships appear relatively consistent. Behavior-related stress symptoms include reductions in productivity, absence, and turnover, as well as changes in eating habits, increased smoking or consumption of alcohol, rapid speech, fidgeting, and sleep disorders.[60]

Managing Stress

Because low to moderate levels of stress can be functional and lead to higher performance, management may not be concerned when employees experience them. Employees, however, are likely to perceive even low levels of stress as undesirable. It's not unlikely, therefore, for employees and management to have different notions of what constitutes an acceptable level of stress on the job. What management may consider to be "a positive stimulus that keeps the adrenaline running" is very likely to be seen as "excessive pressure" by the employee. Keep this in mind as we discuss individual and organizational approaches to managing stress.[61]

INDIVIDUAL APPROACHES An employee can take personal responsibility for reducing stress levels. Individual strategies that have proven effective include time-management techniques, increased physical exercise, relaxation training, and expanded social support networks.

Many people manage their time poorly. The well-organized employee, like the well-organized student, can often accomplish twice as much as the person who is poorly organized. So an understanding and utilization of basic time-management principles can help individuals better cope with tensions created by job demands.[62] A few of the best-known time-management principles are: (1) making daily lists of activities to be accomplished, (2) prioritizing activities by importance and urgency, (3) scheduling activities according to the priorities set, (4) knowing your daily cycle and handling the most demanding parts of your job when you are most alert and productive, and (5) avoiding electronic distractions like frequently checking e-mail, which can limit attention and reduce efficiency.[63] These time-management skills can help minimize procrastination by focusing efforts on immediate goals and boosting motivation even in the face of tasks that are less desirable.[64]

Physicians have recommended noncompetitive *physical exercise*, such as aerobics, walking, jogging, swimming, and riding a bicycle, as a way to deal with excessive stress levels. These activities increase lung capacity, lower the resting heart rate, and provide a mental diversion from work pressures, effectively reducing work-related levels of stress.[65]

Individuals can also teach themselves to reduce tension through *relaxation techniques* such as meditation, hypnosis, and deep breathing. The objective is to reach a state of deep physical relaxation in which you focus all your energy on release of muscle tension.[66] Deep relaxation for 15 or 20 minutes a day releases strain and provides a pronounced sense of peacefulness, as well as significant changes in heart rate, blood pressure, and other physiological factors. A growing body of research shows that simply taking breaks from work at routine intervals can facilitate psychological recovery, and reduce stress significantly, and may improve job performance; these effects are even greater if relaxation techniques are employed.[67]

As we have noted, friends, family, or work colleagues can provide an outlet when stress levels become excessive. Expanding your *social support network* provides someone to hear your problems and offers a more objective perspective on a stressful situation than your own.

ORGANIZATIONAL APPROACHES Several organizational factors that cause stress—particularly task and role demands—are controlled by management and thus can be modified or changed. Strategies to consider include improved employee selection and job placement, training, realistic goal-setting, redesign of jobs, increased employee involvement, improved organizational communication, employee sabbaticals, and corporate wellness programs.

Certain jobs are more stressful than others but, as we've seen, individuals differ in their response to stressful situations. We know that individuals with little experience or an external locus of control tend to be more prone to stress. *Selection and placement* decisions should take these facts into consideration. Obviously, management shouldn't restrict hiring to only experienced individuals with an internal locus, but such individuals may adapt better to high-stress jobs and perform those jobs more effectively. Similarly, *training* can increase an individual's self-efficacy and thus lessen job strain.

We discussed *goal-setting* in Chapter 7. Individuals perform better when they have specific and challenging goals and receive feedback on their progress toward these goals. Goals can reduce stress as well as provide motivation.[68] Employees who are highly committed to their goals and see purpose in their jobs experience less stress, partly because they are more likely to perceive stressors as challenges, rather than hindrances. Specific goals perceived as attainable clarify performance expectations. In addition, goal feedback reduces uncertainties about actual job performance. The result is less employee frustration, role ambiguity, and stress.

Redesigning jobs to give employees more responsibility, more meaningful work, more autonomy, and increased feedback can reduce stress because these factors give employees greater control over work activities and lessen their dependence on others. But as we noted in our discussion of work design, not all employees want enriched jobs. The right redesign for employees with a low need for growth might be less responsibility and increased specialization. If individuals prefer structure and routine, reducing skill variety should also reduce uncertainties and stress levels.

Role stress is detrimental to a large extent because employees feel uncertain about goals, expectations, how they'll be evaluated, and the like. By giving employees a voice in the decisions that directly affect their job performance, management can increase employee control and reduce role stress. Thus, managers should consider *increasing employee involvement* in decision making because evidence clearly shows that increases in employee empowerment reduce psychological strain.[69]

Increasing formal *organizational communication* with employees reduces uncertainty by lessening role ambiguity and role conflict. Given the importance that perceptions play in moderating the stress–response relationship, management can also use effective communications as a means to shape employee perceptions. Remember that what employees categorize as demands, threats, or opportunities at work is an interpretation and that interpretation can be affected by the symbols and actions communicated by management.

Our final suggestion is to create organizationally supported **wellness programs**. These typically provide workshops to help people quit smoking, control alcohol use, lose weight, eat better, and develop a regular exercise program; they focus on the employee's total physical and mental condition.[70] Some help employees improve their psychological health as well. A meta-analysis of 36 programs designed to reduce stress (including wellness programs) showed that interventions to help employees reframe stressful situations and use active coping strategies appreciably reduced stress levels.[71] Most wellness programs assume employees need to take personal responsibility for their physical and mental health and that the organization provides a means to that end.

⊛ WATCH IT

If your professor assigned this, sign in to **mymanagementlab.com** to watch a video titled East Haven Fire Department: Managing Stress to learn more about this topic and respond to questions.

SUMMARY

The need for change has been implied throughout this text. For instance, think about attitudes, motivation, work teams, communication, leadership, organizational structures, human resource practices, and organizational cultures. Change was an integral part in our discussion of each. If environments were perfectly static, if employees' skills and abilities were always up to date and incapable of deteriorating, and if tomorrow were always exactly the same as today, organizational change would have little or no relevance to managers. But the real world is turbulent, requiring organizations and their members to undergo dynamic change if they are to perform at competitive levels. Stress is a natural by-product of work life affecting organizational behavior. Successful organizations recognize the factors that cause undue stress and take an active role in helping employees perform optimally.

IMPLICATIONS FOR MANAGERS

- Consider that, as a manager, you are a change agent in your organization. The decisions you make and your role-modeling behaviors will help shape the organization's change culture.

- Your management policies and practices will determine the degree to which the organization learns and adapts to changing environmental factors.
- Some stress is good. Low to moderate amounts of stress enable many people to perform their jobs better by increasing their work intensity, alertness, and ability to react. This is especially true if stress arises due to challenges on the job rather than hindrances that prevent employees from doing their jobs effectively.
- You can help alleviate harmful workplace stress for you and any employees you supervise by accurately matching workloads to employees, providing employees with stress-coping resources, and responding to their concerns.
- You can identify extreme stress when performance declines, turnover increases, health-related absenteeism increases, and engagement declines. However, by the time these symptoms are visible, it may be too late to be helpful, so stay alert for early indicators and be proactive.

PERSONAL INVENTORY ASSESSMENT

In Personal Inventory Assessment found in MyManagementLab take assessment: Tolerance of Ambiguity Scale

✪ WRITING SPACE

If your professor assigned this, sign in to **mymanagementlab.com** for the following Assisted-graded writing question:

17-1. What do you think are the best organizational responses to employee stress brought on by organizational changes? What are the worst?

EPILOGUE

The end of a book typically has the same meaning to an author that it has to the reader: It generates feelings of both accomplishment and relief. As both of us rejoice at having completed our tour of the essential concepts in organizational behavior, this is a good time to examine where we've been and what it all means.

The underlying theme of this book has been that the behavior of people at work is not a random phenomenon. Employees are complex entities, but their attitudes and behavior can nevertheless be explained and predicted with a reasonable degree of accuracy. Our approach has been to look at organizational behavior at three levels: the individual, the group, and the organization system.

We started with the individual and reviewed the major psychological contributions to understanding why individuals act as they do. We found that many of the individual differences among employees can be systematically labeled and categorized, and therefore generalizations can be made. For example, we know that individuals with a conventional type of personality are better matched to certain jobs in corporate management than are people with investigative personalities. So placing people into jobs that are compatible with their personality types should result in higher-performing and more satisfied employees.

Next, our analysis moved to the group level. We argued that the understanding of group behavior is more complex than merely multiplying what we know about individuals by the number of members in the group, because people act differently in a group than when they are alone. We demonstrated how roles, norms, leadership styles, power relationships, and other similar group factors affect the behavior of employees.

Finally, we overlaid system-wide variables on our knowledge of individual and group behavior to further improve our understanding of organizational behavior. Major emphasis was given to showing how an organization's structure, design, and culture affect both the attitudes and the behavior of employees.

It may be tempting to criticize the stress this book placed on theoretical concepts, but as noted psychologist Kurt Lewin is purported to have said, "There is nothing so practical as a good theory." Of course, it's also true that there is nothing so impractical as a good theory that leads nowhere. To avoid presenting theories that lead nowhere, this book included a wealth of examples and illustrations. And we regularly stopped to inquire about the implications of theory for the practice of management. The result has been the presentation of numerous concepts that, individually, offer some insights into behavior, but which, when taken together, provide a complex system to help you explain, predict, and control organizational behavior.

ENDNOTES

CHAPTER 1

1. Cited in R. Alsop, "Playing Well with Others," *Wall Street Journal* (September 9, 2002).
2. I. S. Fulmer, B. Gerhart, and K. S. Scott, "Are the 100 Best Better? An Empirical Investigation of the Relationship Between Being a 'Great Place to Work' and Firm Performance," *Personnel Psychology* (Winter 2003), pp. 965–993.
3. S. E. Humphrey, J. D. Nahrgang, and F. P. Morgeson, "Integrating Motivational, Social, and Contextual Work Design Features: A Meta-Analytic Summary and Theoretical Extension of the Work Design Literature," *Journal of Applied Psychology* 92, no. 5 (2007), pp. 1332–1356.
4. E. R. Burris, "The Risks and Rewards of Speaking Up: Managerial Responses to Employee Voice," *Academy of Management Journal* 55, no. 4 (2012), pp. 851–875.
5. T. L. Miller, C. L. Wesley II, and D. E. Williams, "Educating the Minds of Caring Hearts: Comparing the Views of Practitioners and Educators on the Importance of Social Entrepreneurship Competencies," *Academy of Management Learning & Education* 2, no. 3 (2012), pp. 349–370.
6. H. Aguinis and A. Glavas, "What We Don't Know About Corporate Social Responsibility: A Review and Research Agenda," *Journal of Management* (July 2012), pp. 932–968.
7. See, for instance, C. Heath and S. B. Sitkin, "Big-B Versus Big-O: What Is *Organizational* about Organizational Behavior?" *Journal of Organizational Behavior* (February 2001), pp. 43–58. For a review of what one researcher believes *should* be included in organizational behavior, based on survey data, see J. B. Miner, "The Rated Importance, Scientific Validity, and Practical Usefulness of Organizational Behavior Theories: A Quantitative Review," *Academy of Management Learning & Education* (September 2003), pp. 250–268.
8. D. M. Rousseau and S. McCarthy, "Educating Managers from an Evidence-Based Perspective," *Academy of Management Learning & Education* 6, no. 1 (2007), pp. 84–101; and S. L. Rynes, T. L. Giluk, and K. G. Brown, "The Very Separate Worlds of Academic and Practitioner Periodicals in Human Resource Management: Implications for Evidence-Based Management," *Academy of Management Journal* 50, no. 5 (2007), pp. 987–1008.
9. M. J. Mauboussin, "Most Companies Use the Wrong Metrics. Don't Be One of Them," *Harvard Business Review* (October 2012), pp. 46–56.
10. See, for instance, M. Workman and W. Bommer, "Redesigning Computer Call Center Work: A Longitudinal Field Experiment," *Journal of Organizational Behavior* (May 2004), pp. 317–337.
11. S. Shellenbarger, "Single and Off the Fast Track," *The Wall Street Journal* (May 23, 2012), pp. D1, D3.
12. F. Luthans and C. M. Youssef, "Emerging Positive Organizational Behavior," *Journal of Management* (June 2007), pp. 321–349; C. M. Youssef and F. Luthans, "Positive Organizational Behavior in the Workplace: The Impact of Hope, Optimism, and Resilience," *Journal of Management* 33, no. 5 (2007), pp. 774–800; and J. E. Dutton and S. Sonenshein, "Positive Organizational Scholarship," in C. Cooper and J. Barling (eds.), *Encyclopedia of Positive Psychology* (Thousand Oaks, CA: Sage, 2007).
13. L. M. Roberts, G. Spreitzer, J. Dutton, R. Quinn, E. Heaphy, and B. Barker, "How to Play to Your Strengths," *Harvard Business Review* (January 2005), pp. 1–6; and L. M. Roberts, J. E. Dutton, G. M. Spreitzer, E. D. Heaphy, and R. E. Quinn, "Composing the Reflected Best-Self Portrait: Becoming Extraordinary in Work Organizations," *Academy of Management Review* 30, no. 4 (2005), pp. 712–736.
14. W. Bailey and A. Spicer, "When Does National Identity Matter? Convergence and Divergence in International Business Ethics," *Academy of Management Journal* 50, no. 6 (2007), pp. 1462–1480; and A. B. Oumlil and J. L. Balloun, "Ethical Decision-Making Differences between American and Moroccan Managers," *Journal of Business Ethics* 84, no. 4 (2009), pp. 457–478.
15. J. Merritt, "For MBAs, Soul-Searching 101," *Business Week* (September 16, 2002), pp. 64–66; and S. Greenhouse, "The Mood at Work: Anger and Anxiety," *The New York Times* (October 29, 2002), p. E1.
16. D. M. Mayer, M. Kuenzi, R. Greenbaum, M. Bardes, and R. Salvador, "How Low Does Ethical Leadership Flow? Test of a Trickle-Down Model," *Organizational Behavior and Human Decision Processes* 108, no. 1 (2009), pp. 1–13; and A. Ardichvili, J. A. Mitchell, and D. Jondle, "Characteristics of Ethical Business Cultures," *Journal of Business Ethics* 85, no. 4 (2009), pp. 445–451.

CHAPTER 2

1. M. Toossi, "A Century of Change: The U.S. Labor Force, 1950–2050," *Bureau of Labor Statistics* (May 2002), www.bls.gov/opub/mlr/2002/05/art2full.pdf.
2. L. Colley, "Not Codgers in Cardigans! Female Workforce Participation and Ageing Public Services," *Gender Work and Organization* (May 2013), pp. 327–238; and M. DiNatale and S. Boraas, "The Labor Force Experience of Women from Generation X," *Monthly Labor Review* (March 2002), pp. 1–15.
3. See, for example, J. D. Fisher and C. A. Houseworth, "The Reverse Wage Gap among Educated White and Black Women," *Journal of Economic Inequality* (December 2012), pp. 449–470; C.-H. Kim and A. Sakamoto, "Have Asian American Men Achieved Labor Market Parity with White Men?," *American Sociological Review* (December 2010), pp. 934–957; A. Sakomoto, K. A. Goyette, and C. Kim, "Socioeconomic Attainments of Asian Americans," *Annual Review of Sociology* 35, (2009), pp. 255–276.
4. M. Toossi, "Labor Force Projections to 2020: A More Slowly Growing Workforce," *Bureau of Labor Statistics* (January 2012), www.bls.gov/opub/mlr/2012/01/art3full.pdf.
5. *SHRM Workplace Forecast* (Alexandria, VA: Society for Human Resource Management, 2013).
6. D. A. Harrison, K. H. Price, J. H. Gavin, and A. T. Florey, "Time, Teams, and Task Performance: Changing Effects of Surface- and Deep-Level Diversity on Group Functioning," *Academy of Management Journal* 45, no. 5 (2002), pp. 1029–1045; and

A. H. Eagly and J. L. Chin, "Are Memberships in Race, Ethnicity, and Gender Categories Merely Surface Characteristics?" *American Psychologist* 65 (2010), pp. 934–935.

7. P. Chattopadhyay, M. Tluchowska, and E. George, "Identifying the Ingroup: A Closer Look at the Influence of Demographic Dissimilarity on Employee Social Identity," *Academy of Management Review* 29, no. 2 (2004), pp. 180–202; and P. Chattopadhyay, "Beyond Direct and Symmetrical Effects: The Influence of Demographic Dissimilarity on Organizational Citizenship Behavior," *Academy of Management Journal* 42, no. 3 (1999), pp. 273–287.

8. L. M. Cortina, "Unseen Injustice: Incivility as Modern Discrimination in Organizations," *Academy of Management Review* 33, no. 1 (2008), pp. 55–75.

9. T. Lytle, "Benefits for Older Workers," *HR Magazine* (March 2012), pp. 53–58.

10. L. Weber, "Americans Rip Up Retirement Plans," *The Wall Street Journal* (January 31, 2013), http://online.wsj.com/article/SB10001424127887323926104578276241741448064.html.

11. K. A. Wrenn and T. J. Maurer, "Beliefs About Older Workers' Learning and Development Behavior in Relation to Beliefs About Malleability of Skills, Age-Related Decline, and Control," *Journal of Applied Social Psychology* 34, no. 2 (2004), pp. 223–242; and R. A. Posthuma and M. A. Campion, "Age Stereotypes in the Workplace: Common Stereotypes, Moderators, and Future Research Directions," *Journal of Management* 35 (2009), pp. 158–188.

12. T. W. H. Ng and D. C. Feldman, "Re-examining the Relationship Between Age and Voluntary Turnover," *Journal of Vocational Behavior* 74 (2009), pp. 283–294.

13. T. W. H. Ng and D. C. Feldman, "The Relationship of Age to Ten Dimensions of Job Performance," *Journal of Applied Psychology* 93 (2008), pp. 392–423.

14. T. W. H. Ng and D. C. Feldman, "Evaluating Six Common Stereotypes about Older Workers with Meta-Analytical Data," *Personnel Psychology* 65 (2012), pp. 821–858.

15. See Ng and Feldman, "The Relationship of Age to Ten Dimensions of Job Performance."

16. T. W. H. Ng and D. C. Feldman, "The Relationship of Age with Job Attitudes: A Meta-Analysis," *Personnel Psychology* 63 (2010), pp. 677–718.

17. F. Kunze, S. A. Boehm, and H. Bruch, "Age Diversity, Age Discrimination Climate and Performance Consequences—A Cross Organizational Study," *Journal of Organizational Behavior* 32 (2011), pp. 264–290.

18. P. L. Roth, K. L. Purvis, and P. Bobko, "A Meta-Analysis of Gender Group Differences for Measures of Job Performance in Field Studies," *Journal of Management* (March 2012), pp. 719–739.

19. See E. M. Weiss, G. Kemmler, E. A. Deisenhammer, W. W. Fleischhacker, and M. Delazer, "Sex Differences in Cognitive Functions," *Personality and Individual Differences* (September 2003), pp. 863–875; and A. F. Jorm, K. J. Anstey, H. Christensen, and B. Rodgers, "Gender Differences in Cognitive Abilities: The Mediating Role of Health State and Health Habits," *Intelligence* (January 2004), pp. 7–23.

20. S. Kolhatkar, "Emasculation Nation," *Bloomberg Businessweek* (September 17–September 23, 2012), pp. 102–103.

21. R. K. Chang, "Bias Persists for Women of Science, A Study Finds," *The New York Times* (September 25, 2012), Science pp. 1, 6.

22. K. Peters, M. Ryan, S. A. Haslam, and H. Fernandes, "To Belong or Not to Belong: Evidence That Women's Occupational Disidentification Is Promoted by Lack of Fit with Masculine Occupational Prototypes," *Journal of Personnel Psychology* 2 (2012), pp. 148–158.

23. R. E. Silverman, "Study Suggests Fix for Gender Bias on the Job," *The Wall Street Journal* (January 9, 2013), p. D4.

24. E. B. King et al., "Benevolent Sexism at Work: Gender Differences in the Distribution of Challenging Developmental Experiences," *Journal of Management* (November 2012), pp. 1835–1866.

25. M. E. Heilman and T. G. Okimoto, "Why Are Women Penalized for Success at Male Tasks? The Implied Communality Deficit," *Journal of Applied Psychology* 92, no. 1 (2007), pp. 81–92.

26. See, for instance, J. Bussey, "How Women Can Get Ahead: Advice from Female CEOs," *The Wall Street Journal* (May 18, 2012), pp. B1–B2; T. Gara, "Sandberg Opens Up on Women and Work," *The Wall Street Journal* (February 6, 2013); and L. Petrecca, "High-Paying Careers Top More Young Women's Lists," *The Wall Street Journal* (April 20, 2012) pp. 1A–2A.

27. D. R. Avery, P. F. McKay, and D. C. Wilson, "What Are the Odds? How Demographic Similarity Affects the Prevalence of Perceived Employment Discrimination," *Journal of Applied Psychology* 93 (2008), pp. 235–249.

28. A. Damast, "She Works Hard for Less Money," *Bloomberg Businessweek* (December 24, 2012–January 6, 2013), pp. 31–32.

29. B. Casselman, "Male Nurses Earn More," *The Wall Street Journal* (February 26, 2013), p. A2.

30. M. A. Belliveau, "Engendering Inequity? How Social Accounts Create vs. Merely Explain Unfavorable Pay Outcomes for Women," *Organization Science* (July–August 2012), pp. 1154–1174.

31. A. J. C. Cuddy, "Increasingly, Juries are Taking the Side of Women Who Face Workplace Discrimination," *Harvard Business Review* (September 2012), pp. 95–100.

32. J. L. Raver and L. H. Nishii, "Once, Twice, or Three Times as Harmful? Ethnic Harassment, Gender Harassment, and Generalized Workplace Harassment," *Journal of Applied Psychology* 95 (2010), pp. 236–254.

33. J. I Hancock, D. G. Allen, F. A. Bosco, K. R. McDaniel, and C. A. Pierce, "Meta-Analytic Review of Employee Turnover as a Predictor of Firm Performance," *Journal of Management* (March 2013), pp. 573–603.

34. J. M. McCarthy, C. H. Van Iddekinge, and M. A. Campion, "Are Highly Structured Job Interviews Resistant to Demographic Similarity Effects?" *Personnel Psychology* 63 (2010), pp. 325–359; and G. N. Powell and D. A. Butterfield, "Exploring the Influence of Decision Makers' Race and Gender on Actual Promotions to Top Management," *Personnel Psychology* 55, no. 2 (2002), pp. 397–428.

35. Avery, McKay, and Wilson, "What Are the Odds? How Demographic Similarity Affects the Prevalence of Perceived Employment Discrimination"; and Raver and Nishii, "Once, Twice, or Three Times as Harmful? Ethnic Harassment, Gender Harassment, and Generalized Workplace Harassment."

36. J. M. Sacco, C. R. Scheu, A. M. Ryan, and N. Schmitt, "An Investigation of Race and Sex Similarity Effects in Interviews: A Multilevel Approach to Relational Demography," *Journal of Applied Psychology* 88, no. 5 (2003), pp. 852–865; and P. F. McKay and M. A. McDaniel, "A Reexamination of Black-White Mean Differences in Work Performance: More Data, More Moderators," *Journal of Applied Psychology* 91, no. 3 (2006), pp. 538–554.

37. T. Vega, "With Diversity Still Lacking, Industry Focuses on Retention," *The New York Times* (September 4, 2012), p. B3.

38. B. R. Ragins, J. A. Gonzalez, K. Ehrhardt, and R. Singh, "Crossing the Threshold: The Spillover of Community Racial Diversity and Diversity Climate to the Workplace," *Personnel Psychology* 65 (2012), pp. 755–787.

39. P. F. McKay, D. R. Avery, and M. A. Morris, "Mean Racial-Ethnic Differences in Employee Sales Performance: The Moderating Role of Diversity Climate," *Personnel Psychology* 61, no. 2 (2008), pp. 349–374.

40. D. R. Avery, J. A. Richeson, M R. Hebl, and N. Ambady, "It Does Not Have to Be Uncomfortable: The Role of Behavioral Scripts in Black-White Interracial Interactions," *Journal of Applied Psychology* 94 (2009), pp. 1382–1393.

41. *Americans with Disabilities Act,* 42 U.S.C. § 12101, et seq. (1990).

42. S. G. Goldberg, M. B. Killeen, and B. O'Day, "The Disclosure Conundrum: How People with Psychiatric Disabilities Navigate Employment," *Psychology, Public Policy, and Law* 11, no. 3 (2005), pp. 463–500; and M. L. Ellison, Z. Russinova, K. L. MacDonald-Wilson, and A. Lyass, "Patterns and Correlates of Workplace Disclosure Among Professionals and Managers with Psychiatric Conditions," *Journal of Vocational Rehabilitation* 18, no. 1 (2003), pp. 3–13.

43. B. S. Bell and K. J. Klein, "Effect of Disability, Gender, and Job Level on Ratings of Job Applicants," *Rehabilitation Psychology* 46, no. 3 (2001), pp. 229–246; and E. Louvet, "Social Judgment Toward Job Applicants with Disabilities: Perception of Personal Qualities and Competences," *Rehabilitation Psychology* 52, no. 3 (2007), pp. 297-303.

44. L. R. Ren, R. L. Paetzold, and A. Colella, "A Meta-Analysis of Experimental Studies on the Effects of Disability on Human Resource Judgments," *Human Resource Management Review* 18, no. 3 (2008), pp. 191–203.

45. S. Almond and A. Healey, "Mental Health and Absence from Work: New Evidence from the UK Quarterly Labour Force Survey," *Work, Employment, and Society* 17, no. 4 (2003), pp. 731–742.

46. T. W. H. Ng and D. C. Feldman, "Organizational Tenure and Job Performance," *Journal of Management* 36, (2010), pp. 1220–1250.

47. I. R. Gellatly, "Individual and Group Determinants of Employee Absenteeism: Test of a Causal Model," *Journal of Organizational Behavior* (September 1995), pp. 469–485.

48. R. W. Griffeth, P. W. Hom, and S. Gaertner, "A Meta-analysis of Antecedents and Correlates of Employee Turnover: Update, Moderator Tests, and Research Implications for the Next Millennium," *Journal of Management* 26, no. 3 (2000), pp. 463–488.

49. M. R. Barrick and R. D. Zimmerman, "Hiring for Retention and Performance," *Human Resource Management* 48 (2009), pp. 183–206.

50. W. van Breukelen, R. van der Vlist, and H. Steensma, "Voluntary Employee Turnover: Combining Variables from the 'Traditional' Turnover Literature with the Theory of Planned Behavior," *Journal of Organizational Behavior* 25, no. 7 (2004), pp. 893–914.

51. E. B. King and A. S. Ahmad, "An Experimental Field Study of Interpersonal Discrimination Toward Muslim Job Applicants," *Personnel Psychology* 63 (2010), pp. 881–906.

52. A. Tilcsik, "Pride and Prejudice: Employment Discrimination against Openly Gay Men in the United States," *American Journal of Sociology* 117 (2011), pp. 586–626.

53. "Facts about Discrimination in Federal Government Employment Based on Marital Status, Political Affiliation, Status as a Parent, Sexual Orientation, or Transgender (Gender Identity) Status," U.S. Equal Employment Opportunity Commission (2013), www.eeoc.gov/federal/otherprotections.cfm.

54. "Sex-Based Discrimination," U.S. Equal Employment Opportunity Commission (2013), www.eeoc.gov/laws/types/sex.cfm.

55. M. Keisling, "No Longer at Zero: An Update on ENDA," *Huffington Post* (March 13, 2013), www.huffingtonpost.com/mara-keisling/no-longer-at-zero-an-upda_b_2861885.html.

56. C. Burns, "The Costly Business of Discrimination," *Center for American Progress* (March 2012), p. 13, www.scribd.com/doc/81214767/The-Costly-Business-of-Discrimination.

57. *HRC Corporate Equality Index,* 2013, www.hrc.org/files/assets/resources/CorporateEqualityIndex_2013.pdf.

58. R. Donadio, "Stuck in Recession, Italy Takes on Labor Laws That Divide the Generations," *The New York Times* (March 19, 2012), pp. A4, A6.

59. P. A. Freund and N. Kasten, "How Smart Do You Think You Are? A Meta-Analysis of the Validity of Self-Estimates of Cognitive Ability," *Psychological Bulletin* 138 (2012), pp. 296–321.

60. R. E. Nisbett et al., "Intelligence: New Findings and Theoretical Developments," *American Psychologist* (February–March 2012), pp. 130–159.

61. L. S. Gottfredson, "The Challenge and Promise of Cognitive Career Assessment," *Journal of Career Assessment* 11, no. 2 (2003), pp. 115–135.

62. M. D. Dunnette, "Aptitudes, Abilities, and Skills," in M. D. Dunnette (ed.), *Handbook of Industrial and Organizational Psychology* (Chicago: Rand McNally, 1976), pp. 478–483.

63. J. W. B. Lang, M. Kersting, U. R. Hülscheger, and J. Lang, "General Mental Ability, Narrower Cognitive Abilities, and Job Performance: The Perspective of the Nested-Factors Model of Cognitive Abilities" *Personnel Psychology* 63 (2010), pp. 595–640.

64. N. Barber, "Educational and Ecological Correlates of IQ: A Cross-National Investigation," *Intelligence* (May–June 2005), pp. 273–284.

65. J. F. Salgado, N. Anderson, S. Moscoso, C. Bertua, F. de Fruyt, and J. P. Rolland, "A Meta-analytic Study of General Mental Ability Validity for Different Occupations in the European Community," *Journal of Applied Psychology* (December 2003), pp. 1068–1081; and F. L. Schmidt and J. E. Hunter, "Select on Intelligence," in E. A. Locke (ed.), *Handbook of Principles of Organizational Behavior* (Malden, MA: Blackwell, 2004).

66. M. E. Beier and F. L. Oswald, "Is Cognitive Ability a Liability? A Critique and Future Research Agenda on Skilled Performance," *Journal of Experimental Psychology: Applied* 18 (2012), pp. 331–345.

67. Y. Ganzach, "Intelligence and Job Satisfaction," *Academy of Management Journal* 41, no. 5 (1998), pp. 526–539; and Y. Ganzach, "Intelligence, Education, and Facets of Job Satisfaction," *Work and Occupations* 30, no. 1 (2003), pp. 97–122.

68. J. J. Caughron, M. D. Mumford, and E. A. Fleishman, "The Fleishman Job Analysis Survey: Development, Validation, and Applications," in M.A. Wilson, W. Bennett Jr., S. G. Gibson, and G.M. Alliger (eds.), *The Handbook of Work Analysis: Methods, Systems, Applications and Science of Work Measurement in Organizations* (New York: Routledge/Taylor & Francis Group, 2012); P. D. Converse, F. L. Oswald, M. A. Gillespie, K. A. Field, and E. B. Bizot, "Matching Individuals to Occupations Using Abilities and the O*Net: Issues and an Application in Career Guidance," *Personnel Psychology* (Summer 2004), pp. 451–487; and E. A. Fleishman, "Evaluating Physical

Abilities Required by Jobs," *Personnel Administrator* (June 1979), pp. 82–92.

69. D. R. Avery, "Reactions to Diversity in Recruitment Advertising: Are the Differences Black and White?" *Journal of Applied Psychology* 88, no. 4 (2003), pp. 672–679; P. F. McKay and D. R. Avery, "What Has Race Got to Do with It? Unraveling the Role of Racioethnicity in Job Seekers' Reactions to Site Visits," *Personnel Psychology* 59, no. 2 (2006), pp. 395–429; and D. R. Avery and P. F. McKay, "Target Practice: An Organizational Impression Management Approach to Attracting Minority and Female Job Applicants," *Personnel Psychology* 59, no. 1 (2006), pp. 157–187.

70. C. C. Miller, "Google Search and Replace," *The New York Times* (August 23, 2012), pp. B1, B5.

71. A. Overholt, "More Women Coders," *Fortune* (February 25, 2013), p. 14.

72. L. Kwoh, "McKinsey Tries to Recruit Mothers Who Left the Fold," *The Wall Street Journal* (February 20, 2013), pp. B1, B7.

73. M. R. Buckley, K. A. Jackson, M. C. Bolino, J. G. Veres, and H. S. Field, "The Influence of Relational Demography on Panel Interview Ratings: A Field Experiment," *Personnel Psychology* 60 (2007), pp. 627–646; J. M. Sacco, C. R. Scheu, A. M. Ryan, and N. Schmitt, "An Investigation of Race and Sex Similarity Effects in Interviews: A Multilevel Approach to Relational Demography," *Journal of Applied Psychology* 88 (2003), pp. 852–865; and J. C. Ziegert and P. J. Hanges, "Employment Discrimination: The Role of Implicit Attitudes, Motivation, and a Climate for Racial Bias," *Journal of Applied Psychology* 90 (2005), pp. 553–562.

74. J. Schaubroeck and S. S. K. Lam, "How Similarity to Peers and Supervisor Influences Organizational Advancement in Different Cultures," *Academy of Management Journal* 45 (2002), pp. 1120–1136.

75. K. Bezrukova, K. A. Jehn, and C. S. Spell, "Reviewing Diversity Training: Where We Have Been and Where We Should Go," *Academy of Management Learning & Education* 2 (2012), pp. 207–227.

76. S. T. Bell, "Deep-Level Composition Variables as Predictors of Team Performance: A Meta–Analysis," *Journal of Applied Psychology* 92, no. 3 (2007), pp. 595–615; S. K. Horwitz and I. B. Horwitz, "The Effects of Team Diversity on Team Outcomes: A Meta-Analytic Review of Team Demography," *Journal of Management* 33, no. 6 (2007), pp. 987–1015; G. L. Stewart, "A Meta-Analytic Review of Relationships Between Team Design Features and Team Performance," *Journal of Management* 32, no. 1 (2006), pp. 29–54; and A. Joshi and H. Roh, "The Role of Context in Work Team Diversity Research: A Meta-Analytic Review," *Academy of Management Journal* 52, no. 3 (2009), pp. 599–627.

77. A. C. Homan, J. R. Hollenbeck, S. E. Humphrey, D. Van Knippenberg, D. R. Ilgen, and G. A. Van Kleef, "Facing Differences with an Open Mind: Openness to Experience, Salience of Intragroup Differences, and Performance of Diverse Work Groups," *Academy of Management Journal* 51, no. 6 (2008), pp. 1204–1222.

78. E. Kearney and D. Gebert, "Managing Diversity and Enhancing Team Outcomes: The Promise of Transformational Leadership," *Journal of Applied Psychology* 94, no. 1 (2009), pp. 77–89.

79. C. L. Holladay and M. A. Quiñones, "The Influence of Training Focus and Trainer Characteristics on Diversity Training Effectiveness," *Academy of Management Learning and Education* 7, no. 3 (2008), pp. 343–354; and R. Anand and M. Winters, "A Retrospective View of Corporate Diversity Training from 1964 to the Present," *Academy of Management Learning and Education* 7, no. 3 (2008), pp. 356–372.

80. Q. M. Roberson and C. K. Stevens, "Making Sense of Diversity in the Workplace: Organizational Justice and Language Abstraction in Employees' Accounts of Diversity-Related Incidents," *Journal of Applied Psychology* 91 (2006), pp. 379–391; and D. A. Harrison, D. A. Kravitz, D. M. Mayer, L. M. Leslie, and D. Lev-Arey, "Understanding Attitudes Toward Affirmative Action Programs in Employment: Summary and Meta-Analysis of 35 Years of Research," *Journal of Applied Psychology* 91 (2006), pp. 1013–1036.

81. A. Kalev, F. Dobbin, and E. Kelly, "Best Practices or Best Guesses? Assessing the Efficacy of Corporate Affirmative Action and Diversity Policies," *American Sociological Review* 71, no. 4 (2006), pp. 589–617.

82. R. J. Crisp and R. N. Turner, "Cognitive Adaptation to the Experience of Social and Cultural Diversity," *Psychological Bulletin* 137 (2011), pp. 242–266.

83. A. Sippola and A. Smale, "The Global Integration of Diversity Management: A Longitudinal Case Study," *International Journal of Human Resource Management* 18, no. 11 (2007), pp. 1895–1916.

CHAPTER 3

1. A. Barsky, S. A. Kaplan, and D. J. Beal, "Just Feelings? The Role of Affect in the Formation of Organizational Fairness Judgments," *Journal of Management* (January 2011), pp. 248–279; S. J. Breckler, "Empirical Validation of Affect, Behavior, and Cognition as Distinct Components of Attitude," *Journal of Personality and Social Psychology* (May 1984), pp. 1191–1205; J. A. Mikels, S. J. Maglio, A. E. Reed, and L. J. Kaplowitz, "Should I Go with My Gut? Investigating the Benefits of Emotion-Focused Decision Making," *Emotion* (August 2011), pp. 743–753; and A. J. Rojas Tejada, O. M. Lozano Rojas, M. Navas Luque, and P. J. Pérez Moreno, "Prejudiced Attitude Measurement Using the Rasch Scale Model," *Psychological Reports* (October 2011), pp. 553–572.

2. A. W. Wicker, "Attitude Versus Action: The Relationship of Verbal and Overt Behavioral Responses to Attitude Objects," *Journal of Social Issues* (Autumn 1969), pp. 41–78.

3. See I. Ajzen, "Nature and Operation of Attitudes," in S. T. Fiske, D. L. Schacter, and C. Zahn-Waxler (eds.), *Annual Review of Psychology,* vol. 52 (Palo Alto, CA: Annual Reviews Inc., 2001), pp. 27–58; L. R. Glasman and D. Albarracín, "Forming Attitudes That Predict Future Behavior: A Meta-Analysis of the Attitude–Behavior Relation," *Psychological Bulletin* (September 2006), pp. 778–822; and M. Riketta, "The Causal Relation Between Job Attitudes and Performance: A Meta-Analysis of Panel Studies," *Journal of Applied Psychology,* 93, no. 2 (2008), pp. 472–481.

4. L. Festinger, *A Theory of Cognitive Dissonance* (Stanford, CA: Stanford University Press, 1957).

5. See, for instance, L. R. Fabrigar, R. E. Petty, S. M. Smith, and S. L. Crites, "Understanding Knowledge Effects on Attitude-Behavior Consistency: The Role of Relevance, Complexity, and Amount of Knowledge," *Journal of Personality and Social Psychology* 90, no. 4 (2006), pp. 556–577; and D. J. Schleicher, J. D. Watt, and G. J. Greguras, "Reexamining

the Job Satisfaction-Performance Relationship: The Complexity of Attitudes," *Journal of Applied Psychology* 89, no. 1 (2004), pp. 165–177.

6. See L. R. Glasman and D. Albarracin, "Forming Attitudes That Predict Future Behavior: A Meta-Analysis of the Attitude-Behavior Relation," *Psychological Bulletin* (September 2006), pp. 778–822; I. Azjen, "Nature and Operation of Attitudes," in S. T. Fiske, D. L. Schacter, and C. Zahn-Waxler (eds.), *Annual Review of Psychology*, vol. 52 (Palo Alto, CA: Annual Reviews, 2001), pp. 27–58; and M. Riketta, "The Causal Relation Between Job Attitudes and Performance: A Meta-Analysis of Panel Studies," *Journal of Applied Psychology* 93, no. 2 (2008), pp. 472–481.

7. D. A. Harrison, D. A. Newman, and P. L. Roth, "How Important Are Job Attitudes? Meta-Analytic Comparisons of Integrative Behavioral Outcomes and Time Sequences," *Academy of Management Journal* 49, no. 2 (2006), pp. 305–325.

8. D. P. Moynihan and S. K. Pandey, "Finding Workable Levers Over Work Motivation: Comparing Job Satisfaction, Job Involvement, and Organizational Commitment," *Administration & Society* 39, no. 7 (2007), pp. 803–832.

9. See, for example, J. M. Diefendorff, D. J. Brown, and A. M. Kamin, "Examining the Roles of Job Involvement and Work Centrality in Predicting Organizational Citizenship Behaviors and Job Performance," *Journal of Organizational Behavior* (February 2002), pp. 93–108.

10. Based on G. J. Blau and K. R. Boal, "Conceptualizing How Job Involvement and Organizational Commitment Affect Turnover and Absenteeism," *Academy of Management Review* (April 1987), p. 290.

11. G. Chen and R. J. Klimoski, "The Impact of Expectations on Newcomer Performance in Teams as Mediated by Work Characteristics, Social Exchanges, and Empowerment," *Academy of Management Journal* 46, no. 5 (2003), pp. 591–607; A. Ergeneli, G. Saglam, and S. Metin, "Psychological Empowerment and Its Relationship to Trust in Immediate Managers," *Journal of Business Research* (January 2007), pp. 41–49; and S. E. Seibert, S. R. Silver, and W. A. Randolph, "Taking Empowerment to the Next Level: A Multiple-Level Model of Empowerment, Performance, and Satisfaction," *Academy of Management Journal* 47, no. 3 (2004), pp. 332–349.

12. B. J. Avolio, W. Zhu, W. Koh, and P. Bhatia, "Transformational Leadership and Organizational Commitment: Mediating Role of Psychological Empowerment and Moderating Role of Structural Distance," *Journal of Organizational Behavior* 25, no. 8 (2004), pp. 951–968.

13. M. Singh and A. Sarkar, "The Relationship Between Psychological Empowerment and Innovative Behavior," *Journal of Personnel Psychology* 2 (2012), pp. 127–137.

14. J. M. Diefendorff, D. J. Brown, A. M. Kamin, and R. G. Lord, "Examining the Roles of Job Involvement and Work Centrality in Predicting Organizational Citizenship Behaviors and Job Performance," *Journal of Organizational Behavior* (February 2002), pp. 93–108.

15. O. N. Solinger, W. van Olffen, and R. A. Roe, "Beyond the Three-Component Model of Organizational Commitment," *Journal of Applied Psychology* 93 (2008), pp. 70–83.

16. B. J. Hoffman, C. A. Blair, J. P. Meriac, and D. J. Woehr, "Expanding the Criterion Domain? A Quantitative Review of the OCB Literature," *Journal of Applied Psychology* 92, no. 2 (2007), pp. 555–566.

17. T. A. Wright and D. G. Bonett, "The Moderating Effects of Employee Tenure on the Relation Between Organizational Commitment and Job Performance: A Meta-Analysis," *Journal of Applied Psychology* (December 2002), pp. 1183–1190.

18. T. W. H. Ng, D. C. Feldman, and S. S. K. Lam, "Psychological Contract Breaches, Organizational Commitment, and Innovation-Related Behaviors: A Latent Growth Modeling Approach," *Journal of Applied Psychology* 95 (2010), pp. 744–751.

19. See, for instance, K. Bentein, C. Vandenberghe, R. Vandenberg, and F. Stinglhamber, "The Role of Change in the Relationship between Commitment and Turnover: A Latent Growth Modeling Approach," *Journal of Applied Psychology* 90 (2005), pp. 468–482; and J. D. Kammeyer-Mueller, C. R. Wanberg, T. M. Glomb, and D. Ahlburg, "The Role of Temporal Shifts in Turnover Processes: It's About Time," *Journal of Applied Psychology* 90 (2005), pp. 644–658.

20. J. P. Hausknecht, N. J. Hiller, and R. J. Vance, "Work-Unit Absenteeism: Effects of Satisfaction, Commitment, Labor Market Conditions, and Time," *Academy of Management Journal* 51 (2008), pp. 1223–1245.

21. D. A. Kaplan, "Salesforce's Happy Workforce," *Fortune* (February 6, 2012), pp. 101–112.

22. L. Rhoades, R. Eisenberger, and S. Armeli, "Affective Commitment to the Organization: The Contribution of Perceived Organizational Support," *Journal of Applied Psychology* 86, no. 5 (2001), pp. 825–836.

23. P. Eder and R. Eisenberger, "Perceived Organizational Support: Reducing the Negative Influence of Coworker Withdrawal Behavior," *Journal of Management* 34, no. 1 (2008), pp. 55–68; and C. Vandenberghe, K. Bentein, R. Michon, J. Chebat, M. Tremblay, and J. Fils, "An Examination of the Role of Perceived Support and Employee Commitment in Employee–Customer Encounters," *Journal of Applied Psychology* 92, no. 4 (2007), pp. 1177–1187.

24. J. Farh, R. D. Hackett, and J. Liang, "Individual-Level Cultural Values as Moderators of Perceived Organizational Support—Employee Outcome Relationships in China: Comparing the Effects of Power Distance and Traditionality," *Academy of Management Journal* 50, no. 3 (2007), pp. 715–729.

25. B. L. Rich, J. A. Lepine, and E. R. Crawford, "Job Engagement: Antecedents and Effects on Job Performance," *Academy of Management Journal* 53 (2010), pp. 617–635.

26. J. K. Harter, F. L. Schmidt, and T. L. Hayes, "Business-Unit-Level Relationship Between Employee Satisfaction, Employee Engagement, and Business Outcomes: A Meta-Analysis," *Journal of Applied Psychology* 87, no. 2 (2002), pp. 268–279.

27. N. R. Lockwood, *Leveraging Employee Engagement for Competitive Advantage* (Alexandria, VA: Society for Human Resource Management, 2007); and R. J. Vance, *Employee Engagement and Commitment* (Alexandria, VA: Society for Human Resource Management, 2006).

28. "Employee Engagement," *Workforce Management* (February 2013), p. 19; and "The Cornerstone OnDemand 2013 U.S. Employee Report," *Cornerstone OnDemand* (2013), www.cornerstoneondemand.com/resources/research/survey-2013.

29. W. H. Macey and B. Schneider, "The Meaning of Employee Engagement," *Industrial and Organizational Psychology* 1 (2008), pp. 3–30; and A. Saks, "The Meaning and Bleeding of Employee Engagement: How Muddy Is the Water?" *Industrial and Organizational Psychology* 1 (2008), pp. 40–43.

30. Y. Brunetto, S. T. T. Teo, K. Shacklock, and R. Farr-Wharton, "Emotional Intelligence, Job Satisfaction, Well-being and Engagement: Explaining Organisational Commitment and Turnover Intentions in Policing," *Human Resource Management Journal* (2012), pp. 428–441.

31. P. Petrou, E. Demerouti, M. C. W. Peeters, W. B. Schaufeli, and Jørn Hetland, "Crafting a Job on a Daily Basis: Contextual Correlates and the Link to Work Engagement," *Journal of Organizational Behavior* (November 2012), pp. 1120–1141.

32. P. W. Hom, T. R. Mitchell, T. W. Lee, and R. W. Griffeth, "Reviewing Employee Turnover: Focusing on Proximal Withdrawal States and an Expanded Criterion," *Psychological Bulletin* 138, no. 5 (2012), pp. 831–858.

33. The Wyatt Company's 1989 national Work America study identified 12 dimensions of satisfaction: Work organization, working conditions, communications, job performance and performance review, co-workers, supervision, company management, pay, benefits, career development and training, job content and satisfaction, and company image and change.

34. See E. Spector, *Job Satisfaction: Application, Assessment, Causes, and Consequences* (Thousand Oaks, CA: Sage, 1997), p. 3.

35. C. L. Dolbier, J. A. Webster, K. T. McCalister, M. W. Mallon, and M. A. Steinhardt, "Reliability and Validity of a Single-Item Measure of Job Satisfaction," *American Journal of Health Promotion* (January–February 2005), pp. 194–198; and J. Wanous, A. E. Reichers, and M. J. Hudy, "Overall Job Satisfaction: How Good Are Single-Item Measures?" *Journal of Applied Psychology* (April 1997), pp. 247–252.

36. N. A. Bowling, M. R. Hoepf, D. M. LaHuis, and L. R. Lepisto, "Mean Job Satisfaction Levels over Time: Are Things Bad and Getting Worse?" *The Industrial-Organizational Psychologist* (April 2013), pp. 57–64.

37. K. Bowman, "Attitudes About Work, Chores, and Leisure in America," *AEI Opinion Studies* (August 25, 2003); A. F. Chelte, J. Wright, and C. Tausky, "Did Job Satisfaction Really Drop During the 1970s?" *Monthly Labor Review* (November 1982), pp. 33–36; "Job Satisfaction High in America, Says Conference Board Study," *Monthly Labor Review* (February 1985), p. 52; and J. Pepitone, "U.S. Job Satisfaction Hits 22-Year Low," *CNNMoney.com* (January 5, 2010).

38. CareerBuilder, "One in Five Workers Plan to Change Jobs in 2014, According to CareerBuilder Survey," CareerBuilder.com press release (January 9, 2014), http://www.careerbuilder.com/share/aboutus/pressreleasesdetail.aspx?sd=1%2F9%2F2014&id=pr797&ed=12%2F31%2F2014, accessed May 8, 2014.

39. W. K. Balzer, J. A. Kihm, P. C. Smith, J. L. Irwin, P. D. Bachiochi, C. Robie, E. F. Sinar, and L. F. Parra, *Users' Manual for the Job Descriptive Index (JDI; 1997 Revision) and the Job in General Scales* (Bowling Green, OH: Bowling Green State University, 1997).

40. M. J. Gelfand, M. Erez, and Z. Aycan, "Cross-Cultural Organizational Behavior," *Annual Review of Psychology* 58 (2007), pp. 479–514; and A. S. Tsui, S. S. Nifadkar, and A. Y. Ou, "Cross-National, Cross-Cultural Organizational Behavior Research: Advances, Gaps, and Recommendations," *Journal of Management* (June 2007), pp. 426–478.

41. World Business Culture, "Doing Business in South Korea," www.worldbusinessculture.com/Business-in-South-Korea.html, accessed June 24, 2013.

42. J. Barling, E. K. Kelloway, and R. D. Iverson, "High-Quality Work, Job Satisfaction, and Occupational Injuries," *Journal of*

Applied Psychology 88, no. 2 (2003), pp. 276–283; and F. W. Bond and D. Bunce, "The Role of Acceptance and Job Control in Mental Health, Job Satisfaction, and Work Performance," *Journal of Applied Psychology* 88, no. 6 (2003), pp. 1057–1067.

43. D. S. Chiaburu and D. A. Harrison, "Do Peers Make the Place? Conceptual Synthesis and Meta-Analysis of Coworker Effect on Perceptions, Attitudes, OCBs, and Performance," *Journal of Applied Psychology* 93, no. 5 (2008), pp. 1082–1103; and S. E. Humphrey, J. D. Nahrgang, and F. P. Morgeson, "Integrating Motivational, Social, and Contextual Work Design Features: A Meta-Analytic Summary and Theoretical Extension of the Work Design Literature," *Journal of Applied Psychology* 92, no. 5 (2007), pp. 1332–1356.

44. T. A. Judge, R. F. Piccolo, N. P. Podsakoff, J. C. Shaw, and B. L. Rich, "The Relationship between Pay and Job Satisfaction: A Meta-Analysis of the Literature," *Journal of Vocational Behavior* 77 (2010), pp. 157-167.

45. E. C. Bianchi, "The Bright Side of Bad Times: The Affective Advantages of Entering the Workforce in a Recession," *Administrative Science Quarterly* (December 2013), pp. 587–623.

46. R. E. Silverman, "Work as Labor or Love?" *The Wall Street Journal* (October 18, 2012), p. D3.

47. See A. Davis-Blake, J. P. Broschak, and E. George, "Happy Together? How Using Nonstandard Workers Affects Exit, Voice, and Loyalty Among Standard Employees," *Academy of Management Journal* 46, no. 4 (2003), pp. 475–485; D. Farrell, "Exit, Voice, Loyalty, and Neglect as Responses to Job Dissatisfaction: A Multidimensional Scaling Study," *Academy of Management Journal* (December 1983), pp. 596–606; J. B. Olson-Buchanan and W. R. Boswell, "The Role of Employee Loyalty and Formality in Voicing Discontent," *Journal of Applied Psychology* (December 2002), pp. 1167–1174; C. E. Rusbult, D. Farrell, G. Rogers, and A. G. Mainous III, "Impact of Exchange Variables on Exit, Voice, Loyalty, and Neglect: An Integrative Model of Responses to Declining Job Satisfaction," *Academy of Management Journal* (September 1988), pp. 599–627; M. J. Withey and W. H. Cooper, "Predicting Exit, Voice, Loyalty, and Neglect," *Administrative Science Quarterly* (December 1989), pp. 521–539; and J. Zhou and J. M. George, "When Job Dissatisfaction Leads to Creativity: Encouraging the Expression of Voice," *Academy of Management Journal* (August 2001), pp. 682–696.

48. A. J. Nyberg and R. E. Ployhart, "Context-Emergent Turnover (CET) Theory: A Theory of Collective Turnover," *Academy of Management Review* 38 (2013), pp. 109–131.

49. T. A. Judge, C. J. Thoresen, J. E. Bono, and G. K. Patton, "The Job Satisfaction–Job Performance Relationship: A Qualitative and Quantitative Review," *Psychological Bulletin* (May 2001), pp. 376–407.

50. J. K. Harter, F. L. Schmidt, and T. L. Hayes, "Business-Unit Level Relationship Between Employee Satisfaction, Employee Engagement, and Business Outcomes: A Meta-Analysis," *Journal of Applied Psychology* (April 2002), pp. 268–279; C. Ostroff, "The Relationship Between Satisfaction, Attitudes, and Performance: An Organizational Level Analysis," *Journal of Applied Psychology* (December 1992), pp. 963–974; and A. M. Ryan, M. J. Schmit, and R. Johnson, "Attitudes and Effectiveness: Examining Relations at an Organizational Level," *Personnel Psychology* (Winter 1996), pp. 853–882.

51. See P. M. Podsakoff, S. B. MacKenzie, J. B. Paine, and D. G. Bachrach, "Organizational Citizenship Behaviors: A

Critical Review of the Theoretical and Empirical Literature and Suggestions for Future Research," *Journal of Management* 26, no. 3 (2000), pp. 513–563.

52. B. J. Hoffman, C. A. Blair, J. P. Maeriac, and D. J. Woehr, "Expanding the Criterion Domain? A Quantitative Review of the OCB Literature," *Journal of Applied Psychology* 92, no. 2 (2007), pp. 555–566.

53. S. L. Blader and T. R. Tyler, "Testing and Extending the Group Engagement Model: Linkages Between Social Identity, Procedural Justice, Economic Outcomes, and Extrarole Behavior," *Journal of Applied Psychology* 94, no. 2 (2009), pp. 445–464.

54. D. S. Chiaburu and D. A. Harrison, "Do Peers Make the Place? Conceptual Synthesis and Meta-Analysis of Coworker Effect on Perceptions, Attitudes, OCBs, and Performance," *Journal of Applied Psychology* 93, no. 5 (2008), pp. 1082–1103.

55. R. Ilies, I. S. Fulmer, M. Spitzmuller, and M. D. Johnson, "Personality and Citizenship Behavior: The Mediating Role of Job Satisfaction," *Journal of Applied Psychology* 94 (2009), pp. 945–959.

56. R. Ilies, B. A. Scott, and T. A. Judge, "The Interactive Effects of Personal Traits and Experienced States on Intraindividual Patterns of Citizenship Behavior," *Academy of Management Journal* 49 (2006), pp. 561–575.

57. See, for instance, D. J. Koys, "The Effects of Employee Satisfaction, Organizational Citizenship Behavior, and Turnover on Organizational Effectiveness: A Unit-Level, Longitudinal Study," *Personnel Psychology* (Spring 2001), pp. 101–114; M. Schulte, C. Ostroff, S. Shmulyian, and A. Kinicki, "Organizational Climate Configurations: Relationships to Collective Attitudes, Customer Satisfaction, and Financial Performance," *Journal of Applied Psychology* 94 (2009), pp. 618–634; and C. Vandenberghe, K. Bentein, R. Michon, J. Chebat, M. Tremblay, and J. Fils, "An Examination of the Role of Perceived Support and Employee Commitment in Employee-Customer Encounters," *Journal of Applied Psychology* 92, no. 4 (2007), pp. 1177–1187.

58. J. M. O'Brien, "Zappos Knows How to Kick It," *Fortune* (February 2, 2009), pp. 55–60.

59. K. D. Scott and G. S. Taylor, "An Examination of Conflicting Findings on the Relationship Between Job Satisfaction and Absenteeism: A Meta-Analysis," *Academy of Management Journal* (September 1985), pp. 599–612; R. P. Steel and J. R. Rentsch, "Influence of Cumulation Strategies on the Long-Range Prediction of Absenteeism," *Academy of Management Journal* (December 1995), pp. 1616–1634; and J. F. Ybema, P. G. W. Smulders, and P. M. Bongers, "Antecedents and Consequences of Employee Absenteeism: A Longitudinal Perspective on the Role of Job Satisfaction and Burnout," *European Journal of Work and Organizational Psychology* 19 (2010), pp. 102–124.

60. J. P. Hausknecht, N. J. Hiller, and R. J. Vance, "Work-Unit Absenteeism: Effects of Satisfaction, Commitment, Labor Market Conditions, and Time," *Academy of Management Journal* 51, no. 6 (2008), pp. 1123–1245.

61. G. Chen, R. E. Ployhart, H. C. Thomas, N. Anderson, and P. D. Bliese, "The Power of Momentum: A New Model of Dynamic Relationships Between Job Satisfaction Change and Turnover Intentions," *Academy of Management Journal* (February 2011), pp. 159–181; R. W. Griffeth, P. W. Hom, and S. Gaertner, "A Meta-Analysis of Antecedents and Correlates of Employee Turnover: Update, Moderator Tests, and

Research Implications for the Next Millennium," *Journal of Management* 26, no. 3 (2000), p. 479; and W. Hom and R. W. Griffeth, *Employee Turnover* (Cincinnati, OH: South-Western Publishing, 1995).

62. D. Liu, T. R. Mitchell, T. W. Lee, B. C. Holtom, and T. R. Hinkin, "When Employees Are Out of Step with Coworkers: How Job Satisfaction Trajectory and Dispersion Influence Individual- and Unit-Level Voluntary Turnover," *Academy of Management Journal* 55, no. 6 (2012), pp. 1360–1380.

63. T. H. Lee, B. Gerhart, I. Weller, and C. O. Trevor, "Understanding Voluntary Turnover: Path-Specific Job Satisfaction Effects and the Importance of Unsolicited Job Offers," *Academy of Management Journal* 51, no. 4 (2008), pp. 651–671.

64. K. Jiang, D. Liu, P. F. McKay, T. W. Lee, and T. R. Mitchell, "When and How Is Job Embeddedness Predictive of Turnover? A Meta-Analytic Investigation," *Journal of Applied Psychology* 97 (2012), pp. 1077–1096.

65. D. S. Chiaburu and D. A. Harrison, "Do Peers Make the Place? Conceptual Synthesis and Meta-Analysis of Coworker Effect on Perceptions, Attitudes, OCBs, and Performance," *Journal of Applied Psychology* 93, no. 5 (2008), pp. 1082–1103; and P. E. Spector, S. Fox, L. M. Penney, K. Bruursema, A. Goh, and S. Kessler, "The Dimensionality of Counterproductivity: Are All Counterproductive Behaviors Created Equal?" *Journal of Vocational Behavior* 68, no. 3 (2006), pp. 446–460.

66. K. Holland, "Inside the Minds of Your Employees," *The New York Times* (January 28, 2007), p. B1; "Study Sees Link Between Morale and Stock Price," *Workforce Management* (February 27, 2006), p. 15; and "The Workplace as a Solar System," *The New York Times* (October 28, 2006), p. B5.

67. E. White, "How Surveying Workers Can Pay Off," *The Wall Street Journal* (June 18, 2007), p. B3.

CHAPTER 4

1. See, for instance, C. D. Fisher and N. M. Ashkanasy, "The Emerging Role of Emotions in Work Life: An Introduction," *Journal of Organizational Behavior,* Special Issue 2000, pp. 123–129; N. M. Ashkanasy, C. E. J. Hartel, and W. J. Zerbe (eds.), *Emotions in the Workplace: Research, Theory, and Practice* (Westport, CT: Quorum Books, 2000); N. M. Ashkanasy and C. S. Daus, "Emotion in the Workplace: The New Challenge for Managers," *Academy of Management Executive* (February 2002), pp. 76–86; and N. M. Ashkanasy, C. E. J. Hartel, and C. S. Daus, "Diversity and Emotion: The New Frontiers in Organizational Behavior Research," *Journal of Management* 28, no. 3 (2002), pp. 307–338.

2. S. G. Barsade and D. E. Gibson, "Why Does Affect Matter in Organizations?" *Academy of Management Perspectives* (February 2007), pp. 36–59.

3. See N. H. Frijda, "Moods, Emotion Episodes and Emotions," in M. Lewis and J. M. Haviland (eds.), *Handbook of Emotions* (New York: Guilford Press, 1993), pp. 381–403.

4. H. M. Weiss and R. Cropanzano, "Affective Events Theory: A Theoretical Discussion of the Structure, Causes and Consequences of Affective Experiences at Work," in B. M. Staw and L. L. Cummings (eds.), *Research in Organizational Behavior,* vol. 18 (Greenwich, CT: JAI Press, 1996), pp. 17–19.

5. See P. Ekman and R. J. Davidson (eds.), *The Nature of Emotions: Fundamental Questions (Oxford, UK: Oxford University Press, 1994).*

6. See, for example, P. Ekman, "An Argument for Basic Emotions," *Cognition and Emotion* (May/July 1992), pp. 169–200; C. E. Izard, "Basic Emotions, Relations Among Emotions, and Emotion–Cognition Relations," *Psychological Bulletin* (November 1992), pp. 561–565; and J. L. Tracy and R. W. Robins, "Emerging Insights into the Nature and Function of Pride," *Current Directions in Psychological Science* 16, no. 3 (2007), pp. 147–150.

7. R. C. Solomon, "Back to Basics: On the Very Idea of 'Basic Emotions,'" *Journal for the Theory of Social Behaviour* 32, no. 2 (June 2002), pp. 115–144.

8. P. Ekman, *Emotions Revealed: Recognizing Faces and Feelings to Improve Communication and Emotional Life* (New York: Times Books/Henry Holt and Co., 2003).

9. Weiss and Cropanzano, "Affective Events Theory," pp. 20–22.

10. Cited in R. D. Woodworth, *Experimental Psychology* (New York: Holt, 1938).

11. D. Watson, L. A. Clark, and A. Tellegen, "Development and Validation of Brief Measures of Positive and Negative Affect: The PANAS Scales," *Journal of Personality and Social Psychology* (1988), pp. 1063–1070.

12. A. Ben-Ze'ev, *The Subtlety of Emotions* (Cambridge, MA: MIT Press, 2000), p. 94.

13. J. T. Cacioppo and W. L. Gardner, "Emotion," in *Annual Review of Psychology,* vol. 50 (Palo Alto, CA: Annual Reviews, 1999), pp. 191–214.

14. D. Holman, "Call Centres," in D. Holman, T. D. Wall, C. Clegg, P. Sparrow, and A. Howard (eds.), *The Essentials of the New Work Place: A Guide to the Human Impact of Modern Working Practices* (Chichester, UK: Wiley, 2005), pp. 111–132.

15. A. Ben-Ze'ev, *The Subtlety of Emotions* (Cambridge, MA: MIT Press, 2000), p. 99.

16. M. Eid and E. Diener, "Norms for Experiencing Emotions in Different Cultures: Inter- and International Differences," *Journal of Personality & Social Psychology* 81, no. 5 (2001), pp. 869–885.

17. O. Burkeman, "The Power of Negative Thinking," *The New York Times* (August 5, 2012), p. 9.

18. E. Jaffe, "Positively Negative," *Association for Psychological Science* (November 2012), pp. 13–17.

19. L. M. Poverny and S. Picascia, "There Is No Crying in Business," Womensmedia.com, October 20, 2009, www .womensmedia.com/new/Crying-at-Work.shtml.

20. M.-A. Reinhard and N. Schwartz, "The Influence of Affective States on the Process of Lie Detection," *Journal of Experimental Psychology* 18 (2012), pp. 377–389.

21. J. Haidt, "The New Synthesis in Moral Psychology," *Science* 316 (May 18, 2007), pp. 998, 1002; I. E. de Hooge, R. M. A. Nelissen, S. M. Breugelmans, and M. Zeelenberg, "What Is Moral about Guilt? Acting 'Prosocially' at the Disadvantage of Others," *Journal of Personality and Social Psychology* 100 (2011), pp. 462–473; and C. A. Hutcherson and J. J. Gross, "The Moral Emotions: A Social-Functionalist Account of Anger, Disgust, and Contempt," *Journal of Personality and Social Psychology* 100 (2011), pp. 719–737.

22. D. C. Rubin, R. M. Hoyle, and M. R. Leary, "Differential Predictability of Four Dimensions of Affect Intensity," *Cognition and Emotion* 26 (2012), pp. 25–41.

23. S. A. Golder and M. W. Macy, "Diurnal and Seasonal Mood Vary with Work, *Sleep*, and Daylength Across Diverse Cultures," *Science* 333 (2011), pp. 1878–1881.

24. Ibid.

25. J. J. A. Denissen, L. Butalid, L. Penke, and M. A. G. van Aken, "The Effects of Weather on Daily Mood: A Multilevel Approach," *Emotion* 8, no. 5 (2008), pp. 662–667; M. C. Keller, B. L. Fredrickson, O. Ybarra, S. Côté, K. Johnson, J. Mikels, A. Conway, and T. Wagner, "A Warm Heart and a Clear Head: The Contingent Effects of Weather on Mood and Cognition," *Psychological Science* 16 (2005) pp. 724–731; and Watson, *Mood and Temperament.*

26. D. Watson, *Mood and Temperament (New York: Guilford Press, 2000).*

27. D. Meinert, "Sleepless in Seattle . . . and Cincinnati and Syracuse," *HR Magazine* (October 2012), pp. 55–57.

28. B. A. Scott and T. A. Judge, "Insomnia, Emotions, and Job Satisfaction: A Multilevel Study," *Journal of Management* 32, no. 5 (2006), pp. 622–645.

29. P. R. Giacobbi, H. A. Hausenblas, and N. Frye, "A Naturalistic Assessment of the Relationship Between Personality, Daily Life Events, Leisure-Time Exercise, and Mood," *Psychology of Sport & Exercise* 6, no. 1 (January 2005), pp. 67–81.

30. L. L. Carstensen, M. Pasupathi, M. Ulrich, and J. R. Nesselroade, "Emotional Experience in Everyday Life Across the Adult Life Span," *Journal of Personality and Social Psychology* 79, no. 4 (2000), pp. 644–655.

31. M. LaFrance and M. Banaji, "Toward a Reconsideration of the Gender–Emotion Relationship," in M. Clark (ed.), *Review of Personality and Social Psychology,* vol. 14 (Newbury Park, CA: Sage, 1992), pp. 178–197; and A. M. Kring and A. H. Gordon, "Sex Differences in Emotion: Expression, Experience, and Physiology," *Journal of Personality and Social Psychology* (March 1998), pp. 686–703.

32. M. G. Gard and A. M. Kring, "Sex Differences in the Time Course of Emotion," *Emotion* 7, no. 2 (2007), pp. 429–437; M. Jakupcak, K. Salters, K. L. Gratz, and L. Roemer, "Masculinity and Emotionality: An Investigation of Men's Primary and Secondary Emotional Responding," *Sex Roles* 49 (2003), pp. 111–120; and M. Grossman and W. Wood, "Sex Differences in Intensity of Emotional Experience: A Social Role Interpretation," *Journal of Personality and Social Psychology* (November 1992), pp. 1010–1022.

33. A. R. Hochschild, "Emotion Work, Feeling Rules, and Social Structure," *American Journal of Sociology* (November 1979), pp. 551–575; W.-C. Tsai, "Determinants and Consequences of Employee Displayed Positive Emotions," *Journal of Management* 27, no. 4 (2001), pp. 497–512; M. W. Kramer and J. A. Hess, "Communication Rules for the Display of Emotions in Organizational Settings," *Management Communication Quarterly* (August 2002), pp. 66–80; and J. M. Diefendorff and E. M. Richard, "Antecedents and Consequences of Emotional Display Rule Perceptions," *Journal of Applied Psychology* (April 2003), pp. 284–294.

34. J. M. Diefendorff and G. J. Greguras, "Contextualizing Emotional Display Rules: Examining the Roles of Targets and Discrete Emotions in Shaping Display Rule Perceptions," *Journal of Management* 35 (2009), pp. 880–898.

35. A. A. Grandey, "When 'The Show Must Go On,'" *Academy of Management Journal* 46 (2003), pp. 86–96.

36. U. R. Hulsheger, H. J. E. M. Alberts, A. Feinholdt, and J. W. B. Lang, "Benefits of Mindfulness at Work: The Role of Mindfulness in Emotion Regulation, Emotional Exhaustion,

and Job Satisfaction," *Journal of Applied Psychology* (March 2013), pp. 310–325.

37. J. P. Trougakos, D. J. Beal, S. G. Green, and H. M. Weiss, "Making the Break Count: An Episodic Examination of Recovery Activities, Emotional Experiences, and Positive Affective Displays," *Academy of Management Journal* 51 (2008), pp. 131–146.

38. H. M. Weiss and R. Cropanzano, "An Affective Events Approach to Job Satisfaction," *Research in Organizational Behavior* 18 (1996), pp. 1–74.

39. J. Basch and C. D. Fisher, "Affective Events–Emotions Matrix: A Classification of Work Events and Associated Emotions," in N. M. Ashkanasy, C. E. J. Hartel, and W. J. Zerbe (eds.), *Emotions in the Workplace* (Westport, CT: Quorum Books, 2000), pp. 36–48.

40. N. M. Ashkanasy, C. E. J. Hartel, and C. S. Daus, "Diversity and Emotion: The New Frontiers in Organizational Behavior Research," *Journal of Management* 28, no. 3 (2002), p. 324.

41. This section is based on Daniel Goleman, *Emotional Intelligence* (New York: Bantam, 1995); P. Salovey and D. Grewal, "The Science of Emotional Intelligence," *Current Directions in Psychological Science* 14, no. 6 (2005), pp. 281–285; M. Davies, L. Stankov, and R. D. Roberts, "Emotional Intelligence: In Search of an Elusive Construct," *Journal of Personality and Social Psychology* (October 1998), pp. 989–1015; D. Geddes and R. R. Callister, "Crossing the Line(s): A Dual Threshold Model of Anger in Organizations," *Academy of Management Review* 32, no. 3 (2007), pp. 721–746.

42. P. A. Vernon, K. V. Petrides, D. Bratko, and J. A. Schermer, "A Behavioral Genetic Study of Trait Emotional Intelligence," *Emotion* 8, no. 5 (2008), pp. 635–642.

43. E. A. Locke, "Why Emotional Intelligence Is an Invalid Concept," *Journal of Organizational Behavior* 26, no. 4 (June 2005), pp. 425–431.

44. J. M. Conte, "A Review and Critique of Emotional Intelligence Measures," *Journal of Organizational Behavior* 26, no. 4 (June 2005), pp. 433–440; and M. Davies, L. Stankov, and R. D. Roberts, "Emotional Intelligence," pp. 989–1015.

45. D. L. Joseph and D. A. Newman, "Emotional Intelligence: An Integrative Meta-Analysis and Cascading Model," *Journal of Applied Psychology* 95 (2010), pp. 54–78.

46. S. L. Koole, "The Psychology of Emotion Regulation: An Integrative Review," *Cognition and Emotion* 23 (2009), pp. 4–41; H. A. Wadlinger and D. M. Isaacowitz, "Fixing Our Focus: Training Attention to Regulate Emotion," *Personality and Social Psychology Review* 15 (2011), pp. 75–102.

47. D. H. Kluemper, T. DeGroot, and S. Choi, "Emotion Management Ability: Predicting Task Performance, Citizenship, and Deviance," *Journal of Management* (May 2013), pp. 878–905.

48. T. L. Webb, E. Miles, and P. Sheeran, "Dealing with Feeling: A Meta-Analysis of the Effectiveness of Strategies Derived from the Process Model of Emotion Regulation," *Psychological Bulletin* 138, no. 4 (2012), pp. 775–808; S. Srivastava, M. Tamir, K. M. McGonigal, O. P. John, and J. J. Gross, "The Social Costs of Emotional Suppression: A Prospective Study of the Transition to College," *Journal of Personality and Social Psychology* 96 (2009), pp. 883–897; Y. Liu, L. M. Prati, P. L. Perrewé, and R. A. Brymer, "Individual Differences in Emotion Regulation, Emotional Experiences at Work, and Work-Related Outcomes: A Two-Study Investigation," *Journal of Applied Social Psychology* 40 (2010), pp. 1515–1538; and H. A. Wadlinger and D. M. Isaacowitz, "Fixing Our Focus: Training Attention to Regulate Emotion," *Personality and Social Psychology Review* 15 (2011), pp. 75–102.

49. J. V. Wood, S. A. Heimpel, L. A. Manwell, and E. J. Whittington, "This Mood Is Familiar and I Don't Deserve to Feel Better Anyway: Mechanisms Underlying Self-Esteem Differences in Motivation to Repair Sad Moods," *Journal of Personality and Social Psychology* 96 (2009), pp. 363–380.

50. S.-C. S. Chi and S.-G. Liang, "When Do Subordinates' Emotion-Regulation Strategies Matter? Abusive Supervision, Subordinates' Emotional Exhaustion, and Work Withdrawal," *Leadership Quarterly* (February 2013), pp. 125–137.

51. R. H. Humphrey, "How Do Leaders Use Emotional Labor?" *Journal of Organizational Behavior* (July 2012), pp. 740–744.

52. P. Totterdell, "Catching Moods and Hitting Runs: Mood Linkage and Subjective Performance in Professional Sports Teams," *Journal of Applied Psychology* 85, no. 6 (2000), pp. 848–859.

53. See A. M. Isen, "Positive Affect and Decision Making," in M. Lewis and J. M. Haviland-Jones (eds.), *Handbook of Emotions,* 2nd ed. (New York: Guilford, 2000), pp. 261–277.

54. L. B. Alloy and L. Y. Abramson, "Judgment of Contingency in Depressed and Nondepressed Students: Sadder but Wiser?" *Journal of Experimental Psychology: General* 108 (1979), pp. 441–485.

55. N. Ambady and H. M. Gray, "On Being Sad and Mistaken: Mood Effects on the Accuracy of Thin-Slice Judgments," *Journal of Personality and Social Psychology* 83, no. 4 (2002), pp. 947–961.

56. S. Lyubomirsky, L. King, and E. Diener, "The Benefits of Frequent Positive Affect: Does Happiness Lead to Success?" *Psychological Bulletin* 131, no. 6 (2005), pp. 803–855; and M. Baas, C. K. W. De Dreu, and B. A. Nijstad, "A Meta-Analysis of 25 Years of Mood-Creativity Research: Hedonic Tone, Activation, or Regulatory Focus," *Psychological Bulletin* 134 (2008), pp. 779–806.

57. M. J. Grawitch, D. C. Munz, and E. K. Elliott, "Promoting Creativity in Temporary Problem-Solving Groups: The Effects of Positive Mood and Autonomy in Problem Definition on Idea-Generating Performance," *Group Dynamics* 7, no. 3 (September 2003), pp. 200–213.

58. S. Lyubomirsky, L. King, and E. Diener, "The Benefits of Frequent Positive Affect: Does Happiness Lead to Success?" *Psychological Bulletin* 131, no. 6 (2005), pp. 803–855.

59. N. Madjar, G. R. Oldham, and M. G. Pratt, "There's No Place Like Home? The Contributions of Work and Nonwork Creativity Support to Employees' Creative Performance," *Academy of Management Journal* 45, no. 4 (2002), pp. 757–767.

60. J. M. George and J. Zhou, "Understanding When Bad Moods Foster Creativity and Good Ones Don't: The Role of Context and Clarity of Feelings," *Journal of Applied Psychology* 87, no. 4 (August 2002), pp. 687–697; and J. P. Forgas and J. M. George, "Affective Influences on Judgments and Behavior in Organizations: An Information Processing Perspective," *Organizational Behavior and Human Decision Processes* 86, no. 1 (2001), pp. 3–34.

61. C. K. W. De Dreu, M. Baas, and B. A. Nijstad, "Hedonic Tone and Activation Level in the Mood-Creativity Link: Toward a Dual Pathway to Creativity Model," *Journal of Personality and Social Psychology* 94, no. 5 (2008), pp. 739–756; J. M. George and J. Zhou, "Dual Tuning in a Supportive Context: Joint Contributions of Positive Mood, Negative Mood, and Supervisory Behaviors to Employee Creativity," *Academy of Management Journal* 50, no. 3 (2007), pp. 605–622.

62. A. Erez and A. M. Isen, "The Influence of Positive Affect on the Components of Expectancy Motivation," *Journal of Applied Psychology* 87, no. 6 (2002), pp. 1055–1067.

63. R. Ilies and T. A. Judge, "Goal Regulation Across Time: The Effect of Feedback and Affect," *Journal of Applied Psychology* 90, no. 3 (May 2005), pp. 453–467.

64. J. E. Bono, H. J. Foldes, G. Vinson, and J. P. Muros, "Workplace Emotions: The Role of Supervision and Leadership," *Journal of Applied Psychology* 92, no. 5 (2007), pp. 1357–1367.

65. S. G. Liang and S.-C. S. Chi, "Transformational Leadership and Follower Task Performance: The Role of Susceptibility to Positive Emotions and Follower Positive Emotions," *Journal of Business and Psychology* (March 2013), pp. 17–19.

66. T. Sy, S. Côté, and R. Saavedra, "The Contagious Leader: Impact of the Leader's Mood on the Mood of Group Members, Group Affective Tone, and Group Processes," *Journal of Applied Psychology* 90, no. 2 (2005), pp. 295–305.

67. V. A. Visser, D. van Knippenberg, G. van Kleef, and B. Wisse, "How Leader Displays of Happiness and Sadness Influence Follower Performance: Emotional Contagion and Creative versus Analytical Performance," *Leadership Quarterly* (February 2013), pp. 172–188.

68. B. E. Ashforth and R. H. Humphrey, "Emotion in the Workplace: A Reappraisal," *Human Relations* (February 1995), pp. 97–125.

69. G. A. Van Kleef, C. K. W. De Dreu, and A. S. R. Manstead, "The Interpersonal Effects of Emotions in Negotiations: A Motivated Information Processing Approach," *Journal of Personality and Social Psychology* 87, no. 4 (2004), pp. 510–528; and G. A. Van Kleef, C. K. W. De Dreu, and A. S. R. Manstead, "The Interpersonal Effects of Anger and Happiness in Negotiations," *Journal of Personality and Social Psychology* 86, no. 1 (2004), pp. 57–76.

70. E. van Dijk, G. A. Van Kleef, W. Steinel, and I. van Beest, "A Social Functional Approach to Emotions in Bargaining: When Communicating Anger Pays and When It Backfires," *Journal of Personality and Social Psychology* 94, no. 4 (2008), pp. 600–614.

71. K. M. O'Connor and J. A. Arnold, "Distributive Spirals: Negotiation Impasses and the Moderating Role of Disputant Self-Efficacy," *Organizational Behavior and Human Decision Processes* 84, no. 1 (2001), pp. 148–176.

72. B. Shiv, G. Loewenstein, A. Bechara, H. Damasio, and A. R. Damasio, "Investment Behavior and the Negative Side of Emotion," *Psychological Science* 16, no. 6 (2005), pp. 435–439.

73. W.-C. Tsai and Y.-M. Huang, "Mechanisms Linking Employee Affective Delivery and Customer Behavioral Intentions," *Journal of Applied Psychology* (October 2002), pp. 1001–1008.

74. See P. B. Barker and A. A. Grandey, "Service with a Smile and Encounter Satisfaction: Emotional Contagion and Appraisal Mechanisms," *Academy of Management Journal* 49, no. 6 (2006), pp. 1229–1238; and S. D. Pugh, "Service with a Smile: Emotional Contagion in the Service Encounter," *Academy of Management Journal* (October 2001), pp. 1018–1027.

75. D. E. Rupp and S. Spencer, "When Customers Lash Out: The Effects of Customer Interactional Injustice on Emotional Labor and the Mediating Role of Emotions, *Journal of Applied Psychology* 91, no. 4 (2006), pp. 971–978; and Tsai and Huang, "Mechanisms Linking Employee Affective Delivery and Customer Behavioral Intentions."

76. R. Ilies and T. A. Judge, "Understanding the Dynamic Relationships Among Personality, Mood, and Job Satisfaction: A Field Experience Sampling Study," *Organizational Behavior and Human Decision Processes* 89 (2002), pp. 1119–1139.

77. T. A. Judge and R. Ilies, "Affect and Job Satisfaction: A Study of Their Relationship at Work and at Home," *Journal of Applied Psychology* 89 (2004), pp. 661–673.

78. Z. Song, M. Foo, and M. A. Uy, "Mood Spillover and Crossover Among Dual-Earner Couples: A Cell Phone Event Sampling Study," *Journal of Applied Psychology* 93, no. 2 (2008), pp. 443–452.

79. See R. J. Bennett and S. L. Robinson, "Development of a Measure of Workplace Deviance," *Journal of Applied Psychology,* June 2000, pp. 349–360; see also P. R. Sackett and C. J. DeVore, "Counterproductive Behaviors at Work," in N. Anderson, D. S. Ones, H. K. Sinangil, and C. Viswesvaran (eds.), *Handbook of Industrial, Work & Organizational Psychology,* vol. 1 (Thousand Oaks, CA: Sage, 2001), pp. 145–164.

80. K. Lee and N. J. Allen, "Organizational Citizenship Behavior and Workplace Deviance: The Role of Affect and Cognition," *Journal of Applied Psychology* 87, no. 1 (2002), pp. 131–142; T. A. Judge, B. A. Scott, and R. Ilies, "Hostility, Job Attitudes, and Workplace Deviance: Test of a Multilevel Model," *Journal of Applied Psychology* 91, no. 1 (2006), 126–138; and S. Kaplan, J. C. Bradley, J. N. Luchman, and D. Haynes, "On the Role of Positive and Negative Affectivity in Job Performance: A Meta-Analytic Investigation," *Journal of Applied Psychology* 94, no. 1 (2009), pp. 162–176.

81. A. K. Khan, S. Ouratulain, and J. R. Cranshaw, "The Mediating Role of Discrete Emotions in the Relationship Between Injustice and Counterproductive Work Behaviors: A Study in Pakistan," *Journal of Business and Psychology* (March 2013), pp. 49–61.

82. R. D. Iverson and P. J. Erwin, "Predicting Occupational Injury: The Role of Affectivity," *Journal of Occupational and Organizational Psychology* 70, no. 2 (1997), pp. 113–128; Kaplan, Bradley, Luchman, and Haynes, "On the Role of Positive and Negative Affectivity in Job Performance: A Meta-Analytic Investigation;" and J. Maiti, "Design for Worksystem Safety Using Employees' Perception About Safety," *Work—A Journal of Prevention Assessment & Rehabilitation* 41 (2012), pp. 3117–3122.

CHAPTER 5

1. G. W. Allport, *Personality: A Psychological Interpretation* (New York: Holt, Rinehart & Winston, 1937), p. 48. For a brief critique of current views on the meaning of personality, see R. T. Hogan and B. W. Roberts, "Introduction: Personality and Industrial and Organizational Psychology," in B. W. Roberts and R. Hogan (eds.), *Personality Psychology in the Workplace* (Washington, DC: American Psychological Association, 2001), pp. 11–12.

2. K. I. van der Zee, J. N. Zaal, and J. Piekstra, "Validation of the Multicultural Personality Questionnaire in the Context of Personnel Selection," *European Journal of Personality* 17, Supl. 1 (2003), pp. S77–S100.

3. S. A. Birkeland, T. M. Manson, J. L. Kisamore, M. T. Brannick, and M. A. Smith, "A Meta-Analytic Investigation of Job Applicant Faking on Personality Measures," *International Journal of Selection and Assessment* 14, no. 14 (2006), pp. 317–335.

4. See R. Illies, R. D. Arvey, and T. J. Bouchard, "Darwinism, Behavioral Genetics, and Organizational Behavior: A Review and Agenda for Future Research," *Journal of Organizational*

Behavior 27, no. 2 (2006), pp. 121–141; and W. Johnson, E. Turkheimer, I. I. Gottesman, and T. J. Bouchard, Jr., "Beyond Heritability: Twin Studies in Behavioral Research," *Current Directions in Psychological Science* 18, no. 4 (2009), pp. 217–220.

5. S. Srivastava, O. P. John, and S. D. Gosling, "Development of Personality in Early and Middle Adulthood: Set Like Plaster or Persistent Change?" *Journal of Personality and Social Psychology* 84, no. 5 (2003), pp. 1041–1053; and B. W. Roberts, K. E. Walton, and W. Viechtbauer, "Patterns of Mean-Level Change in Personality Traits Across the Life Course: A Meta-Analysis of Longitudinal Studies," *Psychological Bulletin* 132, no. 1 (2006), pp. 1–25.

6. S. E. Hampson and L. R. Goldberg, "A First Large Cohort Study of Personality Trait Stability Over the 40 Years Between Elementary School and Midlife," *Journal of Personality and Social Psychology* 91, no. 4 (2006), pp. 763–779.

7. See A. H. Buss, "Personality as Traits," *American Psychologist* 44, no. 11 (1989), pp. 1378–1388; R. R. McCrae, "Trait Psychology and the Revival of Personality and Culture Studies," *American Behavioral Scientist* 44, no. 1 (2000), pp. 10–31; and L. R. James and M. D. Mazerolle, *Personality in Work Organizations* (Thousand Oaks, CA: Sage, 2002).

8. See, for instance, G. W. Allport and H. S. Odbert, "Trait Names, A Psycholexical Study," *Psychological Monographs* no. 47 (1936); and R. B. Cattell, "Personality Pinned Down," *Psychology Today* (July 1973), pp. 40–46.

9. R. B. Kennedy and D. A. Kennedy, "Using the Myers-Briggs Type Indicator in Career Counseling," *Journal of Employment Counseling* 41, no. 1 (2004), pp. 38–44.

10. The Myers & Briggs Foundation, "How Frequent Is My Type?" http://www.myersbriggs.org/my-mbti-personality-type/my-mbti-results/how-frequent-is-my-type.asp, accessed May 14, 2014.

11. A. Grant, "Goodbye to MBTI, the Fad That Won't Die," *Huffington Post* (September 18, 2013), http://www.huffingtonpost.com/adam-grant/goodbye-to-mbti-the-fad-t_b_3947014.html.

12. See, for instance, D. J. Pittenger, "Cautionary Comments Regarding the Myers-Briggs Type Indicator," *Consulting Psychology Journal: Practice and Research* 57, no. 3 (2005), pp. 10–221; L. Bess and R. J. Harvey, "Bimodal Score Distributions and the Myers-Briggs Type Indicator: Fact or Artifact?" *Journal of Personality Assessment* 78, no. 1 (2002), pp. 176–186; R. M. Capraro and M. M. Capraro, "Myers-Briggs Type Indicator Score Reliability Across Studies: A Meta-Analytic Reliability Generalization Study," *Educational & Psychological Measurement* 62, no. 4 (2002), pp. 590–602; and R. C. Arnau, B. A. Green, D. H. Rosen, D. H. Gleaves, and J. G. Melancon, "Are Jungian Preferences Really Categorical? An Empirical Investigation Using Taxometric Analysis," *Personality & Individual Differences* 34, no. 2 (2003), pp. 233–251.

13. See, for example, Oh, Wang, and Mount, "Validity of Observer Ratings of the Five-Factor Model of Personality Traits: A Meta-Analysis"; and M. R. Barrick and M. K. Mount, "Yes, Personality Matters: Moving On to More Important Matters," *Human Performance* 18, no. 4 (2005), pp. 359–372.

14. W. Fleeson and P. Gallagher, "The Implications of Big Five Standing for the Distribution of Trait Manifestation in Behavior: Fifteen Experience-Sampling Studies and a Meta-Analysis," *Journal of Personality and Social Psychology* 97, no. 6 (2009), pp. 1097–1114.

15. See, for instance, I. Oh and C. M. Berry, "The Five-Factor Model of Personality and Managerial Performance: Validity Gains Through the Use of 360 Degree Performance Ratings," *Journal of Applied Psychology* 94, no. 6 (2009), pp. 1498–1513; G. M. Hurtz and J. J. Donovan, "Personality and Job Performance: The Big Five Revisited," *Journal of Applied Psychology* 85, no. 6 (2000), pp. 869–879; J. Hogan and B. Holland, "Using Theory to Evaluate Personality and Job-Performance Relations: A Socioanalytic Perspective," *Journal of Applied Psychology* 88, no. 1 (2003), pp. 100–112; and M. R. Barrick and M. K. Mount, "Select on Conscientiousness and Emotional Stability," in E. A. Locke (ed.), *Handbook of Principles of Organizational Behavior* (Malden, MA: Blackwell, 2004), pp. 15–28.

16. M. K. Mount, M. R. Barrick, and J. P. Strauss, "Validity of Observer Ratings of the Big Five Personality Factors," *Journal of Applied Psychology* 79, no. 2 (1994), p. 272. Additionally confirmed by Hurtz and Donovan, "Personality and Job Performance: The Big Five Revisited"; and Oh and Berry, "The Five-Factor Model of Personality and Managerial Performance."

17. A. E. Poropat, "A Meta-Analysis of the Five-Factor Model of Personality and Academic Performance," *Psychological Bulletin* 135, no. 2 (2009), pp. 322–338.

18. H. Le, I. Oh, S. B. Robbins, R. Ilies, E. Holland, and P. Westrick, "Too Much of a Good Thing: Curvilinear Relationships Between Personality Traits and Job Performance," *Journal of Applied Psychology* 96, no. 1 (2011), pp. 113–133.

19. T. Bogg and B. W. Roberts, "Conscientiousness and Health-Related Behaviors: A Meta-Analysis of the Leading Behavioral Contributors to Mortality," *Psychological Bulletin* 130, no. 6 (2004), pp. 887–919.

20. G. J. Feist, "A Meta-Analysis of Personality in Scientific and Artistic Creativity," *Personality and Social Psychology Review* 2, no. 4 (1998), pp. 290–309; C. Robert and Y. H. Cheung, "An Examination of the Relationship Between Conscientiousness and Group Performance on a Creative Task," *Journal of Research in Personality* 44, no. 2 (2010), pp. 222–231; and M. Batey, T. Chamorro-Premuzic, and A. Furnham, "Individual Differences in Ideational Behavior. Can the Big Five and Psychometric Intelligence Predict Creativity Scores?" *Creativity Research Journal* 22, no. 1 (2010), pp. 90–97.

21. R. J. Foti and M. A. Hauenstein, "Pattern and Variable Approaches in Leadership Emergence and Effectiveness," *Journal of Applied Psychology* 92, no. 2 (2007), pp. 347–355.

22. L. I. Spirling and R. Persaud, "Extraversion as a Risk Factor," *Journal of the American Academy of Child & Adolescent Psychiatry* 42, no. 2 (2003), p. 130.

23. B. Weiss, and R. S. Feldman, "Looking Good and Lying to Do It: Deception as an Impression Management Strategy in Job Interviews," *Journal of Applied Social Psychology* 36, no. 4 (2006), pp. 1070–1086.

24. J. A. LePine, J. A. Colquitt, and A. Erez, "Adaptability to Changing Task Contexts: Effects of General Cognitive Ability, Conscientiousness, and Openness to Experience," *Personnel Psychology* 53, no. 3 (2000), pp. 563–595; S. Clarke and I. Robertson, "An Examination of the Role of Personality in Accidents Using Meta-Analysis," *Applied Psychology: An International Review* 57, no. 1 (2008), pp. 94–108; and M. Baer, "The Strength-of-Weak-Ties Perspective on Creativity: A Comprehensive Examination and Extension," *Journal of Applied Psychology* 95, no. 3 (2010), pp. 592–601.

25. R. Ilies, I. S. Fulmer, M. Spitzmuller, and M. D. Johnson, "Personality and Citizenship Behavior: The Mediating Role of Job Satisfaction," *Journal of Applied Psychology* 94, no. 4 (2009), pp. 945–959.

26. See, for instance, S. Yamagata, A. Suzuki, J. Ando, Y. Ono, K. Yutaka, N. Kijima, et al., "Is the Genetic Structure of Human Personality Universal? A Cross-Cultural Twin Study from North America, Europe, and Asia," *Journal of Personality and Social Psychology* 90, no. 6 (2006), pp. 987–998; H. C. Triandis and E. M. Suh, "Cultural Influences on Personality," *Annual Review of Psychology* 53, no. 1 (2002), pp. 133–160; and R. R. McCrae, P. T. Costa Jr., T. A. Martin, V. E. Oryol, A. A. Rukavishnikov, I. G. Senin, et al., "Consensual Validation of Personality Traits Across Cultures," *Journal of Research in Personality* 38, no. 2 (2004), pp. 179–201.

27. J. F. Rauthmann, "The Dark Triad and Interpersonal Perception: Similarities and Differences in the Social Consequences of Narcissism, Machiavellianism, and Psychopathy," *Social Psychological and Personality Science* 3 (2012), pp. 487–496.

28. P. K. Jonason, S. Slomski, and J. Partyka, "The Dark Triad at Work: How Toxic Employees Get Their Way," *Personality and Individual Differences* 52 (2012), pp. 449–453.

29. E. H. O'Boyle, D. R. Forsyth, G. C. Banks, and M. A. McDaniel, "A Meta-Analysis of the Dark Triad and Work Behavior: A Social Exchange Perspective," *Journal of Applied Psychology* 97 (2012), pp. 557–579.

30. L. Zhang, and M. A. Gowan, "Corporate Social Responsibility, Applicants' Individual Traits, and Organizational Attraction: A Person–Organization Fit Perspective," *Journal of Business and Psychology* 27 (2012), pp. 345–362.

31. D. N. Hartog and F. D. Belschak, "Work Engagement and Machiavellianism in the Ethical Leadership Process," *Journal of Business Ethics* 107 (2012), pp. 35–47.

32. J. J. Sosik, J. U. Chun, and W. Zhu, "Hang On to Your Ego: The Moderating Role of Leader Narcissism on Relationships Between Leader Charisma and Follower Psychological Empowerment and Moral Identity," *Journal of Business Ethics* (February 12, 2013); and B. M. Galvin, D. A. Waldman, and P. Balthazard, "Visionary Communication Qualities as Mediators of the Relationship between Narcissism and Attributions of Leader Charisma," *Personnel Psychology* 63, no. 3 (2010), pp. 509–537.

33. K. A. Byrne and D. A. Worthy, "Do Narcissists Make Better Decisions? An Investigation of Narcissism and Dynamic Decision-Making Performance," *Personality and Individual Differences* (July 2013), pp. 112–117.

34. C. Andreassen, H. Ursin, H. Eriksen, S. Pallesen, "The Relationship of Narcissism with Workaholism, Work Engagement, and Professional Position," *Social Behavior and Personality* 40, no. 6 (2012), pp. 881–890.

35. B. J. Hoffman, S. E. Strang, K. W. Kuhnert, W. K. Campbell, C. L. Kennedy, et al., "Leader Narcissism and Ethical Context: Effects on Ethical Leadership and Leader Effectiveness," *Journal of Leadership & Organizational Studies* 20 (2013), pp. 25–37.

36. L. L. Meier and N. K. Semmer, "Lack of Reciprocity and Strain: Narcissism as a Moderator of the Association Between Feeling Under-benefited and Irritation," *Work & Stress* 26 (2012), pp. 56–67.

37. M. Maccoby, "Narcissistic Leaders: The Incredible Pros, the Inevitable Cons," *The Harvard Business Review* (January-February 2000), pp. 69–77, www.maccoby.com/Articles/NarLeaders.shtml.

38. A. Chatterjee and D. C. Hambrick, "Executive Personality, Capability Cues, and Risk Taking: How Narcissistic CEOs React to Their Successes and Stumbles," *Administrative Science Quarterly* 56 (2011), pp. 202–237.

39. C. J. Resick, D. S. Whitman, S. M. Weingarden, and N. J. Hiller, "The Bright-Side and Dark-Side of CEO Personality: Examining Core Self-Evaluations, Narcissism, Transformational Leadership, and Strategic Influence," *Journal of Applied Psychology* 94, no. 6 (2009), pp. 1365–1381.

40. C. Carpenter, "Narcissism on Facebook: Self-Promotional and Anti-Social Behavior," *Personality and Individual Differences* 52 (2012), pp. 482–486.

41. O'Boyle, Forsyth, Banks, and McDaniel, "A Meta-Analysis of the Dark Triad and Work Behavior: A Social Exchange Perspective," p. 558.

42. B. Wille, F. De Fruyt, and B. De Clercq, "Expanding and Reconceptualizing Aberrant Personality at Work: Validity of Five-Factor Model Aberrant Personality Tendencies to Predict Career Outcomes," *Personnel Psychology* 66 (2013), pp. 173–223.

43. P. K. Jonason, S. Slomski, and J. Partyka, "The Dark Triad at Work: How Toxic Employees Get Their Way," *Personality and Individual Differences* 52 (2012), pp. 449–453; and H. M. Baughman, S. Dearing, E. Giammarco, and P. A. Vernon, "Relationships Between Bullying Behaviours and the Dark Triad: A Study with Adults," *Personality and Individual Differences* 52 (2012), pp. 571–575.

44. J. Concannon, "Mind Matters: Mental Disability and the History and Future of the American with Disabilities Act," *Law & Psychology Review* 36 (2012), pp. 89–114.

45. D. L. Ferris, R. E. Johnson, C. C. Rosen, E. Djurdjevic, C.-H. Chang, et al., "When Is Success Not Satisfying? Integrating Regulatory Focus and Approach/Avoidance Motivation Theories to Explain the Relation Between Core Self-Evaluation and Job Satisfaction," *Journal of Applied Psychology* 98 (2013), pp. 342–353.

46. K. Murayama and A. J. Elliot, "The Competition–Performance Relation: A Meta-Analytic Review and Test of the Opposing Processes Model of Competition and Performance," *Psychological Bulletin* 138 (2012), pp. 1035–1070.

47. S. Nifadkar, A. S. Tsui, and B. E. Ashforth, "The Way You Make Me Feel and Behave: Supervisor-Triggered Newcomer Affect and Approach-Avoidance Behavior," *Academy of Management Journal* 55 (2012), pp. 1146–1168.

48. T. A. Judge and J. E. Bono, "A Rose by Any Other Name . . . Are Self-Esteem, Generalized Self-Efficacy, Neuroticism, and Locus of Control Indicators of a Common Construct?" in B. W. Roberts and R. Hogan (eds.), *Personality Psychology in the Workplace* (Washington, DC: American Psychological Association, 2001), pp. 93–118.

49. A. Erez and T. A. Judge, "Relationship of Core Self-Evaluations to Goal Setting, Motivation, and Performance," *Journal of Applied Psychology* 86, no. 6 (2001), pp. 1270–1279.

50. A. N. Salvaggio, B. Schneider, L. H. Nishi, D. M. Mayer, A. Ramesh, and J. S. Lyon, "Manager Personality, Manager Service Quality Orientation, and Service Climate: Test of a Model," *Journal of Applied Psychology* 92, no. 6 (2007), pp. 1741–1750; B. A. Scott and T. A. Judge, "The Popularity Contest at Work: Who Wins, Why, and What Do They Receive?" *Journal of Applied Psychology* 94, no. 1 (2009), pp. 20–33; and T. A. Judge and C. Hurst, "How the Rich (and Happy) Get Richer (and Happier): Relationship of Core Self-Evaluations to Trajectories in Attaining Work Success," *Journal of Applied Psychology* 93, no. 4 (2008), pp. 849–863.

51. A. M. Grant and A. Wrzesniewksi, "I Won't Let You Down . . . or Will I? Core Self-Evaluations, Other-Orientation, Anticipated Guilt and Gratitude, and Job Performance," *Journal of Applied Psychology* 95, no. 1 (2010), pp. 108–121.

52. U. Malmendier and G. Tate, "CEO Overconfidence and Corporate Investment," *Journal of Finance* 60, no. 6 (2005), pp. 2661–2700.

53. See M. Snyder, *Public Appearances/Private Realities: The Psychology of Self-Monitoring* (New York: W. H. Freeman, 1987); and S. W. Gangestad and M. Snyder, "Self-Monitoring: Appraisal and Reappraisal," *Psychological Bulletin* 126, no. 4 (2000), pp. 530–555.

54. F. J. Flynn and D. R. Ames, "What's Good for the Goose May Not Be as Good for the Gander: The Benefits of Self-Monitoring for Men and Women in Task Groups and Dyadic Conflicts," *Journal of Applied Psychology* 91, no. 2 (2006), pp. 272–281; and Snyder, *Public Appearances/Private Realities.*

55. D. V. Day, D. J. Shleicher, A. L. Unckless, and N. J. Hiller, "Self-Monitoring Personality at Work: A Meta-Analytic Investigation of Construct Validity," *Journal of Applied Psychology* 87, no. 2 (2002), pp. 390–401.

56. H. Oh and M. Kilduff, "The Ripple Effect of Personality on Social Structure: Self-Monitoring Origins of Network Brokerage," *Journal of Applied Psychology* 93, no. 5 (2008), pp. 1155–1164; and A. Mehra, M. Kilduff, and D. J. Brass, "The Social Networks of High and Low Self-Monitors: Implications for Workplace Performance," *Administrative Science Quarterly* 46, no. 1 (2001), pp. 121–146.

57. J. M. Crant, "Proactive Behavior in Organizations," *Journal of Management* 26, no. 3 (2000), p. 436.

58. P. D. Converse, Patrick J. Pathak, A. M. DePaul-Haddock, T. Gotlib, and M. Merbedone, "Controlling Your Environment and Yourself: Implications for Career Success," *Journal of Vocational Behavior* 80 (2012), pp. 148–159.

59. G. Chen, J. Farh, E. M. Campbell-Bush, Z. Wu, and X. Wu, "Teams as Innovative Systems: Multilevel Motivational Antecedents of Innovation in R&D Teams," *Journal of Applied Psychology* (2013).

60. Z. Zhang, M. Wang, J. Shi, Junqi, "Leader-Follower Congruence in Proactive Personality and Work Outcomes: The Mediating Role of Leader-Member Exchange," *Academy of Management Journal* 55 (2012), pp. 111–130.

61. G. Van Hoye and H. Lootens, "Coping with Unemployment: Personality, Role Demands, and Time Structure," *Journal of Vocational Behavior* 82 (2013), pp. 85–95.

62. R. D. Meyer, R. S. Dalal, and R. Hermida, "A Review and Synthesis of Situational Strength in the Organizational Sciences," *Journal of Management* 36 (2010), pp. 121–140.

63. A. M. Grant and N. P. Rothbard, "When in Doubt, Seize the Day? Security Values, Prosocial Values, and Proactivity Under Ambiguity," *Journal of Applied Psychology* (2013).

64. A. M. Watson, T. F. Thompson, J. V. Rudolph, T. J. Whelan, T. S. Behrend, et al., "When Big Brother Is Watching: Goal Orientation Shapes Reactions to Electronic Monitoring During Online Training," *Journal of Applied Psychology* (2013).

65. Y. Kim, L. Van Dyne, D. Kamdar, and R. E. Johnson, "Why and When Do Motives Matter? An Integrative Model of Motives, Role Cognitions, and Social Support as Predictors of OCB," *Organizational Behavior and Human Decision Processes* (2013).

66. M. Rokeach, *The Nature of Human Values* (New York: The Free Press, 1973), p. 5.

67. M. Rokeach and S. J. Ball-Rokeach, "Stability and Change in American Value Priorities, 1968–1981," *American Psychologist* 44, no. 5 (1989), pp. 775–784; and A. Bardi, J. A. Lee, N. Hofmann-Towfigh, and G. Soutar, "The Structure of Intra-individual Value Change," *Journal of Personality and Social Psychology* 97, no. 5 (2009), pp. 913–929.

68. S. Roccas, L. Sagiv, S. H. Schwartz, and A. Knafo, "The Big Five Personality Factors and Personal Values," *Personality and Social Psychology Bulletin* 28, no. 6 (2002), pp. 789–801.

69. B. C. Holtz and C. M. Harold, "Interpersonal Justice and Deviance: The Moderating Effects of Interpersonal Justice Values and Justice Orientation," *Journal of Management* (February 2013), pp. 339–365.

70. J. L. Holland, *Making Vocational Choices: A Theory of Vocational Personalities and Work Environments* (Odessa, FL: Psychological Assessment Resources, 1997).

71. D. A. McKay and D. M. Tokar, "The HEXACO and Five-Factor Models of Personality in Relation to RIASEC Vocational Interests," *Journal of Vocational Behavior* (October 2012), pp. 138–149.

72. See B. Schneider, H. W. Goldstein, and D. B. Smith, "The ASA Framework: An Update," *Personnel Psychology* 48, no. 4 (1995), pp. 747–773; B. Schneider, D. B. Smith, S. Taylor, and J. Fleenor, "Personality and Organizations: A Test of the Homogeneity of Personality Hypothesis," *Journal of Applied Psychology* 83, no. 3 (1998), pp. 462–470; W. Arthur Jr., S. T. Bell, A. J. Villado, and D. Doverspike, "The Use of Person-Organization Fit in Employment Decision-Making: An Assessment of Its Criterion-Related Validity," *Journal of Applied Psychology* 91, no. 4 (2006), pp. 786–801; and J. R. Edwards, D. M. Cable, I. O. Williamson, L. S. Lambert, and A. J. Shipp, "The Phenomenology of Fit: Linking the Person and Environment to the Subjective Experience of Person–Environment Fit," *Journal of Applied Psychology* 91, no. 4 (2006), pp. 802–827.

73. T. A. Judge and D. M. Cable, "Applicant Personality, Organizational Culture, and Organization Attraction," *Personnel Psychology* 50, no. 2 (1997), pp. 359–394; and A. Leung and S. Chaturvedi, "Linking the Fits, Fitting the Links: Connecting Different Types of PO Fit to Attitudinal Outcomes," *Journal of Vocational Behavior* (October 2011), pp. 391–402.

74. M. L. Verquer, T. A. Beehr, and S. E. Wagner, "A Meta-Analysis of Relations Between Person–Organization Fit and Work Attitudes," *Journal of Vocational Behavior* 63, no. 3 (2003), pp. 473–489; and J. C. Carr, A. W. Pearson, M. J. Vest, and S. L. Boyar, "Prior Occupational Experience, Anticipatory Socialization, and Employee Retention, *Journal of Management* 32, no. 32 (2006), pp. 343–359.

75. A. Ramesh and M. J. Gelfand, "Will They Stay or Will They Go? The Role of Job Embeddedness in Predicting Turnover in Individualistic and Collectivistic Cultures," *Journal of Applied Psychology* 95, no. 5 (2010), pp. 807–823.

76. G. Hofstede, *Cultures and Organizations: Software of the Mind* (London: McGraw-Hill, 1991); G. Hofstede, "Cultural Constraints in Management Theories," *Academy of Management Executive* 7, no. 1 (1993), pp. 81–94; G. Hofstede and M. F. Peterson, "National Values and Organizational Practices," in N. M. Ashkanasy, C. M. Wilderom, and M. F. Peterson (eds.), *Handbook of Organizational Culture and Climate* (Thousand Oaks, CA: Sage, 2000), pp. 401–416; and G. Hofstede, *Culture's Consequences: Comparing Values, Behaviors, Institutions, and Organizations Across Nations*, 2nd ed. (Thousand Oaks, CA: Sage, 2001). For criticism of this research, see B. McSweeney, "Hofstede's Model of National Cultural Differences and Their Consequences: A Triumph of Faith—A Failure of Analysis," *Human Relations* 55, no. 1 (2002), pp. 89–118.

77. V. Taras, B. L. Kirkman, and P. Steel, "Examining the Impact of Culture's Consequences: A Three-Decade, Multilevel, Meta-Analytic Review of Hofstede's Cultural Value Dimensions," *Journal of Applied Psychology* 95, no. 5 (2010), pp. 405–439.

78. M. Javidan and R. J. House, "Cultural Acumen for the Global Manager: Lessons from Project GLOBE," *Organizational Dynamics* 29, no. 4 (2001), pp. 289–305; and R. J. House, P. J. Hanges, M. Javidan, and P. W. Dorfman (eds.), *Leadership, Culture, and Organizations: The GLOBE Study of 62 Societies* (Thousand Oaks, CA: Sage, 2004).

79. J. P. Meyer, D. J. Stanley, T. A. Jackson, K. J. McInnis, E. R. Maltin, et al., "Affective, Normative, and Continuance Commitment Levels Across Cultures: A Meta-Analysis," *Journal of Vocational Behavior* 80 (2012), pp. 225–245.

CHAPTER 6

1. H. H. Kelley, "Attribution in Social Interaction," in E. Jones et al. (eds.), *Attribution: Perceiving the Causes of Behavior* (Morristown, NJ: General Learning Press, 1972); and M. J. Martinko, P. Harvey, and M. T. Dasborough, "Attribution Theory in the Organizational Sciences: A Case of Unrealized Potential," *Journal of Organizational Behavior* 32, no. 1 (2011), pp. 144–149.

2. See P. W. Andrews, "The Psychology of Social Chess and the Evolution of Attribution Mechanisms: Explaining the Fundamental Attribution Error," *Evolution and Human Behavior* (January 2001), pp. 11–29; and L. Ross, "The Intuitive Psychologist and His Shortcomings," in L. Berkowitz (ed.), *Advances in Experimental Social Psychology,* vol. 10 (Orlando, FL: Academic Press, 1977), pp. 174–220.

3. T. S. Duval and P. J. Silvia, "Self-awareness, probability of improvement, and the self-serving bias," *Journal of Personality and Social Psychology* (January 2002), pp. 49–61; M. Goerke, J. Moller, S. Schulz-Hardt, U. Napiersky, and D. Frey, "'It's Not My Fault—But Only I Can Change It': Counterfactual and Prefactual Thoughts of Managers," *Journal of Applied Psychology* 89, no. 2 (2004), pp. 279–292; and E. G. Hepper, R. H. Gramzow, and C. Sedikides, "Individual Differences in Self-Enhancement and Self-Protection Strategies: An Integrative Analysis," *Journal of Personality* 78, no. 2 (2010), pp. 781–814.

4. See, for instance, A. H. Mezulis, L. Y. Abramson, J. S. Hyde, and B. L. Hankin, "Is There a Universal Positivity Bias in Attributions: A Meta-Analytic Review of Individual, Developmental, and Cultural Differences in the Self-Serving Attributional Bias," *Psychological Bulletin* 130, no. 5 (2004), pp. 711–747; C. F. Falk, S. J. Heine, M. Yuki, and K. Takemura, "Why Do Westerners Self-Enhance More than East Asians?" *European Journal of Personality* 23, no. 3 (2009), pp. 183–203; and F. F. T. Chiang and T. A. Birtch, "Examining the Perceived Causes of Successful Employee Performance: An East–West Comparison," *International Journal of Human Resource Management* 18, no. 2 (2007), pp. 232–248.

5. S. Nam, "Cultural and Managerial Attributions for Group Performance," unpublished doctoral dissertation, University of Oregon. Cited in R. M. Steers, S. J. Bischoff, and L. H. Higgins, "Cross-Cultural Management Research," *Journal of Management Inquiry* (December 1992), pp. 325–326.

6. T. Menon, M. W. Morris, C. Chiu, and Y. Y. Hong, "Culture and the Construal of Agency: Attribution to Individual Versus Group Dispositions," *Journal of Personality and Social Psychology* 76, no. 5 (1999), pp. 701–717; and R. Friedman, W. Liu, C. C. Chen, and S.-C. S. Chi, "Causal Attribution for Interfirm Contract Violation: A Comparative Study of Chinese and American Commercial Arbitrators," *Journal of Applied Psychology* 92, no. 3 (2007), pp. 856–864.

7. J. Spencer-Rodgers, M. J. Williams, D. L. Hamilton, K. Peng, and L. Wang, "Culture and Group Perception: Dispositional and Stereotypic Inferences about Novel and National Groups," *Journal of Personality and Social Psychology* 93, no. 4 (2007), pp. 525–543.

8. J. D. Brown, "Across the (Not So) Great Divide: Cultural Similarities in Self-Evaluative Processes," *Social and Personality Psychology Compass* 4, no. 5 (2010), pp. 318–330.

9. A. Zhang, C. Reyna, Z. Qian, and G. Yu, "Interpersonal Attributions of Responsibility in the Chinese Workplace: A Test of Western Models in a Collectivistic Context," *Journal of Applied Social Psychology* 38, no. 9 (2008), pp. 2361–2377; and A. Zhang, F. Xia, and C. Li, "The Antecedents of Help Giving in Chinese Culture: Attribution, Judgment of Responsibility, Expectation Change and the Reaction of Affect," *Social Behavior and Personality* 35, no. 1 (2007), pp. 135–142.

10. See P. Rosenzweig, *The Halo Effect* (New York: The Free Press, 2007); I. Dennis, "Halo Effects in Grading Student Projects," *Journal of Applied Psychology* 92, no. 4 (2007), pp. 1169–1176; C. E. Naquin and R. O. Tynan, "The Team Halo Effect: Why Teams Are Not Blamed for Their Failures," *Journal of Applied Psychology* 88, no. 2 (2003), pp. 332–340; and T. M. Bechger, G. Maris, and Y. P. Hsiao, "Detecting Halo Effects in Performance-Based Evaluations," *Applied Psychological Measurement* 34, no. 8 (2010), pp. 607–619.

11. S. E. Asch, "Forming Impressions of Personality," *Journal of Abnormal and Social Psychology* 41, no. 3 (1946), pp. 258–290.

12. J. L. Hilton and W. von Hippel, "Stereotypes," *Annual Review of Psychology* 47 (1996), pp. 237–271; and L. Jia, C. L. Dickter, J. Luo, X. Xiao, Q. Yang, et al., "Different Brain Mechanisms Between Stereotype Activation and Application: Evidence from an ERP Study," *International Journal of Psychology* 47, no. 1 (2012), pp. 58–66.

13. See, for example, C. Ostroff and L. E. Atwater, "Does Whom You Work with Matter? Effects of Referent Group Gender and Age Composition on Managers' Compensation," *Journal of Applied Psychology* 88, no. 4 (2003), pp. 725–740; M. E. Heilman, A. S. Wallen, D. Fuchs, and M. M. Tamkins, "Penalties for Success: Reactions to Women Who Succeed at Male Gender-Typed Tasks," *Journal of Applied Psychology* 89, no. 3 (2004), pp. 416–427; V. K. Gupta, D. B. Turban, and N. M. Bhawe, "The Effect of Gender Stereotype Activation on Entrepreneurial Intentions," *Journal of Applied Psychology* 93, no. 5 (2008), pp. 1053–1061; and R. A. Posthuma and M. A. Campion, "Age Stereotypes in the Workplace: Common Stereotypes, Moderators, and Future Research Directions," *Journal of Management* 35, no. 1 (2009), pp. 158–188.

14. See, for example, N. Dasgupta, D. DeSteno, L. A. Williams, and M. Hunsinger, "Fanning the Flames of Prejudice: The Influence of Specific Incidental Emotions on Implicit Prejudice," *Emotion* 9, no. 4 (2009), pp. 585–591; and J. C. Ziegert and P. C. Hanges, "Strong Rebuttal for Weak Criticisms: Reply to Blanton et al. (2009)," *Journal of Applied Psychology* 94, no. 3 (2009), pp. 590–597.

15. J. L. Eberhardt, P. G. Davies, V. J. Purdic-Vaughns, and S. L. Johnson, "Looking Deathworthy: Perceived Stereotypicality of Black Defendants Predicts Capital-Sentencing Outcomes," *Psychological Science* 17, no. 5 (2006), pp. 383–386.

16. A. S. Rosette, G. J. Leonardelli, and K. W. Phillips, "The White Standard: Racial Bias in Leader Categorization," *Journal of Applied Psychology* 93, no. 4 (2008), pp. 758–777.

17. R. Sanders, *The Executive Decisionmaking Process: Identifying Problems and Assessing Outcomes* (Westport, CT: Quorum, 1999); and K. Tasa and G. Whyte, "Collective

Efficacy and Vigilant Problem Solving in Group Decision Making: A Non-Linear Model," *Organizational Behavior and Human Decision Processes* (March 2005), pp. 119–129.

18. See H. A. Simon, "Rationality in Psychology and Economics," *Journal of Business* (October 1986), pp. 209–224; and E. Shafir and R. A. LeBoeuf, "Rationality," *Annual Review of Psychology* 53 (2002), pp. 491–517.

19. For a review of the rational decision-making model, see M. H. Bazerman and D. A. Moore, *Judgment in Managerial Decision Making*, 7th ed. (Hoboken, New Jersey: Wiley, 2008).

20. J. G. March, *A Primer on Decision Making* (New York: The Free Press, 2009); and D. Hardman and C. Harries, "How Rational Are We?" *Psychologist* (February 2002), pp. 76–79.

21. Bazerman and Moore, *Judgment in Managerial Decision Making*.

22. J. E. Russo, K. A. Carlson, and M. G. Meloy, "Choosing an Inferior Alternative," *Psychological Science* 17, no. 10 (2006), pp. 899–904.

23. D. Kahneman, "Maps of Bounded Rationality: Psychology for Behavioral Economics," *The American Economic Review* 93, no. 5 (2003), pp. 1449–1475; and J. Zhang, C. K. Hsee, and Z. Xiao, "The Majority Rule in Individual Decision Making," *Organizational Behavior and Human Decision Processes* 99 (2006), pp. 102–111.

24. See H. A. Simon, *Administrative Behavior*, 4th ed. (New York: The Free Press, 1997); and M. Augier, "Simon Says: Bounded Rationality Matters," *Journal of Management Inquiry* (September 2001), pp. 268–275.

25. G. Gigerenzer, "Why Heuristics Work," *Perspectives on Psychological Science* 3, no. 1 (2008), pp. 20–29; and A. K. Shah and D. M. Oppenheimer, "Heuristics Made Easy: An Effort-Reduction Framework," *Psychological Bulletin* 134, no. 2 (2008), pp. 207–222.

26. See A. W. Kruglanski and G. Gigerenzer, "Intuitive and Deliberate Judgments Are Based on Common Principles," *Psychological Review* 118 (2011), pp. 97–109.

27. E. Dane and M. G. Pratt, "Exploring Intuition and Its Role in Managerial Decision Making," *Academy of Management Review* 32, no. 1 (2007), pp. 33–54; and J. A. Hicks, D. C. Cicero, J. Trent, C. M. Burton, and L. A. King, "Positive Affect, Intuition, and Feelings of Meaning," *Journal of Personality and Social Psychology* 98 (2010), pp. 967–979.

28. C. Akinci and E. Sadler-Smith, "Intuition in Management Research: A Historical Review," *International Journal of Management Reviews* 14 (2012), pp. 104–122.

29. S. P. Robbins, *Decide & Conquer: Making Winning Decisions and Taking Control of Your Life* (Upper Saddle River, NJ: Financial Times/Prentice Hall, 2004), p. 13.

30. S. Ludwig and J. Natziger, "Beliefs about Overconfidence," *Theory and Decision* (April 2011), pp. 475–500.

31. S. Plous, *The Psychology of Judgment and Decision Making* (New York: McGraw-Hill, 1993), p. 217.

32. C. R. M. McKenzie, M. J. Liersch, and I. Yaniv, "Overconfidence in Interval Estimates: What Does Expertise Buy You," *Organizational Behavior and Human Decision Processes* 107 (2008), pp. 179–191.

33. J. Kruger and D. Dunning, "Unskilled and Unaware of It: How Difficulties in Recognizing One's Own Incompetence Lead to Inflated Self-Assessments," *Journal of Personality and Social Psychology* (November 1999), pp. 1121–1134; and R. P. Larrick, K. A. Burson, and J. B. Soll, "Social Comparison and Confidence: When Thinking You're Better Than Average Predicts Overconfidence (and When It Does Not)"

Organizational Behavior and Human Decision Processes 102 (2007), pp. 76–94.

34. K. M. Hmieleski and R. A. Baron, "Entrepreneurs' Optimism and New Venture Performance: A Social Cognitive Perspective," *Academy of Management Journal* 52, no. 3 (2009), pp. 473–488.

35. See, for instance, J. P. Simmons, R. A. LeBoeuf, and L. D. Nelson, "The Effect of Accuracy Motivation on Anchoring and Adjustment: Do People Adjust from Their Provided Anchors?" *Journal of Personality and Social Psychology* 99 (2010), pp. 917–932.

36. C. Janiszewski and D. Uy, "Precision of the Anchor Influences the Amount of Adjustment," *Psychological Science* 19, no. 2 (2008), pp. 121–127.

37. See E. Jonas, S. Schultz-Hardt, D. Frey, and N. Thelen, "Confirmation Bias in Sequential Information Search after Preliminary Decisions," *Journal of Personality and Social Psychology* (April 2001), pp. 557–571; and W. Hart, D. Albarracín, A. H. Eagly, I. Brechan, M. Lindberg, and L. Merrill, "Feeling Validated Versus Being Correct: A Meta-Analysis of Selective Exposure to Information," *Psychological Bulletin* 135 (2009), pp. 555–588.

38. T. Pachur, R. Hertwig, and F. Steinmann, "How Do People Judge Risks: Availability Heuristic, Affect Heuristic, or Both?" *Journal of Experimental Psychology: Applied* 18 (2012), pp. 314–330; A. Tversky and D. Kahneman, "Availability: A Heuristic for Judging Frequency and Probability," in D. Kahneman, P. Slovic, and A. Tversky (eds.), *Judgment Under Uncertainty: Heuristics and Biases* (Cambridge, U.K.: Cambridge University Press, 1982), pp. 163–178.

39. K. Moser, H.-G. Wolff, and A. Kraft, "The De-escalation of Commitment: Predecisional Accountability and Cognitive Processes," Journal of Applied Social Psychology (February 2013), pp. 363–376; and B. M. Staw, "The Escalation of Commitment to a Course of Action," *Academy of Management Review* (October 1981), pp. 577–587.

40. T. Schultze, F. Pfeiffer, and S. Schulz-Hardt, "Biased Information Processing in the Escalation Paradigm: Information Search and Information Evaluation as Potential Mediators of Escalating Commitment," *Journal of Applied Psychology* 97 (2012), pp. 16–32.

41. See, for example, D. J. Keys and B. Schwartz, "Leaky Rationality: How Research on Behavioral Decision Making Challenges Normative Standards of Rationality," *Psychological Science* 2, no. 2 (2007), pp. 162–180; and U. Simonsohn, "Direct Risk Aversion: Evidence from Risky Prospects Valued Below Their Worst Outcome," *Psychological Science* 20, no. 6 (2009), pp. 686–692.

42. J. K. Maner, M. T. Gailliot, D. A. Butz, and B. M. Peruche, "Power, Risk, and the Status Quo: Does Power Promote Riskier or More Conservative Decision Making," *Personality and Social Psychology Bulletin* 33, no. 4 (2007), pp. 451–462.

43. A. Chakraborty, S. Sheikh, and N. Subramanian, "Termination Risk and Managerial Risk Taking," *Journal of Corporate Finance* 13 (2007), pp. 170–188.

44. R. L. Guilbault, F. B. Bryant, J. H. Brockway, and E. J. Posavac, "A Meta-Analysis of Research on Hindsight Bias," *Basic and Applied Social Psychology* (September 2004), pp. 103–117; and L. Werth, F. Strack, and J. Foerster, "Certainty and Uncertainty: The Two Faces of the Hindsight Bias," *Organizational Behavior and Human Decision Processes* (March 2002), pp. 323–341.

45. J. Bell, "The Final Cut?" *Oregon Business* 33, no. 5 (2010), p. 27.

46. E. Dash and J. Creswell, "Citigroup Pays for a Rush to Risk," *The New York Times* (November 20, 2008), pp. 1, 28;

S. Pulliam, S. Ng, and R. Smith, "Merrill Upped Ante as Boom in Mortgage Bonds Fizzled," *The Wall Street Journal* (April 16, 2008), pp. A1, A14; and M. Gladwell, "Connecting the Dots," *The New Yorker* (March 10, 2003).

47. G. F. Cavanagh, D. J. Moberg, and M. Valasquez, "The Ethics of Organizational Politics," *Academy of Management Journal* (June 1981), pp. 363–374; and G. N. Gotsis and Z. Kortezi, "Ethical Considerations in Organizational Politics: Expanding the Perspective," *Journal of Business Ethics* 93, no. 4 (2010), pp. 497–517.

48. "Is Your Art Killing You?" Investorideas.com (May 13, 2013), downloaded May 14, 2013, from www.investorideas.com/news/2013/renewable-energy/05134.asp.

49. G. Anderson, "Three Tips to Foster Creativity at Your Startup," *ArcticStartup* (May 8, 2013), downloaded May 14, 2013, from http://www.arcticstartup.com/.

50. E. Millar, "How Do Finnish Kids Excel without Rote Learning and Standardized Testing?" *The Globe and Mail* (May 9, 2013), downloaded May 14, 2013, from www.theglobeandmail.com/.

51. Z. Harper, "Mark Cuban Wants You to Design the New Dallas Mavericks Uniforms," CBSSports.com (May 13, 2013), downloaded May 14, 2013, from www.cbssports.com/nba/.

52. C. K. W. De Dreu, B. A. Nijstad, M. Baas, I. Wolsink, and M. Roskes, "Working Memory Benefits Creative Insight, Musical Improvisation, and Original Ideation Through Maintained Task-Focused Attention," *Personality and Social Psychology Bulletin* 38 (2012), pp. 656–669.

53. S. M. Wechsler, C. Vendramini, and T. Oakland, "Thinking and Creative Styles: A Validity Study," *Creativity Research Journal* 24 (April 2012), pp. 235–242.

54. Y. Gong, S. Cheung, M. Wang, and J. Huang, "Unfolding the Proactive Processes for Creativity: Integration of the Employee Proactivity, Information Exchange, and Psychological Safety Perspectives," *Journal of Management* 38 (2012), pp. 1611–1633.

55. S. N. de Jesus, C. L. Rus, W. Lens, and S. Imaginário, "Intrinsic Motivation and Creativity Related to Product: A Meta-Analysis of the Studies Published Between 1990–2010," *Creativity Research Journal* 25 (2013), pp. 80–84.

56. L. Sun, Z. Zhang, J. Qi, and Z. X. Chen, "Empowerment and Creativity: A Cross-Level Investigation," *Leadership Quarterly* 23 (2012), pp. 55–65.

57. J. S. Mueller, S. Melwani, and J. A. Goncalo, "The Bias against Creativity: Why People Desire but Reject Creative Ideas," *Psychological Science* 23 (2012), pp. 13–17.

58. T. Montag, C. P. Maertz, and M. Baer, "A Critical Analysis of the Workplace Creativity Criterion Space," *Journal of Management* 38 (2012), pp. 1362–1386.

CHAPTER 7

1. See, for example, G. P. Latham and C. C. Pinder, "Work Motivation Theory and Research at the Dawn of the Twenty-First Century," *Annual Review of Psychology* 56 (2005), pp. 485–516; and C. C. Pinder, *Work Motivation in Organizational Behavior,* 2nd ed. (London, UK: Psychology Press, 2008).

2. R. Wagner and J. K. Harter, *12: The Elements of Great Managing* (Washington, DC: Gallup Press, 2006).

3. "The 2013 Wasting Time at Work Survey: Everything You've Always Wanted to Know About Wasting Time in the Office," Salary.com (2013), www.salary.com.

4. See, for instance, Pinder, *Work Motivation in Organizational Behavior.*

5. A. Maslow, *Motivation and Personality* (New York: Harper & Row, 1954).

6. See, for example, E. E. Lawler III and J. L. Suttle, "A Causal Correlation Test of the Need Hierarchy Concept," *Organizational Behavior and Human Performance* 7, no. 2 (1972), pp. 265–287; D. Lester, "Measuring Maslow's Hierarchy of Needs," *Psychological Reports* (August 2013), pp. 15–17; and J. Rauschenberger, N. Schmitt, and J. E. Hunter, "A Test of the Need Hierarchy Concept by a Markov Model of Change in Need Strength," *Administrative Science Quarterly* 25, no. 4 (1980), pp. 654–670.

7. D. T. Kenrick, V. Griskcvicius, S. L. Neuberg, and M. Schaller, "Renovating the Pyramid of Needs: Contemporary Extensions Built on Ancient Foundations," *Perspectives on Psychological Science* 5, no. 3 (2010), pp. 292–314.

8. D. McGregor, *The Human Side of Enterprise* (New York: McGraw-Hill, 1960). For an updated analysis of Theory X and Theory Y constructs, see R. E. Kopelman, D. J. Prottas, and D. W. Falk, "Construct Validation of a Theory X/Y Behavior Scale," *Leadership and Organization Development Journal* 31, no. 2 (2010), pp. 120–135.

9. F. Herzberg, B. Mausner, and B. Snyderman, *The Motivation to Work* (New York: Wiley, 1959).

10. R. J. House and L. A. Wigdor, "Herzberg's Dual-Factor Theory of Job Satisfaction and Motivations: A Review of the Evidence and Criticism," *Personnel Psychology* 20, no. 4 (1967), pp. 369–389; T. A. Judge, C. J. Thoresen, J. E. Bono, & G. K. Patton, "The Job Satisfaction-Job Performance Relationship: A Qualitative and Quantitative Review," *Psychological Bulletin* (May 2001), pp. 376–407; D. P. Schwab and L. L. Cummings, "Theories of Performance and Satisfaction: A Review," *Industrial Relations* 9, no. 4 (1970), pp. 403–430; and J. Phillipchuk and J. Whittaker, "An Inquiry into the Continuing Relevance of Herzberg's Motivation Theory," *Engineering Management Journal* 8 (1996), pp. 15–20.

11. D. C. McClelland, *The Achieving Society* (New York: Van Nostrand Reinhold, 1961); J. W. Atkinson and J. O. Raynor, *Motivation and Achievement* (Washington, DC: Winston, 1974); D. C. McClelland, *Power: The Inner Experience* (New York: Irvington, 1975); and M. J. Stahl, *Managerial and Technical Motivation: Assessing Needs for Achievement, Power, and Affiliation* (New York: Praeger, 1986).

12. D. C. McClelland and D. G. Winter, *Motivating Economic Achievement* (New York: The Free Press, 1969); and J. B. Miner, N. R. Smith, and J. S. Bracker, "Role of Entrepreneurial Task Motivation in the Growth of Technologically Innovative Firms: Interpretations from Follow-up Data," *Journal of Applied Psychology* 79, no. 4 (1994), pp. 627–630; and J. Schueler, V. Brandstaetter, and K. M. Sheldon, "Do Implicit Motives and Basic Psychological Needs Interact to Predict Well-Being and Flow? Testing a Universal Hypothesis and a Matching Hypothesis," *Motivation and Emotion* (September 2013), pp. 480–495.

13. McClelland, *Power;* D. C. McClelland and D. H. Burnham, "Power Is the Great Motivator," *Harvard Business Review* (March–April 1976), pp. 100–110; and R. E. Boyatzis, "The Need for Close Relationships and the Manager's Job," in D. A. Kolb, I. M. Rubin, and J. M. McIntyre, *Organizational Psychology: Readings on Human Behavior in Organizations,* 4th ed. (Upper Saddle River, NJ: Prentice Hall, 1984), pp. 81–86.

14. D. G. Winter, "The Motivational Dimensions of Leadership: Power, Achievement, and Affiliation," in R. E. Riggio, S. E. Murphy, and F. J. Pirozzolo (eds.), *Multiple Intelligences and Leadership* (Mahwah, NJ: Lawrence Erlbaum, 2002), pp. 119–138.

15. J. B. Miner, *Studies in Management Education* (New York: Springer, 1965).

16. Ibid.

17. E. Deci and R. Ryan (eds.), *Handbook of Self-Determination Research* (Rochester, NY: University of Rochester Press, 2002); R. Ryan and E. Deci, "Self-Determination Theory and the Facilitation of Intrinsic Motivation, Social Development, and Well-Being," *American Psychologist* 55, no. 1 (2000), pp. 68–78; and M. Gagné and E. L. Deci, "Self-Determination Theory and Work Motivation," *Journal of Organizational Behavior* 26, no. 4 (2005), pp. 331–362.

18. See, for example, E. L. Deci, R. Koestner, and R. M. Ryan, "A Meta-Analytic Review of Experiments Examining the Effects of Extrinsic Rewards on Intrinsic Motivation," *Psychological Bulletin* 125, no. 6 (1999), pp. 627–668; G. J. Greguras and J. M. Diefendorff, "Different Fits Satisfy Different Needs: Linking Person-Environment Fit to Employee Commitment and Performance Using Self-Determination Theory," *Journal of Applied Psychology* 94, no. 2 (2009), pp. 465–477; and D. Liu, X. Chen, and X. Yao, "From Autonomy to Creativity: A Multilevel Investigation of the Mediating Role of Harmonious Passion," *Journal of Applied Psychology* 96, no. 2 (2011), pp. 294–309.

19. R. Eisenberger and L. Rhoades, "Incremental Effects of Reward on Creativity," *Journal of Personality and Social Psychology* 81, no. 4 (2001), 728–741; and R. Eisenberger, W. D. Pierce, and J. Cameron, "Effects of Reward on Intrinsic Motivation—Negative, Neutral, and Positive: Comment on Deci, Koestner, and Ryan (1999)," *Psychological Bulletin* 125, no. 6 (1999), pp. 677–691.

20. M. Burgess, M. E. Enzle, and R. Schmaltz, "Defeating the Potentially Deleterious Effects of Externally Imposed Deadlines: Practitioners' Rules-of-Thumb," *Personality and Social Psychology Bulletin* 30, no. 7 (2004), pp. 868–877.

21. K. M. Sheldon, A. J. Elliot, and R. M. Ryan, "Self-Concordance and Subjective Well-Being in Four Cultures," *Journal of Cross-Cultural Psychology* 35, no. 2 (2004), pp. 209–223.

22. J. E. Bono and T. A. Judge, "Self-Concordance at Work: Toward Understanding the Motivational Effects of Transformational Leaders," *Academy of Management Journal* 46, no. 5 (2003), pp. 554–571.

23. L. M. Graves, M. N. Ruderman, P. J. Ohlott, and Todd J. Webber, "Driven to Work and Enjoyment of Work: Effects on Managers' Outcomes, "*Journal of Management* 38, no. 5 (2012), pp. 1655–1680.

24. J. P. Meyer, T. E. Becker, and C. Vandenberghe, "Employee Commitment and Motivation: A Conceptual Analysis and Integrative Model," *Journal of Applied Psychology* 89, no. 6 (2004), pp. 991–1007.

25. E. A. Locke, "Toward a Theory of Task Motivation and Incentives," *Organizational Behavior and Human Performance* 3, no. 2 (1968), pp. 157–189.

26. P. C. Earley, P. Wojnaroski, and W. Prest, "Task Planning and Energy Expended: Exploration of How Goals Influence Performance," *Journal of Applied Psychology* 72, no. 1 (1987), pp. 107–114.

27. See M. E. Tubbs, "Goal Setting: A Meta-Analytic Examination of the Empirical Evidence," *Journal of Applied Psychology* 71, no. 3 (1986), pp. 474–483; and E. A. Locke and G. P. Latham, "New Directions in Goal-Setting Theory," *Current Directions in Psychological Science* 15, no. 5 (2006), pp. 265–268.

28. E. A. Locke and G. P. Latham, "Building a Practically Useful Theory of Goal Setting and Task Motivation," *American Psychologist* 57, no. 2 (2002), pp. 705–717.

29. C. Gabelica, P. Van den Bossche, M. Segers, and W. Gijselaersa, "Feedback, a Powerful Lever in Teams: A Review," *Educational Research Review* (June 2012), pp. 123–144.

30. K. Dewettinck and H. van Dijk, "Linking Belgian Employee Performance Management System Characteristics with Performance Management System Effectiveness: Exploring the Mediating Role of Fairness," *International Journal of Human Resource Management* (February 1, 2013), pp. 806–825; and M. Erez, P. C. Earley, and C. L. Hulin, "The Impact of Participation on Goal Acceptance and Performance: A Two-Step Model," *Academy of Management Journal* 28, no. 1 (1985), pp. 50–66.

31. T. S. Bateman and B. Bruce, "Masters of the Long Haul: Pursuing Long-Term Work Goals," *Journal of Organizational Behavior* (October 2012), pp. 984–1006; and E. A. Locke, "The Motivation to Work: What We Know," *Advances in Motivation and Achievement* 10 (1997), pp. 375–412.

32. Ibid.

33. J. E. Bono and A. E. Colbert, "Understanding Responses to Multi-Source Feedback: The Role of Core Self-evaluations," *Personnel Psychology* 58, no. 1 (2005), pp. 171–203; and S. A. Jeffrey, A. Schulz, and A. Webb, "The Performance Effects of an Ability-Based Approach to Goal Assignment," *Journal of Organizational Behavior Management* 32 (2012), pp. 221–241.

34. A. M. O'Leary-Kelly, J. J. Martocchio, and D. D. Frink, "A Review of the Influence of Group Goals on Group Performance," *Academy of Management Journal* 37, no. 5 (1994), pp. 1285–1301; and T. Tammemagi, D. O'Hora, and K. A. Maglieri, "The Effects of a Goal Setting Intervention on Productivity and Persistence in an Analogue Work Task," *Journal of Organizational Behavior Management* (March 1, 2013), pp. 31–54.

35. D. F. Crown, "The Use of Group and Groupcentric Individual Goals for Culturally Heterogeneous and Homogeneous Task Groups: An Assessment of European Work Teams," *Small Group Research* 38, no. 4 (2007), pp. 489–508; J. Kurman, "Self-Regulation Strategies in Achievement Settings: Culture and Gender Differences," *Journal of Cross-Cultural Psychology* 32, no. 4 (2001), pp. 491–503; and M. Erez and P. C. Earley, "Comparative Analysis of Goal-Setting Strategies Across Cultures," *Journal of Applied Psychology* 72, no. 4 (1987), pp. 658–665.

36. C. Suc-Chan and M. Ong, "Goal Assignment and Performance: Assessing the Mediating Roles of Goal Commitment and Self-Efficacy and the Moderating Role of Power Distance," *Organizational Behavior and Human Decision Processes* 89, no. 2 (2002), pp. 1140–1161.

37. G. P. Latham and E. A. Locke, "Enhancing the Benefits and Overcoming the Pitfalls of Goal Setting," *Organizational Dynamics* 35, no. 6, pp. 332–340; L. D. Ordóñez, M. E. Schweitzer, A. D. Galinsky, and M. H. Bazerman, "Goals Gone Wild: The Systematic Side Effects of Overprescribing Goal Setting," *Academy of Management Perspectives* 23, no. 1 (2009), pp. 6–16; and E. A. Locke and G. P. Latham, "Has Goal Setting Gone Wild, or Have Its Attackers Abandoned Good Scholarship?" *Academy of Management Perspectives* 23, no. 1 (2009), pp. 17–23.

38. S. J. Perry, L. A. Witt, L. M. Penney, and L. Atwater, "The Downside of Goal-Focused Leadership: The Role of

Personality in Subordinate Exhaustion," *Journal of Applied Psychology* 95, no. 6 (2010), pp. 1145–1153.

39. K. Lanaj, C. D. Chang, and R. E. Johnson, "Regulatory Focus and Work-Related Outcomes: A Review and Meta-Analysis," *Psychological Bulletin* 138, no. 5 (2012), pp. 998–1034.

40. "KEYGroup Survey Finds Nearly Half of All Employees Have No Set Performance Goals," *IPMA-HR Bulletin* (March 10, 2006), p. 1; S. Hamm, "SAP Dangles a Big, Fat Carrot," *BusinessWeek* (May 22, 2006), pp. 67–68; and "P&G CEO Wields High Expectations but No Whip," *USA Today* (February 19, 2007), p. 3B.

41. See, for instance, C. Antoni, "Management by Objectives – An Effective Tool for Teamwork?," *International Journal of Human Resource Management* (February 2005), pp. 174–184; and S. J. Carroll and H. L. Tosi, *Management by Objectives: Applications and Research* (New York: Macmillan, 1973); and R. Rodgers and J. E. Hunter, "Impact of Management by Objectives on Organizational Productivity," *Journal of Applied Psychology* 76, no. 2 (1991), pp. 322–336.

42. A. Bandura, *Self-Efficacy: The Exercise of Control* (New York: Freeman, 1997).

43. A. D. Stajkovic and F. Luthans, "Self-Efficacy and Work-Related Performance: A Meta-Analysis," *Psychological Bulletin* 124, no. 2 (1998), pp. 240–261; and A. Bandura, "Cultivate Self-Efficacy for Personal and Organizational Effectiveness," in E. Locke (ed.), *Handbook of Principles of Organizational Behavior* (Malden, MA: Blackwell, 2004), pp. 120–136.

44. M. Salanova, S. Llorens, and W. B. Schaufeli, "Yes I Can, I Feel Good, and I Just Do It! On Gain Cycles and Spirals of Efficacy Beliefs, Affect, and Engagement," *Applied Psychology* 60, no. 2 (2011), pp. 255–285.

45. P. Tierney and S. M. Farmer, "Creative Self-Efficacy Development and Creative Performance Over Time," *Journal of Applied Psychology* 96, no. 2 (2011), pp. 277–293.

46. A. Bandura and D. Cervone, "Differential Engagement in Self-Reactive Influences in Cognitively-Based Motivation," *Organizational Behavior and Human Decision Processes* 38, no. 1 (1986), pp. 92–113; and A. P. Tolli and A. M. Schmidt, "The Role of Feedback, Causal Attributions, and Self-Efficacy in Goal Revision," *Journal of Applied Psychology* (May 2008), pp. 692–701.

47. Bandura, *Self-Efficacy.*

48. R. C. Rist, "Student Social Class and Teacher Expectations: The Self-Fulfilling Prophecy in Ghetto Education," *Harvard Educational Review* 70, no. 3 (2000), pp. 266–301.

49. D. Eden, "Self-Fulfilling Prophecies in Organizations," in J. Greenberg (ed.), *Organizational Behavior: The State of the Science,* 2nd ed. (Mahwah, NJ: Lawrence Erlbaum, 2003), pp. 91–122.

50. Ibid.

51. C. L. Holladay and M. A. Quiñones, "Practice Variability and Transfer of Training: The Role of Self-Efficacy Generality," *Journal of Applied Psychology* 88, no. 6 (2003), pp. 1094–1103.

52. E. C. Dierdorff, E. A. Surface, and K. G. Brown, "Frame-of-Reference Training Effectiveness: Effects of Goal Orientation and Self-Efficacy on Affective, Cognitive, Skill-Based, and Transfer Outcomes," *Journal of Applied Psychology* 95, no. 6 (2010), pp. 1181–1191; and R. Grossman, and E. Salas, "The Transfer of Training: What Really Matters," *International Journal of Training and Development* 15, no. 2 (2011), pp. 103–120.

53. T. A. Judge, C. L. Jackson, J. C. Shaw, B. Scott, and B. L. Rich, "Self-Efficacy and Work-Related Performance: The Integral Role of Individual Differences," *Journal of Applied Psychology* 92, no. 1 (2007), pp. 107–127.

54. Ibid.

55. See, for example, J. Greenberg, "Cognitive Reevaluation of Outcomes in Response to Underpayment Inequity," *Academy of Management Journal,* March 1989, pp. 174–184; and C. Maslach and M. P. Leiter, "Early Predictors of Job Burnout and Engagement, *Journal of Applied Psychology* (May 2008), pp. 498–512.

56. P. S. Goodman and A. Friedman, "An Examination of Adams' Theory of Inequity," *Administrative Science Quarterly* 16, no. 3 (1971), pp. 271–288; R. P. Vecchio, "An Individual-Differences Interpretation of the Conflicting Predictions Generated by Equity Theory and Expectancy Theory," *Journal of Applied Psychology* 66, no. 4 (1981), pp. 470–481; R. T. Mowday, "Equity Theory Predictions of Behavior in Organizations," in R. Steers, L. W. Porter, and G. Bigley (eds.), *Motivation and Work Behavior,* 6th ed. (New York: McGraw-Hill, 1996), pp. 111–131; R. W. Griffeth and S. Gaertner, "A Role for Equity Theory in the Turnover Process: An Empirical Test," *Journal of Applied Social Psychology* 31, no. 5 (2001), pp. 1017–1037; and L. K. Scheer, N. Kumar, and J.-B. E. M. Steenkamp, "Reactions to Perceived Inequity in U.S. and Dutch Interorganizational Relationships," *Academy of Management* 46, no. 3 (2003), pp. 303–316.

57. See, for example, R. C. Huseman, J. D. Hatfield, and E. W. Miles, "A New Perspective on Equity Theory: The Equity Sensitivity Construct," *Academy of Management Journal* 12, no. 2 (1987), pp. 222–234; K. S. Sauley and A. G. Bedeian, "Equity Sensitivity: Construction of a Measure and Examination of Its Psychometric Properties," *Journal of Management* 26, no. 5 (2000), pp. 885–910; and J. A. Colquitt, "Does the Justice of One Interact with the Justice of Many? Reactions to Procedural Justice in Teams," *Journal of Applied Psychology* 89, no. 4 (2004), pp. 633–646.

58. See, for instance, J. A. Colquitt, D. E. Conlon, M. J. Wesson, C. O. L. H. Porter, and K.-Y. Ng, "Justice at the Millennium: A Meta-Analytic Review of the 25 Years of Organizational Justice Research," *Journal of Applied Psychology* 86, no. 3 (2001), pp. 425–445; T. Simons and Q. Roberson, "Why Managers Should Care About Fairness: The Effects of Aggregate Justice Perceptions on Organizational Outcomes," *Journal of Applied Psychology* 88, no. 3 (2003), pp. 432–443; and B. C. Holtz and C. M. Harold, "Fair Today, Fair Tomorrow? A Longitudinal Investigation of Overall Justice Perceptions," *Journal of Applied Psychology* 94, no. 5 (2009), pp. 1185–1199.

59. C. O. Trevor, G. Reilly, and B. Gerhart, "Reconsidering Pay Dispersion's Effect on the Performance of Interdependent Work: Reconciling Sorting and Pay Inequality," *Academy of Management Journal* (June 2012), pp. 585–610.

60. See, for example, R. Cropanzano, J. H. Stein, and T. Nadisic, *Social Justice and the Experience of Emotion* (New York: Routledge/Taylor and Francis Group, 2011).

61. G. S. Leventhal, "What Should Be Done with Equity Theory? New Approaches to the Study of Fairness in Social Relationships," in K. Gergen, M. Greenberg, and R. Willis (eds.), *Social Exchange: Advances in Theory and Research* (New York: Plenum, 1980), pp. 27–55.

62. J. Brockner and B. M. Wiesenfeld, "An Integrative Framework for Examining Reactions to Decisions: Interactive Effects of Outcomes and Procedures," *Psychological Bulletin* 120 (1996), pp. 189–208; and J. Brockner, B. M. Wiesenfeld, and K. A. Diekmann, "Towards a 'Fairer' Conception of Process Fairness: Why, When, and How More May Not Always Be Better Than Less," *Academy of Management Annals* 3 (2009), pp. 183–216.

63. R. Folger and D. P. Skarlicki, "Fairness as a Dependent Variable: Why Tough Times Can Lead to Bad Management," in R. Cropanzano (ed.), *Justice in the Workplace: From Theory to Practice* (Mahway, NJ: Erlbaum, 2001), pp. 97–118.

64. C. R. Wanberg, L. W. Bunce, and M. B. Gavin, "Perceived Fairness of Layoffs Among Individuals Who Have Been Laid Off," *Personnel Psychology* 52 (1999), pp. 59–84; and B. M. Wiesenfeld, J. Brockner, and V. Thibault, "Procedural Fairness, Managers' Self-Esteem, and Managerial Behaviors Following a Layoff," *Organizational Behavior and Human Decision Processes* (September 2000), pp. 1–32.

65. J. C. Shaw, E. Wild, and J. A. Colquitt, "To Justify or Excuse? A Meta-Analytic Review of the Effects of Explanations," *Journal of Applied Psychology* 88, no. 3 (2003), pp. 444–458.

66. R. J. Bies, "Are Procedural and Interactional Justice Conceptually Distinct?" in J. Greenberg and J. A. Colquitt (eds.), *Handbook of Organizational Justice* (Mahwah, NJ: Erlbaum, 2005), pp. 85–112; and B. A. Scott, J. A. Colquitt, and E. L. Paddock, "An Actor-Focused Model of Justice Rule Adherence and Violation: The Role of Managerial Motives and Discretion," *Journal of Applied Psychology* 94, no. 3 (2009), pp. 756–769.

67. G. A. Van Kleef, A. C. Homan, B. Beersma, D. V. Knippenberg, B. V. Knippenberg, and F. Damen, "Searing Sentiment or Cold Calculation? The Effects of Leader Emotional Displays on Team Performance Depend on Follower Epistemic Motivation," *Academy of Management Journal* 52, no. 3 (2009), pp. 562–580.

68. "Rutgers Fires Mike Rice," 2013, www.espn.com.

69. J. M. Robbins, M. T. Ford, and L. E. Tetrick, "Perceived Unfairness and Employee Health: A Meta-Analytic Integration," *Journal of Applied Psychology* 97, no. 2 (2012), pp. 235–272.

70. J. A. Colquitt, B. A. Scott, J. B. Rodell, D. M. Long, C. P. Zapata, D. E. Conlon, and M. J. Wesson, "Justice at the Millennium, A Decade Later: A Meta-Analytic Test of Social Exchange and Affect-Based Perspectives," *Journal of Applied Psychology* 98, no. 2 (2013), pp. 199–236.

71. B. A. Scott, J. A. Colquitt, and E. L. Paddock, "An Actor-Focused Model of Justice Rule Adherence and Violation: The Role of Managerial Motives and Discretion," *Journal of Applied Psychology* 94, no. 3 (2009), pp. 756–769.

72. Ibid.

73. K. Leung, K. Tong, and S. S. Ho, "Effects of Interactional Justice on Egocentric Bias in Resource Allocation Decisions," *Journal of Applied Psychology* 89, no. 3 (2004), pp. 405–415; and L. Francis-Gladney, N. R. Manger, and R. B. Welker, "Does Outcome Favorability Affect Procedural Fairness as a Result of Self-Serving Attributions," *Journal of Applied Social Psychology* 40, no. 1 (2010), pp. 182–194.

74. L. J. Barlcay and D. P. Skarlicki, "Healing the Wounds of Organizational Injustice: Examining the Benefits of Expressive Writing," *Journal of Applied Psychology* 94, no. 2 (2009), pp. 511–523.

75. R. Fischer and P. B. Smith, "Reward Allocation and Culture: A Meta-Analysis," *Journal of Cross-Cultural Psychology* 34, no. 3 (2003), pp. 251–268.

76. F. F. T. Chiang and T. Birtch, "The Transferability of Management Practices: Examining Cross-National Differences in Reward Preferences," *Human Relations* 60, no. 9 (2007), pp. 1293–1330; A. E. Lind, T. R. Tyler, and Y. J. Huo, "Procedural Context and Culture: Variation in the Antecedents of Procedural Justice Judgments," *Journal of Personality and Social Psychology* 73, no. 4 (1997), pp. 767–780; and M. J. Gelfand, M. Erez, and Z. Aycan, "Cross-Cultural Organizational Behavior," *Annual Review of Psychology* 58 (2007), pp. 479–514.

77. J. K. Giacobbe-Miller, D. J. Miller, and V. I. Victorov, "A Comparison of Russian and U.S. Pay Allocation Decisions, Distributive Justice Judgments, and Productivity Under Different Payment Conditions," *Personnel Psychology* 51, no. 1 (1998), pp. 137–163; and J. K. Giacobbe-Miller, D. J. Miller, W. Zhang, and V. I. Victorov, "Country and Organizational-Level Adaptation to Foreign Workplace Ideologies: A Comparative Study of Distributive Justice Values in China, Russia, and the United States," *Journal of International Business Studies* 23 (2003), pp. 289–406.

78. M. C. Bolino and W. H. Turnley, "Old Faces, New Places: Equity Theory in Cross-Cultural Contexts," *Journal of Organizational Behavior* 29, no. 1 (2008), pp. 29–50.

79. V. H. Vroom, *Work and Motivation* (New York: Wiley, 1964).

80. For criticism, see H. G. Heneman III and D. P. Schwab, "Evaluation of Research on Expectancy Theory Prediction of Employee Performance," *Psychological Bulletin* 78, no. 1 (1972), pp. 1–9; T. R. Mitchell, "Expectancy Models of Job Satisfaction, Occupational Preference and Effort: A Theoretical, Methodological and Empirical Appraisal," *Psychological Bulletin* 81, no. 12 (1974), pp. 1053–1077; and W. Van Eerde and H. Thierry, "Vroom's Expectancy Models and Work-Related Criteria: A Meta-Analysis," *Journal of Applied Psychology* 81, no. 5 (1996), pp. 575–586. For support, see L. W. Porter and E. E. Lawler III, *Managerial Attitudes and Performance* (Homewood, IL: Irwin, 1968); and J. J. Donovan, "Work Motivation," in N. Anderson et al. (eds.), *Handbook of Industrial, Work & Organizational Psychology*, vol. 2 (Thousand Oaks, CA: Sage, 2001), pp. 56–59.

81. Vroom refers to these three variables as expectancy, instrumentality, and valence, respectively.

82. J. Nocera, "The Anguish of Being an Analyst," *The New York Times* (March 4, 2006), pp. B1, B12.

83. R. J. House, H. J. Shapiro, and M. A. Wahba, "Expectancy Theory as a Predictor of Work Behavior and Attitudes: A Reevaluation of Empirical Evidence," *Decision Sciences* 5, no. 3 (1974), pp. 481–506; and Y. Hao and G. Jianping, "Research on Employee Motivation Mechanism in Modern Enterprises Based on Victor H. Vroom's Expectancy Theory," *Proceedings of the 9th International Conference on Innovation and Management* (2012), pp. 988–991.

84. W. A. Kahn, "Psychological Conditions of Personal Engagement and Disengagement at Work," *Academy of Management Journal* 33, no. 4 (1990), pp. 692–724.

85. www.gallup.com/consulting/52/Employee-Engagement.aspx.

86. J. K. Harter, F. L. Schmidt, and T. L. Hayes, "Business-Unit-Level Relationship Between Employee Satisfaction, Employee Engagement, and Business Outcomes: A Meta-Analysis," *Journal of Applied Psychology* 87, no. 2 (2002), pp. 268–279.

87. M. S. Christian, A. S. Garza, and J. E. Slaughter, "Work Engagement: A Quantitative Review and Test of Its Relations with Task and Contextual Performance," *Personnel Psychology* 64, no. 1 (2011), pp. 89–136.

88. W. B. Schaufeli, A. B. Bakker, and W. van Rhenen, "How Changes in Job Demands and Resources Predict Burnout, Work Engagement, and Sickness Absenteeism," *Journal of Organizational Behavior* 30, no. 7 (2009), pp. 893–917; E. R. Crawford, J. A. LePine, and B. L. Rich, "Linking Job Demands and Resources to Employee Engagement and Burnout: A Theoretical Extension and Meta-Analytic Test," *Journal of Applied Psychology* 95, no. 5 (2010), pp. 834–848; and D. Xanthopoulou, A. B. Bakker, E. Demerouti, and W. B. Schaufeli, "Reciprocal Relationships Between Job Resources, Personal Resources, and Work Engagement," *Journal of Vocational Behavior* 74, no 3 (2010), pp. 617–635.

89. B. L. Rich, J. A. LePine, and E. R. Crawford, "Job Engagement: Antecedents and Effects on Job Performance," *Academy of Management Journal* 53, no. 3 (2010), pp. 617–635.

90. M. Tims, A. B. Bakker, and D. Xanthopoulou, "Do Transformational Leaders Enhance Their Followers' Daily Work Engagement?" *Leadership Quarterly* 22, no. 1 (2011), pp. 121–131.

91. D. A. Newman and D. A. Harrison, "Been There, Bottled That: Are State and Behavioral Work Engagement New and Useful Construct 'Wines?'" *Industrial and Organizational Psychology* 1, no. 1 (2008), pp. 31–55; and A. J. Wefald and R. G. Downey, "Job Engagement in Organizations: Fad, Fashion, or Folderol," *Journal of Organizational Behavior* 30, no. 1 (2009), pp. 141–145.

92. J. M. George, "The Wider Context, Costs, and Benefits of Work Engagement," *European Journal of Work and Organizational Psychology* 20, no. 1 (2011), pp. 53–59; and J. R. B. Halbesleben, J. Harvey, and M. C. Bolino, "Too Engaged? A Conservation of Resources View of the Relationship Between Work Engagement and Work Interfere with Family," *Journal of Applied Psychology* 94, no. 6 (2009), pp. 1452–1465.

CHAPTER 8

1. J. R. Hackman and G. R. Oldham, "Motivation Through the Design of Work: Test of a Theory," *Organizational Behavior and Human Performance* 16, no. 2 (1976), pp. 250–279; and J. R. Hackman and G. R. Oldham, *Work Redesign* (Reading, MA: Addison-Wesley, 1980).

2. J. R. Hackman, "Work Design," in J. R. Hackman and J. L. Suttle (eds.), *Improving Life at Work* (Santa Monica, CA: Goodyear, 1977), p. 129.

3. B. M. Meglino and A. M. Korsgaard, "The Role of Other Orientation in Reactions to Job Characteristics," *Journal of Management* 33, no. 1 (2007), pp. 57–83.

4. M. F. Peterson and S. A. Ruiz-Quintanilla, "Cultural Socialization as a Source of Intrinsic Work Motivation," *Group & Organization Management* 28, no. 2 (2003), pp. 188–216.

5. A. Christini and D. Pozzoli, "Workplace Practices and Firm Performance in Manufacturing: A Comparative Study of Italy and Britain," *International Journal of Manpower* 31, no. 7 (2010), pp. 818–842; and K. Kaymaz, "The Effects of Job Rotation Practices on Motivation: A Research on Managers in the Automotive Organizations," *Business and Economics Research Journal* 1, no. 3 (2010), pp. 69–86.

6. T. Silver, "Rotate Your Way to Higher Value," *Baseline* (March/April 2010), p. 12; and J. J. Salopek, "Coca-Cola Division Refreshes Its Talent with Diversity Push on Campus," *Workforce Management Online* (March 2011), www.workforce.com.

7. Skytrax website review of Singapore Airlines, www.airlinequality.com/Airlines/SQ.htm, accessed May 31, 2013.

8. Hackman and Oldham, *Work Redesign*.

9. A. M. Grant, J. E. Dutton, and B. D. Rosso, "Giving Commitment: Employee Support Programs and the Prosocial Sensemaking Process," *Academy of Management Journal* 51, no. 5 (2008), pp. 898–918.

10. See, for example, R. W. Griffin, "Effects of Work Redesign on Employee Perceptions, Attitudes, and Behaviors: A Long-Term Investigation," *Academy of Management Journal* 34, no. 2 (1991), pp. 425–435; and M. Subramony, "A Meta-Analytic Investigation of the Relationship between HRM Bundles and Firm Performance," *Human Resource Management* 48, no. 5 (2009), pp. 745–768.

11. R. D. Pritchard, M. M. Harrell, D. DiazGrandos, and M. J. Guzman, "The Productivity Measurement and Enhancement System: A Meta-Analysis," *Journal of Applied Psychology* 93, no. 3 (2008), pp. 540–567.

12. F. W. Bond, P. E. Flaxman, and D. Bunce, "The Influence of Psychological Flexibility on Work Redesign: Mediated Moderation of a Work Reorganization Intervention," *Journal of Applied Psychology* 93, no. 3 (2008), pp. 645–654.

13. A. M. Grant, "Leading with Meaning: Beneficiary Contact, Prosocial Impact, and the Performance Effects of Transformational Leadership," *Academy of Management Journal,* 55 (2012), pp. 458–476; and A. M. Grant and S. K. Parker, "Redesigning Work Design Theories: The Rise of Relational and Proactive Perspectives," *Annals of the Academy of Management* 3, no. 1 (2009), pp. 317–375.

14. Y. N. Turner, I. Hadas-Halperin, and D. Raveh, "Patient Photos Spur Radiologist Empathy and Eye for Detail." Paper presented at the annual meeting of the Radiological Society of North America (November 2008).

15. A. M. Grant, E. M. Campbell, G. Chen, K. Cottone, D. Lapedis, and K. Lee, "Impact and the Art of Motivation Maintenance: The Effects of Contact with Beneficiaries on Persistence Behavior," *Organizational Behavior and Human Decision Processes* 103, no. 1 (2007), pp. 53–67.

16. Society for Human Resource Management, *2012 Employee Benefits* (Alexandria, VA: Author, 2012).

17. T. Kato, "Work and Family Practices in Japanese Firms: Their Scope, Nature, and Impact on Employee Turnover," *International Journal of Human Resource Management* 20, no. 2 (2009), pp. 439–456; and P. Mourdoukoutas, "Why Do Women Fare Better in the German World of Work than in the US?" *Forbes* (March 25, 2013), www.forbes.com/sites/panosmourdoukoutas/2013/03/25/why-do-women-fare-better-in-the-german-world-of-work-than-in-the-us/.

18. R. Waring, "Sunday Dialogue: Flexible Work Hours," *The New York Times* (January 19, 2013), www.nytimes.com.

19. S. Westcott, "Beyond Flextime: Trashing the Workweek," *Inc.* (August 2008), p. 30.

20. See, for example, D. A. Ralston and M. F. Flanagan, "The Effect of Flextime on Absenteeism and Turnover for Male and Female Employees," *Journal of Vocational Behavior* 26, no. 2 (1985), pp. 206–217; B. B. Baltes, T. E. Briggs, J. W. Huff, J. A. Wright, and G. A. Neuman, "Flexible and Compressed Workweek Schedules: A Meta-Analysis of Their Effects on Work-Related Criteria," *Journal of Applied Psychology* 84, no. 4 (1999), pp. 496–513; K. M. Shockley, and T. D. Allen, "When Flexibility Helps: Another Look at the Availability of Flexible Work Arrangements and Work–Family Conflict," *Journal of Vocational Behavior* 71, no. 3 (2007), pp. 479–493; J. G. Grzywacz, D. S. Carlson, and S. Shulkin, "Schedule Flexibility and Stress: Linking Formal Flexible Arrangements and Perceived Flexibility to Employee Health." *Community, Work, and Family* 11, no. 2 (2008), pp. 199–214; and L. A. McNall, A. D. Masuda, and J. M. Nicklin "Flexible Work Arrangements, Job Satisfaction, and Turnover Intentions: The Mediating Role of Work-to-Family Enrichment," *Journal of Psychology* 144, no. 1 (2010), pp. 61–81.

21. K. M. Shockley and T. D. Allen, "Investigating the Missing Link in Flexible Work Arrangement Utilization: An Individual Difference Perspective," *Journal of Vocational Behavior* 76, no. 1 (2010), pp. 131–142.

22. J. LaReau, "Ford's 2 Julies Share Devotion—and Job," *Automotive News* (October 25, 2010), p. 4.

23. Society for Human Resource Management, *2012 Employee Benefits.*

24. C. B. Mulligan, "What Job Sharing Brings," *Forbes* (May 8, 2013), http://economix.blogs.nytimes.com/2013/05/08/what-job-sharing-brings/.

25. L. Woellert, "U.S. Work Share Program Helps Employers Avoid Layoffs," *Bloomberg Businessweek* (January 24, 2013), www.businessweek.com/articles/2013-01-24/u-dot-s-dot-work-share-program-helps-employers-avoid-layoffs.

26. P. R. Gregory, "Why Obama Cannot Match Germany's Jobs Miracle," *Forbes* (May 5, 2013), www.forbes.com/sites/paulroderickgregory/2013/05/05/why-obama-cannot-match-germanys-jobs-miracle/.

27. See, for example, E. J. Hill, M. Ferris, and V. Martinson, "Does It Matter Where You Work? A Comparison of How Three Work Venues (Traditional Office, Virtual Office, and Home Office) Influence Aspects of Work and Personal/Family Life," *Journal of Vocational Behavior* 63, no. 2 (2003), pp. 220–241; B. Williamson, "Managing Virtual Workers," *Bloomberg Businessweek* (July 16, 2009), www.businessweek.com, and B. A. Lautsch and E. E. Kossek, "Managing a Blended Workforce: Telecommuters and Non-Telecommuters," *Organizational Dynamics* 40, no. 1 (2010), pp. 10–17.

28. B. Belton, "Best Buy Copies Yahoo, Reins in Telecommuting," *USA Today* (March 6, 2013), www.usatoday.com.

29. C. Tkaczyk, "Marissa Mayer Breaks Her Silence on Yahoo's Telecommuting Policy," *CNNMoney.com* (April 19, 2013). Downloaded from http://tech.fortune.cnn.com/2013/04/19/marissa-mayer-telecommuting/ on April 8, 2014.

30. J. Tozzi, "Home-Based Businesses Increasing," *Bloomberg Businessweek* (January 25, 2010), www.businessweek.com.

31. Society for Human Resource Management, *2012 Employee Benefits.*

32. See, for instance, M. Conlin, "The Easiest Commute of All," *BusinessWeek* (December 12, 2005), p. 78; S. Shellenbarger, "Telework Is on the Rise, but It Isn't Just Done from Home Anymore," *The Wall Street Journal* (January 23, 2001), p. B1; and E. O'Keefe, "Teleworking Grows But Still a Rarity," *The Washington Post* (February 22, 2011), p. B3.

33. Conlin, "The Easiest Commute of All."

34. E. E. Kossek, B. A. Lautsch, S. C. Eaton, "Telecommuting, Control, and Boundary Management: Correlates of Policy Use and Practice, Job Control, and Work-Family Effectiveness," *Journal of Vocational Behavior* 68, no. 2 (2006), pp. 347–367.

35. J. Kotkin, "Marissa Mayer's Misstep and the Unstoppable Rise of Telecommuting," *Forbes* (March 26, 2013).

36. J. M. Stanton and J. L. Barnes-Farrell, "Effects of Electronic Performance Monitoring on Personal Control, Task Satisfaction, and Task Performance," *Journal of Applied Psychology* 81, no. 6 (1996), pp. 738–745; and L. Taskin and F. Bridoux, "Telework: A Challenge to Knowledge Transfer in Organizations," *International Journal of Human Resource Management* 21, no. 13 (2010), pp. 2503–2520.

37. J. Welch and S. Welch, "The Importance of Being There," *BusinessWeek* (April 16, 2007), p. 92; Z. I. Barsness, K. A. Diekmann, and M. L. Seidel, "Motivation and Opportunity: The Role of Remote Work, Demographic Dissimilarity, and Social Network Centrality in Impression Management," *Academy of Management Journal* 48, no. 3 (2005), pp. 401–419.

38. See, for example, the increasing body of literature on empowerment, such as D. P. Ashmos, D. Duchon, R. R. McDaniel Jr., and J. W. Huonker, "What a Mess! Participation as a Simple Managerial Rule to 'Complexify' Organizations," *Journal of*

Management Studies 39, no. 2 (2002), pp. 189–206; S. E. Seibert, S. R. Silver, and W. A. Randolph, "Taking Empowerment to the Next Level: A Multiple-Level Model of Empowerment, Performance, and Satisfaction," *Academy of Management Journal* 47, no. 3 (2004), pp. 332–349; M. M. Butts, R. J. Vandenberg, D. M. DeJoy, B. S. Schaffer, and M. G. Wilson, "Individual Reactions to High Involvement Work Processes: Investigating the Role of Empowerment and Perceived Organizational Support," *Journal of Occupational Health Psychology* 14, no. 2 (2009), pp. 122–136; R. Park, E. Applebaum, and D. Kruse, "Employee Involvement and Group Incentives in Manufacturing Companies: A Multi-Level Analysis," *Human Resource Management Journal* 20, no. 3 (2010), pp. 227–243; D. C. Jones, P. Kalmi, and A. Kauhanen, "How Does Employee Involvement Stack Up? The Effects of Human Resource Management Policies in a Retail Firm," *Industrial Relations* 49, no. 1 (2010), pp. 1–21; and M. T. Maynard, L. L. Gilson, and J. E. Mathieu, "Empowerment—Fad or Fab? A Multilevel Review of the Past Two Decades of Research," *Journal of Management* 38, no. 4 (2012), pp. 1231–1281.

39. See, for instance, A. Sagie and Z. Aycan, "A Cross-Cultural Analysis of Participative Decision-Making in Organizations," *Human Relations* 56, no. 4 (2003), pp. 453–473; and J. Brockner, "Unpacking Country Effects: On the Need to Operationalize the Psychological Determinants of Cross-National Differences," in R. M. Kramer and B. M. Staw (eds.), *Research in Organizational Behavior,* vol. 25 (Oxford, UK: Elsevier, 2003), pp. 336–340.

40. C. Robert, T. M. Probst, J. J. Martocchio, R. Drasgow, and J. J. Lawler, "Empowerment and Continuous Improvement in the United States, Mexico, Poland, and India: Predicting Fit on the Basis of the Dimensions of Power Distance and Individualism," *Journal of Applied Psychology* 85, no. 5 (2000), pp. 643–658.

41. Z. X. Chen and S. Aryee, "Delegation and Employee Work Outcomes: An Examination of the Cultural Context of Mediating Processes in China," *Academy of Management Journal* 50, no. 1 (2007), pp. 226–238.

42. G. Huang, X. Niu, C. Lee, and S. J. Ashford, "Differentiating Cognitive and Affective Job Insecurity: Antecedents and Outcomes," *Journal of Organizational Behavior* 33, no. 6 (2012), pp. 752–769.

43. J. J. Caughron and M. D. Mumford, "Embedded Leadership: How Do a Leader's Superiors Impact Middle-Management Performance?" *Leadership Quarterly* (June 2012), pp. 342–353.

44. See, for instance, K. L. Miller and P. R. Monge, "Participation, Satisfaction, and Productivity: A Meta-Analytic Review," *Academy of Management Journal* (December 1986), pp. 727–753; J. A. Wagner III, "Participation's Effects on Performance and Satisfaction: A Reconsideration of Research Evidence," *Academy of Management Review* 19, no. 2 (1994), pp. 312–330; C. Doucouliagos, "Worker Participation and Productivity in Labor-Managed and Participatory Capitalist Firms: A Meta-Analysis," *Industrial and Labor Relations Review* 49, no. 1 (1995), pp. 58–77; J. A. Wagner III, C. R. Leana, E. A. Locke, and D. M. Schweiger, "Cognitive and Motivational Frameworks in U.S. Research on Participation: A Meta-Analysis of Primary Effects," *Journal of Organizational Behavior* 18, no. 1 (1997), pp. 49–65; A. Pendleton and A. Robinson, "Employee Stock Ownership, Involvement, and Productivity: An Interaction-Based Approach," *Industrial and Labor Relations Review* 64, no. 1 (2010), pp. 3–29.

45. D. K. Datta, J. P. Guthrie, and P. M. Wright, "Human Resource Management and Labor Productivity: Does Industry Matter? *Academy of Management Journal* 48, no. 1 (2005), pp. 135–145; C. M. Riordan, R. J. Vandenberg, and H. A. Richardson,

"Employee Involvement Climate and Organizational Effectiveness." *Human Resource Management* 44, no. 4 (2005), pp. 471–488; and J. Kim, J. P. MacDuffie, and F. K. Pil, "Employee Voice and Organizational Performance: Team Versus Representative Influence," *Human Relations* 63, no. 3 (2010), pp. 371–394.

46. J. L. Cotton, *Employee Involvement* (Thousand Oaks, CA: Sage Publications, 1993), p. 114.

47. See, for example, M. Gilman and P. Marginson, "Negotiating European Works Council: Contours of Constrained Choice," *Industrial Relations Journal* 33, no. 1 (2002), pp. 36–51; J. T. Addison and C. R. Belfield, "What Do We Know About the New European Works Council? Some Preliminary Evidence from Britain," *Scottish Journal of Political Economy* 49, no. 4 (2002), pp. 418–444; and B. Keller, "The European Company Statute: Employee Involvement—and Beyond," *Industrial Relations Journal* 33, no. 5 (2002), pp. 424–445.

48. Cotton, *Employee Involvement*, pp. 129–130, 139–140.

49. Ibid., p. 140.

50. E. White, "Opportunity Knocks, and It Pays a Lot Better," *The Wall Street Journal* (November 13, 2006), p. B3.

51. D. A. McIntyre and S. Weigley, "8 Companies That Most Owe Workers a Raise," *USA Today* (May 13, 2013), www.usatoday.com/story/money/business/2013/05/12/8-companies-that-most-owe-workers-a-raise/2144013/.

52. M. Sabramony, N. Krause, J. Norton, and G. N. Burns "The Relationship Between Human Resource Investments and Organizational Performance: A Firm-Level Examination of Equilibrium Theory," *Journal of Applied Psychology* 93, no. 4 (2008), pp. 778–788.

53. See, for example, B. Martinez, "Teacher Bonuses Emerge in Newark," *The Wall Street Journal* (April 21, 2011), p. A.15; and D. Weber, "Seminole Teachers to Get Bonuses Instead of Raises," *Orlando Sentinel* (January 19, 2011), www.orlandosentinel.com.

54. Based on J. R. Schuster and P. K. Zingheim, "The New Variable Pay: Key Design Issues," *Compensation & Benefits Review* (March–April 1993), p. 28; K. S. Abosch, "Variable Pay: Do We Have the Basics in Place?" *Compensation & Benefits Review* (July–August 1998), pp. 12–22; and K. M. Kuhn and M. D. Yockey, "Variable Pay as a Risky Choice: Determinants of the Relative Attractiveness of Incentive Plans," *Organizational Behavior and Human Decision Processes* 90, no. 2 (2003), pp. 323–341.

55. Hay Group, "Hay Group Research Finds Increased Use of Variable Pay for Employees," *Investment Weekly News*, (July 24, 2010), p. 269.

56. S. Miller, "Companies Worldwide Rewarding Performance with Variable Pay," *Society for Human Resource Management* (March 1, 2010), www.shrm.org.

57. S. Miller, "Asian Firms Offer More Variable Pay Than Western Firms," *Society for Human Resource Management* (March 28, 2012), www.shrm.org.

58. H. Kim, K. L. Sutton, and Y. Gong, "Group-Based Pay-for-Performance Plans and Firm Performance: The Moderating Role of Empowerment Practices," *Asia Pacific Journal of Management* (March 2013), pp. 31–52.

59. G. D. Jenkins Jr., N. Gupta, A. Mitra, and J. D. Shaw, "Are Financial Incentives Related to Performance? A Meta-Analytic Review of Empirical Research," *Journal of Applied Psychology* 83, no. 5 (1998), pp. 777–787; and S. L. Rynes, B. Gerhart, and L. Parks, "Personnel Psychology: Performance Evaluation and Pay for Performance," *Annual Review of Psychology* 56, no. 1 (2005), pp. 571–600.

60. C. M. Barnes, J. Reb, and D. Ang, "More Than Just the Mean: Moving to a Dynamic View of Performance-Based Compensation," *Journal of Applied Psychology* 97, no. 3 (2012), pp. 711–718.

61. P. Furman, "Ouch! Top Honchos on Wall Street See Biggest Cuts to Bonuses," *New York Daily News* (February 18, 2013), www.nydailynews.com.

62. S. S. Wiltermuth and F. Gino, "I'll Have One of Each": How Separating Rewards into (Meaningless) Categories Increases Motivation," *Journal of Personality and Social Psychology* (January 2013), pp. 1–13.

63. G. E. Ledford Jr., "Paying for the Skills, Knowledge, and Competencies of Knowledge Workers," *Compensation & Benefits Review,* (July–August 1995), pp. 55–62; B. Murray and B. Gerhart, "An Empirical Analysis of a Skill-Based Pay Program and Plant Performance Outcomes," *Academy of Management Journal* 41, no. 1 (1998), pp. 68–78; J. R. Thompson and C. W. LeHew, "Skill-Based Pay as an Organizational Innovation," *Review of Public Personnel Administration* 20, no. 1 (2000), pp. 20–40; and J. D. Shaw, N. Gupta, A. Mitra, and G. E. Ledford, Jr., "Success and Survival of Skill-Based Pay Plans," *Journal of Management* 31, no. 1 (2005), pp. 28–49.

64. A. Mitra, N. Gupta, and J. D. Shaw, "A Comparative Examination of Traditional and Skill-Based Pay Plans," *Journal of Managerial Psychology* 26, no. 4 (2011), pp. 278–296.

65. E. C. Dierdorff and E. A. Surface, "If You Pay for Skills, Will They Learn? Skill Change and Maintenance under a Skill-Based Pay System," *Journal of Management* 34, no. 4 (2008), pp. 721–743.

66. F. Giancola, "Skill-Based Pay—Issues for Consideration," *Benefits and Compensation Digest* 44, no. 5 (2007), pp. 1–15.

67. C. Vanderborg, "Oracle's Larry Ellison Tops List Of Highest Paid CEO's," *International Business Times* (April 8, 2013), www.ibtimes.com/oracles-larry-ellison-tops-list-highest-paid-ceos-photos-1177217.

68. "Mark Zuckerberg Reaped $2.3 Billion on Facebook Stock Options," *Huffington Post* (April 26, 2013), www.huffingtonpost.com.

69. N. Chi and T. Han, "Exploring the Linkages Between Formal Ownership and Psychological Ownership for the Organization: The Mediating Role of Organizational Justice," *Journal of Occupational and Organizational Psychology* 81, no. 4 (2008), pp. 691–711.

70. See, for instance, D. O. Kim, "Determinants of the Survival of Gainsharing Programs," *Industrial & Labor Relations Review* 53, no. 1 (1999), pp. 21–42; "Why Gainsharing Works Even Better Today Than in the Past," *HR Focus* (April 2000), pp. 3–5; L. R. Gomez-Mejia, T. M. Welbourne, and R. M. Wiseman, "The Role of Risk Sharing and Risk Taking Under Gainsharing," *Academy of Management Review* 25, no. 3 (2000), pp. 492–507; M. Reynolds, "A Cost-Reduction Strategy That May Be Back," *Healthcare Financial Management* (January 2002), pp. 58–64; M. R. Dixon, L. J. Hayes, and J. Stack, "Changing Conceptions of Employee Compensation," *Journal of Organizational Behavior Management* 23, no. 2–3 (2003), pp. 95–116; and I. M. Leitman, R. Levin, M. J. Lipp, L. Sivaprasad, C. J. Karalakulasingam, D. S. Bernard, P. Friedmann, and D. J. Shulkin, "Quality and Financial Outcomes from Gainsharing for Inpatient Admissions: A Three-Year Experience," *Journal of Hospital Medicine* 5, no. 9 (2010), pp. 501–517.

71. T. M. Welbourne and C. J. Ferrante, "To Monitor or Not to Monitor: A Study of Individual Outcomes from Monitoring

One's Peers under Gainsharing and Merit Pay," *Group & Organization Management* 33, no. 2 (2008), pp. 139–162.

72. A. A. Buchko, "The Effects of Employee Ownership on Employee Attitudes: A Test of Three Theoretical Perspectives," *Work and Occupations* 19, no. 1 (1992), 59–78; and R. P. Garrett, "Does Employee Ownership Increase Innovation?" *New England Journal of Entrepreneurship* 13, no. 2, (2010), pp. 37–46.

73. D. McCarthy, E. Reeves, and T. Turner, "Can Employee Share-Ownership Improve Employee Attitudes and Behaviour?" *Employee Relations* 32, no. 4 (2010), pp. 382–395.

74. A. Pendleton and A. Robinson, "Employee Stock Ownership, Involvement, and Productivity: An Interaction-Based Approach," *Industrial and Labor Relations Review* 64, no. 1 (2010), pp. 3–29.

75. X. Zhang, K. M. Bartol, K. G. Smith, M. D. Pfarrer, and D. M. Khanin, "CEOs on the Edge: Earnings Manipulation and Stock-Based Incentive Misalignment," *Academy of Management Journal* 51, no. 2 (2008), pp. 241–258.

76. D. D'Art and T. Turner, "Profit Sharing, Firm Performance, and Union Influence in Selected European Countries," *Personnel Review* 33, no. 3 (2004), pp. 335–350; and D. Kruse, R. Freeman, and J. Blasi, *Shared Capitalism at Work: Employee Ownership, Profit and Gain Sharing, and Broad-Based Stock Options* (Chicago: University of Chicago Press, 2010).

77. A. Bayo-Moriones and M. Larraza-Kintana, "Profit-Sharing Plans and Affective Commitment: Does the Context Matter?" *Human Resource Management* 48, no. 2 (2009), pp. 207–226.

78. C. B. Cadsby, F. Song, and F. Tapon, "Sorting and Incentive Effects of Pay for Performance: An Experimental Investigation," *Academy of Management Journal* 50, no. 2 (2007), pp. 387–405.

79. S. C. L. Fong and M. A. Shaffer, "The Dimensionality and Determinants of Pay Satisfaction: A Cross-Cultural Investigation of a Group Incentive Plan," *International Journal of Human Resource Management* 14, no. 4 (2003), pp. 559–580.

80. See, for instance, M. W. Barringer and G. T. Milkovich, "A Theoretical Exploration of the Adoption and Design of Flexible Benefit Plans: A Case of Human Resource Innovation," *Academy of Management Review* 23, no. 2 (1998), pp. 305–324; D. Brown, "Everybody Loves Flex," *Canadian HR Reporter* (November 18, 2002), p. 1; J. Taggart, "Putting Flex Benefits Through Their Paces," *Canadian HR Reporter* (December 2, 2002), p. G3; and N. D. Cole and D. H. Flint, "Perceptions of Distributive and Procedural Justice in Employee Benefits: Flexible Versus Traditional Benefit Plans," *Journal of Managerial Psychology* 19, no. 1 (2004), pp. 19–40.

81. P. Stephens, "Flex Plans Gain in Popularity," *CA Magazine* (January/February 2010), p. 10.

82. D. Lovewell, "Flexible Benefits: Benefits on Offer," *Employee Benefits* (March 2010), p. S15.

83. L. Shepherd, "Special Report on Rewards and Recognition: Getting Personal," *Workforce Management* (September 2010), pp. 24–29.

84. L. Shepherd, "On Recognition, Multinationals Think Globally," *Workforce Management* (September 2010), p. 26.

85. R. J. Long and J. L. Shields, "From Pay to Praise? Non-Case Employee Recognition in Canadian and Australian Firms," *International Journal of Human Resource Management* 21, no. 8 (2010), pp. 1145–1172.

86. S. E. Markham, K. D. Scott, and G. H. McKee, "Recognizing Good Attendance: A Longitudinal, Quasi-Experimental Field Study," *Personnel Psychology* 55, no. 3 (2002), p. 641; and S. J. Peterson and F. Luthans, "The Impact of Financial and Nonfinancial Incentives on Business Unit Outcomes over Time," *Journal of Applied Psychology* 91, no. 1 (2006), pp. 156–165.

87. A. D. Stajkovic and F. Luthans, "Differential Effects of Incentive Motivators on Work Performance," *Academy of Management Journal* 4, no. 3 (2001), p. 587. See also F. Luthans and A. D. Stajkovic, "Provide Recognition for Performance Improvement," in E. A. Locke (ed.), *Handbook of Principles of Organizational Behavior* (Malden, MA: Blackwell, 2004), pp. 166–180.

CHAPTER 9

1. D. K. Berlo, *The Process of Communication* (New York: Holt, Rinehart & Winston, 1960), pp. 30–32; see also K. Byron, "Carrying Too Heavy a Load? The Communication and Miscommunication of Emotion by Email," *Academy of Management Review* 33, no. 2 (2008), pp. 309–327.

2. J. Langan-Fox, "Communication in Organizations: Speed, Diversity, Networks, and Influence on Organizational Effectiveness, Human Health, and Relationships," in N. Anderson, D. S. Ones, H. K. Sinangil, and C. Viswesvaran (eds.), *Handbook of Industrial, Work and Organizational Psychology*, vol. 2 (Thousand Oaks, CA: Sage, 2001), p. 190.

3. R. L. Simpson, "Vertical and Horizontal Communication in Formal Organizations," *Administrative Science Quarterly* (September 1959), pp. 188–196; A. G. Walker and J. W. Smither, "A Five-Year Study of Upward Feedback: What Managers Do with Their Results Matter," *Personnel Psychology* (Summer 1999), pp. 393–424; and J. W. Smither and A. G. Walker, "Are the Characteristics of Narrative Comments Related to Improvement in Multirater Feedback Ratings Over Time?" *Journal of Applied Psychology* 89, no. 3 (June 2004), pp. 575–581.

4. P. Dvorak, "How Understanding the 'Why' of Decisions Matters," *The Wall Street Journal* (March 19, 2007), p. B3.

5. T. Neeley and P. Leonardi, "Effective Managers Say the Same Thing Twice (or More)," *Harvard Business Review* (May 2011), pp. 38–39.

6. J. Ewing, "Nokia: Bring on the Employee Rants," *BusinessWeek* (June 22, 2009), p. 50.

7. H. A. Richardson and S. G. Taylor, "Understanding Input Events: A Model of Employees' Responses to Requests for Their Input," *Academy of Management Review* 37 (2012), pp. 471–491.

8. E. Nichols, "Hyper-Speed Managers," *HR Magazine* (April 2007), pp. 107–110.

9. See, for example, N. B. Kurland and L. H. Pelled, "Passing the Word: Toward a Model of Gossip and Power in the Workplace," *Academy of Management Review* (April 2000), pp. 428–438; and G. Michelson, A. van Iterson, and K. Waddington, "Gossip in Organizations: Contexts, Consequences, and Controversies," *Group and Organization Management* 35, no. 4 (2010), pp. 371–390.

10. G. Van Hoye and F. Lievens, "Tapping the Grapevine: A Closer Look at Word-of-Mouth as a Recruitment Source," *Journal of Applied Psychology* 94, no. 2 (2009), pp. 341–352.

11. R. L. Rosnow and G. A. Fine, *Rumor and Gossip: The Social Psychology of Hearsay* (New York: Elsevier, 1976).

12. J. K. Bosson, A. B. Johnson, K. Niederhoffer, and W. B. Swann Jr., "Interpersonal Chemistry Through Negativity: Bonding by Sharing Negative Attitudes About Others," *Personal Relationships* 13 (2006), pp. 135–150.

13. T. J. Grosser, V. Lopez-Kidwell, and G. Labianca, "A Social Network Analysis of Positive and Negative Gossip in Organizational

Life," *Group and Organization Management* 35, no. 2 (2010), pp. 177–212.

14. M. Feinberg, R. Willer, J. Stellar, and D. Keltner, "The Virtues of Gossip: Reputational Information Sharing as Prosocial Behavior," *Journal of Personality and Social Psychology* 102 (2012), pp. 1015–1030.

15. L. Dulye, "Get Out of Your Office," *HR Magazine* (July 2006), pp. 99–101.

16. L. S. Rashotte, "What Does That Smile Mean? The Meaning of Nonverbal Behaviors in Social Interaction," *Social Psychology Quarterly* (March 2002), pp. 92–102.

17. C. K. Goman, "5 Body Language Tips to Increase Your Curb Appeal," *Forbes* (March 4, 2013), www.forbes.com/sites/carolkinseygoman/2013/03/14/5-body-language-tips-to-increase-your-curb-appeal/.

18. A. Metallinou, A. Katsamanis, and S. Narayanan, "Tracking Continuous Emotional Trends of Participants During Affective Dyadic Interactions using Body Language and Speech Information," *Image and Vision Computing* (February 2013), pp. 137–152.

19. J. Smith, "10 Nonverbal Cues That Convey Confidence at Work," *Forbes* (March 11, 2013), www.forbes.com/sites/jacquelynsmith/2013/03/11/10-nonverbal-cues-that-convey-confidence-at-work/.

20. See R. L. Daft and R. H. Lengel, "Information Richness: A New Approach to Managerial Behavior and Organization Design," in B. M. Staw and L. L. Cummings (eds.), *Research in Organizational Behavior,* vol. 6 (Greenwich, CT: JAI Press, 1984), pp. 191–233; R. L. Daft and R. H. Lengel, "Organizational Information Requirements, Media Richness, and Structural Design," *Managerial Science* (May 1986), pp. 554–572; R. E. Rice, "Task Analyzability, Use of New Media, and Effectiveness," *Organization Science* (November 1992), pp. 475–500; S. G. Straus and J. E. McGrath, "Does the Medium Matter? The Interaction of Task Type and Technology on Group Performance and Member Reaction," *Journal of Applied Psychology* (February 1994), pp. 87–97; L. K. Trevino, J. Webster, and E. W. Stein, "Making Connections: Complementary Influences on Communication Media Choices, Attitudes, and Use," *Organization Science* (March–April 2000), pp. 163–182; and N. Kock, "The Psychobiological Model: Towards a New Theory of Computer-Mediated Communication Based on Darwinian Evolution," *Organization Science* 15, no. 3 (May–June 2004), pp. 327–348.

21. E. Frauenheim, "Communicating for Engagement During Tough Times," *Workforce Management Online* (April 2010), www.workforce.com.

22. S. Shellenbarger, "Is This How You Really Talk?" *The Wall Street Journal* (April 24, 2013), pp. D1, D3.

23. M. V. Rafter, "Falling from a Cloud," *Workforce Management* (February 2013), pp. 22–23.

24. "At Many Companies, Hunt for Leakers Expands Arsenal of Monitoring Tactics," *The Wall Street Journal* (September 11, 2006), pp. B1, B3; and B. J. Alge, G. A. Ballinger, S. Tangirala, and J. L. Oakley, "Information Privacy in Organizations: Empowering Creative and Extrarole Performance," *Journal of Applied Psychology* 91, No. 1 (2006), pp. 221–232.

25. R. E. Petty and P. Briñol, "Persuasion: From Single to Multiple to Metacognitive Processes," *Perspectives on Psychological Science* 3, no. 2 (2008), pp. 137–147; F. A. White, M. A. Charles, and J. K. Nelson, "The Role of Persuasive Arguments in Changing Affirmative Action Attitudes and Expressed Behavior in Higher Education," *Journal of Applied Psychology* 93, no. 6 (2008), pp. 1271–1286.

26. B. T. Johnson, and A. H. Eagly, "Effects of Involvement on Persuasion: A Meta-Analysis," *Psychological Bulletin* 106, no. 2 (1989), pp. 290–314; and K. L. Blankenship and D. T. Wegener, "Opening the Mind to Close It: Considering a Message in Light of Important Values Increases Message Processing and Later Resistance to Change," *Journal of Personality and Social Psychology* 94, no. 2 (2008), pp. 196–213.

27. See, for example, Y. H. M. See, R. E. Petty, and L. R. Fabrigar, "Affective and Cognitive Meta-Bases of Attitudes: Unique Effects of Information Interest and Persuasion," *Journal of Personality and Social Psychology* 94, no. 6 (2008), pp. 938–955; M. S. Key, J. E. Edlund, B. J. Sagarin, and G. Y. Bizer, "Individual Differences in Susceptibility to Mindlessness," *Personality and Individual Differences* 46, no. 3 (2009), pp. 261–264 and M. Reinhard and M. Messner, "The Effects of Source Likeability and Need for Cognition on Advertising Effectiveness Under Explicit Persuasion," *Journal of Consumer Behavior* 8, no. 4 (2009), pp. 179–191.

28. P. Briñol, R. E. Petty, and J. Barden, "Happiness Versus Sadness as a Determinant of Thought Confidence in Persuasion: A Self-Validation Analysis," *Journal of Personality and Social Psychology* 93, no. 5 (2007), pp. 711–727.

29. R. C. Sinclair, S. E. Moore, M. M. Mark, A. S. Soldat, and C. A. Lavis, "Incidental Moods, Source Likeability, and Persuasion: Liking Motivates Message Elaboration in Happy People," *Cognition and Emotion* 24, no. 6 (2010), pp. 940–961; and V. Griskevicius, M. N. Shiota, and S. L. Neufeld, "Influence of Different Positive Emotions on Persuasion Processing: A Functional Evolutionary Approach," *Emotion* 10, no. 2 (2010), pp. 190–206.

30. J. Sandberg, "The Jargon Jumble: Kids Have 'Skeds,' Colleagues, 'Needs,'" *The Wall Street Journal* (October 24, 2006), http://online.wsj.com/article/SB116165746415401680.html.

31. E. W. Morrison and F. J. Milliken, "Organizational Silence: A Barrier to Change and Development in a Pluralistic World," *Academy of Management Review* 25, no. 4 (2000), pp. 706–725; and B. E. Ashforth and V. Anand, "The Normalization of Corruption in Organizations," *Research in Organizational Behavior* 25 (2003), pp. 1–52.

32. F. J. Milliken, E. W. Morrison, and P. F. Hewlin, "An Exploratory Study of Employee Silence: Issues That Employees Don't Communicate Upward and Why," *Journal of Management Studies* 40, no. 6 (2003), pp. 1453–1476.

33. S. Tangirala and R. Ramunujam, "Employee Silence on Critical Work Issues: The Cross-Level Effects of Procedural Justice Climate," *Personnel Psychology* 61, no. 1 (2008), pp. 37–68; and F. Bowen and K. Blackmon, "Spirals of Silence: The Dynamic Effects of Diversity on Organizational Voice," *Journal of Management Studies* 40, no. 6 (2003), pp. 1393–1417.

34. B. R. Schlenker and M. R. Leary, "Social Anxiety and Self-Presentation: A Conceptualization and Model," *Psychological Bulletin* 92 (1982), pp. 641–669; and L. A. Withers, and L. L. Vernon, "To Err Is Human: Embarrassment, Attachment, and Communication Apprehension," *Personality and Individual Differences* 40, no. 1 (2006), pp. 99–110.

35. See, for instance, S. K. Opt and D. A. Loffredo, "Rethinking Communication Apprehension: A Myers-Briggs Perspective," *Journal of Psychology* (September 2000), pp. 556–570; and B. D. Blume, G. F. Dreher, and T. T. Baldwin, "Examining the Effects of Communication Apprehension within Assessment Centres," *Journal of Occupational and Organizational Psychology* 83, no. 3 (2010), pp. 663–671.

36. See, for example, J. A. Daly and J. C. McCroskey, "Occupational Desirability and Choice as a Function of Communication Apprehension," *Journal of Counseling Psychology* 22, no. 4 (1975), pp. 309–313; and T. L. Rodebaugh, "I Might Look OK, But I'm Still Doubtful, Anxious, and Avoidant: The Mixed Effects of Enhanced Video Feedback on Social Anxiety Symptoms," *Behaviour Research & Therapy* 42, no. 12 (December 2004), pp. 1435–1451.

37. B. M. Depaulo, D. A. Kashy, S. E. Kirkendol, M. M. Wyer, and J. A. Epstein, "Lying in Everyday Life," *Journal of Personality and Social Psychology* 70, No. 5 (1996), pp. 979–995; and K. B. Serota, T. R. Levine, and F. J. Boster, "The Prevalence of Lying in America: Three Studies of Self-Reported Lies," *Human Communication Research* 36, no. 1. (2010), pp. 2–25.

38. DePaulo, Kashy, Kirkendol, Wyer, and Epstein, "Lying in Everyday Life"; and C. E. Naguin, T. R. Kurtzberg, and L. Y. Belkin, "The Finer Points of Lying Online: E-Mail Versus Pen and Paper," *Journal of Applied Psychology* 95, no. 2 (2010), pp. 387–394.

39. A. Vrij, P. A. Granhag, and S. Porter, "Pitfalls and Opportunities in Nonverbal and Verbal Lie Detection," *Psychological Science in the Public Interest* 11, no. 3 (2010), pp. 89–121.

40. R. E. Axtell, *Gestures: The Do's and Taboos of Body Language Around the World* (New York: Wiley, 1991); Watson Wyatt Worldwide, "Effective Communication: A Leading Indicator of Financial Performance—2005/2006 Communication ROI Study," www.watsonwyatt.com/research/resrender.asp?id=w-868; and A. Markels, "Turning the Tide at P&G," *U.S. News & World Report* (October 30, 2006), p. 69.

41. See M. Munter, "Cross-Cultural Communication for Managers," *Business Horizons* (May–June 1993), pp. 75–76; and H. Ren and B. Gray, "Repairing Relationship Conflict: How Violation Types and Culture Influence the Effectiveness of Restoration Rituals," *Academy of Management Review* 34, no. 1 (2009), pp. 105–126.

42. See E. T. Hall, *Beyond Culture* (Garden City, NY: Anchor Press/Doubleday, 1976); W. L. Adair, "Integrative Sequences and Negotiation Outcome in Same- and Mixed-Culture Negotiations," *International Journal of Conflict Management* 14, no. 3–4 (2003), pp. 1359–1392; W. L. Adair and J. M. Brett, "The Negotiation Dance: Time, Culture, and Behavioral Sequences in Negotiation," *Organization Science* 16, no. 1 (2005), pp. 33–51; E. Giebels and P. J. Taylor, "Interaction Patterns in Crisis Negotiations: Persuasive Arguments and Cultural Differences," *Journal of Applied Psychology* 94, no. 1 (2009), pp. 5–19; and M. G. Kittler, D. Rygl, and A. Mackinnon, "Beyond Culture or Beyond Control? Reviewing the Use of Hall's High-/Low-Context Concept," *International Journal of Cross Cultural Management* 11, no. 1 (2011), pp. 63–82.

43. M. C. Hopson, T. Hart, and G. C. Bell, "Meeting in the Middle: Fred L. Casmir's Contributions to the Field of Intercultural Communication," *International Journal of Intercultural Relations* (November 2012), pp. 789–797.

CHAPTER 10

1. This section is based on J. R. Katzenbach and D. K. Smith, *The Wisdom of Teams* (Cambridge, MA: Harvard University Press, 1993), pp. 21, 45, 85; and D. C. Kinlaw, *Developing Superior Work Teams* (Lexington, MA: Lexington Books, 1991), pp. 3–21.

2. J. Mathieu, M. T. Maynard, T. Rapp, and L. Gilson, "Team Effectiveness 1997–2007: A Review of Recent Advancements and a Glimpse into the Future," *Journal of Management* 34, no. 3 (2008), pp. 410–476.

3. J. H. Shonk, *Team-Based Organizations* (Homewood, IL: Business One Irwin, 1992); and M. A. Verespej, "When Workers Get New Roles," *IndustryWeek* (February 3, 1992), p. 11.

4. G. Bodinson and R. Bunch, "AQP's National Team Excellence Award: Its Purpose, Value and Process," *The Journal for Quality and Participation* (Spring 2003), pp. 37–42.

5. See, for example, A. Erez, J. A. LePine, and H. Elms, "Effects of Rotated Leadership and Peer Evaluation on the Functioning and Effectiveness of Self-Managed Teams: A Quasi-experiment," *Personnel Psychology* (Winter 2002), pp. 929–948.

6. See, for instance, C. W. Langfred, "Too Much of a Good Thing? Negative Effects of High Trust and Individual Autonomy in Self-Managing Teams," *Academy of Management Journal* (June 2004), pp. 385–399.

7. G. L. Stewart, S. H. Courtright, and M. R. Barrick, "Peer-Based Control in Self-Managing Teams: Linking Rational and Normative Influence with Individual and Group Performance," *Journal of Applied Psychology* 97, no. 2 (2012), pp. 435–447.

8. C. W. Langfred, "The Downside of Self-Management: A Longitudinal Study of the Effects of Conflict on Trust, Autonomy, and Task Interdependence in Self-Managing Teams," *Academy of Management Journal* 50, no. 4 (2007), pp. 885–900.

9. B. H. Bradley, B. E. Postlethwaite, A. C. Klotz, M. R. Hamdani, and K. G. Brown, "Reaping the Benefits of Task Conflict in Teams: The Critical Role of Team Psychological Safety Climate," *Journal of Applied Psychology*, 97, no. 1 (2012), pp. 151–158.

10. J. Devaro, "The Effects of Self-Managed and Closely Managed Teams on Labor Productivity and Product Quality: An Empirical Analysis of a Cross-Section of Establishments," *Industrial Relations* 47, no. 4 (2008), pp. 659–698.

11. A. Shah, "Starbucks Strives for Instant Gratification with Via Launch," *PRWeek* (December 2009), p. 15.

12. B. Freyer and T. A. Stewart, "Cisco Sees the Future," *Harvard Business Review* (November 2008), pp. 73–79.

13. See, for example, L. L. Martins, L. L. Gilson, and M. T. Maynard, "Virtual Teams: What Do We Know and Where Do We Go from Here?" *Journal of Management* (November 2004), pp. 805–835; and B. Leonard, "Managing Virtual Teams," *HRMagazine* (June 2011), pp. 39–42.

14. A. Malhotra, A. Majchrzak, and B. Rosen, "Leading Virtual Teams," *Academy of Management Perspectives* (February 2007), pp. 60–70; and J. M. Wilson, S. S. Straus, and B. McEvily, "All in Due Time: The Development of Trust in Computer-Mediated and Face-to-Face Teams," *Organizational Behavior and Human Decision Processes* 19 (2006), pp. 16–33.

15. R. S. Gajendran and A. Joshi, "Innovation in Globally Distributed Teams: The Role of LMX, Communication Frequency, and Member Influence on Team Decisions, *Journal of Applied Psychology* 97, no. 6 (2012), pp. 1252–1261.

16. J. R. Mesmer-Magnus, L. A. DeChurch, M. Jimenez-Rodriguez, J. Wildman, and M. Shuffler, "A Meta-Analytic Investigation of Virtuality and Information Sharing in Teams," *Organizational Behavior and Human Decision Processes* 115, no. 2 (2011), pp. 214–225.

17. P. Balkundi and D. A. Harrison, "Ties, Leaders, and Time in Teams: Strong Inference About Network Structure's Effects on Team Viability and Performance," *Academy of Management Journal* 49, no. 1 (2006), pp. 49–68; G. Chen, B. L. Kirkman, R. Kanfer, D. Allen, and B. Rosen, "A Multilevel Study of Leadership, Empowerment, and Performance in Teams," *Journal of*

Applied Psychology 92, no. 2 (2007), pp. 331–346; L. A. DeChurch and M. A. Marks, "Leadership in Multiteam Systems," *Journal of Applied Psychology* 91, no. 2 (2006), pp. 311–329; A. Srivastava, K. M. Bartol, and E. A. Locke, "Empowering Leadership in Management Teams: Effects on Knowledge Sharing, Efficacy, and Performance," *Academy of Management Journal* 49, no. 6 (2006), pp. 1239–1251; and J. E. Mathieu, K. K. Gilson, and T. M. Ruddy, "Empowerment and Team Effectiveness: An Empirical Test of an Integrated Model," *Journal of Applied Psychology* 91, no. 1 (2006), pp. 97–108.

18. R. B. Davison, J. R. Hollenbeck, C. M. Barnes, D. J. Sleesman, and D. R. Ilgen, "Coordinated Action in Multiteam Systems," *Journal of Applied Psychology* 97, no. 4 (2012), pp. 808–824.

19. This model is based on M. A. Campion, E. M. Papper, and G. J. Medsker, "Relations Between Work Team Characteristics and Effectiveness: A Replication and Extension," *Personnel Psychology* (Summer 1996), pp. 429–452; Hyatt and Ruddy, "An Examination of the Relationship Between Work Group Characteristics and Performance," pp. 553–585; S. G. Cohen and D. E. Bailey, "What Makes Teams Work: Group Effectiveness Research from the Shop Floor to the Executive Suite," *Journal of Management* 23, no. 3 (1997), pp. 239–290; L. Thompson, *Making the Team* (Upper Saddle River, NJ: Prentice Hall, 2000), pp. 18–33; and J. R. Hackman, *Leading Teams: Setting the Stage for Great Performance* (Boston: Harvard Business School Press, 2002).

20. See G. L. Stewart and M. R. Barrick, "Team Structure and Performance: Assessing the Mediating Role of Intrateam Process and the Moderating Role of Task Type," *Academy of Management Journal* (April 2000), pp. 135–148.

21. Hyatt and Ruddy, "An Examination of the Relationship Between Work Group Characteristics and Performance," p. 577.

22. P. Balkundi and D. A. Harrison, "Ties, Leaders, and Time in Teams: Strong Inference About Network Structure's Effects on Team Viability and Performance," *Academy of Management Journal* 49, no. 1 (2006), pp. 49–68; G. Chen, B. L. Kirkman, R. Kanfer, D. Allen, and B. Rosen, "A Multilevel Study of Leadership, Empowerment, and Performance in Teams," *Journal of Applied Psychology* 92, no. 2 (2007), pp. 331–346; L. A. DeChurch and M. A. Marks, "Leadership in Multiteam Systems," *Journal of Applied Psychology* 91, no. 2 (2006), pp. 311–329; A. Srivastava, K. M. Bartol, and E. A. Locke, "Empowering Leadership in Management Teams: Effects on Knowledge Sharing, Efficacy, and Performance," *Academy of Management Journal* 49, no. 6 (2006), pp. 1239–1251; and J. E. Mathieu, K. K. Gilson, and T. M. Ruddy, "Empowerment and Team Effectiveness: An Empirical Test of an Integrated Model," *Journal of Applied Psychology* 91, no. 1 (2006), pp. 97–108.

23. J. B. Carson, P. E. Tesluk, and J. A. Marrone, "Shared Leadership in Teams: An Investigation of Antecedent Conditions and Performance," *Academy of Management Journal* 50, no. 5 (2007), pp. 1217–1234.

24. K. T. Dirks, "Trust in Leadership and Team Performance: Evidence from NCAA Basketball," *Journal of Applied Psychology* (December 2000), pp. 1004–1012; M. Williams, "In Whom We Trust: Group Membership as an Affective Context for Trust Development," *Academy of Management Review* (July 2001), pp. 377–396; and J. Schaubroeck, S. S. K. Lam, and A. C. Peng, "Cognition-Based and Affect-Based Trust as Mediators of Leader Behavior Influences on Team Performance," *Journal of Applied Psychology*, Online First Publication (February 7, 2011), doi: 10.1037/a0022625.

25. B. A. De Jong, and K. T. Dirks, "Beyond Shared Perceptions of Trust and Monitoring in Teams: Implications of Asymmetry and Dissensus," *Journal of Applied Psychology* 97, no. 2 (2012), pp. 391–406.

26. See F. Aime, C. J. Meyer, and S. E. Humphrey, "Legitimacy of Team Rewards: Analyzing Legitimacy as a Condition for the Effectiveness of Team Incentive Designs," *Journal of Business Research* 63, no. 1 (2010), pp. 60–66; and P. A. Bamberger and R. Levi, "Team-Based Reward Allocation Structures and the Helping Behaviors of Outcome-Interdependent Team Members," *Journal of Managerial Psychology* 24, no. 4 (2009), pp. 300–327; and M. J. Pearsall, M. S. Christian, and A. P. J. Ellis, "Motivating Interdependent Teams: Individual Rewards, Shared Rewards, or Something in Between?" *Journal of Applied Psychology* 95, no. 1 (2010), pp. 183–191.

27. R. R. Hirschfeld, M. H. Jordan, H. S. Feild, W. F. Giles, and A. A. Armenakis, "Becoming Team Players: Team Members' Mastery of Teamwork Knowledge as a Predictor of Team Task Proficiency and Observed Teamwork Effectiveness," *Journal of Applied Psychology* 91, no. 2 (2006), pp. 467–474; and K. R. Randall, C. J. Resick, and L. A. DeChurch, "Building Team Adaptive Capacity: The Roles of Sensegiving and Team Composition," *Journal of Applied Psychology* 96, no. 3 (2011), pp. 525–540.

28. H. Moon, J. R. Hollenbeck, and S. E. Humphrey, "Asymmetric Adaptability: Dynamic Team Structures as One-Way Streets," *Academy of Management Journal* 47, no. 5 (October 2004), pp. 681–695; A. P. J. Ellis, J. R. Hollenbeck, and D. R. Ilgen, "Team Learning: Collectively Connecting the Dots," *Journal of Applied Psychology* 88, no. 5 (October 2003), pp. 821–835; C. L. Jackson and J. A. LePine, "Peer Responses to a Team's Weakest Link: A Test and Extension of LePine and Van Dyne's Model," *Journal of Applied Psychology* 88, no. 3 (June 2003), pp. 459–475; and J. A. LePine, "Team Adaptation and Postchange Performance: Effects of Team Composition in Terms of Members' Cognitive Ability and Personality," *Journal of Applied Psychology* 88, no. 1 (February 2003), pp. 27–39.

29. S. T. Bell, "Deep-Level Composition Variables as Predictors of Team Performance: A Meta-Analysis," *Journal of Applied Psychology* 92, no. 3 (2007), pp. 595–615; and M. R. Barrick, G. L. Stewart, M. J. Neubert, and M. K. Mount, "Relating Member Ability and Personality to Work-Team Processes and Team Effectiveness," *Journal of Applied Psychology* (June 1998), pp. 377–391.

30. T. A. O'Neill and N. J. Allen, "Personality and the Prediction of Team Performance," *European Journal of Personality* 25, no. 1 (2011), pp. 31–42.

31. Ellis, Hollenbeck, and Ilgen, "Team Learning"; C. O. L. H. Porter, J. R. Hollenbeck, and D. R. Ilgen, "Backing Up Behaviors in Teams: The Role of Personality and Legitimacy of Need," *Journal of Applied Psychology* 88, no. 3 (June 2003), pp. 391–403; J. A. Colquitt, J. R. Hollenbeck, and D. R. Ilgen, "Computer-Assisted Communication and Team Decision-Making Performance: The Moderating Effect of Openness to Experience," *Journal of Applied Psychology* 87, no. 2 (April 2002), pp. 402–410; J. A. LePine, J. R. Hollenbeck, D. R. Ilgen, and J. Hedlund, "The Effects of Individual Differences on the Performance of Hierarchical Decision Making Teams: Much More Than G," *Journal of Applied Psychology* 82 (1997), pp. 803–811; Jackson and LePine, "Peer Responses to a Team's Weakest Link"; and LePine, "Team Adaptation and Postchange Performance."

32. Barrick, Stewart, Neubert, and Mount, "Relating Member Ability and Personality to Work-Team Processes and Team Effectiveness," p. 388; and S. E. Humphrey, J. R. Hollenbeck, C. J. Meyer, and D. R. Ilgen, "Trait Configurations in Self-Managed Teams: A Conceptual Examination of the Use of Seeding for Maximizing and Minimizing Trait Variance in Teams," *Journal of Applied Psychology* 92, no. 3 (2007), pp. 885–892.

33. S. E. Humphrey, F. P. Morgeson, and M. J. Mannor, "Developing a Theory of the Strategic Core of Teams: A Role Composition Model of Team Performance," *Journal of Applied Psychology* 94, no. 1 (2009), pp. 48–61.

34. C. Margerison and D. McCann, *Team Management: Practical New Approaches* (London: Mercury Books, 1990).

35. K. Y. Williams and C. A. O'Reilly III, "Demography and Diversity in Organizations: A Review of 40 Years of Research," in B. M. Staw and L. L. Cummings (eds.), *Research in Organizational Behavior,* vol. 20, (Stamford, CT: Jai Press, 1998) pp. 77–140; and A. Joshi, "The Influence of Organizational Demography on the External Networking Behavior of Teams," *Academy of Management Review* (July 2006), pp. 583–595.

36. W. E. Watson, K. Kumar, and L. K. Michaelsen, "Cultural Diversity's Impact on Interaction Process and Performance: Comparing Homogeneous and Diverse Task Groups," *Academy of Management Journal* (June 1993), pp. 590–602; P. C. Earley and E. Mosakowski, "Creating Hybrid Team Cultures: An Empirical Test of Transnational Team Functioning," *Academy of Management Journal* (February 2000), pp. 26–49; and S. Mohammed and L. C. Angell, "Surface- and Deep-Level Diversity in Workgroups: Examining the Moderating Effects of Team Orientation and Team Process on Relationship Conflict," *Journal of Organizational Behavior* (December 2004), pp. 1015–1039.

37. Watson, Kumar, and Michaelsen, "Cultural Diversity's Impact on Interaction Process and Performance."

38. D. Coutu, "Why Teams Don't Work" *Harvard Business Review* (May 2009), pp. 99–105. The evidence in this section is described in Thompson, *Making the Team*, pp. 65–67. See also L. A. Curral, R. H. Forrester, and J. F. Dawson, "It's What You Do and the Way That You Do It: Team Task, Team Size, and Innovation-Related Group Processes," *European Journal of Work & Organizational Psychology* 10, no. 2 (June 2001), pp. 187–204; R. C. Liden, S. J. Wayne, and R. A. Jaworski, "Social Loafing: A Field Investigation," *Journal of Management* 30, no. 2 (2004), pp. 285–304; and J. A. Wagner, "Studies of Individualism–Collectivism: Effects on Cooperation in Groups," *Academy of Management Journal* 38, no. 1 (February 1995), pp. 152–172.

39. "Is Your Team Too Big? Too Small? What's the Right Number?" *Knowledge@Wharton* (June 14, 2006), pp. 1–5; see also A. M. Carton and J. N. Cummings, "A Theory of Subgroups in Work Teams," *Academy of Management Review* 37, no. 3 (2012), pp. 441–470.

40. Hyatt and Ruddy, "An Examination of the Relationship Between Work Group Characteristics and Performance"; J. D. Shaw, M. K. Duffy, and E. M. Stark, "Interdependence and Preference for Group Work: Main and Congruence Effects on the Satisfaction and Performance of Group Members," *Journal of Management* 26, no. 2 (2000), pp. 259–279; and S. A. Kiffin-Peterson and J. L. Cordery, "Trust, Individualism, and Job Characteristics of Employee Preference for Teamwork," *International Journal of Human Resource Management* (February 2003), pp. 93–116.

41. J. A. LePine, R. F. Piccolo, C. L. Jackson, J. E. Mathieu, and J. R. Saul, "A Meta-Analysis of Teamwork Processes: Tests of a Multidimensional Model and Relationships with Team Effectiveness Criteria," *Personnel Psychology* 61 (2008), pp. 273–307.

42. I. D. Steiner, *Group Processes and Productivity* (New York: Academic Press, 1972).

43. J. A. LePine, R. F. Piccolo, C. L. Jackson, J. E. Mathieu, and J. R. Saul, "A Meta-Analysis of Teamwork Processes: Tests of a Multidimensional Model and Relationships with Team Effectiveness Criteria"; and J. E. Mathieu and T. L. Rapp, "Laying the Foundation for Successful Team Performance Trajectories: The Roles of Team Charters and Performance Strategies," *Journal of Applied Psychology* 94, no. 1 (2009), pp. 90–103.

44. J. E. Mathieu and W. Schulze, "The Influence of Team Knowledge and Formal Plans on Episodic Team Process—Performance Relationships," *Academy of Management Journal* 49, no. 3 (2006), pp. 605–619.

45. A. N. Pieterse, D. van Knippenberg, and W. P. van Ginkel, "Diversity in Goal Orientation, Team Reflexivity, and Team Performance," *Organizational Behavior and Human Decision Processes* 114, no. 2 (2011), pp. 153–164.

46. A. Gurtner, F. Tschan, N. K. Semmer, and C. Nagele, "Getting Groups to Develop Good Strategies: Effects of Reflexivity Interventions on Team Process, Team Performance, and Shared Mental Models," *Organizational Behavior and Human Decision Processes* 102 (2007), pp. 127–142; M. C. Schippers, D. N. Den Hartog, and P. L. Koopman, "Reflexivity in Teams: A Measure and Correlates," *Applied Psychology: An International Review* 56, no. 2 (2007), pp. 189–211; and C. S. Burke, K. C. Stagl, E. Salas, L. Pierce, and D. Kendall, "Understanding Team Adaptation: A Conceptual Analysis and Model," *Journal of Applied Psychology* 91, no. 6 (2006), pp. 1189–1207.

47. A. N. Pieterse, D. van Knippenberg, and W. P. van Ginkel, "Diversity in Goal Orientation, Team Reflexivity, and Team Performance," *Organizational Behavior and Human Decision Processes* 114, no. 2 (2011), pp. 153–164.

48. E. Weldon and L. R. Weingart, "Group Goals and Group Performance," *British Journal of Social Psychology* (Spring 1993), pp. 307–334. See also R. P. DeShon, S. W. J. Kozlowski, A. M. Schmidt, K. R. Milner, and D. Wiechmann, "A Multiple-Goal, Multilevel Model of Feedback Effects on the Regulation of Individual and Team Performance," *Journal of Applied Psychology* (December 2004), pp. 1035–1056.

49. K. Tasa, S. Taggar, and G. H. Seijts, "The Development of Collective Efficacy in Teams: A Multilevel and Longitudinal Perspective," *Journal of Applied Psychology* 92, no. 1 (2007), pp. 17–27; D. I. Jung and J. J. Sosik, "Group Potency and Collective Efficacy: Examining Their Predictive Validity, Level of Analysis, and Effects of Performance Feedback on Future Group Performance," *Group & Organization Management* (September 2003), pp. 366–391; and R. R. Hirschfeld and J. B. Bernerth, "Mental Efficacy and Physical Efficacy at the Team Level: Inputs and Outcomes Among Newly Formed Action Teams," *Journal of Applied Psychology* 93, no. 6 (2008), pp. 1429–1437.

50. A. W. Richter, G. Hirst, D. van Knippenberg, and M. Baer, "Creative Self-Efficacy and Individual Creativity in Team Contexts: Cross-Level Interactions with Team Informational Resources," *Journal of Applied Psychology* 97, no. 6 (2012), pp. 1282–1290.

51. S. Mohammed, L. Ferzandi, and K. Hamilton, "Metaphor No More: A 15-Year Review of the Team Mental Model Construct," *Journal of Management* 36, no. 4 (2010), pp. 876–910.

52. A. P. J. Ellis, "System Breakdown: The Role of Mental Models and Transactive Memory on the Relationships Between Acute Stress and Team Performance," *Academy of Management Journal* 49, no. 3 (2006), pp. 576–589.

53. S. W. J. Kozlowski and D. R. Ilgen, "Enhancing the Effectiveness of Work Groups and Teams," *Psychological Science in the Public Interest* (December 2006), pp. 77–124; and B. D. Edwards, E. A. Day, W. Arthur Jr., and S. T. Bell, "Relationships Among Team Composition, Team Mental Models, and Team Performance," *Journal of Applied Psychology* 91, no. 3 (2006), pp. 727–736.

54. L. A. DeChurch and J. R. Mesmer-Magnus, "The Cognitive Underpinnings of Effective Teamwork: A Meta-Analysis," *Journal of Applied Psychology* 95, no. 1 (2010), pp. 32–53.

55. J. Farh, C. Lee, and C. I. C. Farh, "Task Conflict and Team Creativity: A Question of How Much and When," *Journal of Applied Psychology* 95, no. 6 (2010), pp. 1173–1180.

56. K. J. Behfar, R. S. Peterson, E. A. Mannix, and W. M. K. Trochim, "The Critical Role of Conflict Resolution in Teams: A Close Look at the Links Between Conflict Type, Conflict Management Strategies, and Team Outcomes," *Journal of Applied Psychology* 93, no. 1 (2008), pp. 170–188.

57. K. H. Price, D. A. Harrison, and J. H. Gavin, "Withholding Inputs in Team Contexts: Member Composition, Interaction Processes, Evaluation Structure, and Social Loafing," *Journal of Applied Psychology* 91, no. 6 (2006), pp. 1375–1384.

58. See, for instance, B. L. Kirkman and D. L. Shapiro, "The Impact of Cultural Values on Employee Resistance to Teams: Toward a Model of Globalized Self-Managing Work Team Effectiveness," *Academy of Management Review,* July 1997, pp. 730–757; and B. L. Kirkman, C. B. Gibson, and D. L. Shapiro, "'Exporting' Teams: Enhancing the Implementation and Effectiveness of Work Teams in Global Affiliates," *Organizational Dynamics* 30, no. 1 (2001), pp. 12–29.

59. G. Hertel, U. Konradt, and K. Voss, "Competencies for Virtual Teamwork: Development and Validation of a Web-Based Selection Tool for Members of Distributed Teams," *European Journal of Work and Organizational Psychology* 15, no. 4 (2006), pp. 477–504.

60. T. V. Riper, "The NBA's Most Overpaid Players," *Forbes* (April 5, 2013), downloaded on June 10, 2013, from www.forbes.com.

61. E. Kearney, D. Gebert, and S. C. Voelpel, "When and How Diversity Benefits Teams: The Importance of Team Members' Need for Cognition," *Academy of Management Journal* 52, no. 3 (2009), pp. 581–598.

62. H. M. Guttman, "The New High-Performance Player," *The Hollywood Reporter* (October 27, 2008), www.hollywoodreporter.com.

63. C.-H. Chuang, S. Chen, and C.-W. Chuang, "Human Resource Management Practices and Organizational Social Capital: The Role of Industrial Characteristics," *Journal of Business Research* (May 2013), pp. 678–687; and L. Prusak and D. Cohen, "How to Invest in Social Capital," *Harvard Business Review* (June 2001), pp. 86–93.

64. T. Erickson and L. Gratton, "What It Means to Work Here," *BusinessWeek* (January 10, 2008), www.businessweek .com.

65. M. D. Johnson, J. R. Hollenbeck, S. E. Humphrey, D. R. Ilgen, D. Jundt, and C. J. Meyer, "Cutthroat Cooperation: Asymmetrical Adaptation to Changes in Team Reward Structures," *Academy of Management Journal* 49, no. 1 (2006), pp. 103–119.

66. C. E. Naquin and R. O. Tynan, "The Team Halo Effect: Why Teams Are Not Blamed for Their Failures," *Journal of Applied Psychology,* April 2003, pp. 332–340.

67. E. R. Crawford and J. A. Lepine, "A Configural Theory of Team Processes: Accounting for the Structure of Taskwork and Teamwork," *Academy of Management Review* (January 2013), pp. 32–48; and A. B. Drexler and R. Forrester, "Teamwork—Not Necessarily the Answer," *HR Magazine* (January 1998), pp. 55–58.

CHAPTER 11

1. B. W. Tuckman, "Developmental Sequences in Small Groups," *Psychological Bulletin,* June 1965, pp. 384–399; B. W. Tuckman and M. C. Jensen, "Stages of Small-Group Development Revisited," *Group and Organizational Studies,* December 1977, pp. 419–427; M. F. Maples, "Group Development: Extending Tuckman's Theory," *Journal for Specialists in Group Work* (Fall 1988), pp. 17–23; and K. Vroman and J. Kovacich, "Computer-Mediated Interdisciplinary Teams: Theory and Reality," *Journal of Interprofessional Care* 16, no. 2 (2002), pp. 159–170.

2. J. E. Mathieu and T. L. Rapp, "Laying the Foundation for Successful Team Performance Trajectories: The Roles of Team Charters and Performance Strategies," *Journal of Applied Psychology* 94, no. 1 (2009), pp. 90–103; and E. C. Dierdorff, S. T. Bell, and J. A. Belohlav, "The Power of 'We': Effects of Psychological Collectivism on Team Performance Over Time," *Journal of Applied Psychology* 96, no. 2 (2011), pp. 247–262.

3. M. M. Kazmer, "Disengaging from a Distributed Research Project: Refining a Model of Group Departures," *Journal of the American Society for Information Science and Technology* (April 2010), pp. 758–771.

4. C. J. G. Gersick, "Time and Transition in Work Teams: Toward a New Model of Group Development," *Academy of Management Journal* (March 1988), pp. 9–41; and C. J. G. Gersick, "Marking Time: Predictable Transitions in Task Groups," *Academy of Management Journal* (June 1989), pp. 274–309.

5. Gersick, "Time and Transition in Work Teams"; Gersick, "Marking Time"; M. J. Waller, J. M. Conte, C. B. Gibson, and M. A. Carpenter, "The Effect of Individual Perceptions of Deadlines on Team Performance," *Academy of Management Review* (October 2001), pp. 586–600; and A. Chang, P. Bordia, and J. Duck, "Punctuated Equilibrium and Linear Progression: Toward a New Understanding of Group Development," *Academy of Management Journal* (February 2003), pp. 106–117.

6. Gersick, "Time and Transition in Work Teams"; and Gersick, "Marking Time."

7. M. M. Kazmer, "Disengaging from a Distributed Research Project: Refining a Model of Group Departures," *Journal of the American Society for Information Science and Technology* (April 2010), pp. 758–771.

8. See M. F. Peterson et al., "Role Conflict, Ambiguity, and Overload: A 21-Nation Study," *Academy of Management Journal* (April 1995), pp. 429–452; and I. H. Settles, R. M. Sellers, and A. Damas Jr., "One Role or Two? The Function of Psychological Separation in Role Conflict," *Journal of Applied Psychology* (June 2002), pp. 574–582.

9. For a review of the research on group norms, see J. R. Hackman, "Group Influences on Individuals in Organizations," in M. D. Dunnette and L. M. Hough (eds.), *Handbook of Industrial & Organizational Psychology,* 2nd ed., vol. 3 (Palo Alto, CA: Consulting Psychologists Press, 1992), pp. 235–250. For a more recent discussion, see M. G. Ehrhart and S. E. Naumann, "Organizational Citizenship Behavior in Work Groups: A Group Norms Approach," *Journal of Applied Psychology* (December 2004), pp. 960–974.

10. Adapted from P. S. Goodman, E. Ravlin, and M. Schminke, "Understanding Groups in Organizations," in L. L. Cummings

and B. M. Staw (eds.), *Research in Organizational Behavior,* vol. 9 (Greenwich, CT: JAI Press, 1987), p. 159; and L. Rosh, L. R. Offermann, and R. Van Diest, "Too Close for Comfort? Distinguishing between Team Intimacy and Team Cohesion," *Human Resource Management Review* (June 2012), pp. 116–127.

11. E. Mayo, *The Human Problems of an Industrial Civilization* (New York: Macmillan, 1933); and F. J. Roethlisberger and W. J. Dickson, *Management and the Worker* (Cambridge, MA: Harvard University Press, 1939).

12. C. A. Kiesler and S. B. Kiesler, *Conformity* (Reading, MA: Addison-Wesley, 1969); R. B. Cialdini and N. J. Goldstein, "Social Influence: Compliance and Conformity," *Annual Review of Psychology* 55 (2004), pp. 591–621.

13. S. E. Asch, "Effects of Group Pressure upon the Modification and Distortion of Judgments," in H. Guetzkow (ed.), *Groups, Leadership and Men* (Pittsburgh: Carnegie Press, 1951), pp. 177–190; and S. E. Asch, "Studies of Independence and Conformity: A Minority of One Against a Unanimous Majority," *Psychological Monographs: General and Applied* 70, no. 9 (1956), pp. 1–70.

14. R. Bond and P. B. Smith, "Culture and Conformity: A Meta-Analysis of Studies Using Asch's (1952, 1956) Line Judgment Task," *Psychological Bulletin* (January 1996), pp. 111–137.

15. See S. L. Robinson and A. M. O'Leary-Kelly, "Monkey See, Monkey Do: The Influence of Work Groups on the Antisocial Behavior of Employees," *Academy of Management Journal* (December 1998), pp. 658–672; R. J. Bennett and S. L. Robinson, "The Past, Present, and Future of Workplace Deviance," in J. Greenberg (ed.), *Organizational Behavior: The State of the Science,* 2nd ed. (Mahwah, NJ: Erlbaum, 2003), pp. 237–271; and C. M. Berry, D. S. Ones, and P. R. Sackett, "Interpersonal Deviance, Organizational Deviance, and Their Common Correlates: A Review and Meta-Analysis," *Journal of Applied Psychology* 92, no. 2 (2007), pp. 410–424.

16. C. M. Pearson, L. M. Andersson, and C. L. Porath, "Assessing and Attacking Workplace Civility," *Organizational Dynamics* 29, no. 2 (2000), p. 130; see also C. Pearson, L. M. Andersson, and C. L. Porath, "Workplace Incivility," in S. Fox and P. E. Spector (eds.), *Counterproductive Work Behavior: Investigations of Actors and Targets* (Washington, DC: American Psychological Association, 2005), pp. 177–200.

17. S. Lim, L. M. Cortina, V. J. Magley, "Personal and Workgroup Incivility: Impact on Work and Health Outcomes," *Journal of Applied Psychology* 93, no. 1 (2008), pp. 95–107.

18. M. S. Christian and A. P. J. Ellis, "Examining the Effects of Sleep Deprivation on Workplace Deviance: A Self-Regulatory Perspective," *Academy of Management Journal* 54, no. 5 (2011), pp. 913–934.

19. Robinson and O'Leary-Kelly, "Monkey See, Monkey Do"; and T. M. Glomb and H. Liao, "Interpersonal Aggression in Workgroups: Social Influence, Reciprocal, and Individual Effects," *Academy of Management Journal* 46 (2003), pp. 486–496.

20. P. Bamberger and M. Biron, "Group Norms and Excessive Absenteeism: The Role of Peer Referent Others," *Organizational Behavior and Human Decision Processes* 103, no. 2 (2007), pp. 179–196; and A. Väänänen, N. Tordera, M. Kivimäki, A. Kouvonen, J. Pentti, A. Linna, and J. Vahtera, "The Role of Work Group in Individual Sickness Absence Behavior," *Journal of Health & Human Behavior* 49, no. 4 (2008), pp. 452–467.

21. M. S. Cole, F. Walter, and H. Bruch, "Affective Mechanisms Linking Dysfunctional Behavior to Performance in Work Teams: A Moderated Mediation Study," *Journal of Applied Psychology* 93, no. 5 (2008), pp. 945–958.

22. See J. Berger, M. H. Fisek, R. Z. Norman, and M. Zelditch, *Status Characteristics and Social Interaction: An Expected States Approach* (New York: Elsevier, 1977).

23. Cited in Hackman, "Group Influences on Individuals in Organizations," p. 236.

24. R. R. Callister and J. A. Wall Jr., "Conflict Across Organizational Boundaries: Managed Care Organizations Versus Health Care Providers," *Journal of Applied Psychology* 86, no. 4 (2001), pp. 754–763; and P. Chattopadhyay, W. H. Glick, and G. P. Huber, "Organizational Actions in Response to Threats and Opportunities," *Academy of Management Journal* 44, no. 5 (2001), pp. 937–955.

25. P. F. Hewlin, "Wearing the Cloak: Antecedents and Consequences of Creating Facades of Conformity," *Journal of Applied Psychology* 94, no. 3 (2009), pp. 727–741.

26. B. Groysberg, J. T. Polzer, and H. A. Elfenbein, "Too Many Cooks Spoil the Broth: How High-Status Individuals Decrease Group Effectiveness," *Organization Science* (May–June 2011), pp. 722–737.

27. See J. M. Levine and R. L. Moreland, "Progress in Small Group Research," in J. T. Spence, J. M. Darley, and D. J. Foss (eds.), *Annual Review of Psychology,* vol. 41 (Palo Alto, CA: Annual Reviews, 1990), pp. 585–634; S. D. Silver, B. P. Cohen, and J. H. Crutchfield, "Status Differentiation and Information Exchange in Face-to-Face and Computer-Mediated Idea Generation," *Social Psychology Quarterly* (1994), pp. 108–123; and J. M. Twenge, "Changes in Women's Assertiveness in Response to Status and Roles: A Cross-Temporal Meta-Analysis, 1931–1993," *Journal of Personality and Social Psychology* (July 2001), pp. 133–145.

28. A. M. Christie and J. Barling, "Beyond Status: Relating Status Inequality to Performance and Health in Teams," *Journal of Applied Psychology* 95, no. 5 (2010), pp. 920–934; and L. H. Nishii and D. M. Mayer, "Do Inclusive Leaders Help to Reduce Turnover in Diverse Groups? The Moderating Role of Leader-Member Exchange in the Diversity to Turnover Relationship," *Journal of Applied Psychology* 94, no. 6 (2009), pp. 1412–1426.

29. See, for instance, D. R. Comer, "A Model of Social Loafing in Real Work Groups," *Human Relations* (June 1995), pp. 647–667; S. M. Murphy, S. J. Wayne, R. C. Liden, and B. Erdogan, "Understanding Social Loafing: The Role of Justice Perceptions and Exchange Relationships," *Human Relations* (January 2003), pp. 61–84; and R. C. Liden, S. J. Wayne, R. A. Jaworski, and N. Bennett, "Social Loafing: A Field Investigation," *Journal of Management* (April 2004), pp. 285–304.

30. W. Moede, "Die Richtlinien der Leistungs-Psychologie," *Industrielle Psychotechnik* 4 (1927), pp. 193–207. See also D. A. Kravitz and B. Martin, "Ringelmann Rediscovered: The Original Article," *Journal of Personality and Social Psychology* (May 1986), pp. 936–941.

31. See, for example, J. A. Shepperd, "Productivity Loss in Performance Groups: A Motivation Analysis," *Psychological Bulletin* (January 1993), pp. 67–81; and S. J. Karau and K. D. Williams, "Social Loafing: A Meta-Analytic Review and Theoretical Integration," *Journal of Personality and Social Psychology* (October 1993), pp. 681–706.

32. A. W. Delton, L. Cosmides, M. Guemo, T. E. Robertson, and J. Tooby, "The Psychosemantics of Free Riding: Dissecting the Architecture of a Moral Concept," *Journal of Personality and Social Psychology* 102, no. 6 (2012), pp. 1252–1270.

33. S. G. Harkins and K. Szymanski, "Social Loafing and Group Evaluation," *Journal of Personality and Social Psychology* (December 1989), pp. 934–941.

34. D. L. Smrt and S. J. Karau, "Protestant Work Ethic Moderates Social Loafing," *Group Dynamics-Theory Research and Practice* (September 2011), pp. 267–274.

35. A. Gunnthorsdottir and A. Rapoport, "Embedding Social Dilemmas in Intergroup Competition Reduces Free-Riding," *Organizational Behavior and Human Decision Processes* 101 (2006), pp. 184–199; and E. M. Stark, J. D. Shaw, and M. K. Duffy, "Preference for Group Work, Winning Orientation, and Social Loafing Behavior in Groups," *Group and Organization Management* 32, no. 6 (2007), pp. 699–723.

36. Ibid.

37. Based on J. L. Gibson, J. M. Ivancevich, and J. H. Donnelly Jr., *Organizations,* 8th ed. (Burr Ridge, IL: Irwin, 1994), p. 323; and L. L. Greer, "Group Cohesion: Then and Now," *Small Group Research* (December 2012), pp. 655–661.

38. D. S. Staples and L. Zhao, "The Effects of Cultural Diversity in Virtual Teams versus Face-to-Face Teams," *Group Decision and Negotiation* (July 2006), pp. 389–406.

39. N. Chi, Y. Huang, and S. Lin, "A Double-Edged Sword? Exploring the Curvilinear Relationship Between Organizational Tenure Diversity and Team Innovation: The Moderating Role of Team-Oriented HR Practices," *Group and Organization Management* 34, no. 6 (2009), pp. 698–726.

40. K. J. Klein, A. P. Knight, J. C. Ziegert, B. C. Lim, and J. L. Saltz, "When Team Members' Values Differ: The Moderating Role of Team Leadership," *Organizational Behavior and Human Decision Processes* 114, no. 1 (2011), pp. 25–36; and G. Park and R. P. DeShon, "A Multilevel Model of Minority Opinion Expression and Team Decision-Making Effectiveness," *Journal of Applied Psychology* 95, no. 5 (2010), pp. 824–833.

41. M. Rigoglioso, "Diverse Backgrounds and Personalities Can Strengthen Groups," *Stanford Knowledgebase*, (August 15, 2006), www.stanford.edu/group/knowledgebase/.

42. K. W. Phillips and D. L. Loyd, "When Surface and Deep-Level Diversity Collide: The Effects on Dissenting Group Members," *Organizational Behavior and Human Decision Processes* 99 (2006), pp. 143–160; and S. R. Sommers, "On Racial Diversity and Group Decision Making: Identifying Multiple Effects of Racial Composition on Jury Deliberations," *Journal of Personality and Social Psychology* (April 2006), pp. 597–612.

43. E. Mannix and M. A. Neale, "What Differences Make a Difference? The Promise and Reality of Diverse Teams in Organizations," *Psychological Science in the Public Interest* (October 2005), pp. 31–55.

44. See M. B. Thatcher and P. C. Patel, "Group Faultlines: A Review, Integration, and Guide to Future Research," *Journal of Management* 38, no. 4 (2012), pp. 969–1009.

45. K. Bezrukova, S. M. B. Thatcher, K. A. Jehn, and C. S. Spell, "The Effects of Alignments: Examining Group Faultlines, Organizational Cultures, and Performance," *Journal of Applied Psychology* 97, no. 1 (2012), pp. 77–92.

46. R. Rico, M. Sanchez-Manzanares, M. Antino, and D. Lau, "Bridging Team Faultlines by Combining Task Role Assignment and Goal Structure Strategies," *Journal of Applied Psychology* 97, no. 2 (2012), pp. 407–420.

47. See N. R. F. Maier, "Assets and Liabilities in Group Problem Solving: The Need for an Integrative Function," *Psychological Review* (April 1967), pp. 239–249; G. W. Hill, "Group versus Individual Performance: Are $N + 1$ Heads Better Than One?" *Psychological Bulletin* (May 1982), pp. 517–539;

M. D. Johnson and J. R. Hollenbeck, "Collective Wisdom as an Oxymoron: Team-Based Structures as Impediments to Learning," in J. Langan-Fox, C. L. Cooper, and R. J. Klimoski (eds), *Research Companion to the Dysfunctional Workplace: Management Challenges and Symptoms* (Northampton, MA: Edward Elgar Publishing, 2007), pp. 319–331; and R. F. Martell and M. R. Borg, "A Comparison of the Behavioral Rating Accuracy of Groups and Individuals," *Journal of Applied Psychology* (February 1993), pp. 43–50.

48. D. Gigone and R. Hastie, "Proper Analysis of the Accuracy of Group Judgments," *Psychological Bulletin* (January 1997), pp. 149–167; and B. L. Bonner, S. D. Sillito, and M. R. Baumann, "Collective Estimation: Accuracy, Expertise, and Extroversion as Sources of Intra-Group Influence," *Organizational Behavior and Human Decision Processes* 103 (2007), pp. 121–133.

49. See, for example, W. C. Swap and Associates, *Group Decision Making* (Newbury Park, CA: Sage, 1984).

50. I. L. Janis, *Groupthink* (Boston: Houghton Mifflin, 1982); W.-W. Park, "A Review of Research on Groupthink," *Journal of Behavioral Decision Making* (July 1990), pp. 229–245; J. N. Choi and M. U. Kim, "The Organizational Application of Groupthink and Its Limits in Organizations," *Journal of Applied Psychology* (April 1999), pp. 297–306; and W.-W. Park, "A Comprehensive Empirical Investigation of the Relationships Among Variables of the Groupthink Model," *Journal of Organizational Behavior* (December 2000), pp. 873–887.

51. Janis, *Groupthink*.

52. G. Park and R. P. DeShon, "A Multilevel Model of Minority Opinion Expression and Team Decision-Making Effectiveness," *Journal of Applied Psychology* 95, no. 5 (2010), pp. 824–833.

53. R. Benabou, "Groupthink: Collective Delusions in Organizations and Markets," *Review of Economic Studies* (April 2013), pp.429–462; and M. E. Turner and A. R. Pratkanis, "Mitigating Groupthink by Stimulating Constructive Conflict," in C. K. W. De Dreu and E. Van de Vliert (eds.), *Using Conflict in Organizations* (London: Sage, 1997), pp. 53–71.

54. J. A. Goncalo, E. Polman, and C. Maslach, "Can Confidence Come Too Soon? Collective Efficacy, Conflict, and Group Performance Over Time," *Organizational Behavior and Human Decision Processes* 113, no. 1 (2010), pp. 13–24.

55. See N. R. F. Maier, *Principles of Human Relations* (New York: Wiley, 1952); I. L. Janis, *Groupthink: Psychological Studies of Policy Decisions and Fiascoes,* 2nd ed. (Boston: Houghton Mifflin, 1982); N. Richardson Ahlfinger and J. K. Esser, "Testing the Groupthink Model: Effects of Promotional Leadership and Conformity Predisposition," *Social Behavior & Personality* 29, no. 1 (2001), pp. 31–41; and S. Schultz-Hardt, F. C. Brodbeck, A. Mojzisch, R. Kerschreiter, and D. Frey, "Group Decision Making in Hidden Profile Situations: Dissent as a Facilitator for Decision Quality," *Journal of Personality and Social Psychology* 91, no. 6 (2006), pp. 1080–1093.

56. See P. W. Paese, M. Bieser, and M. E. Tubbs, "Framing Effects and Choice Shifts in Group Decision Making," *Organizational Behavior and Human Decision Processes* (October 1993), pp. 149–165; and I. Yaniv, "Group Diversity and Decision Quality: Amplification and Attenuation of the Framing Effect," *International Journal of Forecasting* (January–March 2011), pp. 41–49.

57. R. D. Clark III, "Group-Induced Shift toward Risk: A Critical Appraisal," *Psychological Bulletin* (October 1971), pp. 251–270; M. Brauer and C. M. Judd, "Group Polarization and Repeated Attitude Expression: A New Take on an Old Topic," *European Review of Social Psychology* 7, (1996), pp. 173–207; and

M. P. Brady and S. Y. Wu, "The Aggregation of Preferences in Groups: Identity, Responsibility, and Polarization," *Journal of Economic Psychology* 31, no. 6 (2010), pp. 950–963.

58. Z. Krizan and R. S. Baron, "Group Polarization and Choice-Dilemmas: How Important Is Self-Categorization?" *European Journal of Social Psychology* 37, no. 1 (2007), pp. 191–201.

59. A. F. Osborn, *Applied Imagination: Principles and Procedures of Creative Thinking,* 3rd ed. (New York: Scribner, 1963). See also R. P. McGlynn, D. McGurk, V. S. Effland, N. L. Johll, and D. J. Harding, "Brainstorming and Task Performance in Groups Constrained by Evidence," *Organizational Behavior and Human Decision Processes* (January 2004), pp. 75–87; and R. C. Litchfield, "Brainstorming Reconsidered: A Goal-Based View," *Academy of Management Review* 33, no. 3 (2008), pp. 649–668.

60. N. L. Kerr and R. S. Tindale, "Group Performance and Decision-Making," *Annual Review of Psychology* 55 (2004), pp. 623–655.

61. See A. L. Delbecq, A. H. Van deVen, and D. H. Gustafson, *Group Techniques for Program Planning: A Guide to Nominal and Delphi Processes* (Glenview, IL: Scott Foresman, 1975); and P. B. Paulus and H.-C. Yang, "Idea Generation in Groups: A Basis for Creativity in Organizations," *Organizational Behavior and Human Decision Processing* (May 2000), pp. 76–87.

62. C. Faure, "Beyond Brainstorming: Effects of Different Group Procedures on Selection of Ideas and Satisfaction with the Process," *Journal of Creative Behavior* 38 (2004), pp. 13–34.

63. A. G. Bedeian and A. A. Armenakis, "A Path-Analytic Study of the Consequences of Role Conflict and Ambiguity," *Academy of Management Journal* (June 1981), pp. 417–424; and P. L. Perrewe, K. L. Zellars, G. R. Ferris, A. M. Rossi, C. J. Kacmar, and D. A. Ralston, "Neutralizing Job Stressors: Political Skill as an Antidote to the Dysfunctional Consequences of Role Conflict," *Academy of Management Journal* (February 2004), pp. 141–152.

64. M. E. Shaw, *Group Dynamics: The Psychology of Small Group Behavior,* 3rd ed. (New York: McGraw-Hill, 1981).

CHAPTER 12

1. See T. A. Judge, J. E. Bono, R. Ilies, and M. W. Gerhardt, "Personality and Leadership: A Qualitative and Quantitative Review," *Journal of Applied Psychology* (August 2002), pp. 765–780.

2. D. R. Ames and F. J. Flynn, "What Breaks a Leader: The Curvilinear Relation Between Assertiveness and Leadership," *Journal of Personality and Social Psychology* 92, no. 2 (2007), pp. 307–324.

3. N. Ensari, R. E. Riggio, J. Christian, and G. Carslaw, "Who Emerges as a Leader? Meta-Analyses of Individual Differences as Predictors of Leadership Emergence," *Personality and Individual Differences* (September 2011), pp. 532–536.

4. R. M. Stogdill and A. E. Coons (eds.), *Leader Behavior: Its Description and Measurement,* Research Monograph no. 88 (Columbus: Ohio State University, Bureau of Business Research, 1951). This research is updated in C. A. Schriesheim, C. C. Cogliser, and L. L. Neider, "Is It 'Trustworthy'? A Multiple-Levels-of-Analysis Reexamination of an Ohio State Leadership Study, with Implications for Future Research," *Leadership Quarterly* (Summer 1995), pp. 111–145; and T. A. Judge, R. F. Piccolo, and R. Ilies, "The Forgotten Ones? The Validity of Consideration and Initiating Structure in Leadership Research," *Journal of Applied Psychology* (February 2004), pp. 36–51.

5. D. Akst, "The Rewards of Recognizing a Job Well Done," *The Wall Street Journal* (January 31, 2007), p. D9.

6. Judge, Piccolo, and Ilies, "The Forgotten Ones?"

7. M. Javidan, P. W. Dorfman, M. S. de Luque, and R. J. House, "In the Eye of the Beholder: Cross Cultural Lessons in Leadership from Project GLOBE," *Academy of Management Perspectives* (February 2006), pp. 67–90.

8. F. E. Fiedler, *A Theory of Leadership Effectiveness* (New York: McGraw-Hill, 1967).

9. S. Shiflett, "Is There a Problem with the LPC Score in LEADER MATCH?" *Personnel Psychology* (Winter 1981), pp. 765–769.

10. F. E. Fiedler, M. M. Chemers, and L. Mahar, *Improving Leadership Effectiveness: The Leader Match Concept* (New York: Wiley, 1977).

11. Cited in R. J. House and R. N. Aditya, "The Social Scientific Study of Leadership," *Journal of Management* 23, no. 3 (1997), p. 422.

12. L. H. Peters, D. D. Hartke, and J. T. Pohlmann, "Fiedler's Contingency Theory of Leadership: An Application of the Meta-Analysis Procedures of Schmidt and Hunter," *Psychological Bulletin* (March 1985), pp. 274–285; C. A. Schriesheim, B. J. Tepper, and L. A. Tetrault, "Least Preferred Coworker Score, Situational Control, and Leadership Effectiveness: A Meta-Analysis of Contingency Model Performance Predictions," *Journal of Applied Psychology* (August 1994), pp. 561–573; and R. Ayman, M. M. Chemers, and F. Fiedler, "The Contingency Model of Leadership Effectiveness: Its Levels of Analysis," *Leadership Quarterly* (Summer 1995), pp. 147–167.

13. House and Aditya, "The Social Scientific Study of Leadership."

14. See, for instance, R. W. Rice, "Psychometric Properties of the Esteem for the Least Preferred Coworker (LPC) Scale," *Academy of Management Review* (January 1978), pp. 106–118; C. A. Schriesheim, B. D. Bannister, and W. H. Money, "Psychometric Properties of the LPC Scale: An Extension of Rice's Review," *Academy of Management Review* (April 1979), pp. 287–290; and J. K. Kennedy, J. M. Houston, M. A. Korgaard, and D. D. Gallo, "Construct Space of the Least Preferred Coworker (LPC) Scale," *Educational & Psychological Measurement* (Fall 1987), pp. 807–814.

15. See E. H. Schein, *Organizational Psychology,* 3rd ed. (Upper Saddle River, NJ: Prentice Hall, 1980), pp. 116–117; and B. Kabanoff, "A Critique of Leader Match and Its Implications for Leadership Research," *Personnel Psychology* (Winter 1981), pp. 749–764.

16. See, for instance, Ibid., pp. 67–84; C. L. Graeff, "Evolution of Situational Leadership Theory: A Critical Review," *Leadership Quarterly* 8, no. 2 (1997), pp. 153–170; and R. P. Vecchio and K. J. Boatwright, "Preferences for Idealized Styles of Supervision," *Leadership Quarterly* (August 2002), pp. 327–342.

17. R. J. House, "A Path-Goal Theory of Leader Effectiveness," *Administrative Science Quarterly* (September 1971), pp. 321–338; R. J. House and T. R. Mitchell, "Path-Goal Theory of Leadership," *Journal of Contemporary Business* (Autumn 1974), pp. 81–97; and R. J. House, "Path-Goal Theory of Leadership: Lessons, Legacy, and a Reformulated Theory," *Leadership Quarterly* (Fall 1996), pp. 323–352.

18. M. Weber, *The Theory of Social and Economic Organization,* A. M. Henderson and T. Parsons (trans.) (New York: The Free Press, 1947).

19. J. A. Conger and R. N. Kanungo, "Behavioral Dimensions of Charismatic Leadership," in J. A. Conger, R. N. Kanungo, and

Associates (eds.), *Charismatic Leadership* (San Francisco: Jossey-Bass, 1988), p. 79; and A.-K. Samnani and P. Singh, "When Leaders Victimize: The Role of Charismatic Leaders in Facilitating Group Pressures," *Leadership Quarterly* (pp. 189–202).

20. J. A. Conger and R. N. Kanungo, *Charismatic Leadership in Organizations* (Thousand Oaks, CA: Sage, 1998); and R. Awamleh and W. L. Gardner, "Perceptions of Leader Charisma and Effectiveness: The Effects of Vision Content, Delivery, and Organizational Performance," *Leadership Quarterly* (Fall 1999), pp. 345–373.

21. R. J. House and J. M. Howell, "Personality and Charismatic Leadership," *Leadership Quarterly* 3 (1992), pp. 81–108; D. N. Den Hartog and P. L. Koopman, "Leadership in Organizations," in N. Anderson and D. S. Ones (eds.), *Handbook of Industrial, Work and Organizational Psychology*, vol. 2 (Thousand Oaks, CA: Sage, 2002), pp. 166–187.

22. P. Balkundi, M. Kilduff, and D. A. Harrison, "Centrality and Charisma: Comparing How Leader Networks and Attributions Affect Team Performance," *Journal of Applied Psychology* 96 (2012), pp. 1209–1222.

23. A. Erez, V. F. Misangyi, D. E. Johnson, M. A. LePine, and K. C. Halverson, "Stirring the Hearts of Followers: Charismatic Leadership as the Transferal of Affect," *Journal of Applied Psychology* 93, no. 3 (2008), pp. 602–615. For reviews on the role of vision in leadership, see S. J. Zaccaro, "Visionary and Inspirational Models of Executive Leadership: Empirical Review and Evaluation," in S. J. Zaccaro (ed.), *The Nature of Executive Leadership: A Conceptual and Empirical Analysis of Success* (Washington, DC: American Psychological Association, 2001), pp. 259–278; and M. Hauser and R. J. House, "Lead Through Vision and Values," in E. A. Locke (ed.), *Handbook of Principles of Organizational Behavior* (Malden, MA: Blackwell, 2004), pp. 257–273.

24. D. N. Den Hartog, A. H. B. De Hoogh, and A. E. Keegan, "The Interactive Effects of Belongingness and Charisma on Helping and Compliance," *Journal of Applied Psychology* 92, no. 4 (2007), pp. 1131–1139.

25. J. C. Pastor, M. Mayo, and B. Shamir, "Adding Fuel to Fire: The Impact of Followers' Arousal on Ratings of Charisma," *Journal of Applied Psychology* 92, no. 6 (2007), pp. 1584–1596.

26. A. H. B. De Hoogh and D. N. Den Hartog, "Neuroticism and Locus of Control as Moderators of the Relationships of Charismatic and Autocratic Leadership with Burnout," *Journal of Applied Psychology* 94, no. 4 (2009), pp. 1058–1067.

27. F. Cohen, S. Solomon, M. Maxfield, T. Pyszczynski, and J. Greenberg, "Fatal Attraction: The Effects of Mortality Salience on Evaluations of Charismatic, Task-Oriented, and Relationship-Oriented Leaders," *Psychological Sciences* (December 2004), pp. 846–851; and M. G. Ehrhart and K. J. Klein, "Predicting Followers' Preferences for Charismatic Leadership: The Influence of Follower Values and Personality," *Leadership Quarterly* (Summer 2001), pp. 153–179.

28. See, for instance, R. Khurana, *Searching for a Corporate Savior: The Irrational Quest for Charismatic CEOs* (Princeton, NJ: Princeton University Press, 2002); and J. A. Raelin, "The Myth of Charismatic Leaders," *Training & Development* (March 2003), pp. 47–54.

29. B. M. Galvin, D. A. Waldman, and P. Balthazard, "Visionary Communication Qualities as Mediators of the Relationship between Narcissism and Attributions of Leader Charisma," *Personnel Psychology* 63, no. 3 (2010), pp. 509–537.

30. See, for instance, B. M. Bass, B. J. Avolio, D. I. Jung, and Y. Berson, "Predicting Unit Performance by Assessing Transformational and Transactional Leadership," *Journal of Applied Psychology* (April 2003), pp. 207–218; and T. A. Judge and R. F. Piccolo, "Transformational and Transactional Leadership: A Meta-Analytic Test of Their Relative Validity," *Journal of Applied Psychology* (October 2004), pp. 755–768.

31. A. M. Grant, "Leading with Meaning: Beneficiary Contact, Prosocial Impact, and the Performance Effects of Transformational Leadership," *Academy of Management Journal* 55 (2012), pp. 458–476.

32. B. M. Bass, "Leadership: Good, Better, Best," *Organizational Dynamics* (Winter 1985), pp. 26–40; and J. Seltzer and B. M. Bass, "Transformational Leadership: Beyond Initiation and Consideration," *Journal of Management* (December 1990), pp. 693–703.

33. T. R. Hinkin and C. A. Schriesheim, "An Examination of 'Nonleadership': From Laissez-Faire Leadership to Leader Reward Omission and Punishment Omission," *Journal of Applied Psychology* 93, no. 6 (2008), pp. 1234–1248.

34. A. E. Colbert, A. E. Kristof-Brown, B. H. Bradley, and M. R. Barrick, "CEO Transformational Leadership: The Role of Goal Importance Congruence in Top Management Teams," *Academy of Management Journal* 51, no. 1 (2008), pp. 81–96.

35. Y. Ling, Z. Simsek, M. H. Lubatkin, and J. F. Veiga, "The Impact of Transformational CEOs on the Performance of Small- to Medium-Sized Firms: Does Organizational Context Matter?" *Journal of Applied Psychology* 93, no. 4 (2008), pp. 923–934.

36. X. Wang and J. M. Howell, "Exploring the Dual-Level Effects of Transformational Leadership on Followers," *Journal of Applied Psychology* 95, no. 6 (2010), pp. 1134–1144.

37. J. R. Baum, E. A. Locke, and S. A. Kirkpatrick, "A Longitudinal Study of the Relation of Vision and Vision Communication to Venture Growth in Entrepreneurial Firms," *Journal of Applied Psychology* (February 2000), pp. 43–54.

38. R. J. House, M. Javidan, P. Hanges, and P. Dorfman, "Understanding Cultures and Implicit Leadership Theories Across the Globe: An Introduction to Project GLOBE," *Journal of World Business* (Spring 2002), pp. 3–10.

39. D. E. Carl and M. Javidan, "Universality of Charismatic Leadership: A Multi-Nation Study," paper presented at the National Academy of Management Conference, Washington, DC (August 2001), p. 29.

40. J. Schaubroeck, S. S. K. Lam, and S. E. Cha, "Embracing Transformational Leadership: Team Values and the Impact of Leader Behavior on Team Performance," *Journal of Applied Psychology* 92, no. 4 (2007), pp. 1020–1030.

41. B. L. Kirkman, G. Chen, J. Farh, Z. X. Chen, and K. B. Lowe, "Individual Power Distance Orientation and Follower Reactions to Transformational Leaders: A Cross-Level, Cross-Cultural Examination," *Academy of Management Journal* 52, no. 4 (2009), pp. 744–764.

42. S. J. Shin and J. Zhou, "Transformational Leadership, Conservation, and Creativity: Evidence from Korea," *Academy of Management Journal* (December 2003), pp. 703–714; V. J. García-Morales, F. J. Lloréns-Montes, and A. J. Verdú-Jover, "The Effects of Transformational Leadership on Organizational Performance Through Knowledge and Innovation," *British Journal of Management* 19, no. 4 (2008), pp. 299–313; and S. A. Eisenbeiss, D. van Knippenberg, and S. Boerner, "Transformational Leadership and Team Innovation: Integrating Team Climate Principles," *Journal of Applied Psychology* 93, no. 6 (2008), pp. 1438–1446.

43. F. O. Walumbwa, B. J. Avolio, and W. Zhu, "How Transformational Leadership Weaves Its Influence on Individual Job Performance: The Role of Identification and Efficacy Beliefs," *Personnel Psychology* 61, no. 4 (2008), pp. 793–825.

44. J. E. Bono and T. A. Judge, "Self-Concordance at Work: Toward Understanding the Motivational Effects of Transformational Leaders," *Academy of Management Journal* (October 2003), pp. 554–571; Y. Berson and B. J. Avolio, "Transformational Leadership and the Dissemination of Organizational Goals: A Case Study of a Telecommunication Firm," *Leadership Quarterly* (October 2004), pp. 625–646; and Schauebroeck, Lam, and Cha, "Embracing Transformational Leadership: Team Values and the Impact of Leader Behavior on Team Performance."

45. H. Hetland, G. M. Sandal, and T. B. Johnsen, "Burnout in the Information Technology Sector: Does Leadership Matter?" *European Journal of Work and Organizational Psychology* 16, no. 1 (2007), pp. 58–75; and K. B. Lowe, K. G. Kroeck, and N. Sivasubramaniam, "Effectiveness Correlates of Transformational and Transactional Leadership: A Meta-Analytic Review of the MLQ Literature," *Leadership Quarterly* (Fall 1996), pp. 385–425.

46. See B. J. Avolio, W. L. Gardner, F. O. Walumbwa, F. Luthans, and D. R. May, "Unlocking the Mask: A Look at the Process by Which Authentic Leaders Impact Follower Attitudes and Behaviors," *Leadership Quarterly* (December 2004), pp. 801–823; W. L. Gardner and J. R. Schermerhorn Jr., "Performance Gains Through Positive Organizational Behavior and Authentic Leadership," *Organizational Dynamics* (August 2004), pp. 270–281; and M. M. Novicevic, M. G. Harvey, M. R. Buckley, J. A. Brown-Radford, and R. Evans, "Authentic Leadership: A Historical Perspective," *Journal of Leadership and Organizational Behavior* 13, no. 1 (2006), pp. 64–76.

47. K. M. Hmieleski, M. S. Cole, and R. A. Baron, "Shared Authentic Leadership and New Venture Performance," *Journal of Management* (September 2012), pp. 1476–1499.

48. R. Ilies, F. P. Morgeson, and J. D. Nahrgang, "Authentic Leadership and Eudaemonic Well-Being: Understanding Leader-follower Outcomes," *Leadership Quarterly* 16 (2005), pp. 373–394; B. Levin, "Raj Rajaratnam Did Not Appreciate Rajat Gupta's Attempt to Leave The Goldman Board, Join 'The Billionaire circle,'" *NetNet with John Carney* (March 14, 2011), downloaded July 26, 2011, from www.cnbc.com/.

49. J. Stouten, M. van Dijke, and D. De Cremer, "Ethical Leadership: An Overview and Future Perspectives," *Journal of Personnel Psychology* 11 (2012), pp. 1–6.

50. J. M. Schaubroeck, S. T. Hannah, B. J. Avolio, S. W. J. Kozlowski, et al., "Embedding Ethical Leadership within and Across Organization Levels," *Academy of Management Journal* 55 (2012), pp. 1053–1078.

51. D. van Knippenberg, D. De Cremer, and B. van Knippenberg, "Leadership and Fairness: The State of the Art," *European Journal of Work and Organizational Psychology* 16, no. 2 (2007), pp. 113–140.

52. B. P. Owens and D. R. Hekman, "Modeling How to Grow: An Inductive Examination of Humble Leader Behaviors, Contingencies, and Outcomes," *Academy of Management Journal* 55 (2012), pp. 787–818.

53. K. M. Kacmar, D. G. Bachrach, K. J. Harris, and S. Zivnuska, "Fostering Good Citizenship Through Ethical Leadership: Exploring the Moderating Role of Gender and Organizational Politics," *Journal of Applied Psychology,* 96, no. 3 (May 2011), pp. 633–642; and F. O. Walumbwa and J. Schaubroeck, "Leader Personality Traits and Employee Voice Behavior: Mediating Roles of Ethical Leadership and Work Group Psychological Safety," *Journal of Applied Psychology* 94, no. 5 (2009), pp. 1275–1286.

54. D. M. Mayer, K. Aquino, R. L. Greenbaum, and M. Kuenzi, "Who Displays Ethical Leadership, and Why Does It Matter? An Examination of Antecedents and Consequences of Ethical Leadership," *Academy of Management Journal* 55 (2012), pp. 151–171.

55. M. E. Brown and L. K. Treviño, "Socialized Charismatic Leadership, Values Congruence, and Deviance in Work Groups," *Journal of Applied Psychology* 91, no. 4 (2006), pp. 954–962.

56. M. E. Brown and L. K. Treviño, "Leader-Follower Values Congruence: Are Socialized Charismatic Leaders Better Able to Achieve It?" *Journal of Applied Psychology* 94, no. 2 (2009), pp. 478–490.

57. S. A. Eisenbeiss and S. R. Giessner, "The Emergence and Maintenance of Ethical Leadership in Organizations," *Journal of Personnel Psychology* 11 (2012), pp. 7–19.

58. D. van Dierendonck, "Servant Leadership: A Review and Synthesis," *Journal of Management* 37, no. 4 (2011), pp. 1228–1261.

59. S. J. Peterson, F. M. Galvin, and D. Lange, "CEO Servant Leadership: Exploring Executive Characteristics and Firm Performance," *Personnel Psychology* 65 (2012), pp. 565–596.

60. F. Walumbwa, C. A. Hartnell, and A. Oke, "Servant Leadership, Procedural Justice Climate, Service Climate, Employee Attitudes, and Organizational Citizenship Behavior: A Cross-Level Investigation," *Journal of Applied Psychology* 95, no. 3 (2010), pp. 517–529.

61. D. De Cremer, D. M. Mayer, M. van Dijke, B. C. Schouten, and M. Bardes, "When Does Self-Sacrificial Leadership Motivate Prosocial Behavior? It Depends on Followers' Prevention Focus," *Journal of Applied Psychology* 2009, no. 4 (2009), pp. 887–899.

62. J. Hu and R. C. Liden, "Antecedents of Team Potency and Team Effectiveness: An Examination of Goal and Process Clarity and Servant Leadership," *Journal of Applied Psychology*, 96, no. 4 (July 2011), pp. 851–862.

63. M. J. Neubert, K. M. Kacmar, D. S. Carlson, L. B. Chonko, and J. A. Roberts, "Regulatory Focus as a Mediator of the Influence of Initiating Structure and Servant Leadership on Employee Behavior," *Journal of Applied Psychology* 93, no. 6 (2008), pp. 1220–1233.

64. T. Menon, J. Sim, J. Ho-Ying Fu, C. Chiu, and Y. Hong, "Blazing the Trail Versus Trailing the Group: Culture and Perceptions of the Leader's Position," *Organizational Behavior and Human Decision Processes* 113, no. 1 (2010), pp. 51–61.

65. D. M. Rousseau, S. B. Sitkin, R. S. Burt, and C. Camerer, "Not So Different After All: A Cross-Discipline View of Trust," *Academy of Management Review* (July 1998), pp. 393–404; and J. A. Simpson, "Psychological Foundations of Trust," *Current Directions in Psychological Science* 16, no. 5 (2007), pp. 264–268.

66. See, for instance, K. T. Dirks and D. L. Ferrin, "Trust in Leadership: Meta-Analytic Findings and Implications for Research and Practice," *Journal of Applied Psychology* 87, no. 4, (2002), pp. 611–628; D. I. Jung and B. J. Avolio, "Opening the Black Box: An Experimental Investigation of the Mediating Effects of Trust and Value Congruence on Transformational and Transactional Leadership," *Journal of Organizational Behavior* (December 2000), pp. 949–964; and A. Zacharatos, J. Barling, and R. D. Iverson, "High-Performance Work Systems and Occupational Safety," *Journal of Applied Psychology* (January 2005), pp. 77–93.

67. Based on L. T. Hosmer, "Trust: The Connecting Link Between Organizational Theory and Philosophical Ethics," *Academy of Management Review* (April 1995), p. 393; R. C. Mayer, J. H. Davis, and F. D. Schoorman, "An Integrative Model of Organizational Trust," *Academy of Management Review* (July 1995), pp. 709–734; and F. D. Schoorman, R. C. Mayer, and J. H. Davis, "An Integrative Model of Organizational Trust: Past, Present, and Future," *Academy of Management Review* 32, no. 2 (2007), pp. 344–354.

68. J. Schaubroeck, S. S. K. Lam, and A. C. Peng, "Cognition-Based and Affect-Based Trust as Mediators of Leader Behavior Influences on Team Performance." *Journal of Applied Psychology* 96, no. 4 (July 2011), pp. 863–871.

69. J. R. Detert and E. R. Burris, "Leadership Behavior and Employee Voice: Is the Door Really Open?" *Academy of Management Journal* 50, no. 4 (2007), pp. 869–884.

70. J. A. Colquitt, B. A. Scott, and J. A. LePine, "Trust, Trustworthiness, and Trust Propensity: A Meta-Analytic Test of Their Unique Relationships with Risk Taking and Job Performance," *Journal of Applied Psychology* 92, no. 4 (2007), pp. 909–927.

71. See, for example, M. Murray, *Beyond the Myths and Magic of Mentoring: How to Facilitate an Effective Mentoring Process*, rev. ed. (New York: Wiley, 2001); K. E. Kram, "Phases of the Mentor Relationship," *Academy of Management Journal* (December 1983), pp. 608–625; R. A. Noe, "An Investigation of the Determinants of Successful Assigned Mentoring Relationships," *Personnel Psychology* (Fall 1988), pp. 559–580; and L. Eby, M. Buits, and A. Lockwood, "Protégés' Negative Mentoring Experiences: Construct Development and Nomological Validation," *Personnel Psychology* (Summer 2004), pp. 411–447.

72. B. R. Ragins and J. L. Cotton, "Easier Said than Done: Gender Differences in Perceived Barriers to Gaining a Mentor," *Academy of Management Journal* 34, no. 4 (1993), pp. 939–951; C. R. Wanberg, E. T. Welsh, and S. A. Hezlett, "Mentoring Research: A Review and Dynamic Process Model," in G. R. Ferris and J. J. Martocchio (eds.), *Research in Personnel and Human Resources Management,* vol. 22 (Greenwich, CT: Elsevier Science, 2003), pp. 39–124; and T. D. Allen, "Protégé Selection by Mentors: Contributing Individual and Organizational Factors," *Journal of Vocational Behavior* 65, no. 3 (2004), pp. 469–483.

73. See, for example, K. E. Kram and D. T. Hall, "Mentoring in a Context of Diversity and Turbulence," in E. E. Kossek and S. A. Lobel (eds.), *Managing Diversity* (Cambridge, MA: Blackwell, 1996), pp. 108–136; B. R. Ragins and J. L. Cotton, "Mentor Functions and Outcomes: A Comparison of Men and Women in Formal and Informal Mentoring Relationships," *Journal of Applied Psychology* (August 1999), pp. 529–550; and D. B. Turban, T. W. Dougherty, and F. K. Lee, "Gender, Race, and Perceived Similarity Effects in Developmental Relationships: The Moderating Role of Relationship Duration," *Journal of Vocational Behavior* (October 2002), pp. 240–262.

74. J. U. Chun, J. J. Sosik, and N. Y. Yun, "A Longitudinal Study of Mentor and Protégé Outcomes in Formal Mentoring Relationships," *Journal of Organizational Behavior* (November 12, 2012), pp. 35–49.

75. Ragins and Cotton, "Mentor Functions and Outcomes"; and C. M. Underhill, "The Effectiveness of Mentoring Programs in Corporate Settings: A Meta-Analytical Review of the Literature," *Journal of Vocational Behavior* 68, no. 2 (2006), pp. 292–307.

76. T. D. Allen, E. T. Eby, and E. Lentz, "The Relationship Between Formal Mentoring Program Characteristics and Perceived Program Effectiveness," *Personnel Psychology* 59 (2006), pp. 125–153; T. D. Allen, L. T. Eby, and E. Lentz, "Mentorship Behaviors and Mentorship Quality Associated with Formal Mentoring Programs: Closing the Gap Between Research and Practice," *Journal of Applied Psychology* 91, no. 3 (2006), pp. 567–578; and M. R. Parise and M. L. Forret, "Formal Mentoring Programs: The Relationship of Program Design and Support to Mentors' Perceptions of Benefits and Costs," *Journal of Vocational Behavior* 72, no. 2 (2008), pp. 225–240.

77. L. T. Eby and A. Lockwood, "Protégés' and Mentors' Reactions to Participating in Formal Mentoring Programs: A Qualitative Investigation," *Journal of Vocational Behavior* 67, no. 3 (2005), pp. 441–458; G. T. Chao, "Formal Mentoring: Lessons Learned from Past Practice," *Professional Psychology: Research and Practice* 40, no. 3 (2009), pp. 314–320; and C. R. Wanberg, J. D. Kammeyer-Mueller, and M. Marchese, "Mentor and Protégé Predictors and Outcomes of Mentoring in a Formal Mentoring Program," *Journal of Vocational Behavior* 69 (2006), pp. 410–423.

78. M. K. Feeney and B. Bozeman, "Mentoring and Network Ties," *Human Relations* 61, no. 12 (2008), pp. 1651–1676; N. Bozionelos, "Intra-Organizational Network Resources: How They Relate to Career Success and Organizational Commitment," *Personnel Review* 37, no. 3 (2008), pp. 249–263; and S. A. Hezlett and S. K. Gibson, "Linking Mentoring and Social Capital: Implications for Career and Organization Development," *Advances in Developing Human Resources* 9, no. 3 (2007), pp. 384–412.

79. Comment by Jim Collins, cited in J. Useem, "Conquering Vertical Limits," *Fortune* (February 19, 2001), p. 94.

80. See, for instance, J. R. Meindl, "The Romance of Leadership as a Follower-Centric Theory: A Social Constructionist Approach," *Leadership Quarterly* (Fall 1995), pp. 329–341; and B. Schyns, J. Felfe, and H. Blank, "Is Charisma Hyper-Romanticism? Empirical Evidence from New Data and a Meta-Analysis," *Applied Psychology: An International Review* 56, no. 4 (2007), pp. 505–527.

81. M. J. Martinko, P. Harvey, D. Sikora, and S. C. Douglas, "Perceptions of Abusive Supervision: The Role of Subordinates' Attribution Styles," *Leadership Quarterly* (August 2011), pp. 751–764.

82. J. R. Meindl, S. B. Ehrlich, and J. M. Dukerich, "The Romance of Leadership," *Administrative Science Quarterly* (March 1985), pp. 78–102; and M. C. Bligh, J. C. Kohles, C. L. Pearce, J. E. Justin, and J. F. Stovall, "When the Romance Is Over: Follower Perspectives of Aversive Leadership," *Applied Psychology: An International Review* 56, no. 4 (2007), pp. 528–557.

83. B. R. Agle, N. J. Nagarajan, J. A. Sonnenfeld, and D. Srinivasan, "Does CEO Charisma Matter?" *Academy of Management Journal* 49, no. 1 (2006), pp. 161–174.

84. Bligh, Kohles, Pearce, Justin, and Stovall, "When the Romance Is Over."

85. Schyns, Felfe, and Blank, "Is Charisma Hyper-Romanticism?"

86. M. Van Vugt and B. R. Spisak, "Sex Differences in the Emergence of Leadership During Competitions Within and Between Groups," *Psychological Science* 19, no. 9 (2008), pp. 854–8

87. R. E. Silverman, "Who's the Boss? There Isn't One," *The Wall Street Journal* (June 20, 2012), pp. B 1, B8.58.

88. S. D. Dionne, F. J. Yammarino, L. E. Atwater, and L. R. James, "Neutralizing Substitutes for Leadership Theory. Leadership

Effects and Common-Source Bias," *Journal of Applied Psychology,* 87 (2002), pp. 454–464; and J. R. Villa, J. P. Howell, P. W. Dorfman, and D. L. Daniel, "Problems with Detecting Moderators in Leadership Research Using Moderated Multiple Regression," *Leadership Quarterly* 14 (2002), pp. 3–23.

89. B. M. Bass, "Cognitive, Social, and Emotional Intelligence of Transformational Leaders," in R. E. Riggio, S. E. Murphy, and F. J. Pirozzolo (eds.), *Multiple Intelligences and Leadership* (Mahwah, NJ: Lawrence Erlbaum, 2002), pp. 113–114.

90. See, for instance, P. Dvorak, "M.B.A. Programs Hone 'Soft Skills,'" *The Wall Street Journal* (February 12, 2007), p. B3.

91. D. S. DeRue, J. D. Nahrgang, J. R. Hollenbeck, and K. Workman, "A Quasi-Experimental Study of After-Event Reviews and Leadership Development," *Journal of Applied Psychology* 97 (2012), pp. 997–1015.

CHAPTER 13

1. R. M. Kanter, "Power Failure in Management Circuits," *Harvard Business Review* (July–August 1979), p. 65.

2. Based on B. M. Bass, *Bass & Stogdill's Handbook of Leadership,* 3rd ed. (New York: The Free Press, 1990).

3. M. Gongloff, "Steve Cohen, Super-Rich and Secretive Trader, Faces Possible SEC Investigation," *Huffington Post* (November 28, 2012), downloaded May 24, 2013 from www.huffingtonpost.com/.

4. J. R. P. French Jr. and B. Raven, "The Bases of Social Power," in D. Cartwright (ed.), *Studies in Social Power* (Ann Arbor, MI: University of Michigan, Institute for Social Research, 1959), pp. 150–167; B. H. Raven, "The Bases of Power: Origins and Recent Developments," *Journal of Social Issues* (Winter 1993), pp. 227–251; and G. Yukl, "Use Power Effectively," in E. A. Locke (ed.), *Handbook of Principles of Organizational Behavior* (Malden, MA: Blackwell, 2004), pp. 242–247.

5. E. A. Ward, "Social Power Bases of Managers: Emergence of a New Factor," *Journal of Social Psychology* (February 2001), pp. 144–147.

6. S. R. Giessner and T. W. Schubert, "High in the Hierarchy; How Vertical Location and Judgments of Leaders' Power Are Interrelated," *Organizational Behavior and Human Decision Processes* 104, no. 1 (2007), pp. 30–44.

7. P. M. Podsakoff and C. A. Schriesheim, "Field Studies of French and Raven's Bases of Power: Critique, Reanalysis, and Suggestions for Future Research," *Psychological Bulletin* (May 1985), pp. 387–411; T. R. Hinkin and C. A. Schriesheim, "Development and Application of New Scales to Measure the French and Raven (1959) Bases of Social Power," *Journal of Applied Psychology* (August 1989), pp. 561–567; and P. P. Carson, K. D. Carson, and C. W. Roe, "Social Power Bases: A Meta-Analytic Examination of Interrelationships and Outcomes," *Journal of Applied Social Psychology* 23, no. 14 (1993), pp. 1150–1169.

8. S. Perman, "Translation Advertising: Where Shop Meets Hip Hop," *Time* (August 30, 2010), www.time.com.

9. See, for example, D. Kipnis and S. M. Schmidt, "Upward-Influence Styles: Relationship with Performance Evaluations, Salary, and Stress," *Administrative Science Quarterly* (December 1988), pp. 528–542; G. Yukl and J. B. Tracey, "Consequences of Influence Tactics Used with Subordinates, Peers, and the Boss," *Journal of Applied Psychology* (August 1992), pp. 525–535; G. Blickle, "Influence Tactics Used by Subordinates: An Empirical Analysis of the Kipnis and Schmidt Subscales," *Psychological Reports* (February 2000), pp. 143–154; and G. Yukl, "Use Power Effectively," pp. 249–252.

10. G. Yukl, *Leadership in Organizations,* 5th ed. (Upper Saddle River, NJ: Prentice Hall, 2002), pp. 141–174; G. R. Ferris, W. A. Hochwarter, C. Douglas, F. R. Blass, R. W. Kolodinsky, and D. C. Treadway, "Social Influence Processes in Organizations and Human Resource Systems," in G. R. Ferris and J. J. Martocchio (eds.), *Research in Personnel and Human Resources Management,* vol. 21 (Oxford, UK: JAI Press/Elsevier, 2003), pp. 65–127; and C. A. Higgins, T. A. Judge, and G. R. Ferris, "Influence Tactics and Work Outcomes: A Meta-Analysis," *Journal of Organizational Behavior* (March 2003), pp. 89–106.

11. C. M. Falbe and G. Yukl, "Consequences for Managers of Using Single Influence Tactics and Combinations of Tactics," *Academy of Management Journal* (July 1992), pp. 638–653.

12. R. E. Petty and P. Briñol, "Persuasion: From Single to Multiple to Metacognitive Processes," *Perspectives on Psychological Science* 3, no. 2 (2008), pp. 137–147.

13. J. Badal, "Getting a Raise from the Boss," *The Wall Street Journal* (July 8, 2006), pp. B1, B5.

14. Yukl, *Leadership in Organizations.*

15. Ibid.

16. Falbe and Yukl, "Consequences for Managers of Using Single Influence Tactics and Combinations of Tactics."

17. A. W. Kruglanski, A. Pierro, and E. T. Higgins, "Regulatory Mode and Preferred Leadership Styles: How Fit Increases Job Satisfaction," *Basic and Applied Social Psychology* 29, no. 2 (2007), pp. 137–149; and A. Pierro, L. Cicero, and B. H. Raven, "Motivated Compliance with Bases of Social Power," *Journal of Applied Social Psychology* 38, no. 7 (2008), pp. 1921–1944.

18. P. P. Fu and G. Yukl, "Perceived Effectiveness of Influence Tactics in the United States and China," *Leadership Quarterly* (Summer 2000), pp. 251–266; O. Branzei, "Cultural Explanations of Individual Preferences for Influence Tactics in Cross-Cultural Encounters," *International Journal of Cross Cultural Management* (August 2002), pp. 203–218; G. Yukl, P. P. Fu, and R. McDonald, "Cross-Cultural Differences in Perceived Effectiveness of Influence Tactics for Initiating or Resisting Change," *Applied Psychology: An International Review* (January 2003), pp. 66–82; and P. P. Fu, T. K. Peng, J. C. Kennedy, and G. Yukl, "Examining the Preferences of Influence Tactics in Chinese Societies: A Comparison of Chinese Managers in Hong Kong, Taiwan, and Mainland China," *Organizational Dynamics* 33, no. 1 (2004), pp. 32–46.

19. C. J. Torelli and S. Shavitt, "Culture and Concepts of Power," *Journal of Personality and Social Psychology* 99, no. 4 (2010), pp. 703–723.

20. Fu and Yukl, "Perceived Effectiveness of Influence Tactics in the United States and China."

21. G. R. Ferris, D. C. Treadway, P. L. Perrewé, R. L. Brouer, C. Douglas, and S. Lux, "Political Skill in Organizations," *Journal of Management* (June 2007), pp. 290–320; K. J. Harris, K. M. Kacmar, S. Zivnuska, and J. D. Shaw, "The Impact of Political Skill on Impression Management Effectiveness," *Journal of Applied Psychology* 92, no. 1 (2007), pp. 278–285; W. A. Hochwarter, G. R. Ferris, M. B. Gavin, P. L. Perrewé, A. T. Hall, and D. D. Frink, "Political Skill as Neutralizer of Felt Accountability–Job Tension Effects on Job Performance Ratings: A Longitudinal Investigation," *Organizational Behavior and Human Decision Processes* 102 (2007), pp. 226–239; and D. C. Treadway, G. R. Ferris, A. B. Duke, G. L. Adams,

and J. B. Tatcher, "The Moderating Role of Subordinate Political Skill on Supervisors' Impressions of Subordinate Ingratiation and Ratings of Subordinate Interpersonal Facilitation," *Journal of Applied Psychology* 92, no. 3 (2007), pp. 848–855.

22. M. C. Andrews, K. M. Kacmar, and K. J. Harris, "Got Political Skill? The Impact of Justice on the Importance of Political Skills for Job Performance." *Journal of Applied Psychology* 94, no. 6 (2009), pp. 1427–1437.

23. C. Anderson, S. E. Spataro, and F. J. Flynn, "Personality and Organizational Culture as Determinants of Influence," *Journal of Applied Psychology* 93, no. 3 (2008), pp. 702–710.

24. Y. Cho and N. J. Fast, "Power, Defensive Denigration, and the Assuaging Effect of Gratitude Expression," *Journal of Experimental Social Psychology* 48, 2012, pp. 778–782.

25. M. Pitesa and S. Thau, "Masters of the Universe: How Power and Accountability Influence Self-Serving Decisions under Moral Hazard," *Journal of Applied Psychology* 98 (2013), pp. 550–558; and N. J. Fast, N. Sivanathan, D. D. Mayer, and A. D. Galinsky, "Power and Overconfident Decision-Making," *Organizational Behavior and Human Decision Processes* 117, 2012, pp. 249–260.

26. A. Grant, "Yes, Power Corrupts, But Power Also Reveals," *Government Executive* (May 23, 2013), downloaded May 23, 2013, from www.govexec.com/.

27. J. K. Maner, M. T. Gaillot, A. J. Menzel, and J. W. Kunstman, "Dispositional Anxiety Blocks the Psychological Effects of Power," *Personality and Social Psychology Bulletin* 38 (2012), pp. 1383–1395.

28. N. J. Fast, N. Halevy, and A. D. Galinsky, "The Destructive Nature of Power without Status," *Journal of Experimental Social Psychology* 48 (2012), pp. 391–394.

29. T. Seppälä, J. Lipponen, A. Bardi, and A. Pirttilä-Backman, Change-Oriented Organizational Citizenship Behaviour: An Interactive Product of Openness to Change Values, Work Unit Identification, and Sense of Power," *Journal of Occupational and Organizational Psychology* 85 (2012), pp. 136–155.

30. K. A. DeCelles, D. S. DeRue, J. D. Margolis, and T. L. Ceranic, "Does Power Corrupt or Enable? When and Why Power Facilitates Self-Interested Behavior," *Journal of Applied Psychology* 97 (2012), pp. 681–689.

31. Mintzberg, *Power In and Around Organizations,* p. 26. See also K. M. Kacmar and R. A. Baron, "Organizational Politics: The State of the Field, Links to Related Processes, and an Agenda for Future Research," in G. R. Ferris (ed.), *Research in Personnel and Human Resources Management,* vol. 17 (Greenwich, CT: JAI Press, 1999), pp. 1–39; and G. R. Ferris, D. C. Treadway, R. W. Kolokinsky, W. A. Hochwarter, C. J. Kacmar, and D. D. Frink, "Development and Validation of the Political Skill Inventory," *Journal of Management* (February 2005), pp. 126–152.

32. S. B. Bacharach and E. J. Lawler, "Political Alignments in Organizations," in R. M. Kramer and M. A. Neale (eds.), *Power and Influence in Organizations* (Thousand Oaks, CA: Sage, 1998), pp. 68–69.

33. A. Drory and T. Romm, "The Definition of Organizational Politics: A Review," *Human Relations* (November 1990), pp. 1133–1154; and R. S. Cropanzano, K. M. Kacmar, and D. P. Bozeman, "Organizational Politics, Justice, and Support: Their Differences and Similarities," in R. Cropanzano and K. M. Kacmar (eds.), *Organizational Politics, Justice and Support: Managing Social Climate at Work* (Westport, CT: Quorum Books, 1995), pp. 1–18; and G. R. Ferris and W A Hochwarter, "Organizational Politics," in S. Zedeck (ed.), *APA Handbook of Industrial and Organizational Psychology,*

vol. 3 (Washington, DC: American Psychological Association, 2011), pp. 435–459.

34. D. A. Buchanan, "You Stab My Back, I'll Stab Yours: Management Experience and Perceptions of Organization Political Behavior," *British Journal of Management* 19, no. 1 (2008), pp. 49–64.

35. J. Pfeffer, *Power: Why Some People Have It—And Others Don't* (New York: Harper Collins, 2010).

36. Drory and Romm, "The Definition of Organizational Politics."

37. S. M. Rioux and L. A. Penner, "The Causes of Organizational Citizenship Behavior: A Motivational Analysis," *Journal of Applied Psychology* (December 2001), pp. 1306–1314; M. A. Finkelstein and L. A. Penner, "Predicting Organizational Citizenship Behavior: Integrating the Functional and Role Identity Approaches," *Social Behavior & Personality* 32, no. 4 (2004), pp. 383–398; and J. Schwarzwald, M. Koslowsky, and M. Allouf, "Group Membership, Status, and Social Power Preference," *Journal of Applied Social Psychology* 35, no. 3 (2005), pp. 644–665.

38. See, for example, G. R. Ferris, G. S. Russ, and P. M. Fandt, "Politics in Organizations," in R. A. Giacalone and P. Rosenfeld (eds.), *Impression Management in the Organization* (Hillsdale, NJ: Lawrence Erlbaum, 1989), pp. 155–156; and W. E. O'Connor and T. G. Morrison, "A Comparison of Situational and Dispositional Predictors of Perceptions of Organizational Politics," *Journal of Psychology* (May 2001), pp. 301–312.

39. D. Farrell and J. C. Petersen, "Patterns of Political Behavior in Organizations," *Academy of Management Review* 7, no. 3 (1982), pp. 403–412.

40. G. R. Ferris and K. M. Kacmar, "Perceptions of Organizational Politics," *Journal of Management* (March 1992), pp. 93–116.

41. See, for example, P. M. Fandt and G. R. Ferris, "The Management of Information and Impressions: When Employees Behave Opportunistically," *Organizational Behavior and Human Decision Processes* (February 1990), pp. 140–158; Ferris, Russ, and Fandt, "Politics in Organizations," p. 147; and J. M. L. Poon, "Situational Antecedents and Outcomes of Organizational Politics Perceptions," *Journal of Managerial Psychology* 18, no. 2 (2003), pp. 138–155.

42. Ferris and Hochwarter, "Organizational Politics."

43. W. A. Hochwarter, C. Kiewitz, S. L. Castro, P. L. Perrewe, and G. R. Ferris, "Positive Affectivity and Collective Efficacy as Moderators of the Relationship Between Perceived Politics and Job Satisfaction," *Journal of Applied Social Psychology* (May 2003), pp. 1009–1035; and C. C. Rosen, P. E. Levy, and R. J. Hall, "Placing Perceptions of Politics in the Context of Feedback Environment, Employee Attitudes, and Job Performance," *Journal of Applied Psychology* 91, no. 1 (2006), pp. 211–230.

44. G. R. Ferris, D. D. Frink, M. C. Galang, J. Zhou, K. M. Kacmar, and J. L. Howard, "Perceptions of Organizational Politics: Prediction, Stress-Related Implications, and Outcomes," *Human Relations* (February 1996), pp. 233–266; and E. Vigoda, "Stress-Related Aftermaths to Workplace Politics: The Relationships among Politics, Job Distress, and Aggressive Behavior in Organizations," *Journal of Organizational Behavior* (August 2002), pp. 571–591.

45. S. Aryee, Z. Chen, and P. S. Budhwar, "Exchange Fairness and Employee Performance: An Examination of the Relationship between Organizational Politics and Procedural Justice," *Organizational Behavior & Human Decision Processes* (May 2004), pp. 1–14; and K. M. Kacmar, D. P. Bozeman, D. S. Carlson, and W. P. Anthony, "An Examination of the Perceptions of Organizational Politics Model," *Human Relations* 52, no. 3 (1999), pp. 383–416.

46. C. Kiewitz, W. A. Hochwarter, G. R. Ferris, and S. L. Castro, "The Role of Psychological Climate in Neutralizing the Effects of Organizational Politics on Work Outcomes," *Journal of Applied Social Psychology* (June 2002), pp. 1189–1207; and M. C. Andrews, L. A. Witt, and K. M. Kacmar, "The Interactive Effects of Organizational Politics and Exchange Ideology on Manager Ratings of Retention," *Journal of Vocational Behavior* (April 2003), pp. 357–369.

47. Kacmar, Bozeman, Carlson, and Anthony, "An Examination of the Perceptions of Organizational Politics Model," p. 389.

48. Ibid., p. 409.

49. K. M. Kacmar, D. G. Bachrach, K. J. Harris, and S. Zivnuska, "Fostering Good Citizenship Through Ethical Leadership: Exploring the Moderating Role of Gender and Organizational Politics," *Journal of Applied Psychology* 96 (2011), pp. 633–642.

50. B. E. Ashforth and R. T. Lee, "Defensive Behavior in Organizations: A Preliminary Model," *Human Relations* (July 1990), pp. 621–648.

51. M. Valle and P. L. Perrewe, "Do Politics Perceptions Relate to Political Behaviors? Tests of an Implicit Assumption and Expanded Model," *Human Relations* (March 2000), pp. 359–386.

52. See, for instance, W. L. Gardner and M. J. Martinko, "Impression Management in Organizations," *Journal of Management* (June 1988), pp. 321–338; M. C. Bolino and W. H. Turnley, "More Than One Way to Make an Impression: Exploring Profiles of Impression Management," *Journal of Management* 29, no. 2 (2003), pp. 141–160; S. Zivnuska, K. M. Kacmar, L. A. Witt, D. S. Carlson, and V. K. Bratton, "Interactive Effects of Impression Management and Organizational Politics on Job Performance," *Journal of Organizational Behavior* (August 2004), pp. 627–640; and M. C. Bolino, K. M. Kacmar, W. H. Turnley, and J. B. Gilstrap, "A Multi-Level Review of Impression Management Motives and Behaviors," *Journal of Management* 34, no. 6 (2008), pp. 1080–1109.

53. M. Snyder and J. Copeland, "Self-Monitoring Processes in Organizational Settings," in R. A. Giacalone and P. Rosenfeld (eds.), *Impression Management in the Organization* (Hillsdale, NJ: Lawrence Erlbaum, 1989), p. 11; Bolino and Turnley, "More Than One Way to Make an Impression"; and W. H. Turnley and M. C. Bolino, "Achieved Desired Images While Avoiding Undesired Images: Exploring the Role of Self-Monitoring in Impression Management," *Journal of Applied Psychology* (April 2001), pp. 351–360.

54. M. R. Leary and R. M. Kowalski, "Impression Management: A Literature Review and Two-Component Model," *Psychological Bulletin* (January 1990), pp. 34–47.

55. J. Ham and R. Vonk, "Impressions of Impression Management: Evidence of Spontaneous Suspicion of Ulterior Motivation," *Journal of Experimental Social Psychology* 47, no. 2 (2011), pp. 466–471; and W. M. Bowler, J. R. B. Halbesleben, and J. R. B. Paul, "If You're Close with the Leader, You Must Be a Brownnose: The Role of Leader–Member Relationships in Follower, Leader, and Coworker Attributions of Organizational Citizenship Behavior Motives," *Human Resource Management Review* 20, no. 4 (2010), pp. 309–316.

56. C. Lebherz, K. Jonas, and B. Tomljenovic, "Are We Known by the Company We Keep? Effects of Name Dropping on First Impressions," *Social Influence* 4, no. 1 (2009), pp. 62–79.

57. J. R. B. Halbesleben, W. M. Bowler, M. C. Bolino, and W. H Turnley, "Organizational Concern, Prosocial Values, or Impression Management? How Supervisors Attribute Motives to Organizational Citizenship Behavior," *Journal of Applied Social Psychology* 40, no. 6 (2010), pp. 1450–1489.

58. C. K. Stevens and A. L. Kristof, "Making the Right Impression: A Field Study of Applicant Impression Management During Job Interviews," *Journal of Applied Psychology* 80 (1995), pp. 587–606; L. A. McFarland, A. M. Ryan, and S. D. Kriska, "Impression Management Use and Effectiveness Across Assessment Methods," *Journal of Management* 29, no. 5 (2003), pp. 641–661; C. A. Higgins and T. A. Judge, "The Effect of Applicant Influence Tactics on Recruiter Perceptions of Fit and Hiring Recommendations: A Field Study," *Journal of Applied Psychology* 89, no. 4 (2004), pp. 622–632; and W. C. Tsai, C.-C. Chen, and S. F. Chiu, "Exploring Boundaries of the Effects of Applicant Impression Management Tactics in Job Interviews," *Journal of Management* (February 2005), pp. 108–125.

59. D. C. Gilmore and G. R. Ferris, "The Effects of Applicant Impression Management Tactics on Interviewer Judgments," *Journal of Management* 15, no. 4 (1989), pp. 557–564.

60. Stevens and Kristof, "Making the Right Impression."

61. C. A. Higgins, T. A. Judge, and G. R. Ferris, "Influence Tactics and Work Outcomes: A Meta-Analysis," *Journal of Organizational Behavior* (March 2003), pp. 89–106.

62. Ibid.

63. K. J. Harris, K. M. Kacmar, S. Zivnuska, and J. D. Shaw, "The Impact of Political Skill on Impression Management Effectiveness," *Journal of Applied Psychology* 92, no. 1 (2007), pp. 278–285; and D. C. Treadway, G. R. Ferris, A. B. Duke, G. L. Adams, and J. B. Thatcher, "The Moderating Role of Subordinate Political Skill on Supervisors' Impressions of Subordinate Ingratiation and Ratings of Subordinate Interpersonal Facilitation," *Journal of Applied Psychology* 92, no. 3 (2007), pp. 848–855.

64. J. D. Westphal and I. Stern, "Flattery Will Get You Everywhere (Especially If You Are a Male Caucasian): How Ingratiation, Boardroom Behavior, and Demographic Minority Status Affect Additional Board Appointments of U.S. Companies," *Academy of Management Journal* 50, no. 2 (2007), pp. 267–288.

65. See T. Romm and A. Drory, "Political Behavior in Organizations: A Cross-Cultural Comparison," *International Journal of Value Based Management* 1 (1988), pp. 97–113; and E. Vigoda, "Reactions to Organizational Politics: A Cross-Cultural Examination in Israel and Britain," *Human Relations* (November 2001), pp. 1483–1518.

66. J. L. T. Leong, M. H. Bond, and P. P. Fu, "Perceived Effectiveness of Influence Strategies in the United States and Three Chinese Societies," *International Journal of Cross Cultural Management* (May 2006), pp. 101–120.

67. Y. Miyamoto and B. Wilken, "Culturally Contingent Situated Cognition: Influencing Other People Fosters Analytic Perception in the United States but Not in Japan," *Psychological Science* 21, no. 11 (2010), pp. 1616–1622.

68. Vigoda, "Reactions to Organizational Politics," p. 1512.

69. Ibid., p. 1510.

70. D. Clark, "A Campaign Strategy for Your Career," *Harvard Business Review* (November 2012), pp. 131–134.

CHAPTER 14

1. See, for instance, D. Tjosvold, "Defining Conflict and Making Choices about Its Management: Lighting the Dark Side of Organizational Life," *International Journal of Conflict Management* 17, no. 2 (2006), pp. 87–95; and M. A. Korsgaard,

S. S. Jeong, D. M. Mahony, and A. H. Pitariu, "A Multilevel View of Intragroup Conflict," *Journal of Management* 34, no. 6 (2008), pp. 1222–1252.

2. K. W. Thomas, "Conflict and Negotiation Processes in Organizations," in M. D. Dunnette and L. M. Hough (eds.), *Handbook of Industrial and Organizational Psychology*, 2nd ed., vol. 3 (Palo Alto, CA: Consulting Psychologists Press, 1992), pp. 651–717.

3. For a comprehensive review of the interactionist approach, see C. K. W. De Dreu and E. Van de Vliert (eds.), *Using Conflict in Organizations* (London: Sage, 1997).

4. J. Yang and K. W. Mossholder, "Decoupling Task and Relationship Conflict: The Role of Intragroup Emotional Processing," *Journal of Organizational Behavior* 25, no. 5 (August 2004), pp. 589–605; and N. Gamero, V. González-Romá, and J. M. Peiró, "The Influence of Intra-Team Conflict on Work Teams' Affective Climate: A Longitudinal Study," *Journal of Occupational and Organizational Psychology* 81, no. 1 (2008), pp. 47–69.

5. N. Halevy, E. Y. Chou, and A. D. Galinsky, "Exhausting or Exhilarating? Conflict as Threat to Interests, Relationships and Identities," *Journal of Experimental Social Psychology* 48 (2012), pp. 530–537.

6. F. R. C. de Wit, L. L. Greer, and K. A. Jehn, "The Paradox of Intragroup Conflict: A Meta-Analysis," *Journal of Applied Psychology* 97 (2012), pp. 360–390.

7. J. Farh, C. Lee, and C. I. C. Farh, "Task Conflict and Team Creativity: A Question of How Much and When," *Journal of Applied Psychology* 95, no. 6 (2010), pp. 1173–1180.

8. B. H. Bradley, A. C. Klotz, B. F. Postlethwaite, and K. G. Brown, "Ready to Rumble: How Team Personality Composition and Task Conflict Interact to Improve Performance," *Journal of Applied Psychology* 98 (2013), pp. 385–392.

9. B. H. Bradley, B. F. Postlethwaite, A. C. Klotz, M. R. Hamdani, and K. G. Brown, "Reaping the Benefits of Task Conflict in Teams: The Critical Role of Team Psychological Safety Climate," *Journal of Applied Psychology* 97 (2012), pp. 151–158.

10. G. A. Van Kleef, W. Steinel, and A. C. Homan, "On Being Peripheral and Paying Attention: Prototypicality and Information Processing in Intergroup Conflict," *Journal of Applied Psychology* 98 (2013), pp. 63–79.

11. S. Benard, "Cohesion from Conflict: Does Intergroup Conflict Motivate Intragroup Norm Enforcement and Support for Centralized Leadership?" *Social Psychology Quarterly* 75 (2012), pp. 107–130.

12. R. S. Peterson and K. J. Behfar, "The Dynamic Relationship Between Performance Feedback, Trust, and Conflict in Groups: A Longitudinal Study," *Organizational Behavior & Human Decision Processes* (September–November 2003), pp. 102–112.

13. T. M. Glomb and H. Liao, "Interpersonal Aggression in Work Groups: Social Influence, Reciprocal, and Individual Effects," *Academy of Management Journal* 46, no. 4 (2003), pp. 486–496; and V. Venkataramani and R. S. Dalal, "Who Helps and Harms Whom? Relational Aspects of Interpersonal Helping and Harming in Organizations," *Journal of Applied Psychology* 92, no. 4 (2007), pp. 952–966.

14. R. Friedman, C. Anderson, J. Brett, M. Olekalns, N. Goates, and C. C. Lisco, "The Positive and Negative Effects of Anger on Dispute Resolution: Evidence from Electronically Mediated Disputes," *Journal of Applied Psychology* (April 2004), pp. 369–376.

15. L. R. Pondy, "Organizational Conflict: Concepts and Models," *Administrative Science Quarterly* (September 1967), p. 302.

16. See, for instance, J. R. Curhan, "What Do People Value When They Negotiate? Mapping the Domain of Subjective Value in Negotiation," *Journal of Personality and Social Psychology* (September 2006), pp. 117–126; R. L. Pinkley, "Dimensions of Conflict Frame: Disputant Interpretations of Conflict," *Journal of Applied Psychology* (April 1990), pp. 117–126; and R. L. Pinkley and G. B. Northcraft, "Conflict Frames of Reference: Implications for Dispute Processes and Outcomes," *Academy of Management Journal* (February 1994), pp. 193–205.

17. A. M. Isen, A. A. Labroo, and P. Durlach, "An Influence of Product and Brand Name on Positive Affect: Implicit and Explicit Measures," *Motivation & Emotion* (March 2004), pp. 43–63.

18. Ibid.

19. P. J. D. Carnevale and A. M. Isen, "The Influence of Positive Affect and Visual Access on the Discovery of Integrative Solutions in Bilateral Negotiations," *Organizational Behavior and Human Decision Processes* (February 1986), pp. 1–13; and C. Montes, D. Rodriguez, and G. Serrano, "Affective Choice of Conflict Management Styles," *International Journal of Conflict Management* 23 (2012), pp. 6–18.

20. Thomas, "Conflict and Negotiation Processes in Organizations."

21. Ibid.

22. Ibid.

23. B. A. Nijstad and S. C. Kaps, "Taking the Easy Way Out: Preference Diversity, Decision Strategies, and Decision Refusal in Groups," *Journal of Personality and Social Psychology* 94, no. 5 (2008), pp. 860–870.

24. M. E. Zellmer-Bruhn, M. M. Maloney, A. D. Bhappu, and R. Salvador, "When and How Do Differences Matter? An Exploration of Perceived Similarity in Teams," *Organizational Behavior and Human Decision Processes* 107, no. 1 (2008), pp. 41–59.

25. For example, see J. A. Wall Jr. and R. R. Callister, "Conflict and Its Management," *Journal of Management* 21, no. 3 (1995) pp. 523–526, for evidence supporting the argument that conflict is almost uniformly dysfunctional. See also P. J. Hinds and D. E. Bailey, "Out of Sight, Out of Sync: Understanding Conflict in Distributed Teams," *Organization Science* (November–December 2003), pp. 615–632.

26. K. A. Jehn, L. Greer, S. Levine, and G. Szulanski, "The Effects of Conflict Types, Dimensions, and Emergent States on Group Outcomes," *Group Decision and Negotiation* 17, no. 6 (2005), pp. 777–796.

27. Zellmer-Bruhn, Maloney, Bhappu, and Salvador, "When and How Do Differences Matter?"

28. J. Fried, "I Know You Are, But What Am I?" *Inc.* (July/August 2010), pp. 39–40.

29. K. J. Behfar, R. S. Peterson, E. A. Mannix, and W. M. K. Trochim, "The Critical Role of Conflict Resolution in Teams: A Close Look at the Links between Conflict Type, Conflict Management Strategies, and Team Outcomes," *Journal of Applied Psychology* 93, no. 1 (2008), pp. 170–188; A. G. Tekleab, N. R. Quigley, and P. E. Tesluk, "A Longitudinal Study of Team Conflict, Conflict Management, Cohesion, and Team Effectiveness," *Group and Organization Management* 34, no. 2 (2009), pp. 170–205; and E. Van de Vliert, M. C. Euwema, and S. E. Huismans, "Managing Conflict with a Subordinate or a Superior: Effectiveness of Conglomerated Behavior," *Journal of Applied Psychology* 80 (1995), pp. 271–281.

30. A. Somech, H. S. Desivilya, and H. Lidogoster, "Team Conflict Management and Team Effectiveness: The Effects of

Task Interdependence and Team Identification," *Journal of Organizational Behavior* 30, no. 3 (2009), pp. 359–378.

31. H. R. Markus and S. Kitayama, "Culture and the Self: Implications for Cognition, Emotion, and Motivation," *Psychological Review* 98, no. 2 (1991), pp. 224–253; and H. Ren and B. Gray, "Repairing Relationship Conflict: How Violation Types and Culture Influence the Effectiveness of Restoration Rituals," *Academy of Management Review* 34, no. 1 (2009), pp. 105–126.

32. M. J. Gelfand, M. Higgins, L. H. Nishii, J. L. Raver, A. Dominguez, F. Murakami, S. Yamaguchi, and M. Toyama, "Culture and Egocentric Perceptions of Fairness in Conflict and Negotiation," *Journal of Applied Psychology* (October 2002), pp. 833–845; and Z. Ma, "Chinese Conflict Management Styles and Negotiation Behaviours: An Empirical Test," *International Journal of Cross Cultural Management* (April 2007), pp. 101–119.

33. P. P. Fu, X. H. Yan, Y. Li, E. Wang, and S. Peng, "Examining Conflict-Handling Approaches by Chinese Top Management Teams in IT Firms," *International Journal of Conflict Management* 19, no. 3 (2008), pp. 188–209.

34. M. H. Bazerman, J. R. Curhan, D. A. Moore, and K. L. Valley, "Negotiation," *Annual Review of Psychology* 51 (2000), pp. 279–314.

35. See, for example, D. R. Ames, "Assertiveness Expectancies: How Hard People Push Depends on the Consequences They Predict," *Journal of Personality and Social Psychology* 95, no. 6 (2008), pp. 1541–1557; and J. R. Curhan, H. A. Elfenbein, and H. Xu, "What Do People Value When They Negotiate? Mapping the Domain of Subjective Value in Negotiation," *Journal of Personality and Social Psychology* 91, no. 3 (2006), pp. 493–512.

36. R. Lewicki, D. Saunders, and B. Barry, *Negotiation,* 6th ed. (New York: McGraw-Hill/Irwin, 2009).

37. J. C. Magee, A. D. Galinsky, and D. H. Gruenfeld, "Power, Propensity to Negotiate, and Moving First in Competitive Interactions," *Personality and Social Psychology Bulletin* (February 2007), pp. 200–212.

38. E. Wilson, "The Trouble with Jake," *The New York Times* (July 15, 2009), www.nytimes.com.

39. J. R. Curhan, H. A. Elfenbein, and H. Xu, "What Do People Value When They Negotiate? Mapping the Domain of Subjective Value in Negotiation," *Journal of Personality and Social Psychology* 91, no. 3 (2006), pp. 493–512.

40. Thomas, "Conflict and Negotiation Processes in Organizations."

41. P. M. Morgan and R. S. Tindale, "Group vs. Individual Performance in Mixed-Motive Situations: Exploring an Inconsistency," *Organizational Behavior & Human Decision Processes* (January 2002), pp. 44–65.

42. C. E. Naquin, "The Agony of Opportunity in Negotiation: Number of Negotiable Issues, Counterfactual Thinking, and Feelings of Satisfaction," *Organizational Behavior & Human Decision Processes* (May 2003), pp. 97–107.

43. M. Giacomantonio, C. K. W. De Dreu, and L. Mannetti, "Now You See It, Now You Don't: Interests, Issues, and Psychological Distance in Integrative Negotiation," *Journal of Personality and Social Psychology* 98, no. 5 (2010), pp. 761–774.

44. F. S. Ten Velden, B. Beersma, and C. K. W. De Dreu, "It Takes One to Tango: The Effect of Dyads' Epistemic Motivation Composition in Negotiation," *Personality and Social Psychology Bulletin* 36, no. 11 (2010), pp. 1454–1466.

45. C. K. W. De Dreu, L. R. Weingart, and S. Kwon, "Influence of Social Motives on Integrative Negotiation: A Meta-Analytic

Review and Test of Two Theories," *Journal of Personality & Social Psychology* (May 2000), pp. 889–905.

46. This model is based on R. J. Lewicki, "Bargaining and Negotiation," *Exchange: The Organizational Behavior Teaching Journal* 6, no. 2 (1981), pp. 39–40.

47. J. R. Curhan, H. A. Elfenbein, and G. J. Kilduff, "Getting Off on the Right Foot: Subjective Value Versus Economic Value in Predicting Longitudinal Job Outcomes from Job Offer Negotiations," *Journal of Applied Psychology* 94, no. 2 (2009), pp. 524–534.

48. M. H. Bazerman and M. A. Neale, *Negotiating Rationally* (New York: The Free Press, 1992), pp. 67–68.

49. R. P. Larrick and G. Wu, "Claiming a Large Slice of a Small Pie: Asymmetric Disconfirmation in Negotiation," *Journal of Personality and Social Psychology* 93, no. 2 (2007), pp. 212–233.

50. T. A. Judge, B. A. Livingston, and C. Hurst, "Do Nice Guys—and Gals—Really Finish Last? The Joint Effects of Sex and Agreeableness on Income," *Journal of Personality and Social Psychology* 102 (2012), pp. 390–407.

51. G. Lelieveld, E. Van Dijk, I. Van Beest, and G. A. Van Kleef, "Why Anger and Disappointment Affect Other's Bargaining Behavior Differently: The Moderating Role of Power and the Mediating Role of Reciprocal Complementary Emotions," *Personality and Social Psychology Bulletin* 38 (2012), pp. 1209–1221.

52. S. Côté, I. Hideg, and G. A. Van Kleef, "The Consequences of Faking Anger in Negotiations," *Journal of Experimental Social Psychology* 49 (2013), pp. 453–463.

53. G. A. Van Kleef and C. K. W. De Dreu, "Longer-Term Consequences of Anger Expression in Negotiation: Retaliation or Spillover?" *Journal of Experimental Social Psychology* 46, no. 5 (2010), pp. 753–760.

54. H. Adam and A. Shirako, "Not All Anger Is Created Equal: The Impact of the Expresser's Culture on the Social Effects of Anger in Negotiations," *Journal of Applied Psychology* (2013).

55. Lelieveld, Van Dijk, Van Beest, and Van Kleef, "Why Anger and Disappointment Affect Other's Bargaining Behavior Differently."

56. M. Olekalns and P. L. Smith, "Mutually Dependent: Power, Trust, Affect, and the Use of Deception in Negotiation," *Journal of Business Ethics* 85, no. 3 (2009), pp. 347–365.

57. A. W. Brooks and M. E. Schweitzer, "Can Nervous Nellie Negotiate? How Anxiety Causes Negotiators to Make Low First Offers, Exit Early, and Earn Less Profit," *Organizational Behavior and Human Decision Processes* 115, no. 1 (2011), pp. 43–54.

58. M. Sinaceur, H. Adam, G. A. Van Kleef, and A. D. Galinsky, "The Advantages of Being Unpredictable: How Emotional Inconsistency Extracts Concessions in Negotiation," *Journal of Experimental Social Psychology* 49 (2013), pp. 498–508.

59. K. Leary, J. Pillemer, and M. Wheeler, "Negotiating with Emotion," *Harvard Business Review* (January–February 2013), pp. 96–103.

60. L. A. Liu, R. Friedman, B. Barry, M. J. Gelfand, and Z. Zhang, "The Dynamics of Consensus Building in Intracultural and Intercultural Negotiations," *Administrative Science Quarterly* 57 (2012), pp. 269–304.

61. M. Liu, "The Intrapersonal and Interpersonal Effects of Anger on Negotiation Strategies: A Cross-Cultural Investigation," *Human Communication Research* 35, no. 1 (2009), pp. 148–169; and H. Adam, A. Shirako, and W. W. Maddux, "Cultural Variance in the Interpersonal Effects of Anger in Negotiations," *Psychological Science* 21, no. 6 (2010), pp. 882–889.

62. P. D. Trapnell and D. L. Paulhus, "Agentic and Communal Values: Their Scope and Measurement," *Journal of Personality Assessment* 94 (2012), pp. 39–52.

63. C. T. Kulik and M. Olekalns, "Negotiating the Gender Divide: Lessons from the Negotiation and Organizational Behavior Literatures," *Journal of Management* 38 (2012), pp. 1387–1415.

64. C. Suddath, "The Art of Haggling," *Bloomberg Businessweek* (November 26, 2012), p. 98.

65. D. A. Small, M. Gelfand, L. Babcock, and H. Gettman, "Who Goes to the Bargaining Table? The Influence of Gender and Framing on the Initiation of Negotiation," *Journal of Personality and Social Psychology* 93, no. 4 (2007), pp. 600–613.

66. E. T. Amanatullah and M. W. Morris, "Negotiating Gender Roles: Gender Differences in Assertive Negotiating Are Mediated by Women's Fear of Backlash and Attenuated When Negotiating on Behalf of Others," *Journal of Personality and Social Psychology* 98, no. 2 (2010), pp. 256–267.

CHAPTER 15

1. L. Garicano and Y. Wu, "Knowledge, Communication, and Organizational Capabilities," *Organization Science* (September–October 2012), pp. 1382–1397.

2. See, for instance, R. L. Daft, *Organization Theory and Design,* 10th ed. (Cincinnati, OH: South-Western Publishing, 2010).

3. T. W. Malone, R. J. Laubacher, and T. Johns, "The Age of Hyperspecialization," *Harvard Business Review* (July–August 2011), pp. 56–65.

4. J. G. Miller, "The Real Women's Issue: Time," *The Wall Street Journal* (March 9–10, 2013), p. C3.

5. C. Woodyard, "Toyota Brass Shakeup Aims to Give Regions More Control," *USA Today* (March 6, 2013), www.usatoday.com/story/money/cars/2013/03/06/toyota-shakeup/1966489/.

6. C. Hymowitz, "Managers Suddenly Have to Answer to a Crowd of Bosses," *The Wall Street Journal* (August 12, 2003), p. B1.

7. See, for instance, "How Hierarchy Can Hurt Strategy Execution," *Harvard Business Review* (July–August 2010), pp. 74–75.

8. See, for instance, J. H. Gittell, "Supervisory Span, Relational Coordination, and Flight Departure Performance: A Reassessment of Postbureaucracy Theory," *Organization Science* (July–August 2001), pp. 468–483.

9. F. A. Csascar, "Organizational Structure as a Determinant of Performance: Evidence from Mutual Funds," *Strategic Management Journal* (June 2013), pp. 611–632.

10. B. Brown and S. D. Anthony, "How P&G Tripled Its Innovation Success Rate," *Harvard Business Review* (June 2011), pp. 64–72.

11. A. Leiponen and C. E. Helfat, "Location, Decentralization, and Knowledge Sources for Innovation," *Organization Science* 22, no. 3 (2011), pp. 641–658.

12. P. Hempel, Z.-X. Zhang, and Y. Han, "Team Empowerment and the Organizational Context: Decentralization and the Contrasting Effects of Formalization," *Journal of Management* (March 2012), pp. 475–501.

13. A. Murray, "Built Not to Last," *The Wall Street Journal* (March 18, 2013), p. A11.

14. L. R. Burns and D. R. Wholey, "Adoption and Abandonment of Matrix Management Programs: Effects of Organizational Characteristics and Interorganizational Networks," *Academy of Management Journal* (February 1993), pp. 106–138; J. R. Galbraith, *Designing Matrix Organizations That Actually Work: How IBM, Procter & Gamble, and Others Design*

for Success (San Francisco: Jossey Bass, 2009); and E. Krell, "Managing the Matrix," *HRMagazine* (April 2011), pp. 69–71.

15. See, for instance, M. Bidwell, "Politics and Firm Boundaries: How Organizational Structure, Group Interests, and Resources Affect Outsourcing," *Organization Science* (November–December 2012), pp. 1622–1642.

16. See, for instance, T. Sy and L. S. D'Annunzio, "Challenges and Strategies of Matrix Organizations: Top-Level and Mid-Level Managers' Perspectives," *Human Resource Planning* 28, no. 1 (2005), pp. 39–48; and T. Sy and S. Cote, "Emotional Intelligence: A Key Ability to Succeed in the Matrix Organization," *Journal of Management Development* 23, no. 5 (2004), pp. 437–455.

17. N. Anand and R. L. Daft, "What Is the Right Organization Design?" *Organizational Dynamics* 36, no. 4 (2007), pp. 329–344.

18. See, for instance, R. E. Miles and C. C. Snow, "The New Network Firm: A Spherical Structure Built on Human Investment Philosophy," *Organizational Dynamics* (Spring 1995), pp. 5–18; D. Pescovitz, "The Company Where Everybody's a Temp," *New York Times Magazine* (June 11, 2000), pp. 94–96; B. Hedberg, G. Dahlgren, J. Hansson, and N. Olve, *Virtual Organizations and Beyond* (New York: Wiley, 2001); N. S. Contractor, S. Wasserman, and K. Faust, "Testing Multitheoretical, Multilevel Hypotheses About Organizational Networks: An Analytic Framework and Empirical Example," *Academy of Management Review* 31, no. 3 (2006) pp. 681–703; and Y. Shin, "A Person-Environment Fit Model for Virtual Organizations," *Journal of Management* (October 2004), pp. 725–743.

19. J. Bates, "Making Movies and Moving On," *Los Angeles Times* (January 19, 1998), p. A1; and T. Hope, "38 Ways the Film Industry Is Failing Today," *Huffington Post The Blog* (May 10, 2010), http://www.huffingtonpost.com/ted-hope/38-ways-the-film-industry_b_569260.html, accessed May 28, 2014.

20. D. Dahl, "Want a Job? Let the Bidding Begin," *Inc.* (March 2011), pp. 94–96.

21. M. Smerconish, "The Pulse: Local Help from Newman's Own," *The Inquirer/Daily News* philly.com website (September 3, 2012), http://articles.philly.com/2012-09-03/news/33549630_1_paul-newman-newman-s-own-foundation-profits-and-royalties, accessed May 28, 2014.

22. J. Schramm, "At Work in a Virtual World," *HRMagazine* (June 2010), p. 152.

23. C. B. Gibson and J. L. Gibbs, "Unpacking the Concept of Virtuality: The Effects of Geographic Dispersion, Electronic Dependence, Dynamic Structure, and National Diversity on Team Innovation," *Administrative Science Quarterly* 51, no. 3 (2006), pp. 451–495; H. M. Latapie and V. N. Tran, "Subculture Formation, Evolution, and Conflict between Regional Teams in Virtual Organizations," *The Business Review* (Summer 2007), pp. 189–193; and S. Davenport and U. Daellenbach, "'Belonging' to a Virtual Research Center: Exploring the Influence of Social Capital Formation Processes on Member Identification in a Virtual Organization" *British Journal of Management* 22, no. 1 (2011), pp. 54–76.

24. "GE: Just Your Average Everyday $60 Billion Family Grocery Store," *IndustryWeek* (May 2, 1994), pp. 13–18.

25. General Electric Company Annual Financials, MarketWatch, *The Wall Street Journal*, www.marketwatch.com/investing/stock/ge/financials, accessed May 28, 2014.

26. J. Scheck, L. Moloney, and A. Flynn, "Eni, CNPC Link Up in Mozambique," *The Wall Street Journal* (March 15, 2013), p. B3.

27. See, for example, U. Wassmer, "Alliance Portfolios: A Review and Research Agenda," *Journal of Management* 36, no. 1 (2010), pp. 141–171; A. M. Hess and F. T. Rothaemel, "When Are Assets Complementary? Star Scientists, Strategic Alliances, and Innovation in the Pharmaceutical Industry," *Strategic Management Journal* 32, no. 8 (2011), pp. 895–909; and J. A. Adegbesan and M. J. Higgins, "The Intra-Alliance Division of Value Created through Collaboration," *Strategic Management Journal* 32, no. 2 (2011), pp. 187–211.

28. Z. Yao, Z. Yang, G. Fisher, C. Ma, and E. Fang, "Knowledge Complementarity, Knowledge Absorption Effectiveness, and New Product Performance: The Exploration of International Joint Ventures in China," *International Business Review* (February 2013), pp. 216–227.

29. S. Constable, "Google's Motorola Starts Layoffs," *The Wall Street Journal* (March 8, 2013), video broadcast with George Stahl, http://online.wsj.com/article/B5AAEF65-2F62-487E-AE7E-EDBD4E0D20F8.html#!B5AAEF65-2F62-487E-AE7E-EDBD4E0D20F8; and R. Yu, "Google's Motorola Mobility to Cut Additional 1,200 Jobs," *USA Today* (March 8, 2013), www.usatoday.com/story/tech/2013/03/08/googles-motorola-mobility-to-cut-jobs/1973007/.

30. S. Brady, "American Express Kicks Off 2013 With Biggest Layoffs in Four Years," *Brand Channel* (January 10, 2013), www.brandchannel.com/home/post/American-Express-Layoffs-011013.aspx; and R. Sidel and A. R. Johnson, "Travel Cuts at AmEx Point to End of Era," *The Wall Street Journal* (January 13, 2013), http://online.wsj.com/article/SB10001424127887324595704578239493843399684.html#articleTabs%3Darticle.

31. "Starbucks Reports 13% Rise in Profit," *The New York Times* (January 24, 2013), www.nytimes.com/2013/01/25/business/starbucks-earnings-increased-13-in-latest-quarter.html?_r=0.

32. See J. P. Guthrie and D. K. Datta, "Dumb and Dumber: The Impact of Downsizing on Firm Performance as Moderated by Industry Conditions," *Organization Science* 19, no. 1 (2008), pp. 108–123; and K. P. De Meuse, T. J. Bergmann, P. A. Vanderheiden, and C. E. Roraff, "New Evidence Regarding Organizational Downsizing and a Firm's Financial Performance: A Long-Term Analysis," *Journal of Managerial Issues* 16, no. 2 (2004), pp. 155–177.

33. L. Alpert, "Can Imported CEO Fix Russian Cars?" *The Wall Street Journal* (March 20, 2013), p. B1.

34. See, for example, C. O. Trevor and A. J. Nyberg, "Keeping Your Headcount When All About You Are Losing Theirs: Downsizing, Voluntary Turnover Rates, and the Moderating Role of HR Practices," *Academy of Management Journal* 51, no. 2 (2008), pp. 259–276; T. M. Probst, S. M. Stewart, M. L. Gruys, and B. W. Tierney, "Productivity, Counterproductivity and Creativity: The Ups and Downs of Job Insecurity," *Journal of Occupational and Organizational Psychology* 80, no. 3 (2007), pp. 479–497; and C. P. Maertz, J. W. Wiley, C. LeRouge, and M. A. Campion, "Downsizing Effects on Survivors: Layoffs, Offshoring, and Outsourcing," *Industrial Relations* 49, no. 2 (2010), pp. 275–285.

35. C. D. Zatzick, and R. D. Iverson, "High-Involvement Management and Workforce Reduction: Competitive Advantage or Disadvantage?" *Academy of Management Journal* 49, no. 5 (2006), pp. 999–1015; A. Travaglione, and B. Cross, "Diminishing the Social Network in Organizations: Does There Need to Be Such a Phenomenon as 'Survivor Syndrome' After Downsizing?" *Strategic Change* 15, no. 1 (2006), pp. 1–13;

and J. D. Kammeyer-Mueller, H. Liao, and R. D. Arvey, "Downsizing and Organizational Performance: A Review of the Literature from a Stakeholder Perspective," *Research in Personnel and Human Resources Management* 20 (2001), pp. 269–329.

36. T. Burns and G. M. Stalker, *The Management of Innovation* (London: Tavistock, 1961); and J. A. Courtright, G. T. Fairhurst, and L. E. Rogers, "Interaction Patterns in Organic and Mechanistic Systems," *Academy of Management Journal* (December 1989), pp. 773–802.

37. This analysis is referred to as a contingency approach to organization design. See, for instance, J. M. Pennings, "Structural Contingency Theory: A Reappraisal," in B. M. Staw and L. L. Cummings (eds.), *Research in Organizational Behavior,* vol. 14 (Greenwich, CT: JAI Press, 1992), pp. 267–309; J. R. Hollenbeck, H. Moon, A. P. J. Ellis, B. J. West, D. R. Ilgen, L. Sheppard, C. O. L. H. Porter, and J. A. Wagner III, "Structural Contingency Theory and Individual Differences: Examination of External and Internal Person–Team Fit," *Journal of Applied Psychology* (June 2002), pp. 599–606; and A. Drach-Zahavy and A. Freund, "Team Effectiveness Under Stress: A Structural Contingency Approach," *Journal of Organizational Behavior* 28, no. 4 (2007), pp. 423–450.

38. The strategy–structure thesis was originally proposed in A. D. Chandler Jr., *Strategy and Structure: Chapters in the History of the Industrial Enterprise* (Cambridge, MA: MIT Press, 1962). For more analysis, see T. L. Amburgey and T. Dacin, "As the Left Foot Follows the Right? The Dynamics of Strategic and Structural Change," *Academy of Management Journal* (December 1994), pp. 1427–1452.

39. See R. E. Miles and C. C. Snow, *Organizational Strategy, Structure, and Process* (New York: McGraw-Hill, 1978); D. C. Galunic and K. M. Eisenhardt, "Renewing the Strategy–Structure–Performance Paradigm," in B. M. Staw and L. L. Cummings (eds.), *Research in Organizational Behavior,* vol. 16 (Greenwich, CT: JAI Press, 1994), pp. 215–255; and S. M. Toh, F. P. Morgeson, and M. A. Campion, "Human Resource Configurations: Investigating Fit with the Organizational Context," *Journal of Applied Psychology* 93, no. 4 (2008), pp. 864–882.

40. M. Mesco, "Moleskine Tests Appetite for IPOs," *The Wall Street Journal* (March 19, 2013), p. B8.

41. See C. Perrow, "A Framework for the Comparative Analysis of Organizations," *American Sociological Review* (April 1967), pp. 194–208; J. Hage and M. Aiken, "Routine Technology, Social Structure, and Organizational Goals," *Administrative Science Quarterly* (September 1969), pp. 366–377; C. C. Miller, W. H. Glick, Y. Wang, and G. P. Huber, "Understanding Technology-Structure Relationships: Theory Development and Meta-Analytic Theory Testing," *Academy of Management Journal* (June 1991), pp. 370–399; and W. D. Sine, H. Mitsuhashi, and D. A. Kirsch, "Revisiting Burns and Stalker: Formal Structure and New Venture Performance in Emerging Economic Sectors," *Academy of Management Journal* 49, no. 1 (2006), pp. 121–132.

42. G. G. Dess and D. W. Beard, "Dimensions of Organizational Task Environments," *Administrative Science Quarterly* (March 1984), pp. 52–73; E. A. Gerloff, N. K. Muir, and W. D. Bodensteiner, "Three Components of Perceived Environmental Uncertainty: An Exploratory Analysis of the Effects of Aggregation," *Journal of Management* (December 1991), pp. 749–768; and O. Shenkar, N. Aranya, and T. Almor,

"Construct Dimensions in the Contingency Model: An Analysis Comparing Metric and Non-metric Multivariate Instruments," *Human Relations* (May 1995), pp. 559–580.

43. C. S. Spell and T. J. Arnold, "A Multi-Level Analysis of Organizational Justice and Climate, Structure, and Employee Mental Health," *Journal of Management* 33, no. 5 (2007), pp. 724–751; and M. L. Ambrose and M. Schminke, "Organization Structure as a Moderator of the Relationship between Procedural Justice, Interactional Justice, Perceived Organizational Support, and Supervisory Trust," *Journal of Applied Psychology* 88, no. 2 (2003), pp. 295–305.

44. See, for instance, Spell and Arnold, "A Multi-Level Analysis of Organizational Justice Climate, Structure, and Employee Mental Health"; J. D. Shaw and N. Gupta, "Job Complexity, Performance, and Well-Being: When Does Supplies–Values Fit Matter? *Personnel Psychology* 57, no. 4 (2004), 847–879; and C. Anderson and C. E. Brown, "The Functions and Dysfunctions of Hierarchy," *Research in Organizational Behavior* 30 (2010), pp. 55–89.

45. T. Martin, "Pharmacies Feel More Heat," *The Wall Street Journal* (March 16–17, 2013), p. A3.

46. See, for instance, R. E. Ployhart, J. A. Weekley, and K. Baughman, "The Structure and Function of Human Capital Emergence: A Multilevel Examination of the Attraction-Selection-Attrition Model," *Academy of Management Journal* 49, no. 4 (2006), pp. 661–677.

47. J. B. Stewart, "A Place to Play for Google Staff," *The New York Times* (March 16, 2013), p. B1.

48. See, for instance, B. K. Park, J. A. Choi, M. Koo, et al., "Culture, Self, and Preference Structure: Transitivity and Context Independence Are Violated More by Interdependent People," *Social Cognition* (February 2013), pp. 106–118.

CHAPTER 16

1. See, for example, E. H. Schein, "Culture: The Missing Concept in Organization Studies," *Administrative Science Quarterly* 41, no. 2 (1996), pp. 229–240.

2. This seven-item description is based on C. A. O'Reilly III, J. Chatman, and D. F. Caldwell, "People and Organizational Culture: A Profile Comparison Approach to Assessing Person-Organization Fit," *Academy of Management Journal* (September 1991), pp. 487–516; and J. A. Chatman and K. A. Jehn, "Assessing the Relationship Between Industry Characteristics and Organizational Culture: How Different Can You Be?" *Academy of Management Journal* (June 1994), pp. 522–553.

3. The view that there will be consistency among perceptions of organizational culture has been called the "integration" perspective. For a review of this perspective and conflicting approaches, see D. Meyerson and J. Martin, "Cultural Change: An Integration of Three Different Views," *Journal of Management Studies* (November 1987), pp. 623–647; and P. J. Frost, L. F. Moore, M. R. Louis, C. C. Lundberg, and J. Martin (eds.), *Reframing Organizational Culture* (Newbury Park, CA: Sage, 1991).

4. See J. M. Jermier, J. W. Slocum Jr., L. W. Fry, and J. Gaines, "Organizational Subcultures in a Soft Bureaucracy: Resistance Behind the Myth and Facade of an Official Culture," *Organization Science* (May 1991), pp. 170–194; and P. Lok, R. Westwood, and J. Crawford, "Perceptions of Organisational Subculture and their Significance for Organisational

Commitment," *Applied Psychology: An International Review* 54, no. 4 (2005), pp. 490–514.

5. D. A. Hoffman and L. M. Jones, "Leadership, Collective Personality, and Performance," *Journal of Applied Psychology* 90, no. 3 (2005), pp. 509–522.

6. T. Hsieh, "Zappos's CEO on Going to Extremes for Customers," *Harvard Business Review* (July/August 2010), pp. 41–45.

7. See, for example, G. G. Gordon and N. DiTomaso, "Predicting Corporate Performance from Organizational Culture," *Journal of Management Studies* (November 1992), pp. 793–798; J. B. Sorensen, "The Strength of Corporate Culture and the Reliability of Firm Performance," *Administrative Science Quarterly* (March 2002), pp. 70–91; and J. Rosenthal and M. A. Masarech, "High-Performance Cultures: How Values Can Drive Business Results," *Journal of Organizational Excellence* (Spring 2003), pp. 3–18.

8. Y. Wiener, "Forms of Value Systems: A Focus on Organizational Effectiveness and Cultural Change and Maintenance," *Academy of Management Review* (October 1988), p. 536; and B. Schneider, A. N. Salvaggio, and M. Subirats, "Climate Strength: A New Direction for Climate Research," *Journal of Applied Psychology* 87 (2002), pp. 220–229.

9. R. T. Mowday, L. W. Porter, and R. M. Steers, *Employee Linkages: The Psychology of Commitment, Absenteeism, and Turnover* (New York: Academic Press, 1982); C. Vandenberghe, "Organizational Culture, Person-Culture Fit, and Turnover: A Replication in the Health Care Industry," *Journal of Organizational Behavior* (March 1999), pp. 175–184; and M. Schulte, C. Ostroff, S. Shmulyian, and A. Kinicki, "Organizational Climate Configurations: Relationships to Collective Attitudes, Customer Satisfaction, and Financial Performance," *Journal of Applied Psychology* 94, no. 3 (2009), pp. 618–634.

10. J. W. Grizzle, A. R. Zablah, T. J. Brown, J. C. Mowen, and J. M. Lee, "Employee Customer Orientation in Context: How the Environment Moderates the Influence of Customer Orientation on Performance Outcomes," *Journal of Applied Psychology* 94, no. 5 (2009), pp. 1227–1242.

11. M. R. Bashshur, A. Hernández, and V. González-Romá, "When Managers and Their Teams Disagree: A Longitudinal Look at the Consequences of Differences in Perceptions of Organizational Support," *Journal of Applied Psychology* 96, no. 3 (2011), pp. 558–573.

12. S. L. Dolan and S. Garcia, "Managing by Values: Cultural Redesign for Strategic Organizational Change at the Dawn of the Twenty-First Century," *Journal of Management Development* 21, no. 2 (2002), pp. 101–117.

13. See C. A. O'Reilly and J. A. Chatman, "Culture as Social Control: Corporations, Cults, and Commitment," in B. M. Staw and L. L. Cummings (eds.), *Research in Organizational Behavior*, vol. 18 (Greenwich, CT: JAI Press, 1996), pp. 157–200. See also M. Pinae Cunha, "The 'Best Place to Be': Managing Control and Employee Loyalty in a Knowledge-Intensive Company," *Journal of Applied Behavioral Science* (December 2002), pp. 481–495.

14. Y. Ling, Z. Simsek, M. H. Lubatkin, and J. F. Veiga, "Transformational Leadership's Role in Promoting Corporate Entrepreneurship: Examining the CEO-TMT Interface," *Academy of Management Journal* 51, no. 3 (2008), pp. 557–576; and A. Malhotra, A. Majchrzak, and B. Rosen, "Leading Virtual Teams," *Academy of Management Perspectives* 21, no. 1 (2007), pp. 60–70.

15. D. Denison, "What Is the Difference Between Organizational Culture and Organizational Climate? A Native's Point of View

on a Decade of Paradigm Wars," *Academy of Management Review* 21 (1996), pp. 519–654; and L. R. James, C. C. Choi, C. E. Ko, P. K. McNeil, M. K. Minton, M. A. Wright, and K. Kim, "Organizational and Psychological Climate: A Review of Theory and Research," *European Journal of Work and Organizational Psychology* 17, no. 1 (2008), pp. 5–32.

16. J. Z. Carr, A. M. Schmidt, J. K. Ford, and R. P. DeShon, "Climate Perceptions Matter: A Meta-Analytic Path Analysis Relating Molar Climate, Cognitive and Affective States, and Individual Level Work Outcomes," *Journal of Applied Psychology* 88, no. (2003), pp. 605–619.

17. Schulte, Ostroff, Shmulyian, and Kinicki, "Organizational Climate Configurations."

18. S. D. Pugh, J. Dietz, A. P. Brief, and J. W. Wiley, "Looking Inside and Out: The Impact of Employee and Community Demographic Composition on Organizational Diversity Climate," *Journal of Applied Psychology* 93, no. 6 (2008), pp. 1422–1428; K. H. Ehrhart, L. A. Witt, B. Schneider, and S. J. Perry, "Service Employees Give as They Get: Internal Service as a Moderator of the Service Climate-Service Outcomes Link," *Journal of Applied Psychology* 96, no. 2 (2011), pp. 423–431; and A. Simha and J. B. Cullen, "Ethical Climates and Their Effects on Organizational Outcomes: Implications from the Past and Prophecies for the Future," *Academy of Management Perspectives* (November 2011), pp. 20–34.

19. J. C. Wallace, P. D. Johnson, K. Mathe, and J. Paul, "Structural and Psychological Empowerment Climates, Performance, and the Moderating Role of Shared Felt Accountability: A Managerial Perspective," *Journal of Applied Psychology* 96, no. 3 (2011), pp. 840–850.

20. J. M. Beus, S. C. Payne, M. E. Bergman, and W. Arthur, "Safety Climate and Injuries: An Examination of Theoretical and Empirical Relationships," *Journal of Applied Psychology* 95, no. 4 (2010), pp. 713–727.

21. J. Bandler and D. Burke, "How HP Lost Its Way," *Fortune* (May 21, 2012), pp. 147–164.

22. R. L. Jepperson, "Institutions, Institutional Effects, and Institutionalism," in W. W. Powell and P. J. DiMaggio (eds.), *The New Institutionalism in Organizational Analysis* (Chicago: University of Chicago Press, 1991), pp. 143–163; G. F. Lanzara and G. Patriotta, "The Institutionalization of Knowledge in an Automotive Factory: Templates, Inscriptions, and the Problems of Durability," *Organization Studies* 28, no. 5 (2007), pp. 635–660; and T. B. Lawrence, M. K. Mauws, B. Dyck, and R. F. Kleysen, "The Politics of Organizational Learning: Integrating Power into the 4I Framework," *Academy of Management Review* (January 2005), pp. 180–191.

23. J. B. Sorensen, "The Strength of Corporate Culture and the Reliability of Firm Performance," *Administrative Science Quarterly* (March 2002), pp. 70–91.

24. See T. Cox Jr., *Cultural Diversity in Organizations: Theory, Research & Practice* (San Francisco: Berrett-Koehler, 1993), pp. 162–170; L. Grensing-Pophal, "Hiring to Fit Your Corporate Culture," *HRMagazine* (August 1999), pp. 50–54; and D. L. Stone, E. F. Stone-Romero, and K. M. Lukaszewski, "The Impact of Cultural Values on the Acceptance and Effectiveness of Human Resource Management Policies and Practices," *Human Resource Management Review* 17, no. 2 (2007), pp. 152–165.

25. S. Cartwright and C. L. Cooper, "The Role of Culture Compatibility in Successful Organizational Marriages," *Academy of Management Executive* (May 1993), pp. 57–70; R. A. Weber and C. F. Camerer, "Cultural Conflict and Merger Failure: An Experimental Approach," *Management Science* (April 2003), pp. 400–412; and I. H. Gleibs, A. Mummendey, and P. Noack, "Predictors of Change in Postmerger Identification During a Merger Process: A Longitudinal Study," *Journal of Personality and Social Psychology* 95, no. 5 (2008), pp. 1095–1112.

26. P. Gumbel, "Return of the Urge to Merge," *Time Europe Magazine* (July 13, 2003), www.time.com/time/europe/magazine/article/0,13005,901030721-464418,00.html.

27. E. H. Schein, "The Role of the Founder in Creating Organizational Culture," *Organizational Dynamics* (Summer 1983), pp. 13–28; and Y. L. Zhao, O. H. Erekson, T. Wang, and M. Song, "Pioneering Advantages and Entrepreneurs' First-Mover Decisions: An Empirical Investigation for the United States and China," *Journal of Product Innovation Management* (December 2012), pp. 190–210.

28. E. H. Schein, "Leadership and Organizational Culture," in F. Hesselbein, M. Goldsmith, and R. Beckhard (eds.), *The Leader of the Future* (San Francisco: Jossey-Bass, 1996), pp. 61–62.

29. See, for example, J. R. Harrison and G. R. Carroll, "Keeping the Faith: A Model of Cultural Transmission in Formal Organizations," *Administrative Science Quarterly* (December 1991), pp. 552–582; and D. E. Bowen and C. Ostroff, "The 'Strength' of the HRM System, Organizational Climate Formation, and Firm Performance," *Academy of Management Review* 29 (2004), pp. 203–221.

30. B. Schneider, H. W. Goldstein, and D. B. Smith, "The ASA Framework: An Update," *Personnel Psychology* (Winter 1995), pp. 747–773; D. M. Cable and T. A. Judge, "Interviewers' Perceptions of Person-Organization Fit and Organizational Selection Decisions," *Journal of Applied Psychology* (August 1997), pp. 546–561; M. L. Verquer, T. A. Beehr, and S. H. Wagner, "A Meta-Analysis of Relations Between Person-Organization Fit and Work Attitudes," *Journal of Vocational Behavior* (December 2003), pp. 473–489; and W. Li, Y. Wang, P. Taylor, K. Shi, and D. He, "The Influence of Organizational Culture on Work-Related Personality Requirement Ratings: A Multilevel Analysis," *International Journal of Selection and Assessment* 16, no. 4 (2008), pp. 366–384.

31. "100 Best Companies to Work For," *Fortune* (2013), http://money.cnn.com/magazines/fortune/best-companies/2013/snapshots/5.html, accessed June 28, 2013.

32. D. C. Hambrick and P. A. Mason, "Upper Echelons: The Organization as a Reflection of Its Top Managers," *Academy of Management Review* (April 1984), pp. 193–206; M. A. Carpenter, M. A. Geletkanycz, and W. G. Sanders, "Upper Echelons Research Revisited: Antecedents, Elements, and Consequences of Top Management Team Composition," *Journal of Management* 30, no. 6 (2004), pp. 749–778, and H. Wang, A. S. Tsui, and K. R. Xin, "CEO Leadership Behaviors, Organizational Performance, and Employees' Attitudes," *The Leadership Quarterly* 22, no. 1 (2011), pp. 92–105.

33. "100 Best Companies to Work For," *Fortune* (2013), http://money.cnn.com/magazines/fortune/best-companies/2013/snapshots/5.html, accessed June 28, 2013.

34. See, for instance, J. P. Wanous, *Organizational Entry*, 2nd ed. (New York: Addison-Wesley, 1992); D. M. Cable and C. K. Parsons, "Socialization Tactics and Person-Organization Fit," *Personnel Psychology* (Spring 2001), pp. 1–23; and T. N. Bauer, T. Bodner, B. Erdogan, D. M. Truxillo, and J. S. Tucker, "Newcomer Adjustment During Organizational Socialization: A Meta-Analytic Review of Antecedents, Outcomes, and Methods," *Journal of Applied Psychology* 92, no. 3 (2007), pp. 707–721.

35. G. Kranz, "Training That Starts Before the Job Begins," *Workforce Management Online* (July 2009), www.workforce.com.

36. R. E. Silverman, "Companies Try to Make the First Day for New Hires More Fun," *The Wall Street Journal* (May 28, 2013), http://online.wsj.com/article/SB10001424127887323 3361045785016314755934850.html.

37. D. C. Feldman, "The Multiple Socialization of Organization Members," *Academy of Management Review* (April 1981), p. 310.

38. C. J. Collins, "The Interactive Effects of Recruitment Practices and Product Awareness on Job Seekers' Employer Knowledge and Application Behaviors," *Journal of Applied Psychology* 92, no. 1 (2007), pp. 180–190.

39. J. D. Kammeyer-Mueller and C. R. Wanberg, "Unwrapping the Organizational Entry Process: Disentangling Multiple Antecedents and Their Pathways to Adjustment," *Journal of Applied Psychology* 88 (2003), pp. 779–794; E. W. Morrison, "Longitudinal Study of the Effects of Information Seeking on Newcomer Socialization," *Journal of Applied Psychology* 78 (2003), pp. 173–183; and M. Wangm Y. Zhan, E. McCune, and D. Truxillo, "Understanding Newcomers' Adaptability and Work-Related Outcomes: Testing the Mediating Roles of Perceived P-E Fit Variables," *Personnel Psychology* 64, no. 1 (2011), pp. 163–189.

40. E. W. Morrison, "Newcomers' Relationships: The Role of Social Network Ties During Socialization," *Academy of Management Journal* 45 (2002), pp. 1149–1160.

41. T. N. Bauer, T. Bodner, B. Erdogan, D. M. Truxillo, and J. S. Tucker, "Newcomer Adjustment During Organizational Socialization: A Meta-Analytic Review of Antecedents, Outcomes, and Methods," *Journal of Applied Psychology* 92, no. 3 (2007), pp. 707–721.

42. W. R. Boswell, A. J. Shipp, S. C., Payne, and S. S. Culbertson, "Changes in Newcomer Job Satisfaction Over Time: Examining the Pattern of Honeymoons and Hangovers," *Journal of Applied Psychology* 94, no. 4 (2009), pp. 844–858.

43. C Vandenberghe, A. Panaccio, K. Bentein, K. Mignonac, and P. Roussel, "Assessing Longitudinal Change of and Dynamic Relationships Among Role Stressors, Job Attitudes, Turnover Intention, and Well-Being in Neophyte Newcomers," *Journal of Organizational Behavior* 32, no. 4 (2011), pp. 652–671.

44. E. Ransdell, "The Nike Story? Just Tell It!" *Fast Company* (January–February 2000), pp. 44–46; and A. Muccino, "Exclusive Interview with Chuck Eichten," *Liquid Brand Summit Blog,* (February 4, 2011), http://blog.liquidbrandsummit.com/.

45. D. M. Boje, "The Storytelling Organization: A Study of Story Performance in an Office-Supply Firm," *Administrative Science Quarterly* (March 1991), pp. 106–126; and M. Ricketts and J. G. Seiling, "Language, Metaphors, and Stories: Catalysts for Meaning Making in Organizations," *Organization Development Journal* (Winter 2003), pp. 33–43l.

46. A. J. Shipp and K. J. Jansen, "Reinterpreting Time in Fit Theory: Crafting and Recrafting Narratives of Fit in Medias Res," *Academy of Management Review* 36, no. 1 (2011), pp. 76–101.

47. See G. Islam and M. J. Zyphur, "Rituals in Organizations: A Review and Expansion of Current Theory," *Group and Organization Management* 34, no. 1 (2009), pp. 114–139.

48. M. Moskowitz and F. Levering, "The 100 Best Companies to Work For," *Fortune* (February 6, 2012), p. 120.

49. M. G. Pratt and A. Rafaeli "Artifacts and Organizations: Understanding Our Objective Reality," in A. Rafaeli and M. G. Pratt, *Artifacts and Organizations: Beyond Mere Symbolism* (Mahwah, NJ: Lawrence Erlbaum, 2006), pp. 279–288.

50. B. Gruley, "Relaxed Fit," *Bloomberg Businessweek* (September 17–23, 2012), pp. 98–99.

51. See B. Victor and J. B. Cullen, "The Organizational Bases of Ethical Work Climates," *Administrative Science Quarterly* (March 1988), pp. 101–125; R. L. Dufresne, "An Action Learning Perspective on Effective Implementation of Academic Honor Codes," *Group & Organization Management* (April 2004), pp. 201–218; and A. Ardichvilli, J. A. Mitchell, and D. Jondle, "Characteristics of Ethical Business Cultures," *Journal of Business Ethics* 85, no. 4 (2009), pp. 445–451.

52. J. P. Mulki, J. F. Jaramillo, and W. B. Locander, "Critical Role of Leadership on Ethical Climate and Salesperson Behaviors," *Journal of Business Ethics* 86, no. 2 (2009), pp. 125–141; M. Schminke, M. L. Ambrose, and D. O. Neubaum, "The Effect of Leader Moral Development on Ethical Climate and Employee Attitudes," *Organizational Behavior and Human Decision Processes* 97, no. 2 (2005), pp. 135–151; and M. E. Brown, L. K. Treviño, and D. A. Harrison, "Ethical Leadership: A Social Learning Perspective for Construct Development and Testing," *Organizational Behavior and Human Decision Processes* 97, no. 2 (2005), pp. 117–134.

53. D. M. Mayer, M. Kuenzi, R. Greenbaum, M. Bardes, and S. Salvador, "How Low Does Ethical Leadership Flow? Test of a Trickle-Down Model," *Organizational Behavior and Human Decision Processes* 108, no. 1 (2009), pp. 1–13.

54. B. Sweeney, D. Arnold, and B. Pierce, "The Impact of Perceived Ethical Culture of the Firm and Demographic Variables on Auditors' Ethical Evaluation and Intention to Act Decisions," *Journal of Business Ethics* 93, no. 4 (2010), pp. 531–551.

55. M. L. Gruys, S. M. Stewart, J. Goodstein, M. N. Bing, and A. C. Wicks, "Values Enactment in Organizations: A Multi-Level Examination," *Journal of Management* 34, no. 4 (2008), pp. 806–843.

56. D. L. Nelson and C. L. Cooper (eds.), *Positive Organizational Behavior* (London: Sage, 2007); K. S. Cameron, J. E. Dutton, and R. E. Quinn (eds.), *Positive Organizational Scholarship: Foundations of a New Discipline* (San Francisco: Berrett-Koehler, 2003); and F. Luthans and C. M. Youssef, "Emerging Positive Organizational Behavior," *Journal of Management* (June 2007), pp. 321–349.

57. J. Robison, "Great Leadership Under Fire," *Gallup Leadership Journal* (March 8, 2007), pp. 1–3.

58. R. Wagner and J. K. Harter, *12: The Elements of Great Managing* (New York: Gallup Press, 2006).

59. M. Mihelich, "2012 Optimas Award Winners: Safelite Auto-Glass," *Workforce Management* (November 2012), p. 27.

60. R. Wagner and J. K. Harter, "Performance Reviews Without the Anxiety," *Gallup Leadership Journal* (July 12, 2007), pp. 1–4; and Wagner and Harter, *12: The Elements of Great Managing*.

61. S. Fineman, "On Being Positive: Concerns and Counterpoints," *Academy of Management Review* 31, no. 2 (2006), pp. 270–291.

62. J. Nicas, "American, US Airways Face Challenges in Integration," *The Wall Street Journal* (February 14, 2013), http://online.wsj.com/article/SB100014241278873244320045783 04192162931544.html.

63. D. J. McCarthy and S. M. Puffer, "Interpreting the Ethicality of Corporate Governance Decisions in Russia: Utilizing Integrative Social Contracts Theory to Evaluate the Relevance of Agency Theory Norms," *Academy of Management Review* 33, no. 1 (2008), pp. 11–31.

64. P. Dvorak, "A Firm's Culture Can Get Lost in Translation," *The Wall Street Journal* (April 3, 2006), pp. B1, B3; K. Kranhold, "The Immelt Era, Five Years Old, Transforms GE," *The Wall Street Journal* (September 11, 2006), pp. B1, B3; and S. McCartney, "Teaching Americans How to Behave Abroad," *The Wall Street Journal* (April 11, 2006), pp. D1, D4.

CHAPTER 17

1. J. Muller, "Why Ford Should Worry," *Forbes* (February 13, 2012), pp. 34–40.

2. P. G. Audia and S. Brion, "Reluctant to Change: Self-Enhancing Responses to Diverging Performance Measures," *Organizational Behavior and Human Decision Processes* 102 (2007), pp. 255–269.

3. M. Fugate, A. J. Kinicki, and G. E. Prussia, "Employee Coping with Organizational Change: An Examination of Alternative Theoretical Perspectives and Models," *Personnel Psychology* 61, no. 1 (2008), pp. 1–36.

4. J. D. Ford, L. W. Ford, and A. D'Amelio, "Resistance to Change: The Rest of the Story," *Academy of Management Review* 33, no. 2 (2008), pp. 362–377.

5. M. T. Hannan, L. Pólos, and G. R. Carroll, "The Fog of Change: Opacity and Asperity in Organizations," *Administrative Science Quarterly* (September 2003), pp. 399–432.

6. J. P. Kotter and L. A. Schlesinger, "Choosing Strategies for Change," *Harvard Business Review* (March–April 1979), pp. 106–114; and R. K. Smollan, "The Multi-Dimensional Nature of Resistance to Change," *Journal of Management & Organization* (November 2011), pp. 828–849.

7. A. E. Rafferty and S. L. D. Restubog, "The Impact of Change Process and Context on Change Reactions and Turnover during a Merger," *Journal of Management* 36, no. 5 (2010), pp. 1309–1338.

8. J. E. Dutton, S. J. Ashford, R. M. O'Neill, and K. A. Lawrence, "Moves That Matter: Issue Selling and Organizational Change," *Academy of Management Journal* (August 2001), pp. 716–736.

9. P. C. Fiss and E. J. Zajac, "The Symbolic Management of Strategic Change: Sensegiving via Framing and Decoupling," *Academy of Management Journal* 49, no. 6 (2006), pp. 1173–1193.

10. Q. N. Huy, "Emotional Balancing of Organizational Continuity and Radical Change: The Contribution of Middle Managers," *Administrative Science Quarterly* (March 2002), pp. 31–69; D. M. Herold, D. B. Fedor, and S. D. Caldwell, "Beyond Change Management: A Multilevel Investigation of Contextual and Personal Influences on Employees' Commitment to Change," *Journal of Applied Psychology* 92, no. 4 (2007), pp. 942–951; and G. B. Cunningham, "The Relationships among Commitment to Change, Coping with Change, and Turnover Intentions," *European Journal of Work and Organizational Psychology* 15, no. 1 (2006), pp. 29–45.

11. R. Peccei, A. Giangreco, and A. Sebastiano, "The Role of Organizational Commitment in the Analysis of Resistance to Change: Co-predictor and Moderator Effects," *Personnel Review* 40, no. 2 (2011), pp. 185–204.

12. J. P. Kotter, "Leading Change: Why Transformational Efforts Fail," *Harvard Business Review* 85 (January 2007), pp. 96–103.

13. K. van Dam, S. Oreg, and B. Schyns, "Daily Work Contexts and Resistance to Organisational Change: The Role of Leader-Member Exchange, Development Climate, and Change Process Characteristics," *Applied Psychology: An International Review* 57, no. 2 (2008), pp. 313–334.

14. S. Oreg and N. Sverdlik, "Ambivalence toward Imposed Change: The Conflict between Dispositional Resistance to Change and the Orientation toward the Change Agent," *Journal of Applied Psychology* 96, no. 2 (2011), pp. 337–349.

15. D. B. Fedor, S. Caldwell, and D. M. Herold, "The Effects of Organizational Changes on Employee Commitment: A Multi-level Investigation," *Personnel Psychology* 59 (2006), pp. 1–29; and R. D. Foster, "Resistance, Justice, and Commitment to Change," *Human Resource Development Quarterly* 21, no. 1 (2010), pp. 3–39.

16. S. Oreg, "Personality, Context, and Resistance to Organizational Change," *European Journal of Work and Organizational Psychology* 15, no. 1 (2006), pp. 73–101.

17. S. M. Elias, "Employee Commitment in Times of Change: Assessing the Importance of Attitudes Toward Organizational Change," *Journal of Management* 35, no. 1 (2009), pp. 37–55.

18. J. W. B. Lang and P. D. Bliese, "General Mental Ability and Two Types of Adaptation to Unforeseen Change: Applying Discontinuous Growth Models to the Task-Change Paradigm," *Journal of Applied Psychology* 94, no. 2 (2009), pp. 411–428.

19. C. O. L. H. Porter, J. W. Webb, and C. I. Gogus, "When Goal Orientations Collide: Effects of Learning and Performance Orientation on Team Adaptability in Response to Workload Imbalance," *Journal of Applied Psychology* 95, no. 5 (2010), pp. 935–943.

20. K. Lewin, *Field Theory in Social Science* (New York: Harper & Row, 1951).

21. P. G. Audia, E. A. Locke, and K. G. Smith, "The Paradox of Success: An Archival and a Laboratory Study of Strategic Persistence Following Radical Environmental Change," *Academy of Management Journal* (October 2000), pp. 837–853; and P. G. Audia and S. Brion, "Reluctant to Change: Self-Enhancing Responses to Diverging Performance Measures," *Organizational Behavior and Human Decision Processes* 102, no. 2 (2007), pp. 255–269.

22. J. B. Sorensen, "The Strength of Corporate Culture and the Reliability of Firm Performance," *Administrative Science Quarterly* (March 2002), pp. 70–91.

23. J. Amis, T. Slack, and C. R. Hinings, "The Pace, Sequence, and Linearity of Radical Change," *Academy of Management Journal* (February 2004), pp. 15–39; and E. Autio, H. J. Sapienza, and J. G. Almeida, "Effects of Age at Entry, Knowledge Intensity, and Imitability on International Growth," *Academy of Management Journal* (October 2000), pp. 909–924.

24. J. P. Kotter, "Leading Changes: Why Transformation Efforts Fail," *Harvard Business Review* (March–April 1995), pp. 59–67; and J. P. Kotter, *Leading Change* (Harvard Business School Press, 1996).

25. For a sampling of various OD definitions, see H. K. Sinangil and F. Avallone, "Organizational Development and Change," in N. Anderson, D. S. Ones, H. K. Sinangil, and C. Viswesvaran (eds.), *Handbook of Industrial, Work and Organizational Psychology*, vol. 2 (Thousand Oaks, CA: Sage, 2001), pp. 332–335; and R. J. Marshak and D. Grant, "Organizational Discourse and New Organization Development Practices," *British Journal of Management* 19, no. 1 (2008), pp. S7–S19.

26. See, for instance, R. Lines, "Influence of Participation in Strategic Change: Resistance, Organizational Commitment and Change Goal Achievement," *Journal of Change Management* (September 2004), pp. 193–215.

27. J. E. Edwards and M. D. Thomas, "The Organizational Survey Process: General Steps and Practical Considerations," in P. Rosenfeld, J. E. Edwards, and M. D. Thomas (eds.), *Improving Organizational Surveys: New Directions, Methods, and Applications* (Newbury Park, CA: Sage, 1993), pp. 3–28; and T. Fauth, K. Hattrub, K. Mueller, and B. Roberts, "Nonresponse in Employee Attitude Surveys: A Group-Level Analysis," *Journal of Business and Psychology* (March 2013), pp. 1–16.

28. F. J. Lambrechts, R. Bouwen, S. Grieten, J. P. Huybrechts, and E. H. Schein, "Learning to Help through Humble Inquiry and Implications for Management Research, Practice, and Education: An Interview with Edgar H. Schein," *Academy of Management Learning & Education* (March 2011), pp. 131–148;

E. H. Schein, *Process Consultation: Its Role in Organizational Development*, 2nd ed. (Reading, MA: Addison-Wesley, 1988), p. 9; and E. H. Schein, *Process Consultation Revisited: Building Helpful Relationships* (Reading, MA: Addison-Wesley, 1999).

29. Schein, *Process Consultation*.

30. W. W. G. Dyer, W. G. Dyer, and J. H. Dyer, *Team Building: Proven Strategies for Improving Team Performance* (Hoboken, NJ: Jossey-Bass, 2007).

31. U. Wagner, L. Tropp, G. Finchilescu, and C. Tredoux (eds.), *Improving Intergroup Relations* (New York: Wiley-Blackwell, 2008).

32. See, for example, R. Fry, F. Barrett, J. Seiling, and D. Whitney (eds.), *Appreciative Inquiry & Organizational Transformation: Reports from the Field* (Westport, CT: Quorum, 2002); J. K. Barge and C. Oliver, "Working with Appreciation in Managerial Practice," *Academy of Management Review* (January 2003), pp. 124–142; and D. van der Haar and D. M. Hosking, "Evaluating Appreciative Inquiry: A Relational Constructionist Perspective," *Human Relations* (August 2004), pp. 1017–1036.

33. A. Harrington, "Who's Afraid of a New Product?" *Fortune* (November 10, 2003), pp. 189–192; and C. C. Manz, F. Shipper, and G. L. Stewart, "Everyone a Team Leader: Shared Influence at W. L. Gore and Associates," *Organizational Dynamics* 38, no. 3 (2009), pp. 239–244.

34. See, for instance, R. M. Kanter, "When a Thousand Flowers Bloom: Structural, Collective and Social Conditions for Innovation in Organizations," in B. M. Staw and L. L. Cummings (eds.), *Research in Organizational Behavior*, vol. 10 (Greenwich, CT: JAI Press, 1988), pp. 169–211.

35. L. Widdicombe, "The End of Food," *The New Yorker* (May 12, 2014), http://www.newyorker.com/reporting/2014/05/12/140512fa_fact_widdicombe?currentPage=all.

36. F. Damanpour, "Organizational Innovation: A Meta-Analysis of Effects of Determinants and Moderators," *Academy of Management Journal* (September 1991), p. 557; and H. W. Volberda, F. A. J. Van den Bosch, and C. V. Heij, "Management Innovation: Management as Fertile Ground for Innovation," *European Management Review* (Spring 2013), pp. 1–15.

37. Damanpour, "Organizational Innovation," pp. 555–590; and G. Westerman, F. W. McFarlan, and M. Iansiti, "Organization Design and Effectiveness over the Innovation Life Cycle," *Organization Science* 17, no. 2 (2006), pp. 230–238.

38. See P. R. Monge, M. D. Cozzens, and N. S. Contractor, "Communication and Motivational Predictors of the Dynamics of Organizational Innovation," *Organization Science* (May 1992), pp. 250–274; P. Schepers and P. T. van den Berg, "Social Factors of Work-Environment Creativity," *Journal of Business and Psychology* 21, no. 3 (2007), pp. 407–428.

39. D. L. Day, "Raising Radicals: Different Processes for Championing Innovative Corporate Ventures," *Organization Science* (May 1994), pp. 148–172; and M. E. Mullins, S. W. J. Kozlowski, N. Schmitt, and A. W. Howell, "The Role of the Idea Champion in Innovation: The Case of the Internet in the Mid-1990s," *Computers in Human Behavior* 24, no. 2 (2008), pp. 451–467.

40. J. M. Howell and C. A. Higgins, "Champions of Change: Identifying, Understanding, and Supporting Champions of Technological Innovations," *Organizational Dynamics* 19, (1990), pp. 40–55; and S. C. Parker, "Intrapreneurship or

Entrepreneurship?" *Journal of Business Venturing* (January 2011), pp. 19–34.

41. M. Cerne, M. Jaklic, and M. Skerlavaj, "Decoupling Management and Technological Innovations: Resolving the Individualism-Collectivism Controversy," *Journal of International Management* (June 2013), pp. 103–117; and S. Shane, S. Venkataraman, and I. MacMillan, "Cultural Differences in Innovation Championing Strategies," *Journal of Management* 21, no. 5 (1995), pp. 931–952.

42. See, for instance, S. Armour, "Rising Job Stress Could Affect Bottom Line," *USA Today* (July 29, 2003), p. 1B; and J. Schramm, "Work/Life on Hold," *HR Magazine* 53 (October 2008), p. 120.

43. B. Mirza, "Workplace Stress Hits Three-Year High," *HR Magazine* (April 2012), p. 15.

44. Adapted from R. S. Schuler, "Definition and Conceptualization of Stress in Organizations," *Organizational Behavior and Human Performance* (April 1980), p. 189. For an updated review of definitions, see C. L. Cooper, P. J. Dewe, and M. P. O'Driscoll, *Organizational Stress: A Review and Critique of Theory, Research, and Applications* (Thousand Oaks, CA: Sage, 2002).

45. See, for instance, M. A. Cavanaugh, W. R. Boswell, M. V. Roehling, and J. W. Boudreau, "An Empirical Examination of Self-Reported Work Stress among U.S. Managers," *Journal of Applied Psychology* (February 2000), pp. 65–74.

46. S. Shellenbarger, "When Stress Is Good for You," *The Wall Street Journal* (January 24, 2012), pp. D1, D5.

47. Ibid.

48. N. P. Podsakoff, J. A. LePine, and M. A. LePine, "Differential Challenge-Hindrance Stressor Relationships with Job Attitudes, Turnover Intentions, Turnover, and Withdrawal Behavior: A Meta-Analysis," *Journal of Applied Psychology* 92, no. 2 (2007), pp. 438–454; and J. A. LePine, M. A. LePine, and C. L. Jackson, "Challenge and Hindrance Stress: Relationships with Exhaustion, Motivation to Learn, and Learning Performance," *Journal of Applied Psychology* (October 2004), pp. 883–891.

49. L. W. Hunter and S. M. B. Thatcher, "Feeling the Heat: Effects of Stress, Commitment, and Job Experience on Job Performance," *Academy of Management Journal* 50, no. 4 (2007), pp. 953–968.

50. J. C. Wallace, B. D. Edwards, T. Arnold, M. L. Frazier, and D. M. Finch, "Work Stressors, Role-Based Performance, and the Moderating Influence of Organizational Support," *Journal of Applied Psychology* 94, no. 1 (2009), pp. 254–262.

51. N. W. Van Yperen and O. Janssen, "Fatigued and Dissatisfied or Fatigued but Satisfied? Goal Orientations and Responses to High Job Demands," *Academy of Management Journal* (December 2002), pp. 1161–1171; and N. W. Van Yperen and M. Hagedoorn, "Do High Job Demands Increase Intrinsic Motivation or Fatigue or Both? The Role of Job Control and Job Social Support," *Academy of Management Journal* (June 2003), pp. 339–348.

52. J. de Jonge and C. Dormann, "Stressors, Resources, and Strain at Work: A Longitudinal Test of the Triple-Match Principle," *Journal of Applied Psychology* 91, no. 5 (2006), pp. 1359–1374.

53. J. Schaubroeck, J. R. Jones, and J. L. Xie, "Individual Differences in Utilizing Control to Cope with Job Demands: Effects

on Susceptibility to Infectious Disease," *Journal of Applied Psychology* (April 2001), pp. 265–278.

54. M. Kivimäki, J. Head, J. E. Ferrie, E. Brunner, M. G. Marmot, J. Vahtera, and M. J. Shipley, "Why Is Evidence on Job Strain and Coronary Heart Disease Mixed? An Illustration of Measurement Challenges in the Whitehall II Study," *Psychosomatic Medicine* 68, no. 3 (2006), pp. 398–401.

55. M. Borritz, K. B. Christensen, U. Bültmann, R. Rugulies, T. Lund, I Andersen, E. Villadsen, F. Didreichsen, and T. S. Krisensen, "Impact on Burnout and Psychosocial Work Characteristics on Future Long-Term Sickness Absence, Prospective Results of the Danish PUMA Study Among Human Service Workers," *Journal of Occupational and Environmental Medicine* 52, no. 10 (2010), pp. 964–970.

56. R. Ilies, N. Dimotakis, and I. E. DePater, "Psychological and Physiological Reactions to High Workloads: Implications for Well-Being," *Personnel Psychology* 63, no. 2 (2010), pp. 407–463.

57. D. Örtqvist and J. Wincent, "Prominent Consequences of Role Stress: A Meta-Analytic Review," *International Journal of Stress Management*, 13, no. 4 (2006), pp. 399–422.

58. J. R. Hackman and G. R. Oldham, "Development of the Job Diagnostic Survey," *Journal of Applied Psychology* (April 1975), pp. 159–170; J. J. Hakanen, A. B. Bakker, and M. Jokisaari, "A 35-Year Follow-Up Study on Burnout among Finnish Employees," *Journal of Occupational Health Psychology* 16, no. 3 (2011), pp. 345 360; Crawford, LePine, and Rich, "Linking Job Demands and Resources to Employee Engagement and Burnout; and G. A. Chung-Yan, "The Nonlinear Effects of Job Complexity and Autonomy on Job Satisfaction, Turnover, and Psychological Well-Being," *Journal of Occupational Health Psychology* 15, no. 3 (2010), pp. 237–251.

59. L. L. Meier, N. K. Semmer, A. Elfering, and N. Jacobshagen, "The Double Meaning of Control: Three-Way Interactions between Internal Resources, Job Control, and Stressors at Work," *Journal of Occupational Health Psychology* 13, no. 3 (2008), pp. 244–258.

60. E. M. de Croon, J. K. Sluiter, R. W. B. Blonk, J. P. J. Broersen, and M. H. W. Frings-Dresen, "Stressful Work, Psychological Job Strain, and Turnover: A 2-Year Prospective Cohort Study of Truck Drivers," *Journal of Applied Psychology* (June 2004), pp. 442–454; R. Cropanzano, D. E. Rupp, and Z. S. Byrne, "The Relationship of Emotional Exhaustion to Work Attitudes, Job Performance, and Organizational Citizenship Behaviors," *Journal of Applied Psychology* (February 2003), pp. 160–169; and S. Diestel and K. Schmidt, "Costs of Simultaneous Coping with Emotional Dissonance and Self-Control Demands at Work: Results from Two German Samples," *Journal of Applied Psychology* 96, no. 3 (2011), pp. 643–653.

61. The following discussion has been influenced J. M. Ivancevich, M. T. Matteson, S. M. Freedman, and J. S. Phillips, "Worksite Stress Management Interventions," *American Psychologist* (February 1990), pp. 252–261; R. Schwarzer, "Manage Stress at Work through Preventive and Proactive Coping," in E. A. Locke (ed.), *Handbook of Principles of Organizational Behavior* (Malden, MA: Blackwell, 2004), pp. 342–355; and K. M. Richardson and H. R. Rothstein, "Effects of Occupational Stress Management Intervention Programs: A Meta-Analysis," *Journal of Occupational Health Psychology* 13, no. 1 (2008), pp. 69–93.

62. T. H. Macan, "Time Management: Test of a Process Model," *Journal of Applied Psychology* (June 1994), pp. 381–391; and B. J. C. Claessens, W. Van Eerde, C. G. Rutte, and R. A. Roe, "Planning Behavior and Perceived Control of Time at Work," *Journal of Organizational Behavior* (December 2004), pp. 937–950.

63. See, for example, G. Lawrence-Ell, *The Invisible Clock: A Practical Revolution in Finding Time for Everyone and Everything* (Seaside Park, NJ: Kingsland Hall, 2002); and B. Tracy, *Time Power* (New York: AMACOM, 2004).

64. R. W. Renn, D. G. Allen, and T. M. Huning, "Empirical Examination of Individual-Level Personality-Based Theory of Self-Management Failure," *Journal of Organizational Behavior* 32, no. 1 (2011), pp. 25–43; and P. Gröpel and P. Steel, "A Mega-Trial Investigation of Goal Setting, Interest Enhancement, and Energy on Procrastination," *Personality and Individual Differences* 45, no. 5 (2008), pp. 406–411.

65. P. Salmon, "Effects of Physical Exercise on Anxiety, Depression, and Sensitivity to Stress: A Unifying Theory," *Clinical Psychology Review* 21, no. 1 (2001), pp. 33–61.

66. K. M. Richardson and H. R. Rothstein, "Effects of Occupational Stress Management Intervention Programs: A Meta-Analysis," *Journal of Occupational Health Psychology* 13, no. 1 (2008), pp. 69–93.

67. V. C. Hahn, C. Binnewies, S. Sonnentag, and E. J. Mojza, "Learning How to Recover from Job Stress: Effects of a Recovery Training Program on Recovery, Recovery-Related Self-Efficacy, and Well-Being," *Journal of Occupational Health Psychology* 16, no. 2 (2011), pp. 202–216; and C. Binnewies, S. Sonnentag, and E. J. Mojza, "Recovery during the Weekend and Fluctuations in Weekly Job Performance: A Week-Level Study Examining Intra-Individual Relationships," *Journal of Occupational and Organizational Psychology* 83, no. 2 (2010), pp. 419–441.

68. E. R. Greenglass and L. Fiksenbaum, "Proactive Coping, Positive Affect, and Well-Being: Testing for Mediation Using Path Analysis," *European Psychologist* 14, no. 1 (2009), pp. 29–39; and P. Miquelon and R. J. Vallerand, "Goal Motives, Well-Being, and Physical Health: Happiness and Self-Realization as Psychological Resources under Challenge," *Motivation and Emotion* 30, no. 4 (2006), pp. 259–272.

69. M. M. Butts, R. J. Vandenberg, D. M. DeJoy, B. S. Schaffer, and M. G. Wilson, "Individual Reactions to High Involvement Work Processes: Investigating the Role of Empowerment and Perceived Organizational Support," *Journal of Occupational Health Psychology* 14, no. 2 (2009), pp. 122–136.

70. L. Blue, "Making Good Health Easy," *Time* (November 12, 2009), www.time.com; and M. Andrews, "America's Best Health Plans," *US News and World Report* (November 5, 2007), pp. 54–60.

71. K. M. Richardson and H. R. Rothstein, "Effects of Occupational Stress Management Intervention Programs: A Meta-Analysis," *Journal of Occupational Health Psychology* 13, no. 1 (2008), pp. 69–93.

GLOSSARY

ability An individual's capacity to perform the various tasks in a job, 49

accommodating The willingness of one party in a conflict to place the opponent's interests above his or her own, 259

adjourning stage The final stage in group development for temporary groups, characterized by concern with wrapping up activities rather than task performance, 198

affect A broad range of feelings that people experience, 71

affect intensity Experiencing the same emotions with different intensities; affectively intense people experience both positive and negative emotions more deeply, 75

affective component The emotional or feeling segment of an attitude, 57

affective events theory (AET) A model that demonstrates employees react emotionally to things at work which influences their job performance and satisfaction, 79

agreeableness A personality dimension that describes someone who is good natured, cooperative, and trusting, 91

anchoring bias A tendency to fixate on initial information, from which one then fails to adequately adjust for subsequent information, 118

anthropology The study of societies for the purpose of learning about human beings and their activities, 28

appreciative inquiry (AI) An approach that seeks to identify the unique qualities and special strengths of an organization, which can then be built on to improve performance, 314

approach-avoidance framework Personality framework that casts personality traits as motivations, 95

attitudes Evaluative statements, either favorable or unfavorable, concerning objects, people, or events, 57

attribution theory An attempt to determine whether an individual's behavior is internally or externally caused, 111

attribution theory of leadership A leadership theory that says that leadership is merely an attribution that people make about other individuals, 230

authentic leaders Leaders who know who they are, know what they believe in and value, and act on those values and beliefs openly and candidly; their followers would consider them to be ethical people, 226

automatic processing A relatively superficial consideration of evidence and information making use of heuristics, 173

authority The rights inherent in a managerial position to give orders and to expect the orders to be obeyed, 274

autonomy The degree to which a job provides substantial freedom and discretion to the individual in scheduling the work and in determining the procedures to be used in carrying it out, 148

availability bias The tendency for people to base their judgments on information that is readily available to them, 119

avoiding The desire to withdraw from or suppress a conflict, 259

BATNA The best alternative to a negotiated agreement; the least the individual should accept, 266

behavioral component An intention to behave in a certain way toward someone or something, 57

behavioral ethics An area of study that analyzes how people behave in ethical dilemmas, 122

behavioral theories of leadership Theories proposing that specific behaviors differentiate leaders from nonleaders, 215

Big Five Model A personality assessment model that taps five basic dimensions, 90

biographical characteristics Personal characteristics—such as age, gender, race, and length of tenure—that are objective and easily obtained from personnel records. These characteristics are representative of surface-level diversity, 42

bonus A way to reward employees for recent performance rather than historical performance, 159

boundaryless organization An organization that seeks to eliminate the chain of command, have limitless spans of control, and replace departments with empowered teams, 281

bounded rationality A process of making decisions by constructing simplified models that extract the essential features from problems without capturing all their complexity, 116

brainstorming An idea-generation process that specifically encourages any and all alternatives while withholding any criticism of those alternatives, 210

bureaucracy An organization structure with highly routine operating tasks achieved through specialization, very formalized rules and regulations, tasks that are grouped into functional departments, centralized authority, narrow spans of control, and decision making that follows the chain of command, 278

centralization The degree to which decision making is concentrated at a single point in an organization, 276

chain of command The unbroken line of authority that extends from the top of the organization to the lowest echelon and clarifies who reports to whom, 274

challenge stressors Stressors associated with workload, pressure to complete tasks, and time urgency, 317

channel richness The degree to which a communication channel can handle multiple cues simultaneously, facilitate feedback, and be personal, 170

charismatic leadership theory A leadership theory that states that followers make attributions of heroic or extraordinary leadership abilities when they observe certain behaviors and give these leaders power, 220

coercive power A power base that is dependent on fear of the negative results from failing to comply, 236

cognitive component The opinion or belief segment of an attitude, 57

cognitive dissonance Any incompatibility between two or more attitudes or between behavior and attitudes, 58

cognitive evaluation theory A version of self-determination theory which holds that allocating extrinsic rewards for behavior that had been previously intrinsically rewarding tends to decrease the overall level of motivation if the rewards are seen as controlling, 132

cohesiveness The degree to which group members are attracted to each other and are motivated to stay in the group, 205

collaborating A situation in which the parties to a conflict each desire to satisfy fully the concerns of all parties, 259

collectivism A tight social framework in which people expect others in groups of which they are a part to look after them and protect them, 104

communication apprehension Undue tension and anxiety about oral communication, written communication, or both, 176

communication process The steps between a sender and a receiver that result in the transfer and understanding of meaning, 165

competing A desire to satisfy one's interests, regardless of the impact on the other party to the conflict, 258

compromising A situation in which each party to a conflict is willing to give up something, 259

confirmation bias The tendency to seek out information that reaffirms past choices and to discount information that contradicts past judgments, 118

conflict A process that begins when one party perceives that another party has negatively affected, or is about to negatively affect, something that the first party cares about, 254

conflict management The use of resolution and stimulation techniques to achieve the desired level of conflict, 260

conflict process A process that has five stages: potential opposition or incompatibility, cognition and personalization, intentions, behavior, and outcomes, 257

conformity Being one of the group and therefore avoiding being visibly different, 201

conscientiousness A personality dimension that describes someone who is responsible, dependable, persistent, and organized, 91

consideration The extent to which a person is likely to have job relationships that are characterized by mutual trust, respect for employees' ideas, and regard for their feelings, 215

contingency variables Situational factors: variables that moderate the relationship between two or more other variables, 29

contrast effects Evaluations of a person's characteristics that is affected by comparisons with other people recently encountered who rank higher or lower on the same characteristics, 113

controlled processing A detailed consideration of evidence and information relying on facts, figures, and logic, 173

core self-evaluations The degree to which an individual likes or dislikes himself or herself, whether the person sees himself or herself as capable and effective, and whether the person feels in control of his or her environment or powerless over the environment; bottom-line conclusions individuals have about their capabilities, competence, and worth as a person, 96

core values Strongly held values, 292

cost-minimization strategy A strategy that emphasizes tight cost controls, avoidance of unnecessary innovation or marketing expenses, and price cutting, 285

creativity The ability to produce novel and useful ideas, 122

cross-functional teams Employees from about the same hierarchical level, but from different work areas, who come together to accomplish a task, 184

Dark Triad Traits of Machiavellianism, narcissism, and psychopathy, 93

decisions Choices made from among two or more alternatives, 114

deep acting Trying to modify one's true inner feelings based on display rules, 78

deep-level diversity Differences in values, personality, and work preferences that become progressively more important for determining similarity as people get to know one another better, 39

defensive behaviors Reactive and protective behaviors to avoid action, blame, or change, 245

demands Responsibilities, pressures, obligations, and even uncertainties that individuals face in the workplace, 317

departmentalization The basis by which jobs are grouped together, 273

dependence B's relationship to A when A possesses something that B requires, 235

deviant workplace behavior Voluntary behavior that violates significant organizational norms and, in so doing, threatens the well-being of the organization or its members. Also called antisocial behavior or workplace incivility, 202

discrimination Noting of a difference between things; often we refer to unfair discrimination which means making judgments about individuals based on stereotypes regarding their demographic group, 40

displayed emotions The emotions that the organization requires workers to show and consider appropriate in a given job, 78

distributive bargaining Negotiation that seeks to divide up a fixed amount of resources; a win/lose situation, 262

distributive justice Perceived fairness of the amount and allocation of rewards among individuals, 140

diversity The degree to which members of the group are similar to, or different from, one another, 206

diversity management The process and programs by which managers make everyone more aware of and sensitive to the needs and differences of others, 52

dominant culture A culture that expresses the core values that are shared by a majority of the organization's members, 292

driving forces Forces that direct behavior away from the status quo, 311

dyadic conflict Conflict between two people, 256

dysfunctional conflict Conflict that hinders group performance, 254

emotional contagion The process by which people's emotions are caused by the emotions of others, 85

emotional dissonance Inconsistencies between the emotions people feel and the emotions they project, 79

emotional intelligence (EI) One's ability to be self-aware, detect emotions in others, and manage emotional cues and information, 80

emotional labor An employee's expression of organizationally desired emotions during interpersonal transactions at work, 78

emotional stability A personality dimension that characterizes someone as calm, self-confident, secure (positive) versus nervous, depressed, and insecure (negative), 91

emotions Intense feelings that are directed at someone or something, 71

employee engagement An individual's involvement with, satisfaction with, and enthusiasm for the work they do, 61

employee involvement A participative process that uses the employees' input and is intended to increase employee commitment to an organization's success, 155

employee-oriented leaders Leaders who emphasize interpersonal relations, take a personal interest in the needs of employees, and accept individual differences among members, 215

employee stock ownership plan (ESOP) A company-established benefit plan in which employees acquire stock, often at below-market prices, as part of their benefits, 160

encounter stage The stage in the socialization process in which a new employee sees what the organization is really like and confronts the possibility that expectations and reality may diverge, 297

environment Institutions or forces outside an organization that potentially affect the organization's performance, 286

equity theory A theory that says that individuals compare their job inputs and outcomes with those of others and then respond to eliminate any inequities, 139

escalation of commitment An increased commitment to a previous decision in spite of negative information, 119

ethical choices Decisions made on the basis of ethical criteria, including the outcomes of the decision, the rights of those affected, and the equitable distribution of benefits and costs, 35

ethical dilemmas Situations in which members of organizations are required to define right and wrong conduct, 35

evidence-based management (EBM) The basing of managerial decisions on the best available scientific evidence, 25

exit response One of the four responses to the exit-voice-loyalty-neglect framework that directs behavior toward leaving the organization, including looking for a new position as well as resigning, 66

expectancy theory A theory that says that the strength of a tendency to act in a certain way depends on the strength of the expectation that the act will be followed by a given outcome and on the attractiveness of that outcome to the individual, 143

expert power Influence based on expertise, special skills, or knowledge, 237

extraversion A personality dimension describing someone who is sociable, gregarious, and assertive, 91

faultlines Perceived divisions that split groups into two or more subgroups based on individual differences, 207

feedback The degree to which carrying out the work activities required by a job results in the individual obtaining direct and clear information about the effectiveness of his or her performance, 148

felt conflict Emotional involvement in a conflict that creates anxiety, tenseness, frustration, or hostility, 258

felt emotions An individual's actual emotions, 78

femininity A national culture attribute that indicates little differentiation between male and female roles; a high rating indicates that women are treated as the equals of men in all aspects of the society, 104

Fiedler contingency model The theory that effective groups depend on a proper match between a leader's style of interacting with subordinates and the degree to which the situation gives control and influence to the leader, 217

filtering A sender's purposely manipulating information so the receiver will see it more favorably, 174

five-stage group-development model The five distinct stages groups go through: forming, storming, norming, performing, and adjourning, 197

fixed pie The belief that there is only a set amount of goods or services to be divvied up between the parties, 262

flexible benefits A benefits plan that allows each employee to put together a benefits package individually tailored to his or her own needs and situation, 161

flextime Flexible schedule in which employees must work a specific number of hours per week but may vary their hours, 152

formal channels Communication channels established by an organization to transmit messages related to the professional activities of members, 165

formal group A designated work group defined by an organization's structure, 197

formalization The degree to which jobs within an organization are standardized, 276

forming stage The first stage in group development, characterized by much uncertainty, 197

functional conflict Conflict that supports the goals of the group and improves its performance, 254

fundamental attribution error The tendency to underestimate the influence of external factors and overestimate the influence of internal factors when making judgments about the behavior of others, 112

gainsharing A formula-based group incentive plan based on improvements in group productivity, 160

general mental ability (GMA) An overall factor of intelligence, as suggested by the positive correlations among specific intellectual ability dimensions, 49

goal-setting theory A theory that says that specific and difficult goals, with feedback, lead to higher performance, 134

grapevine An organization's informal communication network, 168

group Two or more individuals, interacting and interdependent, who have come together to achieve particular objectives, 197

groupshift A change in decision risk between a group's decision and an individual decision that a member within that group would make; the shift can be toward either conservatism or greater risk, interacting and interdependent, who have come together to achieve particular objectives, 208

groupthink A phenomenon in which the norm for consensus overrides the realistic appraisal of alternative courses of action, 208

halo effect The tendency to draw a general impression about an individual on the basis of a single characteristic, 208

heredity Factors determined at conception one's biological, physiological, and inherent psychological makeup, 88

hierarchy of needs Abraham Maslow's hierarchy of five needs—physiological, safety, social, esteem, and self-actualization—in which, as each need is substantially satisfied, the next need becomes dominant, 128

high-context cultures Cultures that rely heavily on nonverbal and subtle situational cues in communication, 178

hindrance stressors Stressors that keep you from reaching your goals (for example, red tape, office politics, confusion over job responsibilities), 317

hindsight bias The tendency for us to believe falsely, after an outcome is actually known, that we would have accurately predicted the outcome, 119

hygiene factors Factors—such as company policy and administration, supervision, and salary—that, when adequate in a job, placate workers. When these factors are adequate, people will not be dissatisfied or satisfied, 131

idea champions People who actively and enthusiastically promote the idea, build support, overcome resistance, and ensure that the innovation is implemented, 315

idea evaluation The process of creative behavior in which we evaluate potential solutions to identify the best one, 123

idea generation The process of creative behavior in which potential solutions are evaluated, 123

illusory correlation The tendency of people to correlate two events when in reality there is no connection, 75

imitation strategy A strategy that seeks to move into new products or new markets only after their viability has already been proven, 285

impression management (IM) The process by which individuals attempt to control the impression others form of them, 246

individualism The degree to which people prefer to act as individuals rather than as members of groups and believe in individual rights above all else, 104

informal channels Communication channels that are created spontaneously and that emerge as responses to individual choices, 165

informal group A group that is neither formally structured nor organizationally determined, 197

information gathering The stage of creative behavior when possible solutions to a problem are sought, 123

informational justice A perception of whether managers provide employees with explanations for key decisions and keep them informed, 141

initiating structure The extent to which a leader is likely to define and structure his or her role and those of subordinates in the search for goal attainment, 215

innovation A new idea applied to initiating or improving a product, process, or service, 315

innovation strategy A strategy that emphasizes the introduction of major new products and services, 285

institutionalization A condition that occurs when an organization takes on a life of its own, apart from any of its members, and acquires immortality, 294

instrumental values Preferable modes of behavior or means of achieving one's terminal values, 101

integrative bargaining Negotiation that seeks one or more settlements that can create a win-win solution, 264

intellectual abilities The capacity to do mental activities—thinking, reasoning, and problem solving, 49

intentions Decisions to act in a given way, 258

interacting groups Typical groups in which members interact with each other face-to-face, 210

interactionist view of conflict The belief that conflict is not only a positive force in a group but also an absolute necessity for a group to perform effectively, 254

intergroup conflict Conflict between groups or teams, 256

intergroup development OD efforts to change the attitudes, stereotypes, and perceptions that groups have of each other, 313

interpersonal justice A perception of whether employees are treated with dignity and respect, 142

intragroup conflict Conflict that occurs within a group or team, 234

intuition A gut feeling not necessarily supported by research, 26

intuitive decision making An unconscious process created out of distilled experience, 116

job characteristics model (JCM) A model that proposes that any job can be described in terms of five core job dimensions: skill variety, task identity, task significance, autonomy, and feedback, 148

job design The way the elements in a job are organized, 148

job engagement The investment of an employee's physical, cognitive, and emotional energies into job performance, 145

job enrichment The vertical expansion of jobs, which increases the degree to which the worker controls the planning, execution, and evaluation of the work, 150

job involvement The degree to which a person identifies with a job, actively participates in it, and considers performance important to self-worth, 59

job rotation The periodic shifting of an employee from one task to another with similar skill requirements at the same organizational level, 150

job satisfaction A positive feeling about one's job resulting from an evaluation of its characteristics, 59

job sharing An arrangement that allows two or more individuals to split a traditional 40-hour-a-week job, 154

leader–member relations The degree of confidence, trust, and respect subordinates have in their leader, 217

leadership The ability to influence a group toward the achievement of a vision or set of goals, 214

least preferred co-worker (LPC) questionnaire An instrument that purports to measure whether a person is task or relationship oriented, 217

legitimate power The power a person receives as a result of his or her position in the formal hierarchy of an organization, 236

long-term orientation A national culture attribute that emphasizes the future, thrift, and persistence, 104

low-context cultures Cultures that rely heavily on words to convey meaning in communication, 178

loyalty response One of the four responses to the exit-voice-loyalty-neglect framework that means passively but optimistically waiting for conditions to improve, including speaking up for the organization in the face of external criticism and trusting the organization and its management to "do the right thing", 66

Machiavellianism The degree to which an individual is pragmatic, maintains emotional distance, and believes that ends can justify means, 93

management by objectives (MBO) A program that encompasses specific goals, participatively set, for an explicit time period, with feedback on goal progress, 136

masculinity A national culture attribute describing the extent to which the culture favors traditional masculine work roles of achievement, 104

material symbols Objects that serve as signals of an organization's culture, including the size of offices, executive perks, and attire, 300

matrix structure A structure that creates dual lines of authority and combines functional and product departmentalization, 278

McClelland's theory of needs A theory that states achievement, power, and affiliation are three important needs that help explain motivation, 131

mechanistic model A structure characterized by extensive departmentalization, high formalization, a limited information network, and centralization, 284

mental models Team members' organized mental representations of how the work gets done by the team, 191

mentor A senior employee who sponsors and supports a less experienced employee, 229

merit-based pay plan A pay plan based on performance appraisal ratings, 159

metamorphosis stage The stage in the socialization process in which a new employee changes and adjusts to the job, work group, and organization, 298

model An abstraction of reality, a simplified representation of some real-world phenomenon, 35

moods Feelings that tend to be less intense than emotions and that lack a contextual stimulus, 71

motivation The process that accounts for an individual's intensity, direction, and persistence of effort toward attaining a goal, 128

movement A change process that transforms the organization from the status quo to a desired end state, 311

multiteam systems Systems in which different teams need to coordinate their efforts to produce a superordinate goal, 186

Myers-Briggs Type Indicator (MBTI) A personality test that taps four characteristics and classifies people into 1 of 16 personality types, 89

narcissism The tendency to be arrogant, have a grandiose sense of self-importance, require excessive admiration, and have a sense of entitlement, 94

need for achievement (nAch) The drive to excel, to achieve in relationship to a set of standards, and to strive to succeed, 131

need for affiliation (nAff) The desire for friendly and close interpersonal relationships, 131

need for power (nPow) The need to make others behave in a way in which they would not have behaved otherwise, 131

negative affect A mood dimension that consists of emotions such as nervousness, stress, and anxiety at the high end and rcontentedness, calmness, and serenity, 72

neglect response One of the four responses to the exit-voice-loyalty-neglect framework that passively allows conditions to worsen and includes chronic absenteeism or lateness, reduced effort, and increased error rate, 66

negotiation A process in which two or more parties decide how to allocate scarce resources, 262

neutralizers Attributes that make it impossible for leader behavior to make any difference to follower outcomes, 231

nominal group technique A group decision-making method in which individuals meet face to face to pool their judgments in a systematic but independent fashion, 210

norming stage The third stage in group development, characterized by close relationships and cohesiveness, 198

norms Acceptable standards of behavior that are shared by the group's members, 200

openness to experience A personality dimension that characterizes someone in terms of imagination, sensitivity, and curiosity, 91

organic model A structure that is flat, uses cross-hierarchical and cross-functional teams, has low formalization, possesses a comprehensive information network, and relies on participative decision making, 284

organizational behavior (OB) A field of study that investigates the impact that individuals, groups, and structures have on a behavior within organizations, for thc purpose of applying such knowledge toward improving an organization's effectiveness, 24

organizational climate The shared perceptions organizational members have about their organization and work environment, 293

organizational commitment The degree to which an employee identifies with a particular organization and its goals and wishes to maintain membership in the organization, 60

organizational culture A system of shared meaning held by members that distinguishes the organization from other organizations, 291

organizational demography The degree to which members of a work unit share a common demographic attribute, such as age, sex, race, educational level, or length of service in an organization, 189

organizational development (OD) A collection of planned change interventions, built on humanistic–democratic values, that seeks to improve organizational effectiveness and employee well-being, 312

organizational justice An overall perception of what is fair in the workplace, composed of distributive, procedural, and interactional justice, 140

organizational structure How job tasks are formally divided, grouped, and coordinated, 272

participative management A process in which subordinates share a significant degree of decision-making power with their immediate superiors, 156

path-goal theory The theory that effective leaders clarify followers' paths to their work goals and reduce work blocks, 219

perceived conflict Awareness by one or more parties of the existence of conditions that create opportunities for conflict to arise, 258

perceived organizational support (POS) The degree to which employees believe the organization values their contributions and cares about their well-being, 60

perception A process by which individuals organize and interpret their sensory impressions to give meaning to their environment, 110

performing The fourth stage of the five-stage group development model where group energy has advanced from understanding each other to performing the task at hand, 198

personality The sum total of ways in which an individual reacts to and interacts with others, 88

personality–job fit theory A theory that identifies six personality types and proposes that the fit between personality type and occupational environment determines satisfaction and turnover, 101

personality traits Enduring characteristics that describe an individual's behavior, 89

physical abilities The capacity to do tasks that demand stamina, dexterity, strength, and similar characteristics, 51

piece-rate pay plan A plan in which employees are paid fixed sum for each unit of production completed, 158

political behavior Activities that are not required as part of one's formal role in the organization but that influence, or attempt to influence, the distribution of advantages and disadvantages within the organization, 241

political skill People's ability to influence others to enhance their own objectives, 239

position power Influence derived from one's formal structural position in the organization; includes power to hire, fire, discipline, promote, and give salary increases, 217

positive affect A mood dimension consisting of positive emotions such as excitement, enthusiasm, and elation on the high end and boredom, depression, and fatigue at the low end, 72

positive organizational culture A culture that emphasizes building on employee strengths, rewards more than punishes, and emphasizes individual vitality and growth, 302

positive organizational scholarship The study of how organizations develop human strengths, foster vitality and resilience, and unlock potential, 34

positivity offset The tendency of most individuals to experience a mildly positive mood at zero input (when nothing in particular is going on), 73

power A capacity that A has to influence the behavior of B so that B acts in accordance with A's wishes, 235

power distance Degree to which people in a country accept that power in institutions and organizations is distributed unequally, 104

power tactics Ways in which individuals translate power bases into specific actions, 238

prearrival stage The period of learning in the socialization process that occurs before a new employee joins the organization, 297

prevention focus In goal-setting theory, the tendency for some people to strive to fulfill duties and obligations and avoid conditions that pull them away from desired goals, 135

proactive personality People who identify opportunities, show initiative, take action, and persevere until meaningful change occurs, 97

problem formulation The stage of creative behavior in which we identify a problem or opportunity which has no known solution, 123

problems Discrepancies between the current state of affairs and some desired state, 114

problem-solving teams Groups of 5 to 12 employees from the same department who meet for a few hours each week to discuss ways of improving quality, efficiency, and the work environment, 183

procedural justice The perceived fairness of the process used to determine the distribution of rewards, 141

process conflict Conflict over how work gets done, 255

process consultation (PC) A meeting in which a consultant assists a client in understanding process events with which he or she must deal and identifying processes that need improvement, 313

production-oriented leader A leader who emphasizes technical or task aspects of the job, 215

profit-sharing plan Organization-wide program that distributes compensation based on some established formula designed around a company's profitability, 160

promotion focus In goal-setting theory, the tendency in some people to strive for advancement and accomplishment, 135

psychological empowerment Employees' belief in the degree to which they affect their work environments, their competence, the meaningfulness of their jobs, and the perceived autonomy in their work, 59

psychology The science that seeks to measure, explain, and sometimes change the behavior of humans and other animals, 28

psychopathy A lack of concern for others, and a lack of guilt or remorse for causing harm, 94

punctuated-equilibrium model A set of phases that temporary groups go through that involves transitions between inertia and activity, 198

rational Characterized by making consistent, value-maximizing choices within specified constraints, 115

rational decision-making model A decision-making model that describes how individuals should behave in order to maximize some outcome, 115

reference groups Important groups to which individuals belong or hope to belong and with whose norms individuals are likely to conform, 202

referent power Influence based on identification with a person who has desirable resources or personal traits, 237

reflexivity A team characteristic of reflecting on and adjusting the master plan when necessary, 191

refreezing Stabilizing a change intervention by balancing and restraining forces, 311

relationship conflict Conflict based on interpersonal relationships, 255

representative participation A system in which workers participate in organizational decision making through a small group of representative employees, 156

resources Things within an individual's control that can be used to resolve demands, 317

restraining forces Forces that hinder movement from the existing equilibrium, 311

reward power Compliance achieved based on the ability to distribute rewards that others view as valuable, 236

risk aversion The tendency to prefer a sure gain of a moderate amount over a riskier outcome, even if the riskier outcome might have a higher expected payoff, 119

rituals Repetitive sequences of activities that express and reinforce the key values of the organization, 300

role A set of expected behavior patterns attributed to someone occupying a given position in a social unit, 199

role conflict When an individual finds that compliance with one role requirement may make it difficult to comply with another, 200

role expectations How others believe a person should act in a given situation, 200

role perception An individual's view of how he or she is supposed to act in a given situation, 199

selective perception Any characteristic that makes a person, object, or event stand out will increase the probability that it will be perceived, 113

self-concordance The degree to which peoples' reasons for pursuing goals are consistent with their interests and core values, 133

self-determination theory A theory of motivation that proposes that prefer to feel they have control over their actions, 132

Self-efficacy theory Also known as *social cognitive theory* or *social learning theory*, refers to an individual's belief that he is capable of performing a task; the higher your self-efficacy, the more confidence you have in your ability to succeed, 136

self-managed work teams Groups of 10 to 15 people who perform highly related or interdependent jobs and take on some supervisory responsibilities, 184

self-monitoring A personality trait that measures an individual's ability to adjust his or her behavior to external situational factors, 97

self-serving bias The tendency for individuals to attribute their own successes to internal factors and put the blame for failures on external factors, 112

servant leadership A leadership style marked by going beyond the leader's own self-interest and instead focusing on opportunities to help followers grow and develop, 227

short-term orientation A national culture attribute that emphasizes the present, 104

simple structure An organization structure characterized by a low degree of departmentalization, wide spans of control, authority centralized in a single person, and little formalization, 277

situational leadership theory The leadership theory that successful leadership depends on the followers, 219

situation strength theory Theoretical framework that proposes the way that personality transfers into behavior depends on the strength of the situation, 98

skill-based pay A pay plan that sets pay levels on the basis of how many skills employees have or how many jobs they can do, 159

skill variety The degree to which a job requires a variety of different activities, 148

social loafing The tendency for individuals to expend less effort when working collectively than when working individually, 204

social psychology Focuses on people's influences on one another, 28

socialization A process that adapts employees to the organization's culture, 296

socialized charismatic leadership A leadership concept that states that leaders convey values that are other-centered versus self-centered and who model ethical conduct, 227

sociology The study of people in relation to their social environment or culture, 28

span of control The number of subordinates a manager directs, 275

status A socially defined position or rank given to groups or group members by others, 203

status characteristics theory A theory that states that differences in status characteristics create status hierarchies within groups, 204

stereotyping When we judge someone on the basis of our perception of the group to which he or she belongs, 113

storming stage The second stage in group development, characterized by intragroup conflict, 198

stress A dynamic condition in which an individual is confronted with an opportunity, a demand, or a resource related to what the individual desires and for which the outcome is perceived to be both uncertain and important, 316

strong culture A culture in which the core values are intensely held and widely shared, 292

subcultures Minicultures within an organization, typically defined by department designations and geographical separation, 292

substitutes Attributes, such as experience and training, that can replace the need for leadership behavior, 231

surface acting Hiding one's inner feelings and foregoing emotional expressions in response to display rules, 78

surface-level diversity Differences in easily perceived characteristics, such as gender, race, ethnicity, age, or disability, that do not necessarily reflect the ways people think or feel but that may activate certain stereotypes, 39

survey feedback The use of questionnaires to identify discrepancies among member perceptions; discussion follows and remedies are suggested, 313

systematic study Looking at relationships, attempting to attribute causes and effects, and drawing conclusions based on scientific evidence, 25

task conflict Conflict over content and goals of the work, 255

task identity The degree to which a job requires completion of a whole and identifiable piece of work, 148

task significance The degree to which a job has a substantial impact on the lives or work of other people, 148

task structure The degree to which the job assignments are procedurized, 217

team building High interaction among team members to increase trust and openness, 313

technology The way in which an organization transfers its inputs into outputs, 285

telecommuting Working from home at least two days a week on a computer that is linked to the employer's office, 154

terminal values Desirable end-states of existence; the goals a person would like to achieve during his or her lifetime, 101

theory X The assumption that employees dislike work, are lazy, dislike responsibility, and must be coerced to perform, 129

theory Y The assumption that employees like work, are creative, seek responsibility, and can exercise self-direction, 129

three-stage model of creativity A model which details the causes and effects of creative behavior, 122

trait activation theory The theory that some situations, events, or interventions activate a trait more than others, 99

traditional view of conflict The belief that all conflict is harmful and must be avoided, 254

trait theories of leadership Theories that consider personal qualities and characteristics that differentiate leaders from non-leaders, 214

transactional leaders Leaders who guide or motivate their followers in the direction of established goals by clarifying role and task requirements, 223

transformational leaders Leaders who inspire followers to transcend their own self-interests and who are capable of having a profound and extraordinary effect on followers, 223

trust A positive expectation that another will not act opportunistically, 228

two-factor theory A theory that relates intrinsic factors to job satisfaction and associates extrinsic factors with dissatisfaction. Also called motivation-hygiene theory, 130

uncertainty avoidance A national culture attribute that describes the extent to which a society feels threatened by uncertain and ambiguous situations and tries to avoid them, 104

unfreezing Changing to overcome the pressures of both individual resistance and group conformity, 311

unity of command The idea that a subordinate should have only one superior to whom he or she is directly responsible, 274

utilitarianism A system in which decisions are made solely on the basis of their outcomes or consequences and to provide the greatest good for the greatest number, 121

value system A hierarchy based on a ranking of an individual's values in terms of their intensity, 100

values Basic convictions that a specific mode of conduct or end-state of existence is personally or socially preferable to an opposite or converse mode of conduct or end-state of existence, 100

variable-pay program A pay plan that bases a portion of an employee's pay on some individual and/or organizational measure of performance, 158

virtual organization A small, core organization that outsources major business functions, 280

virtual teams Teams that use computer technology to tie together physically dispersed members in order to achieve a common goal, 185

vision A long-term strategy for attaining a goal or goals by linking the present with a better future for the organization, 221

vision statement A formal articulation of an organization's vision or mission, 221

voice response One of the four responses to the exit-voice-loyalty-neglect framework that includes actively and constructively attempting to improve conditions, including suggesting improvements, discussing problems with superiors, and undertaking some forms of union activity, 66

wellness programs Organizationally supported programs that focus on the employee's total physical and mental condition, 320

whistle-blowers Individuals who report unethical or illegal practices by their employers to outsiders, 121

work group A group that interacts primarily to share information and to make decisions to help each group member perform within his or her area of responsibility, 182

work specialization The degree to which tasks in an organization are subdivided into separate jobs, 272

work team A group whose individual efforts result in performance that is greater than the sum of the individual inputs, 182

workforce diversity The concept that organizations are becoming more heterogeneous in terms of gender, age, race, ethnicity, sexual orientation, and inclusion of other diverse groups, 33

INDEX

Page references with "e" refer to exhibits.